MACROECONOMIC ANALYSIS AND
STABILIZATION POLICIES

Macroeconomic analysis and stabilization policies

STEPHEN J. TURNOVSKY

Australian National University

CAMBRIDGE UNIVERSITY PRESS

CAMBRIDGE

LONDON-NEW YORK-MELBOURNE

Published by the Syndics of the Cambridge University Press
The Pitt Building, Trumpington Street, Cambridge CB2 1RP
Bentley House, 200 Euston Road, London NW1 2DB
32 East 57th Street, New York, NY 10022, USA
296 Beaconsfield Parade, Middle Park, Melbourne 3206, Australia

First published 1977

Printed in Great Britain at the Alden Press
    Oxford London and Northampton

Library of Congress Cataloguing in Publication Data

Turnovsky, Stephen J
Macroeconomic analysis and stabilization policies.

Includes bibliographical references and index.
1. Macroeconomics – Mathematical models. 2. Economic stabilization.
I. Title.

ISBN 0 521 21520 X

HB171.5.T86   339.5   76-46862

CONTENTS

Preface   xi

1   Introduction and overview   1

   1. Scope of the book   1
   2. Outline of the book   3
   3. Methodology   6

Part I   THE CLOSED ECONOMY   9

2   Review of basic macroeconomic model   10

   1. Some preliminary concepts   10
   2. The output market   13
   3. The money market   17
   4. Equilibrium in product and money markets   20
   5. Monetary and fiscal policy in the simple $IS-LM$ model   21
   6. The balanced-budget multiplier   26
   7. The labour market   26
   8. Equilibrium in the classical model   28
   9. An alternative labour supply function   29
   10. Some Keynesian rigidities   30
   11. Some issues in comparative statics   32
   12. Some final remarks   35

3   The formulation of a consistent macroeconomic model   36

   1. Definition of wealth   36
   2. The private sector budget constraint   38
   3. The government budget constraint   40
   4. The aggregate budget constraint and Walras' law   41
   5. Relationship of savings plans to wealth accumulation   42
   6. Choice between discrete- and continuous-time models   43
   7. A discrete-time model with arbitrary period and imperfect foresight
   A. The household sector   45
   B. Firms   50
   C. The government   50
   D. The total economy   51

8. The continuous-time limit 52
   A. *The household sector* 53
   B. *Firms* 55
   C. *The government* 57
   D. *The total economy* 57
9. The distinction between equity and physical capital 58
10. Some implications for product market relationships 60
11. Some restrictions imposed by budget constraints 62
12. Extension of model to inflationary conditions 64
13. Summary 66

4 The dynamics of the government budget constraint 68
1. Introduction 68
2. Government budget constraint in a simple linear *IS—LM* model 69
3. Analysis of monetary and fiscal policies in simple model 71
4. Extension of model to include wealth effects and interest payments 73
5. First-period effects 75
6. Second-period effects 77
7. Stability and steady-state effects 79
8. Conclusions: some implications for the monetarist debate 84

5 The wage—price sector 86
1. The Phillips curve 87
2. The extended Phillips curve 90
3. A simple model of the wage—price sector 92
4. The 'expectations hypothesis' 94
5. The Phelps hypothesis 98
6. Empirical tests of the expectations hypothesis 98
7. Extension of expectations hypothesis to include bilateral bargaining elements of wage and price determination 102

6 A short-run integrated macroeconomic model 104
1. Introduction 104
2. A simple macroeconomic model incorporating inflationary expectations 105
   A. *The basic model* 105
   B. *Impact of inflationary expectations* 109
   C. *Monetary and fiscal policy* 113
3. Extension of model to include endogenous income tax 114
   A. *Reformulation of model* 114
   B. *Monetary and fiscal policy* 118
   C. *Effects of tax changes* 120
   D. *Impact of inflationary expectations* 122
4. Anticipated and unanticipated government policy 123
5. Summary 126

7 An intermediate-run macroeconomic model 129
1. Introduction 129
2. The Blinder—Solow fixed price model 130

3. An intermediate-run model   132
  A. *Instantaneous relationships*   134
  B. *The dynamics of the system*   137
  C. *Respecification of system in per-unit-of-capital form*   139
  D. *Policy specification in the model*   140
4. Comparative static properties of the instantaneous
   equilibrium   141
  A. *Effects of changes in inflationary expectations*   141
  B. *Effects of changes in financial assets*   143
  C. *Summary*   144
5. The stability of the system   146
  A. *Pure money finance policy*   146
  B. *Pure bond finance policy*   148
6. Intermediate-run equilibrium properties   150
  A. *Some comparative static properties*   151
  B. *The 'Fisher effect'*   154
7. Endogenizing government policy   155
8. Summary   156

8 **A long-run model**   159

1. Introduction   159
2. Adaptive expectations in continuous-time models   159
3. Specification of model   164
  A. *Stock and flow constraints*   164
  B. *The real rate of return on equity*   168
  C. *The production–employment and wage–price
     sectors*   169
  D. *The dynamics of the system*   170
4. Summary of model   172
5. Steady-state equilibrium   175
6. Long-run comparative statics: money-financed deficit   177
  A. *Government expenditure multipliers*   179
  B. *Open market operations*   184
  C. *Change in tax rate*   186
7. Long-run comparative statics: bond-financed deficit   186
8. Conclusion: comparison of money financing with
   bond financing   189

Part II **THE OPEN ECONOMY**

9 **Review of static macroeconomic models of a small
   open economy**   195

1. Introduction   195
2. Domestic product market   196
3. Domestic money market   199
4. The balance of payments   201
5. Equilibrium with fixed prices: fixed exchange
   rate   203
6. Equilibrium with fixed prices: flexible exchange
   rate   206
7. The assignment problem   208

8. Assignments of instruments to targets in an open
economy 211
A. *Fixed exchange rate* 211
B. *Flexible exchange rate* 214
C. *Some general comments* 215
9. Specification of model with variable prices 216

10 **Imported inflation and government policies in a
short-run open macroeconomic model** 217
1. Introduction 218
2. The basic model 218
3. The effects of imported inflation 223
4. Monetary, fiscal and exchange rate policies 230
5. Flexible exchange rates 235
6. Summary and conclusions 237
Appendix 238

11 **The dynamics of an open economy with fixed
exchange rate and fixed prices** 241
1. Introduction 241
2. The model 242
3. Zero capital mobility 251
4. Perfect capital mobility 256
5. The assignment problem 262
6. Summary 264

12 **Imported inflation and government policies in a
dynamic open macroeconomic model** 267
1. Introduction 267
2. The model 268
A. *Domestic output sector* 268
B. *Domestic wage–price sector* 269
C. *Financial sector* 270
D. *Real private disposable income* 272
E. *Dynamics of the system* 272
F. *Summary of model and respecification in real terms* 274
3. Fixed exchange rate 277
A. *Stability* 278
B. *General observations on the short run* 279
C. *Fiscal policy, monetary policy, and imported
inflation in the short run* 280
D. *General observations on the steady state* 282
E. *Fiscal policy, monetary policy and imported
inflation in the steady state* 284
4. Flexible exchange rate 287
A. *Stability* 289
B. *General observations on the short run* 289
C. *Fiscal policy, monetary policy, and imported
inflation in the short run* 291
D. *General observations on the steady state* 293
E. *Fiscal policy, monetary policy, and imported
inflation in the steady state* 293
F. *Steady-state properties: money financing* 297

5. Concluding observations   299
   Appendix   301
   1. Savings and the Marshall–Lerner condition   301
   2. Conditions for local stability of fixed exchange rate
      system   303

Part III   STABILIZATION POLICIES

13   An introduction to stabilization theory and policy   307

   1. Introduction   307
   2. Static Tinbergen theory of stabilization   308
   3. Stabilization in the presence of stochastic disturbances   310
      A. One instrument – one target case   310
      B. Two instruments – one target case   312
   4. Costs of instrument adjustment   313
      A. One instrument – one target case   314
      B. Two instruments – one target case   316
   5. Review of basic multiplier–accelerator model   318
   6. The Phillips stabilization policies   320
      A. Proportional policy   321
      B. Integral policy   323
      C. Derivative policy   324
   7. Introduction to stabilization of dynamic stochastic
      systems   325

14   Optimal stabilization theory   329

   1. Theil static optimal stabilization policy   329
   2. Formulation of dynamic stabilization theory: the
      deterministic case   331
   3. Optimal stabilization policy: deterministic systems   333
   4. Optimal stabilization policies: stochastic systems   337
      A. Uncorrelated multiplicative and additive disturbances   339
      B. Correlated multiplicative and additive disturbances   341
   5. A scalar example   343
   6. Rules versus discretionary stabilization policies   350
   7. An application to the stabilization of a multiplier–
      accelerator model   353
   8. Conclusion   357
   Notes   359

   References   376

   Index   386

PREFACE

This book has evolved from a graduate course in macroeconomics which I have given at the Australian National University over the past five years. Many good books on the subject are now available and the reader may legitimately wonder how this book differs from some of the existing texts in the area.

The main focus of this book is on the construction and analysis of an integrated macroeconomic model. In developing such a model, there are four main aspects which we wish to stress, and which so far have not received adequate attention in existing textbooks.

First, and most important, we emphasize what we call the 'intrinsic dynamics' of the macroeconomic system. This is the dynamics inherent in the system arising from the creation of securities by certain groups in the economy, in order to finance their operations. Typically, the government prints money or issues debt in order to finance its deficit, while firms issue bonds or stocks to finance their investments. These securities are in turn absorbed by households through the process of savings. These relationships necessarily impose a dynamic structure on the macroeconomic system, even if all the underlying behavioural relationships are static. It is the analysis of this dynamic system which forms the central theme of this book and which until now has been conspicuously absent from existing macroeconomic textbooks.

Secondly, a good deal of attention is devoted to developing current ideas in inflation theory — particularly pertaining to the role of inflationary expectations — and incorporating these into a fully integrated macroeconomic model. Thirdly, several chapters are devoted to the international aspects of macroeconomics. These are typically given very brief attention in macroeconomic textbooks, being left to specialist books on international economics. But with increasing international integration, it seems that international macroeconomics should be treated as part of the received body of macroeconomic theory and not just left to specialized books on the subject. Finally, the book discusses in some detail several aspects of stabilization policy, and in particular gives an introduction to optimal stabilization theory.

These four areas reflect the main emphasis of the approach adopted in the present volume and also include what I believe are some of the more important topics neglected by existing books. On the other hand, many books give excellent treatments of the component parts of the macroeconomic system, such as the consumption function, investment function, etc., and these are not discussed in any detail here. Rather, the objective is to take standard forms of such functions and to introduce them into a complete macroeconomic model. In this respect, the present volume can be regarded as complementary to some of the existing texts, which discuss the theoretical and empirical issues relating to these component functions in great detail.

Some of the material appearing in this volume has been adapted from articles which originally appeared in journal form. In particular, I am grateful to the editors and publishers of the *International Economic Review, Australian Economic Papers, Economic Journal, Canadian Journal of Economics* and the *Journal of International Economics* for their kind permission to include material which was originally published in their journals. The paper that I wrote with David H. Pyle, The Dynamics of Government Policy in an Inflationary Economy: An 'Intermediate-Run' Analysis, *Journal of Money, Credit, and Banking,* Vol. VIII, No. 4 (November 1976), copyright ©1976 by the Ohio State University Press, has also been adapted for use in this volume.

In undertaking a project of this size, one necessarily incurs many debts. Many individuals have read parts of the material either in draft form, or in the form of papers which subsequently were revised into chapters. In particular, I would like to express my gratitude to Edwin Burmeister, Geoffrey H. Kingston, Steven W. Kohlhagen, Thomas Mayer, Robert A. Meyer, Frank Milne, John Pitchford, Michael G. Porter, Alan Preston, David H. Pyle, Edward Sieper, Robert M. Solow, Pravin K. Trivedi and W. Murray Wonham, either for reading various parts of the material or for discussions at earlier stages. Comments by graduate students in macroeconomics at the ANU, who were exposed to the manuscript in draft form, were also useful in clarifying various parts. In particular I would like to thank Geoff Carmody and Ian McKenzie for their helpful comments. I would also like to thank Debbie Stoyles for her superb typing of numerous drafts of the manuscript. Thanks are also due to Isobel Everitt who assisted most ably with the typing of two of the chapters and to Lindy Spence for editorial assistance. Finally, I would like to thank my wife, Michelle, and children, Geoffrey and Jacqueline, for their patience and forbearance throughout this long project.

STEPHEN J. TURNOVSKY

NOTE

Throughout this book, where no ambiguity can arise, we shall adopt the convention of letting primes denote total derivatives and denoting partial derivatives by appropriate subscripts. Time derivatives will be denoted by dots about the variable concerned. Thus we shall let

$$f'(x) \equiv \frac{df}{dx}; \quad f_i(x_1, \ldots, x_n) \equiv \frac{\partial f}{\partial x_i} \quad i = 1, \ldots, n,$$

$$f_{ij}(x_1, \ldots, x_n) \equiv \frac{\partial^2 f}{\partial x_i \partial x_j} \quad \text{etc.,} \quad \dot{x} \equiv \frac{dx}{dt}$$

The application of a bar to a letter is used to denote either a stationary equilibrium value to a dynamic system, or the fact that the variable to which it is applied is fixed exogenously. The intended meaning should be quite clear from the particular context.

1

INTRODUCTION AND OVERVIEW

1   Scope of the book

Macroeconomic theory has been a rapidly evolving subject over the past few years. For a long time it was approached in a rather descriptive and non-analytic fashion. While some progress was made in the 1950s at formal macroeconomic model building, the subject was never treated with anything like the rigour with which microeconomics was studied and frequently taught.

This is beginning to change. Much of the recent and current research on the subject has been, and is being, directed at trying to set it in a sounder theoretical framework. In particular, people have become aware of the need for any behavioural relationship embedded in a macroeconomic model to be derivable, at least in principle, from considerations relating to the individual decision-making units within the economy. In other words, the aggregate (macro) system, reflecting the actions of all the individuals (micro units) in the economy, should, in some broad sense, be consistent with their behaviour.

The first area of macroeconomics which economists attempted to derive from underlying microeconomic principles was the analysis of the consumption function. This was the subject of a good deal of theoretical research starting in the late 1940s with the pioneering work of Duesenberry (1948), Modigliani and Brumberg (1954), Friedman (1957), Ando and Modigliani (1963), and Yaari (1964). In this respect, progress in the theory of investment was somewhat slower. It would not be unfair to say that this subject was treated in a rather *ad hoc* manner until well into the 1960s, when the initial appearance of Jorgenson's work (1963, 1965) revolutionized the approach, basing it on the noeclassical micro theory of the firm. Subsequent work by Jorgenson himself, with various co-authors, and more recently by Bischoff (1971), Lucas (1967), Gould (1968), Treadway (1969) and others has continued this development to the point that it has now become the firmly established approach to investment theory. Similar progress has been taking place in the treatment of financial markets in modern macroeconomic theory. For many years, the demand for money was studied in isolation, in terms of the three Keynesian motives, expressed in terms of the transactions, precautionary, and speculative demands. With the appearance of work by Patinkin (1965), Tobin (1969) and others, the more recent approach has been to consider the demand for money, along with the demands for all other financial assets, in the context of a general equilibrium portfolio framework. Finally, the area of employment theory and labour markets provides a further example in which progress is being made to base modern macroeconomic theory on microeconomic principles. However, this is a much more recent development and is a much less settled issue at this stage; see Phelps (1970).

Despite these developments, we do not mean to suggest that it will be possible to treat macroeconomics with the same theoretical rigour with which micro theory is typically studied. It almost certainly will not. Even if a completely general intertemporal, stochastic, theory of microeconomic behaviour were ultimately developed, there would always remain the inherently intractable aggregation problem, whereby the relationships at the aggregate level are obtained from the underlying individual relationships. The intractability of this problem has long been recognized by economists; see Theil (1954). It stems from the fact that it is only under extremely restrictive conditions that the behavioural relations at the aggregate level will be of the same form as functions of the aggregate variables, as they are at the individual level. But recent work by mathematical economists goes much further than this. It has been argued that the restrictions obtained from utility maximizing behaviour for the microeconomic relations provide almost no information as to the likely properties of the corresponding aggregate functions; see Debreu (1974), Sonnenschein (1972). If this view is taken seriously, it would suggest that the advantages in deriving macroeconomic relationships from microeconomic principles may be overstated.

But in spite of these enormous difficulties it would be fair to say that progress has been made in giving macroeconomic theory a firmer theoretical foundation. Particular attention is being devoted to recognizing the existence of budget constraints, which play such a crucial role in microeconomic theory, and to formulating macroeconomic models consistently within these constraints. To this extent at least, a more consistently formulated macroeconomic theory can be said to be emerging.

In this book we attempt to give a fairly rigorous analysis of macroeconomic theory. Our concern is with developing and analysing a consistent, integrated model, rather than with any detailed discussion of particular expenditure functions. Thus we do not devote any attention to discussing such issues as the consumption functions, the investment function, or the demand for money functions. These have all been discussed at length in many excellent textbooks elsewhere; see e.g. Branson (1972), Evans (1969), Lovell (1975), Wonnacott (1974). Rather, our approach is to take some general form of these functions as given (hopefully having reasonably firm microeconomic underpinnings) and to insert them into a complete macroeconomic model. Our purpose is to analyse the behaviour of the model as a whole rather than with a detailed construction of its component parts. We should also emphasize that the book represents a theoretical exercise in macro-economics. Almost no attention is devoted to discussing empirical issues, either pertaining to the empirical estimation of the model, or to the more general empirical literature which has evolved. Again some of this is discussed in other texts; see Evans (1969), Cramer (1971), Kuh and Schmalensee (1973), Bridge (1971). One exception to this is that we do make use of available empirical evidence on certain relevant parameters, insofar as these may be of assistance in determining the likely behaviour of the system, where otherwise no conclusion could be drawn.

Our approach is to develop a succession of models of increasing com-plexity, beginning with relatively simple extensions of the traditional text-book model (see e.g. Branson). In building these models, the main emphasis of our analysis is on what we shall refer to as the *intrinsic* dynamics of the system. By this we mean the dynamic behaviour stemming from certain logical relationships which constrain the system; specifically the relation-ships between stocks and flows. For example, the process of saving gives rise to the accumulation of assets and it is this change in the stock of assets which causes the system to evolve over time. It is only relatively recently that this fundamental dynamic economic process has begun to be incorporated into macroeconomic theory, although it was central to the more specialized subject of economic growth; see Burmeister and Dobell (1970). In any event, it provides a cornerstone to the model we shall develop.

With few exceptions (notably Chapters 13 and 14), we shall abstract from lags in the underlying behavioural relationships. In this respect, our appraoch provides a contrast to what one might regard as the traditional short-run dynamic macroeconomic model, in which the dynamics is often due entirely to the existence of such lags; see Allen (1959, 1967). By abstracting from them, we do not mean to deny their importance, for this is obviously an un-questionable empirical fact. Rather, our reason for neglecting them is that they are not fundamental to the logical consistency of the model in the same way as the intrinsic dynamics clearly are.

2   Outline of the book

The book is divided into three parts. Chapters 2–8 develop and analyse a progression of models for a closed economy; Chapters 9–12 extend these models to allow for international transactions; Chapters 13, 14 deal with problems of stabilization policy.

Our starting point is the traditional textbook static macroeconomic model and in Chapter 2 we begin with a review of the standard *IS–LM* model, to-gether with the various traditional extensions incorporating the labour market. Chapter 3 deals with some of the issues which arise in the formulation of a consistent macroeconomic model. The main point of this chapter is to begin with the underlying constraints facing the various groups in the economy (households, firms, and the government) and to make sure that the behavioural relationships we shall consider are consistent with them. Since throughout this volume we shall use both discrete-time and continuous-time models as convenient, this question is considered for both types of formulations. On the whole, discrete-time analysis is probably more useful where one is concerned with analysing period-by-period effects of various policies, and in particular their short-run impacts. But discrete-time analysis has its drawbacks and continuous-time formulations are generally more useful in longer-run analyses, where the arbitrary choice of time unit may become more critical. In any event, the procedure whereby the continuous-time model is obtained as the limit of an underlying discrete model raises technical issues which require the derivation to be performed with some care. That is the reason why it is necessary to treat the two systems separately.

The first dynamic model is introduced in Chapter 4. This is accomplished by introducing the government budget constraint into the *IS–LM* fixed-price model of Chapter 2. This idea was introduced into macroeconomic theory at a relatively late stage by Ott and Ott (1965), Christ (1967, 1968). The essential idea is the observation that any government deficit needs to be financed. Assuming that tax rates remain constant, this can be achieved either by issuing more debt, or by issuing more money (or both). To the extent that the short-run equilibrium of the economy (the level of income and the rate of interest in the *IS–LM* context) depends upon the stocks of these assets held by the private sector, as these stocks change, this equilibrium will change and the system will evolve over time.

Chapter 5 introduces the wage–price sector, paying particular attention to the role of inflationary expectations. Along with the dynamics of asset accumulation, the evolution of inflationary expectations over time also plays an important role in the dynamics of the overall model. In the following chapter we present our first integrated model. This is obtained by incorporating the analysis of the wage–price sector of Chapter 5 into the conventional static model summarized in Chapter 2. Attention is focused on the short run, although account is taken of the government budget constraint discussed in Chapter 4. Being short run, this model can treat the expected rate of inflation as a given parameter and particular emphasis is placed on analysing the effects of changes in these exogenous anticipations on the short-run equilibrium of the system. The short-run effects of monetary and fiscal policy in an inflationary context are also discussed.

Chapter 7 extends Chapter 6 to what we call the 'intermediate run'. In doing so it introduces several new features. First, we allow for the accumulation of government debt (money and bonds) just as we did for the fixed-price model of Chapter 4. Secondly, we relax the assumption made in our first dynamic model (Chapter 4), that the capital stock remains fixed, and instead allow it to vary as well. This extension of the Ott and Ott and Christ analysis was first undertaken by Blinder and Solow (1973). They noted, quite correctly, that the earlier literature had made a somewhat contradictory assumption, namely, that although net investment was assumed to be taking place, nevertheless the capital stock was treated as remaining constant. This was in direct contrast to the treatment of government debt, the adjustment of which formed the basis for the dynamics of the system. Moreover, in introducing the dynamics of capital accumulation in an inflationary context, it becomes necessary to distinguish between the physical capital itself and the financial claims on capital issued by firms, which we take to be equity. The final modification pertains to our treatment of expectations. Whereas in the short run these could be taken as given, over time they evolve and are determined endogenously.

The model is 'intermediate run' in the following two senses. First, it makes the traditional Keynesian assumption that although capital is accumulated over time, instantaneously it is fixed. Labour is the only short-run variable factor of production which is adjusted to meet the demand-determined output. It therefore does not allow for the substitution of capital for labour (or vice versa) in response to their relative price movements. The second sense in which it is intermediate run is that, unlike the Blinder—Solow model in which the equilibrium they consider is one with a zero rate of investment, the equilibrium for this model is one in which investment is occurring at a positively, endogenously determined rate. The reason for defining it in this way is discussed in Chapter 7 below.

Our final model of the closed economy is presented in Chapter 8. This is a long-run model in which the full capital deepening effects of investment are introduced. In addition, this chapter seeks to integrate some of the more advanced theoretical issues introduced previously in Chapter 3, but which hitherto were not fully treated. For example, in Chapter 3 we will be discussing the implications of stock and flow constraints in continuous time models and their implications for product market equilibrium. We will also be showing how the introduction of capital gains on financial assets, required for the consistent accounting of the system in real terms, also imposes dynamic behaviour on the system. These problems, which are of a somewhat more technical nature, are included in greater generality in this chapter.

Part II introduces international transactions into the model. But we hasten to emphasize at the outset that we do not intend to give a detailed treatment of international economics. Obviously space limitations preclude this and in any event, there are many excellent references available dealing with this subject; see e.g. Takayama (1972), Stern (1973), Mundell (1968), Caves and Jones (1973). Rather, this part should be viewed as an extension of part I to a small open economy, and in many respects our analysis parallels our discussion in earlier chapters quite closely.

Specifically, Chapter 9 reviews the basic static macroeconomic model of a small country. This is the analogue of the *IS—LM* type models discussed in

Chapter 2. Chapter 10 extends this model to allow for variable prices and in particular provides a framework for analysing the short-run effects of foreign inflation on the domestic economy and the appropriate monetary, fiscal, and exchange rate policies to deal with it. This is still a short-run model and can be viewed as an extension to Chapter 6.

Chapters 11 and 12 deal with the longer-run dynamic models of an open economy, incorporating the dynamics of international capital flows, together with that of asset accumulation. Chapter 11 looks at this question within the context of a fixed price — fixed exchange rate economy. It therefore represents the analogue to Chapter 4. Chapter 12 extends this analysis one stage further by introducing the rate of inflation and considers the longer-run effects of monetary and fiscal policies in the context of an inflationary economy. Moreover, it deals with both fixed and flexible exchange rate regimes. On the other hand it is less general than the corresponding chapters for the closed economy, Chapters 7, 8, in that purely for reasons of analytical tractability, we are forced to assume that physical capital remains fixed.

With few exceptions, the analysis of monetary and fiscal policies throughout Parts I and II deals with them in the sense of considering the effects, over various time horizons, of some *fixed* policy, which is maintained throughout. For example, one standard kind of exercise is to consider the short-run and long-run effects of a *sustained* increase in government expenditure, with the only adjustment in the stock of money or bonds being that required to finance the induced government deficits as they occur. This form of analysis is standard practice in modern macroeconomic theory and undoubtedly provides a lot of insight. However, in reality governments do not maintain fixed policies in this way. On the contrary, they are continually changing their monetary and fiscal instruments in order to try and achieve certain specified objectives. Part III therefore takes up the question of stabilization policy, though treating it at a fairly general level. Chapter 13 deals with some of the more traditional aspects of this topic, while some of the more recent developments in optimal stabilization theory are outlined and applied in the concluding chapter.

3   Methodology

We have already remarked that this book is primarily a theoretical exercise. The basic analytical method used is that of comparative statics. Essentially what this involves is to study the economic system at a given state and to see how it is affected by changes in various factors, which at that point of time can be taken as given. Depending upon what is taken as given determines whether we are dealing with a situation of short-run equilibrium or some kind of longer-run steady-rate equilibrium. We also consider the evolution of the system over time and where possible discuss its stability properties. In general our strategy is to proceeed from a consideration of short-run (sometimes instantaneous) equilibrium to the steady-state equilibrium, to which a stable system will converge.

Much of contemporary macroeconomic theory proceeds in this fashion, so in this respect our approach is not very different. However, this mode of analysis does have its limitations. One serious difficulty is that we are restricted to looking only at some kind of equilibrium situation, which typically holds instantaneously (short run) or in the steady state (long run). The problem is — particularly with continuous-time models — that both these extremes may themselves be of limited economic interest. The instantaneous equilibrium is too short in that it allows insufficient time for relevant feedbacks to occur; the long-run steady-state equilibrium is too long, in that it takes an infinite time to be reached. It may be of limited interest, at least for practical policy purposes, to consider a stationary state in which investment and savings has ceased.

While it is essential to be aware of these limitations, comparative statics is still an extremely important and fundamental method of analysis. But it must be used properly, especially if one wishes to use any conclusions obtained in this way, as the basis for policy decisions. For example, one would not want to base policy recommendations too literally on the comparative static properties of some long-run steady-state equilibrium. But nevertheless this kind of analysis can provide a good deal of significant information. Perhaps the most appropriate way to view the role of comparative statics as the basis for policy discussions is the following. Knowing something about the initial effects of some policy (the instantaneous equilibrium) and the terminal effects (the steady-state equilibrium), should yield one a good deal of insight into the likely effects of the policy over some more relevant intermediate finite time horizon. In other words, these two extremes should be treated as reference points, which provide a foundation upon which more practical policy decisions can be based.

A second approach to making steady-state comparative statics more operational is to *define* the system in such a way that its steady-state equilibrium, which, although in theory reached only in infinite time, nevertheless may be approached quite closely in finite time. For this reason, the intermediate-run equilibrium we consider in Chapter 7, in which investment proceeds at a constant (endogenously determined) rate, rather than ceases, may be particularly relevant for policy purposes.

Finally, at a more practical level, an alternative method which is often proposed for analysing the dynamic properties of macroeconomic models such as those we shall be developing, is that of numerical simulation. While this approach is also important, it too has its limitations. The behaviour of a reasonably complex system typically depends rather critically upon the exact parameter values chosen, and only rarely are definitive answers provided to issues pertaining to the dynamics of the system. In assessing these results, it is important to have some idea of the theoretical properties of the model, to serve as background and to which such simulations can be related. In this respect, the two approaches are complements rather than substitutes.

PART I. THE CLOSED ECONOMY

2

REVIEW OF BASIC MACROECONOMIC MODEL

1. Some preliminary concepts

Traditional macroeconomic theory is concerned with analysing certain aggregate economic variables. These include, among other things, such variables as the level of employment, the level of real income and its components, consumption and investment, the quantity of money, the rate of interest, the level of prices and more recently the rate of inflation. In most cases these aggregates are fictions. For example, there is no such thing as *the* rate of interest, or *the* level of prices, or *the* level of real output etc. Rather, there are *many* rates of interest, and millions of different commodities each having its own price. To formulate an economic model capable of studying each individual economic quantity is obviously an impossible task and considerable insight into the economic system can be obtained by analysing these aggregates. However, it should be clearly understood that macroeconomic analysis presupposes a considerable level of aggregation. Specifically, conventional theory tends to aggregate the economy up to four markets namely

      (i) the output or product market,
     (ii) the money market,
    (iii) the bond market,
    (iv) the labour market.

Because of Walras' law, which we shall discuss more fully in Chapter 3 below, only three of these markets are independent. Hence one of them can be eliminated, since its equilibrium is assured by the equilibrium of the other three. Traditionally, it is the bond market which is eliminated, with the analysis focusing on the other three. But there is really no reason why this should be so, and a well defined macroeconomic theory could just as easily be developed in terms of, say, the money market, the bond market and the labour market.

In order to provide a framework for the rest of this book, this chapter is devoted to summarizing the basic macroeconomic model. Because detailed treatment of the underlying relationships can be found in numerous excellent tests, our discussion will necessarily be brief, focusing on those issues most

relevant to subsequent discussion.[1] The model is constructed by first developing the demand side of the system, described by the output and money
markets. To complete the model one must consider the determination of
supply and this involves analysing the labour market.

The starting point for any macroeconomic model is the national income
accounts. These can be looked at from different viewpoints enabling one to
break down gross national product (*GNP*) in several different ways. One basic
way of considering *GNP* is from the point of view of expenditure on final
output. Assuming a closed economy, this is described by the relationship

$$GNP = C + I + G \tag{2.1}$$

where C = consumption expenditure by the private sector,
   I = gross private domestic investment,
   G = total government purchases of goods and services.
That is, output must either be consumed by the private sector, invested by
the private sector, or purchased by the government. Throughout the book we
shall assume that investment goods do not depreciate, so that there is no need
to distinguish between gross and net investment.

In an open economy, the national income accounts must also take account
of transactions involving foreign residents, so that (2.1) must be modified to:

$$GNP = C_d + I_d + G_d + X \tag{2.2}$$

where C_d = private consumption expenditure by domestic residents for
   domestically produced goods,
   I_d = private investment expenditure by domestic residents for
   domestically produced goods,
   G_d = domestic government expenditure on domestically produced
   goods,
   X = exports.
Using the relationships

$$C = C_d + C_m$$

$$I = I_d + I_m$$

$$G = G_d + G_m$$

where the subscript 'm' denotes imports, (measured in terms of domestic
currency) and observing that total imports, *IM* are defined by

$$IM = C_m + I_m + G_m$$

the *GNP* for the open economy can be written in the alternative form

$$GNP = C + I + G + X - IM. \tag{2.3}$$

Since in Part I, we shall be concerned with a closed economy, we shall
not require (2.2), (2.3) for the meantime. We will, however, make extensive

use of them in Part II, where we extend our analysis to deal with problems facing an open economy.

Apart from the break down according to expenditure on final product, there are at least two other ways, in which the flow of *GNP* can be divided. First, there is the relationship

$$GNP = C + S + T + R_f \tag{2.4}$$

where S = total savings,

T = net tax payments,

R_f = transfer payments to foreigners by domestic residents.

This break down of *GNP* describes how the income earned by the sale of production of goods is disposed of. According to (2.4), it can be spent on consumption goods; it can be saved; it can be used to pay taxes; or it can be used for transfer payments to foreigners.

Secondly, income can be considered from the viewpoint of the type of income generated by the production process; that is income may be earned in the form of wages and salaries, corporate profit, rental income, dividend income, interest income etc. All of these ways of looking at income are important and which form one chooses, is dictated largely by the problem one is analysing. In the main, the first two break downs are the most usual in conventional macro theory, although in analysing distributional questions, the income-component break down becomes particularly important.

Before turning to the analysis of the model, we should review the notion of nominal as opposed to real *GNP*. Conventional national income accounts are measured in current dollars; i.e. in nominal terms. Thus an increase in the nominal *GNP* between two time periods may be due either to an increase in prices or to an increase in real output (or both). To get a measure of real activity, which is surely one of the key economic variables with which we are concerned, it is necessary to deflate the nominal *GNP* by an index of the price level. In practice the question of the deflator often poses a nasty statistical problem. In our case, as we shall be aggregating up to a single output, the index number problem implicit in the transition from nominal to real *GNP* largely disappears (or more correctly is side-stepped).

2. The output market

As indicated, the basic asumption underlying our highly aggregated level of analysis is that the economy produces only one commodity. This can be used either for consumption, or it can be invested. In this latter case it is accumulated as a capital good and combined with the other factor of production, labour, to produce more output. Assuming a closed economy, equilibrium in the commodity market is described by the equation

$$Y = C + I + G \tag{2.5}$$

where Y = real output, or national income,
$\quad\quad C$ = real private demand for consumption,
$\quad\quad I$ = real private demand for investment,
$\quad\quad G$ = real government expenditure.

Equation (2.5) must not be confused with the national income identity (2.1). It is an *equilibrium* condition and need not be satisfied; the national income identity, on the other hand, holds definitionally. The distinction between identities and equilibrium relationships has played a prominent role in the history of macroeconomic theory. While we do not wish to discuss this issue here, we will have something to say on it in Chapter 3.

Equation (2.5) has been written in real terms. Given the assumptions of a single output, it must apply whether written in real or nominal terms. With more than one output, the conversion from nominal to real output would involve choosing a numeraire commodity in defining real income. The reason for focusing on real quantities, rather than nominal, is the notion that individuals formulate their underlying demands in real terms. That is they are concerned with *real* consumption or *real* investment, rather than the corresponding nominal quantities. The extent to which this is true is an empirical question, and some evidence, at least for consumption, suggests that individuals may be subject to some degree of 'money illusion'.[2] In any event, if people do formulate their plans in real terms, it is clearly more appropriate to postulate behaviour for C, I in real terms and hence to formulate our product market equilibrium in real terms as well.

It should be further noted that, as well as distinguishing between consumption and investment demand, we have also distinguished government expenditure from private expenditure. The reason for this is that government expenditure decisions are usually motivated by different considerations from private expenditure plans. Consequently, different behavioural relationships are required to explain private and public demand for output. Nevertheless, it does remain true that government expenditure must either take the form of consumption or investment.

If we knew what determined the three components C, I, G, we would have a theory for Y. Thus the first task is to develop behavioural relationships for these demand aggregates. The simplest theory, taught in elementary books on the subject, postulates the consumption function[3]

$$C = C(Y) \qquad 0 < C' < 1 \tag{2.6}$$

with $I = \bar{I}, G = \bar{G}$. That is, consumption depends upon income, while investment and government expenditure are both exogenously determined. Substituting these relationships into (2.5) we obtain

$$Y = C(Y) + \bar{I} + \bar{G} \tag{2.7}$$

so that Y can be solved uniquely in terms of the exogenous values of investment and government expenditure. We thus have a theory of income, but not a very interesting one.

The next level of analysis involves postulating more reasonable, and richer relationships for consumption and particularly investment.

As a first approximation, one might postulate consumption to be a function of real disposable income. That is

$$C = C(Y^D) \qquad 0 < C' < 1 \tag{2.8}$$

where
$$Y^D = Y - T \tag{2.9}$$

and Y^D denotes real disposable income

T denotes real taxes.

Taxes themselves are typically endogenous, varying with the level of income.[4] For the present purposes of review, however, T can be assumed to be constant without causing any difficulty.

Subsequent, more sophisticated, studies of the consumption function have begun their analyses from underlying utility maximization considerations. The upshot of these contributions is that consumption is made to depend on wealth in some form, and possibly the interest rate, as well as disposable income.[5] Thus instead of (2.8) one would postulate

$$C = C(Y^D, r, V) \qquad 0 < C_1 < 1, \quad C_2 \gtrless 0, \quad C_3 > 0 \tag{2.10}$$

where r = rate of interest

V = real wealth of the private sector, defined more precisely in Chapter 3 below.

We do not attempt to justify (2.10) on more rigorous grounds here. This has been done in numerous text books, as well as in the original articles themselves. We will, however, subsequently have occasion to use a form of the consumption function similar to (2.10).

The simplest version of the investment function postulates

$$I = I(r) \qquad I' < 0. \tag{2.11}$$

This can be justified in terms of the discounted present value criterion. Briefly, a profit maximizing firm should invest in those projects yielding a positive discounted present value. As the interest rate rises, the number of projects having this property will fall, so that the amount of investment undertaken by the firm will fall, implying (2.11).[6]

While for present purposes (2.11), will suffice, we will be considering more sophisticated versions of the investment function. Specifically, we postulate

$$I = I(r, Y, K) \qquad I_1 < 0, \quad I_2 > 0, \quad I_3 < 0 \tag{2.12}$$

where investment depends positively on the level of income; negatively on the interest rate and level of existing capital stock K. There is also the question of the form of the interest rate. Much of the analysis of subsequent chapters deals with an inflationary environment when it is the real rather than the nominal, interest rate which is relevant. This will be discussed further at the appropriate places.

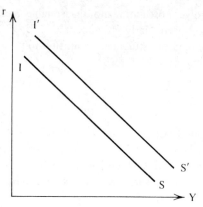

Fig. 2.1 *IS curve*

While (2.12) is still fairly crude, it is nevertheless a significant theoretical improvement over (2.11). Under stringent conditions it can be justified within the framework of the 'neoclassical' theory of investment as developed by Jorgenson.[7] For example, suppose that the desired capital stock K^*, is determined by

$$K^* = F(r, Y) \qquad F_1 < 0, \quad F_2 > 0$$

and that the actual capital stock is adjusted towards K^* at a rate proportional to the gap $(K^* - K)$, (the conventional stock-adjustment relationship) so that,

$$I \equiv \dot{K} = \gamma(K^* - K) \qquad \gamma > 0$$

one immediately derives (2.12).

The conventional macroeconomic model assumes a consumption function and investment function of the form (2.8) and (2.11) respectively. Substituting these relationships into the product market equilibrium relationship (2.5), yields the familiar *IS* curve

$$Y = C(Y - T) + I(r) + G. \tag{2.13}$$

This curve gives the combinations of Y and r which will keep the product market in equilibrium. Differentiating both sides with respect to Y, we have

$$\left(\frac{dr}{dY}\right)_{IS} = \frac{1 - C'}{I'} < 0$$

implying a downward sloping curve as indicated in Figure 2.1. The reason is clear. As income rises, consumption rises, but by less than income. The only way the excess output can be absorbed is by additional investment and for this to be forthcoming, the interest rate must fall.

It is also apparent that the position of the *IS* curve depends upon the positions of the investment function, consumption function and government expenditure. An increase in government expenditure, or equivalently an outward shift in either the *C* or *I* functions will push the *IS* curve outwards to *I' S'* in Figure 2.1

3. The money market

It is clear that equilibrium in the product market alone is insufficient to determine the equilibrium of the system. The *IS* curve only determines pairs of *Y, r* which are consistent with equilibrium in the output market. Even if the price level is held constant, another market is required to determine the unique (Y, r) pair and this market is traditionally taken to be the money market.

The conventional formulation of the real demand for money is

$$\frac{M^D}{P} = L(Y, r) \qquad L_1 > 0, \quad L_2 < 0, \qquad (2.14)$$

where M^D denotes the nominal demand for money and *P* is the price level. The original justification for (2.14) given by Keynes was that money was held partly for transactions purposes, which vary with *Y*, and partly for speculative purposes, which vary inversely with *r*. Initially, these two motives were written as separate functions. More recently it has been recognized that they cannot very usefully be separated in this way. The amount held for transactions purposes will depend upon costs of holding money and therefore, upon the interest rate.[8] Likewise the amount held for speculative purposes is likely to vary with income. More recently, the demand for money has been considered within a more general portfolio framework in which the demand for money is considered along with the elements for all other financial assets. This approach leads to a demand function of the form

$$\frac{M^D}{P} = L(Y, r, V) \qquad L_1 > 0, \quad L_2 < 0, \quad L_3 > 0 \qquad (2.15)$$

where as before $V =$ real wealth in the hands of the private sector.[9]

The nominal supply of money, M^S, say, consists of currency held by the public C^P, plus demand deposits held by the public in the commercial banking system D^P say, so that

$$M^S = C^P + D^P. \qquad (2.16)$$

This is only one definition of the stock of money and in fact it is the narrowest one. There are many other definitions, the most common of which redefines M^S to include time deposits held by the public in the commercial banking system as well.

But, however M^S is defined, the conventional macroeconomic model usually considers it to be exogenous, (*M* say), determined directly by government policy, so that the real money supply is

$$\frac{M^S}{P} = \frac{M}{P}.$$

(2.17)

As a first approximation this may be adequate, but in fact, the total money supply is at best only an indirect policy instrument. The more direct variables of monetary control include the *monetary base,* which is essentially the unborrowed reserves of the commercial banking system, the discount rate, and the reserve requirement ratio. The monetary base tends to be the monetary instrument for short-run stabilization purposes, and is controlled through open market operations, whereby the central bank enters the market for government securities. The other two instruments tend to be longer-run instruments of monetary control and to be adjusted infrequently.

Following Teigen (1964), the total money supply can be related to the volume of base money in the following way. Assuming that the public holds h per cent of its money as currency and the remainder $(1 - h)$ per cent as demand deposits we have

$$C^P = hM^S$$

(2.18a)

$$D^P = (1 - h)M^S.$$

(2.18b)

The central bank sets a required reserve ratio x which determines the fraction of demand deposits that the commercial banks must hold as required reserves R^r, with the central bank. Thus we have

$$R^r = xD^P = x(1 - h)M^S.$$

(2.19)

The total reserves provided by the central bank, R say, consist of the reserves of the commercial banking system, R_1, and currency held in the hands of the non-bank public, so that

$$R = R_1 + C^P$$

(2.20)

There are two ways by which the central bank may provide these reserves. First, it may supply unborrowed reserves through buying government securities on the open market. Such reserves, denoted by R^u say, are often referred to as the monetary base. Secondly, it may provide borrowed reserves R^b by lending to the commercial banks. Thus we have

$$R = R^u + R^b$$

(2.21a)

To the extent that the reserves held by the commercial banks exceed the quantity required, they are said to be holding excess reserves R^e. Hence we must also have

$$R_1 = R^r + R^e.$$

(2.21b)

It therefore follows from (2.20), (2.21) that

$$R^u = R^r + C^P + (R^e - R^b)$$

and substituting (2.19) and (2.18a) yields

$$R^u = [x(1-h)+h] M^S + (R^e - R^b). \tag{2.22}$$

The quantity $R^e - R^b$ is usually referred to as 'free reserves' and can be denoted by R^f say. These free reserves can be used by the banking system to make loans which it views as profitable. Assuming that the banking system can lend at the market rate of interest r, and borrow from the central bank at the discount rate r_d, it seems reasonable to hypothesize that the number of loans made will vary positively with the spread between these two rates of interest. Accordingly, the free reserves — those reserves not loaned out — will vary negatively with $(r - r_d)$, so that

$$R^f = g(r - r_d) \quad \text{where } g' < 0. \tag{2.23}$$

Substituting (2.23) into (2.22), we can solve for M^S in the form

$$M^S = \frac{R^u}{x(1-h)+h} - \frac{g(r-r_d)}{x(1-h)+h}. \tag{2.24}$$

Equation (2.24) thus describes the supply of money in terms of the instrument of monetary control, and an endogenous component, reflecting the profit seeking motives of the commercial banks. Both of these are multiplied by a factor $1/[x(1-h)+h]$ which reflects the familiar multiple expansion of the banking system. Note that if $h = 0$, so that all money consists only of demand deposits, this factor reduces to $1/x$, the inverse of the reserve requirement ratio.

Thus the upshot of the Teigen model is that the money supply is in fact endogenous, bearing a positive relationship to the market rate of interest r. Fortunately, the term $g(r - r_d)$ makes little difference to the conclusions of the conventional model, so that in fact little is lost by abstracting from the commercial banking system.

Thus treating $M^S = M$ as exogenous, the equating $M^S = M^d$, equilibrium in the money market is given by

$$\frac{M}{P} = L(Y, r) \quad L_1 > 0, \quad L_2 < 0. \tag{2.25}$$

Equation (2.25) defines the well known *LM* curve. Given P it determines the combinations of (Y, r) which will keep the money market in equilibrium. Differentiating (2.25) with respect to Y we obtain

$$\left(\frac{dr}{dY}\right)_{LM} = -\frac{L_1}{L_2} > 0$$

implying an upward slope as indicated in Figure 2.2. The reason for this is that an increase in the interest rate leads to a fall in the speculative demand for money as people switch to holding interest-bearing assets. With a fixed supply of money, equilibrium can be maintained only provided people can be

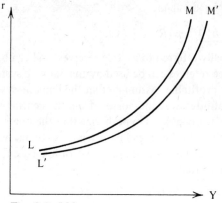

Fig. 2.2. *LM curve*

induced to hold more for transactions purposes and this will be so only if income is increased.

As well as having a positive slope, the *LM* curve traditionally has the convex shape indicated in Figure 2.2. This reflects the notion that at high rates of interest speculative balances have been induced to a minimum. Hence at this point any increase in the level of income must be accompanied by a relatively large increase in the rate of interest, in order to free the necessary money for the additional transactions needs. At the other extreme of a low interest rate, the *LM* curve is relatively flat. This is a consequence of the assumption that at low r, money and bonds become very close substitutes making the demand for money much more interest elastic.

Note that if one was to replace the assumption that $M^S = M$, with the endogenous money supply function (2.24), the *LM* curve would preserve its same upward sloping shape. The only difference would be for the interest elasticity of the supply of money to give it a somewhat flatter slope.

Finally, we should note that the position of the *LM* curve depends upon the supply of money M and the price level P. An increase in M or a decrease in P will cause it to shift to the right as indicated to $L'M'$; a reduction in M or an increase in P will cause the reverse shift.

4.   Equilibrium in product and money markets

The equilibrium level of income and interest rate is determined by combining the *IS* and *LM* curves. Considering the two equations

$$Y - C(Y - T) - I(r) - G = 0 \tag{2.26a}$$

$$\frac{M}{P} - L(Y, r) = 0 \tag{2.26b}$$

where for simplicity taxes T are taken to be exogenous, it is clear that given our assumptions, they can be solved uniquely for Y, r in terms of P, G, M, T.

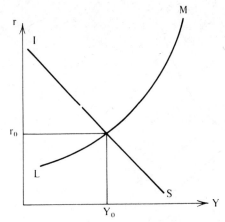

Fig. 2.3 *Determination of equilibrium*

This can be seen graphically in Figure 2.3, where the equilibrium is obtained as the intersection of the *IS* and *LM* curves.

In particular the solution

$$Y = Y(P; \quad G, M, T) \tag{2.27}$$

relating equilibrium income as determined by demand to price can be viewed as an aggregate demand function. Differentiating the pair of equations (2.26) with respect to P we have

$$\begin{pmatrix} 1-C' & -I' \\ \\ -L_1 & -L_2 \end{pmatrix} \begin{pmatrix} \dfrac{\partial Y}{\partial P} \\ \\ \dfrac{\partial r}{\partial P} \end{pmatrix} = \begin{pmatrix} 0 \\ \\ \dfrac{M}{P^2} \end{pmatrix} \tag{2.28}$$

and solving for $\partial Y/\partial P$ yields

$$\frac{\partial Y}{\partial P} = \frac{I'M/P^2}{-L_2(1-C')-L_1I'} < 0 \tag{2.29}$$

so that the aggregate demand curve is indeed downward sloping.

5. Monetary and fiscal policy in the simple IS–LM model

An expansionary fiscal policy in this simple model is typically characterized by an increase in real government expenditure. Like any other expenditure, government expenditure needs to be financed. Broadly speaking, the government can achieve this in three ways;

      (i) by issuing bonds,
      (ii) by printing money,
      (iii) by increasing taxes.

The conventional macroeconomic model typically assumes case (i); i.e. the

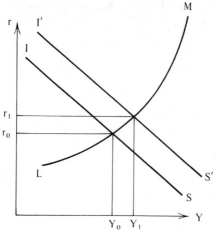

Fig. 2.4 *Expansionary fiscal policy*

government finances its expenditure through borrowing from the public. In the present section we shall do likewise. However, the mode of deficit financing is an important issue and we shall have a lot more to say about it in subsequent chapters, where we shall show that it is crucial to the effectiveness of government expenditure and indeed the overall dynamic behaviour of the economy.

Graphically, a bond-financed increase in government expenditure can be illustrated in Figure 2.4 by an outward shift in the *IS* curve, causing income and the interest rate to rise from their initial levels (Y_0, r_0) to higher levels (Y_1, r_1). With the money supply being held constant, the *LM* curve remains fixed, although it would move if case (ii) was in effect. A simple economic expanation for the shift illustrated in Figure 2.4 runs as follows. With taxes held constant, the immediate effect of the increase in government expenditure is to raise income and with it, the transactions demand for money. At the same time the financing of this increased government expenditure by the issuing of additional bonds forces the interest rate up. The effect of this is to reduce the level of investment demand, tending to partially offset the immediate effects of the increase in G. The ultimate effects are a new equilibrium with a higher level of income, consumption, government expenditure, interest rate, but a lower level of investment.

Algebraically the effect of the increase in government expenditure on the equilibrium levels of income and interest rate can be obtained by differentiating (2.26) with respect to G and solving for $\partial Y/\partial G$, $\partial r/\partial G$. These effects are given by

$$\frac{\partial Y}{\partial G} = \frac{1}{1 - C' + I'L_1/L_2} > 0 \qquad (2.30a)$$

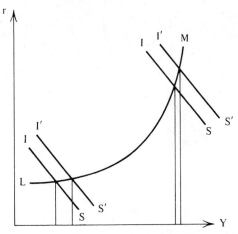

Fig. 2.5 *Effectiveness of fiscal policy*

$$\frac{\partial r}{\partial G} = \frac{-L_1/L_2}{1 - C' + I'L_1/L_2} > 0. \tag{2.30b}$$

Note that (2.30a) is less than the elementary multiplier $1/(1 - C')$, due to the offsetting effects on investment of the higher rate of interest. This phenomenon is often referred to as the (partial) 'crowding out' of private investment by government expenditure; see Blinder and Solow (1973).

The effectiveness of fiscal policy has for a long time been a major policy issue. More recently interest in the topic has revived under the notion of 'monetarism' and we shall have more to say about this later. A first approximation to the question can be answered by considering the fiscal multiplier (2.30). It is seen that $\partial Y/\partial G$ varies inversely with $-L_1/L_2$, which is just the slope of the *LM* curve. In other words if the *LM* curve is relatively flat (i.e. low Y, low r) L_1/L_2 is small and the multiplier is close to $1/(1 - C')$, its value in the absence of a money market. At the other end as the *LM* curve gets steep (i.e. high Y, high r), $-L_1/L_2$ becomes large and the multiplier becomes smaller. In the limiting case where the interest elasticity of the demand for money tends to zero, the government expenditure multiplier tends to zero. In this case the *LM* curve is just

$$\frac{M}{P} = L(Y) \tag{2.25'}$$

implying that the level of income is determined solely by the quantity of money. Equation (2.25') is therefore essentially just a statement of the quantity theory of money. These differences in the effectiveness of fiscal policy are illustrated in Figure 2.5.

It is also possible that the fiscal policy may take the form of a tax change either in conjunction with the change in government expenditure or in

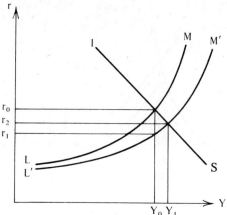

Fig. 2.6 *Expansionary monetary policy*

isolation. These changes can be analysed along similar lines and the special case of the balanced-budget multiplier is briefly considered below.

Monetary policy in this model is formalized by a change in M. Thus an expansionary monetary policy causes the *LM* curve to shift to the right, leading to a higher level of income and lower rate of interest. In economic terms, the immediate impact of the increase in money supply is to lower the rate of interest to r_1 say, in Figure 2.6. This reduction in the interest rate will stimulate investment, raising income and with it the transactions demand for money. With M fixed at its new level, the interest rate is pulled back up partially towards its initial value r_0, with equilibrium being reached at the point r_2. At this point, income, consumption, and investment are all higher than at their original levels; the interest rate on the other hand is lower.

The analytical expressions for the effect of a change in the supply of money on the economy can be calculated by differentiating (2.26) with respect to M and solving for $\partial Y/\partial M$, $\partial r/\partial M$. These are given by

$$\frac{\partial Y}{\partial M} = \frac{I'/PL_2}{1 - C' + I'L_1/L_2} > 0 \qquad (2.31a)$$

$$\frac{\partial r}{\partial M} = \frac{(1 - C')/PL_2}{1 - C' + I'L_1/L_2} < 0. \qquad (2.31b)$$

The effectiveness of monetary policy can be analysed in much the same way as was the effectiveness of fiscal policy. It is clear that the larger I' (numerically), i.e. the flatter the *IS* curve, or the smaller L_2 (numerically), i.e. the steeper the *LM* curve, the more effective is monetary policy. On the other hand as $I' \to 0$ or $L_2 \to \infty$ monetary policy becomes ineffective in influencing income. These cases are illustrated in Figure 2.7.

Consequently, at least at this level of analysis, the relative efficiency of monetary and fiscal policy can be viewed as an empirical matter. Dividing

(2.30a) by (2.31a) we have

$$\frac{\partial Y/\partial G}{\partial Y/\partial M} = \frac{PL_2}{I'}. \tag{2.32}$$

Thus their relative effects depend upon the interest responsiveness of the demand for money on the one hand, and the interest responsiveness of the investment demand on the other. There is, however, a good deal more to the debate than this. Issues like wealth effects, the dynamic properties of monetary and fiscal policy need to be considered and these will be discussed in subsequent chapters below.

It needs to be stressed that we have based this discussion of monetary and fiscal policies on only the simplest behavioural functions. Even within the essentially static framework developed here, the wealth effects just alluded to can be shown to induce further shifts in the *IS* and *LM* curves. However, as we shall argue in Chapter 4 below, to be consistent with the underlying budget constraint of the economy in a discrete-time model, those must in fact operate with a one-period lag. Thus the fiscal and monetary multipliers we have been discussing here in fact turn out to be quite similar to the first period effects obtained in more sophisticated dynamic models.

As a final point, our analysis has thus far treated M, G as exogenous policy variables, which together determine the endogenous variables

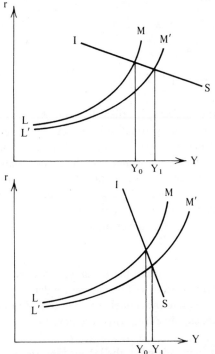

Fig. 2.7 *Effectiveness of monetary policy*

(Y, r). But a possible policy question might be to assign certain desired levels to (Y, r), $(\bar{Y}, \bar{r})$, say, which the policy maker deems as desirable, and consider what combination of (M, G) will succeed in achieving these targets. In other words, the roles of the two pairs of variables (Y, r), (M, G) in (2.26) are reversed; $(\bar{Y}, \bar{r})$ become the exogenously determined policy goals, while (2.26) now determines the endogenous values for (M, G) which will achieve these goals. This of course, is about the simplest formulation of a stabilization problem where the issue is to choose policy instruments in accordance with certain objectives. This topic is discussed at length in Part III, below.

6. The balanced-budget multiplier

We have stated that an increase in government expenditure will need to be financed. Either bond financing or money financing will increase the net indebtedness of the government to the private sector (see Chapter 3 below). An alternative policy which is commonly considered, is one in which the increase in government expenditure is matched by an equal increase in taxes, so that the government budget remains incrementally balanced. In this case no additional increase in net indebtedness is incurred by the government. This form of financial government expenditure yields what is usually referred to as the 'balanced-budget multiplier'.

Algebraically, it is obtained in the present model by letting T and G change simultaneously subject to

$$dT = dG \tag{2.33}$$

Using (2.33), it is readily shown that

$$\frac{\partial Y}{\partial G} = \frac{1 - C'}{1 - C' + I'L_1/L_2} \leqslant 1. \tag{2.34}$$

This consists of two effects; the expansionary effect due to higher government expenditure, and the contractionary effect of higher taxes. However, the tax effect is not fully offsetting. The reason is that it operates through consumption, so that its effectiveness is constrained by the private marginal propensity to consume, which typically is less than one. Note that if investment demand is interest-inelastic, the balanced-budget multiplier is simply unity. Otherwise, it is smaller than one, due to the partial crowding out of private investment as a consequence of the higher interest rate.

7. The labour market

We have already seen how the output market and money market equilibrium conditions can be combined to yield an aggregate demand function for the economy. To complete the model and to determine the price level we must derive an aggregate supply curve. This is achieved by considering the labour market.

Aggregate output is assumed to be related to the labour input N and the level of capital stock K by the aggregate production function

$$Y = F(N, K).$$

The time horizon considered by the macromodel is sufficiently short so that the capital stock is fixed at $\bar{K}$ say, leaving labour as the only variable factor of production. To highlight this we write

$$Y = F(N, \bar{K}) \equiv f(N)$$

where $f' > 0, f'' < 0$ implying that labour has positive but diminishing marginal product.

To determine the demand for labour, we consider a competitive firm, whose objective is to maximize profit Π. Defining

$$\Pi = Pf(N^D) - WN$$

where W denotes the money wage of labour, the demand for labour N^D is determined where

$$Pf'(N^D) = W. \tag{2.35}$$

This is the familar first order condition that the firm should employ labour up to the point where the value of its marginal product equals its wage rate. If the firm is a monopolist, facing a downward sloping demand curve for its product, it is easily shown that its demand for labour is determined where

$$P(1 + 1/e)f'(N^D) = W \tag{2.35'}$$

where e = price elasticity of demand. Assuming the aggregate economy to be some average of competitive and monopolistic elements, this argument suggests an aggregate demand for labour depending on the real wage and of the form

$$\frac{W}{P} = \phi(N^D). \tag{2.36}$$

Moreover, the assumption of diminishing marginal product implies

$$\phi'(N^D) < 0$$

so that the demand for labour curve is in fact downward sloping.

The supply of labour is traditionally determined within the context of an individual's work–leisure choice. Specifically, the individual is assumed to maximize a concave utility function which depends upon real income and leisure L subject to an income constraint.[10] Formally the problem is

$$\text{Max } U(Y, L) \tag{2.37a}$$

subject to

$$\left. \begin{aligned} L &= T - N^S \\ Y &= \frac{W}{P}N^S \end{aligned} \right\} \tag{2.37b}$$

where $T =$ fixed number of hours available to work. N^S thus measures the supply of labour in hours worked (man hours when aggregated). Performing the maximization implies the optimality condition

$$U_1 \frac{W}{P} - U_2 = 0$$

and this implies the labour function

$$\frac{W}{P} = \psi(N^S). \tag{2.38}$$

The assumption that individuals are interested in their real income results in a classical labour supply function in which labour supply depends upon the *real* wage. The restrictions imposed on the utility function U are not sufficient to rule out the possibility of a backward bending portion of the labour supply curve. We, however, do not consider this portion and simply assume an upward sloping supply curve,

$$\psi' > 0$$

in the relevant range.

Equilibrium in the labour market is thus obtained where (2.36), (2.38) hold, and in addition where

$$N^D = N^S = N. \tag{2.39}$$

We can thus write our equilibrium condition in the form

$$\frac{W}{P} = \phi(N) = \psi(N). \tag{2.40}$$

Solving (2.40) with the production function, the labour market implies an aggregate supply function, which is independent of P.

8.   **Equilibrium in the classical model**

Adding the labour market equilibrium condition to the previous *IS* and *LM* equations determines the complete equilibrium in the classical system. Recalling these equations we have

$$Y - C(Y - T) - I(r) - G = 0 \tag{2.41a}$$

$$\frac{M}{P} - L(Y, r) = 0 \tag{2.41b}$$

$$Y - Y(N) = 0 \tag{2.41c}$$

$$\phi(N) = \psi(N) \tag{2.41d}$$

$$\frac{W}{P} = \phi(N). \tag{2.41e}$$

This yields a system of five equations, which in principle can be solved for the five endogenous variables Y, r, P, N, W. However, the solution to this system dichotomizes in a very simple way. Equation (2.41d), equilibrium in the labour market, determines employment N irrespective of the rest of the system. Having determined N the short-run production function (2.41c) then determines output, while the labour demand function (or labour supply function) determines the real wage. With this given value of Y, the output market determines r, while the price level is determined by the money market. Finally given P and the real wage, the money wage immediately follows, completely determining the system.

It is clear that employment, output, and real wages, in this model are determined solely by labour market conditions. In particular, these quantities are independent of G or M. It is thus clear that real activity is independent of fiscal or monetary policy. The effect of an increase in G is to raise the interest rate and to reduce real investment by an amount which exactly offsets the initial increase in G. Put another way, real investment is completely crowded out, being replaced by government expenditure. With a higher interest rate and fixed output, money market equilibrium requires a higher price level. In order to preserve the real wage rate, money wages must rise by the same proportion as prices. The effect of an increase in M on the other hand, is simply to raise P and W by the same proportion, with r, Y, N remaining unchanged. The 'quantity theory of money' is in operation in the sense that the price level moves in proportion to the volume of money.

9. An alternative labour supply function

While it is reasonable to assume that labour demand depends upon the real wage, the assumption that the labour supply also depends upon the real wage is perhaps more questionable. Lack of information etc. suggests that workers may suffer from some degree at least of money illusion and that they do not formulate their labour supply on the basis of the real wage. At the other extreme, we can briefly consider the case where they are interested in their *money* wage so that labour supply is

$$W = \psi(N^S) \qquad \psi'(N^S) > 0. \tag{2.38'}$$

Substituting the labour supply function (2.38') into (2.41), the equilibrium of the system is given by

$$Y - C(Y - T) - I(r) - G = 0 \tag{2.41a}$$

$$\frac{M}{P} - L(Y, r) = 0 \tag{2.41b}$$

$$Y - Y(N) = 0 \tag{2.41c}$$

$$P\phi(N) - \psi(N) = 0 \tag{2.41d}$$

$$\frac{W}{P} - \phi(N) = 0 \tag{2.41e}$$

Now the dichotomy of the classical system breaks down. It is no longer true that labour market alone determines N; instead the entire system is inter-related. In particular, this means that monetary and fiscal policy are now able to influence employment and output. Nevertheless, the model still assumes full employment. The difference is that now the level of employment at which the labour market clears can be shown to be influenced by government policies.

Differentiating the equilibrium equations of the system, one can show in particular

$$\frac{\partial Y}{\partial G} = \frac{1}{(1 - C') + I'L_1/L_2 - I'M(P\phi' - \psi')/L_2 Y'\phi P^2} > 0. \quad (2.42)$$

Comparing (2.42) with (2.30) we see that the multiplier is now reduced from what it was for the pure *IS–LM* model with fixed prices. The reason is that one of the effects of the increase in G is to raise prices, thereby reducing real money balances, raising the interest rate, and providing a partially offsetting contractionary effect. However, unlike the pure classical model of Section 7, the interest rates do not rise sufficiently to lead to an equal reduction in investment demand and the upshot is an increase in income as indicated in (2.42). Put another way, the labour market equilibrium conditions, together with the aggregate production function imply an aggregate supply curve which has the slope

$$\frac{\partial Y}{\partial P} = \frac{Y'\phi}{\psi' - P\phi'} > 0$$

i.e. is upward sloping. It is thus clear that an outward shift in the aggregate demand curve, arising from an increase in G, will lead to a higher level of output and prices. The effects of monetary policy can be similarly analysed, but this is left as an exercise.

10.   Some Keynesian rigidities

The complete models discussed in Section 8 and 9 both share the property that provided money wages, prices and the interest rate are perfectly flexible, the equilibrium of the system will be one with full employment, in the sense that the labour market is cleared. This does not mean, however, that the equilibrium level of employment is necessarily equal to the total labour force. Given the market clearing wage, some people may be quite willing to remain unemployed. In the Classical version of the model, where labour supply depends upon the real wage, the equilibrium level of employ-ment and hence output are determined solely by the labour market and are independent of any monetary or fiscal policies. In the other polar case, where labour supply depends on the money wage, monetary and fiscal policies are generally effective in being able to influence the market clearing level of activity.

Both models, however, exclude the possibility of involuntary unemployment, in the sense of a non-clearing labour market. To incorporate this phenomenon into the model requires some form of rigidity, and inflexibility in money wages, prices, or the rate of interest are capable of explaining it.

For simplicity, we shall return to the case where both labour demand and supply depend upon the real wage.

Formally, the model with rigidities can be described by the following set of equations

$$Y - C(Y - T) - I(r) - G = 0 \tag{2.43a}$$

$$\frac{M}{P} - L(Y, r) = 0 \tag{2.43b}$$

$$W/P = \phi(N^D) \tag{2.43c}$$

$$W/P = \psi(N^S) \tag{2.43d}$$

$$Y = F[\min(N^D, N^S)] \tag{2.43e}$$

$$P = \bar{P}, \quad \text{or} \quad W = \bar{W}, \quad \text{or} \quad r = \bar{r}. \tag{2.43f}$$

Equations (2.43a), (2.43b), just as before are the *IS* and *LM* curves, while (2.43c) and (2.43d) describe labour demand and labour supply respectively. The only difference is that now, since we wish to allow for the possibility of unemployment, we discard the equilibrium condition $N^D = N^S$. The production function (2.43e) relates output to employment, which is given by the smaller of the two quantities N^D, N^S. If $N^D < N^S$ employers hire N^D leaving $N^S - N^D$ involuntarily unemployed; if $N^S < N^D$ employers hire the available supply of labour N^S. The final equation fixes P, W or r, depending upon the rigidity assumed.

The system (2.43) defines six equations determining the six endogenous variables Y, N^D, N^S, P, W, r, and in general these can be uniquely determined. It is clear that there is no reason for $N^D = N^S$, in which case the model will imply either an excess demand for, or excess supply of, labour. The nature of the equilibrium solution, however, depends upon the rigidity assumed. Suppose prices were rigid so that $P = \bar{P}$. In this case Y and r are determined by the *IS* and *LM* curves, just as they are in the simple model discussed in Section 4 above. The production function then determines employment, the smaller of N^D and N^S. Substituting this value of employment into (2.43c), (2.43d) enables one to determine whether $N^D > N^S$ or $N^D < N^S$, as well as the corresponding money wage. The equilibrium is thus determined recursively.

A recursive solution is also obtained when $r = \bar{r}$. In this case, output is determined by product market equilibrium, and given this value of Y, P is now determined so as to equilibrate the money market. Given Y, P, r, the remaining variables N^D, N^S, W are determined through the production function and labour market, just as they are in the rigid price case.

The third case, $W = \bar{W}$, is more complicated. Equilibrium cannot be attained in any simple sequential manner. All variables are determined simultaneously.

11. Some issues in comparative statics

As we discussed in Chapter 1, the basic method of analysis used throughout this book is that of comparative statics. Before proceeding further therefore, it is desirable to consider briefly a couple of issues which arise in connection with this technique.

Much of macroeconomic analysis, whether it be long run or short run, consists of studying relations of the form

$$F^i(x_1, \ldots, x_n; \quad \theta_1, \ldots, \theta_m) \qquad i = 1, \ldots, n \qquad (2.44)$$

where $x = (x_1, \ldots, x_n)$ are n endogenous variables, and $\theta = (\theta_1, \ldots, \theta_m)$ denote m exogenous variables or parameters. In principle we wish to solve for x in terms of the parameters summarized in θ. For this to be possible it is required that there be as many equations (n) as unknowns. Unfortunately, in practice we cannot typically solve explicitly for x in terms of the θ unless the system is of a particularly simple functional form. It is clear that the models we have been discussing in this chapter fit into this general framework.

In considering systems such as (2.44), two important theoretical issues must be considered. First, is the solution unique? In other words, is there only one equilibium which corresponds to a given set of parameters θ? Secondly, what happens to the equilibrium if any of the θs change? This latter question is at the heart of comparative statics.

Let us deal with the uniqueness question first. This can be considered at two levels, namely *locally* and *globally*. We define the solution x^* say, obtained for a given vector of parameters θ^* say, to be *locally* unique if and only if x^* is the only value of x satisfying equations (2.44) for $\theta = \theta^*$, in some neighbourhood of the pair (θ^*, x^*). It is said to be *globally* unique, if the neighbourhood extends over the entire set of feasible pairs (θ, x). These concepts are illustrated for the scalar case in Figure 2.8.

A sufficient condition for the solution of (2.44) for x to be locally unique is that the *Jacobian* of this system defined by the determinant

$$\begin{vmatrix} \dfrac{\partial F^1}{\partial x_1} & \cdots & \dfrac{\partial F^1}{\partial x_n} \\ \vdots & & \vdots \\ \dfrac{\partial F^n}{\partial x_1} & \cdots & \dfrac{\partial F^n}{\partial x_n} \end{vmatrix}$$

be non-zero.

In order to state a sufficient condition for global uniqueness, we must

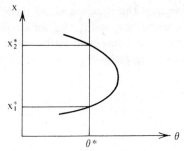

Fig. 2.8 A. *Local but not global uniqueness in neighbourhood of* $(\theta^*, x_1^*), (\theta^*, x_2^*)$.

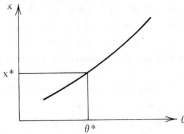

Fig. 2.8 B. *Global uniqueness in neighbourhood of* (θ^*, x^*).

first define the notion of a *P*-matrix. Formally, a real matrix A is a *P*-matrix if all its principal minors (those symmetric around the diagonal) are positive. A sufficient condition for the solution of (2.44) for x to be globally unique is that the *Jacobian matrix*

$$\begin{pmatrix} \dfrac{\partial F^1}{\partial x_1} & \cdots & \dfrac{\partial F^1}{\partial x_n} \\[2ex] \vdots & & \vdots \\[2ex] \dfrac{\partial F^n}{\partial x_1} & \cdots & \dfrac{\partial F^n}{\partial x_n} \end{pmatrix}$$

be a *P*-matrix (see Gale and Nikaido (1965)). In many applications it is often necessary to rearrange the system to get it into this required form.

This latter condition is obviously much more stringent than the non-vanishing of the Jacobian (which it includes as a special case) and in practice will rarely be met. Note, however, from (2.28) that the Jacobian matrix of the *IS–LM* system does meet this requirement, ensuring that the solution is globally unique.

Suppose now for simplicity that $n = 2, m = 1$ so that

$$F^i(x_1, x_2, \theta) = 0 \qquad i = 1, 2 \tag{2.45}$$

and that there is a change in θ (now a scalar). The effect on x_1, x_2 is obtained by partially differentiating (2.45) with respect to θ and solving for $\partial x_1/\partial\theta$, $\partial x_2/\partial\theta$. These are what are often referred to as being comparative static effects. In particular the effect on x_1, say, is given by

$$
\frac{\partial x_1}{\partial \theta} = \frac{\begin{vmatrix} -F_\theta^1 & F_2^1 \\ -F_\theta^2 & F_2^2 \end{vmatrix}}{\begin{vmatrix} F_1^1 & F_2^1 \\ F_1^2 & F_2^2 \end{vmatrix}}
\tag{2.46}
$$

where $F_j^i = \partial F^i/\partial x_j$ as before, and $F_\theta^i = \partial F^i/\partial\theta$. The sign of $\partial x_1/\partial\theta$ is determined by that of the numerator and denominator of (2.46). In particular, the denominator of (2.46) is just the Jacobian of the system. It appears in all comparative static calculations and it is clearly crucial that one be able to attach some sign to it. Sometimes this can be done from the underlying assumptions. This is again the case in the simple *IS–LM* model of (2.26). But in more complex systems, this typically cannot be achieved.

In these instances, restrictions on the denominator can be obtained by appealing to what Samuelson (1947) called the 'correspondence principle'. This refers to the intimate relationship which exists between the comparative static properties of a system on the one hand, and its dynamic stability properties on the other. Consider a change in an exogenous variable which displaces the system from an initial equilibrium. Comparative statics analyses the change in the equilibrium which follows from this initial displacement. While it compares two static situations, it implicitly assumes a stable dynamic adjustment process. The move from one equilibrium to another takes time and will be achieved only as long as the system is stable. Indeed the methods of comparative statics make no sense unless the system is stable, for otherwise any displacement from equilibrium would cause the system to diverge indefinitely. The correspondence principle asserts that we can use the restrictions from dynamic stability considerations to help determine comparative static results.

The simplest way this can be done is to embed the model in a simple dynamic adjustment of the form

$$
\dot{x}_1 = k_1 F^1(x_1, x_2, \theta)
\tag{2.47a}
$$

$$
\dot{x}_2 = k_2 F^2(x_1, x_2, \theta)
\tag{2.47b}
$$

where k_1, k_2 are some arbitrary constants indicating the speed with which x_1 and x_2 change in a disequilibrium situation. Equilibrium is reached when $\dot{x}_1 = \dot{x}_2 = 0$, in which case (2.47) reduce to the static conditions (2.45). In order for (2.47a) to be locally stable we require that (see e.g. Samuelson, 1947, Appendix)

$$k_1 F_1^1 + k_2 F_2^2 < 0 \tag{2.48a}$$

$$k_1 k_2 \begin{vmatrix} F_1^1 & F_2^1 \\ F_1^2 & F_2^2 \end{vmatrix} > 0 \tag{2.48b}$$

Let us assume that we have sufficient information to know the signs (but not the magnitudes) of k_1, k_2, and that without any loss of generality these are both positive. In this case (2.48b) reduces to

$$\begin{vmatrix} F_1^1 & F_2^1 \\ F_1^2 & F_2^2 \end{vmatrix} > 0$$

which it will be observed is precisely the denominator of (2.46). Information on the direction of adjustment, together with stability, enables us to sign the denominator of (2.46). Thus the bulk of our efforts in determining the signs of terms like (2.46) can be focused on the numerator. Notice that we have used only one stability condition. If we knew more about the magnitudes of the k_i we could also use (2.48a) to obtain further restrictions. But this is not commonly possible.

Finally, we should stress that while we have introduced the correspondence principle for two variables, it in fact holds quite generally. We shall have occasion to use it subsequently.

12.   Some final remarks

This completes our summary of the conventional static macro-economic model. Our discussion has been brief, and we have dealt with only relatively simple versions of the model. More complete treatments are available elsewhere and for further discussion the reader is referred to these sources. However, the model we have presented provides an adequate basis on which we can build our subsequent analysis. Throughout subsequent chapters we shall be concerned with the kinds of issues as we have been considering here. We shall be interested in determining equilibrium properties of the system and seeing how these respond to various government policies. We shall be paying particular attention to the dynamic behaviour of the system which, as we show in Chapter 3, is an intrinsic part of these policies.

3

THE FORMULATION OF A CONSISTENT
MACROECONOMIC MODEL

In this chapter we discuss a number of issues relevant for the formulation of a logically consistent macroeconomic theory. As a consequence of considering some of these logical problems we are able to understand more fully some of the assumptions being made, often only implicitly, in the basic *IS–LM* model. Particular attention is devoted to the development of a logically consistent continuous-time model, since it is in the transition to this limiting case where many of the severest problems arise.

1. Definition of wealth

As we discussed at several points in Chapter 2, many of the recent developments in macroeconomic theory place particular emphasis on the role of net wealth. We therefore start our discussion by defining this concept.

Basically the net wealth of an individual consists of the sum of his assets minus the sum of his liabilities. In aggregating over individuals, the assets of persons within the group, which are simultaneously liabilities of other individuals in the same group, cancel out. As a result, the net wealth of the group consists of its *net claims* on persons *outside* that group.

To derive the net wealth of the private sector of the economy, we apply this notion to the separate groups comprising the private sector. For simplicity, we shall confine ourselves to households and firms and shall abstract from the private banking sector.[1]

Consider first the household sector. Their net real wealth at a given point of time is defined by the equation

$$V^h = \frac{M^h}{P} + \frac{B_g^h}{P} + \frac{B_f}{P} + E_f \qquad (3.1)$$

where V^h = net real wealth of households,
        M^h = household sector's holdings of fiat (outside) money (issued by the central bank) in nominal terms,
        B_g^h = household sector's holdings of government bonds, assumed to be fixed-price (variable-interest rate) bonds, in nominal terms,

B_f = household sector's holdings of private bonds, assumed to be
    fixed-price bonds, issued by firms, in nominal terms,

E_f = household sector's holdings of equity issued by firms, in real
    terms,

P = price level.

The real net wealth V^f of the firms in the economy consists of

$$V^f = \frac{M^f}{P} + \frac{B_g^f}{P} - \frac{B_f}{P} - E_f + K. \tag{3.2}$$

The quantities M^f, B_g^f are directly analogous to M^h, B_g^h, defined above for the household sector. Note that the bonds and equities issued by the firms constitute their liabilities. The remaining term K, is the real quantity of physical capital used by firms in production, that is, the economy's physical assets. We are assuming for the present that the unit value of this capital in terms of currently produced goods is unity. Some authors, notably Tobin (1969), allow the unit price of capital to vary from unity. This turns out to have important implications for the logical consistency of certain aspects of macroeconomic model building, which are discussed in Section 7 below and in more detail in Turnovsky (1977a). We should also observe that if one assumes that the market value of the firms' debt and equity just equals the market value of their assets, then the net worth of the firm is zero. This is the typical assumption made in conventional corporate finance theory; see for example Robichek and Myers (1965). We too, shall invoke this assumption in the course of our discussion.

Adding (3.1) and (3.2) yields the real net wealth of the private sector

$$V = \frac{M}{P} + \frac{B}{P} + K \tag{3.3}$$

where
$$V = V^h + V^f$$
$$M = M^h + M^f$$
$$B = B_g^h + B_g^f.$$

This equation defines real private net wealth V, to consist of the total real quantity of outside money M/P, and government bonds B/P, in the hands of the private sector, together with the real physical capital. Observe that private bonds and equity cancel out; so would inside money — the deposit money held in commercial banks — if a private banking sector was included in the model.

Many macroeconomic models work with perpetual bonds, rather than the fixed-price bonds we have introduced above. These have the property that the price of a bond paying $1 perpetually equals the inverse of the interest rate. Thus if the bonds issued by the government are perpetuities, the real net wealth of the private sector is

$$V = \frac{M}{P} + \frac{B}{Pr} + K. \tag{3.3'}$$

The fact that they are never repaid is analytically convenient. On the other hand, the capital gains or losses they involve through changes in the interest rate introduce some complications which are not present with fixed-price bonds. We shall consider both types of bonds in subsequent chapters.

At this point we should make three observations. First, whether or not inside money in fact cancels out in the definition of private wealth has been questioned by Pesek and Saving (1967). The traditional view is that it does, and we shall maintain that position throughout our analysis. Secondly, the extent to which government bonds constitute net private wealth has also been debated. It is sometimes argued that future tax liabilities on the interest earned on these bonds should be netted out. This issue has not yet been resolved.[2] The prevailing conventional view, which we shall adopt here, treats government bonds fully as part of wealth and makes no adjustment for future tax. Thirdly, virtually all of macroeconomic theory holds K constant in defining wealth, but at the same time allows for the full flow effects of investment (changes in K). We too shall do this for much of our analysis. Yet as we shall discuss below, this procedure entails severe logical problems.

2. The private sector budget constraint

Any logically consistent macroeconomic model must have the property that the behavioural relationships it includes are compatible with the underlying budget constraints facing the decision makers in the economy. These constraints apply to both the private and public sectors.

For notational simplicity, we shall assume that firms do not hold money or government bonds. These assets are all held by households. We shall consider the constraints over the unit period $(t, t + 1)$, over which the household sector is assumed to make its decisions subject to the budget constraint,[3]

$$M_t + B_t + B_t^f + E_t^f + r_t(B_t + B_t^f) + Y_{t+1}$$
$$= M_{t+1}^d + B_{t+1}^d + B_{t+1}^{f,d} + E_{t+1}^{f,d} + C_{t+1} + U_{t+1} \quad (3.4)$$

where
M_t = stock of money held by households at time t,
B_t = stock of government bonds held by households at time t,
B_t^f = stock of private bonds issued by firms and held by households at time t,
E_t^f = stock of equity capital held by households at time t,
r_t = rate of interest on government bonds and private bonds at time t,
M_{t+1}^d = planned holding of money by households for time $t + 1$,
B_{t+1}^d = planned holding of government bonds by households for time $t + 1$,

$B_{t+1}^{f,d}$ = planned holding of private bonds by households for time
$t + 1$,

$E_{t+1}^{f,d}$ = planned holding of equity capital by households for time
$t + 1$,

Y_{t+1} = income flow over period, $(t, t + 1)$,

C_{t+1} = planned consumption flow over period $(t, t + 1)$,

U_{t+1} = flow of tax payments, assumed to be exogenous, over period
$(t, t + 1)$.

Following Patinkin (1965) we assume that households make their plans
at time t for time t + 1. They therefore have a unit planning horizon. Formulated in this way we assert that households wish to achieve their objective
at the end of the planning period. We are therefore concerned with what can
be called 'end-of-period equilibrium'.[4] For simplicity, we assume that the
price of output remains constant and is set equal to unity. The extension to
allow for variable prices is discussed in Section 12 below.

Equation (3.4) asserts that the household sector's planned holdings of
money, government bonds, private bonds, equity capital for time $t + 1$,
together with its consumption plans and tax liabilities over the period
$(t, t + 1)$ are constrained by

(i) the value of its wealth at the beginning of the period,
(ii) the interest earned on its holdings of government and private
bonds, $r_t(B_t + B_t^f)$,
(iii) its outside income earned over the period, $(t, t + 1)$.

If we allow the value of the claims to firms' capital to change, then the
changes in value of equity and of private bonds would also need to be taken
into account. This complication is considered in Sections 7–12 below.

We turn now to firms. They operate according to the budget constraint

$$B_{t+1}^f - B_t^f + E_{t+1}^f - E_t^f = I_{t+1} + r_t B_t^f \tag{3.5}$$

where I_{t+1} = investment plans for period $(t, t + 1)$. This equation asserts
that the firms' expenditure commitments over the period $(t, t + 1)$ include
their investment plans, together with the interest owing on their outstanding
debt. In the absence of internal financing, this is financed either by issuing
more bonds, or by issuing additional equity, all of which are held by
households.

The budget constraints (3.4) and (3.5) have two immediate and important
implications. First, if we assume that household demands are determined by
the optimization of some objective function subject to (3.4), it becomes clear
that the appropriate wealth variable determining their decisions at time t, for
time $t + 1$ is V_t^h, their wealth at time t. Likewise, V_t^f is the appropriate
wealth variable determining the firms' decisions for time $t + 1$, being made at
time t. Aggregating (3.4), (3.5) it therefore follows that, apart from the usual
aggregation bias, V_t is the appropriate wealth variable determining the private
sector's decisions for time $t + 1$, (at time t). It therefore follows that wealth

as an explanatory variable in aggregate private expenditure equations should appear with a one period lag. This point, while readily apparent when one considers equations (3.4) and (3.5), has been surprisingly neglected in the literature. There are countless examples of discrete-time models analysing the effects of monetary and fiscal policy in which decisions at time $t - 1$ depend upon terminal wealth V_t. The consequence of this is to allow wealth effects to come into operation immediately, (i.e., during the first period). But as these equations show, this formulation is clearly inconsistent with the underlying private budget constraints.[5] Current wealth is a *consequence* of these decisions, rather than a determinant of them. While this error of specification is of little concern for long-run analysis, its implications for the short run (one period) — most often the period being studied — may be very misleading, since the induced wealth effects of, say, government fiscal policy will come into effect only in the second period. This issue is discussed in further detail in Chapter 4.

The second point, that equation (3.4), or perhaps more appropriately the sum of (3.4) and (3.5), makes explicit, is the implicit assumption being made in much of the traditional *IS–LM* theory when it excludes wealth effects from its analysis. As discussed in Chapter 2, the conventional consumption, investment, and money demand functions do not include wealth as arguments. If this is the case, it then follows from (3.4) and (3.5), that the demand function for private and public bonds and equity, eliminated by Walras' law, (see Section 4 below) must, between them, have a wealth coefficient of unity. In other words, an increase in private wealth is allocated *entirely* to bonds and equity, with no effects on either consumption or money holdings. This extreme behavioural asymmetry, implicit in the standard model, has been criticized at length by authors, most notably Hansen (1970). Once the implications of the private budget constraint are realized, it becomes much more reasonable to allow consumption and the demand for money to share in the wealth effects as well.

3. The government budget constraint

Like private individuals, the government is also constrained in its decision making. Specifically its decisions over the period $(t, t + 1)$ must satisfy the constraint

$$M_{t+1} - M_t + B_{t+1} - B_t = G_{t+1} - U_{t+1} + r_t B_t. \tag{3.6}$$

This equation asserts that the government expenditure on goods and services G_{t+1}, less taxes, plus the interest owing on outstanding government debt, must be financed either by issuing more bonds or by issuing additional money. Note that we are abstracting from other exogenous transfer payments from the government to the private sector. Provided they are given and do not vary with endogenous or policy variables of the system, they clearly do not affect the system in any substantial way. To incorporate them, one would simply add appropriate constant quantities to disposable income and the government deficit.

Bond financing of the deficit occurs when the Treasury covers the deficit by selling bonds either to the non-bank public or to commercial banks. In either case the ultimate consequence of the transaction is an increase in the number of government bonds held by the private sector, with no change in their holdings of money. On the other hand, if the Treasury finances its deficit by selling bonds to the Central Bank in return for deposits at the Bank, the effect of this is to increase the reserves of the banking system and thereby to increase the money supply in the hands of the private sector. This is often referred to as 'printing money'.[6]

We should make it clear that M_t in (3.6) — and indeed throughout this chapter — refers to *fiat* money or the *monetary base* (and in fact in an open economy to just the domestic component, see Chapter 10). This equation describes how the monetary authorities control what we called R^u in Chapter 2. Any increase in M_t in (3.6) will have multiple effects on the total money supply, in accordance with our discussion in Chapter 2.

It seems intuitively clear that the financing of the government deficit will have an important bearing on the impact of government policy. And indeed as we shall show in Chapter 4 and subsequent chapters, this is certainly the case. In view of this it is surprising that it is only recently that economists have explicitly incorporated the government budget constraint into their formal models. The first authors to include it were Ott and Ott (1965), and shortly afterwards Christ (1967, 1968). However, these authors neglected the interest owing on the outstanding debt, defining the constraint by

$$\Delta M_{t+1} + \Delta B_{t+1} = G_{t+1} - U_{t+1}. \tag{3.6'}$$

This version turns out to have significantly different implications from (3.6), and we will indicate them in the next chapter. If, as is usually the case, one treats government expenditure G_{t+1} as the exogenous policy variable then (3.6) is correct and (3.6') is wrong. However, (3.6') can be justified if one treats $G_{t+1} + r_t B_t = G'_{t+1}$ say in (3.6) as the exogenous policy variable. This implies a continual adjustment in G_{t+1} as $r_t B_t$ varies, in order to achieve this exogenously chosen value. This is the procedure adopted by Tobin and Buiter (1976). However, other recent contributions incorporating the government budget constraint (such as Blinder and Solow (1973), Turnovsky (1975b)) specify the constraint by (3.6) and we shall do likewise.

4.   The aggregate budget constraint and Walras' law

To derive the overall constraint confronting the total economy, we add equations (3.4), (3.5), (3.6). This yields, after cancellation,

$$(M_{t+1} - M^d_{t+1}) + (B_{t+1} - B^d_{t+1}) + (B^f_{t+1} + E^f_{t+1} - B^{f,d}_{t+1} + E^{f,d}_{t+1})$$
$$+ (Y_{t+1} - C_{t+1} - I_{t+1} - G_{t+1}) = 0. \tag{3.7}$$

If we assume that private bonds and government bonds are perfect substitutes we can reorganize the terms in (3.7) and write

$$(M_{t+1} - M_{t+1}^d) + (B_{t+1} + B_{t+1}^f - B_{t+1}^d - B_{t+1}^{f,d}) + (E_{t+1}^f - E_{t+1}^{f,d})$$
$$+ (Y_{t+1} - C_{t+1} - I_{t+1} - G_{t+1}) = 0. \quad (3.8)$$

Equation (3.8) is a statement of Walras' Law. It asserts that the sum of the excess demand for money, bonds (private plus government), firms' equity, and current output must equal zero. To any excess demand for one of the quantities there must correspond an excess supply of some other. And equilibrium in any three of these four markets, will necessarily imply equilibrium in the fourth.[7]

Hence under the assumptions we have made, Walras' Law is established for the macroeconomic model. In analysing money, bonds, equity and output, any one of the four markets can be ignored. If, further, we invoke an assumption frequently made, namely that bonds and firms' equity are perfect substitutes in domestic investors' portfolios, we can aggregate E^f in with B and B^f, reducing the model to three markets. Now Walras' Law says that only two of these three markets are independent and hence one may be dropped. Typically this is the bonds-cum-equity market, leaving us with money and output. This is precisely the procedure adopted in conventional macroeconomics when it focuses on *IS* and *LM* curves. But underlying it is the elimination of a market through Walras' Law.

5. **Relationship of savings plans to wealth accumulation**

Retaining the assumption of $P = 1$, the disposable income $Y_{t+1}^{H,D}$ of the household sector is defined by

$$Y_{t+1}^{H,D} = Y_{t+1} + r_t(B_t + B_t^f) - U_{t+1}. \quad (3.9)$$

That is, disposable income equals income earned from current production, plus the interest earned on public and private (firm) bond holdings, less taxes. To derive the disposable income of the total private sector, Y_{t+1}^D say, which is the usual concept adopted, we net out interest income on private bonds, leaving

$$Y_{t+1}^D = Y_{t+1} + r_t B_t - U_{t+1}. \quad (3.10)$$

In a world of changing prices, capital gains or losses on asset holdings would also have to be included (as they would be in the original budget constraints), but we leave this to Sections 7–12 below.

Let us assume that only households save and consume. Then household disposable income must satisfy the constraint

$$Y_{t+1}^{H,D} = C_{t+1} + S_{t+1}. \quad (3.11)$$

That is, after meeting their tax commitments households must either save (S_{t+1}) or consume. Substituting (3.9), together with (3.11) into the household budget constraint (3.4), yields

$$S_{t+1} = M_{t+1}^d + B_{t+1}^d + B_{t+1}^{f,d} + E_{t+1}^{f,d} - (M_t + B_t + B_t^f + E_t^f) \quad (3.12)$$

Let us now add the assumption that the market value of the firms' debt plus equity just equals the value of their assets. Giving an analogous definition for demand, we have

$$B_t^f + E_t^f = K_t$$

$$B_t^{f,d} + E_t^{f,d} = K_t^d$$

where K_t = real quantity of capital at time t,
K_t^d = demand for real capital at time t.

Substituting this into (3.12) we deduce

$$S_{t+1} = M_{t+1}^d + B_{t+1}^d + K_{t+1}^d - (M_t + B_t + K_t). \quad (3.12')$$

Finally defining desired wealth for time t, V_t^d, by

$$V_t^d = M_t^d + B_t^d + K_t^d$$

we obtain

$$S_{t+1} = V_{t+1}^d - V_t. \quad (3.13)$$

Savings plans for period $(t + 1)$ are shown to equal the difference between desired wealth for time $t + 1$ and actual wealth at the beginning of the period. We have, therefore, established the consistency between savings plans and planned or desired wealth accumulation.

6.   **Choice between discrete- and continuous-time models**
    So far we have worked purely in terms of a discrete-time model. While many macroeconomic models are formulated using discrete time, much of macroeconomic theory is formulated using continuous time. Both kinds of models have their place and the choice between them is often dictated by convenience. If one is interested in analysing short-run effects, discrete-time models tend to be more useful. On the other hand, for steady-state and stability analyses, continuous models are usually more practical. We shall use both types of models in subsequent work, selecting whichever is more convenient.
    However, the correct formulation of a continuous-time model involves intricate logical problems, which were first elucidated in an important paper by May (1970). His analysis highlights the crucial distinction between stocks and flows, a distinction which can tend to become obscured in discrete time. Perhaps the most significant conclusion to emerge from his analysis is that the *single* budget constraint for the consolidated household sector in a discrete-time model, gives rise to *two* constraints when one transforms to continuous time. One is a *stock* constraint, the other is a *flow* constraint. May's analysis is based on Patinkin's (1965) model and assumes fixed stocks of all assets. In the latter part of his paper he proceeds to show how some of Patinkin's comparative static conclusions must be modified in the reformulated model.

In order to discuss savings and investment behaviour in a satisfactory way, it is necessary to extend May's analysis to allow for the accumulation of assets over time. This is done in Sections 7 and 8 below. Specifically, we assume that the government issues money and bonds to finance its deficit, while firms issue equity to finance their investment expenditure. Moreover, in introducing the accumulation of physical capital, it turns out to be important to distinguish between the *quantity* of the physical capital on the one hand, and the *market value* of that capital on the other. It is also important to distinguish between actual prices and the expectations of these prices and to allow for the possibility of imperfect foresight.

Before proceeding with the analysis, it may be useful to indicate briefly some further arguments in favour of analysing a macroeconomic model in continuous time.[8] First, there is the important reason already alluded to, of analytical tractability; differential equations are easier to study than difference equations. Secondly, discrete-time analysis suffers from the serious disadvantage of assuming that all decisions of a particular type are perfectly synchronized. In reality, while individual decisions are made at discrete time intervals, they are not coordinated in this way, but instead overlap in time in some stochastic manner. Ideally, one would like to model the true process, although this would obviously be too complex. Thus both discrete and continuous models must be viewed as alternative approximations, and on *a priori* grounds there is no compelling argument in favour of one formulation rather than the other. Thirdly, a related difficulty with discrete-time analysis is that in most economic contexts there is no obvious time interval to serve as the natural unit. Fourthly, while discrete-time analysis is conceptually simpler, it does suffer from the danger that its underlying assumption of a fixed period length may unwittingly yield misleading conclusions. To test whether or not this is the case, it is desirable to allow the period length to vary and ultimately let it shrink to its limit.

7.   A discrete-time model with arbitrary period and imperfect foresight[9]

As a first stage towards formulating a continuous-time model, we reformulate the discrete-time model outlined in Sections 2–4 over an arbitrary finite market period. The reason for giving this case separate treatment is that we also wish to complicate the model by introducing the price of equity and its expectation. The issues this raises can be discussed more satisfactorily using discrete time and without compounding the discussion with a limiting process. Following Sections 2 and 3 the model is developed by considering in turn the constraints facing the three groups of decision makers in the economy, namely households, firms, and the government. These relationships are then aggregated to yield the constraint for the total economy, as in Section 4. The limits of these relationships as the time unit shrinks to zero are then considered in Section 8.

A. *The household sector*

Trading is assumed to occur at the beginning (or end) of Hicksian-like market periods, which we take to be h time units in length. We shall assume further that households have zero transactions costs so that they incur no penalty for trading every period. This implies that households, in making their consumption and savings decisions need plan only one market period ahead. Thus we now assume that households' expenditure plans *for time* $t + h$ are made *at time t*.

The budget constraint facing the household sector over the discrete-time market period $(t, t + h)$, and determining (along with a utility function) its decisions at time t, is given by

$$M(t) + B(t) + p_e(t)E(t) + [p_e^*(t + h, t) - p_e(t)]E(t) + r(t)B(t)h$$

$$+ Y(t + h, t) = M^d(t + h, t) + B^d(t + h, t)$$

$$+ p_e^*(t + h, t)E^d(t + h, t) + C(t + h, t) + U(t + h, t) \qquad (3.14)$$

where

$M(t) =$ stock of money held by households at time t,

$B(t) =$ stock of government bonds held by households at time t,

$E(t) =$ stock of equity capital issued by firms and held by households at time t,

$p_e(t) =$ price of equity capital in terms of currently produced output, at time t,

$p_e^*(t + h, t) =$ expected price of equity capital for time $t + h$, formed at time t,

$r(t) =$ interest rate on government bonds at time t,

$M^d(t + h, t) =$ quantity of money which households plan at time t to hold at time $t + h$,

$B^d(t + h, t) =$ quantity of bonds which households plan at time t to hold at time $t + h$,

$E^d(t + h, t) =$ quantity of equity which households plan at time t to hold at time $t + h$,

$Y(t + h, t) =$ income flow, assumed to be fixed and known, over period $(t, t + h)$,

$C(t + h, t) =$ planned consumption flow over period $(t, t + h)$,

$U(t + h, t) =$ flow of tax payments (net of transfer payments) assumed to be exogenous, over period $(t, t + h)$.

This equation is analogous to (3.4), although there are some significant differences. First, and most importantly, all variables other than current observed quantities are expressed as functions of *two* time variables. This is necessary if one is to specify precise meanings to them. For example to describe expectations exactly, one should indicate

(i) the time *when* they were formed (t),

(ii) the time *for which* they are formed ($t + h$).

The same applies to the specification of plans. Similarly, flow variables should be written as functions of two time variables, indicating the beginning and end of the period over which they are measured. While this distinction is not necessary when, as in the early part of this chapter, one is dealing with a *single fixed* time horizon, it does become important when one lets the time horizon vary and moves to a continuous model.

Secondly, without any essential loss of generality we assume firms employ all equity financing, so that there are no private bonds. Thirdly, although we retain the conventional macroeconomic assumption that output is produced in a single sector, so that the prices of consumption goods and investment goods (new capital) are the same and equal to unity say, the price of equity (claims on capital) in terms of currently produced output is allowed to vary. This reflects the fact that in the short run, with adjustment costs constraining the rate of investment, the real return on holding equity may deviate from the marginal product of physical capital, leading to appropriate movements in the price of the equity claims on that capital. We have also introduced households' expectations of the price of equity, which as we discuss below need not coincide with actual observed prices.

Equation (3.14) asserts the household sector's planned holdings of money, bonds, and equity capital for time $t + h$, together with its consumption plans and tax liabilities over the period $(t, t + h)$ are constrained by,

(i) the value of its assets at the beginning of the period;
(ii) the expected capital gains or losses on its initial holding of equity capital due to changes in its value;
(iii) the interest earned on the holdings of government bonds;
(iv) its outside income earned over the period.

The flow variables, such as consumption, are defined by

$$C(t + h, t) = \int_{t}^{t+h} c(\tau, t)d\tau \tag{3.15}$$

where $c(\tau, t)$ is the (finite) planned consumption rate for time τ, chosen at time t. The other variables $Y(t + h, t)$, $U(t + h, t)$ are defined analogously.[10] It is an immediate consequence of (3.15) that $C(t, t)$ being the accumulation flow over a zero period is zero, with the other flow variables sharing a similar property. For notational convenience we shall define the instantaneous rate of flow at time t by the function of one variable

$$c(t, t) \equiv c(t),$$

with all other flow variables being treated similarly.

We define wealth at time t, $V(t)$, by

$$V(t) = M(t) + B(t) + p_e(t)E(t) \tag{3.16}$$

and let

$$V^d(t + h, t) = M^d(t + h, t) + B^d(t + h, t)$$

$$+ p_e^*(t + h, t)E^d(t + h, t) \tag{3.17}$$

denote analogously the amount of wealth households plan at time t to hold at time $t + h$.

As will become apparent in due course, one consequence of introducing a price differential between claims on capital and new capital is that it becomes essential to distinguish between physical capital and the equity claims on it. This distinction is not usually made in macroeconomic theory where the usual procedure is to associate a single share with a unit of physical capital. Hence physical capital is introduced directly into the household sector's budget constraint, even though in practice, households hold the *securities* issued by firms; see e.g. Tobin (1969), Foley (1975). Without any essential loss of generality these can be taken to consist entirely of equity capital, as we have in fact done. Assuming free entry and perfect competition, the value of equity issued by firms must equal the value of the physical capital they own, so that

$$p_e(t)E(t) = p_k(t)K(t) \tag{3.18}$$

where $p_k(t)$ = unit value of existing capital once installed at time t,
$K(t)$ = stock of physical capital at time t.

Since we are not introducing a market for existing capital, $p_k(t)$ should not be interpreted as a market price. Rather it should be viewed as an *imputed* price, reflecting the rate of earnings attributable to physical capital.

The conventional procedure of setting $E(t) \equiv K(t)$ is usually justified on the grounds that one can choose units so that one unit of equity corresponds to one machine, say. It is clear from (3.18) that for this assumption to be maintained, $p_e(t)$ and $p_k(t)$ must move in proportion and in general this will not be so. In fact, the condition under which it is, and is not, important to distinguish between K and E requires careful discussion. It depends critically upon the nature of the adjustment costs associated with investment and the financing constraint facing the firms. Since these questions can be discussed more satisfactorily after the model has been fully specified, we defer further comments until Section 9 below.

One of the factors entering the household's budget constraint and therefore influencing their decisions are *expected* equity prices. These may or may not equal actual prices depending upon how good they are at forecasting. If they always predict perfectly we say that they have *perfect foresight* and define this formally by

$$p_e^*(t + h, t) = p_e(t + h) \qquad \text{for all } h > 0. \tag{3.19}$$

While we have expressed this concept in terms of equity prices, it is clear that an analogous definition can be given in terms of any variable being predicted. But it is obviously a very restrictive assumption and while we may sometimes invoke it as a limiting case, it is more satisfactory to develop our consistent model on the assumption that it does not hold; that is on the basis of *imperfect foresight*.

On the other hand, we shall require expectations to satisfy the following much weaker condition which we shall describe as a *weak consistency axiom*

$$p_e^*(t, t) = p_e(t) \qquad \text{for all } t. \tag{3.20}$$

That is, (3.20) asserts that the expectation formed at time t for that same instant t must equal the actual price prevailing at that time. This condition is obviously much weaker than perfect foresight. Underlying it is the assumption that forecasters have instantaneous access to information so that they learn $p_e(t)$ the moment it occurs. Under these conditions any rational forecasting process must satisfy (3.20). If such information is not available instantaneously, then (3.20) need not hold.[11]

Utilizing the definitional relationship

$$Y^D(t + h, t) = C(t + h, t) + S(t + h, t), \tag{3.21}$$

where $Y^D(t + h, t), S(t + h, t)$ represent the flows of household disposable income and savings respectively over the period $(t, t + h)$, and are defined analogously to (3.15), it follows from (3.14), (3.16), (3.20), (3.21) that

$$S(t + h, t) = V^d(t + h, t) - V(t) \tag{3.22}$$

if and only if we define

$$Y^D(t + h, t) = Y(t + h, t) + [p_e^*(t + h, t) - p_e(t)]E(t)$$
$$+ r(t)B(t)h - U(t + h, t). \tag{3.22'}$$

That is, planned savings by households will equal their desired accumulation of wealth if and only if household disposable income is defined to include the expected capital gains on equity capital and the interest earned on government bonds.

The budget constraint (3.14) yields a generalization of a point made earlier. If we assume that household demands are determined by the optimization of some objective function subject to (3.14), it becomes clear that provided $h > 0$, the appropriate wealth variable determining decisions (plans) *for* time t say – that is, those decisions made *at* time $(t - h)$ – is the beginning of period wealth $V(t - h)$. But as the market period $h \to 0$, $V(t - h) \to V(t)$, so that in a continuous-time model it is *current* wealth that is appropriate, as is conventionally assumed.

The budget constraint (3.14) refers to *plans* formed at time t. Parallel to it is an *ex post* relationship restricting *actual* behaviour. This can be written as

$$V(t) + [p_e(t + h) - p_e(t)] E(t) + r(t)B(t)h + Y(t + h, t)$$
$$= V(t + h) + C_a(t + h, t) + U(t + h, t) \tag{3.23}$$

where $C_a(t + h, t)$ denotes the actual consumption flow over the period $(t, t + h)$ and is defined analogously to (3.15).

Likewise, analogous to (3.21) the flows of *ex post* disposable income $Y_a^D(t + h, t)$ and savings $S_a(t + h, t)$ satisfy the relationship

$$Y_a^D(t+h, t) = C_a(t+h, t) + S_a(t+h, t). \tag{3.24}$$

Thus provided we define

$$Y_a^D(t+h, t) = Y(t+h, t) + [(p_e(t+h) - p_e(t)]E(t)$$
$$+ r(t)B(t)h - U(t+h, t) \tag{3.25}$$

equations (3.23) and (3.24) imply

$$S_a(t+h, t) = V(t+h) - V(t), \tag{3.26}$$

so that the actual flow of savings equals the actual accumulation of wealth.

Subtracting (3.14) from (3.23), we obtain

$$C_a(t+h, t) - C(t+h, t) + V(t+h) - V^d(t+h, t)$$
$$= [p_e(t+h) - p_e^*(t+h, t)]E(t) \tag{3.27}$$

which describes the implied constraint on the adjustments of consumption and wealth holdings from their respective plans. The quantity $p_e(t+h) - p_e^*(t+h, t)$ measures the forecast error in predicting the price of equity, so that $[p_e(t+h) - p_e^*(t+h, t)] E(t)$ denotes the unanticipated capital gain on holding equity. Since all other components of disposable income are known, this also represents the unanticipated component of *ex post* disposable income. The expression

$$V(t+h) - V^d(t+h, t) = S_a(t+h, t) - S(t+h, t)$$

equals the revision to savings plans, while $C_a(t+h, t) - C(t+h, t)$ similarly denotes the revisions to consumption plans. Thus (3.27) asserts that unanticipated disposable income must be allocated either to the revision of savings or to the revision of consumption plans. Moreover, rewriting (3.27) as

$$C_a(t+h, t) = C(t+h, t) + [p_e(t+h) - p_e^*(t+h, t)]E(t)$$
$$+ V^d(t+h, t) - V(t+h) \tag{3.28}$$

ex post consumption can be expressed as planned consumption plus unanticipated disposable income less the amount of revision to the initial savings plan.

The only difference between the planned and *ex post* budget constraints is that the anticipated capital gain in the former is replaced by the actual capital gain in the latter. Hence, provided the utility function underlying the household sector's allocation decisions remains fixed over the market period, the only reason for initial plans to be revised is through errors in forecasting the price of equity. With perfect foresight, all plans will be realized, so that

$$C_a(t+h, t) = C(t+h, t) \tag{3.29a}$$

$$V(t+h) = V^d(t+h, t) \tag{3.29b}$$

Otherwise, the allocation of the adjustment among consumption and the components of wealth will depend upon the nature of the underlying utility function.

B.   Firms

At a given time t, firms have an accumulated stock of capital $K(t)$. They too plan ahead one market period and determine, by means of some optimization procedure or otherwise, a desired stock of capital $K^d(t + h, t)$, which they wish to hold at time $(t + h)$. Thus assuming zero depreciation, the firms' desired accumulation of capital over the period $(t, t + h)$ — their investment plans — is specified by

$$I(t + h, t) = K^d(t + h, t) - K(t). \tag{3.30}$$

Those investment plans are financed by issuing equity. Specifically, firms plan to issue a sufficient number of additional shares so that when they are sold at the end of the period at the prevailing market price, they expect to obtain precisely the funds required to carry out their investment plans. Since the price of new machines is unity, and the expected market price of equity is $p_e^*(t + h, t)$, this financing–investment constraint is described formally by

$$p_e^*(t + h, t)[E^s(t + h, t) - E(t)] = K^d(t + h, t) - K(t)$$
$$= I(t + h, t) \tag{3.31}$$

where $E^s(t + h, t) =$ total number of shares firms plan at time t to have outstanding at time $(t + h)$.

We assume that the investment process involves adjustment costs, the effects of which are to prevent the desired stock of capital from necessarily being attained in the period, so that typically

$$K(t + h) \neq K^d(t + h, t).$$

Moreover, like households, firms are assumed to possess imperfect foresight so that $p_e^*(t + h, t) \neq p_e(t + h)$, in which case equation (3.31) which is an *ex ante* (planned) relationship, may, or may not, be realized.[12] Corresponding to it is an *ex post* (actual) financing constraint, namely

$$p_e(t + h)[E(t + h) - E(t)] = K(t + h) - K(t) = I_a(t + h, t). \tag{3.32}$$

The left hand side of (3.32) describes the actual amount of finance raised by the additional shares actually issued and this must equal the amount of investment actually undertaken, which we denote by $I_a(t + h, t)$.

C.   The government

Finally, the government is assumed to have expenditure plans $G(t + h, t)$ for the period $(t, t + h)$, as well as owing interest $r(t)B(t)h$ on its outstanding debt over that period. These expenditures are financed through taxes $U(t + h, t)$ (which are fixed), by printing money, or by issuing additional debt. We shall assume that government expenditure plans are a policy decision which is always realized. Thus with taxes and interest payments predetermined, and the government deficit being free of any expectational variables, the government's plans to issue debt will always be realized. Hence its budget constraint, which holds both *ex post* and *ex ante*, is

$$M(t + h) - M(t) + B(t + h) - B(t)$$
$$= G(t + h, t) - U(t + h, t) + r(t)B(t)h.$$

Thus with all government plans being realized, actual government expenditure $G_a(t + h, t)$ must satisfy

$$G_a(t + h, t) = G(t + h, t), \tag{3.34}$$

However, it is easy to relax the assumption in (3.34) and to allow for adjustments to government expenditure plans to be met by revisions in plans to issue debt.

D.   *The total economy*

To obtain the constraint facing the plans of the whole economy over the discrete time period $(t, t + h)$ we add the component *ex ante* budget constraints (3.14), (3.31), (3.33). Cancelling terms this yields the single aggregate constraint

$$M(t + h) - M^d(t + h, t) + B(t + h) - B^d(t + h, t)$$
$$+ p_e^*(t + h, t)[E^s(t + h, t) - E^d(t + h, t)]$$
$$+ Y(t + h, t) - C(t + h, t) - I(t + h, t) - G(t + h, t) = 0 \quad (3.35)$$

Defining the aggregate flow demand for new output over the period $(t, t + h)$ by $Z(t + h, t)$, we have

$$Z(t + h, t) = C(t + h, t) + I(t + h, t) + G(t + h, t). \tag{3.36}$$

Thus equations (3.35) and (3.36) assert that the sum of the excess demands for money, government bonds, equity, and new output must sum to zero. This of course is precisely a statement of Walras' Law.

Adding the *ex post* (actual) budget constraints (3.23), (3.32) and (3.33), and using (3.34), yields the relationship

$$Y(t + h, t) = C_a(t + h, t) + I_a(t + h, t) + G_a(t + h, t). \tag{3.37}$$

This is precisely the familiar identity that *ex post*, income must equal the sum of actual consumption, actual investment, plus actual government expenditure. Substituting from (3.27), (3.32) and (3.34), and using (3.31), this equation can immediately be transformed to (3.35). It is therefore *not* an independent equation, but simply another way of expressing the fact that excess demands must sum to zero.

8. The continuous-time limit

We now proceed to take limits and let the market period (planning horizon) $h \to 0$.[13] In doing so we assume that all functions are continuously differentiable, so that all quantities change smoothly. In particular, this means that plans are revised in a smooth fashion so that the new information that leads to the revision of plans is also acquired smoothly. We are therefore ruling out discontinuous jumps in information, such as that embodied in stochastic disturbances, which would lead to discontinuous jumps in expectations and other variables. This is obviously a restriction, but a complete treatment involving stochastic informational flows goes well beyond the scope of this chapter.

In the course of taking limits, the partial derivatives of $p_e^*, p_{e,1}^*, p_{e,2}^*$, both play an important role and therefore require careful interpretation. Given the weak consistency axiom (3.20), the expected rate of change of price of equity over a finite horizon h is given by

$$\frac{p_e^*(t+h, t) - p_e(t)}{h}.$$

Taking the limit as $h \to 0$ of this expression and using (3.20) yields the *partial* derivative $p_{e,1}^*(t, t)$. This quantity is therefore the correct limiting measure of the *expected* rate of change of price at a given time t; see also Burmeister and Turnovsky (1976).

To consider the other partial derivative $p_{e,2}^*$, we use the first mean value theorem to expand $p_e^*(t+h, t+h)$ about the point $(t+h, t)$. Invoking the consistency axiom (3.20) enables us to write

$$p_e(t+h) - p_e^*(t+h, t) = p_{e,2}^*(t+h, \xi)h \qquad t < \xi < t+h.$$

Thus $p_{e,2}^*(t+h, \xi)$, which measures how the prediction for the fixed time $t+h$ is revised with the variable planning date ξ, is proportional to the forecast error and reflects the extent to which there is imperfect foresight in predicting the price of capital. Asset prices are underestimated or overestimated according as $p_{e,2}^*(t+h, \xi) \gtrless 0$; with perfect foresight $p_{e,2}^*(t+h, \xi) \equiv 0$. Moreover, letting $h \to 0$ we see that perfect *myopic* foresight, a common assumption of macroeconomic theory, is described by $p_{e,2}^*(t, t) = 0$.

The interpretation of the instantaneous partial derivative $p_{e,2}^*(t, t)$ can also be seen another way. Differentiating the weak consistency axiom (3.20) with respect to t yields

$$\dot{p}_e(t) = p_{e,1}^*(t, t) + p_{e,2}^*(t, t). \tag{3.20'}$$

The left hand side of this equation measures the *actual* rate of change of equity price; the quantity $p_{e,1}^*$ measures the *expected* rate of change of price, so that $p_{e,2}^*$ measures the *unanticipated* rate of change of price. With perfect myopic foresight this is always zero. Thus the property of perfect myopic foresight pertains to predicting *rates of change* rather than levels; see Turnovsky and Burmeister (1977).

We now proceed to take the limit as $h \to 0$, of the various budget constraints introduced in Section 7.

A.   *The household sector*
   From the fact that

$$\lim_{h \to 0} C(t + h, t) = C(t, t) = 0$$

and the analogous limits for the other flow quantities $Y(t + h, t)$, $U(t + h, t)$, together with the consistency axiom (3.20) the limit of the household budget constraint (3.14) as $h \to 0$ is

$$M(t) + B(t) + p_e(t)E(t) = M^d(t, t) + B^d(t, t) + p_e^*(t, t)E^d(t, t)$$
$$(3.38)$$

or

$$V(t) = V^d(t, t) \qquad \text{for all } t. \tag{3.38'}$$

Thus if the households' planning horizon shrinks to zero, it follows that their desired and actual wealth must coincide. Put another way, if plans are being made instantaneously, then households must be prepared to hold the existing stock of assets. It is also worth noting that provided $h = 0$, (3.38) and (3.38') hold irrespective of whether t flows continuously or discretely. That is, if households plan at discrete points of time for that very same instant of time, then $V^d(t, t)$ is constrained by $V(t)$. In that case the appropriate wealth variable determining decisions for time t would be $V(t)$. But this instantaneous decision-making horizon would seem to go against the spirit of discrete-time models. It is clearly much more natural to associate an instantaneous planning horizon $h = 0$, with a continuous-time model where plans are being continually made. This will, henceforth, be our interpretation of $h = 0$.

Substituting (3.38') into (3.22), dividing by h and letting $h \to 0$, we obtain

$$\lim_{h \to 0} \left(\frac{S(t + h, t)}{h} \right) = \lim_{h \to 0} \left(\frac{1}{h} \int_t^{t+h} s(\tau, t)d\tau \right)$$

$$= \lim_{h \to 0} \left(\frac{V^d(t + h, t) - V^d(t, t)}{h} \right)$$

from which we deduce

$$s(t) = \left. \frac{\partial V^d(u, t)}{\partial u} \right|_{u=t} \equiv V_1^d(t, t). \tag{3.39}$$

For arbitrary times v, t, the partial derivative $V_1^d(v, t)$ measures the rate of change of desired holding of wealth as the planning horizon increases, at a *given* planning date t. Thus from (3.39) we deduce that the rate of planned savings by households at time t equals their *desired* rate of wealth accumulation at that fixed time. Furthermore, the *single* budget constraint over the discrete time period $(t, t + h)$, given by (3.14), or equivalently (3.22), gives rise to *two* equations when one transforms to continuous time. These include the *stock* constraint (3.38) or (3.38') and the *flow* constraint (3.39). This observation is the thrust of May's important contribution.[14]

But in order for (3.22) to hold, disposable income and savings must satisfy (3.21) and (3.22'). Dividing these two equations by h, and taking limits, we obtain the corresponding continuous-time relationships for rates

$$y^D(t) = c(t) + s(t) \tag{3.40a}$$

$$y^D(t) = y(t) + p_{e,1}^*(t, t)E(t) + r(t)B(t) - u(t). \tag{3.40b}$$

Finally, the above limiting procedures can be applied to the various *ex post* relationships. Dividing (3.26) by h and letting $h \to 0$, implies

$$\lim_{h \to 0} \left(\frac{S_a(t + h, t)}{h} \right) = \lim_{h \to 0} \left(\frac{1}{h} \int_t^{t+h} s_a(\tau, t) d\tau \right)$$

$$= \lim_{h \to 0} \left(\frac{V(t + h) - V(t)}{h} \right)$$

and hence

$$s_a(t) = \dot{V}(t) \tag{3.41}$$

so that the actual rate of savings at time t, $s_a(t)$, equals the actual rate of wealth accumulation. Moreover, differentiating (3.38') and using (3.41) yields

$$s_a(t) = \dot{V}(t) = V_1^d(t, t) + V_2^d(t, t) = s(t) + V_2^d(t, t). \tag{3.42}$$

Thus the actual rate of wealth accumulation at time t in general differs from the desired rate of wealth accumulation at that same instant, and therefore from the planned rate of savings, by the amount $V_2^d(t, t)$, which reflects the rate at which savings plans are being revised instantaneously.

Again (3.26) holds only as long as actual disposable income and savings satisfy (3.24) and (3.25). Dividing these equations by h and taking limits yields the *ex post* relationships

$$Y_a^D(t) = c_a(t) + s_a(t) \tag{3.43a}$$

$$Y_a^D(t) = y(t) + \dot{p}_e(t)E(t) + r(t)B(t) - u(t). \tag{3.43b}$$

Further, applying the same argument to (3.28) (in the process using the consistency axiom (3.20) and the stock constraint (3.38')), yields the analogous continuous-time expression for the actual rate of consumption

$$c_a(t) = c(t) + p_{e,2}^*(t, t)E(t) - V_2^d(t, t). \tag{3.44}$$

This equation can be interpreted as follows. From (3.20'), $p_{e,2}^*(t, t)$ measures the unanticipated rate of change of equity prices, so that $p_{e,2}^*(t, t)E(t)$

denotes the unanticipated rate of capital gains. Since all other components of disposable income are known, this also represents the total unanticipated component of disposable income. Thus the actual rate of consumption equals the planned rate of consumption plus the unanticipated rate of disposable income less the rate at which savings plans are being revised.

The only difference between the planned and actual budget constraints when one moves to the limit is that $p_{e,1}^*$ in the former is replaced by $\dot{p}_e$ in the latter. The difference between these quantities, $p_{e,2}^*$, is the unanticipated component of the rate of change of equity prices. Thus the only reason for the household to modify its initial plans is because of imperfect myopic foresight in predicting equity prices. With perfect myopic foresight, consumption and savings plans will be realized, so that

$$c_a(t) = c(t) \tag{3.45a}$$

$$V_2^d(t, t) = 0. \tag{3.45b}$$

B. Firms

We have argued that because of the adjustment costs and imperfect foresight, firms do not necessarily achieve their desired stock of capital at the end of the market period, so that typically $K^d(t + h, t) \neq K(t + h)$. Moreover, even though by virtue of the consistency axiom (3.20) firms predict current equity prices perfectly, the assumption of adjustment costs still suffices to ensure that firms do not in general own the quantity of capital they would like to hold at that same instant of time (at least for all t) so that $K^d(t, t) \neq K(t)$.

Letting $h \to 0$ in (3.30) yields

$$I(t, t) = K^d(t, t) - K(t)$$

which in turn means that the desired instantaneous rate of investment at time t, $i(t)$, defined by

$$i(t) = \lim_{h \to 0} [I(t + h, t)/h] \tag{3.30'}$$

becomes infinite.

The limiting case in which the desired stock of capital can always be attained instantaneously so that

$$K^d(t, t) = K(t) \qquad \text{for all } t \tag{3.46}$$

occurs if capital is perfectly malleable; that is, there are zero adjustment costs associated with changing the capital stock. In this case

$$i(t) = \lim_{h \to 0} \left(\frac{K^d(t + h, t) - K^d(t, t)}{h} \right) = K_1^d(t, t)$$

and is in general finite. But perfect malleability is a restrictive assumption, which we do not necessarily wish to impose.

The continuous limit of the planned financing–investment constraint (3.31) is obtained as follows. Letting $h \to 0$, we can write

$$p_e^*(t, t)[E^s(t, t) - E(t)] = K^d(t, t) - K(t). \tag{3.31'}$$

Subtracting (3.31') from (3.31), dividing by h and letting $h \to 0$, yields

$$p_e^*(t, t)E_1^s(t, t) + p_{e,1}^*(t, t)[E^s(t, t) - E(t)] = K_1^d(t, t). \tag{3.47}$$

The derivation of (3.47) requires some comment. The expression $K_1^d(t, t)$ equals the rate of change of the desired stock of capital and is a perfectly well defined partial derivative. It does *not* equal the desired rate of investment $i(t)$ (which under our assumption is infinite) unless (3.46) holds, when $i(t)$ becomes finite as well. But despite the fact that we allow $i(t) \to \pm \infty$, (3.47) is perfectly well defined. The reason is that the singularity of $i(t)$ is matched by the singularity in $\lim_{h \to 0} [E^s(t, t) - E(t)]/h$ and as (3.31') indicates, these cancel out in the process of taking derivatives.

The fact that the desired investment rate will typically be infinite may appear to pose severe problems for continuous-time models, where investment plans play such a crucial role. However, this is not really the case. As Tobin (1956) argued many years ago, you really do not need an investment function which is separate from the demand for capital $K^d(t, t)$. The important point is that *this* function, and the associated constraint (3.31') be well defined. The fact that some other related function which we have designated $i(t)$ does not exist, is of little consequence.

The continuous-time analogue of the actual financing relationship (3.32) is obtained by dividing both sides of (3.32) by h and letting $h \to 0$, yielding

$$p_e(t)\dot{E}(t) = \dot{K}(t) = i_a(t) \tag{3.48}$$

where $i_a(t)$ denotes the actual instantaneous rate of investment.

It is worth noting that the problem of the desired instantaneous rate of investment becoming infinite was also encountered by Foley (1975). He resolved it by postulating that investment plans for the period $(t, t + h)$ are set so as to make up some *fraction* of the difference between current and desired capital stock, where the fraction depends upon the length of the market period h. If one follows this approach, (3.30) is modified to

$$I(t + h, t) = \rho h[K^d(t + h, t) - K(t)] \tag{3.30''}$$

where $\rho < 0$ is a constant which measures the rate of adjustment. Letting $h \to 0$, it is clear that $I(t, t) = 0$, irrespective of whether (3.46) holds or not. Furthermore, dividing (3.30'') by h and letting $h \to 0$, we immediately deduce the limiting relationship

$$i(t) = \rho[K^d(t, t) - K(t)] \qquad \rho > 0 \tag{3.49}$$

which in general implies a finite rate of investment demand.

C.   *The government*

The continuous-time limit of the government budget constraint is obtained as usual by dividing (3.33) by h and letting $h \to 0$. This yields

$$\dot{M}(t) + \dot{B}(t) = g(t) - u(t) + r(t)B(t) \tag{3.50}$$

where $g(t) =$ instantaneous rate of flow of planned government expenditure at time t. With government plans being realized, the actual instantaneous rate of flow $g_a(t)$ must be such that

$$g_a(t) = g(t). \tag{3.51}$$

D.   *The total economy*

To obtain the continuous-time limit of the aggregate constraints facing the economy we proceed as follows. Letting $h \to 0$ in (3.35) and using (3.31) yields the aggregate stock constraint

$$M(t) - M^d(t, t) + B(t) - B^d(t, t) + p_e(t)[E(t) - E^d(t, t)] = 0 \tag{3.52}$$

and is identical to the household sector stock constraint (3.38). This reflects the fact that in this model households are the only group whose net worth is positive. Considering (3.52) at time $(t + h)$, subtracting (3.35), dividing by h, and finally letting $h \to 0$, yields the aggregate flow constraint

$$y(t) = c(t) + p_{e,2}^*(t, t)E(t) - V_2^d(t, t) + \dot{K}(t) + g(t) \tag{3.53}$$

Note that if one makes the simplifying assumption of perfect myopic foresight (which implies $p_{e,2}^* = V_2^d = 0$), or that all unexpected income is saved (implying $p_{e,2}^* E = V_2^d$), consumption plans will be realized. In this case (3.53) simplifies to the more familiar relationship

$$y(t) = c(t) + \dot{K}(t) + g(t). \tag{3.53'}$$

These assumptions necessary to obtain (3.53') are in fact the conventional ones typically made in macroeconomics, although they are not usually stated explicitly.

Despite its similarity, equation (3.53) or (3.53') must not be confused with the product market equilibrium condition. It is a *constraint* which in a continuous-time model must hold *for all t*, and as such it is an integral part of such a model. In certain cases, discussed in Section 10 below, it will reduce to the continuous product market equilibrium condition, but in general it will not. Recalling the definitions of the *ex post* rate of consumption, investment, and government expenditure given in (3.44), (3.48), (3.51), this flow constraint is precisely

$$y(t) = c_a(t) + i_a(t) + g_a(t) \tag{3.54}$$

so that it turns out to be the identity that *ex post*, the rate of income must equal the sum of the rates of consumption, investment, and government expenditure. Moreover, the identical constraint can be obtained directly by taking the derivatives of the aggregate *ex post* budget constraint (3.37). It can also be derived (with some manipulation) by summing the component flow constraints (3.39), (3.47), (3.50).

However, unlike the discrete-time model, in which the corresponding constraint (3.37) turns out to be equivalent to (3.35), in the continuous-time limit, the flow constraint (3.54) is *independent* of the stock constraint (3.52). The single aggregate constraint (3.35) gives rise to the two constraints (3.52) and (3.53) as one moves to the limit.

Finally, we may note that our analysis has implications for a common procedure adopted in macroeconomics. As discussed above, a common assumption in formulating such models is to abstract from physical capital in defining wealth (or at least assume that it remains fixed), yet at the same time allow for the flow effects of investment. Following the analysis developed above to the limit in this case yields the flow constraint

$$y(t) = c(t) + g(t) \tag{3.53''}$$

which can never be consistent with product market equilibrium unless investment plans are zero. That is, one cannot formulate a logically consistent continuous-time macroeconomic model which simultaneously postulates positive investment, continuous product market equilibrium, but at the same time assumes physical capital is constant in the definition of wealth. This inconsistency need not arise in discrete time, however.

9. The distinction between equity and physical capital

In developing the model we argued that in general it is necessary to distinguish between capital and the equity claims on that capital. Having specified the basic model, we are now in a position to discuss the economic significance of this distinction — one that is not typically made in macroeconomic theory.

We begin by observing that equilibrium in the equity market requires the real market value of equity at time t to equal the present value of the expected future earnings of the physical capital associated with that equity. In the absence of depreciation and abstracting from taxes on capital we therefore have

$$p_e(t)E(t) = K(t)\int_t^\infty R^*(\tau, t)\exp\left(-\int_t^\tau r_e^*(t', t)dt'\right)d\tau \tag{3.55}$$

where exp denotes exponential and

$\quad R^*(\tau, t) =$ expectation of the marginal physical product of capital formed at time t for time τ,

$\quad r_e^*(t', t) =$ expectation of the cost of equity capital formed at time t for time t'.

Likewise, the expected market value of equity for time $t + h$, formed at time t, must equal the expected real earnings of capital from time $t + h$ on, implying

$$p_e^*(t+h, t)E(t+h)$$

$$= K(t+h)\int_{t+h}^{\infty} R^*(\tau, t)\exp\left(-\int_{t+h}^{\tau} r_e^*(t', t)dt'\right) d\tau \qquad (3.56)$$

where in writing (3.56) we make the simplifying assumption that $E(t+h)$ and $K(t+h)$ are known with certainty at time t. Subtracting (3.56) from (3.55) dividing by h, and letting $h \to 0$, yields

$$r_e(t) = \frac{R(t)K(t)}{p_e(t)E(t)} + \frac{p_{e,1}^*(t, t)}{p_e(t)} + \frac{\dot{E}(t)}{E(t)} - \frac{\dot{K}(t)}{K(t)}. \qquad (3.57)$$

In deriving (3.57) we assume that the forecasts $R^*(\tau, t)$ and $r_e^*(\tau, t)$ satisfy the consistency axiom (3.20), so that

$$R^*(t, t) = R(t)$$

$$r_e^*(t, t) = r_e(t)$$

where $R(t), r_e(t)$ denote the corresponding actual quantities prevailing at time t.

Further, defining $p_k^*(t+h, t)$ to be the expected imputed unit value of capital for time $t+h$, formed at time t, it follows that this must satisfy an analogous equation to (3.18), namely

$$p_e^*(t+h, t)E(t+h) = p_k^*(t+h, t)K(t+h). \qquad (3.18')$$

Taking the partial derivative of (3.18') with respect to h, (3.57) can be written more simply as

$$r_e(t) = \frac{R(t)}{p_k(t)} + \frac{p_{k,1}^*(t, t)}{p_k(t)}. \qquad (3.58)$$

That is, the real rate of return on equity equals the marginal physical product of capital divided by the imputed price of capital, plus the expected percentage rate of change of the imputed price.

From (3.48) together with the imputed valuation equation

$$p_e(t)E(t) = p_k(t)K(t), \qquad (3.18)$$

we immediately deduce that the assumption $E \equiv K$, and hence $\dot{E} = \dot{K}$, implies

$$p_k(t) = p_e(t) = 1 \qquad \text{for all } t.$$

With $p_k(t)$ constant, any rational forecasting mechanism will predict zero rate of change, so that $p_{k,1}^*(t, t) \equiv 0$. Hence it follows from (3.58) that at each instant of time $r_e(t) = R(t)$ for all t. That is, at each instant of time, firms will adjust their actual capital stock so that its marginal product will equal the real rate of return on equity. Assuming profit maximization, this same marginal productivity condition will determine the instantaneous desired stock of capital. Hence we conclude that the assumption $E(t) \equiv K(t)$ implies that

$$K^d(t, t) = K(t) \qquad \text{for all } t,$$

so that capital is perfectly malleable.

However, the argument cannot be reversed unless one imposes additional restrictions. Perfect malleability implies $R(t) \equiv r_e(t)$, but this does not ensure $p_k = p_e = 1$, unless $p_{k,1}^* = 0$. One case in which this does hold is if one assumes

$$R^*(\tau, t) = R(t) \qquad \text{for all } t$$

$$r_e^*(t', t) = r_e(t) \qquad \text{for all } t.$$

This is a situation of static expectations in which the current values of $R(t)$ and $r_e(t)$ are expected to prevail indefinitely. Equation (3.58) now simplifies to

$$r_e(t) = \frac{R(t)}{p_k(t)} \qquad (3.58')$$

and is in fact the expression used by Tobin (1969) and others. In this case perfect malleability implies $p_k = 1$ and hence by appropriate choice of units $E \equiv K$; see (3.18) and (3.48).

With costs of adjusting the capital stock, $r_e(t) \neq R(t)$ in general and the distinction between equity and capital is clearly necessary.

The above argument implies that given our formulation of the financing constraint, then the assumption $E \equiv K$ ensures that the price of equity is *fixed* at unity. Some authors, most notably Tobin, assume $E \equiv K$, and yet allow the price of equity to vary endogenously. This is clearly inconsistent with our formulation of the firms' financing constraint. With the price of new investment goods equal to unity, it can be justified only if one makes the restrictive assumption that the new equity is issued at unity (par) rather than at the prevailing market price.[15] But if this assumption is made, then the capital gains made from the instantaneous revaluation of these assets as the new investment takes place should be included as part of the household sector's disposable income.[16] At the same time it should be realized that this difficulty with identifying capital with equity stems largely from working with a one-sector model. The distinction is not necessary in a two-sector model in which there is a separate market for physical capital, the price of which is free to vary relative to that of consumption.

10. Some implications for product market relationships

Our analysis has implications for the specification of certain relationships often used to characterize the state of product market (dis)-equilibrium. The points can be made most conveniently for the case of perfect myopic foresight, which as we have commented above is the conventional macroeconomic assumption.

The instantaneous rate of aggregate demand $z(t)$ is defined by

$$z(t) = c(t) + i(t) + g(t) \tag{3.59}$$

where $i(t) = \lim_{h \to 0} [K^d(t + h, t) - K(t)]/h$. Hence, if as is typically the case, one postulates continuous product market equilibrium it follows by equating (3.53′) and (3.59) that one must have

$$i(t) = \lim_{h \to 0} \left(\frac{K^d(t + h, t) - K(t)}{h} \right)$$

$$= \lim_{h \to 0} \left(\frac{K(t + h) - K(t)}{h} \right) = \dot{K}(t)$$

from which we deduce

$$K^d(t, t) = K(t) \qquad \text{for all } t. \tag{3.46}$$

Thus, given perfect myopic foresight, continuous product market equilibrium implies that at each instant of time, the desired capital stock firms wish to hold at that instant must equal precisely the actual stock in existence. As we have seen this in turn implies that the instantaneous desired rate of investment $i(t)$ becomes $K_1^d(t, t)$ and is, in general, finite.

On the other hand we have argued above that (3.46) is rather restrictive. Accordingly, if we reject it, we must be prepared to accept product market disequilibrium as a consequence. We should also note that (3.46) is only *necessary* for continuous product market equilibrium. To obtain *sufficient* conditions, as well as (3.46), we require that $K_2^d(t, t) = 0$; that is, firms do not wish to revise their plans instantaneously.

In analysing dynamic models involving product market disequilibrium, one standard approach dating back to Phillips (1954) has been to postulate a lagged output adjustment relationship of the form

$$\dot{y} = \beta(z - y) \quad \text{where} \quad \beta > 0 \text{ is a finite constant.} \tag{3.60}$$

However, if $K^d(t, t) \neq K(t)$, $i(t)$ (as defined by (3.30′)) $\to \pm \infty$, in which case excess demand $z(t) - y(t)$ also becomes infinite. Clearly, since we wish to restrict our attention to finite rates of output adjustment, (3.60) must be modified. If we wish to maintain our assumption $K^d(t, t) \neq K(t)$, the only way a finite adjustment $\dot{y}$ is obtained is if β is postulated to be a function of h, say $\beta = \alpha h$. In this case (3.60) reduces to

$$\dot{y}(t) = \lim_{h \to 0} \alpha h \left(\frac{K^d(t + h, t) - K(t + h)}{h} \right)$$

$$= \alpha \left(K^d(t, t) - K(t) \right). \tag{3.60′}$$

Accordingly, the appropriate adjustment rule is to adjust output in proportion to the instantaneous excess demand for capital rather than output. On the other hand, if one wishes to maintain (3.60) with β constant and independent of h, then for $\dot{y}$ to remain finite, $(z - y)$ must be finite, and this in turn once again requires that (3.46) hold.

Another related form of disequilibrium adjustment processes frequently employed in macroeconomics is the stock adjustment process. Using discrete time this can be written as

$$K(t + h) - K(t) = \beta(h)[K^d(t + h, t) - K(t)] \tag{3.61}$$

where the adjustment parameter is expressed as a function of h. If (3.46) does *not* hold, setting $h = 0$ in (3.61) implies $\beta(0) = 0$. This in turn yields the limiting relationship

$$\dot{K}(t) = \beta'(0) [K^d(t, t) - K(t)] \tag{3.62}$$

and provided the derivative of β at zero, $\beta'(0)$ is finite, $\dot{K}(t)$ is finite. Since under these same conditions $(3.30') \to \pm \infty$, (3.62) implies an infinite rate of product market disequilibrium and accordingly should not be used when the instantaneous rate of investment demand is defined as in $(3.30')$.

In order to obtain plausible implications for the product market one possibility is to again invoke (3.46). In this case provided $\beta(0) > 0$, we derive the continuous relationship

$$\dot{K}(t) = \beta(0)K_1^d(t, t) = \beta(0)i(t) \tag{3.62'}$$

where $i(t)$ is now finite. Once again product market disequilibrium emerges but this time it is finite, with its sign depending upon sgn $(1 - \beta)$.

Finally, we see that if one defines the investment demand function by $(3.30'')$, so that the instantaneous rate of investment demand is given by

$$i(t) = \rho[K^d(t, t) - K(t)] \tag{3.49}$$

the above difficulty associated with (3.62) disappears. Irrespective of whether capital is perfectly malleable or not the conventional continuous time formulation of the stock adjustment process (3.62) is now quite consistent with a *finite* rate of product market disequilibrium, given by

$$z - y = [\rho - \beta'(0)] [K^d(t, t) - K(t)]. \tag{3.63}$$

Furthermore, continuous product market equilibrium is still possible and will occur provided

$$\rho = \beta'(0).$$

Use of the continuous stock adjustment process, with these assumptions in mind, is given in Chapter 8.

11. Some restrictions imposed by budget constraints

So far we have not specified any forms for the underlying demand functions, allowing them to be quite general. But, it is clear that the constraints we have been discussing impose certain restrictions on the household demand functions.

Consider first the stock equilibrium condition (3.38). As a fairly conventional money demand function we postulate

$$M^d = M^d(y, r, r_e, V) \qquad (3.64)$$

where $\quad r$ is the return on holding bonds,
$\qquad r_e$ is the return on holding capital.
Assuming analogous demand functions for B^d, $p_e E^d$, it follows by differentiating (3.64) that

$$M_i^d + B_i^d + p_e E_i^d = 0 \qquad i = y, r, r_e$$
$$M_V^d + B_V^d + p_e E_V^d = 1. \qquad (3.65)$$

These are the 'adding up' conditions stressed by Brainard and Tobin (1968) and Tobin (1969). They imply that instantaneously wealth must be allocated among the three assets, money, bonds, and capital. Moreover, if there is an increase in y, increasing the transactions demand for money ($M_y^d > 0$), this can be achieved instantaneously only by reducing the holding of bonds or capital. Over time, it may also be achieved by saving, but this cannot occur immediately.

The flow constraints (3.39) and (3.40) imply a similar adding up condition for consumption and savings. If one postulates the typical consumption function

$$c = c(y^D, r, r_e, V) \qquad (3.66)$$

it follows from (3.40) that

$$c_i + s_i = 0 \qquad i = r, r_e, V$$
$$c_{y^D} + s_{y^D} = 1 \qquad (3.67)$$

where s_i refers to the partial derivative of the corresponding savings function. Thus, for example, if an increase in wealth increases the rate of consumption it must reduce the rate of savings.

These two sets of constraints can be relaxed somewhat in the discrete-time version of the model where there is a finite planning horizon $h > 0$. For simplicity let us assume that all flows occur at a constant rate $s(t)$ throughout the period, enabling us to write

$$S(t+h, t) = \int_t^{t+h} s(t)d\tau = s(t)h.$$

Thus equation (3.22) can be written as

$$M^d(t+h, t) + B^d(t+h, t) + p_e^*(t+h, t)E^d(t+h, t) - hs(t)$$
$$= M(t) + B(t) + p_e(t)E(t). \qquad (3.22'')$$

Postulating asset demands at time $t + h$, as well as the savings rate over the period, to be functions of the variables at time t, we derive the adding up constraints[17]

$$M_i^d + B_i^d + p_e^*(t + h, t)E_i^d - hs_i = 0 \qquad i = y, r, r_e$$

$$M_V^d + B_V^d + p_e^*(t + h, t)E_V^d - hs_V = 1. \qquad (3.68)$$

It is clear from (3.68) that the constraints (3.65) and (3.67) need not hold. For example, if $s_y > 0$, it is possible to increase the holding of money at time $t + h$, in response to an increase in the transactions motive, without reducing one's holdings of the other assets. This is achieved by the accumulation of new savings. But as the planning horizon $h \to 0$, it is clear that the quantity of savings tends to zero, so that (3.68) converges to (3.65). And this remains true in a discrete model where planning is instantaneous.[18]

12.   Extension of model to inflationary conditions

In extending the model to include variable output prices, one is faced with the problem of maintaining consistency of the system in real terms. Specifically, we wish to ensure that *real* planned (actual) savings equal the *real* desired (actual) accumulation of wealth. For this to be so, we require real disposable income to be appropriately defined.

This problem has concerned economists in their analyses of monetary models of growth. Here two general definitions have been adopted. Some authors, (e.g. Tobin (1967), Stein (1969)) define the rate of real disposable income at time t to be

$$y^D(t) = y(t) + \left(\frac{\dot{M}}{P}\right) = y(t) + \frac{\dot{M}}{P} - \left(\frac{M}{P}\right)\frac{\dot{P}}{P}. \qquad (3.69)$$

That is, ignoring taxes, real disposable income is defined to be real net national income plus the change in the real value of money. Other economists (e.g. Shell, Sidrauski, and Stiglitz (1969); Foley and Sidrauski (1970, 1971)) use the definition

$$y^D(t) = y(t) - \left(\frac{M}{P}\right)\frac{\dot{P}}{P} \qquad (3.70)$$

and include only the capital gains component of changes in M/P (or its expectation) in their definition. The two definitions are obviously identical as long as the nominal money supply remains constant. With a changing money supply which of them is consistent with savings equal to wealth accumulation in real terms, depends upon what assumption is made about net transfer payments from the public to the private sector.[19] This is readily apparent from our model.

Returning to the household budget constraint, in real terms this becomes

$$\frac{M(t) + B(t)}{P(t)} + p_e(t)E(t) + [p_e^*(t + h, t) - p_e(t)]E(t)$$

$$+ r(t)hB(t)/P(t) + (M(t) + B(t)) \left(\frac{1}{P^*(t + h, t)} - \frac{1}{P(t)} \right)$$

$$+ Y(t + h, t) = \frac{M^d(t + h, t) + B^d(t + h, t)}{P^*(t + h, t)}$$

$$+ p_e^*(t + h, t)E^d(t + h, t) + C(t + h, t) + U(t + h, t) \tag{3.71}$$

where $P(t), P^*(t + h, t)$ denote the actual and expected output price respectively. The expectation $P^*(t, t)$ is assumed to satisfy the consistency axiom (3.20). The quantities Y, C, U, E are all now defined in *real* terms, while $M(t), B(t)$ refer to *nominal* stocks of money and bonds respectively. This is virtually the same as (3.14). The only difference is that the real resources of the household sector include the changes in their real holdings of financial assets resulting from expected changes in the output price level. Recalling the definitional relationship (3.21), which we now interpret as holding in real terms, we immediately deduce

$$S(t + h, t) = V^d(t + h, t) - V(t)$$

where S, V, V^d are all in real terms, if and only if we define real disposable income by

$$Y^D(t + h, t) = Y(t + h, t) + [p_e^*(t + h, t) - p_e(t)]E(t)$$

$$+ r(t)hB(t)/P(t) - U(t + h, t)$$

$$+ (M(t) + B(t)) \left(\frac{1}{P^*(t + h, t)} - \frac{1}{P(t)} \right) \tag{3.72}$$

thereby including the expected capital gains or losses on holdings of money and bonds.

Taking the limit of (3.71) as $h \to 0$, yields

$$V(t) = \frac{M(t) + B(t)}{P(t)} + p_e(t)E(t)$$

$$= \frac{M^d(t, t) + B^d(t, t)}{P(t)} + p_e(t)E^d(t, t) = V^d(t, t) \tag{3.73}$$

which is directly analogous to (3.38). Furthermore, following the procedures of Section 8, we immediately obtain the following set of continuous flow relationships

$$y^D(t) = c(t) + s(t) \tag{3.74}$$

$$s(t) = V_1^d(t, t) \tag{3.75}$$

$$y^D(t) = y(t) + p_{e,1}^*(t, t)E(t) + r(t)B(t)/P(t) - u(t)$$

$$- \left(\frac{M+B}{P}\right)\left(\frac{P_1^*(t, t)}{P(t)}\right) \tag{3.76}$$

with (3.75) holding if and only if y^D is defined by (3.76). The partial derivative $P_1^*(t, t)$ has the same interpretation as that given earlier to $p_{e,1}^*(t, t)$. Hence $P_1^*(t, t)/P(t)$ measures the *expected* rate of inflation at time t. With perfect myopic foresight $P_2^*(t, t) = 0$, in which case $\dot{P}(t) = P_1^*(t, t)$ and $P_1^*(t, t)/P(t)$ becomes the *actual* rate of inflation.

From these relationships the flow constraints for the aggregate economy can be readily obtained. With K defined in real terms, the accumulation equation for firms (3.31′) and (3.48) still hold. The budget constraint facing the government in real terms is

$$\frac{\dot{M} + \dot{B}}{P} = g(t) - u(t) + \frac{r(t)B(t)}{P(t)} \tag{3.77}$$

which we can rewrite as

$$\left(\frac{\dot{M}}{P}\right) + \left(\frac{\dot{B}}{P}\right) = g(t) - u(t) + \frac{r(t)B(t)}{P(t)} - \left(\frac{M+B}{P}\right)\frac{\dot{P}}{P}. \tag{3.78}$$

Substituting (3.74), (3.75), (3.78) into (3.76), and using (3.20′) we immediately deduce

$$y(t) = c(t) + p_{e,2}^*(t, t)E(t) - \left(\frac{M+B}{P}\right)\frac{P_2^*(t, t)}{P(t)} - V_2^d(t, t)$$

$$+ \dot{K}(t) + g(t). \tag{3.79}$$

The flow constraint (3.79) is similar to (3.53) derived in Section 8. The only difference is that allowances must be made for $P_2^*(t, t)$, the forecast error made in predicting output price. This constitutes part of unanticipated real disposable income and affects actual consumption. Following the argument of Section 8, this flow constraint can be given an identical interpretation to (3.53) and (3.54), with the identity now holding in real terms. Finally, again following the argument of Section 8, this constraint can be shown to imply the equality of the actual rate of real savings and the actual rate of real wealth accumulation.

13. Summary

The main issues we have been discussing in this chapter have revolved around problems of constructing a logically consistent macroeconomic model. The traditional *IS–LM* model makes several implicit assumptions, which are not fully appreciated until one considers the budget constraints underlying the various behavioural relationships.

These constraints together with some of their implications are first considered using a conventional discrete-time model. However, it is important that the fundamental properties of the model be invariant with respect to the time unit being considered. For this reason, as a test of the logical consistency of the model, it is desirable to allow the time unit to vary. This can be done most conveniently by letting the time horizon shrink to zero and converting the model to continuous time.

The implications of continuous-time models are not very familiar and therefore the general conclusions bear repeating. Letting the period length tend to zero, we obtain in the limit a continuous stock constraint which requires that at each point of time households must be willing to hold the existing stock of assets. For each group we consider (households, firms, government) we obtain a continuous flow constraint asserting that the rate at which it wishes to accumulate (issue) assets equals its desired savings (expenditure) rate. Adding these constraints yields the aggregate flow constraint, which also must hold at all times. This turns out to be the familiar national income identity equating the *ex post* rate of income to the sum of the rates of actual consumption, actual investment, and actual government expenditure. Actual consumption is shown to equal the planned rate of consumption, plus the unanticipated rate of disposable income (due to incorrect forecasts of capital gains) less the rate at which savings plans are revised. The actual rate of investment is simply the *ex post* rate of accumulation of capital, while under our assumptions, government expenditure plans are always realized.

This flow constraint has important consequences for the logical consistency of certain aspects of macroeconomic model building. Some of these were discussed in Section 10 and shall be taken up in later chapters. For example, if investment plans are defined to be the difference between current and desired capital stocks, then given the conventional assumption of perfect myopic foresight, continuous product market equilibrium is shown to imply the restrictive condition that at each point of time firms are able to attain their desired stocks of capital instantaneously; that is, the absence of adjustment costs for investment. If one rejects this condition, product market disequilibrium must result. The flow constraint also has implications for the formulation of disequilibrium adjustment processes in continuous time. Two of the most familiar, the exponential lagged output adjustment mechanism and the capital stock adjustment process, are briefly considered.

Finally, we should note that these issues which we have been discussing pertain to a single sector model. Some of the logical problems we have just been discussing do not necessarily occur when one extends the model to allow for two production sectors, consumption goods and investment goods say. For this reason the kind of two sector model developed by Foley and Sidrauski (1971) represents a significant advance in macroeconomic theory.

4

THE DYNAMICS OF THE GOVERNMENT
BUDGET CONSTRAINT

1.   Introduction

In this chapter we construct and analyse the first of our dynamic models. The essential dynamic relationship we shall introduce is the government budget constraint. Being a relationship between the stocks of financial assets and flows of claims on output, it imposes a dynamic structure on the system even if the underlying behavioural relationships are static. It constitutes part of what one might call the *intrinsic* dynamics of the system. This is in contrast to what could be described as *ad hoc* dynamic models, such as the familiar 'multiplier–accelerator' models, where the dynamic structure is a consequence of assuming arbitrary lags in behaviour.

The model we shall discuss is only a first approximation in that we hold capital constant in our definition of wealth, yet allow for the flow effects of investment. This was the approach followed by the earlier studies which incorporated the dynamics of the government budget constraint into theoretical macroeconomic models. Its justification is usually given in terms of the lags associated with the accumulation of the physical asset capital, as compared to the financial assets issued by the government. While this asymmetric treatment of asset accumulation is really rather unsatisfactory, especially when one looks at long-run steady states, the model nevertheless serves as a convenient starting point.[1]

The analysis of this chapter consists of two basic parts. In Sections 2 and 3 we introduce a simplified version of the government budget constraint into the conventional *IS–LM* model of Chapter 2. We derive the dynamics of the system in terms of past values of the available monetary and fiscal policy instruments. This specification is similar to the early contributions by Ott and Ott (1965) and Christ (1967, 1968), although we place much more emphasis on analysing the difference equation describing the dynamics of the system. By examining this equation, and tracing out the time path of the system we are able to determine exactly when the effects of fiscal policy in this more general dynamic model degenerate to those implied by the conventional static case. This enables us to place the simple model in a broader context.

In sections 4–7 we modify the model to take account of the issues discussed in Chapter 3. First, wealth effects are introduced in a manner which is consistent with the private sector's aggregate budget constraint. Secondly we incorporate interest payments on government bonds into the analysis. As we noted in Chapter 3, practically all of the early studies ignore this in their definitions of the government budget deficit and as will become apparent during the course of this analysis, the recognition of interest payments leads to many fundamental changes to the Ott and Ott and Christ results.

2.   Government budget constraint in a simple linear IS–LM model

We begin by presenting the conventional macroeconomic model, augmented by the inclusion of the government budget constraint. In order to keep the model as close as possible to the conventional text book treatment, we abstract from wealth effects and interest payments on government bonds. Since we wish to solve explicitly for the dynamics of the model we assume all relationships to be linear. Prices are also held constant and set equal to unity say.

Following the discussion of Chapter 2 consumption and investment are specified by the functions[2]

$$C_t = c(1-u)Y_t \quad 0<c<1, \quad 0<u<1 \tag{4.1}$$

$$I_t = iY_t + \gamma r_t \quad i>0, \gamma<0 \tag{4.2}$$

where Y_t = real income in period t,
  C_t = real consumption,
  I_t = real investment,
  r_t = rate of interest.

Consumption depends on disposable income, where for simplicity a constant and proportional income tax structure, specified by a tax rate u, is assumed. Adding government expenditure, G_t, yields the *IS* curve

$$Y_t = c(1-u)Y_t + iY_t + \gamma r_t + G_t \tag{4.3}$$

and imposing the restriction

$$1 - c(1-u) - i > 0 \tag{4.4}$$

ensures that this curve will have the usual downward slope. Similarly equilibrium in the money market yields the *LM* curve

$$M_t = \alpha Y_t + \beta r_t \quad \alpha>0, \quad \beta<0 \tag{4.5}$$

where M_t denotes the real supply of money.

Differentiating the pair of equations (4.3) and (4.5), immediately yields the familiar *IS–LM* multipliers

$$\frac{\partial Y_t}{\partial G_t} = \frac{\beta}{\Omega}>0, \quad \frac{\partial r_t}{\partial G_t} = \frac{-\alpha}{\Omega}>0 \tag{4.6a}$$

$$\frac{\partial Y_t}{\partial M_t} = \frac{\gamma}{\Omega} > 0, \quad \frac{\partial r_t}{\partial M_t} = \frac{1 - c(1-u) - i}{\Omega} < 0 \tag{4.6b}$$

where $\Omega = \beta[1 - c(1-u) - i] + \alpha\gamma < 0$.

These expressions are calculated on the assumption that G_t and M_t can be controlled independently and directly, and ignore the government budget constraint which links these two variables. As we are excluding interest payments for the time being, we assume the simpler formulation of the government budget constraint given in Chapter 3, namely equation (3.6'). That is, in addition to (4.3) and (4.5), we have the relationship

$$\Delta M_t + \frac{\Delta B_t}{r_t} = G_t - uY_t \tag{4.7}$$

where for simplicity we are abstracting from a fractional reserve banking system.[3] This equation asserts that the budget deficit $G_t - uY_t$ must be financed either by printing more money ΔM_t or by issuing more bonds ΔB_t, which for simplicity are assumed to be perpetuities, the price of which is $1/r_t$. Thus given tax rates, the government has three policy variables ΔB_t, ΔM_t, and G_t, any two of which can be chosen independently.[4]

Eliminating M_t from equations (4.3), (4.5) and (4.7), we obtain the following difference equation for Y_t in terms of the two chosen policy instruments,

$$(\Omega + \gamma u)Y_t - \Omega Y_{t-1} = (\gamma + \beta)G_t - \beta G_{t-1} - \gamma(\Delta B/r)_t. \tag{4.8}$$

This is a first order difference equation, implying that in general the government budget constraint imposes a dynamic structure on the static macro model. Solving equation (4.8) yields

$$Y_t = Y_0 \left(\frac{\Omega}{\Omega + \gamma u}\right)^t + \frac{1}{\Omega + \gamma u} \left\{ \sum_{j=0}^{t-1} ((\gamma + \beta)G_{t-j} - \beta G_{t-j-1} \right.$$
$$\left. - \gamma(\Delta B/r)_{t-j})\left(\frac{\Omega}{\Omega + \gamma u}\right)^j \right\} \qquad t \geq 1 \tag{4.9}$$

which gives the time path for Y_t in terms of past values of the policy instruments and the parameters of the system.

We shall analyse the effects of the following two policies on the system.

Policy 1:

$$\left(\frac{\Delta B}{r}\right)_1 > 0, \quad \left(\frac{\Delta B}{r}\right)_t = 0 \quad t \neq 1, \quad G_t \text{ constant for all } t.$$

This represents a pure open market sale of bonds at time 1, financed by decreasing the money supply, except to the extent that induced changes in tax revenues contribute to the financing.

Policy 2:

$$\Delta G_1 > 0, \quad G_t = G_1 \quad t \geqslant 1$$

$$\Delta M_t = \theta(G_t - uY_t) \quad 0 \leqslant \theta \leqslant 1 \qquad \text{for all } t \geqslant 1.$$

This describes a sustained increase in government expenditure at time 1. A fraction θ of the resulting budget deficit is financed by printing money, the remaining $(1 - \theta)$ is financed by issuing bonds.

3. Analysis of monetary and fiscal policies in simple model

Suppose that the system is initially in equilibrium with $Y_t = Y$ $G_t = G, \Delta B_t = 0$. From equation (4.8) this requires

$$uY = G$$

that is, that the government's budget be balanced. Suppose now that in period 1 the monetary authorities engage in an open market sale of bonds. From (4.9) we obtain a first period multiplier

$$\frac{\partial Y_1}{\partial B_1} = \frac{-\gamma}{r(\Omega + \gamma u)} < 0 \tag{4.10}$$

and that for subsequent time periods is

$$\frac{\partial Y_t}{\partial B_1} = \frac{-\gamma}{r(\Omega + \gamma u)} \left(\frac{\Omega}{\Omega + \gamma u}\right)^{t-1}.$$

Note that as $t \to \infty, \partial Y_t / \partial B_1 \to 0$. Hence we see that a single open market sale of bonds will temporarily decrease output, but that this effect will be only transitory. The reason for this is clear. The initial decrease in the money supply resulting from the initial sale of bonds will be contractionary in the conventional manner. However, that is not the end of the story. The first period reduction in income will lead to lower tax revenues and with constant government expenditure a budget deficit will be created. With no further open market operations this deficit will need to be financed through increases in the money supply, which will have an offsetting expansionary effect. Clearly this will continue until the budget is balanced again and income is restored to its original level.

Consequently, a *single* open market operation cannot affect income *permanently*. This is not to say that monetary policy can have no long-run effect. It is certainly possible for *continual* open market operations to have permanent effects on the level of income. For example if the government holds ΔB_t constant for all time, then (4.9) implies a permanent reduction in income of $1/u$ per unit of ΔB. Moreover, if the monetary authorities wish to achieve a permanent reduction in the money supply (which from (4.6b) will certainly lead to a reduction in income) then again it is clear that continual open market sales will be necessary.

We turn now to perhaps the more interesting case of an increase in government expenditure, financed in accordance with Policy 2, described above. Substituting $(\Delta B/r)_t = (1 - \theta)(G_t - uY_t)$ into equation (4.8) yields

$$[\Omega + \gamma u\theta] \, Y_t - \Omega Y_{t-1} \; = \; [\gamma\theta + \beta] \, G_t - \beta G_{t-1} \qquad (4.11)$$

the solution of which is

$$Y_t \; = \; Y_0 \left(\frac{\Omega}{\Omega + \gamma u\theta}\right)^t$$

$$+ \frac{1}{\Omega + \gamma u\theta} \left\{ \sum_{j=0}^{t-1} ([\gamma\theta + \beta]G_{t-j} - \beta G_{t-j-1}) \left(\frac{\Omega}{\Omega + \gamma u\theta}\right)^j \right\}. \qquad (4.12)$$

Consider an increase in government expenditure ΔG_1 at time 1. From equation (4.11) this can be shown to yield the following time path for the change in Y_t from its *original* level

$$Y_t - Y_0 \; = \; \Delta G_1 \left(\frac{1}{u} + \frac{\beta u - \Omega}{u[\Omega + \gamma u\theta]} \left(\frac{\Omega}{\Omega + \gamma u\theta}\right)^{t-1}\right). \qquad (4.13)$$

This equation has several implications. First, the short-run multiplier in period one is

$$\frac{\partial Y_1}{\partial G_1} \; = \; \frac{\beta + \gamma\theta}{\Omega + \gamma u\theta} \; \neq \; \frac{\beta}{\Omega} \qquad (4.14)$$

and therefore in general does not equal the usual expression. This expression will almost certainly (but not necessarily) exceed the multiplier given in (4.6a) and only in very unusual circumstances would this not be so.[5] As long as $0 < \theta \leqslant 1$,

$$0 < \Omega/[\Omega + \gamma u\theta] < 1$$

so that the long-run government expenditure multiplier will converge monotonically to

$$\frac{\partial Y}{\partial G} \; = \; \frac{1}{u} \qquad (4.15)$$

the inverse of the marginal tax rate. This is precisely the result obtained earlier by Ott and Ott (1965) and Christ (1968). The long-run government expenditure multiplier depends solely upon the tax rate and is independent of the other parameters in the system. In particular, it is independent of the financial mix θ, which however does influence the short-run multiplier as well as the speed of adjustment. For $0 < \theta \leqslant 1$, a decrease in θ – that is, an increase in the amount of debt financing – will reduce the speed of adjustment.

The logic of this long-run result is clear. From equations (4.3) and (4.5) Y_t can be seen to be dependent on M_t, so that in order for Y_t to be constant

ΔM_t must be zero. Recalling the specification of Policy 2,

$$\Delta M_t = \theta(G_t - uY_t),$$

we see that long-run equilibrium requires a balanced budget $G_t = uY_t$, from which the multiplier obtained above immediately follows.

Note, however, if $\theta = 0$, the adjustment in income described by (4.13) is completed within the first period, so that the dynamic process described by that equation degenerates to a static response. Setting $\theta = 0$ in (4.13), we obtain

$$\frac{\partial Y_t}{\partial G_1} = \frac{\beta}{\Omega} \qquad \text{for all } t$$

which *is* the conventional multiplier. Thus with complete bond financing, adjustment is immediate and yields the usual result, enabling us to see quite clearly how the conventional result fits into this more general framework.

It is also of interest to consider the implications of the financial mix for equilibrium changes in the rate of interest. The analogous dynamic adjustment equation for r_t is

$$[\Omega + \gamma u\theta] r_t - \Omega r_{t-1} = [\theta[(1-c)(1-u)-i] - \alpha] G_t + \alpha G_{t-1} \qquad (4.16)$$

which yields the long run response to an increase in G_t

$$\frac{\partial r}{\partial G} = \frac{(1-c)(1-u)-i}{\gamma u} \qquad \theta \neq 0 \qquad (4.17a)$$

$$\frac{\partial r}{\partial G} = \frac{-\alpha}{\Omega} > 0 \qquad \theta = 0. \qquad (4.17b)$$

Not surprisingly the conventional result emerges when $\theta = 0$. Note however, that for $\theta \neq 0$, the effect of an increase in government expenditure on the rate of interest is independent of the method of financing chosen by the government. As long as it finances its deficit (surplus) by printing (or withdrawing) *some* money, the effect will be the same, no matter how large or small the change in the money supply. Moreover, none of the restrictions we have imposed on the parameters enable us to sign the numerator of (4.17a) unambiguously. Nevertheless, as long as the tax rate is not too high, it seems almost certain that the condition (4.4) will ensure that $(1-c)(1-u)-i > 0$, in which case $\partial r/\partial G < 0$ – a reversal in sign from the usual result.

4. Extension of model to include wealth effects and interest payments

The analysis of Sections 2 and 3 is restrictive in two important respects. First, by excluding wealth effects from both the demand for money and private expenditure functions, it follows from Walras' law that the implied demand function for bonds must have a wealth coefficient of unity. In other words, an increase in private wealth is spent *entirely* on bonds, with no effect on either consumption or money holdings; see Chapter 3.

Secondly, we have ignored the effects of the interest payments on the bonds issued by the government. Being perpetuities, the value of which at time $(t-1)$ is $(B/r)_{t-1}$ the amount of interest paid during period t by the government to the private sector is simply B_{t-1}. Furthermore, assuming that the interest income is taxed at the same rate u, it follows that the disposable income of the private sector during period t is

$$Y_t^D = (Y_t + B_{t-1})(1-u). \qquad (4.18)$$

However, in incorporating wealth effects into the demand functions, care must be taken to introduce them in a way which is consistent with the underlying budget constraints. This important point has also been discussed at length in Chapter 3. Here we define the relevant wealth variable to be $(M_{t-1} + B_{t-1}/r_t)$. This quantity is just the wealth at the beginning of period, $(M_{t-1} + B_{t-1}/r_{t-1})$, plus $(B_{t-1}/r_t - B_{t-1}/r_{t-1})$, the capital gains or losses incurred during that period. Note that we have incorporated capital gains as revaluations of wealth, rather than as a component of disposable income. This procedure is also consistent with the underlying private sector budget constraint which we write as

$$M_{t-1} + \frac{B_{t-1}}{r_{t-1}} + \left(\frac{B_{t-1}}{r_t} - \frac{B_{t-1}}{r_{t-1}}\right) + (Y_t + B_{t-1})$$

$$= C_t + I_t + M_t^d + \frac{B_t^d}{r_t} + u(Y_t + B_{t-1}). \qquad (4.19)$$

This can be obtained by summing (3.4) and (3.5), on the assumption that firms engage in all bond financing, with B_t^d denoting the private *excess* demand for bonds. We choose to work with perpetual bonds as they turn out to be marginally simpler, without affecting any of the conclusions. Observe also that we are abstracting from the effects of capital accumulation in our definition of wealth, for notational convenience setting the fixed stock of capital $\bar{K}$, say, equal to zero. We have already commented on the problems this raises and will seek to rectify them in subsequent extensions of the model; see Chapters 7 and 8.

In the light of these considerations we postulate the modified consumption and money demand functions

$$\left. \begin{array}{l} C_t = c_1(1-u)(Y_t + B_{t-1}) + c_2(M_{t-1} + B_{t-1}/r_t) \\[4pt] \quad 0 < c_1 < 1, \quad 0 < c_2 < 1 \end{array} \right\} \qquad (4.20)$$

$$\left. \begin{array}{l} M_t^d = \alpha_1 Y_t + \alpha_2(M_{t-1} + B_{t-1}/r_t) + \beta r_t \\[4pt] \quad \alpha_1 > 0, \quad 0 < \alpha_2 < 1, \quad \beta < 0 \end{array} \right\} \qquad (4.21)$$

while the investment function remains unchanged. In addition to the above restrictions on c_2, α_2, the budget constraint (4.19) requires $0 < c_2 + \alpha_2 < 1$, the remaining wealth effect is absorbed by the demand for bonds which is obtained residually from equation (4.19).

It should be pointed out that there are certain asymmetries in these demand functions. For example, consumption is a function of disposable income, while the demand for money depends upon total income. Likewise, wealth effects are assumed absent from the investment function. These assumptions are in no way inconsistent with (4.19). They are the conventional ones and their accuracy is largely an empirical matter. One may justify having different coefficients on the components of Y^D on aggregation grounds and it is clear that we are abstracting from this issue. The fact that money is used for transactions purposes is a further reason for introducing Y rather than Y^D into the demand for money. This assumption could easily be modified without altering the substance of the analysis.[6]

Hence we obtain the modified *IS* and *LM* relationships

$$Y_t - c_1(1-u)(Y_t + B_{t-1}) - c_2(M_{t-1} + B_{t-1}/r_t) - iY_t - \gamma r_t = G_t \quad (4.22)$$

$$M_t = \alpha_1 Y_t + \alpha_2(M_{t-1} + B_{t-1}/r_t) + \beta r_t \quad (4.23)$$

which with the restrictions imposed have the usual slopes.[7]

Finally, the interest payments must also be taken into account in the government budget constraint, which now becomes:

$$\Delta M_t + \frac{\Delta B_t}{r_t} = G_t - uY_t + (1-u)B_{t-1}. \quad (4.24)$$

The extra term measures the interest payments net of taxes which the government must finance in addition to its other commitments. In particular, even if $G_t = uY_t$, the government will need to either print more money or issue additional bonds in order to meet the interest payments on its outstanding debt. Thus it becomes clear that an increase in the quantity of bonds has an income (flow) effect as well as a wealth (stock) effect. While the latter effect is well known, the former effect has essentially been ignored in the existing literature. This turns out to be a particularly serious omission, since as will become apparent from the analysis below, it is this income effect which leads to the major modifications of our earlier results.

Equations (4.22), (4.23) and (4.24) of the modified system specify a dynamic structure. However, since both B_{t-1} and B_{t-1}/r_t appear, the relations are non-linear and thus cannot be readily solved analytically. Consequently, instead of trying to analyse the entire time path as we did in Sections 2 and 3, it is more convenient to examine the first-period, second-period and long-run (equilibrium) comparative statics of the system and these we shall consider in turn. Furthermore, because we are going to consider changes over different time periods, for the sake of clarity, we denote these changes by first differences, rather than partial derivatives.

5. First-period effects

Suppose that initially, in period 0 say, the system is in equilibrium. Since both M_{t-1} and B_{t-1} appear as determinants of equations (4.22), (4.23), this requires $\Delta M_0 = \Delta B_0 = 0$, so that in period 0, the government budget constraint is[8]

$$G_0 - uY_0 + (1-u)B_0 = 0. \tag{4.25}$$

Taking account of this equilibrium condition, it follows that the government budget constraint during period 1 becomes

$$\Delta M_1 + \frac{\Delta B_1}{r_1} = \Delta G_1 - u\Delta Y_1 + (1-u)\Delta B_0 = \Delta G_1 - u\Delta Y_1.$$

Taking first differences of the *IS* and *LM* relations, the first period changes of the system from the original equilibrium are given by the set of equations

$$[1 - c_1(1-u) - i]\Delta Y_1 - (\gamma - c_2 B_0/r_1^2)\Delta r_1 = \Delta G_1 \tag{4.26a}$$

$$\alpha_1 \Delta Y_1 + (\beta - \alpha_2 B_0/r_1^2)\Delta r_1 - \Delta M_1 = 0 \tag{4.26b}$$

$$u\Delta Y_1 + \Delta M_1 = \Delta G_1 - \Delta B_1/r_1. \tag{4.26c}$$

As before, the government has three policy variables $\Delta B_1, \Delta G_1, \Delta M_1$, any two of which can be chosen independently. As written above, we have chosen $\Delta G_1 \, \Delta B_1$ as our independent policy instruments, allowing $\Delta Y_1 \, \Delta r_1, \Delta M_1$ to be endogenously determined.

The system of equations (4.26) readily yield the first period multipliers for the different policies specified above. These turn out to be virtually identical to the corresponding effects obtained in Section 3. The reason is that the additional factors introduced through wealth effects and interest repayments operate with a one period lag and thus do not come into play until period 2.

Thus for example, the first-period effects of a pure open market operation (Policy 1) are given by

$$\frac{\Delta Y_1}{\Delta B_1} = \frac{-(\gamma - c_2 B_0/r_1^2)}{r_1 K_1} < 0 \tag{4.27a}$$

$$\frac{\Delta r_1}{\Delta B_1} = \frac{-[1 - c_1(1-u) - i]}{r_1 K_1} > 0 \tag{4.27b}$$

where $K_1 < 0$ is the Jacobian of (4.26), while the impact on the money supply can be shown to satisfy the inequality

$$-\frac{1}{r_1} < \frac{\Delta M_1}{\Delta B_1} < 0.$$

Likewise, the first-period impact of an increase in G financed in accordance with Policy 2 is

$$\frac{\Delta Y_1}{\Delta G_1} = \frac{(\beta - \alpha_2 B_0/r_1^2) + (\gamma - c_2 B_0/r_1^2)\theta}{K_1 - (1-\theta)u(\gamma - c_2 B_0/r_1^2)} > 0 \tag{4.28}$$

The only differences between these expressions and those obtained in the no-wealth case are due to the capital gains or losses on the outstanding bonds and these do not alter any of the qualitative results. *Consequently, as far as the one period responses are concerned, ignoring the wealth effects does not lead to any seriously misleading implications.* This, however, changes in the second period, when the feedbacks arising from the wealth effects and interest payments begin to operate.

6. Second-period effects

The changes occurring during the second period after the initial displacement from equilibrium are obtained from the set of equations

$$[1 - c_1(1 - u) - i]\Delta Y_2 - (\gamma - c_2 B_1/r_2^2)\Delta r_2$$
$$= c_2 \Delta M_1 + \Delta G_2 + [c_2/r_2 + c_1(1 - u)] \Delta B_1 \qquad (4.29a)$$

$$\alpha_1 \Delta Y_2 + (\beta - \alpha_2 B_1/r_2^2)\Delta r_2 - \Delta M_2 = -\alpha_2 \Delta M_1 - (\alpha_2/r_2)\Delta B_1 \qquad (4.29b)$$

$$u\Delta Y_2 + \Delta M_2 = \Delta G_2 + \Delta G_2 - \Delta B_2/r_2 + (1 - u)\Delta B_1 - u\Delta Y_1 \qquad (4.29c)$$

where ΔY_1, ΔM_1 are the induced first-period changes. Clearly, it would be tedious and of little interest to calculate the second-period multipliers for all the policies specified above. Instead we shall focus on a few specific responses and discuss the issues they raise.

Let us first consider a single open market operation in period 1, which is unsustained during period 2; that is set $\Delta B_2 = \Delta G_2 = \Delta G_1 = 0$. Solving for $\Delta Y_2/\Delta B_1$ we obtain

$$\frac{\Delta Y_2}{\Delta B_1} = \frac{1}{K_2} \left\{ (c_2\beta - \alpha_2\gamma)\frac{\Delta V_1}{\Delta B_1} - (\gamma - c_2 B_1/r_2^2)\frac{\Delta Y_1}{\Delta B_1} \right.$$
$$\left. + (1 - u)[c_1(\beta - \alpha_2 B_1/r_2^2) + (\gamma - c_2 B_1/r_2^2)] \right\} \qquad (4.30)$$

where $K_2 < 0$ is the Jacobian of (4.29) and

$$\frac{\Delta V_1}{\Delta B_1} = \frac{1}{r_2} + \frac{\Delta M_1}{\Delta B_1}$$

is the effect of the increase in bonds on first-period wealth. This can be obtained by solving for the appropriate partial derivatives from (4.26) and to the first order of approximation is positive, by virtue of (4.29c).[9] Similarly, the term $\Delta Y_1/\Delta B_1$ is the first-period income effect which is explicitly reported in (4.27a).

Equation (4.30) describes the change in income occurring in period 2 (from what it was in period 1) arising from the initial change in B_1. It consists of three components. The first is the wealth effect and this is ambiguous in sign. The increase in B_1 increases W_1, thereby increasing consumption expenditure, which is expansionary, while at the same time increasing the demand for money, which is contractionary. In familiar terminology, the *IS* curve shifts to the right and the *LM* curve moves to the left. The net effect on income will depend upon which curve shifts more and this is measured by $(c_2 \beta - \alpha_2 \gamma)$. The second term arises from the interest payments and is strictly positive. It reflects the fact that an increase in B_1 increases interest payments to the private sector, thereby increasing private disposable income. This increases consumption expenditure and provides an expansionary effect, which of course gives rise to further repercussions. The final term is the induced tax effect and as discussed before this is also expansionary. This is because an increase in B_1 by reducing Y_1, lowers tax receipts, thereby creating a budget deficit. With no further open market operations taking place in period 2, this must be financed through increases in the money supply and this of course is an expansionary effect.

Thus the second-period effects of an open market transaction of bonds are not unambiguous. The interest payments and induced tax effects begin to exert expansionary influences, while the wealth effect is indeterminate and depends upon the relative wealth effects in consumption and the demand for money. If the only wealth effect is in consumption then this too will be expansionary; on the other hand the second-period effects may be negative if the wealth effect in the demand for money is sufficiently strong.

The second-period effects of an increase in G_1 ($\Delta G_2 = 0$), where in period 2

$$\frac{\Delta B_2}{r_2} = (1-\theta)[\Delta G_1 - u\Delta Y_1 - u\Delta Y_2 + (1-u)\Delta B_1]$$

are obtained by substituting for this expression into (4.29), yielding

$$\frac{\Delta Y_2}{\Delta G_1} = \frac{1}{K_2 - (1-\theta)u(\gamma - c_2 B_0/r_1^2)} \left\{ (\gamma - c_2 B_1/r_2^2)\theta \right.$$
$$+ (c_2 \beta - \alpha_2 \gamma)\frac{\Delta V_1}{\Delta G_1} + (1-u)[c_1(\beta - \alpha_2 B_1/r_2^2)$$
$$\left. + \theta(\gamma - c_2 B_1/r_2^2)]\frac{\Delta B_1}{\Delta G_1} - u(\gamma - c_2 B_1/r_2^2)\theta\frac{\Delta Y_1}{\Delta G_1} \right\}, (4.31)$$

which consists of a number of components. First, to the extent that the deficit is money financed, there is a continued induced monetary effect given by $(\gamma - c_2 B_1/r_2^2)\theta$. Secondly, there is the wealth effect which is ambiguous for the reasons already discussed. The third term is the effect due to interest payments and it is in general strictly positive. As long as $\theta \neq 0$, an increase in G_1 will increase B_1, thereby raising interest payments in period 2, hence increasing disposable income and consumption. The final term is the tax induced effect and is negative. The increase in G_1 raises Y_1 and hence tax receipts increase. This reduces the budget deficit (or increases the budget surplus) and thereby provides a contractionary effect. Hence overall, the impact of an increase in government expenditure on second-period income contains some indeterminate elements. While one would presumably expect the familiar positive effects to dominate, one cannot rule out the possibility of a drop in second-period income.

Like (4.30), (4.31) gives the change in income in period 2 from what it was in period 1. It therefore measures the *incremental* change occurring in that period resulting from the initial increase in government expenditure. The total *accumulated* change from the initial level of income is given by

$$\frac{Y_2 - Y_0}{G_1} = \frac{\Delta Y_1}{\Delta G_1} + \frac{\Delta Y_2}{\Delta G_1}$$

and is obtained by summing (4.28) and (4.31).

7.   Stability and steady-state effects

We now consider the steady-state (long-run) effects of the various policies, on the assumption that the system starts out from equilibrium. This involves comparing changes in the equilibrium values of the system and can be done only if the dynamic process generated by the policy is stable. With the non-linearities introduced by the wealth effects, only local stability can be examined and to analyse this equation we proceed as follows. Given the policy as specified by B (or ΔB) and G, equation (4.24) describes a dynamic equation for M_t, in terms of the policy instruments, as well as Y_t and r_t. The two equations (4.22) and (4.23) can be solved for Y_t and r_t in terms of M_t, M_{t-1}, B_{t-1} and G_t and upon substitution of these solutions into (4.24) we obtain a difference equation for M_t in terms of the policy variables alone. This equation is then linearized and the stability characteristics of the associated linear system is examined. Since Y_t and r_t both appear contemporaneously in (4.22) and (4.23) they clearly have the same local stability properties and thus the stability of the entire system is determined by the local stability of M_t.

Consider first a single open market operation. Once the initial change in B has occurred and B is held constant at its new level, the money supply must satisfy the difference equation

$$M_t - M_{t-1} + u Y_t = K \tag{4.32}$$

where K is a constant determined by the constant levels of B and G.[10] Linearizing equation (4.32) in the manner indicated above (and recalling that after the initial period B_{t-1} is constant), yields an equation of the form

$$\left(1 + \frac{u \partial Y_t}{\partial M_t}\right) M_t - \left(1 - \frac{u \partial Y_t}{\partial M_{t-1}}\right) M_{t-1} = K'$$

where the partial derivatives are evaluated at equilibrium and the constant K'

depends upon the equilibrium values of M, Y. This equation is locally stable if and only if

$$-(1 + u\partial Y_t/\partial M_t) < 1 - u\partial Y_t/\partial M_{t-1} < (1 + u\partial Y_t/\partial M_t).$$

Substituting for $\partial Y_t/\partial M_t$, $\partial Y_t/\partial M_{t-1}$ one can immediately verify that the left hand inequality is satisfied, while a sufficient (but not necessary) condition for the right hand inequality to hold – and hence for local stability – is

$$(1 - c_1)(1 - u) - i > 0. \tag{4.33}$$

As we have mentioned before, this restriction is stronger than (4.4) imposed on the *IS* curve. Nevertheless it is still rather mild, so that local stability is virtually ensured.[11]

As we have already seen, equilibrium requires $\Delta M_t = \Delta B_t = 0$, that is

$$G - uY + (1 - u)B = 0. \tag{4.34}$$

Thus as an equilibrium condition we still require that the government's budget be balanced. The difference is that now tax receipts and hence income must be sufficient to pay not only for the exogenous government expenditure, but also for the interest net of taxes owing on the outstanding government debt.

The long-run changes of the system resulting from a single open market operation are obtained by taking differences of equations (4.22), (4.23) and (4.34) and solving the system

$$[1 - c_1(1 - u) - i]\Delta'Y - (\gamma - c_2 B/r^2)\Delta'r - c_2 \Delta'M$$
$$= [c_2/r + c_1(1 - u)]\Delta'B \tag{4.35a}$$

$$\alpha_1 \Delta'Y + (\beta - \alpha_2 B/r^2)\Delta'r + (\alpha_2 - 1)\Delta'M = -(\alpha_2/r)\Delta'B \tag{4.35b}$$

$$u\Delta'Y = (1 - u)\Delta'B \tag{4.35c}$$

where Δ' denotes the change in equilibrium values.[12]

From equation (4.35c) we immediately observe that the long-run effect of an open market transaction of bonds on the level of income is

$$\frac{\Delta'Y}{\Delta'B} = \frac{1 - u}{u} > 0. \tag{4.36}$$

This is a rather striking result and is precisely the expression obtained previously by Christ.[13] It asserts that contrary to the conventional view, a *single* open market sale of bonds will eventually lead to a *permanent increase* in the level of income. By now, however, the reason for this seemingly perverse result should be apparent. The initial impact of a sale of bonds is to raise the interest rate, which will tend to reduce income. Next period, the increased interest income resulting from the sale of bonds will have an expansionary effect, which we have already discussed will tend to offset the first effect. As we saw in Section 3, the contractionary effect of the increase in B is only transitory. The decrease in income it generates will create a reduction in tax receipts, which in turn creates a budget deficit. Holding B constant at its new level, this deficit must be financed by printing more money and this is an expansionary policy, eventually completely offsetting the original contraction in activity. On the other hand, the *one-and-for-all* increase in B gives rise to a *permanent* increase in interest payments to the private sector, leading to an increase in disposable income, consumption and expenditure. This latter effect ultimately dominates, so that the long-run effect of an increase in B must indeed be expansionary. By contrast, the long-run multipliers $\partial r/\partial B$, $\partial M/\partial B$ both become indeterminate, implying that in the long run, the monetary authorities may have relatively little ability in influencing monetary variables.

Consider now the stability of a fiscal policy where the budget deficit is financed in accordance with Policy 2. Assuming

$$\Delta B_t/r_t = (1 - \theta)(G_t - uY_t + (1 - u)B_{t-1})$$

the rate of change of money supply and bonds are related by

$$\frac{\Delta B_t}{(1 - \theta)r_t} = \frac{\Delta M_t}{\theta}. \tag{4.37}$$

By taking the first difference of equation (4.23) and eliminating ΔB_t using equation (4.37), we obtain the following first order difference equation in ΔM_t, which however, also involves ΔY_t:

$$\Delta M_t - [1 + (1 - u)(1 - \theta)r_{t-1}]\Delta M_{t-1} = \theta(\Delta G_t - u\Delta Y_t).$$

We must therefore solve for ΔY_t in terms of ΔM_t and ΔM_{t-1} and this can be easily done by taking the first differences of equations (4.22) and (4.23) and eliminating ΔB_{t-1} with (4.37). Performing this calculation yields the solution

$$\Delta Y_t = \frac{1}{\psi}[(\gamma - c_2 B_{t-1}/r_t^2)(\Delta M_t - \Delta M_{t-1}) + \phi\Delta M_{t-1}/\theta]$$

where

$$\phi = \begin{vmatrix} c_2 & -(\gamma - c_2 B_{t-1}/r_t^2) & -(c_2/r_t + c_1(1 - u)) \\ 1 - \alpha_2 & (\beta - \alpha_2 B_{t-1}/r_t^2) & \alpha_2/r_t \\ r_t(1 - \theta) & 0 & \theta \end{vmatrix}$$

$$\psi = (1 - c_1(1 - u) - i)(\beta - \alpha_2 B_{t-1}/r_t^2) + \alpha_1(\gamma - c_2 B_{t-1}/r_t^2) < 0.$$

Substituting for ΔY_t yields the following difference equation in ΔM_t

$$\left(1 + \frac{u\theta}{\psi}\left(\gamma - c_2 B_{t-1}/r_t^2\right)\right) \Delta M_t - \left(1 + \frac{u\theta}{\psi}(\gamma - c_2 B_{t-1}/r_t^2)\right.$$

$$\left. + (1-u)(1-\theta)r_{t-1} - u\phi/\psi\right) \Delta M_{t-1} = \theta \Delta G. \qquad (4.38)$$

After the initial increase in G_t, the right hand side of this equation will be zero; the local stability can be analysed by considering the left hand side of this equation alone.

Accordingly, Policy 2 will be stable if and only if

$$-2\psi - 2u\theta(\gamma - c_2 B/r^2) > (1-u)(1-\theta)r\psi - u\phi > 0. \qquad (4.39)$$

Note that this stability analysis is in terms of ΔM_t. When the system is stable, equation (4.38) implies $\Delta M_t \to 0$, that is M_t tends to a constant. This constant level is not determined by the adjustment equation (4.38) but will be dependent upon initial conditions.[14]

Thus a fiscal policy, financed in accordance with Policy 2 may be unstable. Taking limiting cases, we can show that if $\theta = 1$, so that the entire budget deficit is financed by printing money, then it is almost certainly stable. The inequality (4.33) provides a weak sufficiency condition which ensures this will be the case.[15] On the other hand, for $\theta = 0$, this policy may quite plausibly be unstable, depending upon the parameters of the system. Stability under bond-financing thus becomes essentially an empirical matter.

This result is consistent with that obtained by Blinder and Solow (1973). In their fixed capital stock model they show that fiscal policy may quite plausibly be unstable when the resulting government deficit is financed entirely by debt, although when the capital stock is allowed to vary, instability is much less likely to occur.

The fact that with complete debt financing the system may be unstable is not surprising. As we have been stressing the most important reason is the interest payments on the outstanding debt which continually need to be financed. Suppose that the system is initially in equilibrium and that there is an increase in G with the resulting budget deficit being financed completely by issuing new debt the initial effect of which is to raise income. Moreover, the interest paid by the government to the private sector on the new debt will increase disposable income, thereby increasing consumption expenditure and causing income to rise further. If the additional tax receipts induced by the increase of income are less than the additional interest payments, the government's budget deficit will increase. This will lead the government to increase the rate at which it is issuing new bonds, thereby increasing the rate of growth of interest payments, and income, and thus generating an unstable situation.

However, we now suppose that the system is stable and examine the long-run responses resulting from an increase in government expenditure. As we have already seen, this policy defines a relationship between ΔM_t and ΔB_t, given by (4.37). The adjustment imposes a relationship between $\Delta'M$ and $\Delta'B$, the long-run equilibrium changes in these two variables. Integrating equation (4.37), it follows that to the first order approximation[16]

$$\theta\Delta'B = (1-\theta)r\Delta'M. \tag{4.40}$$

Hence with this relationship, the long-run changes in the equilibrium values of the system are now obtained by solving

$$[1-c_1(1-u)-i]\Delta'Y-[\gamma-c_2B/r^2]\Delta'r-c_2\Delta'M$$
$$-[(c_2/r+c_1(1-u)]\Delta'B = \Delta'G \tag{4.41a}$$

$$\alpha_1\Delta'Y+[\beta-\alpha_2B/r^2]\Delta'r+(\alpha_2-1)\Delta'M+(\alpha_2/r)\Delta'B = 0 \tag{4.41b}$$

$$(1-\theta)r\Delta'M-\theta\Delta'B = 0 \tag{4.41c}$$

$$u\Delta'Y-(1-u)\Delta'B = \Delta'G \tag{4.41d}$$

The important thing to observe about this system is that *all the multipliers – and in particular* $\partial Y/\partial G$ *– will depend upon all the parameters of the system and not just the tax parameters as is the case when interest payments are ignored.* How Y responds to changes in G now depends upon how the government deficit is financed, since this determines $\Delta'B$, which in turn is jointly determined with $\Delta'r$, $\Delta'M$.

$$\frac{\Delta'Y}{\Delta'G} = \frac{\phi-(1-u)r(1-\theta)(\beta-\alpha_2B/r^2)}{u\phi-(1-u)r(1-\theta)\psi} \tag{4.42}$$

where the terms ϕ, ψ have been defined above. With all money financing $(\theta=1)$, $\Delta'Y/\Delta'G = 1/u$, just as it is when interest payments are ignored. This is the case considered by Christ, and indicate that his results are, in fact, very special; see Christ (1969, pp. 698–9). The stability conditions ensure that the denominator of (4.42) – which is just the Jacobian of the system (4.41) – is negative (see (4.39)). However, the numerator of this expression cannot be signed unambiguously and one cannot eliminate the possibility that $\Delta'Y/\Delta'G$ may be negative. Nevertheless, this is an extremely unlikely occurrence and if we add the weak restriction (4.33) then we can easily show

$$\frac{\Delta'Y}{\Delta'G}>\frac{1}{u}>0. \tag{4.43}$$

In this case, not only is the multiplier positive, but it is *larger* than the corresponding expression obtained for the simple model. Furthermore, provided $\partial Y/\partial G>0$ one can immediately deduce from (4.41c) and (4.41d) that both $\partial B/\partial G$, $\partial M/\partial G>0$. The effect on the interest rate however, is indeterminate.

8.   Conclusions: some implications for the monetarist debate

This chapter has extended the basic Keynesian macroeconomic model to incorporate the government budget constraint. It demonstrates that in general, this constraint imposes a dynamic structure on the model, which only in very restrictive cases degenerates to the usual static case. The most important results emerging from the analysis are as follows.

First, taking a simple model which abstracts from wealth effects and interest payments on the outstanding bonds (and therefore coincides most closely with the usual *IS–LM* model), we show that in general, neither the single period, nor the long-run multipliers equal the usual expressions. In particular, a single open market sale or purchase of bonds while having a short-run effect, will in the long run be only transitory. The increase in income generated by an initial purchase of bonds by the monetary authorities will create a budget surplus, the effects of which will be to reduce the money supply and cause an offsetting reduction in income.

The government expenditure multiplier was calculated on the assumption that the government decides to finance a certain fraction of its budget deficit by issuing bonds (and the rest by increasing the supply of money). In this case, the long-run government expenditure multiplier simply equals the inverse of the tax rate and is independent of all other parameters in the system; in particular, (with one exception) it is invariant with respect to the financial mix chosen. This, is precisely one of the main results previously obtained by Ott and Ott and Christ. However, the proportion of the deficit financed by bonds, θ, does influence the speed of adjustment to equilibrium. For $\theta \neq 0$, the rate of convergence varies inversely with θ; for $\theta = 0$, complete adjustment occurs within a single period, in which case the dynamic structure degenerates and the standard, static case emerges. The effects of G on r are also examined and a similar dichotomy of cases is obtained. As long as $\theta = 0$, so that some money is being issued, we find that an increase in G will most likely, but not necessarily, lower the interest rate and that this reduction in r is independent of θ. For $\theta = 0$, the usual result of an increase in r is obtained.

Introducing wealth effects and interest payments into the analysis leaves the first-period responses virtually unchanged. However, the second period and long-run equilibrium effects alter dramatically. Almost all second-period multipliers have indeterminacies. For example, while the immediate impact of an open market sale of bonds by the government is to raise interest rates and to lower income, it does have an offsetting expansionary effect which comes into effect in the next period. The increase in bonds held by the public, raises interest income and hence disposable income, thereby increasing consumption and expenditure. Furthermore, while the contractionary effect of a once-and-for-all increase in B will dominate in the short run, in the long run it will disappear. On the other hand, the increase in private bond holdings resulting from such a sale, gives rise to a *permanent* increase in interest payments to the public, creating a permanent increase in disposable income. Thus we obtain the rather paradoxical result that a once-and-for-all open market sale of bonds will lead to a long-run increase in income, with the magnitude of the impact depending purely on the tax rate.

A striking difference is also obtained for the long-run government expenditure multiplier, where a fraction θ of the deficit is financed through additional bonds. Unlike a single open market operation, this policy may, quite plausibly, be unstable, especially if the proportion financed by bonds is very high. However, assuming that the system is stable, an increase in G will almost certainly increase income, *although (unless $\theta = 1$) the increase in income will depend upon all the parameters of the system – not just the tax rate.* In this respect, the introduction of interest payments fundamentally alters the early Ott and Ott and Christ result. While in equilibrium the government budget must still be balanced, one of the items in the budget is interest payments, which depend upon the rest of the system.

In contrast to the short run, this analysis suggests that the traditional macroeconomic model which ignores the government budget constraint, has very misleading implications for the longer-run effects of policy changes. While we have chosen to focus on the complications arising from interest payments and wealth effects within the conventional model, it is clear that this analysis can be extended in other directions as well. Some of these are pursued in subsequent chapters.

Finally, we conclude the present discussion by summarizing briefly its implications for the monetarist debate and in particular for the effectiveness of fiscal policy. This question has been taken up at length by Blinder and Solow (1973) using a similar (continuous-time) model to that presented here. Their conclusions (and ours) are that the economy will almost certainly be stable under all money financing, in which case the steady-state government expenditure multiplier equals the inverse of the tax rate, as we have shown. If the economy is stable under all bond financing, then fiscal policy is normally effective and in that case will be *more* expansionary than a money-financed deficit. Hence for fiscal policy to be ineffective, the system must almost certainly be unstable. In that case a bond-financed increase in the government deficit will have a perverse effect on income, driving it down indefinitely! As we have seen, the stability under bond financing is essentially an empirical matter and the possibility of instability certainly cannot be ruled out.

5

THE WAGE–PRICE SECTOR

It will be recalled from Chapter 2 that the traditional macroeconomic model can be reduced to an aggregate demand curve and an aggregate supply curve. These two relationships between them determine, among other things, the equilibrium price level. Early discussions of inflation were conducted in terms of shifts in these aggregate demand and supply curves. An exogenous upward shift in the aggregate demand curve by increasing equilibrium output and equilibrium price would create what is known as a 'demand-pull' inflation. Similarly an exogenous upward shift in the aggregate supply curve, by reducing equilibrium output and raising equilibrium price would give rise to 'cost-push' inflation, reflecting the fact that the upward shift in the supply curve was a consequence of increased costs.

The traditional discussion of inflation fully recognized the interaction between 'demand-pull' and 'cost-push' effects. Higher prices resulting from an exogenous increase in demand say, would cause workers to seek higher wages. To the extent these claims are granted, costs would be increased, thereby shifting the aggregate supply curve upwards. These higher wages would in turn mean higher income for labour, increasing their demand and leading to further outward shifts in the aggregate demand curve. Further price increases would result and this cycle would be repeated.[1]

But the discussion was basically in static terms, using a static model, and focusing on price levels. Inflation is generally defined to be a situation of rising prices, and to be concerned with (percentage) *rates of change* of prices, rather than price levels. It can therefore be more usefully analysed within a dynamic framework rather than in purely comparative static terms. This is the standpoint we shall adopt throughout our analysis. The two views are not inconsistent. An increase in the equilibrium price level implies that the price must be changing over some period at least. And the larger the increase in the price level, the larger is the rate of change of prices in some average sense.

In this chapter we analyse the wage–price sector. While inflation is sometimes considered in terms of only the interaction of wages and prices, in fact the behaviour of wages and prices constitutes only one aspect of the inflationary process and ultimately must be integrated with the rest of the macroeconomic system. This synthesis is undertaken in the following chapters. We should also make it very clear that we are not attempting to provide a comprehensive discussion of wage and price determination. With the recent inflationary conditions a voluminous literature has developed on this subject and several theories have evolved; for a survey of this recent literature see Trevithick and Mulvey (1975), Laidler and Parkin (1975). Our concern will be on one main aspect of this literature, which has been central to the discussion and which we regard as particularly relevant, namely the role of inflationary expectations. We shall exposit this theory in sufficient detail to enable us to incorporate it eventually into a complete macroeconomic model.

1.   The Phillips curve

Much of modern theory of inflation owes its origins to the so-called 'Phillips curve'. This relationship is due to A.W. Phillips (1958) who discovered the existence of an inverse empirical relationship between the percentage rate of change of money wages on the one hand, and the rate of unemployment on the other. Stimulated by his findings, other researchers have investigated this trade-off using data for a number of countries. In general, the inverse relationship originally obtained by Phillips for the United Kingdom over the period 1861–1957 was confirmed, at least initially, although subsequent work has indicated that other variables are also important determinants of money wage changes.[2] This observation has led to the so-called 'extended Phillips curve' which we shall discuss further below.

In algebraic terms, the simplest Phillips curve can be written as

$$w \equiv \frac{\dot{W}}{W} = f(U) \qquad f'(U) < 0 \tag{5.1}$$

where W = level of money wages,
         w = percentage rate of change of money wages; i.e. the rate of money wage inflation,
         U = rate of unemployment.

While it is often convenient to assume a linear relationship for f, much of the available empirical evidence tends to favour a hyperbolic relationship such as

$$\frac{\dot{W}}{W} = a_0 + a_1 U^{-1} \qquad a_1 > 0. \tag{5.1'}$$

In this case the trade-off relationship between money wage inflation and the rate of unemployment becomes steeper the lower the level of unemployment; see Figure 5.1.

The term 'Phillips curve' is often used to describe the relationship between the rate of change of *prices* and unemployment. This definition and the one given above in (5.1) are intimately related. Let us assume the simple pricing relationship

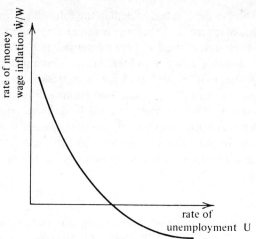

Fig. 5.1 *The Phillips curve*

$$P = mULC \tag{5.2}$$

where P = price of output,
             m = mark-up factor, assumed to be constant $\geqslant 1$,
             ULC = unit labour costs.

Equation (5.2) asserts that price is set as a mark-up on unit labour costs where

$$ULC = \frac{WN}{Y} \tag{5.3}$$

        N = employment of labour,
        Y = output.

Taking percentage changes of (5.2) and (5.3) yields

$$p \equiv \frac{\dot{P}}{P} = \frac{\dot{ULC}}{ULC} = \frac{\dot{W}}{W} + \left(\frac{\dot{N}}{Y}\right) \bigg/ \left(\frac{N}{Y}\right) \tag{5.4}$$

where p = rate of price inflation. If average labour productivity (Y/N) grows at a rate ρ say, (5.4) can be written as

$$p = w - \rho \tag{5.5}$$

implying the rate of price inflation/unemployment trade-off relationship

$$p = f(U) - \rho. \tag{5.6}$$

Of course (5.6) and its intimate relationship to (5.1), is a consequence of the extremely simple pricing rule (5.2); a more complex rule will give rise to a more complex relationship.

The wage–unemployment trade-off as presented by Phillips was not founded on any particularly rigorous theory. The problem of providing the relationship with some theoretical underpinnings has occupied the attention of many economists. One of the first attempts at rationalizing the relationship was given by Lipsey (1960). He viewed it in terms of a Walrasian price adjustment relationship of the type specified earlier by Samuelson (1947) and others and applied to commodity markets in various contexts.

This suggests a wage adjustment relationship of the form

$$\frac{\dot{W}}{W} = f\left(\frac{D-S}{N}\right) \qquad f' > 0 \tag{5.7}$$

where D = demand for labour,
S = supply of labour,
so that wages are assumed to move in proportion to excess labour demand. Since the demand for labour must equal amount of labour employed plus unfilled vacancies, while the supply of labour equals the amount of labour employed plus unemployed workers, we have by definition

$$D = N + V_a$$
$$S = N + U_n$$

where U_n = number of workers unemployed,
V_a = number of job vacancies.

Thus

$$\frac{D-S}{N} = \frac{V_a - U_n}{N}$$

so that the excess demand for labour (relative to employment) depends upon the difference between the vacancy rate V_a/N and the unemployment rate U_n/N.

This Walras–Samuelson approach to the wage adjustment relationship suggests that the appropriate excess demand variable is the vacancy rate less the unemployment rate. Wage equations using the vacancy rate either together with, or instead of, the unemployment rate as the demand variable have been estimated, but in general these prove to be no better than simply using the unemployment variable alone.[3] One of the reasons is that vacancy data are often of rather poor quality since firms tend to be unreliable in reporting unfilled jobs. Thus the vast bulk of empirical literature simply uses U (or some function of it) as the proxy variable for excess demand.

As a further development of Phillips' work, Lipsey suggested that money wage changes depend not only on unemployment, but also on its changes. Specifically, he postulated an equation of the form

$$\frac{\dot{W}}{W} = a_0 + a_1 U^{-1} + a_2 U^{-2} + a_3 \Delta U \tag{5.8}$$

and found $a_1 > 0, a_2 > 0, a_3 < 0$. The negative coefficient on ΔU implies that changes in money wage rates are greater than would otherwise be so when unemployment is falling and less when it is rising.

Recent work on labour markets has attempted to explain the Phillips curve in terms of more sophisticated theoretical issues. These include the time and cost associated with job search and with looking for suitable employees. This literature is still very much in its early stages of development, and we do not discuss it further here.[4]

The Phillips curve as described by (5.1) or (5.6) is not a complete theory of inflation. The reason is that it involves the unemployment rate, which is an endogenous variable and itself needs to be explained. To provide a complete explanation of the inflationary process a relationship such as (5.1) or (5.6) must be considered as part of a larger system explaining U. The development of this integrated model is the task of Chapters 6–8.

Thus rather than providing a theory of inflation, the Phillips curve describes the trade-off possibilities which are available to the economy between the two *endogenous* variables, price stability and unemployment. With a downward sloping curve, a lower level of unemployment can be achieved only at the expense of a higher rate of inflation and vice versa. The dilemma posed by this trade-off relationship has been a central point in recent policy debates. These have been discussed at length elsewhere and we need not pursue them further here; see e.g., Tobin (1972).

While our interpretation of the Phillips curve stresses the nature of the trade-off between the rate of price or wage inflation, and the level of unemployment, the equation is also interpreted in other ways. As already suggested, Lipsey tended to view it as an equation describing the dynamics of price adjustment. He treated it as a structural relationship and as such it represents one of the first attempts to introduce some explicitly dynamic considerations into modern macroeconomic theory. Our reason for emphasising the trade-off aspects, rather than the price dynamics, is that our subsequent analysis tends to focus on the dynamics of the *rate of inflation* rather than that of the *price level*. If one's concern is with the evolution of rates of inflation, the Phillips curve can be more appropriately regarded as a *static* relationship between say $p \, (\equiv \dot{P}/P)$ and U. Further issues pertaining to the interpretation of the Phillips curve are discussed in a recent paper by Desai (1975).

2. The extended Phillips curve

Early empirical estimation of Phillips curve relationships indicated that money wage changes depend on more than just the rate of unemployment. Empirical work by Eckstein and Wilson (1962) and Perry (1964) found the percentage change of prices and the rate of profit to be significant explanatory variables, suggesting an extended Phillips curve of the form

$$w = \alpha_0 + \alpha_1 U + \alpha_2 p + \alpha_3 \Pi \tag{5.9}$$

where Π = rate of profit.

The change in prices was interpreted as reflecting the impact of cost of living increases on money wages. The rate of profit was justified as a measure of the effects of unions in determining wage increases. If profits increase, unions press for higher wage increases, which employers are presumably able to grant, at least in part, implying that $\alpha_3 > 0$.

Equations such as (5.9), which have formed the basis for much of the existing empirical work must be viewed as being rather *ad hoc*. There is no satisfactory rigorous theory at present which explains how unions bargain for higher wages. Yet it is this kind of behaviour which Π is supposed to capture. In Section 7 below we summarize a bilateral bargaining model of wage–price behaviour but this does not assign any explicit role of profits.

One further point should be made regarding equation (5.9). This equation, which as just commented is very typical of applied work, asserts that current wage changes at time t say, are determined solely by current explanatory variables at that same point of time t. This specification overlooks one crucial institutional factor – the existence of multi-period contracts. The effect of such contracts is to introduce a rather complex distributed lag structure into the determination of current wages. To see the nature of the issue involved, suppose that the workforce consists of two groups of people. Half have their wages determined by contracts signed at periods, $t, t + 2, t + 4 \ldots$, the other half sign contracts at time $t + 1, t + 3, t + 5, \ldots$ These contracts typically specify a wage increase for the period in which it is signed and also something for the next period. The period after that it is renegotiated. The average wage change taking place over the period $(t + 1, t + 2)$ say consists partly of the wage changes of workers who sign their contract at time $t + 2$, and partly of the wage changes of workers whose contracts were signed in the previous period, $t + 1$. It seems reasonable to suppose, at least as a first approximation, that contracts signed at any point of time t will depend upon economic conditions prevailing at that time. This means that the wage changes for workers signing contracts at time $t + 1$, specified for the following time period $(t + 1, t + 2)$ will be determined by conditions at time $t + 1$. If this is the case, it becomes intuitively clear that the wage change over period $(t + 1, t + 2)$ will depend partly upon factors at time $t + 1$, and partly on factors at time $t + 2$. When one generalizes this argument to contracts lasting several periods it is apparent that the existence of multi-period contracts creates a rather complex distributed lag structure in the determination of current wages, with the lag being intimately related to the percentage of workers who sign contracts at each point of time.

This important institutional fact is extremely difficult to incorporate in applied work and on the whole has been neglected. The conventional assumption, implicit in (5.8), is that *all* wages are adjusted each period. A detailed development of a model incorporating such contracts in empirical work is given in Taylor, Turnovsky and Wilson (1973), while a somewhat simpler version is given in Black and Kelejian (1972).[5] It is even more cumbersome to incorporate into a formal model and we do not attempt to do so. But it is important to realize the institutional assumptions implicit in conventional macroeconomic wage equations.

3.　　A simple model of the wage–price sector

One of the first integrated theories of the wage–price sector, which is also convenient for expository purposes is the model developed by Eckstein (1964).[6] This was constructed for an oligopolistic sector in which prices were determined by a form of target return pricing. In simplified form the Eckstein model can be described by the following set of equations

$$w \equiv \frac{\dot{W}}{W} = \alpha_0 + \alpha_1 U + \alpha_2 p + \alpha_3 \Pi \tag{5.9}$$

$$P = mULC \qquad m \geqslant 1 \tag{5.10}$$

$$ULC = AWe^{-\rho t} \tag{5.11}$$

Equation (5.9) is of course just the extended Phillips curve. Assuming that there is only one variable factor of production, labour, (5.10) asserts that prices are set as a constant mark-up on unit labour costs. Eckstein actually applies the mark-up to *normal* unit labour costs; that is those unit labour costs incurred when the firm is operating at some standard or normal rate. This hypothesis differs from a mark-up on *actual* unit labour costs in that it assumes that pricing behaviour is not influenced by short-run changes in labour productivity resulting from random fluctuations in output. Finally, equation (5.11) specifies (actual) unit labour costs to be an exponentially declining function of time, reflecting the growth in average labour productivity.

Taking percentage changes of (5.10) and (5.11) and assuming m, A, ρ remain constant, the system can be rewritten as:

$$w = \alpha_0 + \alpha_1 U + \alpha_2 p + \alpha_3 \Pi$$

$$p = w - \rho$$

which can be reduced to a single equation

$$p = \frac{\alpha_0}{1 - \alpha_2} + \frac{\alpha_1 U}{1 - \alpha_2} + \frac{\alpha_3 \Pi}{1 - \alpha_2} - \frac{\rho}{1 - \alpha_2}. \tag{5.12}$$

This equation is a reduced form of the wage–price sector and gives the rate of price inflation in terms of U, Π, ρ, and the parameters of the wage equation.

The pricing relationship (5.10) is the simplest one possible. It may be a reasonable representation of pricing behaviour in oligopolistic sectors, but it is not an adequate description of pricing in competitive industries. It completely neglects any demand effects which surely play an important role in price determination in this sector. As a first approximation, it would seem reasonable to replace (5.10), (5.11) by

$$p = \beta_0 + \beta_1 X + \beta_2 (w - p) \qquad \beta_1 > 0, \quad \beta_2 > 0 \qquad (5.13)$$

where X denotes some measure of excess product demand. Several such measures have been adopted. These include the degree of capacity utilization, measure of inventory disequilibria, and unfilled orders disequilibria; see e.g., Eckstein and Fromm (1968), Nordhaus (1972) for further discussion. The measure we shall adopt is the deviation between actual output Y and full employment output $\bar{Y}$, (possibly as a ratio of $\bar{Y}$), so that we write

$$p = \beta_0 - \beta_2 \rho + \beta_1 (Y - \bar{Y}) + \beta_2 w. \qquad (5.13')$$

Equation (5.13) thus represents a combination of cost pricing and competitive pricing, the latter being dominated by demand effects. It is analogous to the Phillips curve (5.9), but just like the Phillips curve it lacks any really firm theoretical underpinning.

Combining (5.13′) with (5.9) yields the following pair of equations for p and w:

$$p = \frac{(\beta_0 + \alpha_0 \beta_2) + \beta_1 (Y - \bar{Y}) + \beta_2 \alpha_1 U + \beta_2 \alpha_3 \Pi - \beta_2 \rho}{1 - \beta_2 \alpha_2} \qquad (5.13a)$$

$$w = \frac{(\alpha_0 + \beta_0 \alpha_2) + \alpha_1 U + \alpha_2 \beta_1 (Y - \bar{Y}) + \alpha_3 \Pi - \alpha_2 \beta_2 \rho}{1 - \beta_2 \alpha_2}. \qquad (5.13b)$$

Given U, $(Y - \bar{Y})$ and Π, equations (5.13) determine the rates of wage and price inflation. Note that while there are two excess demands $(Y - \bar{Y})$, U, these are not unrelated, especially in the short run. This can be seen as follows.

Suppose output is given by the production function

$$Y = F(\bar{K}, N)$$

where K denotes capital which in the short run is fixed at $\bar{K}$. Letting $\bar{N}$ denote the full employment level of labour, it follows that to a first order approximation

$$Y - \bar{Y} = \frac{\partial F}{\partial N} (N - \bar{N}).$$

Defining the unemployment rate U by

$$U = \frac{N - \bar{N}}{\bar{N}}$$

it follows that excess product demand, as measured by $(Y - \bar{Y})$ is related to U by a linear relationship of the form

$$U = \delta_0 + \delta_1 (Y - \bar{Y}) \qquad (5.14)$$

in which case one of the two variables can be immediately eliminated. This kind of relationship has obtained some empirical support from work by Okun

(1970). He found a reasonably stable relationship to exist between output and the rate of unemployment over the business cycle assuming that $\bar{Y}$ is exogenous. A one percent increase in the unemployment rate was associated with about a three percent decrease in real output. This short-run relationship has become known as *Okun's Law*.

For longer run models the relationship (5.14) is not likely to be satisfactory. Over the longer run, capital can be varied so that any increase in output may be met by more intensive use of capital rather than through increased employment. This issue is taken up at greater length in Chapter 8.

Finally, we should emphasize that equations (5.13) yield the simplest model of the wage–price sector. Eckstein's model is more complex in that it allows for other factors of production (notably raw materials) and for varying labour productivity. His model is extended further by Taylor, Turnovsky and Wilson, who as well as including these factors incorporate the distributed lags arising from the existence of multi-period contracts.

4.   The 'expectations hypothesis'

About the middle of the 1960s, the simple Phillips curve appeared to break down. The degree of explanatory power tended to decline and the empirical estimates were typically very unstable. This was a matter of some concern to economists and a good deal of effort was devoted to trying to explain these phenomena. One explanation was that shifts in the Phillips curve were due to changes in the price or wage expectations; see Friedman (1968), Phelps (1968). This proposition has received increasing attention over the past few years, and is discussed in some detail in the remaining sections of this chapter. However, other explanations were also given and these should be briefly mentioned. One of these suggested that the reason for the breakdown was due to the fact that the unemployment rate was an inadequate measure of excess demand. The evidence for this view tends to be inconclusive and we shall not discuss it further; see Trevithick and Mulvey (1975) for a summary. Another emphasized the monetary aspects of inflation and suggested that for an open economy, the domestic variables such as the unemployment rate would be dominated by international monetary develop- ments in their effects on domestic inflation. This view can be investigated only within the context of a complete model of an open economy such as the one developed in Chapter 12.

In its simplest form, the expectations hypothesis can be described by

$$w_t = a_0 + a_1 U_t + a_2 p_t^* \qquad a_1 < 0, \quad 0 \leqslant a_2 \leqslant 1 \qquad (5.15)$$

where p_t^* = expected rate of inflation during period t; i.e. over the time interval $(t-1, t)$. This equation asserts that current money wage changes depend upon the expected rate of inflation rather than the actual rate of price increase. It can be rationalized as a Walrasian price adjustment process if one assumes that the excess demand for labour leads to adjustments in the expected *real* wage. This interpretation yields a money wage equation of the form

$$w_t = a_0 + a_1 U_t + p_t^*$$ (5.15′)

where the coefficient of p_t^* is unity. Under this rationalization a 1 per cent increase in the expected rate of inflation should be reflected by a 1 per cent increase in the rate of money wage inflation.

The magnitude of the expectations coefficient a_2 turns out to be of crucial importance in determining the slope of the long-run Phillips curve. Hence interest in this question has inspired an extensive body of empirical literature which we discuss in more detail in Section 6.

To complete the formulation of the expectations hypothesis, we must postulate a price equation, together with some expectations formation relationship. For illustrative purposes we shall retain the simple price mark-up relationship

$$p = w - \rho$$ (5.5)

enabling us to write (5.15) as

$$p_t = a_0 - \rho + a_1 U_t + a_2 p_t^*.$$ (5.16)

As an expectations hypothesis we shall take the simplest 'static hypothesis',

$$p_t^* = p_{t-1}$$ (5.17)

according to which the anticipated rate of inflation for period t equals the previous rate of inflation p_{t-1}.

Equation (5.16) describes the short-run trade-off between the current inflation rate and unemployment for a given level of inflationary expectations p_t^*. As these expectations change, the position of this short-run Phillips curve shifts. Thus equations (5.16) and (5.17) together determine the evolution of the rate of price inflation over time. Substituting (5.17) into (5.16) yields

$$p_t = a_0 - \rho + a_1 U_t + a_2 p_{t-1}$$ (5.18)

which is a difference equation in p_t, and describes how the Phillips curve shifts over time. Provided $0 \leqslant a_2 \leqslant 1$, (5.18) converges to the long-run stationary trade-off

$$p = \frac{a_0 - \rho}{1 - a_2} + \frac{a_1}{1 - a_2} U.$$ (5.19)

The two trade-off curves (5.16) and (5.19) are illustrated in Figure 5.2. As long as $0 \leqslant a_2 < 1$, the long-run curve has a finite negative slope $a_1/(1 - a_2)$, implying the existence of a long-run trade-off between inflation and unemployment. Moreover, this long-run Phillips curve is steeper than the short-run curve whose slope is a_1. It is also interesting to note that the position of the long-run curve depends upon the rate of growth of labour

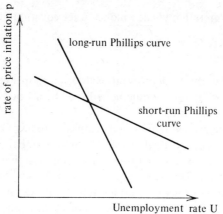

Fig. 5.2 *Short-run and long-run Phillips curves*

productivity. Differentiating (5.19) with respect to ρ yields

$$\frac{\partial p}{\partial \rho} = -\frac{1}{1-a_2} < 0$$

so that an increase in ρ lowers the rate of inflation for given U, thereby
shifting the long-run Phillips curve towards the origin.

If $a_2 = 1$, as would be the case if wages were negotiated in real terms, the
long-run Phillips curve is vertical. This means that there is no long-run trade-
off between the rate of inflation and the rate of unemployment. This has
important policy implications. It means that the government is unable to
reduce, say, the level of unemployment permanently by settling on a higher
rate of inflation. On the contrary, whatever the current rate of inflation
happens to be, after expectations have adjusted, the system will tend towards
the same rate of unemployment which for this reason has been termed the
'natural rate of unemployment'; see Friedman (1968).

To understand the 'natural rate' case ($a_2 = 1$), and its associated dynamics
more fully, let us consider the steady-state (long-run) equilibrium of the
difference equation (5.18). By substitution, this immediately implies

$$a_0 - \rho + a_1 U = 0$$

the solution to which defines the 'natural rate of unemployment' $\bar{U}$. Thus in
this model, the only way the government can influence the long-run rate of
unemployment is by shifting the long-run vertical Phillips curve and this
involves changing the parameters a_0, a_1, ρ. In particular, an increase in
labour productivity will shift the curve to the left and thus reduce $\bar{U}$.

To analyse the dynamics of (5.18) in the natural rate case, we rewrite
this equation in the form

$$p_t - p_{t-1} = a_1 (U_t - \bar{U}) \qquad a_1 < 0. \tag{5.20}$$

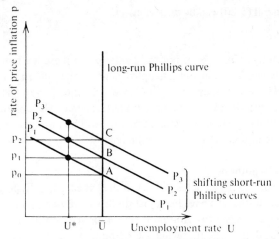

Fig. 5.3 *The vertical long-run Phillips curve and the natural rate of unemployment*

Suppose that the initial rate of inflation is p_0 and that the economy is at its natural rate of unemployment $\bar{U}$, in Figure 5.3. The short-run Phillips curve for period 1, $P_1 P_1$, is given by

$$p_1 = a_1(U_1 - \bar{U}) + p_0$$

and passes through the point $(\bar{U}, p_0)$. Suppose now the government attempts to reduce the level of unemployment below $\bar{U}$, to U^* say. The effect of this policy is to raise the rate of inflation in period one, to p_1 say, above p_0. This in turn raises expectations and shifts the short-run Phillips curve for period two to $P_2 P_2$. This curve is parallel to $P_1 P_1$ but passes through the point $(\bar{U}, p_1)$. If the government ceases to set $U = U^*$, the economy will return to its natural rate of unemployment, but this time at a higher rate of inflation. The effect of this one period policy will be to shift the economy from A to B on the vertical long-run Phillips curve through $\bar{U}$. That is, a *once-and-for-all* reduction in U leads to a *permanent* increase in the rate of inflation.

However, if the government sustains U at U^*, below $\bar{U}$, the rate of inflation in period two will rise further to $p_2 > p_1$ and the short-run Phillips curve in period three will shift out to $P_3 P_3$, passing through the point $(\bar{U}, p_2)$. Indeed as long as $U^* < \bar{U}$, the rate of inflation will continue to increase and the short-run Phillips curves will continue to shift outwards without limit. For this reason, the case $a_2 = 1$ is often referred to as the 'acceleration hypothesis' since unless U is held constant at U^*, the rate of inflation will not settle down to any stable value, but instead, price increases will continually accelerate (or decelerate if $U > \bar{U}$).

While we have illustrated the acceleration hypothesis for the case of static expectations, the same argument applies for more general forms of expectations. In general (5.20) can be written as

$$p_t - p_t^* = a_1(U_t - \bar{U}). \qquad (5.20')$$

In the short run, as long as inflation is not fully anticipated there is a temporary trade-off between inflation and unemployment. In the long run, however, inflation will be correctly anticipated in which case $p_t^* = p_t$ and (5.20') reduces once again to a vertical long-run Phillips curve. The only difference is that the actual dynamic adjustment process will be more complicated and will depend upon how p_t^* is formulated.

5.   The Phelps hypothesis

The approach taken by Phelps (1968) to the expectations hypothesis is somewhat different to that we have been just discussing. By analysing a model in which firms are trying to maintain their competitive position in the labour market, Phelps derives the following wage equation

$$w_t = f(U, V) + w_t^* \qquad (5.21)$$

where
$\qquad w_t^*$ = expected percentage change in money wages,
$\qquad V$ = vacancy rate.

This theory attributes most of the thrust of money wage dynamics to the attempts by individual firms to maintain a desired wage differential. Thus, given the excess demand for labour $f(U, V)$, the rate of change of money wages is dependent upon the expected rate of change of money wages. The reason for this is that if entrepreneurs expect money wages paid by their competitors to rise at a given rate and if they expect firms to pass on these higher wages in the form of higher prices, then they too will wish to raise their own money wages at the same rate if they are to maintain their competitive position in the labour market.

To complete the dynamics of (5.21) requires the addition of some expectations hypothesis for w_t^* and once this is done the story is similar to that discussed in Section 4. Indeed as long as prices and wages are growing at constant rates which differ by only a productivity growth factor, there is little difference between the two approaches.

As written in (5.21), the Phelps hypothesis implies a natural rate of unemployment determined where

$$f(U, V) = 0.$$

However, if we prefer to allow for the possible existence of a long-run trade-off curve, we can modify (5.21) to

$$w_t = f(U, V) + a_2 w_t^* \qquad 0 \leqslant a_2 \leqslant 1. \qquad (5.21')$$

6.   Empirical tests of the expectations hypthesis

The expectations hypothesis has given rise to a substantial body of empirical testing and analysis. Of particular importance in view of the foregoing discussion is the magnitude of the expectations coefficient and much of the emphasis of the applied work has been to see how it compares to unity.

To estimate an equation such as

$$w_t = a_0 + a_1 U_t + a_2 p_t^* \tag{5.15}$$

directly it is necessary to have observations on all variables, including the expected rates of inflation p_t^*. Unfortunately, direct observations on expectations are not widely available in which case a proxy variable needs to be substituted for it. In the literature, the typical solution to this problem is to assume that expectations are generated by a distributed lag on past values of the variable. In general terms one postulates

$$p_t^* = \sum_{i=0}^{\infty} \phi_i p_{t-1} \quad \sum_{i=0}^{\infty} \phi_i = 1 \tag{5.22}$$

and substitutes (5.22) into (5.15) obtaining the equation

$$w_t = a_0 + a_1 U_t + a_2 \sum_{i=0}^{\infty} \phi_i p_{t-i} \tag{5.23}$$

which is now in terms of observable variables. In practice in order to reduce the number of lagged variables in (5.23), one imposes restrictions on the lag structure described by the ϕ_i. This can be done in various ways. One method is to hypothesize some simple relationship for p_t^* involving only one or two parameters which can then be estimated from the data.

Two simple and widely used hypotheses include

$$p_t^* = p_{t-1} + \theta(p_{t-1} - p_{t-2}) \tag{5.22a'}$$

$$p_t^* = p_{t-1}^* + \gamma(p_{t-1} - p_{t-1}^*). \tag{5.22b'}$$

Hypothesis (5.22a') is often described as the *extrapolative* hypothesis. It asserts that expected inflation equals the immediate past rate of inflation, together with a correction which allows for the trend in the inflation rate over the previous period. If $\phi > 0$, the forecaster extrapolates these trends, expecting them to continue. If $\phi < 0$, he expects past trends to reverse themselves, in which case they are said to be *regressive*. If $\phi = 0$ this hypothesis reduces to the static hypotheses considered in Section 4. Hypothesis (5.22b') is the *adaptive* expectations hypothesis, according to which the forecast for the past period is corrected by some fraction of that period's forecast error; see Cagan (1956), Nerlove (1958). Other methods include constraining the ϕ_i to lie on certain specified low order polynomials by using the 'Almon lag' technique; see Almon (1965).

Substituting these hypotheses into (5.15) yields the wage equations

$$w_t = a_0 + a_1 U_t + a_2(1 - \theta) p_{t-1} - a_2 p_{t-2} \tag{5.23a'}$$

$$w_t = \gamma a_0 + a_1 U_t - a_1(1 - \gamma) U_{t-1} + a_2 \gamma p_{t-1} + (1 - \gamma) w_{t-1}. \tag{5.23b'}$$

The coefficient θ in (5.22a$'$) can be estimated from (5.23a$'$), together with the other coefficients a_0, a_1, a_2. Similarly, the rate of adaptation γ can be estimated from (5.23b$'$), although this equation does impose a simple non-linear constraint on the coefficients of U_t, U_{t-1} and w_{t-1}.

A related method of proceeding is to construct 'pseudo-expectational' data explicitly. This can be done by assuming different weights for ϕ_i in (5.22) and applying these to past observations p_{t-i}. The most common procedure is to take different values for γ in the adaptive expectations hypothesis (5.22a$'$) and for some initial starting value p_0^* construct series of expectational data which can then be inserted directly into (5.15).

However, these general procedures have several limitations. Distributed lags on past price changes can arise for different reasons. On the one hand, they may indeed reflect expectations as we have postulated in (5.23). But they may equally well reflect a 'catching up' of current wage changes to past inflation as well as other institutional lags in adjustment. One might argue that workers, in bargaining over current wage contracts, are more concerned with being compensated for past price increases which have occurred since their last contract, rather than worrying about the future, although this view may be less accurate in highly inflationary times. In any event, autoregressive hypotheses such as (5.22) are indeed extremely naive and imply that forecasters are locked in by the past and ignore current conditions in making their predictions (except insofar as these are reflected by past price changes). While some empirical evidence for the United States suggests that these hypotheses are reasonably accurate during the inflationary period of the latter half of the 1960s, they were unsatisfactory in explaining the inflationary expectations held in the 1950s; see Turnovsky (1970).

For these various reasons it is desirable, if possible, to test the role of expectations by the direct use of expectations data. One such set of survey data which have been used were compiled by Mr Joseph A. Livingston of the *Philadelphia Bulletin*. While these data also have their drawbacks, they nevertheless provide supporting evidence for the distributed lag approach.[7]

The earliest tests of the expectations hypothesis were carried out by Solow (1968), and Gordon (1970) using US data. They did not have direct observations on expectations, but instead used the kinds of proxy procedures described above. Both these studies yielded expectations coefficients of about 0.4, implying the existence of a long-run Phillips curve. These results were confirmed by Turnovsky and Wachter (1972), who, as well as using the proxy variable approach, also used the Livington survey data. Moreover, in addition to estimating (5.23) they also estimated the 'Phelps equation' and again both methods yielded coefficients well below unity (about 0.3).[8]

Results for other countries tend to be somewhat higher. For example Bodkin, Bond, Reuber, Robinson (1966), Vanderkamp (1972), Turnovsky (1972) obtain expectations coefficients for Canada of about 0.8–0.9. While the reason for the difference between the two countries is not clear, one explanation for it is given in Chapter 6. There it is argued that because the wage–price sector is only part of a larger system, the expectations coefficients obtained from it alone are in fact usually downwardly biased estimates of the total effects of expectations on inflation. Furthermore, the downward bias varies inversely with the magnitude of the coefficient. Hence the difference between the Canadian and US expectations coefficients may really be much smaller than the estimates of 0.4 and 0.9 suggest.

The studies we have mentioned were conducted before the recent experience of accelerating inflation was fully underway. It seems likely that in periods of very rapid inflation, wages are likely to reflect expectations more fully than they are when inflation is proceeding at only a mild rate. This hypothesis was first tested by Eckstein and Brinner (1972) who introduced a 'threshold' variable, whereby wages were fully adjusted once inflation exceeded a specified level. When they introduced this variable into the relationship, they found the expectations coefficient to be much closer to unity, implying nearly complete adjustment of inflation to expectations, once inflation is above a certain level.

As the period of estimation is extended to include the more recent inflationary experience, the coefficient of price expectations in (5.15) has tended to increase steadily towards unity. This suggests hypothesizing a relationship in which a_2 increases with p_t^*, in which case the estimation of (5.15) may involve non-linear techniques. While this hypothesis does not seem to have been tested (except in a rather specific form by Eckstein and Brinner) it would seem to be a reasonably useful one, worth further investigation.

Another related hypothesis advanced by Turnovsky (1972) and Turnovsky and Wachter (1972) is what they call the 'error-adjusted expectations' hypothesis. The expectations hypothesis, as we have described it, does not allow for any errors in forecasting. If actual price inflation grows more rapidly than was anticipated, real wages will not have risen by as much as was bargained. Workers will feel cheated and will try to capture at least part of the difference in their current negotiations and an analogous argument in the reverse case. This is formalized by hypothesizing

$$w_t = a_0 + a_1 U_t + a_2 p_t^* + a_3(p_{t-1} - p_{t-1}^*) \tag{5.24}$$

where $a_3 > 0$. The term $(p_{t-1} - p_{t-1}^*)$ represents the catching-up effect, where workers try to adjust their current money wages to compensate for past forecast errors. Equations of this form, estimated using both Canadian and US data found the 'catching-up coefficient' to be highly statistically significant, providing some support for the hypothesis.

7. **Extension of the expectations hypothesis to include bilateral bargaining elements of wage and price determination**

Virtually all of the existing literature analysing the 'expectations hypothesis' is based on competitive output and labour markets, and hence tends to ignore, or at least downplay, the non-competitive elements of price and wage determination. In the light of the increase in unionization which has occurred in many industries in recent years, this assumption would seem to be unwarranted. It is therefore desirable to extend this analysis by constructing a model which stresses the bilateral bargaining context within which many wages and prices are determined, as well as incorporating the conventional competitive factors.

Such models have been constructed by various authors; see e.g. Pitchford (1963, 1977), Turnovsky and Pitchford (1977), Johnston (1972), Desai (1973). While it would take us too far afield to develop any such model in detail, it is worth briefly outlining the approach and indicating the kinds of qualitative conclusions they yield.

For example, Turnovsky and Pitchford consider an economy in which price and wage movements are determined in part by excess demand conditions (together with appropriate expectational variables) and in part by the competing claims for income shares by entrepreneurs and wage earners. Given excess demand conditions, prices in the non-competitive sector are assumed to adjust towards a target price set by entrepreneurs and wage earners. Given excess demand conditions, prices in the non-competitive sector are assumed to adjust towards a target price set by entrepreneurs as a mark-up on expected unit labour costs, which in turn depend upon the expected rate of wage inflation. The mark-up which is taken as exogenous, embodies the desired share of income which profit earners (entrepreneurs) wish to obtain. Similarly, movements in money wages are determined partly by the wage claims of unions. These are specified in terms of target money wages which, given expected price movements, would ensure a desired real wage share for labour. The claims by these two groups may by no means be compatible and indeed their degree of inconsistency plays a crucial role in the inflationary process generated by the model. The main focus of the analysis is to determine how these non-competitive elements affect the steady-state trade-off between excess demand and the rate of inflation, and for this reason we take the level of excess demand to be an exogenous variable, determined by government policy.

The main conclusions of this analysis can be summarized as follows. First, in this model the rate of inflation and the distribution of income become jointly determined variables and must therefore be analysed simultaneously. Leaving aside polar cases, and provided the system is stable, the most likely outcome of the model is a steady-state relationship between price (and wage) movements and excess demand having both a *positive* and *finite* slope. However, the possibility that the inflationary process may be unstable is quite plausible and definitely *cannot* be ruled out. This is likely to be the case if,

(i) the non-competitive sectors are significant in the economy;

(ii) the adjustment of money wages and prices in non-competitive sectors to their respective targets is complete or nearly so;

(iii) price and wage movements in the competitive sector fully or nearly fully incorporate inflationary expectations;

(iv) income claims are excessive, in the sense that the sum of the claimed shares of output by workers and entrepreneurs exceeds unity.

While the model is capable of yielding the borderline case of a natural rate of unemployment, this is much less likely to be so than in the more conventional models involving expectations. In general, the natural rate requires rather stringent relations among the parameters of the system to be satisfied. These include not only speeds of adjustment of money wages and prices to expectations, but also the consistency of income claims as well. However, at one extreme the model reduces to the Phelps case, in which case the conditons for a natural rate are correspondingly weakened.

6

A SHORT-RUN INTEGRATED
MACROECONOMIC MODEL

1.   Introduction[1]

In this chapter we present the first stage towards the development of
an integrated macroeconomic model. Specifically we shall incorporate our
analysis of the wage—price sector into the traditional macroeconomic model
summarized in Chapter 2. Yet while the model is restricted to the short run,
nevertheless we do take account of the existence of the government budget
constraint discussed in Chapter 4, and the dynamic structure it imposes. In
effect, the present analysis can be viewed as introducing prices into the first
period effects of the simple dynamic model studied in Chapter 4.

As we discussed in Chapter 5, our analysis of the wage—price sector
emphasizes the role of inflationary expectations. And that is one aspect
which we wish to stress in the first integrated model as well. Indeed during
recent years increasing attention has been devoted to analysing the role of
inflationary expectations in macroeconomic problems. Much of the recent
work has focused on two specific, and seemingly unrelated questions. On the
one hand, there is the growing body of literature dealing with the role of inflationary expectations in wage and price determination. This has been
reviewed at some length in Chapter 5. Secondly, many economists have been
concerned with analysing the relationship between the nominal rate of
interest and anticipated inflation. This relationship has a long history in
economics, going back to Irving Fisher (1930). He advanced the proposition
that the real interest rate is essentially determined by real phenomena and is
independent of the rate of anticipated inflation. Hence a one percent increase
in the expected rate of price inflation leads to a one percent increase in the
nominal rate of interest. Recently there has been a revival of this Fisherian
proposition and many economists have been concerned with analysing the
extent to which this adjustment in fact takes place.[2,3]

By and large these two bodies of literature have been developed in isolation and have not been considered within the context of an integrated
macroeconomic model. This is obviously a shortcoming since unless one
examines these kinds of questions within a unified framework one is able to
analyse only partial effects.[4]

Indeed the construction of such a model is desirable for several reasons. First, it enables us to identify the channels through which inflationary expectations influence the economy and to see the feedbacks to which each gives rise. As a consequence of this, the model provides considerable insight into the interpretation of some of the related empirical literature and as discussed below, helps reconcile some differences that have been obtained. Secondly, the analysis reveals that, at least for the model we develop, the relationship between the nominal rate of interest and inflationary expectations on the one hand, and the relationship between the actual rate of inflation and the anticipated rate of inflation on the other, are themselves related in a rather simple way. Finally, by specifically introducing inflationary expectations and price adjustments, we are able to readily modify the traditional macro model so as to give a more satisfactory analysis of the impacts of monetary and fiscal policy on inflation and output.

The chapter consists of three basic parts. The first, described in Section 2 outlines a simple model in which total income taxes are fixed in real terms and analyses the kind of issues just mentioned, treating inflationary expectations as exogenously determined. In Section 3 this model is extended to allow for endogenously varying income taxes. This is very important, since, as shown below, one of the ways in which income taxes influence the economy is through their interaction with price expectations. With a progressive tax structure, workers have to be compensated by more than any anticipated inflation in order to maintain their expected real wage.[5] This exerts additional inflationary effects on the economy, leading to further feedbacks. Consequently the impact of taxation on the economy cannot be adequately analysed without the proper treatment of anticipated inflation, and in fact the comparative static implications of tax changes are far more indeterminate that the traditional textbook analysis would suggest. Furthermore, the presence of progressive taxes coupled with inflationary expectations leads to a substantial modification of the effects of monetary policy and government expenditure on inflation. The third part discusses a relatively simple way of endogenizing price expectations in this model and introduces the distinction between anticipated and unanticipated government policy.

2.   A simple macroeconomic model incorporating inflationary expectations

A.   *The basic model*

The analysis is based on a simple extension of the traditional *IS–LM* macroeconomic model, which of course is based on a number of restrictive assumptions. Specifically, since we shall be concerned with short-run equilibrium we shall ignore technological change, as well as the growth of capital stock and other wealth effects. Also, total taxes are held constant in *real* terms and are therefore unrelated to current real income. This assumption can be justified by supposing for example, that nominal taxes are based on the previous period's nominal income, with the current tax rates being appropriately adjusted for current inflation. The implications of the model will be developed on the basis of these assumptions.

The real side of our simple model consists of the following simple consumption and investment functions:

$$C = C(Y - T) \qquad 0 < C'(Y - T) < 1 \tag{6.1}$$

$$I = I(r - \pi) \qquad I'(r - \pi) < 0 \tag{6.2}$$

where C, I, Y denote real consumption, investment and income respectively, r denotes the nominal rate of interest, while π denotes the anticipated rate of inflation.[6] T denotes real taxes, which are assumed to be constant. These two functions are of the standard variety discussed in Chapter 2, the only modification being that real investment is a function of the *real* rate of interest, $r - \pi$, as implied by neoclassical investment theory in a context of inflationary expectations.[7] Denoting real government expenditure by G we have the product market equilibrium condition

$$Y = C(Y - T) + I(r - \pi) + G. \tag{6.3}$$

The demand for real money balances is assumed to be given by the relation

$$\frac{M^d}{P} = L(Y, r, \pi), \quad L_1 > 0, \quad L_2 < 0, \quad L_3 < 0. \tag{6.4}$$

where P denotes the price level. This again is perfectly standard except for the fact that following Friedman and others, the demand for money is assumed to vary inversely with the anticipated rate of inflation.[8]

Some authors, notably Tobin (1969) postulate asset demand functions which depend positively on their own real rates of return and negatively on the real rates of return of other assets. With bonds the only alternative asset to money, this implies a money demand function of the form

$$\frac{M^d}{P} = L'(Y, r - \pi, -\pi), \quad L_1' > 0, \quad L_2' < 0, \quad L_3' > 0. \tag{6.4'}$$

Hence the assumption $L_3 < 0$ in (6.4) is equivalent to

$$L_2' + L_3' > 0$$

in (6.4').

In order to focus on the current rate of inflation, p, rather than the current price level, it is convenient to utilize the relationship

$$P = P_{-1}(1 + p) \tag{6.5}$$

where -1 refers to the previous period. Substituting this into (6.4) yields[9]

$$\frac{M^d}{P_{-1}(1 + p)} = L(Y, r, \pi) \tag{6.4''}$$

and assuming equilibrium in the money market, we obtain

$$L(Y, r, \pi) = \frac{M}{P_{-1}(1+p)}. \tag{6.6}$$

Even treating π as a given parameter, and taking M as given, equations (6.3) and (6.6) are underdetermined in that there are only two equations to determine the three endogenous variables Y, r, P (or p). As discussed at length by Friedman (1970) one crucial difference between Keynesians and Monetarists is the manner in which they close the model. Keynes regarded the money wage rate as being exogenously determined and assumed that firms set prices equal to or proportional to marginal costs. Assuming constant short-run marginal costs this implies constant prices and thus subsequent post Keynesian macroeconomic models have tended to treat P as exogenously given solving equations (6.3) and (6.6) for Y and r. This is basically the *IS–LM* model of Chapter 2, Section 5. Monetarists assume output equals the exogenously given full-employment level and treat r and P as the endogenous variables; see the classical full-employment model in Chapter 2, Section 7. Both of these models represent extremes. The present model takes an intermediate position by positing a price adjustment equation of the type discussed in the previous chapter. As a result, it contains elements of both extremes in that both Y and P (as well as r) become endogenously determined.

Letting w denote the percentage change in money wages, we introduce a Phillips curve embodying the 'expectations hypothesis' of wage determination; (see 5.15):

$$w = a_0 + \alpha_1 U + b\pi \tag{6.7}$$

where

$$\alpha_1 < 0, \quad 0 \leqslant b \leqslant 1.$$

The coefficient α_1 defines the short-run trade-off between the unemployment rate U and the rate of wage inflation w for a given π, while b measures the extent to which inflationary expectations are reflected in current wage changes. Since we are dealing with a short-run model in which capital stock is given, we may assume that real income and employment N are related by

$$Y = F(N) \quad \text{where} \quad F'(N) > 0. \tag{6.8}$$

Assuming that the unemployment rate is sufficiently small so that $F(N)$ can be adequately represented by a linear approximation about the full employment level $\bar{N}$, we obtain

$$U = \frac{\bar{N} - N}{\bar{N}} = k(Y - \bar{Y}) \tag{6.9}$$

where $k < 0$ and $\bar{Y}$ is the corresponding full-employment level of output.[10] Finally prices are assumed to be set in accordance with a constant mark-up on unit labour costs. Given our assumption of zero technological change, labour productivity remains constant, so that we simply have

$$p = w. \tag{6.10}$$

Eliminating w, and U from (6.7) we derive the price adjustment equation

$$p = a_0 + a_1(Y - \bar{Y}) + b\pi \tag{6.11}$$

where $a_1 > 0, 0 \leqslant b \leqslant 1$, and which describes how current price changes in response to current disequilibrium in the product market and inflationary expectations. This equation is virtually identical to (5.16) derived in Chapter 5.

For simplicity we abstract from the commercial banking sector so that all money is 'outside money', issued by the central bank. To complete the model we must describe its supply and this involves introducing the government's budget constraint. In the absence of interest payments, this is described by the equation

$$\Delta M + \frac{\Delta B}{r} = P(G - T) = P_{-1}(1 + p)(G - T). \tag{6.12}$$

This asserts that the nominal government deficit must be financed either by increasing the monetary base or by issuing additional bonds (B), which for simplicity are assumed to be perpetuities, the price of which is $1/r$. Note that equation (6.12) describes the simplified version of the government budget constraint discussed in Chapter 3 (see (3.6′)) in that it abstracts from the interest payments on outstanding government bonds. For a one period analysis this is not serious, especially if we assume that interest is paid with a one period lag. In any event, (6.12) indicates quite clearly that the government has *four* policy instruments; M (or ΔM), B (or ΔB), and G and T, any *three* of which can be chosen independently. The fourth is then determined by the budget constraint. In our analysis we take G and T to be exogenously specified, we postulate an adjustment rule for M, and allow B to adjust endogenously.

Clearly there are numerous assumptions one might make about how the monetary base is adjusted and whichever hypothesis is adopted, the given G, T, (6.12) defines a corresponding adjustment in bonds. Following the discussion of Chapter 4 we specify the following plausible hypothesis

$$\Delta M = \theta P_{-1}(1 + p)(G - T) + m \qquad 0 \leqslant \theta \leqslant 1. \tag{6.13}$$

The first term on the right hand side of (6.13) represents the increase in the monetary base induced by the government deficit. The parameter θ indicates the proportion of the nominal government deficit $P(G - T)$ financed through increases in high powered money. If $\theta = 0$ the entire deficit is financed by borrowing; if $\theta = 1$ it is wholly financed by increasing the monetary base. The remaining term describes any exonenous changes in the money supply and thus can be used to characterize exogenous monetary policy.

Finally, we must consider the expectational variable π. Since we wish to focus on how the system responds to given inflationary expectations, for most of the chapter we choose to treat π as a given parameter. As our analysis is strictly short run and provided π is determined in *prior* periods, that is a perfectly valid procedure. In the longer-run extensions of this model undertaken in subsequent chapters it becomes necessary to treat π as endogenous, in which case the system has to be closed by postulating some expectations generating mechanism for π. However, even within this short-run framework it is possible to endogenize π and some extensions in this direction are undertaken in the latter part of the chapter.

Thus the complete system is described by the set of equations

$$Y - C(Y - T) - I(r - \pi) - G = 0 \tag{6.14a}$$

$$L(Y, r, \pi) - \frac{M}{P_{-1}(1 + p)} = 0 \tag{6.14b}$$

$$a_0 + a_1(Y - \bar{Y}) - p + b\pi = 0 \tag{6.14c}$$

$$M - M_1 - \theta P_{-1}(1 + p)(G - T) - m = 0. \tag{6.14d}$$

These equations define four relationships involving the four endogenous variables Y, r, p, M, the exogenous variables $G, P_{-1}, M_{-1}, \pi, m, T$ and the constant parameters such as a_0, a_1, b, which characterize the economy. The Jacobian of this system is the determinant

$$J = \begin{vmatrix} 1 - C' & -I' & 0 & 0 \\ L_1 & L_2 & \dfrac{M}{P_{-1}(1 + p)^2} & \dfrac{-1}{P_{-1}(1 + p)} \\ a_1 & 0 & -1 & 0 \\ 0 & 0 & -\theta P_{-1}(G - T) & 1 \end{vmatrix}$$

which using (6.5), simplifies to

$$-I'L_1 - (1 - C')L_2 - \frac{I'a_1}{P(1 + p)} [M - \theta P(G - T)] \tag{6.15}$$

and is almost certainly strictly positive.[11] Thus at any point of time t we can uniquely determine Y_t, r_t, p_t and M_t in terms of the exogenous variables and given parameters.

B. Impact of inflationary expectations
  Looking at the system equations (6.14), it can be seen that inflationary expectations affect the system via three channels

  (i) the investment demand function;
  (ii) the money demand function;
  (iii) the price adjustment process.

Each one of these direct effects gives rise to further repercussions and feedbacks, all of which contribute towards determining the ultimate response of the system.

Differentiating the system with respect to π, we obtain the response in the short-run equilibrium values of the endogenous variables Y, r, and p to an increase in inflationary expectations. The various responses can be most conveniently expressed in the form

$$\frac{\partial Y}{\partial \pi} = \frac{I'M}{PJ}\left(\frac{e_r}{r} + \frac{e_\pi}{\pi} + \frac{b}{1+p} - \frac{b\theta P_{-1}(G-T)}{M}\right) \tag{6.16a}$$

$$\frac{\partial r}{\partial \pi} - 1 = \frac{(1-C')M}{PJ}\left(\frac{e_r}{r} + \frac{e_\pi}{\pi} + \frac{b}{1+p} - \frac{b\theta P_{-1}(G-T)}{M}\right) \tag{6.16b}$$

$$\frac{\partial p}{\partial \pi} - b = \frac{a_1 I'M}{PJ}\left(\frac{e_r}{r} + \frac{e_\pi}{\pi} + \frac{b}{1+p} - \frac{b\theta P_{-1}(G-T)}{M}\right) \tag{6.16c}$$

where

e_r = interest elasticity of the demand for real money balances;
e_π = elasticity of the demand for real money balances with respect to inflationary expectations.

Hence we obtain the interesting result that

$$\frac{\partial Y}{\partial \pi} \gtrless 0 \quad \text{if and only if} \quad \frac{\partial r}{\partial \pi} \lessgtr 1,$$

$$\text{and if and only if} \quad \frac{\partial p}{\partial \pi} \gtrless b. \tag{6.17}$$

The key element in determining the sign of these responses is the term

$$\Omega \equiv \left(\frac{e_r}{r} + \frac{e_\pi}{\pi} + \frac{b}{1+p} - \frac{b\theta P_{-1}(G-T)}{M}\right).$$

Taking plausible values for these parameters and elasticities suggests that the expression is most likely negative, at least in periods of moderate inflation in which case

$$\frac{\partial Y}{\partial \pi} > 0, \quad \frac{\partial r}{\partial \pi} < 1, \quad \frac{\partial p}{\partial \pi} > b. \tag{6.17'}$$

However, a reversal of all signs in (6.17') certainly cannot be ruled out and may indeed occur under more inflationary conditions.[12]

These results have several important implications. First, in general changes in inflationary expectations *do* exert an influence on the real behaviour of the economy. Moreover, the nominal rate of interest does not in general adjust exactly to changes in inflationary expectations; typically there is some compensating adjustment (usually downwards, at least in moderately inflationary circumstances) in the real rate of interest. Thirdly, the total effect of the anticipated rate of inflation on the actual rate of inflation generally differs from (and usually exceeds) the partial response determined from the expectations coefficient b of the Phillips curve. Furthermore, we see that the factors determining whether or not the nominal interest rate under- or over-adjusts to inflationary expectations are *precisely the same as* those which determine whether the partial effect of inflationary expectations, b, under- or over-states the true response and whether anticipated inflation exerts an expansionary or contractionary effect on income. The crucial factors include[13]

     (i) the interest elasticity of the demand for money;

     (ii) the inflationary expectations elasticity of the demand for money;

     (iii) the inflationary expectations coefficient in the price adjustment equation;

     (iv) the proportion of government expenditure financed by increasing the monetary base.

The reason for the relationships among the responses is clear. If the nominal rate of interest adjusts only partially to an increase in expected inflation, the real rate of interest must fall, causing investment to rise. Given a marginal propensity to consume between zero and one, income will rise via the multiplier, excess demand will be created, so that from (6.11) prices must rise by *more* than the direct effect b. Conversely if $\partial p / \partial \pi > b$, (6.11) implies that Y must rise, which in turn means an increase in savings matched by an increase in investment required to maintain equilibrium in the product market. This increase in investment can be induced only provided the real rate of interest falls, that is so long as there is only partial adjustment in the nominal rate of interest to anticipated inflation.[14]

These results throw considerable light on the findings of two bodies of empirical literature which analyse the role of inflationary expectations. The first deals with the question of empirically determining the extent to which the nominal rate of interest r incorporates inflationary expectations, and does so by estimating equations of the form

$$r_t = c_0 + c_1 \pi_t. \tag{6.18}$$

According to the Fisherian proposition, r_t fully adjusts to inflationary expectations, in which case $c_1 = 1$. Accordingly, the estimated coefficient of π_t can serve as a test for that hypothesis. The majority of empirical studies yield estimates of c_1 well below unity and these are taken to reject the hypothesis.[15] However, given plausible parameter values, this finding is perfectly consistent with the present theoretical analysis when the full repercussions of inflationary expectations are taken into account.

Perhaps more important is the contribution equation (6.16c) can provide to a better understanding of some of the empirical results recently obtained in tests of the 'expectations hypothesis' of wage determination. As discussed in Chapter 5, in the strict version of this theory, wages and prices should fully adjust to inflationary expectations, implying a value of $b = 1$ in the price adjustment equation (6.11). However, very few of the existing empirical studies (certainly of those using US data prior to say 1973) yield estimates of b close to unity and for most countries (with the possible exception of Canada) the typical estimates are in the range 0.3–0.8. While estimates of this magnitude may be viewed as a refutation of the stringent expectations hypothesis (i.e. $b = 1$), they may also be due at least in part to statistical problems. Errors in variables, arising from the use of poor proxy variables for expectations, together with the simultaneity of wage and price determination may cause the estimated coefficient b to be downwardly biased.[16]

However, equation (6.16c) suggests an alternative explanation for these low estimates. This equation asserts that in general b is a biased measure of the true impact of inflationary expectations π, on the actual rate of inflation, p, and that with plausible parameter values, b will *understate* the true response. Hence, if in fact p does totally adjust to anticipated inflation so that $\partial p / \partial \pi = 1$, equation (6.16c) implies that the coefficient b *should be less than unity*. In other words, an empirically estimated coefficient $b < 1$ is consistent with the absence of money illusion and the stringent expectations hypothesis. The balance of the adjustment in the actual rate of inflation occurs in response to the increase in real output, which itself is a consequence of the increase in inflationary expectations. Moreover, equation (6.16c) provides assistance in reconciling some puzzling differences with regard to the expectations coefficients obtained for the United States and Canadian wage equations. In two papers Turnovsky (1972), Turnovsky and Wachter (1972) wage equations (basically equation (6.7)) were estimated for these two countries and yielded expectations coefficients (essentially b) of about 0.4 and 0.8–0.9 respectively. These results are most consistent with those obtained by other researchers and appear to be quite robust with respect to the precise specification of the estimating equation; see Chapter 5. They imply that, (at least over the period of estimation) US wage earners were subject to money illusion, whereas their Canadian counterparts were not. In view of the similarities between the two countries, the difference is hard to explain, although some of it may be due to the relative openness of the Canadian economy.[17]

Equation (6.16c) indicates that not only does b in general underestimate the true response $\partial p / \partial \pi$, but also that the magnitude of the downward bias varies *inversely* with b. This follows immediately from (6.16c), when it is recognized that J is independent of b. Thus, if one obtains $b = 0.4$ for the US and $b = 0.9$ for Canada, the downward bias in the former case is much larger than in the latter, so that a comparison of the partial responses as measured by b overstates the true difference. In fact, with quite plausible parameter values one can generate overall responses for $\partial p / \partial \pi$ for the two countries which are not too different from one another.

The reason for the bias is quite clear. If inflationary expectations increase by $\Delta\pi$ say, the direct effect is to increase p by $b\Delta\pi$. This lowers real money balances, leading to an increase in the nominal interest rate of say Δr. Assuming $\Delta r < \Delta\pi$, this in turn causes an increase in investment and consequently an increase in income, yielding an additional effect on the actual rate of inflation via the excess demand term in the Phillips curve. The strength of this additional effect varies proportionately with the initial direct effect, which in turn is proportional to b. Consequently, the striking differences obtained in these empirical studies may in fact be illusory. It may simply be that in one country, Canada, the responses occur through more direct channels than in the other.

C. Monetary and fiscal policy

We shall define an increase in m, the exogenous rate of growth of the money supply (monetary base), to characterize an expansionary monetary policy. Thus differentiating the system of equations (6.14) with respect to m we obtain the following effects of an increase in the growth of the monetary base.

$$\frac{\partial Y}{\partial m} = \frac{-I'}{PJ} > 0, \quad \frac{\partial p}{\partial m} = \frac{-a_1 I'}{PJ} > 0. \tag{6.19}$$

The income effect is essentially the same as it is in the conventional model where prices are held constant. The only difference is that when inflation is introduced, the impact of changes in m is less expansionary than when it is ignored. A negative feedback is introduced via the price adjustment relationship.[18] On the one hand, an increase in the rate of growth of the money supply decreases r, thereby increasing investment, which in turn leads to an increase in real income. This higher level of real income raises the demand for money causing a partially offsetting increase in r and fall in Y. This much is well known from standard macroeconomic theory. However, at the same time, the initial increase in income creates a higher rate of inflation, which in turn leads to a partially offsetting decrease in real money balances resulting in a further partially offsetting increase in r and decrease in Y.

We turn now to the effects of fiscal policy. Differentiating (6.13) with respect to G we obtain for given P

$$\frac{\partial M}{\partial G} = \theta P \tag{6.20}$$

which is the partial induced monetary effect of a change in government expenditure.

Using (6.20) we can readily obtain the following expressions

$$\frac{\partial Y}{\partial G} = -\frac{(L_2 + \theta I')}{J} > 0, \quad \frac{\partial p}{\partial G} = -\frac{a_1(L_2 + \theta I')}{J} > 0. \tag{6.21}$$

Thus an expansionary fiscal policy will increase output (employment) only at the expense of a concurrent increase in the rate of inflation. It is clear that the strength of the expansionary and inflationary effects of an increase in government expenditure will increase, the larger is the proportion of G financed by an increase in the stock of high powered money. This result is of course in accordance with one's expectations. Nevertheless, one should point out that the fact that an increase in government expenditure is necessarily inflationary is in part a consequence of assuming fixed taxes. As shown in Section 3 below, a progressive tax structure weakens the inflationary impact of government expenditure and may actually cause it to be deflationary.

Taking ratios of the terms in (6.19) and (6.21) we see that the relative impact of monetary and fiscal policy on output is the same as it is on inflation. Just as in the conventional model, the potency of monetary policy relative to fiscal policy as a stimulus for output expansion varies positively with the interest elasticity of investment demand and inversely with the interest elasticity of the demand for money. In the light of the fact that r is likely to have a much more immediate impact on the money market than on investment demand, these results tend to favour the use of fiscal policy as being more effective in the short run.

Finally, it is of some interest to determine the effects of an increase in G on r. The conventional model discussed in Chapter 2 argues that an increase in G raises output, increasing the transactions demand for money and that if we assume a given money supply this forces up the rate of interest. However, from the present analysis we find

$$\frac{\partial r}{\partial G} = \frac{1}{PJ} \left(\frac{a_1 [M - \theta(G - T)P]}{1 + p} + [L_1 - \theta(1 - C')]P \right) \qquad (6.22)$$

which is ambiguous in sign. If $\theta = 0$, (the traditional assumption) then this expression is unambiguously positive. On the other hand, an increase in government expenditure may lower the rate of interest if the proportion of the expenditure financed by increasing the monetary base is sufficiently large.

3.   **Extension of model to include endogenous income tax**
A.   *Reformulation of model*
        One crucial assumption we made was that taxes were independent of current economic activity, being fixed in real terms. This is rather restrictive, since taxes are typically specified in nominal terms and usually vary with money income. We therefore extend the model to allow for the existence of such taxes. This introduces some complications into the analysis due to the fact that typically, income tax rates vary progressively with *money* income, preventing *real* disposable income from being expressed in terms of real income alone (and tax parameters). Consequently, it becomes necessary to work in terms of money income and price separately.

For simplicity, we assume that taxes are levied according to the linear relationship[19]

$$T_n = t_0 + t_1 X \qquad (6.23)$$

where

T_n = nominal tax receipts,
t_0 = base tax rate,
t_1 = constant marginal tax rate, $0 < t_1 < 1$,
X = money income ($= PY$).

A tax structure is said to be progressive, proportional or regressive, according as the marginal tax rate exceeds, equals, or is less than, the average rate. With the linear tax function, these three cases correspond to[20]

$$t_0 < 0, \quad t_0 = 0, \quad t_0 > 0$$

respectively. Since typical tax structures tend to be progressive, we shall assume $t_0 < 0$.

Assuming that consumption is a function of real disposable income, the product market equilibrium relation becomes

$$\frac{X}{P} - C\left(\frac{X(1 - t_1) - t_0}{P}\right) - I(r - \pi) - G = 0 \qquad (6.24)$$

where, because of the non-homogeneity of the tax function, we must express these real quantities in terms of X and P separately, rather than in terms of real income Y. Similarly, money market equilibrium is described by

$$L\left(\frac{X}{P}, r, \pi\right) = \frac{M}{P}$$

while the price level P and the current rate of inflation p are related by the identity

$$P = P_{-1}(1 + p).$$

As before, we must close the system by formulating a price-adjustment relationship and here the introduction of taxes leads to two significant modifications. Letting

Q = number of man hours worked by labour,
W = money wage rate,
P^* = expected price level,

it follows that money income before taxes earned by labour is QW. Let us assume that the proportion of total income going to labour is constant, λ say, so that

$$QW = \lambda X, \qquad 0 < \lambda < 1.$$

The after-tax real income which workers expect to receive is

$$\frac{WQ(1 - t_1) - t_0}{P^*} = \frac{\lambda X(1 - t_1) - t_0}{P^*}$$

Assume first that workers and unions negotiate their wages so as to maintain the constancy of their after-tax income rate following any changes that occur in expected prices and tax parameters. To ensure this, the money wage rate W must adjust so as to satisfy the equation[21]

$$\Delta\left(\frac{WQ(1-t_1)-t_0}{P^*}\right) = 0. \tag{6.25}$$

Assuming Q is constant, equation (6.25) implies the following first order approximation describing the required percentage change in the money wage rate

$$w = \left(1 - \frac{t_0}{\lambda X(1-t_1)}\right)\pi + \left(\frac{\Delta t_0}{\lambda(1-t_1)X} + \frac{\Delta t_1}{1-t_1}\right) \tag{6.26}$$

where all symbols are as previously defined. In addition, money-wage inflation is also influenced by the unemployment rate, which as before, we approximate by $k(Y-\bar{Y})$. Thus retaining the constant mark-up pricing assumption, we obtain a price adjustment relationship of the form

$$p = a_0 + a_1(Y-\bar{Y}) + b\left(1 - \frac{t_0}{\lambda X(1-t_1)}\right)\pi$$
$$+ d\left(\frac{\Delta t_0}{\lambda(1-t_1)X} + \frac{\Delta t_1}{(1-t_1)}\right) \tag{6.27}$$

which reduces to (6.11) in the absence of taxes.

The first term is the familiar excess demand effect and requires no further comment. The other two terms indicate that income taxes have two direct effects on the rate of price inflation.[22] The first, captured by the term

$$\left(1 - \frac{t_0}{\lambda X(1-t_1)}\right)\pi$$

we call the 'expectations-progressivity effect'. This describes the fact that with a progressive tax structure, workers have to be compensated by *more* than the anticipated rate of inflation if they are to maintain their after-tax real wage. If they are able to fully capture this then $b=1$; however, we permit $0 \leqslant b \leqslant 1$, in order to allow for only partial compensation. Note that this effect *increases* with t_1 and *decreases* with t_0, reflecting the fact that an increase in the marginal tax rate increases the progressivity of the tax structure, while an increase in the base rate decreases it.

The final term we call the 'income claims effect'. This reflects the fact that an increase in either the base rate or the marginal rate leads to a direct reduction in after-tax real income.[23] The interesting point about this effect is its transitional nature. It exists only during the period of the tax increase, since in the typical period when tax rates are unchanging both Δt_0 and Δt_1 will be zero. Complete compensation for this effect would require $d=1$, but again we permit $0 \leqslant d \leqslant 1$, in order to allow for only partial adjustment.

Finally, we must consider the government budget constraint which with endogenous income taxes becomes

$$\Delta M + \frac{\Delta B}{r} = PG - t_0 - t_1 X. \tag{6.28}$$

Note that the government now has five policy variables, any four of which can be chosen independently. We shall assume that the government chooses M, G, t_0 and t_1, letting B make the endogenous adjustments required by the budget constraint. Analogous to (6.13) we postulate the money supply adjustment equation

$$M - M_1 = m + \theta (PG - t_0 - t_1 X)$$

where as before θ refers to the proportion of the budget deficit that is financed by increasing the monetary base.

Thus the complete system with income taxes is described by

$$\frac{X}{P} - C\left(\frac{X(1 - t_1) - t_0}{P}\right) - I(r - \pi) - G = 0 \tag{6.29a}$$

$$L(X/P, r, \pi) - \frac{M}{P} = 0 \tag{6.29b}$$

$$a_0 + a_1 \left(\frac{X}{P} - \bar{Y}\right) + b\left(1 - \frac{t_0}{\lambda X(1 - t_1)}\right)\pi$$

$$+ d\left(\frac{\Delta t_0}{\lambda(1 - t_1)X} + \frac{\Delta t_1}{(1 - t_1)}\right) - p = 0 \tag{6.29c}$$

$$P - (1 + p)P_{-1} = 0 \tag{6.29d}$$

$$M - M_{-1} - m - \theta(PG - t_0 - t_1 X) = 0 \tag{6.29e}$$

which now consistes of the five endogenous variables X, r, P, p, M. The Jacobian of this system is

$$K = \begin{vmatrix} \dfrac{1 - C'(1 - t_1)}{P} & -I' & \dfrac{-X + C'(X - T)}{P^2} & 0 & 0 \\[3mm] \dfrac{L_1}{P} & L_2 & \dfrac{M - L_1 X}{P^2} & 0 & \dfrac{-1}{P} \\[3mm] \phi & 0 & \dfrac{-a_1 X}{P^2} & -1 & 0 \\[3mm] 0 & 0 & 1 & -P_{-1} & 0 \\[3mm] \theta t_1 & 0 & -\theta G & 0 & 1 \end{vmatrix} \tag{6.30}$$

where

$$\phi = \frac{a_1}{P} + \frac{b\pi t_0 - d\Delta t_0}{\lambda X^2 (1 - t_1)}. \tag{6.31}$$

Evaluating (6.30), we obtain

$$K = \frac{L_2 [1 - C'(1 - t_1)] + I'(L_1 + \theta t_1)}{P}$$

$$+ \frac{P_{-1} a_1 [I'(M - \theta GP + \theta t_1 X) - L_2 C' t_0]}{P^3}$$

$$+ \frac{P_{-1} (b\pi t_0 - d\Delta t_0)}{\lambda P^2 X^2 (1 - t_1)} \{I'(M - \theta GP - L_1 X) + L_2 [-X + C'(X - T)]\} \tag{6.32}$$

Recalling that $0 < C' < 1, I' < 0, t_0 < 0, 0 < t_1 < 1, L_1 > 0, L_2 < 0$ and using the result $M - \theta GP + \theta t_1 X > 0$, the first and second terms of (6.32) are both unambiguously negative.[24] The third term is indeterminate in sign, although for a proportional tax structure ($t_0 = 0$) it is zero, in which case $K < 0$. However, it is clear from (6.32) that provided the other terms are sufficiently negative, $K < 0$ under a progressive tax structure as well, and henceforth we shall assume this to be so.

B.   *Monetary and fiscal policy*
      The impact of an increase in the stock of money on the current rate of inflation p for a given tax structure ($\Delta t_0 = \Delta t_1 = 0$) is given by the expression

$$\frac{\partial p}{\partial m} = \frac{I'\phi}{PK} = \frac{I'}{PK}\left(\frac{a_1}{P} + \frac{b\pi t_0}{\lambda X^2(1 - t_1)}\right) \tag{6.33}$$

so that $\partial p / \partial m \gtrless 0$ according as $\phi \gtrless 0$. Thus the response is seen to consist of two parts, the first of which

$$\frac{I'a_1}{P^2 K}$$

is essentially the same as that obtained in the no tax case of Section 2C.
      This component is inflationary and operates via the excess demand terms in the price adjustment equation. As shown below, an increase in the rate of growth of the money supply increases Y, thereby raising excess demand (or reducing excess supply) and exerting an upward inflationary pressure. The second term reflects the interaction of taxes and inflationary expectations and with a progressive tax structure ($t_0 < 0$) is negative. An increase in m can readily be shown to increase nominal income X, which for given tax

parameters t_0, t_1 implies a decrease in the ratio of the marginal to the average tax rate.That is, the income tax becomes less progressive thereby weakening the expectations-progressivity effect and exerting a downward pressure on the rate of price inflation. Which effect will dominate will depend upon the relative strengths of (a) the response of current prices to excess demand on the one hand, and (b) the degree of progressivity of taxes, the amount of inflationary expectations, and the extent to which these are reflected in increased inflation on the other.[25]

The important feature of equation (6.33) is its implication that an expansionary monetary policy (in the form of increasing the rate of growth of the money supply) may actually be *deflationary* if the factors enumerated under (b) are sufficiently strong. Furthermore, it implies that any monetary policy (either expansionary or contractionary) will be ineffective in dealing with inflation if the factors mentioned in (a) and (b) are of roughly comparable strength and tend to cancel out.

Given a constant tax structure, the response in real output (employment) to an increase in m is

$$\frac{\partial Y}{\partial m} = \frac{I'}{P^2 K} \left(1 - \frac{b\pi t_0}{\lambda(1-t_1)(1+p)X} \right) \tag{6.34}$$

which again consists of two terms, the first of which is essentially as in Section 2C. The second effect also originates from the expectations-progressivity effect of the price adjustment equation and reinforces the first. The reason is that this latter effect exerts a downward pressure on prices, thereby increasing the real value of any increase in nominal income.

The impacts of an increase in government expenditure (for t_0, t_1 constant) are analogous, the corresponding expressions being

$$\frac{\partial p}{\partial G} = \frac{L_2 + I'\theta}{K} \left(\frac{a_1}{P} + \frac{b\pi t_0}{\lambda X^2 (1-t_1)} \right) \tag{6.35}$$

$$\frac{\partial Y}{\partial G} = \frac{L_2 + I'\theta}{PK} \left(1 - \frac{b\pi t_0}{\lambda(1-t_1)(1+p)X} \right) \tag{6.36}$$

so that the same remarks made earlier regarding monetary policy apply to fiscal policy as well. Furthermore, provided $\phi \neq 0$, we see that the relative potency of monetary and fiscal policy in affecting the level of output (employment) is the same as their relative effects on inflation namely

$$\frac{\partial Y/\partial m}{\partial Y/\partial G} = \frac{I'}{P[L_2 + I'\theta]} = \frac{\partial p/\partial m}{\partial p/\partial G}. \tag{6.37}$$

These expressions are identical to those obtained in the no-tax case and are seen to be independent of any tax parameters.

Hence, while relative effects are unaffected by income taxes, we have seen that the existence of progressive taxes may lead to a reversal in the impact of expansionary monetary and fiscal policies on the actual rate of inflation. Thus, when tax effects are recognized, it becomes possible for an increase in G or m to increase output and employment, while at the same time actually reducing the rate of inflation.

C.   Effects of tax changes

We now turn to the important question of analysing the effects of changes in the income tax rate upon the level of income (employment) and the rate of inflation. This became a topical issue when the US Government imposed a 10 per cent surtax during 1968–69 in an attempt to provide a short-run remedy for the increased inflation occurring at that time. The failure of the surtax to curb the inflation led to lively debate, and interest in the use of taxation as an anti-inflationary policy measure has continued as the prevailing inflationary conditions have intensified. The role of inflationary expectations which have tended to be neglected in the discussion so far, introduces another dimension that should be taken into account.[26]

We shall consider two kinds of tax changes:

(i) changes in the base tax level t_0;

(ii) changes in the marginal rate t_1.

To simplify the analysis somewhat we shall assume $\theta = 0$. That is, any budget surplus or deficit resulting from the tax change is totally financed by issuing additional bonds.

Differentiating the system equations (6.29) with respect to t_0, yields

$$\frac{\partial p}{\partial t_0} = \frac{-\phi L_2 C'}{PK} - \frac{(b\pi - d)}{\lambda K(1 - t_1)PX} \{[1 - C'(1 - t_1)]L_2 + I'L_1\}$$

$$(6.38)$$

which consists of three components. The first, described by the term

$$\frac{-\phi L_2 C'}{PK}$$

is the 'total demand effect'. Recalling that $L_2 < 0$, $C' > 0$, $K < 0$ the sign of this term is seen to vary inversely with that of ϕ. An increase in t_0 will, *ceteris paribus*, reduce aggregate demand Y, which in turn will have two effects on p. The first is the familiar deflationary effect resulting from the decrease in excess demand; the second is an inflationary effect due to the fact that the decrease in nominal income X, which can be shown to occur, increases the progressivity of the tax structure.

Secondly, there is the direct expectations-progressivity effect

$$\frac{-b\pi}{\lambda K(1 - t_1)PX} \{[1 - C'(1 - t_1)]L_2 + I'L_1\}$$

and this is always deflationary. This is because the direct effect of an increase in the base tax rate t_0 is to reduce the progressivity of the tax structure, thereby reducing the pressure on prices resulting from any inflationary expectations.

Finally, there is the income claims effect, given by the remaining term and which is always inflationary. As taxes increase, workers and unions will attempt to be compensated correspondingly, thereby pressuring firms to raise prices. As discussed earlier, this effect is strictly transitory and will persist only for the period during which taxes are being increased. Thereafter it becomes zero and ceases to have any effect.[27]

The upshot of the above discussion is that the net effect of an increase in the basic tax rate is complex and highly indeterminate. In the very short run the income claims effect will be inflationary, as will the total demand effect, if inflationary expectations are high and taxes are highly progressive (i.e. $\phi < 0$). To offset that, the direct expectations-progressivity effect will tend to be deflationary. In the intermediate run, the inflationary income claims effect becomes zero, so that some of the inflationary impact will disappear.

If $\theta > 0$, there will be a further effect operating through the money supply. Raising t_0 will probably (but not necessarily) raise tax receipts, reduce the budget deficit, and thus reduce the rate of growth of the money supply. As shown in (6.34) this will probably (but again not necessarily) have a deflationary impact, depending upon the parameters of the system. Consequently, this additional effect adds a further degree of indeterminacy to the ultimate response.

The impact of t_0 on real output is (for $\theta = 0$)

$$\frac{\partial Y}{\partial t_0} = \frac{-C'}{KP^2} L_2 \left(1 - \frac{b\pi t_0}{\lambda(1-t_1)(1+p)X}\right)$$
$$- \frac{(b\pi - d)}{\lambda KP^2 (1-t_1)(1+p)X} [C't_0 - I'M] \qquad (6.39)$$

which again consists of a variety of effects. The first term is the total demand effect, which is unambiguously negative, and itself consists of two components. The first, the direct demand effect, ignores taxes; the second takes account of the fact that an increase in t_0 lowers X, thereby increasing the progressivity of the tax structure, exerting an upward pressure on prices and further lowering real output. The second term in (6.39) represents the expectations-progressivity and incomes claims effects of the tax. As we have seen, the former has a deflationary, and the latter an inflationary, effect on prices and both in turn influence the *real* value of any nominal change in income arising from a tax change. The net effect of this second term is ambiguous, thereby making the overall partial derivative $\partial Y/\partial t_0$ indeterminate in sign. The ambiguity increases in the second period, when the transitory negative incomes claims effect ceases to operate.

These calculations can be repeated for increases in the marginal tax rate t_1 and the expressions obtained are very similar. Thus, we have

$$\frac{\partial p}{\partial t_1} = \frac{-\phi X C' L_2}{PK} - \frac{\omega}{PK} \{L_2 [1 - C'(1 - t_1)] + I' L_1\} \qquad (6.40)$$

where

$$\omega = \frac{b\pi t_0}{\lambda(1 - t_1)^2 X} - \frac{d[(1 - t_1) + \Delta t_1]}{(1 - t_1)^2} < 0$$

and again there are three components. The important difference worth noting, however, is that the expectations-progressivity effect is now inflationary. An increase in the marginal rate t_1 raises the progressivity of taxes and with given inflationary expectations increases the upward pressure on prices. The other two effects are as before, so that one can conclude that an increase in the marginal tax rate is more inflationary than an increase in the basic tax level. Finally, it can be shown that all effects of an incease in the marginal tax rate on output operate in the same direction, implying that unambiguously

$$\frac{\partial Y}{\partial t_1} < 0. \qquad (6.41)$$

The expressions given in (6.38)–(6.41) describe the effects of changes in the various tax parameters and thus can provide the basis for discussing tax policies directed at improving the inflation–unemployment situation. They suggest that the effects of changing the marginal tax rate are likely to be more determinate than those resulting from adjusting the base tax level. Moreover, in some circumstances it may be possible for a cut in the marginal tax rate to both increase output and reduce the current rate of inflation simultaneously. It must be remembered, however, that these are only partial responses, and to determine an overall government policy one would need to consider these tax effects in conjunction with the monetary and government expenditure effects discussed earlier. By combining policies in this way one should in principle be able to derive composite policies capable of achieving desired objectives for both output and inflation.

D.   *Impact of inflationary expectations*

As might be expected in the light of the interaction between anticipated inflation and taxes, the responses of the short run equilibrium values of Y, r, and p to changes in anticipated inflation are much more complicated than in the no-tax model. There seems little point in reporting the formulae, but the results indicate that in general the symmetric relationships contained in (6.17) cease to hold. The one instance where they do continue to apply is in the case of a proportional tax rate (where $t_0 = 0$). This is hardly surprising, since in this case, the interaction of taxes with anticipated inflation, which enters through the term

$$b \left(1 - \frac{t_0}{\lambda X(1 - t_1)} \right) \pi$$

in the price adjustment equation (6.27) vanishes.

4.   **Anticipated and unanticipated government policy**
      The models analysed in Sections 2 and 3 have treated expectations as an exogenous variable, completely independent of any of the government policy instruments. Specifically we solve for the short-run rate of inflation p and level of income Y in the form

$$p = f(\pi, Z) \tag{6.42a}$$

$$Y = g(\pi, Z) \tag{6.42b}$$

where in general Z denotes a vector of government policy variables. For our present purposes it suffices to assume that there is just a single policy variable, government expenditure say, so that Z is taken to be the scalar G. We shall therefore restrict our comments to the simpler model of Section 3, although the principle we wish to consider generalizes quite readily. In terms of the present notation, the various effects reported in (6.16), (6.21) are described by the partial derivatives

$$f_1 > 0, \quad f_2 > 0,$$
$$g_1 > 0, \quad g_2 > 0.$$

It will be recalled that we justified our assumption of treating π as a constant parameter on the grounds that it is determined by events occurring in prior periods. This assumption is often employed in the macroeconomic modelling of expectations and we discussed some the simpler hypotheses describing the formation of expectations in the previous chapter. All of these mechanisms, which treat π as predetermined at a given time t say, constitute what are sometimes referred to as *autoregressive* hypotheses. This name arises because of the fact that they assume the forecast value to be determined by past values of the variable being predicted.

Despite their widespread use in a variety of contexts, these autoregressive hypotheses have periodically come under severe criticism, especially when applied to predicting *endogenous* variables. These objections have been along the following lines. By forecasting an endogenous variable on the past values of that variable alone, one is clearly disregarding a considerable volume of available information relevant to that variable. In particular one is ignoring any knowledge one might have of the economic structure being analysed, the very purpose of which is to provide predictions of the endogenous variable. Indeed there is no reason to suppose that the predictions generated from the autoregressive scheme will be consistent with those implied by the model. Hence it has been argued that if forecasters are aware of the structure of the relevant economic system, the rational way for them to form their expectations is to base them on the predictions of the economic model. Of course, these comments do not apply to predictions of exogenous variables, since by definition these are not explained within the framework of the model. This hypothesis, known as the rational expectations hypothesis originated with Muth (1961). Formally it requires the forecaster's predicted value of a given variable for period t say to equal the value predicted by the system, conditional on all the information available at time $(t-1)$ when the forecast is made. The formal application of the hypothesis requires the specification of a full stochastic model and we do not plan to pursue this further. Nevertheless, it is possible to extract some of the ideas underlying the rational hypothesis within our deterministic framework.

Consider the determination of current inflation in the simplified model. This is given by

$$p = f(\pi, G). \tag{6.43}$$

Let us now invoke the basic idea underlying the rational expectations hypothesis, namely that forecasters base their predictions of inflation on the structural relationships of the economic system. We describe this by

$$\pi = f(\pi, G^*) \tag{6.44}$$

where G^* is their prediction of government expenditure, and is taken to be exogenous. Since actual government expenditure G is taken to be an exogenous policy variable it is perfectly consistent and reasonable for its prediction to be treated similarly.

Thus (6.44) asserts that forecasters use, as their predictive mechanism for π, the same structure as that determining the actual rate of inflation p. If $G^* = G$, then since there are no exogenous random variables in the model, $\pi = p$, and predictions are perfect. Thus forecast errors in this model are due *solely* to errors in predicting the *exogenous* policy variable G. In one sense this is more general than the Muth hypothesis in that we allow for the incorrect predictions of these exogenous variables. On the other hand it is also less general in that it abstracts from exogenous random disturbances. Note also as a weaker form of this hypothesis one could postulate

$$p = f(\pi, G) \qquad f_1 > 0, \quad f_2 > 0$$
$$\pi = f'(\pi, G^*) \qquad f_1' > 0, \quad f_2' > 0$$

where the function f' is not identical to f. This alternative hypothesis asserts that π responds in the same direction as p to changes in its arguments, but not necessarily by the same amount.

Let us now take differentials of (6.43) and (6.44). These are

$$dp = f_1 d\pi + f_2 dG$$
$$(1 - f_1)d\pi = f_2 dG^*$$

from which we deduce

$$dp = \frac{f_1 f_2 dG^*}{1 - f_1} + f_2 dG. \qquad (6.45)$$

Equation (6.45) gives the change in current inflation due to
  (i) changes in *actual* government policy dG,
  (ii) changes in *anticipated* government policy dG^*.
It immediately yields the following partial derivatives

$$\frac{\partial p}{\partial G} = f_2 > 0 \qquad (6.46a)$$

$$\frac{\partial p}{\partial G^*} = \frac{f_1 f_2}{1 - f_1} > 0. \qquad (6.46b)$$

The first effect is the impact of an increase in government expenditure on the rate of inflation when no increase is anticipated. This is precisely the expression discussed in Sections 2 and 3. The second effect describes the impact of an increase in *anticipated* government expenditure on the current rate of inflation, with *actual* government expenditure held constant. This operates through the price expectations variable. An increase in anticipated government expenditure, even if unrealized, raises the anticipated rate of inflation which in turn raises the actual rate of inflation, for reasons discussed earlier. Indeed the impact of changes in anticipated government expenditure can be large relative to the changes in actual government expenditure. Comparing (6.46a), (6.46b) we see

$$\frac{\partial p}{\partial G} \gtrless \frac{\partial p}{\partial G^*} \quad \text{according as} \quad f_1 \lessgtr \tfrac{1}{2}.$$

Thus if one takes as a reasonable estimate of $\partial p / \partial \pi$ say 0.6 (recalling that the estimated expectations coefficients are downwardly biased), we deduce

$$\frac{\partial p}{\partial G^*} \bigg/ \frac{\partial p}{\partial G} = 1.5. \qquad (6.47)$$

More generally we might assume

$$dG^* = \lambda dG$$

where λ describes the accuracy with which exogenous increases in government expenditure are predicted; with perfect forecasting $\lambda = 1$. Substituting (6.47) into (6.45) yields

$$\frac{\partial p}{\partial G} = \frac{f_1 f_2 \lambda + f_2 (1 - f_1)}{1 - f_1} \tag{6.48}$$

and when $\lambda = 1$ this becomes

$$\frac{\partial p}{\partial G} = \frac{f_2}{1 - f_1}$$

while if $\lambda = 0$, it again reduces to (6.46a). It is clear that as long as $\lambda > 0$, so that forecasters are predicting in the right direction, the total effect of an increase in G on p will be larger than that discussed in Sections 2 and 3. To the extent that the increase in government expenditure is anticipated, inflationary expectations will increase and this will add further stimulus to the actual rate of inflation.

It is clear that we can calculate the same kind of effect for actual output Y, or the interest rate r. It is also apparent that we can generalize the argument to more complex models and more government instruments. While in the present example we have found the effect of anticipated government policy to reinforce unambiguously the direct effect of actual increased expenditure, this need not always be the case. For instance, it is easy to show that as far as the effects of an expansionary monetary policy on the nominal interest rate are concerned, the induced expectations effects tend to offset the conventional direct effects. In such a case it would pay the government to mislead the public as to its policies, if it wishes to have maximum impact. However, its ability to deceive the public can only be temporary. Ultimately individuals would learn and in the long run would predict the government's behaviour perfectly. But to model this process adequately involves the introduction of a learning process into the analysis and it would take us too far afield to pursue this interesting question further here.

5. Summary

This chapter has developed a short-run macroeconomic model analysing the role of inflationary expectations. Particular attention has been devoted to questions dealing with the extent to which the nominal interest rate and the actual rate of inflation adjust to changes in inflationary expectations. After developing the basic model under the simplifying assumption of having total taxes fixed in real terms, the analysis is extended to allow for endogenous income taxes and to investigate the manner in which their interaction with inflationary expectations influences the system.

With fixed real taxes the relationships describing how

(1) the nominal interest rate,
(2) the actual rate of inflation,
(3) real income,

respond to inflationary expectations are symmetrical in the following sense.

The nominal interest rate under-(over-)adjusts to inflationary expectations if and only if the partial effect of inflationary expectations on actual inflation (as measured by the expectations coefficient b in the price-adjustment equations) under-(over-)states the true effect. Furthermore, both these responses will be as just indicated if and only if anticipated inflation exerts an expansionary (contractionary) effect on real income.

Thus, in general, the Fisherian proposition that the nominal interest rate adjusts to exactly incorporate changes in inflationary expectations does not hold. While over-adjustment in the short run is possible, plausible parameter values indicate that only partial adjustment is much more likely to occur. The crucial factors determining the direction of adjustment of the real rate of interest include,

    (i) the interest elasticity of the demand for money;
    (ii) the inflationary expectations elasticity of the demand for money;
    (iii) the expectations coefficient in the price adjustment equation;
    (iv) the proportion of government expenditure financed by increasing the monetary base.

Similarly, plausible parameter values imply that the partial effect of inflationary expectations on actual inflation understates the full short-run impact and that the magnitude of the bias varies inversely with the size of the expectations coefficient. Both these results yield important insights into some of the empirical findings related to this issue. Most significantly, we see that complete adjustment of actual inflation to anticipated inflation in general implies an expectations coefficient of less than unity.

With the introduction of taxes, the symmetric relationships referred to above cease to hold. The complicating factor is the interaction of taxes and price expectations, which appears in the price adjustment equation. This is a consequence of a progressive (or regressive) tax structure and we refer to it as the 'expectations-progressivity effect'. This interaction has implications for monetary and fiscal policy as well. For example, unlike the no-tax case, it is now possible for an expansionary monetary policy, or an increase in government expenditure, to have a deflationary effect on prices, provided the interaction is sufficiently strong.

The impact of an increase in the base and marginal tax rate on the rate of inflation in particular gives rise to several effects. First there is a demand effect which consists of the traditional deflationary component, together with an inflationary component, due to the fact that the decrease in income resulting from the tax increase increases the progressivity of the tax structure. Secondly, there is the direct expectations-progressivity effect which is deflationary for increases in the base tax rate and inflationary for increases in the marginal rate. Thirdly, there is the direct cost, or income claims effect which is inflationary but strictly transitory. Fourthly, if the government finances part of its budget deficit through increases in the money supply, this will give rise to a further effect which probably, but not necessarily, will be deflationary.

The fact that these effects operate in opposite directions makes the overall impact of a tax increase on the rate of inflation difficult to assess. The most important conclusion of these results is that the implementation of an appropriate tax policy as a means of controlling inflation is much more complicated than a simple textbook analysis would suggest and that an increase in the marginal tax rate in particular, is likely to be inflationary. Indeed, unless one takes careful account of the interactions we have been discussing, it is quite possible for a particular tax policy to be ineffective or to even lead to perverse effects.

Finally, we have indicated how the model can be extended to allow for endogenous price expectations. This has been done by utilizing the idea of rational expectations and requiring the expectations to be determined in a manner which is consistent with the structure of the underlying model. This in turn enables us to distinguish between the effects of anticipated and unanticipated government policies. It is shown how, at least within the short run, a considerable amount of the effect of government policy can be through its impact on anticipations.

7

AN INTERMEDIATE-RUN MACROECONOMIC MODEL

1.   Introduction[1]

It will be recalled from the discussion of Chapter 4, that our first dynamic model was based solely on the dynamics imposed by the government budget constraint. This arises from the fact that in order to finance its deficit, the government issues financial assets (bonds or money) thereby changing the net worth of the private sector and that these changes in turn give rise to dynamic adjustments in the other endogenous variables such as the level of income and the rate of interest. In contrast to the explicit dynamic treatment of financial assets, the model we developed assumed that physical capital remains fixed, despite the fact that net investment is continually taking place. In the introduction to Chapter 4 we remarked on the rather unsatisfactory nature of this asymmetric treatment of asset accumulation, but justified our procedure largely on the pedagogical grounds of serving as a useful starting point.

It is time now to move to the next stage of our dynamic analysis and to modify this rather unpalatable assumption. Specifically, we shall explicitly introduce the fact that investment leads to the accumulation of capital and that this affects wealth and other variables in a parallel fashion to the accumulation of financial assets. We shall extend the model in two stages. First, we shall outline briefly the approach adopted by Blinder and Solow (1973), who were the first authors to incorporate the accumulation of physical capital into such a macroeconomic model. But, as we shall see below, while their analysis is an important advance over previous models, it too suffers from certain defects. Our second stage therefore, is to develop in some detail a somewhat different formulation, which circumvents the difficulties of the Blinder–Solow analysis, yet captures the crucial dynamic behaviour. Moreover, their analysis is based on the assumption of fixed prices. In our model we relax this assumption by allowing the rate of inflation to be determined by a Phillips curve embodying the 'expectations hypothesis', along the lines developed in Chapter 5. In this respect the present chapter can be viewed as a dynamic extension of Chapter 6, allowing us to extend our discussion of the issues raised in that chapter to a genuine dynamic context.

2.   **The Blinder–Solow fixed price model**
        The Blinder–Solow model was formulated using continuous time
and since this is more convenient for longer run analysis, which is now our
main concern, we shall follow this approach. Their model consists of the
following four equations

$$Y = C[(1-u)(Y+B), M + B/r + K] + I(r, K) + G$$
$$0 < C_1 < 1, \quad C_2 > 0, \quad I_1 < 0, \quad I_2 < 0 \qquad (7.1a)$$

$$M = L(Y, r, M + B/r + K) \qquad L_1 > 0, \quad L_2 < 0, \quad L_3 > 0$$
$$(7.1b)$$

$$\dot{M} + \frac{\dot{B}}{r} = G + B - u(Y + B) \qquad (7.1c)$$

$$\dot{K} = I(r, K) \qquad (7.1d)$$

where all variables are as defined in Chapter 4, and as before K denotes the
stock of physical capital. The dot denotes the derivative with respect to time.
If one assumes that K is constant and considers the subsystem defined by
(7.1a)–(7.1c) for given K, the model is the direct continuous-time analogue
of our model analysed at some length in Chapter 4. Equations (7.1a), (7.1b)
define the instantaneous IS and LM curves respectively, while (7.1c) defines
the dynamics due to the government budget constraint. Since these have all
been discussed at length earlier, there is no need to elaborate on them again
now.

    The new element is equation (7.1d) which recognizes the fact that the
investment process gives rise to the accumulation of capital. This equation
asserts that increases in either the interest rate or the existing stock of capital
exert downward effects on the rate of investment, as one would expect. Note
that with the introduction of (7.1d), the dynamics of physical capital accumulation play a parallel role to that of financial asset accumulation in their
effects on wealth accumulation and the ultimate development of the system.

    One further point we should note at least parenthetically at this stage, is
that $I(r, K)$ denotes investment *demand,* while $\dot{K}$ is the *actual* rate of capital
accumulation. As we discussed in Chapter 3, in a continuous-time model such
as this, these two quantities can be equated to ensure continuous product
market equilibrium if and only if rather stringent conditions are met; see e.g.
(3.46). For the purposes of the present chapter we shall assume that these
conditions are met and we shall delay to Chapter 8 a consideration of what
happens when they are violated, so that the product market may be in
continuous disequilibrium.

    The formal analysis of the Blinder–Solow model takes place in two stages.
First, the restrictions introduced in (7.1) ensure that the static equations

(7.1a), (7.1b) can be solved uniquely for Y, r, in terms of K, M, B, G to yield

$$Y = F(M, B, K, G) \tag{7.2a}$$

$$r = H(M, B, K, G). \tag{7.2b}$$

These values are then substituted into the dynamic equations (7.1c), (7.1d) to give the dynamic relationships

$$\dot{M} + \frac{\dot{B}}{r} = G + B - u[F(M, B, K, G) + B] \tag{7.3a}$$

$$\dot{K} = I[H(M, B, K, G), K]. \tag{7.3b}$$

These equations are now in terms of M, B, K alone (treating G as a fixed parameter), and as in Chapter 4 to completely specify the system one must postulate policies for the variables M and B. Once this is done, the dynamics of the system are uniquely determined. Blinder and Solow consider the two extremes of

(i) all money financing, in which $B = \bar{B}$;
(ii) all bond financing, in which $M = \bar{M}$.

They then go on to consider the local stability of the system under these two modes of financing and some long-run steady-state government expenditure multipliers. The methodology is very similar to that given in Chapter 4, and since we shall do this in some detail for the model we propose to develop in the following sections of this chapter, it suffices to simply summarize their conclusions.

They show that given their assumptions, under all money financing the system will definitely be stable. By contrast, with all bond financing, instability becomes possible, although they argue that for plausible parameter values, stability should still prevail. They also consider the long-run effects of changes in government expenditure and show directly from (7.1c) that with all money financing $(\partial Y/\partial G)_m = 1/u$, just as it was in Chapter 4. With all bond financing it follows from the same equation that

$$\left(\frac{\partial Y}{\partial G}\right)_b = \frac{1}{u} + \frac{1-u}{u} \frac{\partial B}{\partial G} \tag{7.4}$$

so that if $\partial B/\partial G > 0$, then not only is $(\partial Y/\partial G)_b > 0$, but in fact it exceeds $(\partial Y/\partial G)_m$, the government expenditure multiplier obtained with money-financed deficits. While Blinder and Solow do not attempt to draw any strong conclusions about $\partial B/\partial G$ they nevertheless argue that given plausible parameter values (7.4) should be positive.

Despite the fact that the Blinder–Solow analysis is clearly an important advance over previous models, such as the analysis of Chapter 4, it nevertheless does suffer from two rather disturbing difficulties. First, from the stationary solutions to (7.1c), (7.1d) it will be seen that equilibrium is reached when the accumulation of real capital (net investment), as well as the accumulation of financial assets, ceases, so that savings have been reduced to zero. This is somewhat unsatisfactory as an equilibrium for a model which makes the usual Keynesian assumption that output is demand-determined and capital is fixed instantaneously (i.e. labour is the only short-run variable factor of production). For example, if one makes the common assumption of zero wealth effects in consumption, the long-run equilibrium of zero net investment in such a model is obtained by *driving down* aggregate demand and income to the level where savings, and hence net investment, are reduced to zero. Although this may appear to be consistent with the equilibrium of neoclassical growth theory, in which the equilibrium capital stock grows at the rate of growth of population, there is an important difference. The neoclassical equilibrium is reached via a process of *capital deepening,* in which the capital–labour ratio can be continuously adjusted in response to changing relative factor prices, with the constant equilibrium per capita savings being achieved because of the resulting *increase* in per capita income. In a recent paper, Tobin and Buiter (1976) undertake the analysis of a full-employment long-run model of this sort, in which the equilibrium rate of investment is zero. In Chapter 8 we shall develop a similar kind of model, which in addition, allows for the possibility of both short-run and long-run unemployment.

The second difficulty with the Blinder–Solow model is that its consistency depends crucially upon the existence of wealth effects in consumption. If these wealth effects are zero, then it is easily seen that in the steady-state, when $G - uY + (1 - u)B = 0$, (7.1a) implies a steady-state national income multiplier for money-financed deficits of unity, while the steady-state government budget constraint (7.1c) implies a corresponding multiplier of $1/u$. In the case of bond-financed deficits, the consistency of the national income multipliers from these two equations requires each unit of government expenditure to stimulate the economy sufficiently so that the induced tax receipts allow outside bonds to be *reduced* by one unit. If one allows for positive wealth effects in consumption, as Blinder and Solow do, these extreme difficulties do not occur, but the implied constraint on the long-run effect of government expenditure on wealth becomes an empirical question which cannot be decided clearly in favour of consistency, given plausible empirical estimates of the relevant parameters. In any event, while few economists would deny the importance of these wealth effects, it is nevertheless somewhat disturbing to have the *logical consistency* of the model so crucially dependent upon them.

3.   An intermediate-run model

Because of these limitations of the Blinder–Solow model, and because it is felt that a model which anticipates a somewhat shorter time horizon that the neoclassical 'golden age' in which all investment ceases, is of prime relevance for policy analysis, in this chapter we analyse the dynamics and equilibrium properties of what we shall call an 'intermediate-run' model. The intermediate-run we shall consider has the following general characteristics. On the one hand, we recognize that investment implies a change in the capital stock and generates financial assets, which must be absorbed in savers' portfolios. This capital is used in production and, along with the demand-determined output, determines labour demand in the short run. In both these regards, we follow Blinder and Solow in making the traditional Keynesian assumption of treating capital as fixed instantaneously (in determining labour demand) and in recognizing the supply effects of increasing the capital stock. We differ from Blinder and Solow in that we do not require the accumulation of capital to cease in the steady state of our model. As we have suggested, to do so, within a Keynesian framework, implies driving down aggregate income to reach a zero savings rate in the steady state. Thus the analysis is intermediate run in the sense that it does not allow for the full capital deepening effects that would ultimately lead to a golden age and does not require the accumulation of capital to cease in the steady state. To obtain a steady state, in which positive savings occur, we adopt a technique used previously by Sargent (1973a) and work with appropriate quantities relative to the stock of capital. Thus, in equilibrium, all real quantities grow at the same rate as capital.[2]

As we have already indicated, the second modification we make to the Blinder–Solow model is to relax their assumption of fixed prices. This is done by postulating the rate of price inflation to be determined by a Phillips curve embodying the 'expectations hypothesis', with the expectations endogenously determined. We also include an expanded financial sector along the lines developed by Tobin (1969), in which bonds, money, and equity capital are, in general, imperfect substitutes in portfolio allocation. Extending the model in this way enables us to integrate the Blinder–Solow analysis which stresses the dynamics of the system, with a more adequate portfolio model, and with the Friedman (1968) and Phelps (1968) analysis of the long-run rate of inflation. But the integration of these various developments in macroeconomic theory has its price. Results are inevitably more complex and indeterminate; few neat, clear-cut propositions emerge. Nonetheless, we are able to provide some insight into stability conditions and steady-state comparative static properties of various government policies over a time horizon relevant to policy decisions.

The development of the model proceeds in several stages. First, we consider a number of relationships describing the instantaneous equilibrium of the system in terms of a number of variables, such as the supplies of the assets and expectations, which describe the state of the system. Next, we consider the intrinsic dynamics of the system arising from the financing of the government budget deficit, the accumulation of capital, and the formation of expectations. These relationships describe the evolution of the system over time. Third, for the reasons already given, we rewrite the system in terms of quantities per unit of physical capital, and, finally, we specify the government policies we wish to consider.

A. *Instantaneous relationships*

At every instant of time, the following relationships must hold:

$$Y = C[(Y+B/P)(1-u), V] + I(r_e, Y, K) + G$$
$$0 < C_1 < 1, \quad C_2 > 0, \quad I_1 < 0, \quad I_2 > 0, \quad I_3 < 0 \tag{7.5}$$

$$p = \alpha_0 + \alpha_1 \left(\frac{Y-\bar{Y}}{\bar{Y}}\right) + \beta\pi$$
$$\alpha_1 > 0 \quad 0 \leqslant \beta \leqslant 1 \tag{7.6}$$

$$M/P = L(Y, r_e, r-\pi, -\pi, V)$$
$$L_1 > 0, \quad L_2 \leqslant 0, \quad L_3 \leqslant 0, \quad L_4 > 0, \quad 0 < L_5 < 1 \tag{7.7}$$

$$B/Pr = J(Y, r_e, r-\pi, -\pi, V)$$
$$J_1 < 0, \quad J_2 \leqslant 0, \quad J_3 > 0, \quad J_4 \leqslant 0, \quad 0 < J_5 < 1 \tag{7.8}$$

$$qE = N(Y, r_e, r-\pi, -\pi, V)$$
$$N_1 = 0, \quad N_2 > 0, \quad N_3 \leqslant 0, \quad N_4 \leqslant 0,$$
$$0 < N_5 < 1 \tag{7.9}$$

$$V = M/P + B/Pr + qE \tag{7.10}$$

$$r_e = \frac{R(Y/K)K}{qE}$$
$$R' > 0 \tag{7.11}$$

where for convenience we redefine the notation we shall use as follows:
- Y = real output
- $\bar{Y}$ = full employment real output
- C = real consumption
- I = real investment
- G = real government expenditure
- K = quantity of real capital
- B = nominal value of interest payments on government debt (assumed to be perpetual bonds paying \$1 per bond)
- M = nominal stock of money
- E = quantity of real equity, i.e., number of shares outstanding
- q = price of equity in terms of currently produced goods
- V = real net private wealth
- L = demand for real balances of outside money
- J = demand for real outside bonds
- N = demand for real equity
- u = proportional tax rate
- r_e = real rate of return on equity

r = nominal rate of interest on bonds
P = price level
$p \equiv \dot{P}/P$ = rate of price inflation
π = expected rate of inflation
R = marginal physical product of capital.

Consumption is assumed to be a function of real disposable income and real wealth. Real disposable income itself consists of two components; ordinary after-tax personal income and the capital gains on the existing assets. However, these may have differential effects on consumption and, indeed, the available empirical evidence suggests that the marginal propensity to consume out of accrued capital gains is less than 0.01.[3] Thus, we make the simplifying assumption that all capital gains are saved, thereby having their effects on consumption through the process of wealth accumulation. Accordingly, consumption is specified to depend on only the ordinary-income component, which is defined to be the after-tax value of the sum of real output and the real interest payments on government debt, where, for simplicity, a proportional tax rate, u, is assumed. Investment is specified as a function of the real return of equity, real income, and the quantity of physical capital. The fact that it is independent of the cost of any debt capital can be justified under the assumption of all equity financing of the firm, or alternatively if the conditions of the Modigliani and Miller theorem on capital structure with no corporate taxes apply; see Modigliani and Miller (1958).[4] The final component of aggregate demand is real governmental expenditures, which we take to be a policy instrument.

Equation (7.5) describes the condition for continuous product market equilibrium. The restrictions on the functions $C(\quad)$ and $I(\quad)$ given in that equation are self-explanatory and, in addition to these, we require

$$1 - c_1(1 - u) - c_2 R'/r_e - i_2 > 0,$$

ensuring that the economy's *IS* curve has the usual downward slope. The other requirement we introduce is for C to be homogeneous of degree one in disposable income and wealth, and for I to have a similar property with respect to Y and K. This is necessary to enable us to work in per unit of capital terms.

Equation (7.6) is the price-adjustment equation. It postulates that the current rate of inflation depends upon the disequilibrium in the product market and the rate of inflationary expectations. It is a standard version of the 'expectations hypothesis' as developed in Chapter 5 and introduced into a one-period model in Chapter 6. As we have seen, it can be viewed as a 'reduced form' for the wage–price sector.

The financial sector draws heavily on the monetary framework discussed by Tobin (1969). There are three financial assets, so that real private wealth is the sum of the real value of equity (which must also equal the real imputed value of physical capital), the real value of government bonds, and the real value of money. Real asset demands are assumed to be functions of real income before taxes, expected real rates of return on assets, and real wealth. The notion that the level of real wealth, the own real rate of return, and the real rates of return on other assets influence the demand for assets is straight-forward. Real income is introduced as a determinant of the transactions demand for assets.

Equations (7.7) to (7.9) assert that the three asset markets are continuously in equilibrium although, because of the wealth constraint (7.10), only two of the markets are in fact independent. Indeed this equation is precisely the 'stock constraint' discussed in Chapter 3.

As pointed out by Tobin and indicated in Chapter 3, this constraint imposes the following 'adding up' restrictions on the partial derivatives of the asset demand functions

$$\text{(i)} \begin{cases} L_i + J_i + N_i = 0 & i = 1, \ldots, 4 \\ L_5 + J_5 + N_5 = 1. \end{cases}$$

Conditions (i) assert that any increase in wealth must be allocated to some asset. On the other hand any increase in the demand for a particular asset in response to a change of income or a real rate of return must be met by a com-pensating reduction in demand for some other asset.

In addition to (i) we follow Tobin and assume

> (ii) The demand for each asset varies positively with its own real rate of return and nonpositively with the rates on other assets; that is, all assets are gross substitutes.
>
> (iii) Equity is not a transactions substitute for money, so that

$$N_1 = 0, \quad \text{and} \quad L_1 = -J_1.$$

In other words, any increase in the demand for money for transactions pur-poses is met by instantaneously reducing bond holdings, not by adjusting holdings of equity. Both the sets of assumptions (ii) and (iii) are embodied in the restrictions on the partial derivatives reported in equations (7.7)–(7.9). Finally, we require

> (iv) the asset demand functions to be homogeneous of degree one in income and wealth.

Money in the model is outside money and is non-interest-bearing, so that its expected rate of return is the negative of the expected rate of inflation. The supply of money in nominal terms is M, so that its real value is M/P. Because we abstract from a fractional reserve banking system, M refers to 'high-powered money'. The interest-bearing government debt is assumed to be in the form of perpetual bonds paying \$1 per bond. With the number of bonds outstanding being B, their real quantity, and hence the real amount of total interest paid on the government debt, is B/P, as already noted above. Moreover, letting the nominal interest rate on bonds be r, the real value of bonded debt is B/Pr. The nominal value of a claim on one unit of equity is $P_e = qP$. Thus the real value of equity shares is qE.

The total return on physical capital is obtained by multiplying the marginal physical product of capital (which we specify to be an increasing function of the output–capital ratio) by the number of units of capital, and therefore equals RK. Thus equation (7.11) defines the real rate of return on equity to be RK, divided by the total real value of equity. This formula is derived from the fact that in equilibrium the real value of equity claims on capital must equal the discounted present value of the expected real future earnings from owning the physical capital stock; see (3.55). That is

$$q(t) E(t) = K(t) \int_t^\infty R^*(\tau)e^{-r_e^*(\tau)\,(\tau-t)}d\tau \qquad (7.12)$$

where $R^*(\tau)$ denotes the expected marginal physical product of capital and $r_e^*(\tau)$ is the expected discount rate for time τ. The expression (7.12) is obtained on the assumption that the expectations R^* and r_e^* are uniform with respect to all future periods. If further these constant expectations equal their *current* values, integrating (7.12) immediately yields (7.11). If this condition is not met, the expected percentage rate of change in qE/K would also need to be taken into account. This additional term is a severe complication and is not incorporated into the present analysis. However, the necessary modifications it entails are described in some detail in our more general model developed in Chapter 8.

Equations (7.5), (7.6), (7.7), (7.8), (7.10) and (7.11) define six independent, instantaneous, equilibrium conditions. Provided that the Jacobian of this system is non-zero, the set of equations can be solved for the six variables: Y, qE, r_e, r, V, and p, in terms of M, B, K, π, and other exogenous variables and parameters.

B.   *The dynamics of the system*

To complete the model, we need to describe its evolution over time. Recalling the investment function, it is clear that the accumulation of capital is given by

$$\dot{K} = I(r_e, Y, K). \qquad (7.13)$$

As mentioned in Chapter 6, in a dynamic analysis such as we are now developing, it is necessary to endogenize the inflationary expectations π. There are several ways this might be done. We assume that their dynamics is generated by the adaptive process

$$\dot{\pi} = \gamma(p - \pi) \qquad (7.14)$$

where $\gamma > 0$ is constant. This equation is the continuous-time analogue to the hypothesis specified by equation (5.22b'). It asserts that the instantaneous anticipated rate of inflation at time t is adjusted at a rate which is a constant proportion of the instantaneous forecast error. Integrating (7.14), $\pi(t)$ can be written as

$$\pi(t) = \gamma \int_{-\infty}^{t} p(\tau)e^{-\gamma(t-\tau)}d\tau \tag{7.15}$$

from which it can be seen that the current anticipated rate of inflation is an exponentially-weighted average of all past actual rates of inflation. Thus inflationary expectations are responsive to policy changes or any other changes in the system insofar as these changes affect the actual rate of inflation and therefore the distributed lag in (7.15).

It is perhaps worth noting at this point that if one invokes the *weak consistency* axiom (3.20) introduced in Chapter 3, the interpretation of the adaptive expectations hypothesis as described by (7.14) encounters certain logical difficulties when applied to predicting levels. These difficulties do *not* arise if, as is the case here, one is predicting rates of change, so that our formulation is quite consistent with this axiom. This problem is discussed at length in Burmeister and Turnovsky (1976) and also is taken up in Chapter 8.

Finally, the accumulation of government debt is described by the government budget constraint (expressed in real terms):

$$\frac{\dot{M}}{P} + \frac{\dot{B}}{Pr} = G - uY + (1-u)\frac{B}{P}. \tag{7.16}$$

This equation asserts that the sum of government expenditures, plus interest payments on the government's bonded debt, less tax receipts, must be financed either by changes in the stock of outside money, or outside bonds, or both. Thus, the system still possesses one degree of freedom and, to close it, we must specify a policy describing how the government finances its deficit. Once this is done, the dynamics of the model and its ultimate equilibrium will be uniquely determined, assuming there are no singularities.

There is, in fact, one additional dynamic relationship in the model – namely:

$$P_e\dot{E} = P\dot{K} \quad \text{or} \quad q\dot{E} = \dot{K}. \tag{7.17}$$

This equation is the financial constraint facing firms and describes the number of additional shares they need to issue at the current market price, P_e, to raise the money necessary to purchase the new machines at their market price, P. Integrating this equation enables us to determine the separate components, q, E. These quantities, even at equilibrium, turn out to depend upon initial conditions, which, of course, is a direct consequence of the singularity (7.17) imposes on the system. But since we are not interested in determining q and E separately, there is no need to concern ourselves further with this equation.

C.   *Respecification of system in per-unit-of-capital form*
For reasons we have already discussed (chiefly because we wish to focus on the intermediate run), it is convenient to analyse the system relative to the stock of capital. The homogeneity assumptions we have introduced for the C, I, L, J, N functions enable us to scale the income and wealth variables in this way. Using these homogeneity assumptions and the following redefinitions of variables,

$$Y/K = y, \quad \bar{Y}/K = \bar{y}, \quad V/K = v, \quad M/KP \equiv m, \quad B/KP = b,$$

$$E/K = e, \quad G/K = g, \quad C/K = c, \quad L/K = l, \quad J/K = j,$$

$$N/K = n, \quad I/K = i,$$

the system of equations describing the instantaneous equilibrium, and the price-adjustment mechanism may be written as:

$$y - c\,[(1 - u)\,(y + b),\, v] - i(r_e, y) - g = 0 \qquad (7.18\text{a})$$

$$l(y, r_e, r - \pi, -\pi, v) - m = 0 \qquad (7.18\text{b})$$

$$j(y, r_e, r - \pi, -\pi, v) - b/r = 0 \qquad (7.18\text{c})$$

$$v = qe + m + b/r \qquad (7.18\text{d})$$

$$qe = \frac{R(y)}{r_e} \qquad (7.18\text{e})$$

$$p = \alpha_0 + \alpha_1 \left(\frac{y - \bar{y}}{\bar{y}}\right) + \beta\pi. \qquad (7.18\text{f})$$

where the various functions have been rewritten using lower case letters for the purposes of notational conformity.

These six equations determine $y, r_e, r, v, qe,$ and p in terms of $m, b, g,$ and π. With quantity variables being expressed in per unit of capital form, it is necessary to transform the dynamic equations into a comparable form, yielding:[5]

$$\dot{k} = \frac{\dot{K}}{K} = i(r_e, y) \qquad (7.19\text{a})$$

$$\dot{\pi} = \gamma(p - \pi) \qquad (7.19\text{b})$$

$$\dot{m} + \frac{\dot{b}}{r} = g - uy + (1 - u)b - (m + b/r)(p + \dot{k}) \qquad (7.19\text{c})$$

together with the policy specification for $\dot{m}$ and/or $\dot{b}$. In equation (7.19c) the quantity, $g - uy + (1 - u)b$, is the government budget deficit, including interest payments on outstanding bonds, expressed in real terms per unit of physical capital. The remaining term, $-(m + b)/r)\,(p + \dot{k})$, measures what might be loosely called a 'real inflationary and growth tax' levied on the real stock of existing outside government debt. Thus, equation (7.19c) asserts that, even if the government's budget is balanced, in the sense that $G - uY + (1 - u)B/P = 0$, so that nominal debt ceases to be issued, the real value per unit of physical capital of this debt will fall as long as capital is being accumulated and/or prices are rising. However, for convenience, we refer to the entire right-hand side of (7.19c) as the real budget deficit in capital units, since this is the amount to be financed by changes in $\dot{m}$ or $\dot{b}/r$.

Equations (7.18) and (7.19) provide the complete model.

D.   *Policy specification in the model*

As noted above, to close the model we must specify a policy describing how the government finances its deficit. There are many ways this might be done, and the policies we consider — although quite plausible — are chosen partly for their analytical convenience.

The dynamics of financial asset accumulation are expressed in terms of $\dot{m}$ and $\dot{b}$, the rates of change of the real supplies of financial assets per unit of capital, and we shall specify our policies in terms of these real quantities as well. In practice, the monetary authorities may tend to formulate their policies in terms of the nominal supplies of their financial liabilities, namely, $\dot{M}$ and $\dot{B}$, although $\dot{m}$ and $\dot{M}$ (and likewise $\dot{b}$ and $\dot{B}$) are related by:

$$\frac{\dot{m}}{m} = \frac{\dot{M}}{M} - \frac{\dot{P}}{P} - \frac{\dot{K}}{K} = \frac{\dot{M}}{M} - (p + i).$$

It should be realized that while we are perfectly at liberty to specify our policies directly in terms of $\dot{m}$ and/or $\dot{b}$, by doing so we are implicitly imposing an adjustment on the nominal supply of the asset. Likewise, government expenditure policy is now described by g and is therefore relative to the stock of capital.[6]

In specifying how the government finances its deficit, we shall define the deficit to be *purely bond financed* if $\dot{m} = 0$, so that

$$\frac{\dot{b}}{r} = g - uy + (1 - u)b - (m + b/r)(p + i).$$

Thus, pure bond financing does *not* mean that the nominal supply of money is held constant; on the contrary, it grows at the rate,

$$\frac{\dot{M}}{M} = p + i(r_e, y).$$

Clearly, in an inflationary economy, in which capital is accumulating, the natural base for defining a neutral or passive monetary growth policy is one which, in equilibrium, would maintain portfolio balance. Given our specification of the asset-demand functions, portfolio balance in equilibrium requires m to be constant, thus suggesting $\dot{m} = 0$ as the appropriate benchmark policy.[7]

At the other extreme, we shall define the deficit to be *purely money financed* if $\dot{b} = 0$, so that

$$\dot{m} = g - uy + (1 - u)b - (m + b/r)(p + i),$$

with identical remarks applying to this notion as just given for the pure-bond case.

4   **Comparative static properties of the instantaneous equilibrium**
        By substituting for v and qe into equations (7.18a) to (7.18c), the instantaneous equilibrium of the system can be reduced to three equations, determining the three variables, y, r_e, and r, in terms of the dynamically evolving variables m, b and π, as well as other exogenous variables, such as g. Once these variables are determined, the instantaneous rate of price adjustment can then be determined recursively from (7.18f). The comparative static properties of this instantaneous equilibrium are needed for the stability and steady-state equilibrium analysis undertaken later in this chapter.

A.   *Effects of changes in inflationary expectations*
        The instantaneous response of the system to a change in the expected rate of price inflation is given by the following system of equations.[8]

$$\begin{pmatrix} c_y & c_{r_e} & c_r \\ l_y & l_{r_e} & l_r \\ j_y & j_{r_e} & j_r \end{pmatrix} \begin{pmatrix} \partial y/\partial \pi \\ \partial r_e/\partial \pi \\ \partial r/\partial \pi \end{pmatrix} = \begin{pmatrix} 0 \\ l_\pi \\ j_\pi \end{pmatrix} \qquad (7.20)$$

which we write as

$$Dx = z$$

where

$$c_y = 1 - c_1(1 - u) - c_2 R'/r_e - i_2 > 0,$$

$$c_{r_e} = c_2 R/r_e^2 - i_1 > 0,$$

$$c_r = c_2 b/r^2 > 0,$$

$$l_y = l_1 + l_5 R'/r_e > 0,$$

$$l_{r_e} = l_2 - l_5 R/r_e^2 < 0,$$

$$l_r = l_3 - l_5 b/r^2 < 0,$$

$$j_y = j_1 + j_5 R'/r_e \gtrless 0,$$

$$j_{r_e} = j_2 - j_5 R/r_e^2 < 0,$$

$$j_r = j_3 + (1 - j_5)b/r^2 > 0,$$

$$l_\pi = l_3 + l_4 \gtrless 0,$$

$$j_\pi = j_3 + j_4 \gtrless 0.$$

The signs of all the elements of D follow from the restrictions given earlier.[9] With these assumptions, the only indeterminate elements are j_y in the matrix D, and l_π, j_π, in the vector z.

Let $|D|$ denote the determinant of the matrix D. Five of the six terms in the sum that gives its value are negative. Alternative sufficient conditions to ensure that $|D|$ is negative — and hence ensure that the instantaneous equilibrium can be solved uniquely for y, r, r_e — are

> (*A* 1*a*) The elasticity of the demand for money with respect to income is greater than or equal to the absolute value of the elasticity of the demand for money with respect to the rate of return on equity,
>
> $$\left(\text{i.e. } \frac{\partial m}{\partial y} \frac{y}{m} \geqslant \left| \frac{\partial m}{\partial r_e} \frac{r_e}{m} \right| \right) \quad \text{or}$$
>
> (*A*1*b*) The impact of wealth on consumption is negligible (i.e., $c_2 = 0$).

Since the first of these two conditions in particular is most likely to be met, one can assume with some confidence that $|D| < 0$, and henceforth we assume this to be so.

Given either of the above conditions, sufficient conditions for $\partial y / \partial \pi$ to be positive are

> (*A*2) The partial effect of an increase in the expected rate of inflation on the demand for money is non-positive (i.e. $l_3 + l_4 \geqslant 0$) *and* (*A*.1*b*) holds.

Since $A2$ is quite a plausible condition, on balance one would expect $\partial y / \partial \pi$ to be positive, consistent with the results of the one-period model of Chapter 6.

Next, consider the sign of $\partial r / \partial \pi$. One would expect this derivative to be positive, and a sufficient condition to ensure this will be so is:

> (*A*3) $l_3 + l_4 = 0$.

This condition is much more stringent than the inequality in $A2$ and is not likely to be met precisely. However, it is not a necessary condition and $\partial r / \partial \pi$ will be positive as long as the difference between the own-rate derivative of money demand and the absolute value of the derivative of money demand with respect to the bond rate is small. It is also likely that $\partial r / \partial \pi$ will be less than unity, implying that an increase in inflationary expectations will lead to a lower real return on bonds (instantaneously). Tobin (1969) with his assumption of fixed output, was able to show that this result always holds. In our case, however, where output is endogenously determined, this result requires the imposition of additional restrictions. One reasonably mild sufficient condition which will ensure $\partial r / \partial \pi < 1$ is:

(A4) The elasticity of bond demand with respect to wealth is greater than or equal to its elasticity with respect to income

$$\left(\text{i.e. } \frac{\partial b}{\partial v}\frac{v}{b} \geqslant \frac{\partial b}{\partial y}\frac{y}{b}\right).$$

On the other hand it is not possible, on the basis of simple sufficiency conditions such as those we have been considering, to determine the effect of a change in inflationary expectations on the real return to claims on capital. The reason for this inherent indeterminacy is as follows. As we have just seen, it is likely that $\partial y/\partial\pi$ is positive. It can be shown that the relative price of claims on capital, q, is also likely to increase with anticipated inflation. Since r_e depends directly on y and inversely on q [see (7.11)], it is thus not surprising that the sign of $\partial r_e/\partial\pi$ is indeterminate and will depend upon which of these effects dominates. This is again in contrast to the Tobin fixed output model, in which only the q effect operates, implying $\partial r_e/\partial\pi < 0$, unambiguously.

Finally, from the price adjustment equation (7.18f), it is clear that given our assumptions on α, β,

$$\text{sgn} \,(\partial p/\partial\pi) \;=\; \text{sgn} \,(\partial y/\partial\pi).$$

B. *Effects of changes in financial assets*
The partial derivatives with respect to changes in the stocks of the financial assets can be obtained analogously by differentiating the instantaneous equilibrium conditions. Since these calculations are similar to those given in (7.20) there is no need to report the full system. Assuming $|D| < 0$, it can be shown, without further restrictions, that $\partial y/\partial m$, and hence $\partial p/\partial m$ are both positive, as one would expect. Perhaps rather surprisingly, one cannot show $\partial r/\partial m < 0$, without further assumptions. The simplest sufficient — but by no means necessary — condition is $A1b$, namely, that the impact of wealth on consumption is negligible. Finally, the instantaneous effect of an increase in the money supply on the real return to capital is ambiguous, although intuitively one would expect $\partial r_e/\partial m < 0$. This, however, cannot be established without imposing several restrictions on the elasticities.

As one might expect, the partial derivative of the bond rate with respect to the bond–capital ratio b is likely to be positive. Sufficient conditions to ensure that is so are given by assumptions $A1a$ and $A4$ above. However, the sign of $\partial y/\partial b$, and hence that of $\partial p/\partial b$, is indeterminate. The reason for this is that on the one hand an increase in b has, as we have just seen, the contractionary effect of raising r. On the other hand, more bonds means higher interest payments and thus higher disposable income, and this is expansionary. It also gives rise to wealth effects, the net effects of which are ambiguous and add to the overall indeterminacy. As in previous cases, the effect on r_e is ambiguous, although if bonds and equity are close substitutes one would expect $\partial r_e/\partial b > 0$.

C.   Summary
         The results of the above comparative static analysis of the instan-
taneous equilibrium are summarized in the following table, in which the
probable signs of the various derivatives are reported. We have also included
the instantaneous derivatives with respect to government expenditure g, as
these are required in subsequent analysis. These, however, are self-
explanatory, and we do not discuss them further.

Table 1. Summary of probable signs

Derivative of	With respect to			
	π	m	b	g
y	+	+	?	+
p	+	+	?	+
r	+	−	+	+
$r_b = r - \pi$	−	−	+	+
r_e	?	?	?	+

   As we have suggested, the main purpose in considering these partial derivatives is because they are needed in the subsequent analysis. They are of
limited economic interest in their own right, since, as the government's
budget constraint makes clear, a change in any one policy variable necessarily
leads to a change in at least one of the other policy variables. But, by combining these partial derivatives, it is possible to consider the instantaneous
effects of economically feasible policies.
   Consider the instantaneous effects of an open market operation that is consistent with the government's budget constraint. In the context of this model
this policy is defined by the equation

$$dm + \frac{db}{r} = 0. \tag{7.21}$$

Note that this is not the usual definition of an open market operation as an
exchange of a *nominal* quantity of outside money for a *nominal* value of
outside bonds; see Chapter 4. But it is the natural definition in our context.
As we noted earlier, when there is capital growth and inflation, a neutral or
passive monetary policy requires nominal outside money balances to grow at
the rate $p + i$. Similarly, a passive bond growth policy requires nominal outside bond balances to grow at this same rate. To undertake active monetary
policy by an open market operation, nominal outside money growth must be
at a rate greater or less than $p + i$ with the nominal outside bond growth rate
making a compensating adjustment, so that total outside debt in nominal
terms continues to grow at the equilibrium rate. These requirements are met
by our definition.
   The net effect of a change in m and b on the nominal rate of interest is

given by the total derivative

$$dr = \frac{\partial r}{\partial m} dm + \frac{\partial r}{\partial b} db$$

and substituting from equation (7.21), the instantaneous effect of an open-market purchase of bonds is seen to be:

$$\frac{dr}{db} = \frac{\partial r}{\partial b} - \frac{1}{r} \frac{\partial r}{\partial m}. \qquad (7.22)$$

From Table 1 we can see that dr/db is most likely to be positive, and an explicit evaluation of equation (7.22) shows that this is unambiguously true, given our basic assumptions.

By a similar analysis, we may write analogous expressions for the effect of an open market purchase on the other two endogenous variables of the instantaneous equilibrium.

Although the partial effects of money and bonds on the real rate of return on equity are ambiguous (as shown in Table 1), the instantaneous effect of an open market purchase of bonds is likely to be negative. A sufficient condition for this to be the case is that wealth effects in consumption are negligible.

Somewhat surprisingly, the instantaneous effect of an open market purchase of bonds on output is ambiguous. This indeterminacy does not depend on having positive wealth effects in consumption. Rather, it results from the conflict between increased investment due to the decrease in the real rate of return on equity and decreased consumption due to reduced bond interest payments to the private sector.

The instantaneous effects of a change in the rate of government expenditure are given by the partial derivatives with respect to g in Table 1. This is the case since the induced effects of this change in the rate of expenditure on the stock of outstanding government debt occur over time and are zero instantaneously. The instantaneous effect is therefore independent of the type of financing that is ultimately undertaken in response to the induced change in the deficit.

The instantaneous time interval is too short to be of interest for practical policy purposes. The effects of alternative government policies for some finite period will be dependent on the time period chosen and on induced events during that time period.

To illustrate this point, consider a change of government policy. Suppose at time t, when the policy is introduced, the government's budget $d(t)$ is in balance, so that $d(t) = 0$. At time $t + h$, the induced change in the stock of government debt is approximately.

$$dm + db/r = d(t + h)h$$

where $d(t + h)$ is the deficit resulting from the policy change. The change in government debt outstanding clearly depends upon the time interval h and tends to zero as $h \to 0$, reducing the equation above to $dm + db/r = 0$ (cf. (7.21)) to obtain the instantaneous effects. Given the inherent intractability of this kind of analysis for finite $h > 0$, we shall proceed to the steady state.

5. The stability of the system

It will be recalled from the second section that the dynamics of the system are specified by equations (7.19). However, since we are concerned with the system expressed per unit of physical capital, the evolution of K itself does not concern us, except as it affects the real budget deficit expressed in terms of units of capital. Therefore, substituting (7.19a) into (7.19c) we can analyse the dynamics in terms of equations (7.19b) and (7.19c). Provided the system is stable, capital stock — and thus real income and the real supplies of financial assets — will all be growing at the same rate in the intermediate-run equilibrium that we are considering. That rate is $i(r_e^*, y^*)$, where * denotes the equilibrium values of the endogenous variables that are arguments of i.

We can restrict our discussion of stability to the evolution of price expectations and the dynamics of financial asset accumulation. As indicated in Section 3D, the policy specifications we shall use are *pure money finance* $(\dot{b} = 0)$ and *pure bond finance* $(\dot{m} = 0)$.

One could consider the intermediate case in which some fraction of the deficit is financed by bonds (over and above that required to maintain $\dot{b} = 0$), with the rest financed by money. As one would expect, this turns out to be an average of the two extremes being considered, and we do not give it separate treatment.

A. *Pure money finance policy*

Solving the instantaneous equilibrium conditions for y, r_e, r the real government deficit per unit of capital, which we shall denote by d, can be expressed in the form:

$$g - uy + (1 - u)b - s(p + i) \equiv d[m, b, \pi, g],$$

where $s \geq 0$ denotes the real stock of government debt, per unit of capital. In the case where the government's deficit is purely money-financed, the dynamics can be described by the following pair of differential equations in m, π:

$$\dot{m} = d[m, \bar{b}, \pi, g] \tag{7.23a}$$

$$\dot{\pi} = \gamma[p(m, \bar{b}, \pi, g) - \pi] \tag{7.23b}$$

where $\bar{b}$ denotes the fact that b is held constant.

Linearizing the pair of equations (7.23) about their equilibrium, the sufficient conditions for this system to be locally stable are:

$$\frac{\partial d}{\partial m} + \gamma\left(\frac{\partial p}{\partial \pi} - 1\right) < 0 \tag{7.24a}$$

$$\frac{\partial d}{\partial m}\left(\frac{\partial p}{\partial \pi} - 1\right) - \frac{\partial p}{\partial m}\frac{\partial d}{\partial \pi} > 0. \tag{7.24b}$$

All the partial derivatives in (7.24) can, with the aid of (7.22), be obtained from the instantaneous comparative static analysis reported earlier. These earlier results fall short of ensuring that these inequalities will be satisfied. Nevertheless, one would expect the system to be stable.[10]

One set of conditions sufficient for stability, which the previous comparative statics suggest are likely to be met is

$$\left.\begin{array}{ll} \dfrac{\partial p}{\partial m} > 0, & \dfrac{\partial p}{\partial \pi} \leqslant 1 \\[2ex] \dfrac{\partial d}{\partial m} < 0, & \dfrac{\partial d}{\partial \pi} < 0 \end{array}\right\} \tag{7.25}$$

The positive sign of $\partial p/\partial m$ is obtained directly from Table 1 and always applies. The incomplete adjustment of instantaneous price movements to changes in inflationary expectations, while tending to be supported by available empirical evidence, need not hold. In particular, given $\partial y/\partial \pi \geqslant 0$, it will cease to be true if the coefficient on price expectations in the price equation (i.e. β) approaches one. In this case, $\partial d/\partial m < 0$ becomes a necessary condition for (7.24a) to hold and $\partial d/\partial m$ is in turn necessary to ensure that (7.24b) holds.

Differentiating d, with respect to m, π, we can express $\partial d/\partial m$, $\partial d/\partial \pi$, in terms of the instantaneous derivatives from the previous section

$$\frac{\partial d}{\partial m} = -u\frac{\partial y}{\partial m} - s\left(\frac{\partial p}{\partial m} + i_1\frac{\partial r_e}{\partial m} + i_2\frac{\partial y}{\partial m}\right)$$

$$- (p+i)\left(1 - \frac{b}{r^2}\frac{\partial r}{\partial m}\right) \tag{7.26a}$$

$$\frac{\partial d}{\partial \pi} = -u\frac{\partial y}{\partial \pi} - s\frac{\partial(p+i)}{\partial \pi} - (p+i)\frac{\partial s}{\partial \pi}$$

$$\tag{7.26b}$$

$$= -u\frac{\partial y}{\partial \pi} - s\left(\frac{\partial p}{\partial \pi} + i_1\frac{\partial r_e}{\partial \pi} + i_2\frac{\partial y}{\partial \pi}\right) + (p+i)\frac{b}{r^2}\frac{\partial r}{\partial \pi}.$$

On intuitive grounds, one would expect an increase in the supply of money with government bonds held constant to reduce the government deficit, and (7.26a) indicates that this will almost certainly be so. Given the signs reported in Table 1, and introducing the mild restriction, $p + i \geqslant 0$, all partial derivatives in (7.26a) are negative, with the exception of $\partial r_e/\partial m$, which is ambiguous. However, as was argued earlier, if claims on physical capital are a sufficiently close substitute for bonds in investors' portfolios, $\partial r_e/\partial m$ will be negative as well, in which case $\partial d/\partial m < 0$ unambiguously.

The sign of $\partial d/\partial \pi$ is somewhat less determinate. On the one hand, an increase in π raises income and with it tax receipts. It also raises the current rate of inflation and almost certainly the rate of investment, thereby raising the 'real inflationary and growth tax' on existing debt. However, for given levels of m and b, it will also almost certainly raise the nominal interest rate on bonds, thereby reducing the value of existing bonds, and hence the base on which this 'inflationary and growth tax' is levied. On balance, it still seems reasonable to expect $\partial d/\partial \pi < 0$, as we have suggested.

By evaluating the terms involved in (7.25), the following alternative set of sufficient conditions for stability can be obtained:

$$\frac{\partial r_e}{\partial m} < 0, \quad \frac{\partial r_e}{\partial \pi} < 0$$

$$\frac{\partial p}{\partial \pi} \leqslant 1, \quad r > (\pi + i)\frac{b/r}{s} > 0, \tag{7.27}$$

None of the constraints on the derivatives appearing in (7.27) are ensured by the instantaneous comparative static results, although it does seem reasonable that they should be met. The constraint on the nominal rate of interest on bonds also seems likely to be satisfied for a plausible choice of parameters.

One may conclude with some confidence that the pure money finance policy will be stable. However, the possibility of instability cannot be ruled out, especially if the coefficient of price expectations, β, in the price equation tends to unity and expectations adjust rapidly to actual price changes (γ large). Note, however, as $\gamma \to \infty$, so that inflation is perfectly anticipated, we do not necessarily get instability, as is the case in some (but not all) long-run models of money and growth.[11] In this case, $\partial d/\partial m$ would have to be negative and sufficiently large in absolute value to offset the destabilizing behaviour of prices. In either case, the stability conditions (7.25) highlight the role played by price movements and expectations in determining the stability of a purely money-financed government deficit.

Before leaving our discussion of the pure money finance policy, it is worth pointing out that essentially the same analysis also holds for a single open market operation. For example, an open market sale of bonds implies a once-and-for-all increase in b; thereafter, b stays constant at its new level, with all subsequent government deficits or surpluses so generated being financed by changes in the money supply. The dynamics are thus virtually identical to that of our pure money finance policy.

B. *Pure bond finance policy*

The other extreme, where the government deficit is financed by a pure bond policy, can be similarly analysed. In this case, the dynamic equations are:

$$\frac{\dot{b}}{r} = d(\bar{m}, b, \pi, g) \tag{7.28a}$$

$$\dot{\pi} = \gamma(p(\bar{m}, b, \pi, g) - \pi) \tag{7.28b}$$

with $\bar{m}$ now referring to the fixed stock of money per unit of capital. The sufficient conditions for local stability in the neighbourhood of equilibrium are:

$$r\frac{\partial d}{\partial b} + \gamma\left(\frac{\partial p}{\partial \pi} - 1\right) < 0 \tag{7.29a}$$

$$\frac{\partial d}{\partial \pi}\left(\frac{\partial p}{\partial \pi} - 1\right) - \frac{\partial p}{\partial b}\frac{\partial d}{\partial \pi} > 0 \tag{7.29b}$$

and again the relevant partial derivatives can be obtained from the previous section. Now, however, one can be much less certain that these conditions will be met.

Analogous to (7.25), the following are sufficient conditions for stability:

$$\frac{\partial p}{\partial b} > 0, \quad \frac{\partial p}{\partial \pi} \leqslant 1$$

$$\frac{\partial d}{\partial b} < 0, \quad \frac{\partial d}{\partial \pi} < 0 \tag{7.30}$$

two of which are the same as in the pure money policy, but the other two are quite indeterminate. As discussed previously, $\partial y/\partial b$ (and $\partial p/\partial b$) cannot be signed on a priori grounds, as an increase in bonds has several offsetting effects on aggregate income. It will almost certainly raise r_e (contractionary), increase interest payments to the private sector and thus raise disposable income (expansionary), and increase wealth (indeterminate). Consequently, its net effect on output and inflation cannot be determined unambiguously without further knowledge of relevant parameter values.

Also, while it may seem reasonable to suppose that an increase in b with m held constant will reduce the government deficit, the effect is again more in doubt than is the corresponding effect of an increase in the supply of money. This can be readily seen from the following expression for this effect:

$$\frac{\partial d}{\partial b} = (1 - u) - u\frac{\partial y}{\partial b} - s\left(\frac{\partial p}{\partial b} + i_1\frac{\partial r_e}{\partial b} + i_2\frac{\partial y}{\partial b}\right)$$

$$- (p + i)\left(\frac{1}{r} - \frac{b}{r^2}\frac{\partial r}{\partial b}\right). \tag{7.31}$$

One of the key destabilizing factors is the net interest payment on the outstanding government debt. It is clear that this will be increased by an increase in b, thereby tending to raise the deficit. It is also apparent that, given the likely signs for $\partial r_e/\partial b$, $\partial r/\partial b$, it is almost certainly necessary for $\partial y/\partial b > 0$ in order to ensure $\partial d/\partial b < 0$.

Without going into the stability conditions (7.30) in any more detail, it is clear that pure bond financing is much more likely to be unstable than is a purely money-financed budget deficit. If $\partial y/\partial b > 0$, and if the interest payments from the public to the private sector are not too large, then one may be reasonably confident that bond financing will be stable. This, however, is an open empirical question about which relatively little information is currently available.[12]

6. Intermediate-run equilibrium properties

The steady-state solution to this intermediate-run model consists of the six instantaneous equilibrium conditions (7.18), together with the stationary solutions to the two dynamic equations (7.19b), (7.19c) and the policy specification. The latter relationships provide three extra equations:

$$p = \pi$$

$$g - uy + (1 - u)b - (m + b/r)(p + i) = 0$$

$$m = \bar{m}, \quad \text{or} \quad b = \bar{b},$$

giving a total of nine independent equations to be solved for the nine variables, $y, r_e, r, qe, v, p, \pi, m$ and b. Eliminating p, qe, v, the equilibrium (for which (7.25) and (7.30) are sufficient conditions for uniqueness) can be written more compactly as:

$$y - c[(1-u)(y+b), R(y)/r_e + m + b/r] - i(r_e, y) - g = 0 \quad (7.32a)$$

$$l[y, r_e, r-\pi, -\pi, R(y)/r_e + m + b/r] - m \qquad = 0 \quad (7.32b)$$

$$j[y, r_e, r-\pi, -\pi, R(y)/r_e + m + b/r] - b/r \qquad = 0 \quad (7.32c)$$

$$(1-\beta)\pi = \alpha_0 + \alpha_1 \left(\frac{y-\bar{y}}{\bar{y}}\right) \qquad (7.32d)$$

$$g - uy + (1-u)b - (m+b/r)(\pi+i) \qquad = 0 \quad (7.32e)$$

together with $b = \bar{b}$ or $m = \bar{m}$, depending upon whether a pure money or pure bond policy is being specified. The first three equations are just the condensed instantaneous equilibrium conditions; (7.32d) is the steady-state equilibrium price (and price expectations) adjustment relationship, while (7.32e) is the requirement that, in equilibrium, the real stock of financial assets per unit of physical capital must be constant.

There are several features of this equilibrium to which attention should be drawn. First, unlike the Blinder and Solow (1973) long-run equilibrium, our intermediate-run equilibrium is one in which positive savings and investment is occurring. Second, the stationary solution is what is sometimes referred to as a 'quasi-equilibrium', in that it is characterized by a constant *rate of inflation*, rather than a constant price level. Furthermore, because of the normalization we have adopted, all real quantities are also growing at the constant rate, $i(r_e, y)$.

Third, rewriting (7.32e) in the form:

$$p = \pi = \frac{g - uy + (1 - u)b}{m + b/r} - i(r_e, y) = \frac{\dot{M} + \dot{B}/r}{M + B/r} - \frac{\dot{K}}{K} \quad (7.32e')$$

it becomes apparent that the equilibrium rate of inflation equals the difference between the rate of growth of *nominal* government debt and the rate of growth of *real* physical capital. This relationship is an immediate consequence of our steady-state definition. Intuitively, the reason for it is that, in the steady-state portfolio, balance can be maintained only if the supplies of all assets grow at the same *real* rate. From this it follows that the equilibrium rate of inflation must equal the difference in growth rates between the nominal supplies of assets — and, in particular, the nominal government debt — and their common growth rate. But looked at in this way, we see that the only way the rate of inflation can be reduced is if the rate of growth of nominal government debt, relative to that of the real physical capital stock, is reduced.

The fourth property of some interest is the fact that even if $\beta = 1$, so that (7.32d) implies a natural rate of unemployment and thus the absence of a steady-state trade-off between inflation and unemployment (or excess demand), the system still implies a determinate equilibrium rate of inflation. This is again given by (7.32e'), with y set equal to $\tilde{y} = (\alpha_1 - \alpha_0)\bar{y}/\alpha_1$, the corresponding 'natural rate of output'.

A.   *Some comparative static properties*
        To analyse the equilibrium comparative static behaviour of the system, we can differentiate (7.32) with respect to the parameter of interest and solve for the resulting set of partial derivatives. This turns out to be a cumbersome exercise and, for the properties with which we are most concerned — namely, the comparative inflationary and expansionary effects of the two alternative extreme means of financing increases in government expenditure — it is more convenient to work in terms of the stationary solutions to the dynamic functions described in (7.23) and (7.28). These equations, which of course embody implicitly the instantaneous equilibrium conditions (7.32a) to (7.32c), yield equilibrium solutions for the pairs (π, m), (π, b), respectively. The corresponding value of output can then be readily obtained from the steady-state price relationship (7.32d) (except, of course, when $\beta = 1$, when we know it is fixed).

Looking first at the case of a purely money-financed government deficit, the equilibrium levels of π, m, are given by the stationary solutions to (7.23), namely:

$$d(m, \bar{b}, \pi, g) = 0 \quad (7.33a)$$

$$p(m, \bar{b}, \pi, g) - \pi = 0. \quad (7.33b)$$

For simplicity, let us assume that the sufficient conditions for stability (7.25) which we have already argued are likely to be met, are in fact satisfied, so that

$$d_1 < 0, \quad d_3 < 0, \quad p_1 > 0, \quad (p_3 - 1) \leqslant 0. \tag{7.34}$$

We have already seen from Table 1 that an increase in government expenditure will increase the instantaneous level of output and rate of inflation. Moreover, it seems reasonable to expect that, for given m and b, it will not decrease the instantaneous government deficit, although this result cannot be established unambiguously. Accepting the latter result, we have the further restrictions:

$$d_4 \geqslant 0, \quad p_4 > 0. \tag{7.35}$$

Using (7.34) and (7.35), we can readily show that with pure money financing, an increase in government expenditure will be unambiguously inflationary, the effect being:

$$\left(\frac{\partial \pi}{\partial g} \right)_m = \frac{p_1 d_4 - p_4 d_1}{d_1 (p_3 - 1) - p_1 d_3} > 0. \tag{7.36}$$

The corresponding impact on the equilibrium supply of money is given by:

$$\frac{\partial m}{\partial g} = \frac{p_4 d_3 - d_4 (p_3 - 1)}{d_1 (p_3 - 1) - p_1 d_3} \gtreqless 0 \tag{7.37}$$

and is ambiguous. Although one would intuitively expect $\partial m / \partial g > 0$, it is interesting to note that in the 'natural rate' case, where $\beta = 1$ and, hence, $p_3 > 1$ (but the system is stable), (7.37) implies $\partial m / \partial g < 0$. The reason for this rather counterintuitive result is that, starting from equilibrium, an increase in g will raise the rate of inflation, both directly (see (7.35)) and indirectly, through its induced effects on inflationary expectations. Moreover, the latter indirect effects are now destabilizing, so that the only way for equilibrium to be restored is if m is ultimately reduced, thereby providing an offsetting deflationary and stabilizing effect. This can be seen immediately by differentiating (7.33b) with respect to g.

With pure bond financing, the equilibrium levels of π, b are determined by the stationary solutions to (7.28) – namely,

$$d(\bar{m}, b, \pi, g) = 0 \tag{7.38a}$$

$$p(\bar{m}, b, \pi, g) - \pi = 0 \tag{7.38b}$$

so that:

$$\left(\frac{\partial \pi}{\partial g} \right)_b = \frac{d_4 p_2 - d_2 p_4}{d_2 (p_3 - 1) - p_2 d_3} \gtreqless 0 \tag{7.39}$$

where the stability condition (7.29b) implies $d_2 (p_3 - 1) - p_2 d_3 > 0$. If we now add the conditions, $p_2 > 0, d_2 < 0$, which we showed in (7.30) form part of a set of sufficient conditions for stability, but which we nevertheless argued are somewhat tenuous, then we have unambiguously,

$$\left(\frac{\partial \pi}{\partial g}\right)_b > 0. \tag{7.39'}$$

The effect on the equilibrium supply of bonds is:

$$\frac{\partial b}{\partial g} = \frac{p_4 d_3 - d_4(p_3 - 1)}{d_2(p_3 - 1) - p_2 d_3} \tag{7.40}$$

implying $\text{sgn}\left(\dfrac{\partial b}{\partial g}\right) = \text{sgn}\left(\dfrac{\partial m}{\partial g}\right)$ if both methods of financing are stable.

A related question of some importance is to determine the comparative inflationary effects of the two modes of deficit financing. This is obtained by subtracting (7.39) from (7.37), yielding:

$$\left(\frac{\partial \pi}{\partial g}\right)_m = \left(\frac{\partial \pi}{\partial g}\right)_b = \frac{[d_4(p_3 - 1) - p_4 d_3][p_1 d_2 - d_1 p_2]}{[d_2(p_3 - 1) - p_2 d_3][d_1(p_3 - 1) - p_1 d_3]},$$

from which it follows that:

$$\text{sgn}\left(\left(\frac{\partial \pi}{\partial g}\right)_m - \left(\frac{\partial \pi}{\partial g}\right)_b\right) = \text{sgn}\left\{\frac{\partial m}{\partial g}\left(\frac{\partial d}{\partial m}\frac{\partial y}{\partial b} - \frac{\partial y}{\partial m}\frac{\partial d}{\partial b}\right)\right\}. \tag{7.41}$$

Let us consider the more plausible case where $\partial m/\partial g > 0$ (and equivalently $\partial b/\partial g > 0$). In this case, the comparison reduces to:

$$\left(\frac{\partial \pi}{\partial g}\right)_m - \left(\frac{\partial \pi}{\partial g}\right)_b \gtreqless 0 \quad \text{according as} \quad \frac{\partial d}{\partial m}\frac{\partial y}{\partial b} \gtreqless \frac{\partial y}{\partial m}\frac{\partial d}{\partial b} \tag{7.42}$$

which, recalling the fact that $\partial y/\partial m > 0$ and adding the further weak restriction, $\partial d/\partial m < 0$, can be written in relative form:

$$\left(\frac{\partial \pi}{\partial g}\right)_m - \left(\frac{\partial \pi}{\partial g}\right)_b \gtreqless 0 \quad \text{according as} \quad \frac{\partial d}{\partial b}\bigg/\frac{\partial d}{\partial m} \gtreqless \frac{\partial y}{\partial b}\bigg/\frac{\partial y}{\partial m}. \tag{7.43}$$

In economic terms, this says that if the instantaneous impact of bond financing on the deficit, relative to the impact of money financing on the deficit, is algebraically greater than (less than) the impact of bond financing on output relative to the output effect of money financing then money financing will be more (less) inflationary than bond financing. The inequalities in (7.43) can go either way, so that one cannot conclude on *a priori* grounds which is the more inflationary mode of government finance. While it is commonly thought that money financing is more inflationary, by taking special cases it can be readily shown that in fact this need not be so; bond financing may quite plausibly be the more inflationary policy.

The various conclusions stemming from (7.43) would of course all need to be reversed as $\beta \to 1$ and the sign of $\partial m/\partial g$ changes.

The effects of increased government expenditure on the equilibrium rate of inflation can be used to determine corresponding impacts on output. First, provided $\beta \neq 1$ so that a steady-state trade-off exists between inflation and output, we immediately deduce

$$\text{sgn}\left(\frac{\partial y}{\partial g}\right) = \text{sgn}\left(\frac{\partial \pi}{\partial g}\right) \tag{7.44}$$

with the comparative effects satisfying

$$\text{sgn}\left\{\left(\frac{\partial y}{\partial g}\right)_m - \left(\frac{\partial y}{\partial g}\right)_b\right\} = \text{sgn}\left\{\left(\frac{\partial \pi}{\partial g}\right)_m - \left(\frac{\partial \pi}{\partial g}\right)_b\right\}. \tag{7.45}$$

Thus, the comments made with respect to the impact of increased government expenditure on inflation apply to output as well.[13] With $\beta = 1$, we know $y = \tilde{y}$, implying

$$\frac{\partial y}{\partial g} = 0 \tag{7.46}$$

irrespective of how the deficit is financed.

B.   *The 'Fisher effect'*

Another comparative static question which has attracted recent attention from monetary economists is the Fisherian proposition that nominal interest rates fully incorporate inflationary expectations. We have already discussed this proposition within the context of the short-run model developed in Chapter 6. There we showed that, consistent with much of the empirical literature on this topic, the nominal interest rate adjusts only partially to inflationary expectations, at least within the short run. Thus, real rates of return tend to fall with increases in inflationary expectations, a conclusion which also tends to be confirmed by the instantaneous comparative statics we presented in Section 4.

However, Fisher was probably concerned with a longer run relationship than that considered by these models and certainly longer than that given by an instantaneous model. We therefore briefly consider the relationship between inflationary expectations and interest rates within the context of the steady-state equilibrium of our model. In considering such steady-state relationships, it should be realized that, in equilibrium, both the rate of inflation (and equivalently its expectation) and the rate of interest are endogenously determined. It therefore makes no sense to calculate and interpret derivatives such as $\partial r/\partial \pi$ in the usual comparative static way. Recognizing this, authors such as Sargent (1973b) have reinterpreted the Fisher proposition to assert that in equilibrium the real rate of interest is independent of the systematic part of the money supply.

To consider this hypothesis, one can differentiate the equilibrium system (7.32) with respect to an exogenous shift $(d\phi)$ in the supply of an asset, say money, and calculate $\partial r_e / \partial \phi$, $\partial r_b / \partial \phi$ (where $r_b = r - \pi$). From the general structure of this system we can see that there is no reason for $\partial r_e / \partial \phi = \partial r_b / \partial \phi = 0$ and there is little point in reporting the actual calculations. Some idea of the issues involved can be obtained by considering the example where $\beta = 1$ (so that $y = \tilde{y}$) and where there are no wealth effects in consumption ($c_2 = 0$). These, incidentally, were two of the critical assumptions made by Sargent, who showed that the existence of a natural rate of unemployment and the validity of this version of the Fisherian proposition are intimately related.

In this case, differentiating (7.32a) with respect to the exogenous shift parameter ϕ, we have

$$c_1(1 - u) \frac{\partial b}{\partial \phi} + i_1 \frac{\partial r_e}{\partial \phi} = 0.$$

Thus, with pure money financing $\partial b / \partial \phi = 0$, which implies $\partial r_e / \partial \phi = 0$ so that the real return on capital is indeed independent of systematic shifts in the supply of money. With pure bond financing, however, $\partial b / \partial \phi$ is presumably non-zero, in which case $\partial r_e / \partial \phi$ will be non-zero. The effect on the real rate of interest on bonds is somewhat more complex and involves differentiating the asset demand functions, together with the steady-state government budget constraint. Even with the special assumptions we are making, we deduce that in general $\partial r_b / \partial \phi \neq 0$; moreover the effect on the real rate of interest will vary with the mode of government finance. One case in which $\partial r_b / \partial \phi = 0$ is if bonds and equity are perfect substitutes and all incremental government debt is money financed.

7. **Endogenizing government policy**

The analysis of this chapter (and the literature it follows) has been predicated on the assumption that the government does not react to the evolving economic conditions. Government expenditure is held constant (relative to capital stock) in real terms, while the only adjustment of money or bonds is to finance deficits as they occur and not for any active stabilization purposes. While this analysis is instructive, it is clear that the government will not play such a passive role. If inflation exceeds some acceptable rate, or if the level of unemployment gets too high, it will respond with what it regards as appropriate policies. This question leads directly into the topic of stabilization policy which is taken up at length in Part III. Nevertheless it seems useful at this stage to at least hint at the issues it raises within the context of the present model.

There are various ways one might model this policy response. One plausible possibility is to assume that it specifies target levels for real income (y^*) and the rate of inflation (p^*) say, which it regards as desirable. In order to preserve consistency within the model we assume that these target values are chosen so as to lie on the long-run Phillips curve which acts as a constraint on the set of feasible steady-state choices. They therefore satisfy (7.18f); other-wise an inconsistency may occur.[14]

Given these objectives, we specify the following policy adjustment relations

$$\dot{g} = \epsilon(y^* - y) \qquad \epsilon > 0 \tag{7.47a}$$

$$\dot{m} = \theta d - \eta(p - p^*) \qquad 0 \leqslant \theta \leqslant 1 \quad \eta > 0 \tag{7.47b}$$

$$\frac{\dot{b}}{r} = (1 - \theta)d + \eta(p - p^*) \tag{7.47c}$$

Equation (7.47a) is one of the policy adjustment rules introduced by Phillips (1954) and widely used since. It asserts that if real income is below its target, the government increases its expenditure and vice versa. The other two adjust-ment equations assert that apart from issuing assets to finance the deficit, the government decreases the growth in the money supply if the rate of inflation exceeds the target rate and increases it otherwise. Any changes in the supply of money must be appropriately compensated for by changes in bonds, so as to satisfy the budget constraint (7.19c). Thus, in this model, fiscal policy is directed at the output objective, while monetary policy is used to deal with inflation. This assignment of policy instruments accords in essence with current US policy.

The dynamics of the system now consists of these three policy adjustment equations, together with the evolution of π. Provided that the system is stable, it is clear that from the stationary solutions to (7.47a) to (7.47c) that the sys-tem will converge to its target values y^*, p^*. In contrast to our earlier analy-sis, g, m, and b are now all endogenous. Their equilibrium values can be ob-tained by inserting y^*, p^* into the set of steady-state equations (7.32) and solving these five equations for g, m, b, r, and r_e. However, stability cannot be taken for granted; in fact it becomes the central issue. One of the main points of Phillips' contribution was to show how even in his extremely simple multiplier model the policy adjustment rule (7.47a), if not appropriately implemented, could destabilize the system. The same proposition applies in the present model, with stability now depending, among other things, on the three policy parameters ϵ, θ, η. Further discussion of these stabilization issues is postponed until Part III.

8.   Summary
In this chapter we have analysed the dynamics of an 'intermediate-run' model of an inflationary economy. It is intermediate run in the sense that the model takes full account of the dynamics of physical capital accumu-lation on demand and on productive capacity, as well as of the associated equity accumulation on portfolio behaviour, in a way analogous to the treat-ment of financial assets. But it does not incorporate longer run capital deepening effects. At any point of time labour demand is determined by the demand-determined output and the inherited capital stock. Moreover, in the

steady state which we consider the accumulation of capital does not cease, but proceeds at a constant endogenously determined rate. This is incorporated into the analysis by normalizing appropriate quantities relative to the stock of physical capital. The most important conclusions of our analysis can be summarized as follows.

The stability of the system depends crucially upon how the government finances its deficit, as well as upon the degree to which price changes incorporate inflationary expectations and the speed with which these expectations respond to past price changes. With what we call pure money financing (a policy in which the real supply of government bonds per unit of capital is held constant), one can be reasonably sure that the system will be stable provided inflationary expectations are not fully reflected in current price changes. However, it is possible for the price adjustment to be destabilizing, in which case the instability of the entire system cannot be dismissed. This possibility arises as the coefficient of price expectations in the price equation tends to unity and expectations adjust rapidly to actual price changes. In this case, the dynamics describing the accumulation of assets would have to be 'strongly stable' in order to compensate for the destabilizing influence of price behaviour.

On the other hand, even with a stable price adjustment equation, stability becomes less clear when the deficit is entirely bond financed. One of the destabilizing factors is the interest paid on outstanding bonds. This interest needs to be continually financed. A further destabilizing element is the fact that the impact of an increase in bonds on output is indeterminate. This is due to the fact that, while an increase in bonds will have a contractionary effect through higher interest rates, they also have an expansionary effect in the form of higher interest payments and larger disposable income. If these expansionary effects dominate, one can again be reasonably confident that the system will be stable.

Assuming that the system is stable, its steady state is one in which there is a constant rate of inflation and all real quantities grow at the same constant rate as capital. This equilibrium rate of price change is shown to equal the difference in the growth rate of *nominal* government debt and the rate of growth of *real* physical capital. Moreover, even when $\beta = 1$ so that there is no steady-state trade-off between inflation and output, a determinate equilibrium rate of inflation is obtained; equilibrium conditions in the asset markets determine a unique point on the vertical steady-state Phillips curve.

In considering the comparative static properties of this equilibrium, we show that under plausible conditions a money-financed increase in government expenditure will be unambiguously inflationary, although the corresponding effect under bond financing is somewhat less determinate. However, with some added restrictions, notably that $\partial y/\partial b > 0$, one can be fairly confident that this latter case will be inflationary as well. The comparative inflationary effects of these two modes of finance are also considered. We have shown that in the steady state it is by no means certain that government expenditures with money-financed deficits are more expansionary than equal expenditures with bond-financed deficits. In fact, there are plausible circumstances in which the opposite would be true.

We have also considered the equilibrium 'Fisher Effects' and reach the following conclusions. In general the real rates of return depend crucially upon the mode of government finance. Where bonds and equity are imperfect substitutes, the real rate of interest on bonds will respond to shifts in the money supply. With negligible wealth effects in consumption and expectations fully incorporated in current price changes, the Fisherian proposition will hold with respect to the real return on capital in the case where the incremental debt is money financed; it will not hold with bond financing. This same proposition applies to the real rate of interest on bonds, in the limiting case where bonds and physical capital are perfect substitutes in investors' portfolios.

Finally, we briefly examined the effect on the model of endogenizing government policy to meet certain specified objectives. If the resulting system is stable, it will converge to the government's output and inflation targets as long as those targets are consistent with the long-run Phillips curve. However, stability with endogenous government policies of the type we have specified is by no means ensured. Indeed it becomes the critical question and will depend to a large extent upon the policy adjustment parameters chosen by the government.

8

A LONG-RUN MODEL

1. Introduction

We now proceed to develop a third dynamic macroeconomic model. The main objective of the present chapter is to integrate in a consistent manner some of the issues which we have raised in previous chapters, but which we have so far not incorporated into our formal analysis. There are several such questions we wish to consider. First, the model we shall construct is long run in the sense that we allow for the full capital deepening effects of the investment process. These have been explicitly excluded from our analysis up to this stage. Secondly, the model will be formulated using continuous time so as to incorporate consistently the stock and flow constraints developed in Chapter 3. It will be recalled that Chapter 7 was based on the assumption of continuous product market equilibrium, and as we discussed previously, only under extremely restrictive conditions is this consistent with the flow constraint. It is time to consider the implications of relaxing these conditions. Thirdly, we wish to include the dynamics associated with *expected* capital gains. These appear both as a component of disposable income and as part of the real rate of return on equity and have not been dealt with adequately to date. The introduction of expectations involves the specification of an expectations hypothesis and we assume, as we have done throughout, that these are formed adaptively. Thus as a final, and closely related matter, we want to consider some of the issues pertaining to the consistent formulation of adaptive expectations in a continuous-time model. These questions are alluded to in Chapter 7, but again we have delayed giving a full treatment until now.

2. Adaptive expectations in continuous-time models

Since expectations form such a crucial element of the theory, we shall begin with this aspect first.

As noted in Chapter 7, the adaptive expectations hypothesis implies that the forecast at time t, say, depends upon an exponentially declining weighted average of all past values of the variable being predicted. From time to time autoregressive forecasting mechanisms such as these have been criticised as being *ad hoc.* It has been contended that the rational way to form expectations is to base them on the underlying economic model. We briefly explored the implications of this approach within the context of a short-run model in Chapter 6. However, in view of the information required to formulate rational expectations, it too has also come under some criticism recently. Moreover, authors such as Friedman (1975b) have shown how under certain assumptions regarding the accumulation of information, the rational hypothesis can be reduced to an adaptive hypothesis. Thus, since the adaptive process can in fact be supported on fairly rigorous grounds, we shall continue to adopt it.

But as we have suggested in Chapter 7, the use of the adaptive hypothesis in continuous-time models can encounter certain logical difficulties when aplied to predicting *levels,* although these problems need not arise when *rates* of change or percentage changes are being forecast. Since we wish to apply the hypothesis to predicting *both* kinds of variables we must derive its continuous limit carefully.

(a)   *Application to levels forecasting*
        We begin by postulating the following discrete-time version of the adaptive hypothesis

$$\left.\begin{array}{c} P^*(t+h,t) - P^*(t,t-h) = \gamma(h)\,[P(t) - P^*(t,t-h)] \\[2mm] 0 < \gamma(h) < 1 \end{array}\right\} \qquad (8.1)$$

where

$P(t)$ = actual *level* of some economic variable (say a price) at time t,

$P^*(t+h,t)$ = expectation formed at time t for the variable at time $(t+h)$.

Equation (8.1) asserts that the expectations formed at time t for time $t+h$ equals the most recent forecast plus a correction for the last forecasting error. This formulation assumes that forecasts are made every h time units for h time units ahead so that the time interval between predictions and the time horizon over which predictions are made are equal. While this assumption is the one usually made, the two time periods need not be equal. Burmeister and Turnovsky (1976) develop the appropriate limiting expressions in that case, but for our purposes the simpler formulation suffices. Thus equation (8.1) is identical to the hypothesis as specified in Chapter 5, the only difference being that the time unit h is arbitrary rather than unity.

Let us suppose that the forecast satisfied the *weak consistency axiom* (3.20), so that

$$P^*(t,t) = P(t), \qquad (8.2)$$

It will be recalled that this asserts that the expectation formed at time t for that same instant t equals the actual prevailing value at that time. This will be satisfied if forecasters have instantaneous access to current information.

Letting $h \to 0$ in (8.1) and invoking (8.2), it follows that

$$\lim_{h \to 0} \gamma(h) = \gamma(0) \text{ and is } finite.$$

Dividing (8.1) by h yields

$$\frac{P^*(t+h, t) - P^*(t, t-h)}{h} = \frac{\gamma(h)}{h} [P(t) - P^*(t, t-h)]. \qquad (8.3)$$

Expanding the left hand side of (8.1) in a Taylor expansion about $(t, t-h)$ we have

$$P^*(t+h, t) - P^*(t, t-h) = P_1^*(t, t-h)h + P_2^*(t, t-h)h + o(h) \qquad (8.4)$$

where $P_i^*(t, t-h)$ denotes the partial derivative of P^* with respect to its ith argument, evaluated at the point $(t, t-h)$ and $o(h)$ denotes 'terms of order smaller than h'; i.e.

$$\lim_{h \to 0} [o(h)/h] = 0.$$

Equations (8.3) and (8.4) together imply

$$[P_1^*(t, t-h) + P_2^*(t, t-h)] + \frac{o(h)}{h} = \frac{\gamma(h)}{h} [P(t) - P^*(t, t-h)] \qquad (8.5)$$

and taking limits as $h \to 0$ yields

$$P_1^*(t, t) + P_2^*(t, t) = \lim_{h \to 0} \left\{ \gamma(0) \frac{[P(t) - P^*(t, t-h)]}{h} \right\}. \qquad (8.6)$$

Now consider the left hand side of (8.6). This can be written as

$$\frac{\partial P^*(u, t)}{\partial u}\bigg|_{u=t} + \frac{\partial P^*(t, v)}{\partial v}\bigg|_{v=t}$$

which is precisely the *total* time derivative

$$\dot{P}^*(t, t) \equiv \frac{dP^*(t, t)}{dt}.$$

To obtain the limit of the right hand side of (8.6) we must consider $\lim_{h \to 0} [P(t) - P^*(t, t-h)]/h$. Invoking the consistency condition (8.2), this can be written as

$$\lim_{h \to 0} \left(\frac{P^*(t, t) - P^*(t, t-h)}{h} \right) = P_2^*(t, t).$$

Thus defining for convenience the function of one variable

$$P^*(t) \equiv P^*(t, t) \tag{8.7}$$

the limiting equation (8.6) becomes

$$\dot{P}^*(t) = \gamma(0) P_2^*(t, t). \qquad 0 < \gamma(0) < 1. \tag{8.8}$$

Equation (8.8) is the correct limit of (8.1) as $h \to 0$, based on the assumption that the weak consistency axiom holds. It is a mixed total–partial differential equation, and as we shall show in Sections 3 and 4 below, it can be combined with other dynamic equations in the system to yield a total differential equation for $P^*(t)$.

The conventional formulation of the adaptive expectations hypothesis in continuous time is of the form

$$\dot{P}^*(t) = \eta [P(t) - P^*(t)] \tag{8.9}$$

where $\eta > 0$ is finite. This is inconsistent with the weak consistency axiom (8.2). From this axiom, $P^*(t) = P(t)$ for all t, so that (8.9) implies $\dot{P}^*(t) = 0$ for all t, and it follows further from (8.2) that $\dot{P}(t) = 0$ for all t. But $P(t)$ is exogenous and will typically vary with t, so that $\dot{P}(t) \neq 0$, implying a contradiction. Alternatively, the only conditions under which the conventional continuous time formulation can be justified is if one discards the weak consistency axiom (8.2).

(b)   *Application to forecasting percentage changes*
As we shall be applying the adaptive hypothesis to predicting the percentage rate of change, we define

$$p(t, t - h) \equiv \frac{P(t) - P(t - h)}{hP(t - h)} \tag{8.10a}$$

$$\pi(t, t - h) \equiv \frac{P^*(t, t - h) - P(t - h)}{hP(t - h)} \tag{8.10b}$$

Equation (8.10a) defines the actual percentage rate of change of $P(t)$ over the period $(t - h, t)$ measured at a rate per unit period. Likewise, (8.10b) measures the expected percentage rate of change of P over the same period. Note that the prediction of the rate of change is formed by calculating the predicted minus the actual value of $P(t)$. This of course is the appropriate measure on the assumption implicit in the weak axiom, that forecasters have the latest actual data on $P(t)$ available to them at the time they make their prediction. It is certainly the way expected rates of change have been calculated in the empirical literature.[1]

Taking the limit of (8.10a) as $h \to 0$, we obtain

$$p(t) \equiv p(t, t) = \frac{\dot{P}(t)}{P(t)} \tag{8.11}$$

so that $p(t, t)$ is the instantaneous rate of change. Similarly, letting $h \to 0$ in (8.10b) and invoking (8.2), we see

$$\pi(t) \equiv \pi(t, t) = \frac{1}{P(t)} \lim_{h \to 0} \left(\frac{P^*(t, t-h) - P^*(t-h, t-h)}{h} \right)$$

$$= \frac{P_1^*(t, t)}{P(t)} \tag{8.12}$$

i.e. $\pi(t)$ denotes the expected instantaneous percentage rate of change. Thus interpreting $P(t)$ as denoting the price *level*, (8.12) is the formal definition of the instantaneous expected rate of inflation as used for example in Chapter 7.

Given the definitions in (8.10), there are two possible notions of consistency of forecasts one might want to consider. The first is the weak consistency axiom (8.2), namely

$$P^*(t, t) = P(t)$$

which requires that the forecast of the *level* implicit in (8.10b) to equal the actual current level. Secondly, one might assume, what we shall call the *strong consistency axiom*

$$\pi(t) = p(t). \tag{8.13}$$

This requires the forecasts of the current rate of change to equal the actual current rate of change. These two notions of consistency are not equivalent; as our terminology suggests (8.13) implies (8.2) but not conversely.

Subtracting (8.10b) from (8.10a) and taking the limit as $h \to 0$, we obtain

$$p(t) - \pi(t) = \frac{1}{P(t)} \lim_{h \to 0} \left(\frac{P(t) - P^*(t, t-h)}{h} \right) \tag{8.14}$$

Assuming the weak consistency axiom (8.2) to hold, it follows that the limit in brackets on the right hand side of (8.14) equals the partial derivative $P_2^*(t, t)$, so that

$$p(t) - \pi(t) = \frac{P_2^*(t, t)}{P}. \tag{8.14'}$$

Thus for strong consistency to hold we require in addition that $P_2^*(t, t) = 0$, which in (3.20') we showed to be equivalent to perfect myopic foresight.

On the other hand, consistency in rates of change certainly implies that the left hand side of (8.14) = 0, which in turn ensures that (8.2) must hold.

Thus consistency in forecasting rates of change implies consistency in forecasting levels, although the converse is not true. While one might argue that the weak axiom is a plausible assumption which should hold, one might also argue that the strong consistency axiom is perhaps overly stringent and should not necessarily be imposed. This is the position we shall take.

When applied to percentage rates of change, the adaptive hypothesis is

$$\pi(t+h,\,t) - \pi(t,\,t-h) \;=\; \delta(h)[p(t,\,t-h) - \pi(t,\,t-h)] \left.\right\} $$
$$ 0 < \delta(h) < 1 \qquad\qquad (8.15)$$

Letting $h \to 0$ and following an identical argument to that given in Section 2(a) above, implies

$$\dot{\pi}(t) \equiv \dot{\pi}(t,\,t) \;=\; \lim_{h \to 0}\left(\frac{\delta(h)}{h}\,[p(t) - \pi(t)] \right). \qquad (8.16)$$

Provided

$$\lim_{h \to 0}\left(\frac{\delta(h)}{h} \right) \;=\; \delta'(0)$$

is finite, then

$$\dot{\pi}(t) \;=\; \delta'(0)\,[p(t) - \pi(t)] \qquad\qquad (8.17)$$

which is the conventional continuous time version of the adaptive hypothesis. Thus since under the weak consistency axiom, $p(t) \not\equiv \pi(t)$, one can derive a well defined continuous adaptive expectations hypothesis for anticipated rates of change as defined above. Moreover, since we are now dealing with percentage rates of change, $\delta'(0)$ is dimensionally equivalent to $\gamma(0)$ defined in Section 2(a) above for levels. Equations (8.8) and (8.17) are therefore quite consistent with one another.

Thus to summarize the discussion thus far, given the weak consistency axiom, the correct limiting version of the adaptive expectations hypothesis when applied to levels is

$$\dot{P}^*(t) \;=\; \gamma P_2^*(t,\,t); \qquad 0 < \gamma < 1 \qquad\qquad (8.8)$$

when applied to percentage rates of change, the conventional continuous time version

$$\dot{\pi}(t) \;=\; \rho\,[p(t) - \pi(t)] \qquad \rho > 0 \qquad\qquad (8.17)$$

where $\rho \equiv \delta'(0)$ is consistent with the underlying assumptions.

3. Specification of model
A. Stock and flow constraints

The most significant aspect of the analysis developed in Chapter 3 was to show how a consistently formulated continuous-time model requires both a stock constraint and a flow constraint to hold at each instant of time.

To develop the stock constraint we shall assume as before that there are three financial assets, outside money, government bonds, and equity issued by firms. The instantaneous demand functions for these assets are described as follows:

$$\frac{M^d(t,\,t)}{P} \;=\; L(Y,\, r_e(1-u),\, r(1-u) - \pi,\, -\pi,\, V) \qquad (8.18a)$$

$$\frac{B^d(t, t)}{P} = J(Y, r_e(1 - u), r(1 - u) - \pi, - \pi, V) \qquad (8.18b)$$

$$p_e(t)E^d(t, t) = N(Y, r_e(1 - u), r(1 - u) - \pi, - \pi, V) \qquad (8.18c)$$

where $\dfrac{M^d(t, t)}{P}$ = instantaneous demand for real money balances at time t; i.e. the demand for money *at* time t *for* time t,

$\dfrac{B^d(t, t)}{P}$ = instantaneous demand for real government bonds at time t,

$p_e(t)E^d(t, t)$ = instantaneous demand for real equity at time t

and

P = price of output at time t,
p_e = price of equity in terms of currently produced goods at time t,
Y = real income (expressed as a rate) at time t,
r_e = real rate of return on holding equity at time t,
r = nominal interest rate at time t,
π = expected rate of inflation at time t,
V = real net private wealth at time t,
u = rate of income tax (taken to be proportional).

The properties of the asset demand functions $L(\quad)$, $J(\quad)$, and $N(\quad)$ have all been discussed in Chapter 7 and we shall assume that these continue to hold. There is, however, one important difference. That is, the rates of return are introduced net of taxes, reflecting the assumption that, in allocating their portfolios, individuals are concerned with real after-tax returns. Moreover, in introducing taxes, care must be taken to ensure that consistency is preserved with the form of taxation implicit in the definition of disposable income given in (8.22) below. There we assume that nominal taxes are levied proportionally on nominal current factor income, so that real taxes depend upon real current income. Insofar as physical capital contributes to current production, this implies that the real marginal product of capital is being taxed. Hence to the extent that the real rate of return on equity reflects the real marginal physical product of capital (see (8.25) below), the real return on equity is also being taxed. On the other hand, consistent with factor income, and in accordance with conventional taxation practices, we are assuming that nominal taxes are levied on nominal interest income. The real net of tax rate of return on holding government bonds is therefore given by $r(1 - u) - \pi$. There are of course, other conventions which may also be considered, such as the taxation of capital gains. The adjustment of rates of return for taxes is not usually introduced into most macroeconomic models (see, however, Tobin and Buiter (1976)). While it does not affect any of the qualitative results significantly, it is of some importance in a model such as the one we are developing in the present chapter, in which its logical consistency is being emphasized.

Real net private wealth is still defined by

$$V = \frac{M + B}{P} + p_e E \tag{8.19}$$

where

M = nominal stock of money

B = nominal stock of bonds, taken to be variable interest rate bonds,

E = quantity of real equity, i.e. number of shares outstanding.

Defining

$$V^d(t, t) = \frac{M^d(t, t) + B^d(t, t)}{P(t)} + p_e(t) E^d(t, t)$$

the wealth constraint is simply

$$V^d(t, t) = V(t) \tag{8.20}$$

which asserts that at each instant of time the household sector must be willing to hold the existing stock of assets. As a result of this constraint only two of the asset demand functions (8.18) can be independent; equilibrium in any two asset markets ensures equilibrium in the third. Focusing on the money and bond markets and assuming that these are in equilibrium, yields

$$\frac{M}{P} = L(Y, r_e(1 - u), r(1 - u) - \pi, -\pi, V) \tag{8.18a'}$$

$$\frac{B}{P} = J(Y, r_e(1 - u), r(1 - u) - \pi, -\pi, V) \tag{8.18b'}$$

The aggregate flow constraint was derived in Chapter 3 by aggregating the flow constraints facing households, firms, and the government. In the most general case we considered this turned out to be (see (3.79))

$$Y(t) = C(t) + p_{e,2}^*(t, t)E(t) - \left(\frac{M + B}{P}\right)\frac{P_2^*(t, t)}{P(t)}$$
$$- V_2^d(t, t) + \dot{K}(t) + G(t) \tag{8.21}$$

where

$C(t)$ = rate of consumption at time t,

$K(t)$ = stock of capital at time t,

$G(t)$ = rate of flow of government expenditure at time t,

$P^*(t, t), p_e^*(t, t)$ denote the instantaneous expectations of $P(t)$ and $p_e^*(t)$ respectively.

In Chapter 3 this equation was interpreted as the familiar *ex post* identity that the rate of income must equal the sum of the rates of actual consumption, actual investment and actual government expenditures. The quantity

$p^*_{e,2}(t, t)E(t) - [(M + B)/P]\,(P^*_2(t, t)/P$ was shown to equal the unanticipated component of disposable income, with $V^a_2(t, t)$ representing the rate at
which this is being saved. Since unanticipated disposable income must either
be consumed or saved, the difference $p^*_{e,2}E - [(M + B)/P]\,(P^*_2/P) - V^d_2$ is
the rate at which consumption plans are being revised at time t. Thus, since
by definition actual consumption equals planned consumption plus unanticipated consumption, it follows that we can interpret $C(t) + p^*_{e,2}E -$
$[(M + B)/P]\,(P^*_2/P) - V^d_2$ as measuring the rate of *ex post* consumption. The
rate of ex post investment is obviously given by the rate of actual accumulation of capital, $\dot{K}(t)$. Finally, $G(t)$ measures the rate of government expenditure plans, which by assumption equals the rate of actual government
expenditure.[2]

By making the conventional assumption that consumption plans are
realized, we have $V^d_2(t, t) = p^*_{e,2}E - [(M + B)/P]\,(P^*_2/P)$, so that (8.21)
reduces to the simpler relationship

$$Y = C + \dot{K} + G. \tag{8.21'}$$

To avoid excessive complication this is the version of the flow constraint we
shall use throughout the rest of this chapter. We shall take G to be an
exogenous policy variable, while $\dot{K}$ is determined by the dynamics of asset
accumulation specified more fully below. Consumption is assumed to depend
upon real disposable income (Y^D) and wealth, so that

$$Y = C(Y^D, V) + \dot{K} + G, \quad 0 < C_1 < 1, \quad C_2 \geqslant 0. \tag{8.21''}$$

The relationship between (8.21'') and the more familiar product market equilibrium condition

$$Y = C + I + G$$

where I denotes the planned rate of investment, was discussed at length in
Chapter 3. There we showed that (8.21'') is a *constraint*. It follows from the
underlying budget constraints facing the individuals in the economy as one
moves to the continuous limit. It does not in general ensure continuous
product market equilibrium, unless of course investment plans, as well as consumption plans, are realized. For simplicity this is the assumption we make,
but in principle it can easily be relaxed to allow for disequilibrium in the
transition to the steady state.

In order to ensure the consistency between savings plans and the desired
accumulation of wealth, both in real terms, we showed in Chapter 3 that this
requires real disposable income to be defined appropriately as follows

$$Y^D = \left(Y + \frac{Br}{P}\right)(1 - u) + p^*_{e,1}E - \left(\frac{M + B}{P}\right)\pi \tag{8.22}$$

Hence, real disposable income consists of income from current production (labour plus capital), plus interest income, both net of taxes, together with the expected capital gains on holding equity and government debt (bonds and money), which we assume are not taxed. Moreover, our formulation of the consumption function in (8.21″) assumes that the marginal propensity to consume out of capital gains equals that out of the ordinary income component. In Chapter 7, we circumvented the complications introduced by capital gains by assuming that the *MPC* out of them was negligible.

B.   The real rate of return on equity

As discussed in Chapter 3, the current value of equity at time t (in terms of new consumption goods) must equal the discounted present value of the expected future earnings of the real capital associated with that equity. As we are presently allowing for taxes on capital, the relationship must now hold after-taxes, so that (3.50) becomes

$$p_e(t)E(t) = K(t)\int_t^\infty (1-u)R^*(\tau, t)\exp\left(-\int_t^\tau r_e^*(t', t)(1-u)dt'\right)d\tau$$

(8.23)

where exp denotes exponential

and $R^*(\tau, t)$ = expected marginal physical product of capital for time τ formed at time t,

$r_e^*(t', t)$ = expected rate of return on equity for time t', formed at time t.

Likewise the expected value of equity for time $(t + h)$, formed at time t, must equal the after-tax expected discounted earnings of real capital from time $(t + h)$ on, yielding

$$p_e^*(t + h, t)E(t + h)$$

$$= K(t + h)\int_{t+h}^\infty (1-u)R^*(\tau, t)\exp\left(-\int_{t+h}^\tau r_e^*(t', t)(1-u)dt'\right)d\tau \qquad (8.24)$$

where we are making the simplifying assumption that the quantity of equity and physical capital in existence at time $(t + h)$ are both known with perfect certainty at time t. Subtracting (8.23) from (8.24), dividing by h and letting $h \to 0$ we obtain

$$r_e(t)(1-u) = \frac{R(t)(1-u)K(t)}{p_e(t)E(t)} + \frac{p_{e,1}^*(t, t)}{p_e(t)} + \frac{\dot{E}(t)}{E(t)} - \frac{\dot{K}(t)}{K(t)}. \qquad (8.25)$$

In deriving (8.25) we invoke two consistency conditions analogous to (8.2)

$$R^*(t, t) = R(t)$$

$$r_e^*(t, t) = r_e(t)$$

where $R(t)$ denotes the actual marginal physical product of capital at time t and $r_e(t)$ has been defined above.

On the assumption that physical capital is paid its marginal physical product, $R(t)K(t)$ represents the quantity of income attributable to capital, so that $R(t)(1-u)K(t)/p_e(t)E(t)$ is the after-tax rate of return on a dollar invested in equity. The total after-tax real rate of return on holding equity consists, not only of this component, but also of the expected change in the value of equity per unit of physical capital. This is assumed to be non-taxable and is given by the remaining three terms in (8.25).

C.   *The production–employment and wage–price sectors*
        Output is determined in accordance with the production function

$$Y = F(K, N) \tag{8.26}$$

where N is the employment of labour. We assume that F possesses the usual neoclassical properties of positive, but diminishing marginal product of each factor, together with constant returns to scale. Formally, these properties are summarized by

$$\left. \begin{array}{l} F_i > 0, F_{ii} < 0 \qquad i = 1, 2 \\ F_{11}F_{22} - F_{12}^2 = 0. \end{array} \right\} \tag{8.27}$$

The linear homogeneity of the production function enables us to write

$$Y = NF(K/N, 1) = Nf(K/N) \tag{8.28}$$

where

$$F(K/N, 1) = f(K/N).$$

From equations (8.26) and (8.28) we derive the following well known facts, used in subsequent derivations

$$\left. \begin{array}{l} F_1 = f'(K/N), \quad F_2 = f(K/N) - f'(K/N)K/N \equiv g(K/N) \\ F_{11} = f''/N, \quad F_{12} = -f''K/N^2, \quad F_{22} = f''K^2/N^3. \end{array} \right\} \tag{8.29}$$

The production side of the economy is assumed to operate as follows. At any point of time t say, firms have accumulated a given stock of capital $K(t)$. Given this stock of capital, their demand for labour is then determined so as to equate the marginal physical product of labour to the given real wage rate W/P, so that

$$F_2(K, N) = g(K/N) = W/P \equiv v. \tag{8.30}$$

Given the employment of labour determined by (8.30) and the real cost of equity capital issued to finance their investment, the firms' instantaneous desired stock of physical capital at time t, $K^d(t, t)$ is determined by the marginal productivity condition

$$F_1(K^d, N) \equiv f'(K^d/N) = r_e. \tag{8.31}$$

Likewise, given K and N, the actual marginal physical product of capital, which we have thus far denoted by R, is determined by

$$R = F_1(K, N) = f'(K/N) \qquad (8.32)$$

Production decisions are thus made in a kind of recursive fashion, similar to that proposed by Jorgenson (1963). As well as having a certain intuitive appeal, this scenario preserves the spirit of Keynesian theory in viewing labour as a short-run variable factor of production, with the adjustments in capital taking a longer period to complete. It should be noted, however, that this process has been criticized by certain authors as not being necessarily optimal; see e.g. Gould (1969), Coen (1971). Despite this weakness, it suffices for our purposes, especially since our main concern will be with the steady state, when these difficulties disappear.

As was discussed at some length in Chapter 3, there is no need for $K^d(t, t) \equiv K(t)$ and indeed from (8.31) and (8.32) they will be equal if and only if $r_e = R$ − a condition which in general will not hold for all t. But as we have seen, any difference between $K^d(t, t)$ and $K(t)$ typically implies a disequilibrium in the product market, which forms a component part of the subsequent dynamic evolution of the system.

Given the level of employment determined by (8.30), the rate of money wage inflation w, is assumed to be determined by the Phillips curve

$$w = \alpha_0 + \alpha_1 \left(\frac{N - \bar{N}}{\bar{N}} \right) + \beta\pi \qquad \alpha_1 > 0, \quad 0 \leqslant \beta \leqslant 1 \qquad (8.33)$$

where $\bar{N}$ denotes the full employment supply of labour. This equation is identical to the expectations hypothesis developed in Chapter 5, with the unemployment rate being explicitly written in the form $-(N - \bar{N})/\bar{N}$. This relationship requires no further comment at this point.

Finally, an expression for the rate of price inflation $p \equiv \dot{P}/P$ can be obtained by differentiating the real wage v with respect to t, to yield

$$\frac{\dot{v}}{v} = w - p. \qquad (8.34)$$

D.   The dynamics of the system

The relationships we have outlined above involve several variables which are subject to dynamic adjustments. To close the model and to determine its path over time, these must be determined. In fact the model includes three types of dynamic relationships; those arising from

(i) the evolution of expectations,
(ii) the financial flow constraints,
(iii) the accumulation of physical capital.

We shall discuss these in turn.

Two expectational variables have been introduced. These are (i) the expected *rate* of inflation $\pi(t)$, and (ii) the expected *level* of equity prices $p_e^*(t)$ (expressed in terms of new goods). These are assumed to be generated according to the adaptive hypothesis. Given the weak consistency axiom (8.2), and as a consequence of the discussion of Section 2, the appropriate continuous time versions of the hypothesis for these two expectational variables are

$$\dot{\pi}(t) = \rho\,[p(t) - \pi(t)] \qquad \rho > 0 \tag{8.35}$$

$$\dot{p}_e^*(t) = \gamma p_{e,2}^*(t, t). \qquad 0 < \gamma < 1 \tag{8.36}$$

Differentiating the weak consistency axiom (as applied to $p_e(t)$) with respect to t,

$$\dot{p}_e(t) = \dot{p}_e^*(t, t) = p_{e,1}^*(t, t) + p_{e,2}^*(t, t)$$

and substituting into (8.36), enables us to write this expression in the equivalent and slightly more convenient form

$$p_{e,1}^* = \left(\frac{\gamma - 1}{\gamma}\right)\dot{p}_e(t). \tag{8.36'}$$

The financial relationships consist of the flow constraints faced by the firms and the government, who issue securities to finance their respective operations. Letting P_e denote the nominal price of equity, $p_e = P_e/P$, and hence the financial constraint facing firms is

$$P_e\dot{E} = P\dot{K} \quad \text{or} \quad p_e\dot{E} = \dot{K} \tag{8.37}$$

This equation determines the number of additional shares firms need to issue at the current nominal market price P_e in order to be able to finance their purchase of new machines at their current market price P. In addition, assuming free entry and perfect competition, the value of equity issued by firms must equal the value of the physical capital, so that

$$p_e E = p_k K \tag{8.38}$$

where p_k is the unit value of existing capital once installed. Note, that as remarked in Chapter 3, since we are not introducing a separate market for existing capital, p_k should be interpreted as an *imputed* rather than a market price.

The financial constraint facing the government is its familiar budget constraint

$$\frac{\dot{M} + \dot{B}}{P} = G + r\frac{B}{P} - u\left(Y + \frac{B}{P}r\right) \tag{8.39}$$

This equation has been discussed at length in earlier chapters and does not require further comment at this stage.

As we have remarked at several points, we have distinguished explicitly between $K^d(t, t)$ and $K(t)$ and have argued that in general there is no need for them to be identically equal. As a consequence of this, continuous product market disequilibrium is implied, the adjustment of which needs to be modelled. There are several ways in which this might be done. In Chapter 3 we demonstrated that under our assumptions one appropriate hypothesis is

$$\dot{Y} = \theta \left[K^d(t, t) - K(t) \right], \quad \theta > 0, \tag{8.40}$$

This hypothesis was shown to be one correct limiting version of the conventional lagged adjustment process which specifies output to adjust in proportion to the rate of excess demand for output; see Chapter 3. Alternatively, under appropriate conditions one can specify the adjustment in terms of the conventional stock adjustment process.

The actual rate of capital accumulation consists of planned investment I, and unintended investment I_u. If we assume that investment plans are given by

$$I = \lambda [K^d(t, t) - K(t)] \qquad \lambda > 0$$

and that investment plans are realized, we obtain

$$\dot{K}(t) = \lambda [K^d(t, t) - K(t)]. \tag{8.41}$$

Primarily on the grounds of its familiarity, we choose to adopt (8.41). But the entire consequence of this choice is on the short-run dynamic behaviour of the system. It has no impact on the steady-state equilibrium.

4.   **Summary of model**

The model we have developed in Section 3 is a rather complex one. In order to comprehend its structure more readily, two modest modifications are desirable. First, it is convenient to combine equation (8.25), which describes the real rate of return on equity, with the adaptive expectations equation (8.36), thereby eliminating the partial derivatives $p_{e,1}^*(t, t)$, $p_{e,2}^*(t, t)$. Secondly, with asset demands specified in real terms, it is necessary to express the dynamics of the government budget constraint in terms of the real quantities $m = M/P$, $b = B/P$, as well. This in turn makes it convenient to specify government financial policy directly in terms of $\dot{m}$ and $\dot{b}$. Because of the simple fact that

$$\frac{\dot{m}}{m} = \frac{\dot{M}}{M} - \frac{\dot{P}}{P}$$

any policy specification for $\dot{m}$ implies a corresponding adjustment for the change in the nominal money supply $\dot{M}$. And the same is true for $\dot{b}$ and $\dot{B}$.

As one extreme benchmark policy, we define the government deficit to be purely *bond-financed* if $\dot{m} = 0$, in which case the nominal money supply grows at the rate of inflation. In an inflationary context such as we are considering, the natural base for defining neutral growth in the stock of money is one which in equilibrium would maintain portfolio balance. Given the present specification of the asset demand functions, $\dot{m} = 0$ is the appropriate choice. At the other extreme, and for the same reasons, we shall define the deficit to be purely *money-financed* if $\dot{b} = 0$.

Substituting from (8.25) for the partial derivative $p^*_{e,1}(t, t)$, using (8.36′), the flow constraint (8.37), and substituting for $\dot{K}$ from (8.41), the anticipated and unanticipated components of the capital gains associated with holding equity can be expressed as

$$p^*_{e,1}E = (p_eEr_e - RK)(1 - u) + \lambda(K^* - K)(p_eE/K - 1) \quad (8.42a)$$

$$p^*_{e,2}E = \frac{1}{\gamma - 1}(p_eEr_e - RK)(1 - u)$$

$$+ \frac{\lambda}{\gamma - 1}(K^* - K)(p_eE/K - 1) \quad (8.42b)$$

Thus the system can be reduced to the following two sets of equations:

$$Y = C[(Y + br)(1 - u) + (p_eEr_e - RK)(1 - u)$$
$$+ \lambda(K^* - K)(p_eE/K - 1) - (m + b)\pi, V] + \lambda(K^* - K) + G \quad (8.43a)$$

$$m = L(Y, r_e(1 - u), r(1 - u) - \pi, -\pi, V) \quad (8.43b)$$

$$b = J(Y, r_e(1 - u), r(1 - u) - \pi, -\pi, V) \quad (8.43c)$$

$$m + b + p_eE = V \quad (8.43d)$$

$$Y = Nf(K/N) \quad (8.43e)$$

$$w = \alpha_0 + \alpha_1\left(\frac{N - \bar{N}}{\bar{N}}\right) + \beta\pi \quad (8.43f)$$

$$v \equiv \frac{W}{P} = G(K/N) \quad (8.43g)$$

$$R = f'(K/N) \quad (8.43h)$$

$$f'(K^*/N) = r_e \quad (8.43i)$$

$$\frac{\dot{v}}{v} = w - p \quad (8.44a)$$

$$\dot{\pi} = \rho(p - \pi) \quad (8.44b)$$

$$\dot{K} = \lambda(K^* - K) \quad (8.44c)$$

$$\dot{m} + \dot{b} = G + br - u(Y + br) - p(m + b) \quad (8.44d)$$

$$(\dot{p_eE}) = \left(\frac{\gamma(1 - u)}{\gamma - 1}\right)[p_eEr_e - RK] + \frac{\gamma(K^* - K)}{\gamma - 1}\left(\frac{\gamma p_eE}{K} - 1\right) \quad (8.44e)$$

where for notational simplicity K^* denotes the desired stock of capital.

The development of the model proceeds as follows. At any point of time, the stock of capital K, the value of equity $p_e E$, the real stock of money m, the real stock of government bonds, b, and the rate of inflationary expectations can all be taken as given instantaneously. Given these fixed values of $K, p_e E, m, b$, and π, wealth is then determined from (8.43d). Given V, the flow constraint (8.43a), the financial market equilibrium conditions (8.43b) and (8.43c), the production function (8.43e) and the marginal productivity conditions (8.43h) and (8.43i) jointly determine the desired stock of capital, K^*, the level of output Y, the level of employment N, the real rate of return on equity r_e, the nominal rate of interest on bonds r, and the marginal product of capital R. Furthermore, given K and N, the marginal product condition (8.43g) determines the real wage v. Finally, the instantaneous rate of money wage inflation w is determined from the Phillips curve.

Equations (8.44) describe the dynamic adjustment of the system. Equations (8.44a), (8.44b), (8.44c) are unchanged from Section 3 and require no further comment. Equation (8.44d) is simply the government budget constraint transformed in terms of the real quantities m and b. The final equation describes the dynamics of the value of real equity $(p_e E)$. This equation, obtained by combining (8.25) with (8.36) and eliminating $\dot{K}$ from (8.41), embodies the rate at which expectations of equity prices p_e^* are adapted. Note also, that all the system determines is the *value* of equity $p_e E$. To obtain the separate components p_e, E one would need to integrate the firms' financial constraint (8.37). This would yield solutions for E, and p_e which, even in equilibrium, would depend upon initial conditions and are of little interest in their own right; see Chapter 7.

The evolution of the system can be discussed more formally as follows. Defining the vectors

$$z = (V, Y, N, r_e, r, K^*, v, R, w)$$

$$x = (K, p_e E, m, b, \pi)$$

the nine equations contained in (8.43) can, at least in principle, be solved for the nine components of z in terms of x and p to yield

$$z = H(x, p) \tag{8.45}$$

where H is a vector-valued function. Further, differentiating (8.45) with respect to t yields

$$\dot{z} = H_1(x, p)\dot{x} + H_2(x, p)\dot{p} \equiv G(x, p, \dot{x}, \dot{p}). \tag{8.45'}$$

The equation set (8.44) provides five equations involving the six variables

$$(\dot{K}, (\dot{p_e E}), \dot{m}, \dot{b}, \dot{\pi}, p) \equiv (\dot{x}, p).$$

To close the system and thus determine unique values for $(\dot{x}, p)$ at each instant of time, requires a final equation. This is provided by the policy specification for $\dot{m}$ and $\dot{b}$ and for simplicity we focus on the two extremes of (i) pure money financing ($\dot{b} = 0$); pure bond financing ($\dot{m} = 0$).

The set of differential equations (8.44b)–(8.44e), together with the policy specification is of the general form

$$\dot{x} = J(x, z, p)$$

and substituting from (8.45) can be written as

$$\dot{x} = J[x, H(x, p), p] \equiv A(x, p) \tag{8.46a}$$

The final differential equation to determine the system is obtained from (8.44a). From this equation it is seen that p being a function of w, v and $\dot{v}$ depends upon terms included in z and $\dot{z}$. Thus by virtue of (8.45) and (8.45$'$) p can in general be expressed in the form

$$p = \phi[H(x, p), G(x, p, \dot{x}, \dot{p})]$$

so that

$$\dot{p} = \psi(x, \dot{x}, p).$$

Substituting for $\dot{x}$ from (8.46a) yields the final dynamic equation

$$\dot{p} = \psi[x, A(x, p), p] \equiv B(x, p). \tag{8.46b}$$

Thus equations (8.46a) and (8.46b) specify the complete dynamics of the system; from any given value of x the evolution of the system is determined.

In one important respect our discussion of the dynamics is incomplete. In writing equations such as (8.45) and (8.46), we have assumed that at each instant of time the system can be solved uniquely for z in terms of x and p and for $\dot{x}$ in terms of x and p. This may or may not be the case. Local uniqueness can be obtained provided the appropriate Jacobian matrices are non-singular. Global uniqueness requires the much stronger property that these matrices be so-called P-matrices.[3] In general, the restrictions we have imposed on the underlying functions do not suffice to rule out the singularity of the relevant matrices and therefore the possibility of local non-uniqueness. But without meaning to downgrade the importance of this issue, apart from a few comments in Section 6, we do not pursue this question further.

5.   **Steady-state equilibrium**

The dynamics of the model, as summarized by (8.46), is determined by a sixth order differential equation system in the six variables (K, $p_e E$, m, b, p, π) although it does reduce to a fifth order system when the polar cases $\dot{m} = 0$, $\dot{b} = 0$ are considered. Its stability properties can in principle be established by applying the Routh–Hurwitz conditions, although for a fifth order system of this complexity, this would obviously be a hopelessly intractable task.[4] Thus, although we are able to make some statements below about certain *necessary* conditions for stability, apart from that, the question must simply be taken for granted. With this in mind we turn to the steady-state (long-run) equilibrium of the system.

Steady-state equilibrium is reached when

$$\dot{K} = (\dot{p_e E}) = \dot{\pi} = \dot{m} = \dot{b} = \dot{v} = 0$$

Setting these quantities equal to zero in (8.44) implies

$$p = \pi = w \qquad (8.47\text{a})$$

$$K^* = K \qquad (8.47\text{b})$$

$$G + br - u(Y + br) - p(m + b) = 0 \qquad (8.47\text{c})$$

$$Y = C[(Y + br)(1 - u) - (m + b)\pi, V] + G \qquad (8.47\text{d})$$

$$p_e E r_e = RK \qquad (8.47\text{e})$$

$$R = r_e. \qquad (8.47\text{f})$$

Hence in equilibrium the rates of money-wage inflation, price inflation, and expected rate of price inflation all converge to a common constant value. The instantaneous stock of capital equals the actual existing stock, thereby ensuring that the real rate of return on equity equals the marginal physical product of capital. Moreover, the capital gains associated with changing equity prices are transitory and disappear in the steady state. By contrast, capital gains (or more likely losses) associated with holding real money balances and bonds equal to $-(m + b)\pi$ persist indefinitely. Finally, equations (8.45e), (8.45f), together with (8.38), imply

$$p_e E = K, \quad \text{so that} \quad p_k = 1.$$

That is, in long-run equilibrium the imputed price of existing capital should equal the price of new output. We have therefore provided a rigorous proof of a proposition asserted some years ago by Tobin (1969).

Inserting the equilibrium conditions (8.47) into (8.43) and (8.44), the stationary equilibrium of the system can be reduced to the following set of equations

$$Y = C[(Y + br)(1 - u) - (m + b)\pi, V] + G \qquad (8.48\text{a})$$

$$m = L(Y, f'(K/N)(1 - u), r(1 - u) - \pi, -\pi, V) \qquad (8.48\text{b})$$

$$b = J(Y, f'(K/N)(1 - u), r(1 - u) - \pi, -\pi, V) \qquad (8.48\text{c})$$

$$V = m + b + K \qquad (8.48\text{d})$$

$$Y = Nf(K/N) \qquad (8.48\text{e})$$

$$(1 - \beta)\pi = \alpha_0 + \alpha_1 \left(\frac{N - \bar{N}}{\bar{N}}\right) \qquad (8.48\text{f})$$

$$G + rb - u(Y + br) - \pi(m + b) = 0 \qquad (8.48\text{g})$$

$$m = \bar{m} \quad \text{or} \quad b = \bar{b}. \qquad (8.48\text{h})$$

This is a set of eight equations which determine the eight endogenous variables Y, b, r, m, π, K, N, and V. From these values, the equilibrium of other variables such as $R, p_e E, v$, etc. can be computed.

But before considering some of the comparative static properties of (8.48), it is worthwhile noting some of its general characteristics. First, as in the Blinder–Solow (1973) model long-run equilibrium is characterized by a zero rate of savings and investment. But in contrast to their analysis, this stationary state occurs through a process of capital deepening in which the capital–labour ratio is adjusted in accordance with changes in the relative factor prices. Secondly, the steady state is one with a non-zero rate of inflation, which from (8.48g) can be written as

$$\pi = \frac{G + rb - u(Y + br)}{m + b} = \frac{\dot{M} + \dot{B}}{M + B}.$$ (8.48g')

This equation is analogous to (7.32e'). It asserts that the long-run equilibrium rate of inflation equals the rate of growth of nominal government debt. As in Chapter 7, this is an immediate consequence of our steady state definition and reflects the fact that with asset demands formulated in real terms, long-run portfolio balance requires the supplies of all financial assets to grow at the rate of inflation. Finally, the result obtained in Chapter 7 continues to hold; namely that even if $\beta = 1$, so that (8.48f) implies a natural rate of unemployment and the absence of a long-run trade-off between unemployment and inflation, asset market equilibrium conditions will still ensure a determinate rate of inflation.

6.   **Long-run comparative statics: money-financed deficit**
To analyse the equilibrium properties of (8.48) in further detail is another extremely tedious task. Therefore to render this exercise more manageable, we shall introduce the following two simplifying assumptions:
  (i) zero wealth effects in consumption, i.e. $C_2 = 0$,
  (ii) bonds and equities are perfect substitutes in the portfolios of
       investors.
These assumptions – particularly (ii) – are in fact standard ones in modern macroeconomic theory and so do not require any elaborate justification on our part. The effect of (ii) is to impose the steady-state constraint

$$r(1 - u) - \pi = r_e(1 - u) = R(1 - u) = f'(K/N)(1 - u)$$ (8.49)

the after-tax real rate of interest must equal the after-tax real return on equity, both of which in long-run equilibrium must equal the after-tax real marginal physical product of capital. Moreover, as a further consequence of (ii), only a composite demand function for the sum of bonds plus equity can be formulated, so that from the wealth constraint the equilibrium condition (8.48d) is now eliminated. Thus letting $b = \bar{b}$ denote the fact that bonds are fixed in real terms, (all money financing as defined in Section 4), and substituting (8.48f) into (8.48a), the equilibrium relationships can be simplified to

$$Y - C(Y-G) - G = 0 \tag{8.50a}$$

$$m - L(Y, f'(K/N)(1-u), -\pi, m + \bar{b} + K) = 0$$
$$(L_1 > 0, \quad L_2 < 0, \quad L_3 > 0, \quad 0 < L_4 < 1) \tag{8.50b}$$

$$Y - Nf(K/N) = 0 \tag{8.50c}$$

$$\pi(1-\beta) - \alpha_0 - \alpha_1 \left(\frac{N - \bar{N}}{\bar{N}}\right) = 0 \tag{8.50d}$$

$$G + f'(K/N)\bar{b}(1-u) - uY - \pi m = 0 \tag{8.50e}$$

This system of five equations determines the equilibrium levels of the five endogenous variables $Y, m, K, N,$ and π.

Note that in the important case of a natural rate of unemployment, when $\beta = 1$, this system of equations dichotomizes in a simple way. The amount of labour employed is determined from (8.50d); output is determined by G from the product equilibrium condition (8.50a); the production function (8.50c) then determines the amount of capital used. Given N, K, Y, the steady-state rate of inflation, and real money supply are determined jointly by the conditions for money market equilibrium (8.50b) and budget balance (after allowing for the inflation tax); see (8.50e).

We shall consider the effects of changes in the three exogenous policy variables $G, \bar{b}$ and u. These are contained in the differential of (8.50), namely

$$\begin{bmatrix} 1 - C_1 & 0 & 0 & 0 & 0 \\ -L_1 & -(L_2 f''(1-u)/N + L_4) & L_2 f''(1-u)K/N^2 & L_3 & 1 - L_4 \\ 1 & -f' & -(f - f'K/N) & 0 & 0 \\ 0 & 0 & -\alpha_1/\bar{N} & 1 - \beta & 0 \\ -u & \bar{b}(1-u)f''/N & -f''\bar{b}(1-u)K/N^2 & -m & -\pi \end{bmatrix} \begin{bmatrix} dY \\ dK \\ dN \\ d\pi \\ dm \end{bmatrix}$$

$$= \begin{bmatrix} (1 - C_1)dG \\ L_4 d\bar{b} - L_2 f' du \\ 0 \\ 0 \\ -dG - f'(1-u)d\bar{b} + (Y + f'\bar{b})du \end{bmatrix} \tag{8.51}$$

Denoting the determinant on the left hand side of (8.51) by D_1, we have

$$D_1 = (1 - C_1)[(1 - L_4)\omega_1 - \pi\omega_2] \tag{8.52}$$

where $\quad \omega_1 = \alpha_1 mf'/\bar{N} + (1-\beta)\bar{b}(1-u)ff''/N$

$\qquad \omega_2 = (1-\beta)ff''L_2(1-u)/N + (1-\beta)L_4[f-f'K/N]$

$\qquad\qquad + L_3 f'\alpha_1/\bar{N} > 0.$

The quantity D_1 can be shown to be equal to the value of the determinant associated with the matrix of coefficients describing the dynamics of the system over time. For the system to be stable it is *necessary* but not sufficient for $D_1 < 0$. Evaluating the terms of D_1, it is seen that on the basis of the previous sign restrictions, D_1 is indeterminate in sign. It is interesting to note, furthermore, that if $\beta = 1$ and $\pi \leqslant 0$, then $D_1 > 0$, so that the system is in fact *unstable*. In economic terms this means that if the system starts from an equilibrium in which the rate of inflation is non-positive, and if increases in inflationary expectations are fully reflected in the rate of wage inflation, then with a money-financed deficit, the system will be unstable. The existence of a natural rate of unemployment need not be destabilizing in the neighbourhood of an equilibrium with a positive rate of inflation.

Upon reflection, the instability of the system when $\beta = 1$ and $\pi = 0$ is really not very surprising. This corresponds to a long-run equilibrium with full employment and stable prices and accords most closely with the standard one-sector neoclassical growth model; see e.g. Solow (1956). It is a well known result that the equilibrium of such a model will be stable if and only if

$$sf'(K/N) < n$$

where
$\qquad s = $ constant savings rate,
$\qquad n = $ rate of growth of population.

With constant population $(n = 0)$ as we are assuming here, the neoclassical model is therefore also unstable, so that the two sets of instability results are in fact quite consistent.

If $\pi < 0$, the term $-\pi(m+\bar{b}) > 0$, which we can loosely refer to as an 'inflation tax on government debt' becomes an 'inflation subsidy' and provides a further destabilizing influence. On the other hand, if $\pi > 0$, it reverts to being an 'inflation tax', thereby providing a stabilizing effect which could even be sufficiently strong to stabilize the entire system.

A.   *Government expenditure multipliers*
The effect of an increase in government expenditure on income is obtained directly from (8.50a) and is simply

$$\frac{dY}{dG} = 1. \tag{8.53}$$

That is, the long-run equilibrium effect of an increase in government expenditure of \$1 is to raise national income by \$1. Consumption is unaffected (as is investment which by definition is zero); the net impact is simply to increase the size of the government sector. It is interesting to note that (8.53) is identical to the expression for the balanced budget multiplier in the elementary *IS–LM* model in which the level of investment is exogenously determined; see Chapter 2, Section 6. Upon reflection this is hardly surprising, since the long-run equilibrium of the present model is one in which the budget is balanced in real terms.

Moreover, since (8.53) is obtained from (8.50a) alone, which does not involve either m or b, this long-run government expenditure multiplier is *independent* of the mode of deficit financing. That is, irrespective of whether the government uses money or bond financing, in the absence of wealth effects in consumption, the long-run government expenditure multiplier is unity. Therefore, any multiplier effects which deviate from unity in the long run must be attributable to wealth effects in consumption.

Turning now to the other derivatives, these are in general all rather complex. From the production function and the result that $dY/dG = 1$, it follows that

$$1 = F_1 \frac{\partial K}{\partial G} + F_2 \frac{\partial N}{\partial G} \tag{8.54}$$

so that an increase in G must increase the demand for at least one of the factors of production. But in general which of the two factors (or possibly both) experiences the increase in demand depends critically on the expectations coefficient β. If $\beta = 1$, so that the economy is one with a natural rate of unemployment, $N = \bar{N}$ and hence

$$\frac{\partial N}{\partial G} = 0.$$

In this case the full-employment effect of the expansionary government expenditure policy is experienced by capital, the demand for which increases by

$$\frac{\partial K}{\partial G} = \frac{1}{F_1} > 0.$$

Moreover, in order to induce the increase in employment of capital, the net real rate of interest (and net real return on equity) must fall

$$(1-u)\frac{\partial R}{\partial G} = (1-u)\frac{\partial r_e}{\partial G} = \frac{\partial}{\partial G}[r(1-u) - \pi]$$

$$= (1-u)f''/\bar{N}\frac{\partial K}{\partial G} < 0.$$

To see what happens to the steady-state rate of inflation and real money supply under the assumption $\beta = 1$, it is convenient to substitute the

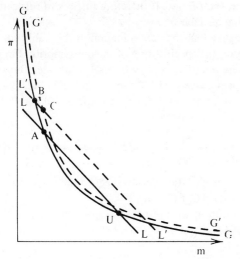

Fig. 8.1 *Relationship between equilibrium rate of inflation and real money stock when β = 1 and government deficit is money financed.*

expressions for $\partial Y/\partial G$ etc. into (8.50). The resulting changes in π and m are now given by

$$L_3 d\pi + (1 - L_4)dm = [L_1 + L_2 f''(1 - u)/f'\bar{N} + L_4/f']dG$$

(8.55a)

$$md\pi + \pi dm = [(1 - u) + f''\bar{b}(1 - u)/f'\bar{N}]dG \qquad (8.55b)$$

which involves only two endogenous variables and can be easily analysed graphically. This is done in Fig. 8.1.

The line LL is the combination of rates of inflation and real money supply, which given the predetermined values of Y, N, K will keep the money market in equilibrium. Because of the fact that an increase in m will increase supply more than it increases demand, this must be accompanied by a decrease in π, in order to generate sufficient additional demand to restore equilibrium to the money market. This is a direct consequence of (8.55a). Likewise, the line GG is the combination of m, and π, which will maintain government budget balance (allowing for the inflationary tax). This too is negatively sloped. Given Y, N, K, the real government deficit net of inflationary tax is given. This determines the amount of additional inflationary tax required to balance the budget. It is clear that the higher the rate of inflation, the lower the real money balances which are needed to achieve this. Moreover, from (8.50e) it is seen that GG is in fact a rectangular hyperbola, so that typically it will intersect LL (at least) twice as indicated. (We ignore the possibility of no intersection) Hence in general there will be two equilibria. The stability condition $D_1 < 0$, together with $C_1 < 1$, requires that the slope of the GG curve must be steeper than that of the LL line. It therefore suffices to rule out the lower equilibrium U as being unstable.

But it is important to realize that the determination of the stable equilibrium depends crucially upon the specification of the consumption function. For example, suppose it were modified to vary inversely with the after-tax real rate of return, as well as positively with disposable income. Steady-state consumption is then $C[Y-G, f'(K/N)(1-u)]$, $C_2 < 0$, and if $\beta = 1$, the stability condition $D_1 < 0$ can be written as

$$\frac{\alpha_1 f'}{\bar{N}} \left[1 - C_1 - \frac{e_1 C}{\sigma Y} \left(1 - \frac{1}{e_2} \right) \right] [(1 - L_4)m - L_3 \pi] < 0 \qquad (8.52')$$

where

$\quad e_1 = $ elasticity of consumption with respect to the real after-tax
$\qquad\qquad$ rate of return, $(= C_2 f'(1-u)/Y < 0)$,
$\quad e_2 = $ elasticity of output with respect to capital, $(= f'K/fN > 0)$,
$\quad \sigma = $ elasticity of substitution (defined below).

It is now conceivable that

$$\left[1 - C_1 - \frac{e_1 C}{\sigma Y} \left(1 - \frac{1}{e_2} \right) \right] < 0 \qquad (8.52'')$$

in which case U would become the stable equilibrium. Empirical evidence on e_1 (see Weber (1970) who found that $e_1 > 0$) suggests that $(8.52'')$ is unlikely to be met and accordingly we shall treat A as the stable equilibrium. However, if $(8.52'')$ were to hold, the analysis below would need to be modified appropriately.

With this in mind, consider an increase in government expenditure. This will shift the LL curve out to $L'L'$ and provided $f' + f''b/N > 0$ the GG curve will shift similarly outwards to $G'G'$. But suppose initially that there is no shift in the GG curve. In this case, for the reasons just noted, (the maintenance of a balanced budget), m and π must move in opposite directions. Because of the fact that a high rate of inflation tends to be stabilizing (through the inflation tax) this will require the changes to be in the form of a higher rate of inflation, accompanied by a reduction in the real money supply. This is shown by the move from A to B in Figure 8.1. To the extent that the budget balance line shifts outwards, this increase in the rate of inflation and reduction in the money supply will be reduced somewhat; see the move from A to B to C. But on balance one would still expect $\dfrac{\partial \pi}{\partial G} > 0$, $\dfrac{\partial m}{\partial G} < 0$. Sufficient conditions to ensure that this will be so are:

$$\pi > 0 \qquad (8.56a)$$

$$\theta \equiv \pi L_4 - (1 - L_4)[(1-u)r - \pi] > 0 \qquad (8.56b)$$

which are almost certainly likely to be met in periods of high inflation, when the net real rate of interest tends to be low. For example, taking as plausible parameters, $u = 0.25, r = 0.11, \pi = 0.08$, (8.56b) requires $L_4 > 0.03$, a value of the wealth coefficient which tends to be supported by the available empirical evidence; see e.g. Goldfeld (1973). For a low rate of inflation, however, $\theta < 0$ is much more likely, in which case the signs could be reversed.

If $\beta < 1$, the impact of an increase in G on K, N becomes less clear-cut. For example, the employment effect is

$$\frac{\partial N}{\partial G} = \frac{(1 - \beta)(1 - C_1)}{D_1} [-\pi(L_1 f' + L_2 f''(1 - u)/N + L_4)$$

$$+ (1 - L_4)(1 - u)(f' + \bar{b} f''/N)] \tag{8.57}$$

the sign of which cannot be decided from the restrictions we have so far imposed. While an increase in government expenditure will expand output, it is not clear that this will necessarily stimulate the demand for labour. Furthermore, in this case, a money-financed deficit is more likely to result in an increase in the steady-state real money supply. This in turn is likely to lead to a reduction in the nominal and real rates of interest, the effect of which is to stimulate the demand for capital relative to that of labour. Indeed if the capital deepening effect is sufficiently strong, it is possible for the increase in output to lead to so much substitution of capital for labour that the demand for labour actually falls. But while a fall in the demand for labour remains a definite theoretical possibility, the more usual increase in the demand for labour is the more probable outcome. Sufficient conditions to ensure $\partial N/\partial G > 0$ are given by (8.56).

By virtue of the long-run Phillips curve, the effect of an increase in government expenditure on the equilibrium rate of inflation is proportional to its effect on employment

$$\frac{\partial \pi}{\partial G} = \frac{\alpha_1}{1 - \beta} \left(\frac{\partial N}{\partial G} \right).$$

Thus irrespective of the magnitude of β the conditions (8.56) suffice to ensure that an increase in G will be inflationary. However, since for the reasons discussed above, the increase in G may reduce the level of employment, the possibility of it actually lowering the rate of inflation cannot be dismissed.

As one further exercise, it is of some interest to consider briefly the effects of an increase in government expenditure on income distribution. Denoting the capital–labour ratio K/L by k, the impact on the real wage v is

$$\frac{\partial v}{\partial G} = -kf''(k) \frac{\partial k}{\partial G} \tag{8.58}$$

implying

$$\text{sgn} \left(\frac{\partial v}{\partial G} \right) = -\text{sgn} \left(\frac{\partial R}{\partial G} \right).$$

While in general $\partial R/\partial G$ is ambiguous, it is always true that any increase in the real rate of interest will be accompanied by a reduction in the real wage. Further, if $\beta = 1$, we know that $\partial R/\partial G < 0$, in which case the real wage rate will rise.

The relative share of output obtained by labour and capital is

$$s = \frac{vN}{RK} = \frac{f(k) - kf'(k)}{kf'(k)}$$

so that

$$\frac{\partial s}{\partial G} = \frac{[-ff''k - ff' + kf'^2]}{k^2 f'^2} \frac{dk}{dG}.$$

Using the fact that for a constant returns to scale production function, the elasticity of substitution σ is given by[5]

$$\sigma = \frac{F_1 F_2}{FF_{12}} = \frac{f'[f - kf']}{-ff''k}$$

the effect on relative shares can be written as

$$\frac{\partial s}{\partial G} = \frac{ff''(\sigma - 1)}{kf'^2} \frac{dk}{dG} \tag{8.59}$$

which depends crucially on both dk/dG and the magnitude of σ. Thus if $\beta = 1$, $dk/dG > 0$, and in this case an increase in government expenditure will increase the relative share of income provided the elasticity of substitution is low ($\sigma < 1$); otherwise its relative share will decline.

B.   *Open market operations*

The second policy we wish to consider is an open market transaction of bonds, which we define by a change in $\bar{b}$. Because of the fact that income is determined solely by the level of G in the product market equilibrium condition (8.50a), it immediately follows that

$$\frac{\partial Y}{\partial \bar{b}} = 0. \tag{8.60}$$

An open market transaction of bonds therefore has no effect on the steady-state level of income.

Moreover, provided $\beta = 1$, we can also show

$$\frac{\partial N}{\partial \bar{b}} = \frac{\partial K}{\partial \bar{b}} = \frac{\partial R}{\partial \bar{b}} = \frac{\partial [r(1 - u) - \pi]}{\partial \bar{b}} = 0 \tag{8.61}$$

That is, in the natural rate case, an open market operation will have no effect on the level of employment, the demand for capital, or the net real rate of interest. This last conclusion is essentially the Fisherian proposition that in the long run nominal interest rates fully incorporate inflationary expectations, and which we have discussed in previous chapters. It will be recalled that while in general the Fisherian proposition did not hold, we showed that it did apply if we assumed (i) zero wealth effects in consumption; (ii) $\beta = 1$; (iii) bonds and equity are perfect substitutes; (iv) all money financing – all of which are precisely the conditions being assumed to derive (8.61). Hence the present result is completely consistent with our previous conclusions; see Chapter 7.

In economic terms the reason is straightforward. Since a change in $\bar{b}$ has no effect on equilibrium income, and since with $\beta = 1$ it can have no effect on equilibrium employment (which is tied to the natural rate), it follows from the production function that it can have no effect on the demand for capital. Thus given that the capital–labour ratio remains constant, the marginal physical product of capital and hence the real rate of interest must also remain fixed.

For $\beta < 1$, the impacts of an open market operation on K, N, R and π are all intimately related. Recalling the definition of θ given in (8.56b), these effects are

$$\frac{\partial K}{\partial \bar{b}} = \frac{(1 - C_1)(f - kf')(1 - \beta)\theta}{D_1} \tag{8.62a}$$

$$\frac{\partial N}{\partial \bar{b}} = \frac{-(1 - C_1)(1 - \beta)f'\theta}{D_1} \tag{8.62b}$$

$$\frac{\partial R}{\partial \bar{b}} = \frac{ff''(1 - C_1)(1 - \beta)\theta}{D_1} \tag{8.62c}$$

$$\frac{\partial \pi}{\partial \bar{b}} = \frac{-(1 - C_1)f'\theta}{D_1} \tag{8.62d}$$

so that all the signs depend crucially on that of θ. While on *a priori* grounds we are unable to sign θ, we have argued above that under inflationary conditions one could plausibly expect $\theta > 0$, in which case

$$\frac{\partial K}{\partial \bar{b}} < 0 \tag{8.63a}$$

$$\frac{\partial N}{\partial \bar{b}} > 0 \tag{8.63b}$$

$$\frac{\partial R}{\partial \bar{b}} > 0 \tag{8.63c}$$

$$\frac{\partial \pi}{\partial \bar{b}} > 0. \tag{8.63d}$$

Under these conditions an open market sale of bonds to the public will force up the real rate of interest, thereby causing producers to substitute labour for capital, in turn driving up the rate of money-wage inflation and with it the long-run rate of price inflation.

But we must also be aware that this scenario is highly tentative, particularly if the rate of inflation is low. Indeed if $\pi = 0$, then $\theta < 0$ and all of the signs in (8.63) would have to be reversed.

C.   *Change in tax rate*

The effects of an increase in the tax rate u turn out to be quite determinate in sign; provided $\pi > 0$ they are given by

$$\frac{\partial Y}{\partial u} = 0, \quad \frac{\partial m}{\partial u} < 0, \quad \frac{\partial K}{\partial u} \leqslant 0, \quad \frac{\partial N}{\partial u} \geqslant 0, \quad \frac{\partial \pi}{\partial u} > 0. \tag{8.64}$$

The economic explanation behind these responses is also rather simple. By providing additional revenue to the government, an increase in the tax rate reduces the deficit and hence the need to print money, thereby lowering the steady-state stock of money.[6] As a consequence, the real rate of interest will rise leading to a fall in the demand for physical capital. With output being independent of the level of taxes (being determined by G), this fall in the use of capital must be offset by an increase in the employment of labour, the effect of which is to increase both the rate of money-wage and price inflation.

The fact that an increase in the tax rate u is associated with an increase in the steady-state rate of inflation is counter-intuitive and requires further comment. Essentially it stems from the conditions for money-market equilibrium. The reduction in the real quantity of money following from a tax increase must be accompanied by a reduction in demand. While the increase in the real rate of interest generates some reduction in demand, it is insufficient to restore equilibrium. This can be accomplished only if in addition, the real return on holding money falls; i.e. the rate of inflation rises.

7.   Long-run comparative statics: bond-financed deficit

Our treatment of this case shall be quite brief. All the steady-state multipliers are contained in the differential of the system

$$\begin{bmatrix} 1-C_1 & 0 & 0 & 0 & 0 \\ -L_1 & -(L_2 f''(1-u)/N + L_4) & L_2 f''(1-u)K/N^2 & L_3 & -L_4 \\ 1 & -f' & -(f-f'K/N) & 0 & 0 \\ 0 & 0 & -\alpha_1/\bar{N} & 1-\beta & 0 \\ -u & b(1-u)f''/N & -f''b(1-u)K/N^2 & -\bar{m} & f'(1-u) \end{bmatrix} \begin{bmatrix} dY \\ dK \\ dN \\ d\pi \\ db \end{bmatrix}$$

$$= \begin{bmatrix} (1-C_1)dG \\ -(1-L_4)d\bar{m} \\ 0 \\ 0 \\ -dG + \pi d\bar{m} + (Y + f'b)du \end{bmatrix} \tag{8.65}$$

We have already commented on the fact that due to the absence of wealth effects in consumption, (8.65) implies a long-run government expenditure multiplier for income of

$$\frac{dY}{dG} = 1$$

just as it does for pure money financing. The determinant of the matrix on the left hand side of (8.65) equals

$$D_2 = (1 - C_1) [-L_4 \omega_1 + f'(1-u)\omega_2] \qquad (8.66)$$

where ω_1, ω_2, are defined in (8.52). A necessary condition for stability is that $D_2 < 0$. Note that in contrast to D_1, the case $\beta = 1, \pi \leqslant 0$, does not necessarily imply instability. Nevertheless, just as in earlier models, the presence of net interest payments provides a highly destabilizing influence. This can be seen from the government budget constraint

$$\dot{b} = G - uY + f'(K/\bar{N})b(1-u) - \bar{m}\pi.$$

Suppose that the marginal product of capital is constant. If in the neighbourhood of equilibrium income is unresponsive to a change in b, the accumulated interest payments are potentially highly destabilizing. Indeed it is the restrictions required to avoid this instability which are the cause for some seemingly anomalous results we shall discuss below. One condition which is now *necessary* for stability is the existence of positive wealth effects in the demand for money. Again, however, all these conclusions are highly dependent upon the specification of the consumption function and would require significant modification if (8.52″) held.

Turning now to the other multipliers, we begin with the case $\beta = 1$. The effects of an increase in government expenditure on equilibrium employment, demand for capital, and the real net rate of interest are precisely as they are when the deficit is money financed, namely

$$\frac{\partial N}{\partial G} = 0; \quad \frac{\partial K}{\partial G} = \frac{1}{F_1} > 0, \quad \frac{\partial R}{\partial G} < 0.$$

The effect on the rate of inflation is now different and requires further discussion.

Just as before the system dichotomizes, so that the effects on b, π, are determined jointly from the condition for money market equilibrium and budget balance. These changes are given by

$$L_3 d\pi - L_4 db = [L_1 + L_2 f''(1-u)/f'\bar{N} + L_4/f'] dG \qquad (8.67a)$$

$$\bar{m} d\pi - f'(1-u)db = [(1-u) + f''b(1-u)/f'\bar{N}]dG. \qquad (8.67b)$$

Again we can proceed graphically.

In Figure 8.2, the line LL is the combination of π and b, which given the

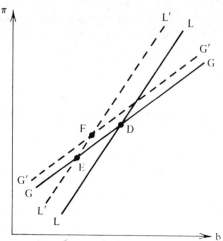

Fig. 8.2 *Relationship between equilibrium rate of inflation and real stock of bonds when* β = 1 *and government deficit is bond financed.*

predetermined values of Y, N, K, will maintain money market equilibrium. Because of the fact that an increase in b will increase demand through the wealth effect, leaving the supply unaltered, this must be accompanied by an increase in π, in order to restore equilibrium. Similarly, the line GG is the locus of pairs of π and b which will maintain government budget balance. Since an increase in b will increase the deficit, this must be matched by an appropriate increase in π, in order to generate sufficient inflation tax to maintain a balanced budget. Hence both curves are upward sloping and unlike the previous case there is nothing in (8.67) to suggest that there need be more than one equilibrium. Moreover, because of the stability condition, and the fact $C' < 1$, the slope of the LL curve is steeper than that of the GG curve; if (8.52″) holds these relative slopes would be reversed with the discussion below requiring the appropriate amendments.

Consider now an increase in government expenditure. As before, this will shift the LL curve out. If the GG curve remains fixed, the result would be a reduction in both the rate of inflation and the real stock of bonds. To the extent that the GG curve shifts out as well, these reductions in π and b will be smaller; see the move from D to E to F in Figure 8.2. While these results may appear surprising, they are a consequence of the severe restrictions imposed by stability. The reduction in bonds is required in order to avoid the destabilizing effects of higher interest payments, which would accompany an increased supply of bonds. The lower rate of inflation is then in turn necessary, in order to maintain equilibrium in the money market.

For $\beta < 1$, these results are subject to some modification. In this case, interest payments tend to be even more destabilizing (see (8.66)), requiring any increase in G to give rise to an even larger reduction in b (than when

$\beta = 1$). The effect of this is for the reduction in the real net interest rate to be larger, increasing the use of capital even more. Given that $dY/dG = 1$ and is independent of β, it follows that with $\beta < 1$, an increase in government expenditure will actually lead to a *reduction* in employment and in the rate of inflation. This can be seen directly from the following expression,

$$\frac{\partial N}{\partial G} = \frac{(1-\beta)(1-C_1)(1-u)}{D_2} \{f'[L_1 f' + L_2 f''(1-u)/N] - L_4 b f''/N\}$$

$$(8.68)$$

which given stability, is necessarily negative.

Again these results are counter-intuitive. But as we have stressed, pure bond financing is highly unstable. The destabilizing effects of higher interest payments can only be avoided, provided these seemingly perverse results prevail.

The effects of an increase in the tax rate u are again rather simple. Qualitatively, they are

$$\frac{\partial Y}{\partial u} = 0, \quad \frac{\partial b}{\partial u} < 0, \quad \frac{\partial K}{\partial u} \geqslant 0, \quad \frac{\partial N}{\partial u} \leqslant 0, \quad \frac{\partial \pi}{\partial u} < 0 \qquad (8.69)$$

which it will be observed are qualitatively opposite to those obtained with a money-financed deficit. The economic rationale is straightforward. By providing additional revenue, an increase in the tax rate reduces the deficit and therefore the need to issue additional bonds, thereby lowering the steady-state stock of bonds. As a consequence the real rate of interest will fall, leading to a rise in the demand for physical capital. With fixed output, this reduces the demand for labour and with it the rate of inflation. This response is of course the more conventional one; an increase in the tax rate is deflationary.

8.   Conclusion: comparison of money financing with bond financing

To conclude this discussion it is useful to compare briefly some of the main features of the policy implications contained in the two preceding sections, and to relate them to the conclusions derived in earlier chapters. Recalling the definitions of D_1 and D_2 (and our specification of the consumption function), one necessary condition for stability in each case is

Money-financing: $(1 - L_4)\omega_1 - \pi\omega_2 < 0$ (8.70a)

Bond-financing: $-L_4\omega_1 + f'(1-u)\omega_2 < 0.$ (8.70b)

These conclusions contain the following interest result. For $\pi \leqslant 0$, (8.70a) implies that $\omega_1 < 0$ is necessary for stability, while for (8.70b) to hold $\omega_1 > 0$ is required. It is therefore impossible for *both* sets of conditions to be met simultaneously. In other words, if initially $\pi \leqslant 0$, it is impossible for both bond financing and money financing to be stable policies. At least one of them must be unstable. Which one it is, cannot be determined on *a priori* grounds; it depends upon the empirical magnitudes of the parameters included in ω_1. But it does mean that starting from a situation of zero inflation or deflation, the method of government finance must be chosen carefully if an unstable time path is to be avoided. For $\pi > 0$, both (8.70a) and (8.70b) may hold over appropriate ranges. Thus in comparing steady-state multipliers over which both these conditions are assumed to hold, we must restrict ourselves to this (positive) range of π.

One of the most striking results to emerge from the present analysis is the proposition that, in the absence of wealth effects in consumption, the two modes of finance both yield long-run government expenditure multipliers of unity. In this respect our results also bear a close resemblance to the conclusions obtained in the simplest dynamic model discussed in Chapter 4. There it was shown that when interest payments on government debt were ignored, the long-run government expenditure multiplier equals the inverse of the marginal tax rate, $1/u$, and is also invariant with respect to the mode of deficit financing chosen by the government. In both models, the long-run government expenditure multipliers are independent of any parameters which characterize consumption, investment, or asset demands.

If the assumption of zero wealth effects in consumption is relaxed, the long-run government expenditure multipliers are no longer the same. They become respectively (identified by appropriate subscripts)

$$\left(\frac{\partial Y}{\partial G}\right)_m = 1 + \frac{C_2}{1 - C_1}\left(\frac{\partial V}{\partial G}\right)_m \tag{8.71a}$$

$$\left(\frac{\partial Y}{\partial G}\right)_b = 1 + \frac{C_2}{1 - C_1}\left(\frac{\partial V}{\partial G}\right)_b \tag{8.71b}$$

so that the difference between them

$$\left(\frac{\partial Y}{\partial G}\right)_m - \left(\frac{\partial Y}{\partial G}\right)_b = \frac{C_2}{1 - C_1}\left[\left(\frac{\partial V}{\partial G}\right)_m - \left(\frac{\partial V}{\partial G}\right)_b\right] \tag{8.72}$$

is due entirely to their differential induced effects on private wealth.

A further example of how the unitary multiplier depends crucially on the specification of consumption can be seen by modifying it to vary inversely with the after-tax real rates of return on assets. In this case, taking $\beta = 1$, it can be easily seen that $dY/dG > 1$, whichever method of finance is adopted. The reason is that with employment fixed, the additional output resulting from the increase in government expenditure must be produced by the more intensive use of capital. For this to occur, the real rates of return must be reduced, thereby providing an additional stimulus to consumption.

With $\beta = 1$, the direction and magnitude of the effects of an increase in government expenditure on some of the other endogenous variables are also invariant with respect to government financial policy. An increase in government expenditure will have no effect on employment; it will increase the demand for capital. and lower the after-tax real rate of interest. The impact on the equilibrium rate of inflation, however, is crucially dependent upon whether the deficit is money-financed or bond-financed. In the former case, we have shown that an increase in government expenditure will almost certainly lead to a higher rate of inflation; in the latter case the equilibrium rate of inflation will be reduced. While this last result is counter-intuitive, it is a consequence of the highly destabilizing effects of higher interest payments. As a consequence of these, if pure bond-financing is to be stable it must result in a lower supply of real bonds, accompanied by a reduction in the rate of inflation.

If $\beta < 1$, the results become somewhat less determinate. While under money-financing, the expansionary effect of an increase in government expenditure on the equilibrium level of income will probably stimulate employment, this need not occur. Because of the capital deepening effects now being considered, it is possible that capital may be substituted for labour to such an extent that the demand for labour actually falls. On the other hand, for a pure bond-finance policy to be stable, an expansion in government expenditure *must* lead to a reduction in employment. Again the cause for this phenomenon is the existence of interest payments which become even more destabilizing when $\beta < 1$. As a result an even larger reduction in bonds is required, leading to a larger reduction in the real interest rate, a bigger increase in the use of capital, and the reduction in employment. As a further consequence of this, the result that an increase in government expenditure will be inflationary or deflationary according to whether the deficit is money-financed or bond-financed will most probably continue to hold. At the same time we must emphasize, that the potential instability of bond-financing may in fact create an unstable situation of accelerating inflation.

We have also seen that in the absence of wealth effects a tax change will have no effect on output. Its effects on all other variables will depend crucially on how the associated government deficit is financed. In particular, a tax increase will be deflationary as long as the deficit is bond-financed; it will be inflationary if money-financing is used. This conclusion is of some importance for the appropriate use of taxation as an instrument of inflationary control.

Finally, we should draw attention once again to the fact that the stability conditions (8.52), (8.66), so crucial to these comparative static results, are highly dependent upon the form of the consumption function. In many cases, our conclusions would be subject to severe modification if (8.52″) were to hold.

PART II. THE OPEN ECONOMY

9

REVIEW OF STATIC MACROECONOMIC
MODELS OF A SMALL OPEN ECONOMY

1.   Introduction

In the first part of this book we have treated the economy as being
in isolation and have neglected any transactions it may have with the rest of
the world. In practice there are few economies in which the volume of international transactions is so low that it may be neglected in this way. Possibly
the United States is one such country, although even there the relative
importance of trade has increased over the post war years. In virtually all
other Western economies international trade represents a significant proportion
of their economic activity and certainly should not be ignored.

In extending the macroeconomic model to include foreign transactions
there are various issues that are raised. The first is the size of the country
being considered. The question is whether or not it is small enough to ignore
any repercussions it may have on the rest of the world. In particular, can it
treat such variables as the level of income in the rest of the world, the foreign
interest rate, the foreign price level, the foreign level of wealth as given
parameters? Or are these determined, at least in part, by its own domestic
activities? If these variables can be viewed as exogenously determined, then
we can refer to the country as being 'small'. This is the assumption we shall
maintain throughout our discussion of the open economy. By contrast, a
'large' economy is one in which these foreign variables are influenced by the
state of the domestic economy. In this case the equilibrium of the domestic
economy, together with that of the rest of the world, are determined simultaneously by solving a 'world-wide' general equilibrium model. While a good
deal of work has been devoted by international economists to these 'two-
country' macroeconomic models, the development of such a model is beyond
our scope.[1] Despite that, it is to be hoped that the development we shall give
of the small country model in the following chapters, will provide a basic
framework for extending the analysis to the two-country case.

A second general issue one must consider in incorporating international
aspects into a macroeconomic model is the assumption one makes about
the nature of the exchange rate system. Two polar assumptions are almost
invariably made. First, is the case of the *fixed exchange rate* in which all

disequilibrium in foreign transactions is reflected in the balance of payments. Secondly, there is the assumption of a perfectly *flexible exchange rate* system, in which the exchange rate adjusts continuously so as to maintain balance of payments equilibrium. In principle, intermediate cases embodying both kinds of adjustments simultaneously also exist, but we shall follow tradition and deal with the two polar cases. Before proceeding, we should make it clear that our purpose in Part II is to incorporate international transactions into the macroeconomic model developed in Part I. It is not our intention to give a detailed discussion of international economics. There are may excellent text-books available which deal with this subject and the reader is referred to them for detailed discussion.[2]

2.   Domestic product market
We shall assume that the economy produces a single homogeneous good, the real aggregate demand for which is defined by

$$Z = C_d + I_d + G_d + X \tag{9.1}$$

where

C_d = real private consumption demand by domestic residents for the domestically produced good,

I_d = real private investment demand by domestic residents for the domestically produced good,

G_d = real domestic government expenditure on the domestically produced good,

X = real export demand.

Letting C_m denote the real quantity of consumption goods imported, its real volume measured in terms of the domestic good is $C_m QE/P$ where

P = domestic price level,

Q = foreign price level,

E = exchange rate, defined to be the price of foreign exchange in terms of domestic currency.

The quantity QE measures the price of foreign goods in terms of domestic currency, so that P/QE measures the domestic price level relative to that abroad. In a single good economy this will also measure the terms of trade. Thus total real domestic private consumption, measured in terms of the domestic good as numeraire is

$$C = C_d + C_m \frac{QE}{P}.$$

Similarly, total real domestic private investment and total real domestic government expenditure, both with the domestic good as numeraire, are

$$I = I_d + I_m \frac{QE}{P}$$

$$G = G_d + G_m \frac{QE}{P}.$$

Noting that total real imports M are given by

$$M = C_m + I_m + G_m$$

aggregate demand in an open economy can be written in the equivalent form

$$Z = C + I + G + X - \frac{QE}{P} M \tag{9.2}$$

or defining M' say to be $\frac{QE}{P} M$, this in turn can be written as

$$Z = C + I + G + X - M'. \tag{9.2'}$$

Thus product market equilibrium in which demand Z equals output Y, can be expressed in the alternative forms

$$Y = C_d + I_d + G_d + X \tag{9.3}$$

$$Y = C + I + G + X - \frac{QEM}{P}. \tag{9.4}$$

Because of the fact that (9.3) is in terms of the domestic good only, whereas (9.4) is in terms of total demand functions and hence involves the relative price, the former is clearly the more convenient formulation. However, as many treatments use (9.4) (or a variant of it in which M' replaces QEM/P) we also present this version for the sake of completeness.

In expositing the basic static model, we shall retain, with only appropriate minor modifications, the simple consumption and investment functions used in Chapter 2. Specifically, we postulate

$$C_d = C_d(Y - T, QE/P) \qquad 0 < C_{d,1} < 1, C_{d,2} > 0 \tag{9.5a}$$

$$C_m = C_m(Y - T, QE/P) \qquad 0 < C_{m,1} < 1, C_{m,2} < 0 \tag{9.5b}$$

$$I_d = I_d(Y, r) \qquad I_{d,1} > 0, I_{d,2} < 0 \tag{9.6a}$$

$$I_m = I_m(Y, r) \qquad I_{m,1} > 0, I_{m,2} < 0 \tag{9.6b}$$

where $T(=$ real taxes$)$ is assumed to be fixed.

Equations (9.5) postulate that the consumptions of domestically produced goods and imported goods depend upon both the real domestic disposable income and the relative price level home and abroad. The fact that C_d and C_m are functions of the same variables is a consequence of the underlying assumption that the decisions to consume these two alternative consumption goods are made jointly, subject to the same budget constraint.

Strictly speaking, in introducing domestic prices, we should distinguish between (i) the price of domestically produced goods; (ii) the overall domestic price level, which will include a component reflecting imported goods. Since this distinction is not typically made in the basic models we are considering, we postpone further elaboration of this question until we develop the more detailed models in subsequent chapters.[3]

Investment expenditure on domestic and imported goods are both hypothesized to vary inversely with the domestic interest rate and positively with the level of real income. But for most purposes, it is convenient to combine C_d and I_d into real private domestic expenditure on domestically produced goods. Aggregating (9.5a) and (9.6a) this is defined by

$$H = H(Y, r, QE/P, T), \ 0 < H_1 < 1, H_2 < 0, H_3 > 0, H_4 < 0$$

(9.7)

Note that we have entered Y, T as separate arguments. The reason for doing so is to reflect the assumption that, whereas consumption depends upon disposable income $(Y - T)$, investment depends upon total income Y.

From the definition of M it follows that

$$M = C_m(Y - T, QE/P) + I_m(Y, r) + G_m.$$

If we treat G_m as an exogenous policy variable, it follows that the import demand function can be written as

$$M = M(Y, r, QE/P, T), \quad M_1 > 0, M_2 < 0, M_3 < 0, M_4 < 0.$$

(9.8)

That is, imports increase with domestic income but decrease with the domestic interest rate and relative prices. Note that as a consequence of its definition, M is specified to depend upon the same arguments as H, again reflecting the fact that these are jointly determined decision variables.

It is worth commenting, however, that this consistency is not always followed in the literature. It is common practice to define real private domestic expenditures on domestically produced goods as in (9.7) above and to postulate an import demand function of the form say

$$M = M(Y, QE/P)$$

(9.8')

This can be justified only if one makes very restrictive assumptions about the nature of the underlying import goods. For example, given the investment demand functions (9.6), imports must consist of only consumption goods.

The domestic country's exports are the imports of the rest of the world and are therefore determined by its import demand function. If we assume that this is of the form (9.8), with foreign income, tax, and interest rate in place of Y, T, r, and if we maintain our small country assumption which enables us to treat these as exogenous, the export function can be written as

$$X = X(QE/P) \qquad X' > 0.$$

(9.9)

Thus exports of the domestic economy are hypothesized to vary positively with relative prices, as of course one would expect.

Inserting these demand functions into (9.3), the domestic economy's *IS* curve can be written as

$$Y = H(Y, r, QE/P, T) + X(QE/P) + G_d. \qquad (9.10)$$

Alternatively defining

$$C = C_d + C_m \frac{QE}{P} \equiv C(Y - T, QE/P)$$

$$I = I_d + I_m \frac{QE}{P} \equiv I(Y, r, QE/P)$$

yields the equivalent relationship for the *IS* curve

$$\left. \begin{array}{l} Y = C(Y - T, QE/P) + I(Y, r, QE/P) + X(QE/P) \\[2mm] \quad - M'(Y, r, QE/P, T) + G \end{array} \right\} \qquad (9.10')$$

where M' is defined in (9.2) and the term QE/P in C and M' measures in part a substitution effect and in part an aggregation effect. In order to ensure that the economy's *IS* curve is downward sloping we require the restriction

$$1 > C_1 + I_1 - \frac{QE}{P} M_1.$$

3.   Domestic money market

The demand for real money balances follows the conventional form specified in Chapter 2

$$\frac{L^D}{P} = L(Y, r) \qquad L_1 > 0, \quad L_2 < 0. \qquad (9.11)$$

For simplicity, since we wish to abstract from a banking sector, we shall interpret this as referring to *base* money.

The nominal supply of the monetary base, in terms of the domestic currency, L, consists of two components

$$L = D + F \qquad (9.12)$$

where

   D = domestic component of the nominal money stock, expressed in terms of the domestic currency

   F = volume of foreign reserves, expressed in terms of the domestic currency.

That is, the reserves of the domestic banking system consist not only of the liabilities of the domestic central bank, D, but also of the liabilities of foreign central banks, through holding foreign reserves, F, (assumed to be held in the form of foreign currency).

Taking first differences of (9.12), it follows that

$$L = L_{-1} + \Delta D + \Delta F. \tag{9.13}$$

The change in the level of foreign reserves is by definition equal to the balance of payments, so that

$$\Delta F = B \tag{9.14}$$

where the balance of payments, B, is expressed in terms of the domestic currency.

Changes in the domestic component of the money supply, ΔD, are under the control of the domestic monetary authorities. In choosing ΔD they are constrained by the government budget constraint

$$\Delta D + \Delta A = PG_d + QEG_m - PT. \tag{9.15}$$

This is the simplified version of the constraint which abstracts from interest payments on outstanding debt. It asserts that the nominal government expenditure on domestic goods as well as imports less nominal tax receipts are financed either by printing money or by issuing new securities (ΔA), which we take to be variable interest rate bonds. For simplicity we shall assume that the monetary authorities adjust the domestic component of the monetary base according to:

$$\Delta D = -(1-s)\,\Delta F + \gamma \qquad 0 \leqslant s \leqslant 1 \tag{9.16}$$

Given (9.16), the budget constraint (9.15) implies a compensating adjustment in the quantity of government bonds outstanding.

Equation (9.16) asserts that the domestic monetary authorities engage in open market operations directed at offsetting any changes in the money supply originating from fluctuations in the balance of payments. This process is known as *sterilization* of the surplus (or deficit) in the balance of payments. The extent to which this is done is described by the parameter s. If $s = 0$ the monetary authorities completely sterilize a balance of payments surplus say ($\Delta F > 0$), by selling bonds on the open market to domestic residents, thereby reducing their own liabilities ΔD. If $s = 1$, no such offsetting adjustment is taking place. The parameter γ describes any exogenous changes in the money supply and thus can be used to characterize exogenous monetary policy.

Substituting for (9.14) and (9.16) into (9.13), equilibrium in the domestic money market is given by

$$L(Y, r) = \frac{L_{-1} + sB + \gamma}{P}. \tag{9.17}$$

Equation (9.17) is in essence the open economy *LM* curve. Note that to the extent changes in the foreign reserves are *not* sterilized, any balance of payments surplus or deficit feeds into the domestic supply of money. Indeed, as we shall discuss in Chapter 10 below, this is one of the key channels through which foreign inflationary conditions may impinge on the domestic economy.

4. The balance of payments

The balance of payments summarizes the net flow of foreign reserves into or out of the country over a given specified period, as a result of its foreign transactions over that period. It is a *flow* concept. Basically, these transactions can be divided into *two* categories. First, there are the *current* account transactions. These include the foreign exchange earned and spent in the process of exporting and importing commodities; the provision or purchases of services such as shipping etc; and the receipt or payment of current income earned from the use of capital equipment abroad. This last item consists principally of interest income earned from, or paid, overseas. If one ignores these last two components, the balance of payments on current accounts consists of just the balance of trade, B_T. Expressed in terms of the domestic currency this equals

$$B_T = PX - QEM. \tag{9.18}$$

Much of the early literature dealing with the effects of devaluation on the balance of payments restricted itself to the balance of trade components. The 'elasticity approach', as it is called, was concerned with determining the conditions under which a devaluation, say, would lead to an improvement in the balance of payments, on the assumption that prices, income and interest rates remain fixed.[4] Setting $P = Q = 1$, and ignoring Y and r

$$B_T = X(E) - EM(E) \qquad X'(E) > 0, M'(E) < 0. \tag{9.18'}$$

Differentiating B_T with respect to E

$$\frac{dB_T}{dE} = X'(E) - EM'(E) - M(E). \tag{9.19}$$

Assuming that before devaluation the balance of payments (trade) is in equilibrium, so that

$$X(E) = EM(E)$$

(9.19) can be written in the elasticity form

$$\eta_X + \eta_M > 1 \tag{9.20}$$

where

$$\eta_X = \text{price elasticity of demand for exports} \left(= \frac{X'E}{X} \right)$$

$$\eta_M = \text{price elasticity of demand for imports} \left(= -\frac{M'E}{M} \right).$$

Thus (9.20) is the familiar Marshall–Lerner condition, asserting that a devaluation will lead to an improvement in the balance of trade, provided the sum of these two elasticities exceeds unity.[5]

Secondly, there is the balance on *capital* account. This consists of the net flow of foreign reserves resulting from domestic residents' purchases of foreign assets and reciprocally, foreigners' investments in the domestic economy. As a first approximation, this has traditionally been specified by the relationship[6]

$$K = K(Y, r - \bar{r}) \qquad K_1 > 0, K_2 > 0 \tag{9.21}$$

where
$K = $ net capital inflow
$\bar{r} = $ foreign (exogenous) rate of interest.

The function (9.21) is justified on the argument that if the domestic interest rate rises relative to that abroad, foreigners will be encouraged to invest domestically, while domestic residents will also be stimulated to do the same. The net effect of this will be to increase the flow of foreign exchange into the domestic economy. If the interest differential falls, the opposite adjustments will take place.

One limiting case which is often discussed is that of perfect capital mobility in which the domestic bond market is perfectly integrated with that in the rest of the world. In this case, the domestic interest rate is pegged to the foreign rate so that $r = \bar{r}$. Analytically, this is embodied in (9.21) by letting the partial derivative $K_2 \to \infty$.

The other variable, income, is usually justified on heuristic grounds. It is argued that if domestic income goes up this is likely to encourage investment and hence attract foreign capital.

In any event, while (9.21) represents the first attempts to specify capital flows, it has been criticized increasingly as being rather *ad hoc*. It also has the undesirable implication that if Y, r are constant, but not necessarily such that $K(Y, r) = 0$, positive or negative capital flows at a constant rate will occur, which ultimately would lead to an infinite accumulation or decumulation of foreign reserves. Thus (9.21) must be rejected for long-run analysis. The modern approach to capital flows, correctly views them as part of a portfolio adjustment process, which incorporates the underlying demand for the stocks of assets explicitly. This aspect of the theory is developed in detail in Chapters 11 and 12. For the moment, we shall work with (9.21) which, suppressing $\bar{r}$, we shall write more simply as

$$K = K(Y, r). \tag{9.21'}$$

Substituting (9.18) and (9.21') into the definition of the balance of payments, yields

$$B = PX(QE/P) - QEM(Y, r, QE/P, T) + K(Y, r). \tag{9.22}$$

At this point we need to distinguish the two polar assumptions we are making regarding the exchange rate system. Under the fixed exchange rate system E is fixed exogenously at $\bar{E}$ say in which case

$$B = PX(Q\bar{E}/P) - Q\bar{E}M(Y,r,Q\bar{E}/P,T) + K(Y,r) \qquad (9.22')$$

and by appropriate choice of units $\bar{E} = 1$. With flexible rates, the exchange rate adjusts endogenously to maintain the balance of payments in equilibrium so that (9.22) becomes

$$0 = PX(QE/P) - QEM(Y,r,QE/P,T) + K(Y,r). \qquad (9.22'')$$

Note then in this case $\Delta F \equiv 0$, in which case there is no feedback from the balance of payments to the domestic money supply.

5. Equilibrium with fixed prices: fixed exchange rate[7]

We shall assume for the present that the price level, both domestically and overseas, is fixed, so that with appropriate choice of units $P = Q = 1$. We shall also consider a fixed exchange rate regime, enabling us to treat E as exogenously given. Under these conditions, the simple model outlined in Sections 2–4 can be summarized as:

$$Y - H(Y,r,E,T) - X(E) - G_d = 0 \qquad (9.23a)$$
$$0 < H_1 < 1, \quad H_2 < 0, \quad H_3 > 0, \quad H_4 < 0, \quad X' > 0$$

$$- L(Y,r) + (L_{-1} + sB + \gamma) = 0 \qquad (9.23b)$$

$$B - X(E) + EM(Y,r,E,T) - K(Y,r) = 0 \qquad (9.23c)$$
$$0 < M_1 < 1, \quad M_2 < 0, \quad M_3 < 0, \quad M_4 < 0.$$

Equations (9.23a)–(9.23c) provide three equations which can be solved to determine the three endogenous variables Y, r, B. The effects of changes in the various policy variables can then be derived by taking differentials of the system. We shall consider the effects of three policy variables; government expenditure on domestic goods, G_d, exogenous monetary policy γ, and the exchange rate E, the incremental effects of which are contained in

$$\begin{pmatrix} 1 - H_1 & -H_2 & 0 \\ L_1 & -L_2 & s \\ (EM_1 - K_1) & (EM_2 - K_2) & 1 \end{pmatrix} \begin{pmatrix} dY \\ dr \\ dB \end{pmatrix} = \begin{pmatrix} dG_d + (H_3 + X')dE \\ -d\gamma \\ (X' - EM_3 - M)dE \end{pmatrix} \qquad (9.24)$$

In order to sign the determinant, D_1 say, of the matrix on the left hand side of (9.24) (the Jacobian of the system), we introduce one mild restriction

$$EM_1 - K_1 > 0. \qquad (9.25)$$

This asserts that the increase in imports resulting from an increase in income outweighs the possible inflow of capital, so that *ceteris paribus* the net effect of an increase in domestic income, is a deterioration in the balance of payments. With this restriction

$$D_1 = -L_2(1 - H_1) - H_2 L_1$$

$$-s[H_2(EM_1 - K_1) + (EM_2 - K_2)(1 - H_1)] > 0.$$

The various multipliers included in (9.24) are as follows:

$$\frac{\partial Y}{\partial G_d} = \frac{-[L_2 + s(EM_2 - K_2)]}{D_1} > 0;$$

$$\left. \frac{\partial r}{\partial G_d} = \frac{L_1 + s(EM_1 - K_1)}{D_1} > 0 \quad \right\} \quad (9.26a)$$

$$\frac{\partial B}{\partial G_d} = \frac{-L_1(EM_2 - K_2) + L_2(EM_1 - K_1)}{D_1} \gtrless 0$$

$$\frac{\partial Y}{\partial \gamma} = \frac{-H_2}{D_1} > 0; \quad \frac{\partial r}{\partial \gamma} = \frac{-(1 - H_1)}{D_1} < 0$$

$$\left. \frac{\partial B}{\partial \gamma} = \frac{(1 - H_1)(EM_2 - K_2) + H_2(EM_1 - K_1)}{D_1} < 0 \quad \right\} \quad (9.26b)$$

$$\frac{\partial Y}{\partial E} = \frac{-\omega s H_2 - (H_3 + X')[L_2 + s(EM_2 - K_2)]}{D_1}$$

$$\frac{\partial r}{\partial E} = \frac{-s(1 - H_1)\omega + (H_3 + X')[s(EM_1 - K_1) + L_1]}{D_1} \quad \left. \right\} \quad (9.26c)$$

$$\frac{\partial B}{\partial E} = \frac{\omega[-L_2(1 - H_1) - H_2 L_1]}{D_1}$$

$$+ \frac{(H_3 + X')[-L_1(EM_2 - K_2) + L_2(EM_1 - K_1)]}{D_1}$$

where $\quad \omega = X' - EM_3 - M.$

If initially the trade balance is zero $(X = EM)$,

$$\text{sgn } \omega = \text{sgn } [\eta_X + \eta_M - 1]$$

so that $\omega \gtrless 0$, according to whether or not the Marshall–Lerner condition is met. The results may be summarized as follows. An increase in government expenditure (with a bond-financed deficit) will increase the level of domestic income and the domestic rate of interest. Given the restriction (9.25), the former of these effects will tend to create a balance of payments deficit. At the same time, the increase in interest rate will both discourage imports and stimulate the capital inflow, thereby causing a balance of payments surplus. As a consequence the net impact on the balance of payments is ambiguous, as indicated in (9.26a).

An exogenous increase in the supply of money domestically will stimulate domestic income and reduce the domestic rate of interest. Both of these effects will contribute to an unambiguous deterioration in the balance of payments.

As long as $s \neq 0$, so that some foreign reserves are feeding into the domestic money supply, the effect of a devaluation on the domestic economy depends in part on the Marshall–Lerner condition. If this is satisfied, a devaluation will increase the level of income unambiguously, while its effect on the domestic interest rate is indeterminate. Its impact on the balance of payments is also ambiguous; indeed it is now possible for a devaluation to lead to an improvement in the balance of payments even if the Marshall–Lerner condition is violated.

As mentioned above, one case which is often discussed in the literature is that of perfect capital mobility. Formally this is obtained by letting $K_2 \to \infty$. In this case the various multipliers become

$$\frac{\partial Y}{\partial G_d} = \frac{1}{1 - H_1} > 0; \quad \frac{\partial r}{\partial G_d} = 0; \quad \frac{\partial B}{\partial G_d} = \frac{L_1}{s(1 - H_1)} > 0 \qquad (9.27\text{a})$$

$$\frac{\partial Y}{\partial \gamma} = 0; \quad \frac{\partial r}{\partial \gamma} = 0; \quad \frac{\partial B}{\partial \gamma} = -\frac{1}{s} < 0 \qquad (9.27\text{b})$$

$$\frac{\partial Y}{\partial E} = \frac{(H_3 + X')}{1 - H_1} > 0; \quad \frac{\partial r}{\partial E} = 0; \quad \frac{\partial B}{\partial E} = \frac{L_1(H_3 + X')}{s(1 - H_1)} > 0. \qquad (9.27\text{c})$$

The government expenditure multiplier is simply

$$\frac{1}{1 - H_1} = \frac{1}{1 - C_1 + QEM_1/P - I_1}$$

and equals the elementary 'small country open economy' multiplier which abstracts from any monetary feedbacks; see e.g. Takayama (1972). The effect on the interest rate is zero, an immediate consequence of the fact that the domestic interest rate is determined abroad. The balance of payments, on the other hand, will increase. The reason is that the increase in income generated by the increase in government expenditure will raise the demand for money. With the domestic rate of interest fixed, the only way equilibrium can be restored to the money market is if the balance of payments surplus is increased.

The effect of an increase in domestic monetary expansion will have no effect on the domestic interest rate and hence no effect on the domestic level of income. This confirms the well known result that under perfect capital mobility and fixed exchange rates, a small country can have no independent monetary policy. Any exogenous increase in the money supply is exactly offset by an equal outflow of capital, reducing the level of the balance of payments, but leaving the domestic money supply fixed.

The impact of a devaluation has an unambiguously expansionary impact on the level of domestic income, while simultaneously creating a balance of payments surplus. The reason is that with r fixed abroad, the increase in aggregate demand resulting from the devaluation must be accompanied by an increase in output. This in turn increases the transactions demand for money, which can only be accommodated provided the balance of payments surplus is increased.

6.   Equilibrium with fixed prices: flexible exchange rate

We shall now consider the other extreme where the exchange rate is perfectly flexible, and adjusts continually to ensure a zero balance of payments. We shall maintain the assumption of fixed prices both domestically and overseas, again setting $P = Q = 1$. Strictly speaking, in a world of flexible exchange rates, this is a somewhat anomalous assumption. One component of the domestic price level is the price of imported goods (in domestic currency) and if this is allowed to fluctuate, the domestic price level itself should be variable. However, as this assumption is made in much of the early literature we are reviewing, we too shall invoke it for illustrative purposes. It can be justified, at least in the short run, by appealing to lags in price adjustment.

The simple model now becomes

$$Y - H(Y, r, E, T) - X(E) - G_d = 0 \tag{9.28a}$$

$$-L(Y, r) + L_{-1} + \gamma = 0 \tag{9.28b}$$

$$-X(E) + EM(Y, r, E, T) - K(Y, r) = 0 \tag{9.28c}$$

the endogenous variables of which are now Y, r, E. The differential of the system in response to policy changes $dG_d, d\gamma$ is now given by

$$\begin{pmatrix} 1 - H_1 & -H_2 & -(H_3 + X') \\ -L_1 & -L_2 & 0 \\ (EM_1 - K_1) & (EM_2 - K_2) & -[X' - EM_3 - M] \end{pmatrix} \begin{pmatrix} dY \\ dr \\ dE \end{pmatrix} = \begin{pmatrix} dG_d \\ -d\gamma \\ 0 \end{pmatrix} \tag{9.29}$$

while the Jacobian of (9.29) is

$$D_2 = [L_2(1 - H_1) + L_1 H_2] [X' - EM_3 - M]$$
$$+ (H_3 + X') [L_1(EM_2 - K_2) - L_2(EM_1 - K_1)]$$

and in general cannot be signed unambiguously. Note that D_2 is precisely the negative of the term appearing in the numerator of $\partial B/\partial E$, given in (9.26c). Thus, if we assume that in the associated fixed exchange rate system a devaluation will have its conventional positive impact on the balance of payments,

$$D_2 < 0.$$

The effects of changes in the two policy variables, G_d, γ are thus given by

$$\frac{\partial Y}{\partial G_d} = \frac{L_2 \omega}{D_2}; \quad \frac{\partial r}{\partial G_d} = \frac{-L_1 \omega}{D_2},$$

$$\frac{\partial E}{\partial G_d} = \frac{-L_1(EM_2 - K_2) + L_2(EM_1 - K_1)}{D_2} \tag{9.30a}$$

$$\frac{\partial Y}{\partial \gamma} = \frac{(H_3 + X')(EM_2 - K_2) + H_2 \omega}{D_2};$$

$$\frac{\partial r}{\partial \gamma} = \frac{(1 - H_1)\omega - (H_3 + X')(EM_1 - K_1)}{D_2} \tag{9.30b}$$

$$\frac{\partial E}{\partial \gamma} = \frac{H_2(EM_1 - K_1) + (1 - H_1)(EM_2 - K_2)}{D_2} > 0$$

Provided the Marshall–Lerner condition is satisfied, ($\omega > 0$), an expansion of government expenditure will raise the level of both domestic income and the rate of interest. The effect on the exchange rate, however, is indeterminate. Under the same conditions on ω, an expansion in the domestic money supply will raise domestic income, but have an indeterminate effect on the domestic rate of interest. The net effect of the increase in income together with the change in the rate of interest turns out to lead to a downward pressure on the balance of payments, through increased imports and/or reduced capital inflows. The consequence of this is an unambiguous devaluation of the domestic currency. In fact the devaluation will occur irrespective of whether or not the Marshall–Lerner condition holds.

With perfect capital mobility

$$\frac{\partial Y}{\partial G_d} = 0; \quad \frac{\partial r}{\partial G_d} = 0 \quad \frac{\partial E}{\partial G_d} = \frac{-1}{(H_3 + X')} < 0 \tag{9.31a}$$

$$\frac{\partial Y}{\partial \gamma} = \frac{1}{L_1} > 0, \quad \frac{\partial r}{\partial \gamma} = 0 \quad \frac{\partial E}{\partial \gamma} = \frac{(1 - H_1)}{(H_3 + X')L_1} > 0. \tag{9.31b}$$

Note that in this limiting case fiscal policy is ineffective in controlling the level of domestic income. The reason is that with the rate of interest determined abroad, the level of income is determined solely by the domestic money supply; see (9.28b). As a consequence of domestic output being independent of fiscal policy, an increase in G_d must be met by a reduction in private demand for domestic goods. With r fixed, this can occur only through a revaluation of the domestic currency, inducing a substitution of foreign for domestic goods.

An expansionary monetary policy, on the other hand, by raising income increases domestic demand H, but by a smaller amount. In order to restore equilibrium, further stimulus for the demand for the domestic product is required and this is achieved by a devaluation of the domestic currency.

7. The assignment problem

Originating with the early contributions by Mundell (1962, 1964), much of the discussion of monetary and fiscal policy in an open economy has centred around the so-called 'assignment problem'. In its simplest form this problem can be formulated as follows. Suppose that the policy makers have two separate policy targets which they wish to achieve. Suppose also that they have available to them two policy instruments which they can control to achieve their two objectives. The question, as posed originally by Mundell, is whether or not it is possible to assign *one* target to *one* instrument in such a way that the target variables will ultimately converge to their desired values, irrespective of the speed with which the instruments are adjusted.

The advantage of such an assignment, if it exists, is that it permits the decentralization of decision making. Each decision maker need focus on only one objective — his assigned target — and on one instrument, which he adjusts in some assigned direction whenever the target is not at its chosen value. Because of the imperfect information with which policy makers typically operate, it is obviously desirable for each decision maker to focus his attention on only one target variable, rather than having to consider all objectives simultaneously. For fairly apparent reasons, the assignment problem had its genesis in policy discussions of the open economy. In such economies there are two central policy objectives which come immediately to mind:

(a) an internal objective, such as the level of income;

(b) an external objective, such as the balance of payments.

While there are many policy variables, again two main ones stand out — monetary policy and fiscal policy. Phrased in the context of an open economy, the assignment problem asks whether it is possible to direct one of the policy variables, say fiscal policy, to the internal objective and the other policy variable to the external target in such a way that a stable adjustment to the desired target values is assured.

But despite the fact that the assignment discussion has taken place almost entirely within the internal—external balance framework, it is a general kind of question that could be asked about any economy in which more than one policy objective is stipulated. For example, one could consider the problem of assigning monetary and fiscal policies to the twin policy goals of inflation and unemployment; or to controlling the level and distribution of income etc.

Before applying the analysis to the specific open economy discussed in Sections 1—6 of this chapter, we shall first consider the assignment rules in general terms. These can then be applied to the specific problem of internal and external balance.

Consider the two policy instruments X_1, X_2 and the two target variables Y_1, Y_2. At any point of time, it is assumed that the system can be solved uniquely for Y_1, Y_2 in terms of X_1, X_2 (and vice versa) so that

$$Y_1 = F(X_1, X_2) \qquad (9.32a)$$

$$Y_2 = G(X_1, X_2) \tag{9.32b}$$

Equations (9.32) are typical reduced form solutions, expressing the endogenous variables in terms of the exogenous variables. These are taken to be purely *static* relationships. The short-run equilibria we have been considering throughout this chapter, can, in principle, be solved in this form. The decision makers are assumed to know the *signs* of the partial derivatives F_1, F_2, G_1, G_2, but *not* their magnitudes. Again this is the information normally provided by the kind of comparative static analysis we have been undertaking.

Let us assume that the policy maker has some specified goals $\bar{Y}_1, \bar{Y}_2$. Corresponding to them are values of the policy variables $\bar{X}_1, \bar{X}_2$, satisfying

$$Y_1 = F(X_1, X_2) \tag{9.32a'}$$

$$Y_2 = G(X_1, X_2) \tag{9.32b'}$$

Choosing these values of the policy instruments ensures that the target objectives will be met.

Suppose for the moment we postulate a general or centralized policy adjustment rule of the form

$$\dot{X}_1 = \alpha_{11}(Y_1 - \bar{Y}_1) + \alpha_{12}(Y_2 - \bar{Y}_2) \tag{9.33a}$$

$$\dot{X}_2 = \alpha_{21}(Y_1 - \bar{Y}_1) + \alpha_{22}(Y_2 - \bar{Y}_2) \tag{9.33b}$$

As they are written, equations (9.33) assert that *both* policy variables X_1, X_2 are adjusted in accordance with the discrepancies of *both* target variables from their respective goals. A policy assignment in the sense discussed above is obtained by setting either α_{11} and $\alpha_{22} = 0$, or α_{12} and $\alpha_{21} = 0$.

Because of (9.32), Y_1, Y_2 are functions of the policy varibles X_1, X_2. Linearizing (9.33) about the equilibrium defined in (9.32') yields

$$\dot{X}_1 = \alpha_{11}[F_1(X_1 - \bar{X}_1) + F_2(X_2 - \bar{X}_2)]$$
$$\quad + \alpha_{12}[G_1(X_1 - \bar{X}_1) + G_2(X_2 - \bar{X}_2)]$$
$$\dot{X}_2 = \alpha_{21}[F_1(X_1 - \bar{X}_1) + F_2(X_2 - \bar{X}_2)]$$
$$\quad + \alpha_{22}[G_1(X_1 - \bar{X}_1) + G_2(X_2 - \bar{X}_2)],$$

where the partial derivatives F_i, G_i are evaluated at the equilibrium $(\bar{X}_1, \bar{X}_2)$. Letting $x_1 = X_1 - \bar{X}_1, x_2 = X_2 - \bar{X}_2$, the adjustment system can be written in *deviation* form as

$$\begin{pmatrix} \dot{x}_1 \\ \dot{x}_2 \end{pmatrix} = \begin{pmatrix} \alpha_{11}F_1 + \alpha_{12}G_1 & \alpha_{11}F_2 + \alpha_{12}G_2 \\ \alpha_{21}F_1 + \alpha_{22}G_1 & \alpha_{21}F_2 + \alpha_{22}G_2 \end{pmatrix} \begin{pmatrix} x_1 \\ x_2 \end{pmatrix} \tag{9.34}$$

This equation describes the adjustment of the system in the neighbourhood of equilibrium when *both* policy variables are adjusted simultaneously to *both* targets.

The necessary and sufficient condition for the linearized system to be stable is that

(i) $\text{tr } \Delta < 0$

(ii) $\det \Delta > 0$

where tr denotes trace, det denotes determinant, and Δ denotes the matrix of coefficients in (9.34). Thus in general (9.34) is stable if and only if[8]

$$\alpha_{11} F_1 + \alpha_{12} G_1 + \alpha_{21} F_2 + \alpha_{22} G_2 < 0 \tag{9.35a}$$

$$(\alpha_{11}\alpha_{22} - \alpha_{12}\alpha_{21})(F_1 G_2 - F_2 G_1) > 0. \tag{9.35b}$$

We have assumed that the policy maker knows the signs of F_i, G_i. Suppose, without loss of generality, these are all positive. The question is can we set either $\alpha_{12} = \alpha_{21} = 0$ or $\alpha_{11} = \alpha_{22} = 0$ and have both (9.35a), (9.35b) met?

Consider the first assignment. If $\alpha_{12} = \alpha_{21} = 0$, (9.35a) will be met for *any* arbitrary *negative* values α_{11}, α_{22}. Moreover for these chosen arbitrary negative values, (9.35b) will be met provided $(F_1 G_2 - F_2 G_1) > 0$. In this case the adjustment of the system will be stable for all magnitudes of the adjustment speeds $\alpha_{11} < 0, \alpha_{22} < 0$.

Alternatively, setting $\alpha_{11} = \alpha_{22} = 0$, (9.35a) will hold for any arbitrary negative values of α_{12}, α_{21}. For these chosen values, (9.36b) will be satisfied provided $(F_1 G_2 - F_2 G_1) < 0$. In this case the adjustment of the system will be stable irrespective of the magnitude of the adjustment speeds α_{12}, α_{21}.

Since one of these two cases *must* obtain, a stable assignment is possible. Under our assumptions $F_i > 0, G_i > 0$, the stable assignment is as follows

(a) if $F_1 G_2 - F_2 G_1 > 0$

$$\left.\begin{array}{ll} \dot{X}_1 = \alpha_{11}(Y_1 - \bar{Y}_1) & \alpha_{11} < 0 \\ \dot{X}_2 = \alpha_{22}(Y_2 - \bar{Y}_2) & \alpha_{22} < 0 \end{array}\right\} \tag{9.36}$$

(b) if $F_1 G_2 - F_2 G_1 < 0$

$$\left.\begin{array}{ll} \dot{X}_1 = \alpha_{12}(Y_2 - \bar{Y}_2) & \alpha_{12} < 0 \\ \dot{X}_2 = \alpha_{21}(Y_1 - \bar{Y}_1) & \alpha_{21} < 0. \end{array}\right\} \tag{9.37}$$

If the signs of any of the partial derivatives F_i, G_i are negative, then the corresponding direction of adjustment would need to be reversed. But an assignment such as (a) or (b) can always be found. If a sufficient number of the F_i, G_i are indeterminate in sign, a stable assignment which is independent of speeds of adjustment cannot be specified without additional information. An example of this is given in Section 8.

These assignment rules can be given an intuitive interpretation. The condition

$$F_1 G_2 - F_2 G_1 > 0$$

can be written as (assuming $F_i > 0, G_i > 0$)

$$\frac{\partial Y_1/\partial X_1}{\partial Y_2/\partial X_1} > \frac{\partial Y_1/\partial X_2}{\partial Y_2/\partial X_2}.$$

This asserts that the first instrument is relatively more effective in influencing the first target than is instrument two. In other words X_1 has a *comparative advantage* in influencing target Y_1. Likewise if $F_1 G_2 - F_2 G_1 < 0$, X_2 has the comparative advantage with respect to the first target variable Y_1. Thus the assignment rule asserts that a stable adjustment will be achieved by assigning each instrument to the target with respect to which it has a comparative advantage. This rule has become known as the *Principle of Effective Market Classification* (PEMC), Mundell (1962, 1964).

Recently Patrick (1973) has attempted to extend this two instrument – two target policy assignment problem to more general cases. Unfortunately no such simple general assignment propositions emerge. More detailed information of the structure of the system is required before a stable convergence can be assured.

8. Assignments of instruments to targets in an open economy

We now apply the PEMC discussed in Section 7 to the assignment of instruments in the small open economy. We shall consider the fixed and flexible exchange rate regimes in turn.

A. *Fixed exchange rate*

We assume that the policy makers have two objectives; an internal objective expressed by some level of income $\bar{Y}$ which is desirable, and an external objective, which is described by a target level of the balance of payments $\bar{B}$. We shall consider the two policy variables, government expenditure G_d, and monetary policy γ, and consider how these should be assigned so as to ensure a stable adjustment to $(\bar{Y}, \bar{B})$.

The short-run solution to the fixed rate system can be viewed as yielding solutions for Y, B of the form

$$Y = Y(G_d, \gamma) \tag{9.38a}$$

$$B = B(G_d, \gamma) \tag{9.38b}$$

where the partial derivatives $\partial Y/\partial G_d$, $\partial Y/\partial \gamma$, $\partial B/\partial G_d$, $\partial B/\partial \gamma$ are given in (9.26). Following (9.34), the general policy adjustment rule can be expressed as

$$\begin{pmatrix} \dot{G}_d \\ \dot{\gamma} \end{pmatrix} = \begin{pmatrix} \alpha_{11} \partial Y/\partial G_d + \alpha_{12} \partial B/\partial G_d & \alpha_{11} \partial Y/\partial \gamma + \alpha_{12} \partial B/\partial \gamma \\ \alpha_{21} \partial Y/\partial G_d + \alpha_{22} \partial B/\partial G_d & \alpha_{21} \partial Y/\partial \gamma + \alpha_{22} \partial B/\partial \gamma \end{pmatrix} \begin{pmatrix} G_d - \bar{G}_d \\ \gamma - \bar{\gamma} \end{pmatrix} \tag{9.39}$$

where $(\bar{G}_d, \bar{\gamma})$ are the values of the instruments which correspond to the equilibrium values of the target variables $(\bar{Y}, \bar{B})$; see (9.32').

Given the signs of the partial derivatives $\partial Y/\partial G_d$ etc., it is clear that the trace of the matrix of coefficients in (9.39) will certainly be negative if one sets

$$\alpha_{11} < 0, \quad \alpha_{22} > 0, \quad \alpha_{12} = \alpha_{21} = 0.$$

Furthermore, from (9.26) we can show

$$\frac{\partial Y}{\partial G_d}\frac{\partial B}{\partial \gamma} - \frac{\partial Y}{\partial \gamma}\frac{\partial B}{\partial G_d} = \frac{(EM_2 - K_2)}{D_1} < 0 \tag{9.40}$$

in which case with the α_{ij} chosen as above, the determinant of the matrix will certainly be positive.

Thus a stable assignment is obtained by setting

$$\dot{G}_d = \alpha_{11}(Y - \bar{Y}) \qquad \alpha_{11} < 0 \tag{9.41a}$$

$$\dot{\gamma} = \alpha_{22}(B - \bar{B}) \qquad \alpha_{12} > 0. \tag{9.41b}$$

In economic terms this says that a stable adjustment towards the objective will be ensured if: (i) the fiscal authorities decrease (increase) the rate of government expenditure whenever income is above (below) its target level, and (ii) the monetary authorities increase (decrease) the money supply whenever the balance of payments exceeds (is less than) its desired target.

This policy adjustment rule is often summarized by saying that under a fixed exchange rate system fiscal policy should be assigned to the internal objective; monetary policy to the external objective.

Note that the other assignment of targets to instruments,

$$\dot{G}_d = \alpha_{12}(B - \bar{B})$$

$$\dot{\gamma} = \alpha_{21}(Y - \bar{Y})$$

need not be unstable. Given the PEMC as summarized in (9.40), the determinantal stability condition requires

$$\alpha_{12}\alpha_{21} > 0$$

i.e. α_{12}, α_{21} be of the same sign. The trace condition requires

$$\alpha_{12}\frac{\partial B}{\partial G_d} + \alpha_{21}\frac{\partial Y}{\partial \gamma} < 0.$$

If $\partial B/\partial G_d > 0$, a stable adjustment is assured for any $\alpha_{12} < 0, \alpha_{21} < 0$. However, $\partial B/\partial G_d$ is indeterminate in sign and, in general, stability depends crucially on the speeds of adjustment with which policy makers adjust their respective instruments being chosen appropriately.

Further insight into the stable policy assignment (9.41) can be obtained from a graphical consideration of the adjustment rule.

The internal objective $\bar{Y}$ is achieved when

$$Y(G_d, \gamma) = \bar{Y} \tag{9.42a}$$

so that provided the function $Y(\quad)$ is continuous, there is a whole locus of combinations of G_d, γ for which the economy is in this state of internal balance. Differentiating (9.42a)

$$\left(\frac{\partial \gamma}{\partial G_d}\right)_{Y=\bar{Y}} = -\frac{\partial Y/\partial G_d}{\partial Y/\partial \gamma} < 0 \tag{9.43a}$$

so that when this locus is graphed in $G_d - \gamma$ space, it has a negative slope. Fiscal expansion must be accompanied by monetary contraction if the desired level of income $\bar{Y}$ is to be maintained.

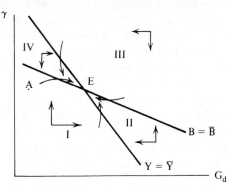

Fig. 9.1 *Stable assignment: fixed exchange rate*
Region I: domestic recession, balance of payments surplus
     II: domestic excess demand, balance of payments surplus
    III: domestic excess demand, balance of payments deficit
    IV: domestic recession, balance of payments deficit.

Likewise the external objective is achieved when

$$B(G_d, \gamma) = \bar{B} \tag{9.42b}$$

so again there is a whole locus of combinations of the policy variables which will ensure the attainment of external balance. The slope of this curve in $G_d - \gamma$ space is

$$\left(\frac{\partial \gamma}{\partial G_d}\right)_{B=\bar{B}} = -\frac{\partial B/\partial G_d}{\partial B/\partial \gamma} \gtrless 0 \tag{9.43b}$$

which is of either sign, due to the fact that $\partial B/\partial G_d \gtrless 0$. In any event, because of the PEMC, its slope is less negative than that of (9.43a).

These two equilibrium curves are shown in Figure 9.1 where to be specific we have drawn the external balance curve, $B = \bar{B}$, with a negative slope. This, however, is no restriction and the same conclusions obtain if it has a positive slope. These curves cut the $G_d - \gamma$ plane into four regions having the characteristics indicated in Figure 9.1. For example, Region 1, which lies below both the YY curve and BB curve, is one of domestic recession and balance of payments surplus. With $Y < \bar{Y}$ and $B > \bar{B}$, the adjustment rule (9.41) calls for both domestic government expenditure and domestic money supply to be increased. This is indicated by the direction of the arrow in Figure 9.1. The other regions require the policy variables to be adjusted in the indicator direction.

To illustrate the adjustment process, suppose the economy is initially at point A in region 1. The simultaneous expansion of both monetary and fiscal policy will move it into Region IV, in which the initial domestic recession is now accompanied by a balance of payments deficit. This has been created largely by the capital outflow resulting from the lower domestic interest rate, which in turn is a consequence of the initial expansionary monetary policy. To correct this situation now requires the expansionary fiscal policy to be accompanied by a contractionary monetary policy, thereby adjusting the system towards E. It is possible that this adjustment will proceed monotonically, so that the system remains in Region IV. Alternatively in the process of transition it may move out of IV to say III and then II. But in any event, it will ultimately converge to the equilibrium level.

It should be clearly understood that the reason we have found a stable assignment so easily, stems largely from the simplicity of the model and the fact that most of the relevant partial derivatives in (9.26) are determinate in sign. As soon as one complicates the model so that these effects become ambiguous, a stable assignment is much less readily apparent; see Levin (1972), Helliwell (1969).

B. Flexible exchange rate

The traditional discussion of this case views the external objective as being some desired target level of the exchange rate $\bar{E}$. It is not so clear why policy makers should be particularly concerned with this as a policy objective, but for illustrative purposes we shall treat this as the external target variable.

The short-run solutions to the flexible case can be expressed as

$$Y = Y(G_d, \gamma)$$

$$E = E(G_d, \gamma)$$

with the adjustments of the policy variables being

$$\begin{pmatrix} \dot{G_d} \\ \dot{\gamma} \end{pmatrix} = \begin{pmatrix} \alpha_{11} \dfrac{\partial Y}{\partial G_d} + \alpha_{12} \dfrac{\partial E}{\partial G_d} & \alpha_{11} \dfrac{\partial Y}{\partial \gamma} + \alpha_{12} \dfrac{\partial E}{\partial \gamma} \\ \alpha_{21} \dfrac{\partial Y}{\partial G_d} + \alpha_{22} \dfrac{\partial E}{\partial G_d} & \alpha_{21} \dfrac{\partial Y}{\partial \gamma} + \alpha_{22} \dfrac{\partial E}{\partial \gamma} \end{pmatrix} \begin{pmatrix} G_d - \bar{G}_d \\ \gamma - \bar{\gamma} \end{pmatrix} \qquad (9.44)$$

In general, because of the ambiguities of the partial derivatives in (9.30), it is not possible to determine a stable assignment without introducing some additional information or restrictions. With perfect capital mobility, however, a stable assignment can be immediately determined from (9.31). The condition on the trace will be met by setting $\alpha_{11} = 0 = \alpha_{22}$, $\alpha_{12} > 0$, $\alpha_{21} < 0$.

Since in this limiting case

$$\frac{\partial Y}{\partial G_d}\frac{\partial E}{\partial \gamma} - \frac{\partial Y}{\partial \gamma}\frac{\partial E}{\partial G_d} > 0$$

the determinantal condition is also certainly met.

Thus a stable assignment is obtained by setting

$$\dot{G}_d = \alpha_{12}(E - \bar{E}) \qquad \alpha_{12} > 0 \tag{9.45a}$$

$$\dot{\gamma} = \alpha_{21}(Y - \bar{Y}) \qquad \alpha_{21} < 0. \tag{9.45b}$$

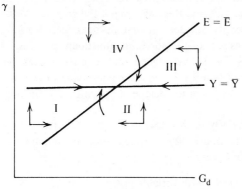

Fig. 9.2 *Stable assignment: flexible exchange rate and perfect capital mobility*

Region I: domestic recession, price of foreign exchange too high
II: domestic recession, price of foreign exchange too low
III: domestic excess demand, price of foreign exchange too low
IV: domestic excess demand, price of foreign exchange too high.

Note that in this case the assignment is reversed from the fixed rate case. Under flexible exchange rates (at least in the limiting case of perfect capital mobility) monetary policy should be directed to the internal objective and fiscal policy to the external goal. When income is below (above) its target, an expansionary (contractionary) monetary policy should be adopted. When the price of foreign exchange is too high ($E > \bar{E}$) government expenditure should be increased. This will increase the level of aggregate demand for domestic goods. With domestic output independent of the level of government expenditure (see (9.31a)), the effect is to force up the relative price of domestic goods; i.e. to lead to an upward revaluation of the domestic currency. Events are reversed when initially $E < \bar{E}$.

A graphical illustration of the stable policy assignment in the limiting case of perfect capital mobility is given in Figure 9.2. The dynamics of the adjustment from any initial point can be discussed as in the fixed rate case, but that exercise is left for the reader.

C.   *Some general comments*
        The application of the assignment problem to the problem of
achieving internal and external balance has given rise to a voluminous literature
since its first appearance by Mundell (1962, 1964); see e.g. Johnson (1966),
Jones (1968), Sohmen (1967), Cooper (1969), Takayama (1969), Levin
(1972).
        Virtually all of this literature assumes that the underlying economic
relations are all static. The only dynamics of the system are due to the adjustment of the policy instruments. It ignores the 'intrinsic' dynamics of the
system stemming from the fact that the financing of the government deficit
creates changes in the quantity of assets, or that a proper specification of
capital flows treats them as part of the portfolio adjustment process.[9] Moreover, as Aghevli and Borts (1973) have argued, once one recognizes the
inherent dynamics of the system it is much more reasonable to regard the
level of foreign reserves rather than the balance of payments as the appropriate external objective.
        We propose to return briefly to this issue in Chapter 11, after we have
developed a more complete model, which encompasses the dynamics of
capital flows and deficit financing.

9.   **Specification of model with variable prices**
        The simplest extension of the basic model which allows for a variable
price level is obtained by adding a domestic supply function. The complete
model thus becomes

$$Y = H(Y, r, QE/P, T) + X(QE/P) + G_d \qquad (9.10)$$

$$L(Y, r) = \frac{L_{-1} + sB + \gamma}{P} \qquad (9.17)$$

$$B = PX(QE/P) - QEM(Y, r, QE/P, T) + K(Y, r) \qquad (9.22)$$

$$P = S(Y) \qquad S'(Y) > 0 \qquad (9.46)$$

$$E = \bar{E} \text{ (fixed)} \quad \text{or} \quad B = 0 \text{ (flexible)}.$$

The new equation (9.46) is a simple supply function, specifying the price
level to be an increasing function of the level of output. Thus the four
equations (9.10), (9.17), (9.22) and (9.46) determine the four endogenous
variables Y, r, P, B (fixed exchange rate) or Y, r, P, E (flexible exchange rate).
        This system is a somewhat simplified version of the static model considered
by Krueger (1965), Helliwell (1969), Takayama (1969). It can be used to
analyse the kinds of questions discussed in earlier sections. In particular,
Helliwell (1969) has used it to consider the allocation of instruments to targets at some length. Rather than consider this model any further, we shall
proceed to develop in some detail an alternative short-run model which
focuses more on the rate of inflation, rathen than the price level. The
problems of monetary and fiscal policy, and their assignment can then be
discussed within this inflationary context.

10

IMPORTED INFLATION AND GOVERNMENT POLICIES IN A SHORT-RUN OPEN MACROECONOMIC MODEL

1.   Introduction[1]

With the recent acceleration of inflation throughout the Western world, the topic of 'imported inflation' has become an important one for many smaller economies. Policy makers and economists in these countries have begun to assess the extent to which their domestic inflation is being imported from abroad and to consider appropriate policy measures to deal with it. As a result of the interest the subject has generated, it has begun to receive detailed theoretical study by a number of economists.

Broadly speaking, one can distinguish two general approaches to this problem. First, there is the traditional Keynesian, or what might now more appropriately be referred to as the Keynes–Phillips approach; see e.g. Takayama (1969), Helliwell (1969) and more recently Turnovsky and Kaspura (1974) and Branson (1975). These models tend to be short run (or at least one period) and to focus usually on the price level rather than the rate of inflation (although in a one-period context these are essentially the same). Typically, the effects of fiscal and monetary policy are also studied in this literature, and indeed have received somewhat more attention than the imported inflation question. On the other hand, there is the recent 'Monetary' approach developed by Mundell (1971, 1972), Johnson (1973), Dornbusch (1973), and others.[2] This approach is in fact not new. Its origins can be traced back to David Hume's 'price-specie-flow' mechanism. It differs from the more familiar Keynesian approach in two essential respects. First, central to it is the notion that the balance of payments, being a flow of money, is basically a monetary phenomenon. Secondly, it tends to focus much more on stock rather than flow equilibrium relationships, and on the accumulation of assets, part of which takes place through the balance of payments.

In analysing the problem of imported inflation it is important to identify explicitly the various channels through which foreign inflation influences the domestic economy and to consider the feedbacks to which each gives rise. Only by considering the question within an integrated framework are we able to assess fully the significance of imported inflation and to discuss satisfactorily the relevant policy issues it raises.

The present chapter follows the first of the above approaches and analyses the question within the context of the conventional short-run Keynesian macroeconomic model. The model we use is an appropriate extension of that developed in Chapter 9. In Chapter 12 we present a longer-run dynamic analysis and at that time attempt to incorporate some of the monetarist notions.

2.   The basic model

The model makes several important simplifying assumptions. First, since we shall be concerned with short-run equilibrium we shall ignore technological change, as well as the growth of capital stock and other wealth effects. Secondly, the behavioural relationships are basically static, although certain elements of the model — namely the price adjustment equation, the government budget constraint, and the balance of payments adjustment — all impose an intrinsically dynamic structure on the system. In particular the fact that capital flows and monetary expansion involve changes in stocks is ignored in the analysis. Thirdly, the country is sufficiently competitive in the market for its imports to take the price of imports as given. On the other hand, we assume that export prices are determined in the domestic output market, being the same as the prices of domestically produced non-traded goods. This enables us to focus on a single price level of all domestically produced goods. While this is a limiting case, it does seem to approximate a multi-country situation where each country tends to import a large number of commodities, while being rather specialized in its exports.[3] Finally, exchange rates are assumed to be fixed, although Section 5 briefly treats the alternative flexible exchange rate case.

For simplicity we assume no domestic production of the imported good and no imported inputs. Given our assumption of export prices, equilibrium in the domestic output market is[4]

$$\left. \begin{aligned} Y &= H(Y, r - \pi, QE/P_1, u) + X(QE/P_1) + G_d \\ 0 &< H_1 < 1, \quad H_2 < 0, \quad H_3 > 0, \quad H_4 < 0, \quad X' > 0 \end{aligned} \right\} \quad (10.1)$$

where Y = real domestic output (income) in terms of the price of domestically produced goods;

H = real private domestic expenditure on domestically produced goods;

X = real exports of domestically produced goods;

G_d = real government expenditure on domestically produced goods;

r = domestic rate of interest;

π = expected overall rate of domestic inflation, so that $(r - \pi)$ is a measure of the real rate of interest;[5]

P_1 = market price of domestically produced goods (in terms of domestic currency);

Q = money price of foreign goods (in terms of foreign currency);

E = the price of foreign exchange in terms of domestic currency;
u = the domestic rate of income tax, taken to be constant.

There are several aspects of this equation which deserve comment. First, for the same reasons as in Chapter 9 (essentially aggregation reasons), we include u as a separate argument, rather than as a component of disposable income. Secondly, as we are analysing an inflationary situation, the rate of interest is introduced in real rather than nominal terms. Thirdly, the ratio of the price of foreign goods, in terms of domestic currency, to the price of domestically produced goods is included to reflect the possible substitution between domestic and foreign goods as their relative prices change. Fourthly, while the export function is written in terms of relative prices, with P_1 being determined domestically, we do not mean to imply that export prices are independent of foreign demand. On the contrary, foreign demand plays a crucial role in their determination. As is clear from equation (10.5) below, P_1 is determined partly by the total level of demand – which includes foreign demand – in the domestic output market and partly by import costs, which are also likely to reflect foreign demand conditions. Moreover, we could also introduce foreign demand explicitly into the export function, by specifying $X(EQ/P_1, Z)$ where Z measures foreign income and $X_2 > 0$. In this case Z would clearly play a role in determining P_1. However, as we are dealing with a country which is sufficiently small so as to take foreign demand Z as given, we choose to delete this as an argument, absorbing it in the function X.

In order to focus on current rates of inflation, rather than price levels, it is convenient to substitute[6]

$$P_1 = P_{1,-1}(1 + p_1) \tag{10.2a}$$

$$Q = Q_{-1}(1 + q) \tag{10.2b}$$

where lower case letters p_1, q, denote the current rates of inflation of domestically produced goods and foreign goods respectively, while the subscript -1 refers to the previous period. Without loss of generality we can define $P_{1,-1} = Q_{-1} = 1$ enabling us to rewrite (10.1) as

$$Y = H\left(Y, r - \pi, \frac{(1+q)E}{1+p_1}, u\right) + X\left(\frac{(1+q)E}{1+p_1}\right) + G_d \tag{10.1'}$$

The overall domestic price level P is a weighted average of the price of domestically produced goods, and the domestic price of foreign goods, their weights being the proportion of domestic absorption consisting of domestically produced goods and imports respectively. That is

$$P = \frac{P_1[H(Y, r - \pi, QE/P_1, u) + G_d] + QEM(Y, r - \pi, QE/P_1, u)}{H + G_d + M}$$

$$M_1 > 0, \quad M_2 < 0, \quad M_3 < 0, \quad M_4 < 0 \tag{10.3}$$

denotes the total volume of real imports. Note that since some portion of imports are investment goods, which are assumed to be interest elastic, $r - \pi$ is included as an argument of M; see Chapter 9.

Equation (10.3), while the true expression for P, is rather complicated and it is necessary for our subsequent work to approximate it with a simpler one. To this end we adopt the following argument. Since Y, u, and $r - \pi$ affect H and M in the same direction, while P_1 and QE have opposite effects, it seems reasonable that P will be much more sensitive to price changes than to changes in Y, u, or $r - \pi$. Indeed as a limiting case, if one assumes that the elasticity of import demand with respect to Y, u, or $(r - \pi)$ equals the corresponding elasticity of domestic expenditure on domestically produced goods, then $\partial P/\partial Y = \partial P/\partial u = \partial P/\partial(r - \pi) = 0$. Since there is no reason to suppose that there should be any systematic differences between corresponding elasticities, it does not seem unreasonable to assume that at an aggregate level they should be of roughly comparable magnitude. Certainly this assumption is not violently contradicted by any empirical evidence.

Hence, assuming that P is dominated by price effects, we approximate (10.3) by

$$P = C(P_1, QE) \tag{10.4}$$

where $C_1 > 0, C_2 > 0, C_1 + C_2 = 1$, and C is homogenous of degree one in its two arguments. Choosing units so that the exchange rate in the previous period E_{-1} is unity, it follows from the homogeneity of (10.4), together with the normalization $P_{1,-1} = Q_{-1} = 1$, that $P_{-1} = 1$. Hence, (10.4) can be written in terms of current rates of inflation as

$$1 + p = C[(1 + p_1), (1 + q)E] \tag{10.4'}$$

where p is defined analogously to p_1, q.

The rate of inflation of domestically produced goods is determined by the relationship

$$\left. \begin{array}{l} p_1 = \alpha_0 + \alpha_1 (Y - \bar{Y}) + \alpha_2 w + \alpha_3 \Delta(QE)/(QE)_{-1} \\ \alpha_1 > 0, \quad 0 \leqslant \alpha_2 \leqslant 1, \quad 0 \leqslant \alpha_3 \leqslant 1, \quad 0 \leqslant \alpha_1 + \alpha_2 \leqslant 1. \end{array} \right\} \tag{10.5}$$

Equations similar to this have formed the basis for many of the empirical studies investigating price determination in open economies.[7] It asserts that the percentage change in the price of domestically produced goods depends partly on demand pressures in the domestic output market, partly on changes in costs and partly on the relative competitive position of domestic producers *vis à vis* their foreign counterparts. The first effect is approximated by $(Y - \bar{Y})$, the deviation of actual output from its full employment level. As we are abstracting from imported inputs, and assuming the price of domestic inputs to grow at the same rate as that of output, p_1, the net effects of changes in costs on p_1 are measured by the percentage change in unit labour costs. In the absence of any change in labour productivity this is equal to the percentage change in domestic money wages w. The third effect is reflected by the term $\Delta(QE)/(QE)_{-1}$. In general any price increase overseas will increase the scope for domestic producers to raise prices without jeopardizing their competitive position.[8]

Following previous chapters, the percentage rate of change of domestic money wages are determined by an 'extended Phillips curve' of the form

$$w = \beta_0 + \beta_1 U + \beta_2 \pi \qquad \beta_1 < 0, \quad 0 \leqslant \beta_2 \leqslant 1. \tag{10.6}$$

That is, the rate of money wage inflation domestically depends partly upon labour market conditions, as reflected by the rate of unemployment U, and partly by the expected percentage change in the domestic cost of living. As argued in Chapter 5, in a short-run analysis such as this, it is reasonable to suppose that the state of excess demand in the domestic labour market will be closely related to the conditions in the domestic output market. Assuming a simple linear approximation

$$U = \delta_0 + \delta_1 (Y - \bar{Y}) \tag{10.7}$$

we can eliminate, w, U from equations (10.5), (10.6), (10.7) to obtain a single reduced form equation of the domestic wage–price sector. Given our normalizing assumptions on $P_{1,-1}, Q_{-1}, E_{-1}$ this can be expressed in the form

$$\left. \begin{array}{l} p_1 = a_0 + a_1 (Y - \bar{Y}) + a_2 [(1 + q)E - 1] + a_3 \pi \\[2mm] a_1 > 0, \quad 0 \leqslant a_2 \leqslant 1, \quad 0 \leqslant a_3 \leqslant 1, \quad 0 \leqslant a_2 + a_3 \leqslant 1 \end{array} \right\} \tag{10.8}$$

and with E constant ($= 1$), this simply reduces to

$$p_1 = a_0 + a_1 (Y - \bar{Y}) + a_2 q + a_3 \pi. \tag{10.8'}$$

Turning to the monetary sector, the demand for real money balances is of the form specified in Chapter 6, namely

$$\frac{L^d}{P} = L(Y, r, \pi) \quad L_1 > 0, \quad L_2 < 0, \quad L_3 < 0 \tag{10.9}$$

in which the demand for money varies inversely with the anticipated rate of inflation. Note that since the transactions demand for money is to finance imports as well as domestically produced goods, the relevant deflator is P, the overall domestic price level.

Following the discussion of Chapter 9, the nominal supply of money, L, consists of two components

$$L = D + F \tag{10.10}$$

where $D =$ the domestic component of the nominal money stock,
      $F =$ the volume of foreign reserves,
from which it follows that

$$L = L_{-1} + \Delta D + \Delta F. \tag{10.11}$$

In general changes in the domestic component of the money supply ΔD must satisfy the government budget constraint

$$\Delta D + \Delta A = P_1 G_d + QEG_m - uP_1 Y \tag{10.12}$$

where G_m denotes government imports and ΔA denotes the additional securities issued by the government to help finance its deficit. These are taken to be variable interest rate bonds. This is the simplified version of the government budget constraint which omits the interest payments on the government bonds outstanding. For the present short-run analysis this is not serious, but for the longer-run models of Chapters 11 and 12 this component becomes important and cannot be ignored.

For simplicity, and without essential loss of generality, we shall abstract from government imports, so that henceforth $G_m \equiv 0$. Hence analogous to Chapter 9 we specify the following equation for ΔD

$$\Delta D = \theta P_1 (G_d - uY) - (1-s)\Delta F + \gamma \qquad \left. \begin{array}{l} 0 \leqslant \theta \leqslant 1 \\[2mm] 0 \leqslant s \leqslant 1 \end{array} \right\} \tag{10.13}$$

with (10.12) implying a corresponding adjustment for ΔA. This equation postulates three factors which contribute to the change in the domestic component of the supply of money. First, the government finances a fraction θ of its deficit by the creation of new money. Secondly, the monetary authorities are assumed to engage in open market operations directed at offsetting changes in their holdings of foreign reserves. Thirdly, the parameter γ describes any exogenous changes in the money supply reflecting exogenous changes in monetary policy through open market operations.

Equilibrium in the money market is given by

$$L(Y, r, \pi) = \frac{L_{-1} + \theta P_1 (G_d - uY) + s\Delta F + \gamma}{P} \tag{10.14}$$

which in terms of rates of inflation becomes

$$L(Y, r, \pi) = \frac{L_{-1} + \theta(1 + p_1)(G_d - uY) + s\Delta F + \gamma}{1 + p}. \tag{10.14'}$$

To close the model we must explain $\Delta F \equiv B$, the balance of payments. This is just the sum of the balance of trade and net capital movements, both being valued in terms of domestic currency. Hence we write

$$B \equiv \Delta F = (1 + p_1)X\left(\frac{(1+q)E}{1+p_1}\right)$$

$$- (1+q)EM\left(Y, r - \pi, \frac{(1+q)E}{1+p_1}, u\right) + K(Y, r) \tag{10.15}$$

where $K_1 \geqslant 0$, $K_2 \geqslant 0$ and all other derivatives have been signed above. The first two terms together make up the balance of trade, while $K(Y, r)$ measures the capital inflow. The rationale for the function $K(Y, r)$ has been given in the previous chapter.[9]

Before writing down the complete system we must consider π, the expected rate of change of the overall domestic cost of living. As our analysis is strictly for one period, and as π is presumably determined by past events, such as the p_{t-1}, we can treat it as a given parameter.[10] A longer run analysis would require us to treat π as endogenous, in which case the system would have to be closed by postulating some expectations generating mechanism for π.

Thus the complete system is described by the set of equations

$$Y - H\left(Y, r - \pi, \frac{(1+q)E}{1+p_1}, u\right) - X\left(\frac{(1+q)E}{1+p_1}\right) - G_d = 0 \quad (10.16a)$$

$$L(Y, r, \pi) - \frac{L_{-1} + \theta(1+p_1)(G_d - uY) + sB + \gamma}{1+p} = 0 \quad (10.16b)$$

$$(1+p_1)X\left(\frac{(1+q)E}{1+p_1}\right) - (1+q)EM\left(Y, r - \pi, \frac{(1+q)E}{1+p_1}, u\right)$$

$$+ K(Y, r) - B = 0 \quad (10.16c)$$

$$a_0 + a_1(Y - \bar{Y}) + a_2[(1+q)E - 1] + a_3\pi - p_1 = 0 \quad (10.16d)$$

$$C[(1+p_1), (1+q)E] - (1+p) = 0. \quad (10.16e)$$

These equations define five relationships involving the five endogenous variables Y, r, p_1, p, and B ($= \Delta F$); the exogenous variables, E, L_{-1}, G_d, γ, q, u, π; and the constant parameters which characterize the system. Note that the model contains two measures of domestic inflation, one relating to domestically produced goods alone, the other to the overall domestic price level. Also, as long as the exchange rate does not change and given our choice of units, $E = 1$. However, as we do consider the effects of changing E in our policy discussion below, we prefer to include it explicitly throughout. While the Jacobian of the system (J) cannot be signed unambiguously, imposing the restrictions in (10.19) below, ensures that $J > 0$. Thus at any point of time t we can determine Y_t, r_t, p_{1t}, p_t and B_t in terms of the exogenous variables and given parameters.

3.   **The effects of imported inflation**

Examining the system (10.16) it can be seen that the rate of foreign inflation impinges directly on the system via four channels. First, an increase in q will lower the relative price of domestic goods, thereby raising demand for these goods. Secondly, it will affect the balance of payments, thereby directly influencing the domestic money supply. Thirdly, a rise in prices abroad will cause domestic producers to raise prices. Finally, an increase in the price of imported goods will, *ceteris paribus*, raise the overall cost of living p. We shall refer to these four channels as:

(i) the direct demand effect $(H^*(q))$;
(ii) the direct balance of payments effects $(B^*(q))$;
(iii) the direct price effects $(P^*(q))$;
(iv) the direct cost of living effects $(C^*(q))$.

As this section is devoted to studying the effects of changes in q, holding all other exogenous factors constant, we shall delete them from the functional relationships. Thus, for example, we may write the solution for p_1, in the form

$$p_1 = p_1 [H^*(q), B^*(q), P^*(q), C^*(q)] \qquad (10.17)$$

with similar solutions for Y, r, p, and B. Writing the solution in this form stresses the fact that q enters the system through the four channels enumerated above.

But it should be appreciated that by treating all foreign variables other than q as constant we are abstracting from any effects that a change in q may have on the foreign economy. Most important of these is its effect on the foreign interest rate. Typically one could expect an increase in the foreign rate of inflation to be accompanied by an increase in the foreign rate of interest. This will in turn create monetary effects which in a complete analysis should be discussed in conjunction with the direct foreign inflationary effects we are considering. This is particularly true in the long run after the foreign interest rate has had time to adjust. As a consequence this effect is taken into account in the steady-state analysis of Chapter 12.

Differentiating (10.17) with respect to q, we obtain

$$\frac{\partial p_1}{\partial q} = \frac{\partial p_1}{\partial H^*}\frac{\partial H}{\partial q} + \frac{\partial p_1}{\partial B^*}\frac{\partial B^*}{\partial q} + \frac{\partial p_1}{\partial P^*}\frac{\partial P^*}{\partial q} + \frac{\partial p_1}{\partial C^*}\frac{\partial C^*}{\partial q} \qquad (10.17')$$

with, again, similar equations holding for the other endogenous responses. This equation shows that the overall effect of an increase in the foreign rate of inflation on the system consists of the four direct effects, together with the resulting repercussions and feedbacks to which each gives rise. Thus, for example, $\partial H^*/\partial q$ measures the direct effect of an increase in q on demand, while $\partial p_1/\partial H^*$ reflects the impact of a unit increase in demand on the rate of inflation of domestically produced goods.

Differentiating the system of equations (10.16) with respect to q we obtain

$$
\begin{pmatrix}
1-H_1 & -H_2 & 0 & \lambda & 0 \\[2mm]
\omega & L_2 & \dfrac{-s}{1+p} & \rho & \phi \\[2mm]
K_1-(1+q)EM_1 & K_2-(1+q)EM_2 & -1 & \psi & 0 \\[2mm]
a_1 & 0 & 0 & -1 & 0 \\[2mm]
0 & 0 & 0 & C_1 & -1
\end{pmatrix}
\begin{pmatrix}
\dfrac{\partial Y}{\partial q} \\[2mm]
\dfrac{\partial r}{\partial q} \\[2mm]
\dfrac{\partial B}{\partial q} \\[2mm]
\dfrac{\partial p_1}{\partial q} \\[2mm]
\dfrac{\partial p}{\partial q}
\end{pmatrix}
=
\begin{pmatrix}
\dfrac{\partial H^*}{\partial q} \\[2mm]
0 \\[2mm]
-\dfrac{\partial B^*}{\partial q} \\[2mm]
-\dfrac{\partial P^*}{\partial q} \\[2mm]
-\dfrac{\partial C^*}{\partial q}
\end{pmatrix}
$$

$$(10.18)$$

where

$$\frac{\partial H^*}{\partial q} = \frac{(H_3+X')E}{1+p_1} > 0$$

$$\frac{\partial B^*}{\partial q} = E\left(X'-M-\frac{(1+q)EM_3}{(1+p_1)}\right)$$

$$\frac{\partial P^*}{\partial q} = a_2 E > 0$$

$$\frac{\partial C^*}{\partial q} = C_2 E > 0$$

$$\phi = \frac{L}{(1+p)^2} > 0, \quad \lambda = \left(\frac{1+q}{1+p_1}\right)\frac{\partial H^*}{\partial q}$$

$$\omega = L_1 + \frac{\theta u(1+p_1)}{1+p} > 0, \quad \rho = \frac{-\theta(G_d-uY)}{1+p}$$

$$\psi = \left(X-\frac{(1+q)EX'}{1+p_1}+\frac{(1+q)^2 E^2 M_3}{(1+p_1)^2}\right).$$

The direct effects can each be identified with an equation in (10.16) and hence with the right hand side vector in (10.18). Of these $\partial H^*/\partial q$, $\partial P^*/\partial q$, $\partial C^*/\partial q$ are all unambiguously positive, and the same is true for $\partial B^*/\partial q$ provided the Marshall–Lerner condition holds.[11] Henceforth we shall take this to be the case, enabling us to define all the direct effects to be positive. The determinant of the matrix appearing in equation (10.18) is precisely the Jacobian J of the system (10.16) and adding the restrictions

$$\psi < 0 \qquad\qquad\qquad (10.19a)$$

$$K_1 - (1+q)EM_1 < 0 \qquad\qquad (10.19b)$$

$$G_d - uY \qquad\quad < 0 \qquad\qquad (10.19c)$$

certainly suffices to ensure that it is positive. The first condition again follows from the Marshall–Lerner condition. The second asserts that the increase in imports resulting from an increase in income outweighs the possible inflow of capital, so that the net effect is a deterioration in the balance of payments. These two restrictions are rather mild. By contrast, the third requirement, that there be a government budget surplus, is obviously much more restrictive. Indeed it is *much* more stringent than necessary and the condition $J > 0$ will almost certainly be met even if (10.19c) is violated. The feedback terms (the terms $\partial p_1 / \partial H^*$, $\partial p_1 / \partial B^*$, $\partial p_1 / \partial P^*$, $\partial p_1 / \partial C^*$ in (10.17′)) can be readily obtained by calculating appropriate cofactors of J. For example, $\partial p_1 / \partial H^*$ $= J_{14}/J$, where J_{14} is the cofactor of the $(1, 4)$ element of J and other indirect effects are obtained analogously.[12]

The overall impact of a change in the foreign rate of inflation on the endogenous variables of the system (i.e. the solutions to (10.18)) are, as one might expect, rather complex expressions. Accordingly, the actual formulae are relegated to an Appendix. Most of the information is summarized in Table 1, where we report the signs of the feedbacks originating with the four direct effects, all of which themselves have been taken to be positive.

Table 1.

Sign of feedbacks originating from			
Direct demand effect	Direct balance of payments effect	Direct price effect	Direct cost of living effect
$\dfrac{\partial Y}{\partial q}$ +	+	−	−
$\dfrac{\partial r}{\partial q}$ +	−	?	+
$\dfrac{\partial B}{\partial q}$?	−	?	+
$\dfrac{\partial p_1}{\partial q}$ +	+	+	−
$\dfrac{\partial p}{\partial q}$ +	+	+	+

We should stress that the feedbacks we refer to and discuss are only those which occur within the *single* period we are considering. They are the net effects completed within that time interval, taking into account the inter-actions between the various sectors of the model. But even in describing these one period effects, one tends to regard them as taking place in a time sequence (which we loosely refer to below as 'initial' and 'secondary' feed-backs), although this really cannot be done without breaking down the single period into a number of sub-periods. More importantly, because of the intrinsic dynamics of the system it is clear that any changes occurring in a given period will give rise to further feedbacks throughout subsequent periods until a new state of equilibrium is reached. These longer run repercussions are not discussed in our analysis, although that is not to deny their importance.

Consider an increase in q. One direct effect is to lower the relative price for domestically produced goods, thereby raising demand for them. This increase in demand stimulates output, forcing up p_1, and thus the overall rate of inflation p. It will also raise the transactions demand for money, forcing up the domestic interest rate, the increase in which will be accentuated somewhat by the fact that the increased domestic inflation rate will reduce the real value of money balances. While the higher interest rates will encourage a capital inflow and lower imports, the higher level of income will tend to increase imports (while possibly encouraging more capital), making the overall effects on the balance of payments ambiguous. These are just the initial feedbacks and in turn give rise to secondary feedbacks, even within the first period. However, these do not change the ultimate direction of response, the signs of which are given in column 1.

The repercussions arising from the balance of payments effects are given in column 2, which are based on the assumption of $s \neq 0$, so that the government is assumed not to sterilize completely the inflow of foreign reserves. If this is the case, the increase in balance of payments resulting from the increase in q will increase the domestic money supply, thereby lowering r and raising domestic activity and output. Excess demand will be increased, forcing up the rate of inflation of domestically produced goods as well as p. Moreover the increase in real demand, coupled with a decrease in r will lead to an unambiguous deterioration in the balance of payments. If $s = 0$, however, the domestic money supply is not increased as a result of the initial balance of payments increase and all these repercussions disappear.

The feedbacks originating with the direct price effect (see column 3) are to some extent offsetting and somewhat more ambiguous. The higher q encourages domestic producers to raise p_1, thereby reducing demand and lowering output. The transactions demand for money falls, lowering the rate of interest. At the same time the higher rate of overall domestic inflation will lower the real values of money balances, exerting an upward pressure on the rate of interest. The conflicting effects tend to make the overall impact on the balance of payments indeterminate and this in turn introduces further indeterminacies into the monetary sector.

Finally, the cost of living feedbacks (column 4) operate as follows. An increase in the overall rate of domestic inflation p (originating with a higher q), reduces the value of domestic real balances, the effects of which are to raise r, lower Y and to reduce the pressure on p_1. This yields an offsetting effect on p, which nevertheless can be shown to be dominated by the initial inflationary impact. The lower level of income, together with the higher interest rates yield an unambiguous improvement in the balance of payments.

We must stress that what we have been discussing are the *feedbacks* – and indeed mainly the initial feedbacks – associated with the four direct effects. All of these give rise to secondary and even subsequent effects within the first period and it is the signs of the full first-period repercussions (originating with a particular effect) which are given in Table 1. The overall impact of an increase in inflation abroad on any one of the endogenous variables consists of the sum of these effects; see e.g. equation (10.17') in general and the Appendix (10.A.1)–(10.A.5) in particular. As Table 1 makes clear, only one of these total effects – the effect on the overall rate of domestic inflation p – can be signed unambiguously. In all other cases some repercussions are off-setting, making their signs indeterminate. While it is possible to select parameter values which yield $\partial p_1/\partial q < 0$, this can be ruled out as an extreme, and highly implausible case. However, some of the other responses are not so clear cut and could go either way. Perhaps the most indeterminate is the over-all response in the domestic rate of interest where the demand effect and balance of payments effect act in opposite directions, while the price effect is ambiguous. In this case, quite plausible parameters could yield a response of either sign.

As we have already commented equation (10.8), or some variant of it, has formed the basis for much of the empirical work on price determination in open economies. In these studies the coefficient a_2, the estimated elasticity of domestic prices with respect to a change in foreign prices, is often taken to be a measure of the extent to which inflation is imported. This coefficient is of course just the direct price effect we have been discussing, and as our analysis has shown it is not in general the total effect. Assuming that the exchange rate remains fixed so that $E = E_{-1} = 1$, equation (10.16a) immediately implies

$$\frac{\partial p_1}{\partial q} - a_2 = a_1 \frac{\partial Y}{\partial q}.$$

That is, the direct effect of an increase in q on p_1 differs from the true effect by an amount which depends upon the responsiveness of income. Accordingly, the direct effect under-(over-)states the true effect according to whether the effect on income is positive or negative. While we have not been able to sign $\partial Y/\partial q$ unambiguously, it seems most likely to be positive, in which case the magnitude of a_2 *understates* the extent to which inflation abroad is reflected in the price rises of domestic goods. Part of the impact of inflation abroad is to stimulate demand for domestic goods, thereby exerting an additional upward pressure on domestic prices, which is not reflected in the direct coefficient a_2.

With the model containing two indices of domestic inflation, p and p_1, it may be of some interest to compare their responsiveness to increases in q. Differentiating (10.16e), using $C_1 + C_2 = 1$ and holding E constant at its initial value of unity, one immediately obtains

$$\frac{\partial p}{\partial q} - \frac{\partial p_1}{\partial q} = C_2 \left(1 - \frac{\partial p_1}{\partial q}\right).$$

This expression yields the expected result that as long as $\partial p_1/\partial q < 1$ (which one would presumably expect to be the case), then an increase in the rate of foreign inflation, with its full impact on imported prices, has a larger effect on the overall inflation rate than it does on that of domestically produced goods alone. To the extent that this occurs estimates of a_2, which are based on equations using some kind of price index of domestically produced goods as the dependent variable, further understate the total inflationary impact of a rise in q.

In view of the many indeterminate elements contained in the general results, further insight into likely responses can be obtained by considering the polar case of perfect capital mobility. This case is obtained by letting $K_2 \to \infty$, implying that an infinitesimal change in r will lead to an infinite movement of capital, so that the domestic rate of interest is in fact equal to the foreign rate of interest, $\bar{r}$ say. Under this limiting assumption, the effects of a rise in the foreign rate of inflation on the endogenous variables simplify drastically to the following:

$$\frac{\partial Y}{\partial q} = \frac{[(1+p_1)-(1+q)a_2E]\partial H^*/\partial q}{(1+p_1)J'} \tag{10.20a}$$

$$\frac{\partial r}{\partial q} = 0 \tag{10.20b}$$

$$\frac{\partial p_1}{\partial q} = \frac{a_1 \partial H^*/\partial q + (1-H_1)\partial P^*/\partial q}{J'} > 0 \tag{10.20c}$$

$$\frac{\partial p}{\partial q} = C_1 \frac{\partial p_1}{\partial q} + C_2 E > 0 \tag{10.20d}$$

$$\frac{\partial B}{\partial q} = \frac{1+p}{sJ'} \left\{ \frac{\partial H^*/\partial q}{1+p_1} [\phi a_1(1+p) + \omega[(1+p_1) - a_2E(1+q)] + a_1 \rho] \right.$$
$$\left. + (1-H_1)[\phi \partial C^*/\partial q + (\rho + \phi C_1)\partial P^*/\partial q] \right\} \tag{10.20e}$$

where
$$J' = 1 - H_1 + a_1 \left(\frac{1+q}{1+p_1}\right) \frac{\partial H^*}{\partial q} > 0.$$

Taking plausible values for a_2 (say in the range 0.2–0.6) and E constant ($= 1$) one can confidently expect $\partial Y/\partial q > 0$, while for all parameter values both $\partial p_1/\partial q$, $\partial p/\partial q$ are unambiguously positive.[13] With $r = \bar{r}$, which the model takes as given, one immediately obtains $\partial r/\partial q = 0$. As a result of this, the feedbacks which originate with the impact of the balance of payments on the supply of money all disappear. If the model were extended to allow the foreign interest rate to reflect foreign inflationary conditions, then under reasonable assumptions one could show $\partial r/\partial q = \partial \bar{r}/\partial q > 0$, in which case the monetary feedbacks would reappear. Finally, under the same conditions that ensure $\partial Y/\partial q > 0$, an increase in the foreign rate of inflation will lead to an improvement in the domestic balance of payments and can also be shown to imply a deterioration in the terms of trade.[14]

4.   Monetary, fiscal and exchange rate policies

We turn now to an analysis of some of the policy options open to a country operating under a fixed exchange rate system and confronted with inflationary pressures from abroad. While the discussion of monetary and fiscal policies for an open economy has by now grown into a voluminous literature, little attention has been devoted to questions involving inflationary control. As noted in Chapter 9, starting with Mundell's early contributions (1962, 1964), much of the discussion has identified two policy objectives — an internal target (real income), and an external target (balance of payments) — and has been concerned with designing policy packages and assignments of instruments to attain these objectives. For a fixed exchange rate system, Mundell's work suggested assigning fiscal policy to the internal objective and a monetary instrument to the external objective. Much of the subsequent work has been concerned with reappraising these propositions; see Chapter 9 for references to this literature.

The apparent neglect of inflationary considerations from this discussion can no doubt be attributed largely to the fact that much of this work was done during a period of relative price stability. However, in an inflationary environment, it becomes natural to view the country as having (at least) three policy objectives:

(i) the level of domestic real income;
(ii) the domestic rate of inflation;
(iii) the balance of payments or level of foreign reserves.

Applying the Tinbergen target-instrument proposition, to achieve the desired goals for three targets requires, in general, the use of three policy instruments.[15] This also raises the question of the assignment problem in a three instrument–three target context. However, as it appears that no general solution to the 3×3 case can be found (see Patrick (1973)), we do not dwell on this issue, although our results do yield some conclusions relevant to this discussion.

In order to consider the question of an overall policy package aimed at achieving a set of desired policy objectives, we must first analyse the impacts of the various instruments on the different objectives in turn. In the discussion we shall take the three target variables to be Y, p and B.[16] We should note that in a recent article Aghevli and Borts (1973) have criticized much of the literature for focusing on the balance of payments as the external policy objective. They argue that, because of the implicit dynamics involved in the balance of payments adjustment, the appropriate target should be formulated in terms of the *level* of foreign reserves. If one is concerned with the multi-period impacts of policies this argument is quite correct, and indeed our equation (10.15) fully incorporates the dynamics. However, as we are dealing with only a short-run (one-period) model, it makes no difference whether the objective is formulated in terms of $B = \Delta F$, or F itself.

As policy instruments we shall take:

(i) Real government expenditure on domestic production, G_d;
(ii) The exogenous component of the domestic money supply, γ;
(iii) the exchange rate, E.

There are several points worthy of comment. First, the fiscal instrument refers to only the domestically-produced component of real government expenditure. While many authors refer to an expansionary policy as being an increase in G, without specifying which component has increased, this is in fact the implicit assumption being made. An increase in government expenditure on imported goods would have a direct effect on imports which would also have to be taken into account. Secondly, apart from γ, the model contains two other parameters which reflect aspects of monetary policy. These are θ, the proportion of the government deficit financed by printing additional money and s, the extent to which changes in foreign reserves are being sterilized. These parameters shall be taken as given, but it would be a straightforward exercise to consider how they affect the system.

The expressions describing the effects of changes in the three policy variables on the three target variables are given in equations (10.A.6)–(10.A.8) of the Appendix. Here we merely note that they have the following signs:

$$\frac{\partial Y}{\partial G_d} > 0, \quad \frac{\partial p}{\partial G_d} > 0, \quad \frac{\partial B}{\partial G_d} \gtrless 0 \tag{10.21a}$$

$$\frac{\partial Y}{\partial \gamma} > 0, \quad \frac{\partial p}{\partial \gamma} > 0, \quad \frac{\partial B}{\partial \gamma} < 0 \tag{10.21b}$$

$$\frac{\partial Y}{\partial E} \gtrless 0, \quad \frac{\partial p}{\partial E} > 0, \quad \frac{\partial B}{\partial E} \gtrless 0 \tag{10.21c}$$

An increase in the domestic money supply will increase both the level of income and the rate of domestic inflation, while resulting in a deterioration in the balance of payments. An expansionary fiscal policy will similarly increase output and inflation, although its effect on the balance of payments is indeterminate. The income and balance of payments effects are essentially the same as those obtained previously in the literature and require no further comment; the fact that the price effects follow the income effects is an immediate consequence of the price-adjustment equation. One point worth noting is that, as one might expect, the expansionary and inflationary effects of an increase in G_d increase with θ, the proportion of the government budget deficit financed by increases in the money supply.

As the relevant foreign prices in the model are always expressed in terms of the domestic currency, the impact of an increase in the exchange rate E (a devaluation) is proportional to an increase in the rate of foreign inflation q, the effects of which we have already considered in some detail. Thus, in general, a devaluation can be broken down into four effects, some of which are offsetting. Nevertheless, while all responses have some ambiguities, one would expect a devaluation to be both inflationary and expansionary.

In the limiting case of perfect capital mobility, the impacts of the various policy instruments become much more determinate. Taking plausible values for a_2 (say 0.2–0.6; see Section 3), yields

$$\frac{\partial Y}{\partial G_d} = \frac{1}{J'} > 0; \qquad \frac{\partial p}{\partial G_d} = \frac{C_1 a_1}{J'} > 0;$$

$$\frac{\partial B}{\partial G_d} = \frac{(1+p)}{sJ'} \left(\omega + a_1 C_1 \phi - \frac{\theta(1+p_1)J'}{(1+p)} \right) \gtrless 0 \tag{10.22a}$$

$$\frac{\partial Y}{\partial \gamma} = 0; \qquad \frac{\partial p}{\partial \gamma} = 0; \qquad \frac{\partial B}{\partial \gamma} = -\frac{1}{s} < 0 \tag{10.22b}$$

$$\frac{\partial Y}{\partial E} = \frac{1+q}{E}\frac{\partial Y}{\partial q} > 0; \qquad \frac{\partial p}{\partial E} = \frac{1+q}{E}\frac{\partial p}{\partial q} > 0;$$

$$\frac{\partial B}{\partial E} = \frac{1+q}{E}\frac{\partial B}{\partial q} > 0 \tag{10.22c}$$

with the only ambiguous effect being that of an increase in G_d on B. Note that monetary policy now becomes ineffective in dealing with output or domestic inflation. The reason is that while the immediate effect of an increase in γ may be to lower the interest rate and thus be expansionary, this situation cannot last. With perfect capital mobility, the lower rate of interest will encourage an immediate outflow of capital which exactly offsets the initial increase, thereby restoring the system to its original level.

The impacts given in (10.A.6)–(10.A.8) form the basis for considering the question of choosing the policy mix to attain desired short-run objectives. The solutions for the target variables in terms of the policy instruments can be written in the form

$$Y = f(G_d, \gamma, E) \tag{10.23a}$$

$$p = g(G_d, \gamma, E) \tag{10.23b}$$

$$B = h(G_d, \gamma, E). \tag{10.23c}$$

Suppose that the policy maker has specified desired short-run changes in the policy objectives of dY, dp, dB, respectively. Taking differentials of (10.23) we have

$$dY = f_1 dG_d + f_2 d\gamma + f_3 dE \tag{10.24a}$$

$$dp = g_1 dG_d + g_2 d\gamma + g_3 dE \qquad (10.24b)$$

$$dB = h_1 dG_d + h_2 d\gamma + h_3 dE \qquad (10.24c)$$

where f_i, g_i, h_i, are partial derivatives and are precisely the set of multipliers given in (10.A.6)–(10.A.8). Solving these three equations for $dG_d, d\gamma$, and dE, yields the appropriate one-period adjustments in the policy instruments necessary to achieve the objectives. By making use of the simple relationships between g_i and f_i (see (10.A.6)–(10.A.8)), we can eliminate the g_i and obtain the solutions in the form:

$$dE = \frac{dp - \mu_1 dY}{\mu_2} \qquad (10.25a)$$

$$dG_d = \frac{1}{\mu_2 \Delta} \{ [\mu_1(f_2 h_3 - f_3 h_2) - \mu_2 h_2] dY \\ + (f_3 h_2 - f_2 h_3)dp + f_2 \mu_2 dB \} \qquad (10.25b)$$

$$d\gamma = \frac{1}{\mu_2 \Delta} \{ [\mu_1(f_3 h_1 - f_1 h_3) + \mu_3 h_1] dY \\ + (f_1 h_3 - f_3 h_1)dp - f_1 \mu_2 dB \} \qquad (10.25c)$$

where $\mu_1 = C_1 a_1, \mu_2 = (1 + q)(C_1 a_2 + C_2), \Delta = f_2 h_1 - f_1 h_2 > 0$. These results have some interesting implications. First, the exchange rate should be directed at internal objectives only. That is, it should be adjusted in accordance with its targets for domestic inflation and domestic real income. Somewhat paradoxically, it should *not* be used to meet a balance of payments target. This result is a direct consequence of the fact that our model implies

$$\frac{\partial Y}{\partial G_d} \bigg/ \frac{\partial Y}{\partial \gamma} = f_1/f_2 = g_1/g_2 = \frac{\partial p}{\partial G_d} \bigg/ \frac{\partial p}{\partial \gamma} \qquad (10.26)$$

which asserts that the relative impact of monetary and fiscal policy on domestic output is the same as it is on domestic inflation. It means that if the exchange rate is directed towards the balance of payments, monetary policy and fiscal policy used together are unable to achieve the simultaneous attainment of independent goal for dp and dY. Secondly, fiscal and monetary policies should in general be directed at all three objectives. In view of the indeterminacies in the signs of f_3, h_3 and h_1 we cannot determine unambiguously the direction of adjustment, except to note that if the objective is to improve the balance of payments, this calls for an expansionary fiscal policy coupled with a contraction of the money supply.

More definite results can be obtained by considering the case in which capital is perfectly mobile. In this case $f_2 = g_2 = 0$, so that (10.25b) simplifies to

$$dG_d = \frac{\mu_1 f_3}{\mu_2 f_1} dY - \frac{f_3}{f_1} dp. \qquad (10.25b')$$

Thus we obtain a decomposition in the allocation of instruments to targets. The exchange rate and government expenditure should both be directed towards the two internal policy goals of inflation and output. Having appropriately chosen these, monetary policy should then be applied to achieve the desired balance of payments objective. Hence these results yield a kind of 'block assignment rule' in which subsets of instruments are directed at subsets of targets in a manner which is a direct generalization of Mundell's original assignment.

Furthermore, the limiting case is much more conclusive regarding the direction of policy adjustment. For example, suppose that the policy maker wishes to increase real domestic output, holding p and B constant. This calls for an expansionary fiscal policy coupled with a contraction in the money supply and a revaluation of the domestic currency. Likewise, the same set of policies will be appropriate if the aim is to reduce inflation, while maintaining the other objectives constant. Finally, if the government wishes to improve its balance of payments, it should adopt a tighter monetary policy. Note that using the exchange rate as one of its instruments, the government is able to achieve simultaneously a reduction in the domestic rate of inflation and an increase in domestic output. This cannot be done by the use of conventional domestic monetary and fiscal policy instruments alone, due to the fact that the relative effects of these two instruments on domestic output are the same as on domestic inflation; see (10.26).

To give one final example, suppose that the set of policy objectives is to set $dY > 0, dp < 0, dB > 0$. In this case, the set of equations (10.25) call for an unambiguous revaluation, together with an increase in government expenditure and tighter monetary policy. Note, however, that if instead the authorities wish to reduce the balance of payments, the overall direction of monetary adjustment becomes ambiguous. While the internal objective would require a contractionary policy, the external target would require an expansion of the money supply.

It needs to be stressed that these specific policy adjustment rules apply to the limiting case where capital is perfectly mobile. Nevertheless they provide some insight into the appropriate use of the three instruments and illustrate how appropriate coordination of policies enable the three objectives to be simultaneously attained. They also highlight the crucial role that the use of the exchange rate may play in the attainment of the domestic policy goals, at least in the short run.

Finally, we should emphasize that the question we have been discussing of how the policy mix should be chosen, pertains to the attainment of *short-term* objectives. We have not considered whether this yields a stable adjustment so that any prescribed set of *long-term* objectives can be reached. Our concern has therefore been with a somewhat different issue than the 'assignment problem' as outlined in Chapter 9.

5. Flexible exchange rates

We turn now to a brief discussuion of the flexible exchange rate case. This requires minor modification to the previous model, arising from the fact that the exchange rate now becomes an endogenous variable, adjusting to ensure the maintenance of balance of payments equilibrium. Thus the complete system becomes

$$Y - H\left(Y, r - \pi, \frac{(1+q)E}{1+p_1}, u\right) - X\left(\frac{(1+q)E}{1+p_1}\right) - G_d = 0 \quad (10.16a)$$

$$L(Y, r, \pi) - \frac{L_{-1} + \theta(1+p_1)(G_d - uY) + \gamma}{1+p} = 0 \quad (10.16b)$$

$$(1+p_1)X\left(\frac{(1+q)E}{1+p_1}\right) - (1+q)EM\left(Y, r - \pi, \frac{(1+q)E}{1+p_1}, u\right)$$
$$+ K(Y, r) = 0 \quad (10.16c)$$

$$a_0 + a_1(Y - \bar{Y}) + a_2[(1+q)E - 1] + a_3\pi - p_1 = 0 \quad (10.16d)$$

$$C[(1+p_1), (1+q)E] - (1+p) = 0 \quad (10.16e)$$

which is to be solved for the five endogenous variables Y, r, p, p_1 and E.

To determine the impact of an increase in foreign inflation on the domestic economy, we differentiate the system with respect to q and obtain

$$\frac{\partial Y}{\partial q} = \frac{\partial r}{\partial q} = \frac{\partial p_1}{\partial q} = \frac{\partial p}{\partial q} = 0 \quad (10.27a)$$

$$\frac{\partial E}{\partial q} = -\frac{E}{1+q} < 0. \quad (10.27b)$$

These equations yield the conclusion that with flexible exchange rates, the country is able to insulate itself completely from inflationary pressures abroad. Any rise in prices overseas is offset exactly by an appreciation of the exchange rate, leaving the price of imported goods in terms of domestic currency constant. This result is a consequence of the fact that q and E enter together through the factor $(1+q)E$. However, one might argue that with a floating exchange rate, people base their decisions on what they regard as 'permanent' rates, rather than changing their behaviour in response to short-run fluctuations. This has been suggested by some empirical studies of pricing behaviour for Canada during the period that the Canadian dollar was floating.[17] If this is so, and individuals construct their estimates of permanent exchange rates by taking averages of past rates, and if further the relevant averaging is not formed uniformly throughout the economy, then the domestic economy may no longer be completely insulated from inflation abroad, especially in the very short run.[18]

But it also should be pointed out at this stage that the perfect insulation provided by flexible exchange rates in this model is partly a consequence of the incomplete specification of the financial markets. As we shall show in Chapter 12, once these are specified properly flexible exchange rates need *not* insulate the domestic economy completely from foreign inflationary pressures. With perfect capital mobility, perfect insulation will be achieved if and only if the foreign rate of interest fully adjusts to the foreign rate of inflation; see Chapter 12.

The fact that a floating exchange rate tends to insulate the domestic economy from foreign price movements (at least in this model) does not necessarily mean that it ensures a lower rate of domestic inflation. Inflation is a consequence of many influences and a floating exchange rate merely eliminates one of these, namely foreign effects. At the same time it is possible for a flexible exchange rate to intensify some of the domestic causes of inflation. To compare formally the rates of inflation under the two systems would involve comparing the solutions to the model under the two regimes. While we do not intend to pursue this in detail, it is nevertheless of some interest to indicate how this might occur.

Consider an exogenous increase in the domestic demand for domestically produced goods. This will raise domestic output, at the same time forcing up p_1 and r. These effects will also have repercussions in the international sector and in general these will be indeterminate. On balance one might expect the initial effect to be a balance of payments deficit. If this is so, then under a fixed exchange rate system foreign reserves will be reduced, while if the exchange rate is flexible, there will be a tendency for a devaluation of the domestic currency. While the first case leads to an offsetting deflationary effect, the second adds further upward pressures on domestic prices, illustrating how a flexible system may indeed be more inflationary overall.

The short-run effects of changes in monetary and fiscal policy on an economy operating with a flexible exchange rate system can be analysed along the lines in Section 4. These calculations are straightforward and are left as an exercise for the interested reader. The policy options open to such an economy can also be studied along similar lines, although under a flexible regime, the exchange rate is of course unavailable as a policy instrument. Because of the differential effects monetary and fiscal policies have on the exchange rate E, the proportionality between them given by (10.26), ceases to hold. This means that it is now possible to achieve given independent target values for Y, p (or dY and dp) by the use of the two conventional monetary and fiscal instruments. This was shown to be impossible in the fixed exchange rate case, due to the linear dependence implied by (10.26).

However, any policies which are directed at the two goals for Y and P will have endogenous impacts on the exchange rate and these may cause policy makers to consider E as a third policy objective. The costs to importers and exporters of having to continually adjust their plans to constantly changing exchange rates may in the short run be high. Moreover, changes in E

imply distributional changes between importers and exporters which the government may or may not regard as desirable. But if the policy makers do wish to achieve a desired short-run target for E (and indeed it is frequently viewed as an external objective), then an additional instrument must be introduced.

In principle, several instruments could be added to G_d and γ. One possibility would be to use the tax rate u. In this case one could solve for the target variables in the form

$$Y = f'(G_d, u, \gamma) \tag{10.28a}$$

$$p = g'(G_d, u, \gamma) \tag{10.28b}$$

$$E = h'(G_d, u, \gamma). \tag{10.28c}$$

Differentiating (10.28) with respect to the three arguments, one can show that the Jacobian is non-vanishing, thereby ensuring that any desired combination of (Y, p, E) can be achieved by the appropriate choice of (G_d, u, γ). Moreover one can show that

$$f'_i/f'_j \neq g'_i/g'_j \qquad \text{for any pair } i, j$$

so that in general the *three* instruments will all be directed at the *three* targets. In other words, the 'block assignment rule' obtained as a limiting case for fixed exchange rates, does not apply here. However, details of these statements are omitted.

6.   Summary and conclusions

This chapter has analysed the role of imported inflation within the framework of a conventional short-run open macroeconomic model. We have identified four channels through which foreign inflation impinges on the domestic economy and have shown how each of these creates subsequent repercussions throughout the system. Some of the feedbacks operate in offsetting ways, with the result that the only determinate effect of an increase in foreign inflation is on the overall domestic rate of inflation, which will increase. The effects on other endogenous variables all contain ambiguous elements making their total responses indeterminate. On balance one would clearly expect an increase in foreign inflation to raise the price of domestically produced goods and to increase domestic output, although one can quite readily choose feasible parameters for which this would not be true. In the limiting case of perfect capital mobility the responses of the system become much more determinate. An increase in foreign inflation raises both the rate of inflation of domestically produced goods, as well as the overall domestic inflation. Moreover, for any plausible value of a_2, the domestic country will experience an increase in output and an improvement in its balance of payments. Its terms of trade, however, will deteriorate.

In discussing the policy implications of the model, we focus on three policy objectives. These consist of two internal objectives — domestic output and domestic inflation — together with an external balance of payments target. As a consequence, it is necessary to consider three policy instruments and particular emphasis is placed upon the use of the exchange rate as a strategic variable for achieving domestic stability. We show that while monetary and fiscal policies should in general be directed at all three objectives, exchange rate policy should be directed at only the internal policy goals. In the limiting case of perfect capital mobility we obtain a complete decomposition of the allocation of instruments to targets; government expenditure and the exchange rate should both be directed at only the two internal objectives, while the monetary instrument alone should be directed at the balance of payments target.

With flexible exchange rates we obtain the result that a country is able to insulate itself completely from inflationary pressures abroad, although this conclusion is in part a consequence of the incomplete specification of the financial sector of the model. In any event this insulation does not necessarily imply an overall reduction in domestic inflation. The policy implications of this case are also rather different; in particular all instruments should be directed at all targets.

In conclusion, we must draw attention to two limitations of this analysis. First, we have assumed the prices of export goods to be determined domestically. While this assumption may approximate a large number of situations, for many small countries the prices of these goods are likely to be determined largely on world markets. If that is the case, export prices become a further source of imported inflation and to incorporate them the model needs to be appropriately modified. Secondly, we must emphasize that these results refer to first period effects only and hence are most relevant for short-run stabilization policy questions. We have abstracted from such things as wealth effects and have not traced through the intrinsic dynamic structure imposed upon the system by some of the behavioural relationships. It is clear that these factors will have an impact on behaviour in subsequent periods and any longer-run analysis of imported inflation would need to take them into account. This second set of issues is taken up in Chapters 11 and 12.

Appendix

1. *Effects of a change in foreign inflation on the endogenous variables in a fixed exchange rate system*

$$
\begin{aligned}
\frac{\partial Y}{\partial q} = & \frac{\partial H^*/\partial q}{J}\left(\frac{s[K_2 - (1+q)EM_2]}{1+p} - L_2\right) - \frac{\partial B^*/\partial q}{J}\left(\frac{sH_2}{1+p}\right) \\
& + \frac{\partial P^*/\partial q}{J}\left(\phi C_1 H_2 - \frac{sH_2\psi}{1+p} - \lambda\left(\frac{s[K_2 - (1+q)EM_2]}{1+p} - L_2\right)\right. \\
& \left. + H_2\rho\right) + \frac{H_2\phi\partial C^*/\partial q}{J}
\end{aligned}
\quad (10.\text{A}.1)
$$

$$
\frac{\partial r}{\partial q} = \frac{\partial H^*/\partial q}{J}\left(\phi a_1 C_1 - \frac{a_1 \psi s}{1+p} + a_1 \rho + \omega - \frac{s}{1+p}\,[K_1\right.
$$

$$
\left. - (1+q)EM_1]\right) - \frac{s\partial B^*/\partial q}{J(1+p)}\,[(1-H_1) + a_1\lambda]
$$

$$
+ \frac{\partial P^*/\partial q}{J}\left(\phi C_1(1-H_1) - \lambda\left\{\omega - \frac{s}{1+p}[K_1 - (1+q)EM_1]\right\}\right.
$$

$$
\left. - \frac{\psi s}{1+p}(1-H_1) + \rho(1-H_1)\right) + \frac{\phi\partial C^*/\partial q}{J}[(1-H_1)+a_1\lambda]
$$

(10.A.2)

$$
\frac{\partial B}{\partial q} = \frac{\partial H^*/\partial q}{J}\left(\phi C_1 a_1[K_2 - (1+q)EM_2] - a_1 L_2\psi\right.
$$

$$
\left. + (a_1\rho + \omega)[K_2 - (1+q)EM_2] - L_2[K_1 - (1+q)EM_1]\right)
$$

$$
- \frac{\partial B^*/\partial q}{J}\left(\phi C_1 a_1 H_2 + a_1 L_2\lambda + L_2(1-H_1) + H_2\omega + H_2 a\rho\right)
$$

$$
+ \frac{\partial P^*/\partial q}{J}\left(\phi C_1\{[K_2 - (1+q)EM_2]\,(1-H_1) + H_2\,[K_1\right.
$$

$$
- (1+q)EM_1]\} - \lambda\{[K_2 - (1+q)EM_2]\,\omega - L_2\,[K_1
$$

$$
- (1+q)EM_1]\} + \rho\{H_2\,[K_1 - (1+q)\,EM_2]
$$

$$
\left. + (1-H_1)\,[K_2 - (1+q)EM_2]\} - \psi[L_2(1-H_1) + H_2\omega]\right)
$$

$$
+ \frac{\partial C^*/\partial q}{J}\left(\phi a_1\{H_2\psi + [K_2 - (1+q)EM_2]\,\lambda\} + \phi\{[K_2\right.
$$

$$
\left. - (1+q)EM_2]\,(1-H_1) + [K_1 - (1+q)EM_1]\,H_2\}\right)
$$

(10.A.3)

$$
\frac{\partial p_1}{\partial q} = \frac{\partial H^*/\partial q}{J}\left(\frac{sa_1[K_2 - (1+q)EM_2]}{1+p} - a_1 L_2\right) - \frac{\partial B^*/\partial q}{J}\left(\frac{sa_1 H_2}{1+p}\right)
$$

$$
+ \frac{\partial P^*/\partial q}{J}\left(\frac{s}{1+p}\{(1-H_1)\,[K_2 - (1+q)EM_2]\right.
$$

$$
\left. + H_2\,[K_1 - (1+q)EM_1] - L_2(1-H_1) - H_2\omega\}\right)
$$

$$
+ \frac{\partial C^*/\partial q}{J}[a_1\phi H_2]
$$

(10.A.4)

$$
\frac{\partial p}{\partial q} = C_1\,\frac{\partial p_1}{\partial q} + C_2 E > 0.
$$

(10.A.5)

2. *Effects of changes in policy instruments on target variables*

$$\frac{\partial Y}{\partial G_d} = \frac{1}{J}\left(\frac{s\left[K_2 - (1+q)EM_2\right]}{1+p} - L_2 - \frac{\theta(1+p_1)}{1+p}H_2 \right) > 0;$$

$$\frac{\partial p}{\partial G_d} = C_1 a_1 \frac{\partial Y}{\partial G_d} > 0$$

$$\frac{\partial B}{\partial G_d} = \frac{1}{J}\left(\phi C_1 a_1 \left[K_2 - (1+q)EM_2\right] - a_1 L_2 \psi + \left[K_2 \right.\right.$$

$$- (1+q)EM_2\right](\omega + a_1\rho) - L_2\left[K_1 - (1+q)EM_1\right]$$

$$- \frac{\theta(1+p_1)}{1+p}\left[a_1 H_2 \psi + \left[a_1\lambda + (1-H_1)\right]\left[K_2 \right.\right.$$

$$\left.\left. - (1+q)EM_2\right] + H_2(K_1 - (1+q)EM_1)\right]\right)$$

(10.A.6)

$$\frac{\partial Y}{\partial \gamma} = \frac{H_2}{(1+p)J} > 0; \quad \frac{\partial p}{\partial \gamma} = C_1 a_1 \frac{\partial Y}{\partial \gamma} > 0$$

$$\frac{\partial B}{\partial \gamma} = -\frac{1}{(1+p)J}\left(a_1 H_2 \psi + (a_1\lambda + 1 - H_1)\left[K_2 - (1+q)EM_2\right] \right.$$

$$\left. + H_2\left[K_1 - (1+q)EM_1\right] \right) < 0$$

(10.A.7)

$$\frac{\partial Y}{\partial E} = \frac{(1+q)}{E}\frac{\partial Y}{\partial q}; \quad \frac{\partial p}{\partial E} = \frac{(1+q)}{E}\frac{\partial p}{\partial q}; \quad \frac{\partial B}{\partial E} = \frac{(1+q)}{E}\frac{\partial B}{\partial q}.$$

(10.A.8)

11

THE DYNAMICS OF AN OPEN ECONOMY WITH FIXED EXCHANGE RATE AND FIXED PRICES

1.   Introduction[1]

In Chapters 9 and 10 we have developed two short-run (one-period) macro models of a small open economy. The first of these assumed, for the most part, that prices are fixed and is in effect a direct open economy generalization of the basic *IS–LM* model reviewed in Chapter 2. The second model introduced endogenous prices, focusing particularly on the short-run rate of inflation, and in many respects can be viewed as an appropriate extension of Chapter 6. In both cases we have been concerned with assessing the short-run effects of various policies, without considering any repercussions throughout subsequent periods.

It is time now to extend this analysis and to allow for the intrinsic dynamics of the system stemming from the interaction between stocks and flows. In the present chapter we shall present the simplest such dynamic model in which all prices, including the exchange rate, are fixed. The model is therefore the direct open-economy analogue of Chapter 4 and the first Blinder–Solow (1973) model. The dynamics we shall consider contains two essential components. First, as in the closed economic model, there is the accumulation of assets arising from the financing of the government deficit. Secondly, there is the dynamics associated with capital flows and the balance of payments and their impact on the domestic money supply. Our concern will therefore be with the longer-run (steady-state) effects of fiscal and financial policy in such an economy.

There is by now a voluminous literature dealing with monetary and fiscal policy in an open economy. Much of the analysis, like much of the work for the closed economy, is essentially static, ignoring the intrinsic dynamics of the system.[2] Certainly, previous authors such as Oates (1966), McKinnon and Oates (1966), McKinnon (1969) recognized the role of the government budget constraint in an open economy, although they discussed only the equilibrium of the system and did not consider the dynamics. As we show below, a result of this is that their conclusions regarding the equilibrium conditions of the system in fact hold only in some special cases. Other authors, such as Floyd (1969), Tower (1972) explicitly consider the dynamics of capital flows and the balance of payments adjustment, but they essentially ignore how the government deficit is financed, or make very simple assumptions regarding it. Further, they do not consider the stability of the dynamic adjustment process itself. Another example is a recent paper by Allen (1973), which takes the government's monetary and debt policies to be independent policy decisions, unrelated to the endogenous variables of the model. By contrast, Agehvli and Borts (1973) focus explicitly on the stability of the balance of payments adjustment process and assume that the entire government budget deficit is financed by selling bonds. Moreover, they abstract from interest payments in the budget, a factor which our previous analysis for the closed economy shows to be crucial. Similarly, the recent extension of this work by Sakakibara (1975) also downplays the role of the government budget constraint.

In attempting to integrate some of these recent developments in international monetary theory into the fixed-price dynamic model, there are three aspects to which we wish to give particular emphasis. First we introduce the mix of money and debt financing of the government budget deficit on the one hand, and the extent to which monetary authorities sterilize changes in foreign reserves through open market operations on the other, as policy parameters. Both these decisions have impacts on the supply of domestic financial assets, thereby endogenizing the government's monetary and debt policies. These policy decisions in turn influence the dynamics of the system and indeed much of the emphasis of our discussion is on the stability of the resulting adjustment process. One of the important conclusions emerging from the analysis is that in general this depends crucially, yet in a rather simple way, upon how these policy parameters are chosen. Secondly, the model is developed under the assumption that domestic residents treat domestic and foreign bonds as distinct assets, having a separate demand for each. This contrasts with much of the recent literature investigating capital flows which takes capital to be perfectly mobile internationally; see, for example, Aghevli and Borts (1973), Allen (1973). We too consider this as one limiting case and show how the equilibrium and stability properties it implies differ significantly from those where capital is imperfectly mobile. Thirdly, we also incorporate interest payments into the model. As in the closed economy, these have an important effect on both the stability and long-run equilibrium properties of the system.

2.   The model

As in the formulation of our previous dynamic models, particular attention is paid to the interactions between stocks and flows in the system. The country's exchange rate is assumed to be fixed and equal to unity. All prices, both domestic and foreign, are constant, and by appropriate choice of units can also be set equal to unity. Also, as was the case for the dynamic analysis of earlier chapters, the development of the model takes place in two stages. First, we describe a number of static or instantaneous equilibrium and definitional relationships, which are required to hold continuously. Secondly, we consider the intrinsic dynamics of the system, arising from the financing of the government budget deficit and the endogenous impact of the balance of payments on the domestic money supply.[3] Since we are now concerned with longer-run effects we shall present the analysis using continuous time.

We begin with the domestic output market, which in equilibrium is described by the relationship

$$Y = H(Y^D, r, V) + X + G_d \qquad 0 < H_1 < 1, \quad H_2 < 0, \quad H_3 > 0$$

$$(11.1)$$

where
Y = real domestic output,
Y^D = real domestic disposable income,
r = domestic rate of interest,
V = real net domestic wealth,
H = real domestic private expenditure on domestically produced goods,
X = real volume of exports
G_d = real domestic government expenditure on domestically produced goods.

Equation (11.1) is virtually identical to the specification of domestic product market equilibrium in Chapters 9 and 10. The only substantive modification is that the wealth effects are included in H. Also, since the country is small, we take exports to be exogenously given, being determined by foreign economic factors.

The monetary sector is also straightforward. We assume that domestic residents demand only domestic currency, specifying their demand L^d by

$$L^d = L(Y, r, V) \qquad L_1 > 0, \quad L_2 < 0, \quad 0 < L_3 < 1. \qquad (11.2)$$

The supply of money, L, consists of two components

$$L = D + F \qquad (11.3)$$

where
D = domestic component of the money stock,
F = volume of foreign reserves.

Equilibrium in the money market is thus described by[4] $\qquad (11.4)$

$$L = D + F = L(Y, r, V)$$

Apart from money, there are two other financial assets in the economy, namely domestic bonds and foreign bonds. For simplicity, we assume that the only issuer of debt in either country is the government.[5] Both these assets may be demanded and held by both domestic residents and foreigners, who except in the case of perfect capital-market integration discussed in Section 4, do not regard them as perfect substitutes. Thus we specify the following private demand functions for bonds, both of which for simplicity, are taken to be perpetuities,

$$\frac{A^{D,d}}{r} = J^D(Y,r,V,r^*) \qquad J_1^D \gtrless 0, \quad J_2^D > 0, \quad 0 < J_3^D < 1, \quad J_4^D < 0$$

$$(11.5a)$$

$$\frac{A^{F,d}}{r} = J^F(Y^*,r^*,V^*,r) \qquad J_1^F \gtrless 0, \quad J_2^F < 0, \quad 0 < J_3^F < 1, \quad J_4^F > 0$$

$$(11.5b)$$

$$\frac{C^d}{r^*} = N(Y,r,V,r^*) \qquad N_1 \gtrless 0, \quad N_2 < 0, \quad 0 < N_3 < 1, \quad N_4 > 0,$$

$$(11.5c)$$

where Y^*, r^*, V^*, denote foreign income, interest, and wealth respectively, all of which by our small country assumption are taken to be exogenously determined.[6] Equation (11.5a) describes the domestic demand for domestic bonds, and we shall let A^D signify the number of these bonds held by domestic residents. Likewise, (11.5b) describes the foreign demand for domestic bonds, with A^F analogously denoting the number of domestic bonds held by foreigners. Equation (11.5c) describes the domestic demand for foreign bonds, with the number held being C. There is also a foreign demand for such bonds, but this is of no concern here. The partial derivatives of the demand functions are indicated in (11.5) and are self explanatory. In particular as in earlier chapters the two assets are treated as gross substitutes for one another. Since the variables Y^*, r^*, V^* are all treated as exogenous to the small country, they can be omitted from the demand functions which we rewrite more simply as[7]

$$\frac{A^{D,d}}{r} = J^D(Y,r,V) \qquad J_1^D \gtrless 0, \quad J_2^D > 0, \quad 0 < J_3^D < 1 \ (11.5a')$$

$$\frac{A^{F,d}}{r} = J^F(r) \qquad (J^F)' > 0 \qquad\qquad\qquad (11.5b')$$

$$\frac{C^d}{r^*} = N(Y,r,V) \qquad N_1 \gtrless 0, \quad N_2 < 0, \quad 0 < N_3 < 1. \ (11.5c')$$

Throughout the chapter we shall abstract from net investment in the domestic economy, so that the physical stock of domestic capital remains fixed at $\bar{K}$ say. We shall assume that it is not traded internationally and that it is a perfect substitute for bonds in the portfolios of domestic investors, enabling its demand to be subsumed in the function J. But even though $\bar{K}$ remains fixed, its *value* (expressed in terms of the fixed price of output) will change. As we shall show presently, if the marginal physical product of capital is expected to remain constant over time, then allowing for the variable value of fixed capital does not affect the qualitative properties of the results for the two limiting cases we consider in detail. Hence without essential loss of generality, we can set $\bar{K} = 0$. The reason for abstracting from investment is basically to avoid some of the inconsistencies we draw attention to in Chapter 3. Specifically, we remarked on the unsatisfactory procedure adopted in much of macroeconomic theory of allowing for the flow effects of investment, yet abstracting from the resulting growth of capital. Unfortunately, to introduce capital accumulation complicates what is already a fairly complex model. We therefore prefer to exclude it at the outset.

The net national wealth of the domestic economy, V_n say, is defined to consist of its physical capital, its foreign reserve holdings, and its net holding of foreign securities (that is, the difference between the domestic holding of foreign bonds and the foreign holding of domestic bonds). With $\bar{K} = 0$, we thus have

$$V_n = R + C/r^* - A^F/r.$$

The net wealth of the domestic private sector thus consists of V_n plus the net claims on the domestic government, namely

$$\left.\begin{aligned}
V &= V_n + D + A/r \\
&= L + A^D/r + C/r^*.
\end{aligned}\right\} \tag{11.6}$$

Hence apart from its fixed stock of physical capital, domestic private wealth consists of three components; domestic money, the value of domestic government bonds held by domestic residents, and the value of foreign bonds held by domestic residents.

For a continuous-time model such as this, the aggregate budget constraint for the private sector of the domestic economy has been shown to imply *two* constraints on private demand; see Chapter 3. One of these is the stock constraint

$$V = L + \frac{A^D}{r} + \frac{C}{r^*} = L^d + \frac{A^{D,d}}{r} + \frac{C^d}{r^*}, \tag{11.7}$$

The other is a flow constraint. Under the restrictive conditions discussed in Chapter 3, this reduces to the product market equilibrium condition (11.1). We shall assume that these conditions apply in the present context. The important implication of (11.7) is that only two of the three domestic asset demand functions can be independent.[8] Given equilibrium in the domestic money market, and by substitution, (11.7) becomes

$$\frac{A^D}{r} + \frac{C}{r^*} = J^D(Y, r, V) + N(Y, r, V). \tag{11.7'}$$

An analogous equation to (11.7) also holds in the rest of the world. Adding (11.7) to its foreign counterpart, it follows that three of the four asset markets (domestic money, domestic bonds, foreign money, foreign bonds) are independent. Assuming the domestic (and foreign) money market to be in equilibrium we are still free to impose equilibrium in the domestic bonds market as an additional independent equilibrium condition. This is described by

$$\frac{A^D}{r} + \frac{A^F}{r} = J^D(Y, r, V) + J^F(r). \qquad (11.7'')$$

Furthermore, since the domestic government bonds must be held either by the domestic public or by foreigners, A^D, A^F must satisfy the constraint

$$A = A^D + A^F. \qquad (11.8)$$

From equations (11.6) and (11.7) we can see why setting $\bar{K} = 0$ results in little loss of generality. Assuming that the marginal physical product of capital is expected to remain constant, and that domestic capital and bonds are perfect substitutes, the value of the capital stock $\bar{K}$ is given by

$$q\bar{K} = \frac{R(Y)\bar{K}}{r} \qquad R'(Y) > 0$$

where q is the price of a unit claim on capital in terms of new output, and $R(Y)$ is the marginal physical product of capital; see (3.58'). Wealth of domestic private residents now becomes

$$V = L + \frac{A^D}{r} + \frac{C}{r^*} + \frac{R(Y)\bar{K}}{r}. \qquad (11.6')$$

The inclusion of the extra term $R(Y)\bar{K}/r$ in the definition of wealth, and also in the constraints (11.7') and (11.7'') turns out to have no effect on the qualitative effect on the results in the two limiting cases of zero capital mobility and perfect capital mobility. The reason is that in both these cases the only asset demand function that we need consider is the demand for money $L(Y, r, V)$ and the signs of the partial derivatives of this function remain unaffected by the inclusion of the extra term. The same holds true for the commodity demand function $H(Y^D, r, V)$. Hence, at least as far as these two extreme cases are concerned, nothing is lost by our simplification $\bar{K} = 0$.

To complete the static relationships we must define disposable income Y^D. This is defined to equal national income, plus the interest earned by domestic residents on both their domestic government and foreign bond holdings, all net of taxes, where for simplicity, we assume a proportional tax rate u. Hence we write

$$Y^D = (1 - u)(Y + A^D + C). \qquad (11.9)$$

Note that the definition of disposable income given in (11.9) abstracts from the capital gains on the holding of bonds due to changes in the domestic interest rate and hence in their price. Strictly speaking, for complete consistency these should be included in (11.9); see Chapter 3. However, since they are only transitory we feel that the analytical convenience obtained by ignoring them is justified. In any event our simplification can be maintained if we assume, as in Chapter 7, that all capital gains are saved so that their effect on current consumption is zero.

We turn now to the dynamic relation intrinsic in the system. The first of these is the government budget constraint

$$\dot{D} + \frac{\dot{A}}{r} = G + A - u(Y + A^D + C) \equiv g \qquad (11.10)$$

where G denotes total government expenditure on goods and services (on imports G_m, and domestically produced goods G_d), so that

$$G = G_d + G_m.$$

The quantity $G + A$ represents total government expenditure commitments, including the interest A, on the outstanding bonded debt A/r. The remaining term $u(Y + A^D + C)$ is the government's total tax receipts.[9] This equation asserts that any government deficit is financed either by increasing the domestic monetary base, or by issuing more bonds.

Changes in the foreign component of the total domestic money supply are given by the equation

$$\dot{F} = B \qquad (11.11)$$

where B denotes the balance of payments. Adding (11.10) and (11.11), and noting from (11.3) that

$$\dot{L} = \dot{D} + \dot{F}$$

yields

$$\dot{L} + \dot{A}/r = g + B \qquad (11.12)$$

At this point several authors (particularly McKinnon and Oates) argue that for the system to be in a stationary state requires $\dot{L} + \dot{A} = 0$, implying that in steady state equilibrium[10]

$$g + B = 0. \qquad (11.13)$$

That is, in a steady state neither the government budget nor the balance of payments need be in balance. A surplus (deficit) in the government budget can be offset by running a balance of payments surplus (deficit).

However, by reasoning in this way, they are neglecting to consider any dynamic adjustment describing the transition to a stationary equilibrium. While an equation such as (11.13) is a necessary condition for a stationary equilibrium as will become clear in the course of the present analysis, the conditions under which it is also sufficient to ensure a steady state in a fully specified dynamic system are in fact fairly restrictive.[11] One case in which a similar (but not identical) equation is obtained is if capital is perfectly mobile internationally. With less than perfect capital mobility the same equation may be also obtained if both $\dot{D}$ and $\dot{A}$ are taken to be exogenous, and tax receipts are not related exclusively to income, but contain an autonomous component, which can be continually adjusted so as to satisfy the budget constraint (11.10).

If, as is more reasonable, one wishes to specify *endogenous* adjustments for the policy variables D and A, then the adjustments which, on the one hand are consistent with the budget constraint and on the other ensure that in equilibrium $g + B = 0$ without requiring the separate components g, B themselves to be zero, are most restrictive. Assuming linear policy adjustment this will be so if and only if

$$\dot{L} = \theta(g + B) \qquad 0 \leqslant \theta \leqslant 1$$

$$\dot{A}/r = (1 - \theta)(g + B)$$

that is, if and only if,

$$\dot{D} = \theta g - (1 - \theta)B$$
$$\dot{A}/r = (1 - \theta)g + (1 - \theta)B. \tag{11.14}$$

Written in this way, we see that it requires the proportion of the government budget deficit financed by increases in the domestic component of the money stock to equal the extent to which monetary authorities do *not* seek to offset changes in foreign reserves through open market operations. As these decisions are presumably quite distinct, made by different sections of the government, it would be only by pure chance if they happened to coincide in this way.

We postulate the following adjustment for the domestic component of the money supply

$$\dot{D} = \theta g - (1 - s)B \qquad 0 \leqslant \theta \leqslant 1, \quad 0 \leqslant s \leqslant 1. \tag{11.15}$$

This equation is the continuous-time analogue of (10.13) (with $\gamma = 0$). It asserts that as above, the government finances a fraction θ of its deficit by the creation of new money. Secondly, the monetary authorities engage in open market operations directed at sterilizing, at least in part, changes in their holdings of foreign reserves. Adding $\dot{F}$ to (11.15) implies an adjustment in the total money supply

$$\dot{L} = \theta g + sB \tag{11.16}$$

with (11.12) implying a corresponding adjustment in A

$$\frac{\dot{A}}{r} = (1 - \theta)g + (1 - s)B. \tag{11.17}$$

To complete the model, we must describe B, the balance of payments. This is made up of the sum of the balance of trade, together with net capital movements and is described by

$$B = T(Y^D, r, V) - G_m + \frac{\dot{A}^F}{r} - \frac{\dot{C}}{r^*} + C - A^F \left.\begin{matrix} \\ \\ \end{matrix}\right\} \quad (11.18)$$

$$T_1 < 0, \quad T_2 > 0, \quad T_3 < 0, \quad 1 > H_1 - T_1 > 0.$$

The balance of trade consists of private net exports, denoted by $T(Y^D, r, V)$, less government imports. It will be observed that T depends upon the same variables as H (although with all signs reversed). This reflects the assumption that while exports are exogenous, imports are presumably determined jointly with H, and therefore depend upon the same factors. The constraint $1 > H_1 - T_1 > 0$ follows directly from the fact that disposable income must be either saved, spent on domestic consumption, or spent on imported consumption goods.

Capital flows consist of two components. First there is the net inflow of new capital. This consists of the net change in the quantity of domestic bonds held by foreigners, purchased at their current price $1/r$ less the net change in the quantity of foreign bonds held by domestic residents, purchased at their current price $1/r^*$. The sum of these net effects is given by $[(\dot{A}^F/r - \dot{C}/r^*)]$. This is the quantity which in earlier literature was usually (incorrectly) specified by the function $K(Y, r)$; see Chapter 9. Taking the derivatives of $\dot{A}^F$ and $\dot{C}$ it is clear that the *rates* of change of Y, r, V, etc. are the appropriate explanatory variables in explaining new capital flows. Secondly, any outstanding debt must be serviced. That is, domestic residents' holdings of foreign bonds valued at C/r^* earns them interest of C, while the interest earned by foreigners on their holdings of domestic securities is A^F. The net flow of interest payments is therefore $(C - A^F)$ and tends to offset the flow of new capital. This component has most frequently been ignored in the earlier discussion, one of the few authors to incorporate it being Levin (1972).

Substituting for Y^D, the instantaneous equilibrium relationships can be reduced to the following six equations

$$Y = H[(1-u)(Y + A^D + C), r, V] + X + G_d \qquad (11.19a)$$

$$L = L(Y, r, V) \qquad (11.19b)$$

$$A^D/r + C/r^* = J^D(Y, r, V) + N(Y, r, V) \qquad (11.19c)$$

$$A^D/r + A^F/r = J^D(Y, r, V) + J^F(r) \qquad (11.19d)$$

$$A = A^D + A^F \qquad (11.19e)$$

$$V = L + \frac{A^D}{r} + \frac{C}{r^*} \qquad (11.19f)$$

which, provided the Jacobian of the system is non-zero, can be solved locally for the six variables, Y, V, r, A^F, C, A^D, in terms of A, L and exogenous variables and parameters. The dimensionality of the system can be further reduced by substitution and subsequently we shall in fact do this.

The dynamics describing the evolution of L and A are given by

$$\dot{L} + s\left(\frac{\dot{C}}{r^*} - \frac{\dot{A}^F}{r}\right) = \theta g + sb \tag{11.20a}$$

$$\frac{\dot{A}}{r} + (1-s)\left(\frac{\dot{C}}{r^*} - \frac{\dot{A}^F}{r}\right) = (1-\theta)g + (1-s)b \tag{11.20b}$$

where g is defined above and

$$b = T[(1-u)(Y + A^D + C), r, V] - G_m + C - A^F \tag{11.21}$$

defines the balance of payments on current account. Note that the dynamic equations (11.20) include $\dot{C}$ and $\dot{A}^F$, as well as $\dot{L}$ and $\dot{A}$. However, the system can be reduced to a pair of differential equations in L and A alone. This can be done as follows. First solve the instantaneous equilibrium equations (11.19) for Y, V, r, A^F, C, A^D in terms of L, A, thereby enabling us to write the functions g, b, as functions of L, A, alone. Secondly, differentiating (11.19) with respect to t, we can solve for $\dot{C}$ and $\dot{A}^F$ in particular, in terms of $\dot{L}$ and $\dot{A}$. Substituting for these quantities into (11.20), the dynamic behaviour of the general system can be summarized by a pair of equations of the form

$$\psi_1(\dot{L}, \dot{A}) = \theta g(L, A) + sb(L, A) \tag{11.22a}$$

$$\psi_2(\dot{L}, \dot{A}) = (1-\theta)g(L, A) + (1-s)b(L, A) \tag{11.22b}$$

where $\psi_1(0, 0) = \psi_2(0, 0) = 0$. The local stability properties of the system can then be investigated by analysing (11.22). In the general case these turn out to be highly complex and most of the insights can be obtained by considering the polar cases of zero capital mobility and perfect capital mobility. We shall therefore confine ourselves to these cases, but before doing so it is worth noting the implications of (11.22) for steady-state equilibrium.

Setting $\dot{L} = 0 = \dot{A}$ in (11.22), these equations imply

$$\theta g + sb = 0$$

$$(1-\theta)g + (1-s)b = 0$$

and provided $\theta \neq s$, it follows from this last pair of equations that *both*

$$g = 0 \tag{11.23a}$$

$$b = 0. \tag{11.23b}$$

Thus, as long as $\theta \neq s$, steady state equilibrium requires that *both* the government's budget be balanced *and* the balance of payments be in equilibrium. Furthermore, all flows of new capital, $\dot{A}^F$ and $\dot{C}$ must cease, with the only capital flows being the interest payments on the debt outstanding. Hence the balance of payments equilibrium condition requires the *current account* to be in balance, with the balance of trade just offsetting the net interest payments.

The requirement that all new capital flows must cease, and not just balance, is due to the fact that domestic bonds and foreign bonds are imperfect substitutes, for which there are separate demands. Hence for the system to be in equilibrium, each of the three asset markets separately must be in stationary equilibrium. As we shall see in Section 4 below, this equilibrium condition of zero new capital flows is not required if capital is perfectly mobile. In that case, all that is needed is that any change in the holding of domestic bonds by domestic residents must be offset exactly by changes in their holdings of foreign bonds.

The result that with $\theta \neq s$, equilibrium requires both $g = 0$ and $b = B = 0$, is considerably more stringent than the McKinnon–Oates equilibrium condition that $g + B = 0$. But the reason for it is clear. Suppose $g + B = 0$ and $\theta > s$. Then from (11.20) we must have $\dot{L} > 0$ and $\dot{A} < 0$, and as long as these assets are changing, expenditure and income will change, so that the system cannot be in equilibrium.

With $\theta = s$, both (11.20a) and (11.20b) reduce to the same equilibrium condition namely

$$g + b = 0 \tag{11.23'}$$

which is essentially the McKinnon–Oates result, asserting that a government surplus can be offset by a deficit in the balance of payments on current account. However, now, the special assumptions under which this will in fact be the case, are apparent.

3.   Zero capital mobility

As a first polar case let us assume that there is zero mobility of capital internationally. That is, there are no capital flows, with all bonds being held by the citizens of the country in which they are issued.

The static equilibrium conditions (11.19) can be reduced to

$$Y - H[(1-u)(Y+A), r, V] - X - G_d = 0 \tag{11.24a}$$

$$L(Y, r, V) - L = 0 \tag{11.24b}$$

$$L + A/r - V = 0 \tag{11.24c}$$

which can be solved for the three endogenous variables Y, r, V, while the two dynamic equations for L and A, (11.20), simplify to

$$\dot{L} = \theta[G - uY + (1-u)A] + s\{T[(1-u)(Y+A), r, V] - G_m\} \tag{11.25a}$$

$$\frac{\dot{A}}{r} = (1-\theta)[G - uY + (1-u)A]$$

$$+ (1-s)\{T[(1-u)(Y+A), r, V] - G_m\}. \tag{11.25b}$$

Differentiating g and b (the latter in the absence of capital flows being just $T - G_m$), we have

$$\frac{\partial g}{\partial L} = -u \frac{\partial Y}{\partial L} < 0, \qquad \frac{\partial g}{\partial A} = -u \frac{\partial Y}{\partial A} + (1-u)$$

$$\frac{\partial b}{\partial L} = T_1 (1-u) \frac{\partial Y}{\partial L} + T_2 \frac{\partial r}{\partial L} + T_3 \left(1 - \frac{A}{r^2}\frac{\partial r}{\partial L}\right) \qquad (11.26)$$

$$\frac{\partial b}{\partial A} = T_1 (1-u) \frac{\partial Y}{\partial A} + T_2 \frac{\partial r}{\partial A} + T_3 \left(1 - \frac{A}{r^2}\frac{\partial r}{\partial A}\right)$$

where the partial derivatives appearing in (11.26) are readily calculated from (11.24).

Sufficient conditions for the local stability of the dynamic system (11.25) are given by the pair of equations

$$\theta \frac{\partial g}{\partial L} + s \frac{\partial b}{\partial L} + r(1-\theta) \frac{\partial g}{\partial A} + r(1-s) \frac{\partial b}{\partial A} < 0 \qquad (11.27a)$$

$$(\theta - s) \left(\frac{\partial g}{\partial L}\frac{\partial b}{\partial A} - \frac{\partial g}{\partial A}\frac{\partial b}{\partial L} \right) > 0 \qquad (11.27b)$$

where $\frac{\partial g}{\partial L}$ etc. are given in (11.26). Necessary conditions for local stability require the absence of instability of the linearized system associated with (11.25) and this will be met provided[12]

$$\theta \frac{\partial g}{\partial L} + s \frac{\partial b}{\partial L} + r(1-\theta) \frac{\partial g}{\partial A} + r(1-s) \frac{\partial b}{\partial A} \leqslant 0 \qquad (11.27a')$$

$$(\theta - s) \left(\frac{\partial g}{\partial L}\frac{\partial b}{\partial A} - \frac{\partial g}{\partial A}\frac{\partial b}{\partial L} \right) \geqslant 0. \qquad (11.27b')$$

In particular, (11.27b') highlights the important conclusion that the stability of the system depends crucially upon how the policy parameters are chosen. Under most reasonable conditions, the derivative appearing in (11.26) can be shown to almost certainly ensure that $\left(\frac{\partial g}{\partial L}\frac{\partial b}{\partial A} - \frac{\partial g}{\partial A}\frac{\partial b}{\partial L} \right) > 0$. Sufficient conditions for this to be include $T_3 = 0$, and either $T_2 = 0$ or $\partial r/\partial L < 0$ but it will also be true under other conditions as well. In this case (11.27b') reduces to

$$\theta \geqslant s. \qquad (11.27b'')$$

That is, in order for the system to be stable, we require that the proportion of the government budget deficit financed by increasing the domestic monetary base should be at least as great as the degree to which foreign reserves entering the country are *not* sterilized through open market operations. Thus, for example, a policy in which the entire government deficit is financed by issuing bonds ($\theta = 0$) and no sterilization of foreign reserves takes place

$(s = 1)$, would be unstable. In the highly unlikely case that $\dfrac{\partial g}{\partial L}\dfrac{\partial b}{\partial A} - \dfrac{\partial b}{\partial L}\dfrac{\partial g}{\partial A} < 0$
the relative magnitudes of θ and s would need to be reversed.

If $\theta = s$, (11.27b) is not satisfied strictly. Provided (11.27a) holds the system will be stable, but in the somewhat weaker sense in that the equilibrium to which it converges depends upon the initial conditions.

In the present general case, the stability condition (11.27b′) is rather hard to interpret economically. In formal terms, the reason for the necessity of (11.27b′) for stability is that if this inequality is violated the dynamic system will have eigenvalues of opposite sign, implying that the equilibrium is a saddle point. Nevertheless some idea of the economic reasoning behind this condition can be obtained by considering the special case $T_2 = T_3 = 0$, so that the balance of trade depends upon only disposable income. Evaluating the terms in (11.26), this assumption implies

$$\frac{\partial g}{\partial L}\frac{\partial b}{\partial A} - \frac{\partial g}{\partial A}\frac{\partial b}{\partial L} = -T_1(1-u)\frac{\partial Y}{\partial L} > 0$$

in which case (11.27b″) applies. It is also helpful for expository purposes to focus on the two polar cases $\theta = 0$, $s = 1$ (unstable), $\theta = 1$, $s = 0$ (stable).

Let us consider the former case first and suppose that an initial equilibrium in which $g = b = 0$ is disturbed by an increase in government expenditure. This gives rise to two instantaneous effects. First, it will raise income, thereby increasing import demand and creating a balance of trade deficit. Secondly, since the instantaneous increase in income does not generate sufficient additional tax receipts to finance the additional government expenditure, a government budget deficit is also immediately created. With all debt financing, this deficit will lead to an increase in A, thereby increasing the government interest payments to the private sector. But the balance of trade deficit also has its consequences. It will lead to a loss of foreign reserves, which in the absence of sterilization will cause a reduction in the domestic money supply. The effect of this will be to reduce income (i.e. to offset the initial expansion), thereby lowering tax receipts. One result of these two secondary effects (which in turn feed back on one another) is that the size of budget deficit created by the original increase in expenditure will tend to increase. Moreover, this increase will tend to grow over time, as the interest payments on the increasing stock of existing debt needs to be financed by further increases in debt. This is clearly an unstable process.

On the other hand, suppose $\theta = 1$, $s = 0$. The instantaneous effects of an increase in government expenditure remain as described above but now the responses to them are different. The instantaneous budget deficit is financed through increases in the supply of money, while with complete sterilization, the government responds to the instantaneous balance of trade deficit by engaging in an open market purchase of bonds. Both of these actions have stabilizing influences. The increase in L will tend to increase income further, thereby increasing tax receipts and tending to reduce the government deficit. At the same time the purchase of bonds will tend to reduce the interest payments of the government and this too will tend to reduce the size of the original deficit and thereby slow the growth of the money supply and prevent the kind of instability discussed above.

These results may appear to be at variance with the more usual view in the international monetary literature that sterilization leads to *instability*. But any apparent conflict can be immediately explained by the fact that this conclusion has been based on models which ignore interest payments and as we have seen these are the key destabilizing element. If we ignore interest payments in our model, then under the usual assumption made in this literature $T_2 = T_3 = 0$, we too reach the same conclusion. In this case we find $\dfrac{\partial g}{\partial L}\dfrac{\partial b}{\partial A} - \dfrac{\partial g}{\partial A}\dfrac{\partial b}{\partial L} = 0$, so that (11.27b′) holds with equality irrespective of the relative sizes of θ and s; these are now irrelevant. Furthermore, as s increases, it turns out that the likelihood of (11.27a) being met also increases, leading to the conclusion that less sterilization is likely to lead to stability.

But interest payments should *not* be ignored and by incorporating them, our results tend to confirm the results of Chapter 4 obtained for the analogous model of a closed economy. One of the main conclusions derived there is that while a money-financed deficit tends to be stable, bond financing may quite plausibly lead to instability. As in the present analysis the crucial destabilizing factor is the interest payments on the outstanding government debt. In a sense our stability condition (11.27b′) can be viewed as an open-economy analogue of the previous result.

On the presumption that the system is stable, we now turn to a consideration of its equilibrium properties. As discussed in Section 2, the stationary conditions resulting from these dynamic relations will depend upon whether $\theta \neq s$ or $\theta = s$, and hence it is necessary to consider each case separately.

(a) $\theta \neq s$

In this case the equilibrium of the system consists of the three instantaneous equilibrium equations (11.24), together with the two stationary equations

$$G + A - u(Y + A) = 0 \tag{11.28a}$$

$$T[(1-u)(Y^D + A), r, V] - G_m = 0 \tag{11.28b}$$

where it will be recalled $G = G_d + G_m$. These five equations determine equilibrium values of Y, r, V, A, L, given G_d, G_m, u, and other exogenous parameters.

For a stable system one can take derivatives of the equilibrium relationships (11.24), (11.28) and calculate various equilibrium multipliers. One point worth noting is that all multipliers, and in particular the government expenditure multipliers, are *independent* of θ, s, the mode of government finance and sterilization policy. The fact that they are independent of θ, is a significant difference from the analogous result for a closed economy. While early work by Christ (1967) and others did in fact imply the same result for a closed economy, the more recent paper by Blinder and Solow (1973) shows that this is because the earlier authors ignored interest payments on the outstanding debt. When these are included, it turns out that the long run bond-financed government expenditure multiplier tends to exceed that for money-financed deficit spending; see Chapter 4. This proposition is no longer true here; as in the simplified Christ system (although for obviously different reasons), it is *independent* of the mode of finance.

From (11.28a) we see that the effect of an increase in government expenditure (on domestic goods) on domestic income is

$$\frac{\partial Y}{\partial G_d} = \frac{1}{u} + \frac{1-u}{u}\frac{\partial A}{\partial G_d}. \tag{11.29}$$

Equation (11.29) is formally identical to the analogous result obtained by Blinder–Solow (see equation (7.4)); the one difference is that in our context, the induced bond effect is always necessarily endogenous. Unless $\theta = s = 1$, a situation ruled out by our assumption $\theta \neq s$, A must be changing until equilibrium is reached. Evaluating (11.29), we can show that $\partial Y/\partial G_d > 0$ under quite weak conditions. For example, one simple condition which ensures this will be so is if $T_2 = 0$. But there are many weaker conditions as well, although these involve more complex expressions. Similarly, $\partial Y/\partial G_m$ is most likely negative, a sufficient condition for this to be so being $T_3 = 0$.

(b) $\theta = s$

In this case, the three equations (11.24) still apply. However, recalling (11.23'), (11.28) no longer holds and is replaced by

$$G_d + A - u(Y + A) + T[(1-u)(Y+A), r, V] = 0. \tag{11.30}$$

The final equation is obtained as follows. With $\theta = s$, the two dynamic equations imply proportional adjustments in A and L, in the sense that

$$\theta\frac{\dot{A}}{r} = (1-\theta)\dot{L}. \tag{11.20'}$$

Integrating this equation yields (in the neighbourhood of equilibrium)

$$\frac{\theta}{r}(A - A_0) - (1 - \theta)(L - L_0) = 0 \qquad (11.31)$$

where A_0, L_0 denote initial values. Thus the equilibrium values of the system are now determined by the static relations (11.24) together with (11.30) and (11.31).

This equilibrium differs in two important respects from that in the previous case. The first is that it depends upon the initial state L_0, A_0. The reason for this, is that the linear dependence between $\dot{A}$ and $\dot{L}$ implied by (11.20') makes the dynamic system singular.[13] A and L are not free to vary independently and as is well known, the equilibrium of such a degenerate system depends upon the starting point. The second difference is that θ, which now represents both the proportion of the government deficit financed by money and the degree of sterilization, will influence the comparative static properties of the equilibrium and in particular will affect the government expenditure multiplier.

Finally, we note that while this section has dealt with zero capital mobility, the qualitative nature of the equilibrium conditions hold in the more general conditions where capital is partially, but imperfectly mobile internationally. Furthermore, the crucial role played by the policy parameters θ, s, in the stability of the system also continues to apply. Results, however, change drastically when we make the other polar assumption of perfect capital mobility.

4.   Perfect capital mobility

Consider now the opposite extreme where the capital market of the small country is perfectly integrated with that in the rest of the world. This means that domestic and foreign bonds are perfect substitutes, with the domestic rate of interest, r, being determined abroad, and thus equal to the foreign rate r^*. One can no longer specify separate demand functions for the two types of bonds; they are indistinguishable. Moreover, given the demand for money L^d, the total domestic demand for the single bond is now determined from the stock constraint (11.6).

Thus the instantaneous equilibrium conditions simplify to

$$Y - H[(1-u)(Y + A^D + C), r^*, V] - X - G_d = 0 \qquad (11.32a)$$

$$L(Y, r^*, V) - L = 0 \qquad (11.32b)$$

$$L + (A^D + C)/r^* - V = 0 \qquad (11.32c)$$

which can be solved for total domestic holdings of the *single* bond $(A^D + C)$, as well as Y and V in terms of L and exogenous factors. The foreign holding of domestic bonds is determined residually by

$$A^F = A - A^D.$$

Differentiating this set of equations with respect to L, A yields

$$\frac{\partial Y}{\partial L} = \frac{H_3 - H_1(1-u)r^*(L_3 - 1)}{\Delta} > 0$$

$$\frac{\partial V}{\partial L} = \frac{[1 - H_1(1-u)] + L_1 H_1(1-u)r^*}{\Delta} > 0$$

$$\frac{\partial(A^D + C)}{\partial L} = -\frac{r^*[(1 - H_1(1-u))(L_3 - 1) + H_3 L_1]}{\Delta}$$

$$\frac{\partial g}{\partial L} = -u \left(\frac{\partial Y}{\partial L} + \frac{\partial(A^D + C)}{\partial L} \right) \qquad\qquad (11.33)$$

$$\frac{\partial b}{\partial L} = (1-u)T_1 \frac{\partial Y}{\partial L} + [T_1(1-u) + 1] \frac{\partial(A^D + C)}{\partial L} + T_3 \frac{\partial V}{\partial L}$$

$$\frac{\partial Y}{\partial A} = \frac{\partial V}{\partial A} = \frac{\partial(A^D + C)}{\partial A} = 0, \quad \frac{\partial A^D}{\partial A} = -\frac{\partial C}{\partial A}$$

$$\frac{\partial g}{\partial A} = 1, \quad \frac{\partial b}{\partial A} = -1$$

where $\Delta = H_3 L_1 + L_3[1 - H_1(1-u)] + L_1 H_1(1-u)r^* > 0$. These results as well as being of some interest in their own right, are important in under-standing the stability (or instability) of the adjustment process. They there-fore merit some comment. An increase in the total domestic money supply raises income and wealth, having an ambiguous effect on the domestic hold-ings of the single bond. The expressions for responses to changes in A are perhaps more interesting. The instantaneous effect of a change in A on out-put is zero. Furthermore, an increase in A has no effect on total domestic bond holdings so that with a given money supply domestic wealth is unchanged. As a result, interest income also remains unaltered implying that total personal income, and hence tax revenues received by the domestic government, stay constant. The net effect on the government deficit is to raise it by the additional number of bonds, this being its additional interest commitments. On the other hand, the balance of payments on current account deteriorates by precisely the amount of increase in A. The lower holding of foreign bonds, coupled with the increased holding of domestic bonds by foreigners, results in a net reduction in interest earnings from abroad, while imports, and thus the balance of trade, remain unaffected.

However, it should be clearly understood that these derivatives are purely instantaneous comparative static effects and do not consider the processes whereby these changes occur. For example, $\partial Y/\partial A$ does not describe exactly the effects of an open market operation as such, since in that process L would be changing as well. Hence the expressions in (11.33) must be interpreted with some caution.

In order to analyse the dynamics of the system, we must first consider the steady state equilibrium conditions implied by (11.32). With r being determined exogenously by r^*, we shall consider the system to be in an equilibrium stationary state when $\dot{Y} = 0$. Differentiating (11.32) with respect to t and setting $\dot{Y} = 0$, we obtain the following stationary conditions

$$\dot{A}^D + \dot{C} = \dot{V} = \dot{L} = 0.$$

The most important fact emerging from these conditions is that since $\dfrac{\partial Y}{\partial A} = 0$, it is *not* necessary to have $\dot{A} = 0$, in order for output to be stationary; the number of bonds issued by the domestic government may be changing. If $\dot{A} > 0$ say, then equilibrium will be maintained provided the rate at which domestic residents increase their holdings of domestic bonds is just offset by the rate at which they reduce their holdings of foreign bonds. This will ensure that domestic wealth and interest income remain constant, hence making it possible for domestic income to be stationary.

Differentiating the static equilibrium conditions (11.32) with respect to t, and using (11.33), yields the linear approximation

$$\dot{A}^D + \dot{C} = \alpha \dot{L}$$

where $\alpha \equiv \dfrac{\partial (A^D + C)}{\partial L}$. Also differentiating (11.19e) with respect to t

$$\dot{A}^F = \dot{A} - \dot{A}^D$$

and abstracting these two expressions, we obtain

$$\dot{C} - \dot{A}^F = \alpha \dot{L} - \dot{A}.$$

Substituting for $(\dot{C} - \dot{A}^F)$ into (11.20), the dynamic system becomes

$$\begin{pmatrix} 1 + s\alpha/r^* & -s/r^* \\ \alpha(1-s)/r^* & s/r^* \end{pmatrix} \begin{pmatrix} \dot{L} \\ \dot{A} \end{pmatrix} = \begin{pmatrix} \theta g + sb \\ (1-\theta)g + (1-s)b \end{pmatrix} \tag{11.34}$$

In order for this pair of equations to imply consistent expressions for $\dot{L}, \dot{A}$ we require $s \neq 0$.[14] If $s = 0$, the two equations degenerate into two mutually inconsistent equations for $\dot{L}$. This reflects the fact that with perfect capital mobility, any attempt to sterilize capital inflows *completely* by open market operations is necessarily an infeasible policy. If $B > 0$ say, and the monetary authorities attempt to sterilize this completely by an open market sale of bonds, we will have $\dot{D} = -B < 0$. With perfect capital mobility this will induce a net inflow of capital equal to $(\dot{A}^F - \dot{C})/r^* = + B > 0$, so that the domestic money supply will in fact remain unchanged.

Consequently, it is necessary throughout this section to assume $s \neq 0$, in which case the dynamic system can be expressed in the form

$$(1 + \alpha/r^*)\dot{L} = g(L, A) + b(L, A) \qquad (11.34a')$$

$$\frac{s}{r^*}(1 + \alpha/r^*)\dot{A} = [(1 - \theta) + \alpha(s - \theta)/r^*] g(L, A)$$

$$+ (1 - s)b(L, A). \qquad (11.34b')$$

Linearizing the right hand side of $(11.34')$ and utilizing the fact that $g_2 = 1$, $b_2 = -1$, equation $(11.34a')$ is seen to be *independent of A and thus is a differential equation in L alone.* Consequently, as the stationarity conditions for Y have been shown above not to depend upon A, *the equilibrium and stability of Y depends only upon that of equation (11.34a');* the corresponding properties of $(11.34b')$ are irrelevant.

It immediately follows from the stationarity requirement $\dot{L} = 0$, that in equilibrium

$$g(L, A) + b(L, A) = 0. \qquad (11.23')$$

This of course, is the McKinnon–Oates equilibrium condition that the deficit in the government's budget must equal the deficit in the balance of payments on current account. Any increase in L resulting from a balance of payments surplus, say, is exactly offset, after taking into account portfolio adjustment, by an equal reduction in L resulting from the government running a surplus.

It is also illuminating to express the equilibrium condition $(11.23')$ in terms of B. Substituting for $\dot{C}, \dot{A}^F$, and b into (11.18) yields

$$B = b + (\dot{A} - \alpha\dot{L})/r^*$$

In equilibrium, when $\dot{L} = 0$, and $(11.23')$ holds, $\dot{A}$ must satisfy

$$s\dot{A}/r^* = (s - \theta)g$$

from which we immediately deduce that $(11.23')$ is equivalent to

$$B + \theta g/s = 0. \qquad (11.23'')$$

In particular if the government's deficit is completely debt-financed ($\theta = 0$), we see that in equilibrium, the total balance of payments (current account plus capital) will equal zero. On the other hand, if part of the deficit is financed by money-creation ($\theta \neq 0$) the stationary solution implies an overall disequilibrium in the balance of payments proportional to the size of the deficit.

Returning to (11.23a'): since it is easily shown that $(1 + \alpha/r^*) > 0$, it follows from the fact that this equation is independent of A, that the sufficient condition for the local stability of L, and consequently of output Y, is simply

$$g_1 + b_1 < 0 \tag{11.35}$$

while the necessary condition is the corresponding weak inequality

$$g_1 + b_1 \leqslant 0. \tag{11.35'}$$

Substituting from (11.33) for the partial derivatives g_1, b_1 we obtain $g_1 + b_1$

$$
= \frac{H_3[T_1(1-u) - u - L_1(1-u)(1+T_1)r^*] - r^*(L_3 - 1)(1-u)(1-H_1+T_1)}{\Delta}
$$

$$
+ \frac{T_3[1 - H_1(1-u) + L_1 H_1(1-u)r^*]}{\Delta} \tag{11.36}
$$

which can be seen to be indeterminate in sign. On the basis of typical empirical estimates one would expect $(g_1 + b_1) < 0$. Taking plausible values such as $H_3 = 0.06, r^* = 0.05, H_1 = 0.70, T_1 = -0.20, u = 0.24$, (11.36) is certainly negative for all values of the remaining parameters T_3, L_1, L_3, lying in their respective ranges $T_3 \leqslant 0, L_1 \geqslant 0, 0 \leqslant L_3 \leqslant 1$.[15] In this case, which we regard as quite realistic, the system will certainly be stable.

However, we must also point out that if wealth effects are absent from both real private domestic expenditure and import demand (i.e. $H_3 = T_3 = 0$), $(g_1 + b_1)$ is unambiguously positive, thereby making the system unstable. As we shall discuss below, the source of the instability is the interest payments on debt, which form a component of disposable income. If, as is typically done, one (incorrectly) ignores these, then one can show that stability is again restored to the system.[16]

To see why (11.35) is necessary and sufficient for stability, consider the dynamics of the system starting from a situation in which *both* the government budget and the balance of payments are in equilibrium so that $[g(0) = b(0) = \dot{C}(0) = \dot{A}^F(0) = 0]$, and which is suddenly displaced by an increase in government expenditure, say, so that $g(0 +) > 0$. From equation (11.15) this is financed by an increase in domestic money θg, together with an increase in domestic government bonds $(1 - \theta)g$. Concurrently with this, the increase in these two domestic assets results in a net capital inflow of $-(\alpha\theta/r^* - (1 - \theta))g$. This in turn creates a balance of payments surplus which with $s \neq 0$ will also involve a change in domestic assets. After the portfolio adjustment is completed — all of which in our continuous-time model takes place instantaneously — the net effect is that the domestic money supply increases by $g/(1 + \alpha/r^*)$. This is seen from (11.34') where we also see that the net increase in domestic bonds is

$$r^*g[(1-\theta) + \alpha(s-\theta)/r^*]/s(1 + \alpha/r^*).$$

The initial increases in L and A in turn affect g and b and hence have further effects on both $\dot{A}$ and $\dot{L}$. But, as the differential equation describing L has been shown to be a function of L alone, the stability of L (and Y) does not depend on what happens to A. The subsequent dynamics of A can therefore be ignored, enabling us to focus on the movements of L alone.

To further understand (11.35), and more particularly to see the destabilizing nature of interest payments, it is useful to consider the limiting case $H_3 = T_3 = 0$, when, as we have already seen, the system will be unstable. In this case, the initial increase in L raises income and domestic wealth, resulting in an increased holding of bonds, which for given A must be obtained from abroad. This in turn raises interest income received from abroad, creating a balance of payments surplus on current account. This is offset partly by higher imports which result from the higher level of domestic income. But the net effect is a balance of payments surplus on current account, leading to further increases in the domestic money supply.

At the same time, the increase in interest earnings from abroad, together with the increase in domestic income, raises tax receipts, thereby reducing the domestic government budget deficit. To the extent that this occurs, this is stabilizing, tending to offset the increase in L resulting from the balance of payments surplus. With $H_3 = T_3 = 0$ the unstable interest payments effect can be shown to dominate the other stabilizing adjustments. Moreover, the smaller is L_3, the more the increase in wealth resulting from the increase in L is held in the form of additional bonds.[17] Consequently, the larger are the interest earnings from abroad and hence the larger is the increase (or at least the smaller the decrease) in the overall domestic money supply, the more unstable the system becomes. Conversely, while the interest earnings from abroad are destabilizing, the wealth effects in domestic expenditure, balance of trade and domestic money demand (H_3, T_3 and L_3) are stabilizing.[18]

It is clear from the foregoing analysis that unlike the previous case of zero (imperfect) capital mobility, the stability condition for L (and Y) is independent of the financial policy parameters θ and s. The reason for this is that these determine the stability of A, which as we have seen is unnecessary for that of L. If, on the contrary, we wish to have the system stable in A as well as in L, then it follows from (11.34′) that sufficient conditions for this to be so are given by the pair of equations

$$g_1 + b_1 < 0$$

and

$$\theta > s.$$

The latter condition arises from the effects of the initial increase in A and $\dot{L}$ on $\dot{A}$. The increase in L may tend to either increase A further, or to restore it towards its equilibrium depending upon the sign of $(1 - \theta)g_1 + (1 - s)b_1$. However, whatever happens in the short run, in the long run its effect disappears. The reason for this is simply that as we have just seen, provided (11.35) holds, L must ultimately stabilize, in which case there are no further changes in L to influence A.[19]

The crucial element in determining the stability of A is the stabilizing or destabilizing effect of the increase in A on $\dot{A}$. This is given by the term $(1-\theta)g_2 + (1-s)b_2 = (s-\theta)$. On the one hand a unit increase in bonds increases the government deficit by one unit, resulting in an issue of a further $(1-\theta)$ bonds, on the other hand, a unit increase in bonds reduces the balance of payments on current account by one unit, which with a sterilization coefficient s, results in a withdrawal of $(1-s)$ bonds. If $\theta - s > 0$, the net effect of an increase in $\dot{A}$ is to lower A and thereby to be stabilizing; however if $\theta - s \leqslant 0$ the process is destabilizing.

Assuming the system is stable, we turn briefly to a consideration of its equilibrium properties. These can be most conveniently reduced to the three static equations (11.32a)–(11.32c), together with the stationary solution to (11.34a$'$), namely (11.23$'$), which we can then solve for the equilibrium values of the four variables $Y, (A^D + C), V, L$. By differentiating this set of four equations we can calculate various long-run (equilibrium) responses to parameter changes. Of these, probably the most interesting is the government expenditure multiplier

$$\frac{\partial r}{\partial G_d} = \frac{(T_3 - H_3) - r^*(L_3 - 1)(1-u)(1-H_1+T_1)}{\Delta_1} \qquad (11.37)$$

where the denominator of (11.37), Δ_1, is precisely the numerator of (11.36), the sign of which determined the stability of the system. Thus provided the system is stable, this expression is negative. For the same plausible parameters which ensured $g_1 + b_1 < 0$, the numerator of (11.37) is also negative implying $\dfrac{\partial Y}{\partial G_d} > 0$. However, it is certainly possible for the numerator and denominator of this expression to be of opposite signs, in which case a perverse multiplier cannot be ruled out. But whatever the sign of (11.37), the magnitude of the multiplier is independent of θ, s.

5.   The assignment problem

The model we have been studying has important implications for the 'assignment problem', outlined in Chapter 9. Recalling the discussion, it was shown that given two targets, and two policy instruments, the stability of adjustment is assured if each instrument is assigned to the target for which it has a comparative advantage. This was known as the 'principle of effective market classification' (PEMC). In applying this principle to the open economy, Mundell's early work suggested that under fixed exchange rates, fiscal policy has a comparative advantage over monetary policy in attaining the domestic objective. Hence he showed that a stable assignment calls for directing fiscal policy towards the income objective and monetary policy towards the balance of payments goal. His model was based on the simplest behavioural assumptions and subsequent work has been concerned with determining whether these propositions continue to hold in more complex models.

In adopting the PEMC (which applies to purely *static* systems), virtually all of the literature makes the error of ignoring the inherent dynamics of the system arising from the government budget constraint and the balance of payments adjustment. In our model these are described by the $\dot{A}, \dot{F}, \dot{D}$ equations. The conventional approach takes the static equations such as (11.19) and simply embeds them in conventional dynamic adjustment functions; see (9.33). It does not take into account the consequent repercussions on the money supply and flow of capital.

It is clear from the present discussion that the dynamics of policy instrument adjustment must be considered *within the context of the entire dynamic model.* Moreover, as Aghevli and Borts (1973) have argued recently, once one recognizes the inherent dynamics of the system, it is much more reasonable to regard the level of foreign reserves F, rather than the balance of payments B, as the appropriate external objective.

Thus suppose that the government policy makers have an internal income objective $\bar{Y}$ and a foreign reserve objective $\bar{F}$. Assume further, that following Mundell and others it assigns fiscal policy to the former, monetary policy to the latter. Thus we postulate[20]

$$\dot{D} = \theta g - \gamma_1 (\bar{F} - F) \qquad \gamma_1 > 0 \qquad (11.38a)$$

$$\dot{A}/r = (1 - \theta)g + \gamma_1 (\bar{F} - F) \qquad (11.38b)$$

$$\dot{F} = B \qquad (11.38c)$$

$$\dot{G} = \gamma_2 (\bar{Y} - Y) \qquad \gamma_2 > 0 \qquad (11.38d)$$

where the coefficients γ_1, γ_2, describe the policy assignment.

Equation (11.38a) asserts that the domestic monetary base is adjusted partly to finance the government deficit and also for purposes of achieving the external policy objective. We could also include a sterilization component as we did before, but this would seem to be unnecessary where the external objective is explicitly stated in terms of F. Equations (11.38b) and (11.38c) are straightforward, having been discussed in Section 2. The final equation gives the fiscal policy adjustment; government expenditure is adjusted to move Y towards $\bar{Y}$.

Note that with F being introduced as an explicit objective it is necessary to consider D and F separately, rather than their sum L, as was done above. Following the procedure outlined in Section 2, we can solve for the terms $\dot{C}, \dot{A}^F$ which appear in B, in terms of $\dot{D}, \dot{A}/r$, and $\dot{F}$, yielding a dynamic system of the form

$$\dot{D} = \theta g(D + F, A, G) - \gamma_1 (\bar{F} - F) \qquad \gamma_1 > 0 \qquad (11.38a')$$

$$\frac{\dot{A}}{r} = (1 - \theta)g(D + F, A, G) + \gamma_1(\bar{F} - F) \qquad (11.38c')$$

$$\dot{F} = \lambda_1 b(D + F, A, G) + \lambda_2 g + \lambda_3(F - \bar{F}) \qquad (11.38c')$$

$$\dot{G} = \gamma_2[\bar{Y} - Y(D + F, A, G)] \qquad \gamma_2 > 0 \qquad (11.38d')$$

where g, b are defined as before and are now written explicitly as functions of G as well. Provided the system is stable, it is clear that its equilibrium is given by

$$F = \bar{F}, \quad Y = \bar{Y}, \quad g = 0 = b$$

so that both the government budget and the balance of payments on current account must balance when the target variables attain their objectives.

The key issue in the assignment problem is the stability of the adjustment (11.38'), and this requires the eigenvalues of the following matrix

$$\begin{pmatrix} \theta g_1 & \theta g_2 & \theta g_1 + \gamma_1 & \theta g_3 \\ r(1 - \theta)g_1 & r(1 - \theta)g_2 & r(1 - \theta)g_1 - \gamma_1 r & r(1 - \theta)g_3 \\ \lambda_1 b_1 + \lambda_2 g_1 & \lambda_1 b_2 + \lambda_2 g_2 & \lambda_1 b_1 + \lambda_2 g_1 + \lambda_3 & \lambda_1 b_3 + \lambda_2 g_3 \\ -\gamma_2 Y_1 & -\gamma_2 Y_2 & -\gamma_2 Y_1 & -\gamma_2 Y_3 \end{pmatrix}$$

to have negative real parts.[21] To determine the restrictions this implies is a tedious exercise and we do not pursue it here. But it is apparent that since the adjustment of the policy instruments is only *part* of a larger, more complex dynamic system, stability does not depend only upon choosing γ_1, γ_2 appropriately. These would need to be chosen in conjunction with θ, so that the PEMC alone, is likely to be neither necessary nor sufficient for equilibrium.

6.   **Summary**

Despite the rather complicated analysis, the most important conclusions of this chapter can be summarized quite simply.

Assuming domestic bonds and foreign bonds are imperfect substitutes, then provided the proportion of the government deficit financed by the creation of new money (θ), does *not* equal the proportion of changes in foreign reserves which the domestic monetary authorities do not seek to sterilize (s), equilibrium requires *both* the government's budget deficit (g) *and* the balance of payments on current account (b) to be in equilibrium ($= 0$). All new issues of domestic bonds and changes in the domestic money supply must cease (i.e. $\dot{L} = \dot{A} = 0$), as must all international flows of new capital. The only flows of capital remaining are the interest payments on the outstanding debt. While typically one would expect $\theta \neq s$, it is, of course, possible for $\theta = s$, in which case equilibrium requires only that $g + b = 0$. That is, any deficit (surplus) in the government budget must just equal the deficit (surplus) in the current account of the balance of payments.

Considering first the case of zero capital mobility, stability is shown to

depend crucially upon the sign of $(\theta - s)$. Provided $\left(\dfrac{\partial g}{\partial L} \dfrac{\partial b}{\partial A} - \dfrac{\partial g}{\partial A} \dfrac{\partial b}{\partial L} > 0 \right)$ —

which we argue will almost certainly be met — a *necessary* condition for local stability is that $\theta \geqslant s$. If $\theta = s$, the system becomes singular, and if stable, converges to an equilibrium which depends upon initial conditions. Consequently a significant result of the analysis is to highlight how the appropriate choice of the policy parameters θ, s, is of central importance to the stability of the model. For $\theta \neq s$, the equilibrium multipliers are shown to be independent of these policy parameters. Most notably, the government expenditure multiplier is thus independent of the method of finance, a result which is significantly different from that for a closed economy. When $\theta = s$, on the other hand, the equilibrium comparative static properties of the system do once again depend upon the (common) value of these policy parameters.

The above conclusions, while obtained for the limiting case of zero capital mobility, can be shown to apply in the general case where international capital is *imperfectly* mobile. Results for the other polar case of perfect capital mobility, however, differ quite substantially. First, equilibrium does not require the issue of new domestic bonds to cease. All that is needed is that the rate at which domestic residents increase their holding of domestic bonds be exactly offset by the rate at which they reduce their holdings of foreign bonds. As a result equilibrium requires only that $g + b = 0$, irrespective of how θ, s are chosen. If the government's deficit is completely debt financed this implies that the total balance of payments (current account plus capital account) is zero. For $\theta \neq 0$, however, it yields an overall balance of payments deficit proportional to the government's deficit.

Taking plausible parameter values, suggests that in this limiting case the system will be stable, although the possibility of instability certainly cannot be dismissed. Indeed it is shown how interest payments tend to be destabilizing, while wealth effects in real private domestic expenditure and the domestic demand for money tend to be offsetting stabilizing influences. Furthermore, in this case the stability of output is independent of how θ, s are chosen, as are the equilibrium multipliers of the system. These parameters are important in determining the stability of A, but as this is not required for the stability of the rest of the system, and in particular for output, their selection is not constrained as it is when capital is imperfectly mobile.

Finally, we discussed briefly the implications of the analysis for the assignment problem. It becomes clear that since the adjustment of policy instruments is only part of a larger dynamic system, the principle of effective market classification alone will in general be neither necessary nor sufficient for a stable assignment.

12

IMPORTED INFLATION AND GOVERNMENT POLICIES IN A DYNAMIC OPEN MACROECONOMIC MODEL

1. Introduction[1]

We turn now to our final model of the open economy in which we consider some of the longer-run aspects of monetary and fiscal policies in an inflationary environment. Specifically, our concern is to introduce the rate of inflation and its associated dynamics into a model incorporating the dynamics of asset accumulation and capital flows. In effect, the analysis we shall undertake can be viewed as an extension of both Chapter 10, which dealt with the short-run aspects of monetary and fiscal policies in inflationary conditions, and Chapter 11, which introduced the dynamics of asset accumulation in a world of fixed prices, and fixed exchange rates. The present model, however, shall deal with both fixed and flexible exchange rate regimes, although because of the complexity of the analysis we restrict ourselves to the limiting case of perfect capital mobility throughout.

Our approach to this problem draws upon both Keynes—Phillips and monetary elements. It is Keynesian in the sense that, as in our previous models, it assumes Keynesian-type expenditure functions and determines output endogenously by means of a flow equilibrium relationship in the product market. It includes a Phillips curve, augmented to allow for the impact of inflationary expectations, as one of the relationships explaining the domestic rate of inflation. On the other hand we pay particular attention to the relationship between stocks and flows in the system. As in Chapter 11, we explicitly incorporate the fact that a balance of payments surplus or deficit generally involves changes in the domestic money supply. Similarly, a government deficit or surplus must be financed, and this too involves changes in the outside wealth of the private sector. In this respect the analysis is in the spirit of the monetary approach, and indeed our general conclusions turn out to be quite consistent with many monetarist propositions.

The formal method of analysis we adopt follows our previous dynamic models closely. Essentially we embed an instantaneous equilibrium (the Keynesian model) into a longer-run dynamic system, in which the dynamic forces are the accumulation of assets, the evolution of price expectations, and the movement of relative prices. It is thus very much in the spirit of Chapters 7, 8 for the closed ecconomy as well as Chapter 11.

2. The model

For the most part, our model is developed in sufficient generality to apply to either a fixed or a flexible exchange rate system. In the latter stages of the section we indicate the extra assumptions necessary to apply the model to the two separate cases. As in Chapter 10 we assume that the country is sufficiently competitive in the markets for its imports to take the price of imports as given. On the other hand, we assume that export prices are determined in the domestic output market, being the same as the prices of domestically produced non-traded goods. We therefore associate imported inflation with rising import prices.[2]

As indicated above, the development of the model follows our earlier dynamic models. First we consider a number of static or instantaneous relationships describing the output sector, the wage–price sector, the financial sector, and the disposable income concept of the model. These together provide a set of equations describing the instantaneous equilibrium of the system in terms of a number of variables, such as the stock of assets, the terms of trade, and the level of inflationary expectations, which together describe the state of the system. We then consider the dynamics of the system as these variables evolve over time.

A. Domestic output sector

The specification of the domestic output sector, is virtually the same as that given in Chapters 10 and 11. Specifically, we assume no domestic production of the imported good and no imported inputs. Given our assumption for export prices, equilibrium in the domestic output market is

$$Z = H(Y^D, r - \pi, QE/P_1, V) + X(QE/P_1) + G_d \\ 0 < P_1 H_1/P < 1, \quad H_2 < 0, \quad H_3 > 0, \quad H_4 > 0, \quad X' > 0 \right\} \quad (12.1)$$

where

Z = real domestic output; i.e., nominal output deflated by the price of domestically produced goods P_1,

H = real private domestic demand for domestically produced goods,

X = real exports of domestically produced goods,

G_d = real government expenditure on domestically produced goods,

Y^D = real private domestic disposable income; i.e. nominal income deflated by the overall domestic price index P (defined below),

r = domestic nominal rate of interest,

π = expected rate of inflation of the domestic cost of living P, so that $(r - \pi)$ is a measure of the expected real rate of interest,

P_1 = price of domestically produced goods (in terms of domestic currency),

Q = price of foreign goods (in terms of foreign currency),

P = domestic cost of living (in terms of domestic currency),

E = price of foreign exchange in terms of domestic currency,

V = real private domestic wealth; i.e., nominal wealth deflated by P.

In one important respect this equation differs from our previous specification. Both Y^D, V are obtained by deflating by P (rather than P_1 as before) reflecting the fact that consumers are concerned with the overall purchasing power of their income and wealth. As a consequence, to the extent to which a devaluation results in changes in P, it gives rise to both an income effect and a wealth effect. These have been discussed elsewhere in the international trade literature; see Machlup (1956), Dornbusch (1973).

B. *Domestic wage–price sector*

We shall specify the domestic cost of living (CPI) by the following index

$$P = \phi(P_1, QE) \tag{12.2}$$

where $\phi_1 > 0$, $\phi_2 > 0$ and ϕ is homogeneous of degree one in its two arguments. If we assume further that the domestic residents' utility function, defined with domestic goods and imports as its arguments, is Cobb–Douglas, then the associated 'true' cost-of-living index is of the form[3]

$$P = P_1^\delta (QE)^{1-\delta}. \tag{12.2'}$$

Taking the logarithmic derivative of (12.2') with respect to time t yields the corresponding percentage change relationship

$$p = \delta p_1 + (1 - \delta)(q + e) \tag{12.3}$$

where

$p_1 = \dot{p}_1/p_1$ = rate of inflation of the price of the domestic good, (in terms of domestic currency),

$q = \dot{Q}/Q$ = rate of inflation of the price of foreign goods (in terms of foreign currency),

$e = \dot{E}/E$ = rate of exchange depreciation,

$p = \dot{P}/P$ = rate of inflation of domestic cost of living (in terms of domestic currency).

Since our concern is with analysing the rate of inflation, the multiplicative fixed-weight index assumed in (12.2'), as well as being of some theoretical merit, is most convenient. We shall therefore assume that (12.2'), and therefore (12.3), holds throughout.

It will be noted in equation (12.1) that demands depend upon the relative price QE/P_1. Denoting this ratio by σ, it follows that $1/\sigma$ measures the terms of trade. Furthermore, because of the homogeneity of (12.2) we have

$$P/P_1 \equiv \phi(\sigma) = \sigma^{1-\delta} \tag{12.4}$$

a relationship we shall use subsequently.

The rate of inflation of domestically produced goods is explained by the equation

$$\left.\begin{array}{l} p_1 = a_0 + a_1(Z - \bar{Z}) + a_2 w + a_3(q + e) \\ a_1 > 0, \quad 0 < a_2 \leqslant 1, \quad 0 \leqslant a_3 < 1, \quad 0 < a_2 + a_3 \leqslant 1 \end{array}\right\} \tag{12.5}$$

where w denotes the rate of money wage inflation and $\bar{Z}$ is the capacity level of output. This equation is the continuous-time analogue of (10.5). The comments made in Chapter 10 thus apply here as well. Assuming that the rate of money-wage inflation is generated by the extended Phillips curve (10.6) and that the rate of unemployment is related to the degree of product market disequilibrium by the linear equation (10.7), we are able to obtain the following reduced form equation for the domestic wage–price sector,

$$\left.\begin{array}{l} p_1 = \alpha_0 + \alpha_1(Z - \bar{Z}) + \alpha_2 \pi + \alpha_3(q + e) \\ \alpha_1 > 0, 0 \leqslant \alpha_2 \leqslant 1, 0 \leqslant \alpha_3 < 1, 0 < \alpha_2 + \alpha_3 \leqslant 1. \end{array}\right\} \tag{12.6}$$

C. Financial sector

We assume that two assets are held in the portfolios of the domestic private sector; domestic money and a single bond, which is taken to be a variable interest rate bond. Private citizens at home and abroad do not hold foreign currencies as assets. The bond may be issued either by the domestic government or by the foreign government, with investors viewing these as perfect substitutes. This assumption of perfect capital mobility is of course, a limiting one, which greatly simplifies the analysis. While the assumption can be shown to influence significantly the comparative statics of the model, it does not affect the general properties of the steady state in any substantial way. An outline of the model for the more general case of imperfect capital mobility is given in Kingston and Turnovsky (1976).

In order for domestic and foreign bonds to be perfect substitutes, their (expected) rates of return in terms of domestic currency must be equal. Hence the domestic rate of interest and the foreign rate of interest r^*, which we take to be exogenously given, must be related by

$$r = r^* + e^* \tag{12.7}$$

where

$e^* =$ expected rate of exchange depreciation of the domestic currency

For simplicity, we assume that exchange rate changes are perfectly anticipated so that $e^* \equiv e$, in which case[4]

$$r = r^* + e. \tag{12.7'}$$

Given the fact that information on exchange rate changes is usually readily available, this assumption does not seem too unreasonable. With fixed exchange rates, (12.7') reduces to the more familiar expression

$$r = r^*. \tag{12.7''}$$

Following the discussion of Chapters 7 and 8 we assume that real asset demands are functions of real output, expected real rates of return, and real wealth. For expositional simplicity we follow convention by introducing the rates of return in pre-tax form. This does not alter the substance of the analysis, but in this connection the comments made in Chapter 8 should be borne in mind.[5] Hence we specify the following equilibrium relationship for asset demand,[6]

$$\frac{L}{P} = L(Z, r^* + e - \pi, -\pi, V) \qquad L_1 > 0, \quad L_2 < 0, \quad L_3 > 0,$$

$$0 < L_4 < 1 \tag{12.8a}$$

$$\frac{N}{P} = J(Z, r^* + e - \pi, -\pi, V) \qquad J_1 < 0, \quad J_2 > 0, \quad J_3 < 0,$$

$$0 < J_4 < 1 \tag{12.8b}$$

where

L = nominal stock of domestic money held by domestic residents (denominated in domestic currency),

N = nominal stock of bonds held by domestic residents (valued in domestic currency).

As in Chapter 11, we shall abstract from net investment in the domestic economy, so that the physical stock of domestic capital remains fixed at $\bar{K}$ say. For notational simplicity we shall set $\bar{K} = 0$. The conditions under which this simplification can be justified without any essential loss of generality are discussed in Chapter 11, Section 2 and the same arguments apply here as well.[7]

Bearing this assumption in mind, the demand functions (12.8) are subject to the wealth constraint

$$\frac{L + N}{P} = V. \tag{12.9}$$

The following points should be noted about (12.8) and (12.9). First, because of the wealth constraint, only one of the two functions (12.8) can be specified independently, enabling us to eliminate (12.8b) say. Secondly, as in earlier chapters, differentiating the wealth constraint imposes the following 'adding-up' restrictions on the partial derivatives of the asset demand functions

$$L_i + J_i = 0 \qquad i = 1, 2, 3$$

$$L_4 + J_4 = 1.$$

Finally, the signs of the partial derivatives given in (12.8) include the assumption that the demand for each asset varies positively with its own real rate of return and negatively with the return on the other assets; the two assets are gross substitutes.

D. Real private disposable income

The final instantaneous relationship we must consider is real private disposable income. Following the discussion of Chapter 3, we define this by

$$Y^D = (1-u)\left(\frac{P_1 Z}{P} + (r^* + e)\,\frac{N}{P}\right) - \pi V \tag{12.10}$$

where u = domestic rate of income tax, taken to be constant. That is, real private disposable income, measured in domestic cost-of-living units, equals the nominal value of factor income $(1-u)P_1 Z$, plus nominal interest income both deflated by the overall cost of living P, and net of taxes, as well as the expected capital gain or loss on the private holding of financial wealth. Since each component of pV appears as a revenue item in the real budget constraint of the domestic or foreign government, we shall refer to πV as the '(expected) inflation tax on financial wealth'.

E. Dynamics of the system

We turn now to the dynamic equations of the model. These describe the accumulation of assets, the adjustments in the terms of trade, and the evolution of inflationary expectations.

The first relationship is the domestic government budget constraint. This is described by

$$\dot{D} + \dot{A} = P_1 G_d + QEG_m + (r^* + e)A - u[P_1 Z + (r^* + e)N] \tag{12.11}$$

where

$\quad G_m$ = real government demand for imports,

$\quad A$ = outstanding stock of bond debt of the domestic government, in nominal units of the domestic currency,

$\quad D$ = domestic component of the monetary base, expressed in nominal units of the domestic currency.

Equation (12.11) is the analogue to (11.10). It asserts that total goverment expenditure plus interest payments, less tax receipts, all expressed in nominal domestic currency, must be financed either by selling government bonds or by increasing the domestic component of the monetary base.

Secondly, there is the identity relating the accumulation of foreign reserves to the balance of payments. We express this by

$$\dot{F} = B \tag{12.12}$$

where

F = level of foreign reserves, expressed in terms of domestic currency,

B = balance of payments, expressed in terms of nominal units of the domestic currency.

We assume that foreign reserves are held in foreign currency and do not earn interest. Domestic government debt is not held in the reserve portfolios of foreign governments. Under a flexible exchange rate system (12.12) is, of course, identically zero, but as we have already mentioned, we are developing the model in sufficient generality to cover the two exchange rate systems. The balance of payments is defined by the relationship

$$\left. \begin{aligned} B &= P_1 X - QE\left[M(Y^D, r^* + e - \pi, \sigma, V) + G_m\right] \\ &\quad + \dot{A} - \dot{N} + (r^* + e)(N - A) \\ 0 &< \frac{QE}{P} M_1 < 1, \quad M_2 < 0, \quad M_3 < 0, \quad M_4 > 0 \end{aligned} \right\} \tag{12.13}$$

where M denotes real private domestic demands for imports. The balance of payments therefore consists of the balance of trade $[P_1 X - QE(M + G_m)]$, the net inflow of new capital $(\dot{A} - \dot{N})$, together with the offsetting movements of interest payments on the existing debt, $(r^* + e)(N - A)$.

Differentiating the definitional relationship,

$$L = D + F$$

yields,

$$\dot{L} = \dot{D} + \dot{F}. \tag{12.14}$$

Adding (12.11) and (12.12), and using (12.13) and (12.14), it follows that

$$\dot{L} + \dot{N} = \{P_1 G_d + QEG_m + (r^* + e)A - u[P_1 Z + (r^* + e)N]\}$$
$$+ [P_1 X - QE(M + G_m) + (r^* + e)(N - A)]. \tag{12.15}$$

That is, the accumulation of nominal wealth of the domestic private sector equals the nominal government deficit, plus the nominal balance of payments on current account.

The dynamics of relative prices is obtained by differentiating σ with respect to time, yielding

$$\dot{\sigma} = (q + e - p_1)\sigma. \tag{12.16}$$

Finally, the evolution of inflationary expectations is assumed to be generated by a simple adaptive process

$$\dot{\pi} = \rho(p - \pi) \tag{12.17}$$

where $\rho > 0$ is constant and describes the speed of expectations adjustment.

F.   *Summary of model and respecification in real terms*
This completes our description of the basic relationships underlying the model. However, before embarking on any analysis we shall summarize it and transform it to real terms.
Letting

$$l \equiv \frac{L}{P} = \text{real stock of domestic money}$$

$$n \equiv \frac{N}{P} = \text{real stock of bonds held by domestic private sector,}$$

the instantaneous relationships discussed in Sections A–D can be reduced to

$$Z = H(Y^D, r^* + e - \pi, \sigma, V) + X(\sigma) + G_d \tag{12.18a}$$

$$p_1 = \alpha_0 + \alpha_1(Z - \bar{Z}) + \alpha_2 \pi + \alpha_3(q + e) \tag{12.18b}$$

$$p = \delta p_1 + (1 - \delta)(q + e) \tag{12.18c}$$

$$V = l + n \tag{12.18d}$$

$$l = L(Z, r^* + e - \pi, -\pi, V) \tag{12.18e}$$

$$Y^D = (1 - u)\left(\frac{Z}{\phi(\sigma)} + (r^* + e)n\right) - \pi V. \tag{12.18f}$$

Similarly, defining

$$b_T = \frac{X(\sigma) - \sigma[M(Y^D, r^* + e - \pi, \sigma, V) + G_m]}{\phi(\sigma)} \tag{12.19a}$$

$$g_T = \frac{G_d + \sigma G_m - uZ}{\phi(\sigma)} \tag{12.19b}$$

(12.15) can be expressed in real terms as

$$\dot{V} = g_T + b_T + (1 - u)(r^* + e)n - pV \tag{12.20a}$$

b_T denotes the balance of trade in domestic cost of living units. g_T is seen to be an analogous item in the government current accounts; it would seem however, that g_T does not have a generally accepted name. We shall describe it as the *fiscal deficit*. Thus, real wealth accumulation of the domestic private sector equals the fiscal deficit, plus the trade surplus, plus the net asset income of the domestic private sector. The other two equations remain as before, namely,

$$\dot{\sigma} = (q + e - p_1) \tag{12.20b}$$

$$\dot{\pi} = \rho(p - \pi). \tag{12.20c}$$

The logical structure of the model is now clear. Let us first consider the case of a fixed exchange rate, in which case $e \equiv 0$. The instantaneous relationships (12.18) can be viewed as defining six independent equations in the six variables Z, Y^D, p_1, p, n, l. Provided the Jacobian of the system is non-zero, these equations can be solved locally for these six variables in terms of V, σ, π, and any exogenous variables and parameters. These solutions can then be inserted into the dynamic relationships (12.19). The resulting differential equations in V, σ, π, then describe the evolution of the complete system over time.

One interesting feature of this system is that (barring singularities in the Jacobian) its dynamics is completely determined without specifying any government policy for financing its deficit or target level of foreign reserves. This is entirely a consequence of our assumption of perfect capital mobility; it ceases to be true in the more general case of imperfect capital mobility. In this case to close the model one must specify some government policy for describing the adjustment of l and a. Moreover, the dynamic properties of the system are highly sensitive to the policies chosen; see Chapter 11.

With flexible exchange rates, on the other hand, the rate of exchange depreciation e is also an endogenous variable. The instantaneous equations (12.18) are therefore insufficient to determine solutions for Z, Y^D, p, p_1, n, l, e, in terms of the dynamic variables. An additional relationship is needed to close the system and this is obtained by postulating some government policy for l, say. As soon as this is specified, the instantaneous part of the system can be solved, enabling the dynamics to be analysed. Thus, analogous to the closed economy, (and the fixed exchange rate system under imperfect capital mobility), the flexible rate system is not fully determinate until some government policy is specified.

Another observation worth noting about the flexible case is that the differential equation (12.20a) is perfectly consistent with the condition of zero balance of payments, which we know must always hold. This can be easily seen as follows. Setting (12.12) equal to zero, noting from (12.14) that this implies $\dot{D} = \dot{L}$, and applying (12.11) again yields (12.15), from which (12.20a) again follows.

The final point we wish to check is that our system as defined implies the consistency of savings and wealth accumulation *in real terms*. It will be recalled that this issue was discussed in general at some length in Chapter 3.

From the identity

$$PY^D = P_1 H + QEM + PS \tag{12.21}$$

where S denotes real savings plans, we deduce

$$S = Y^D - \frac{H + \sigma M}{\phi(\sigma)}.$$ (12.21')

Substituting for Y^D from (12.18f) and using (12.18a), this yields

$$S = \frac{G_d - uZ + X - \sigma M}{\phi(\sigma)} + (r^* + e)(1 - u)n - \pi V$$

which from the definitions (12.19), and equation (12.20a) implies

$$S = g_T + b_T + (1 - u)(r^* + e)n - \pi V.$$ (12.22)

Now taking equation (12.20a) and (12.22) together we obtain

$$\dot{V} = S + (\pi - p)V.$$ (12.23)

This equation is entirely consistent with our analysis of Chapter 3. The left hand side of (12.23) is the *actual (ex post)* rate of wealth accumulation. The term $(\pi - p)V$ denotes the unanticipated component of the capital gains (or losses) associated with holding financial wealth and therefore is the unanticipated component of real private disposable income. Because we have expressed the flow constraint in the form of continuous product market equilibrium, we are making the implicit assumption that all consumption plans are realized. Hence any unanticipated component of disposable income must be allocated to savings. Thus $(\pi - p)V$ is the revision to the original savings plans S, so that the entire right hand side of (12.23) denotes the *ex post* rate of savings, thereby ensuring that the *ex post* equality of the actual rate of savings and wealth accumulation holds.

Indeed it turns out to be more convenient to substitute savings directly into the dynamic equation (12.20a). Since S is determined jointly with H and M subject to the flow budget constraint (12.21), it will presumably depend upon the same variables. Differentiating (12.21) with respect to Y^D, $r^* + e - \pi$, V, it follows from the previous assumptions on the corresponding partial derivatives of H, M, that

$$0 < \frac{\partial S}{\partial Y^D} < 1, \qquad \frac{\partial S}{\partial (r^* + e - \pi)} > 0, \qquad \frac{\partial S}{\partial V} < 0.$$ (12.24)

The derivative with respect to σ, is much less determinate. But since it is conventional to assume that real aggregate consumption is independent of relative prices, we shall retain this assumption, setting $\partial S/\partial \sigma = 0$. Accordingly we write

$$S = S(Y^D, r^* + e - \pi, V) \qquad 0 < S_1 < 1, \quad S_2 > 0, \quad S_3 < 0.$$ (12.25)

The assumption that savings is independent of relative prices imposes a restriction on the price elasticities of demand for goods which is intimately related to the Marshall–Lerner condition. This is discussed further in the Appendix.

While in retrospect it may appear more convenient and natural to posulate the process of asset accumulation by the relationship (12.23) directly, the problem with doing this is that it obscures the nature of the underlying dynamics. As we have already commented it is only in very special cases that the dynamics can be described in terms of wealth accumulation alone without considering the growth of the separate component assets. Indeed in the flexible exchange rate case, discussed in Section 4 below, the dynamics are not fully specified until the accumulation of the separate assets is described, and for this reason we need to know the underlying dynamic relationships such as (12.11).

3. Fixed exchange rate

We turn now to an analysis of the fixed exchange rate case. To do this it is convenient to reduce further the set of equations (12.18) to the following four equations involving Z, Y^D, p, n, as well as V, σ, π,

$$Z - H(Y^D, r^* - \pi, \sigma, V) - X(\sigma) - G_d = 0 \tag{12.26a}$$

$$Y^D - (1 - u)\left(\frac{Z}{\phi(\sigma)} + r^*n\right) + \pi V = 0 \tag{12.26b}$$

$$V - n - L(Z, r^* - \pi, -\pi, V) = 0 \tag{12.26c}$$

$$p - \gamma_0 - \gamma_1(Z - \bar{Z}) - \gamma_2 \pi - \gamma_3 q = 0 \tag{12.26d}$$

where

$$\gamma_i = \delta\alpha_i \qquad i = 0, 1, 2$$

$$\gamma_3 = \alpha_3\delta + (1 - \delta)$$

with the dynamics being described by

$$\dot{V} = S(Y^D, r^* - \pi, V) + (\pi - p)V \tag{12.27a}$$

$$\dot{\sigma} = [q - \alpha_0 - \alpha_1(Z - \bar{Z}) - \alpha_2\pi - \alpha_3 q]\sigma \tag{12.27b}$$

$$\dot{\pi} = \rho(p - \pi). \tag{12.27c}$$

In considering the stability and steady-state properties of this system, we can, without loss of generality, choose units so that in equilibrium $P_1 = QE$. This means that in the steady state

$$\sigma = \phi(\sigma) = 1, \quad \phi'(\sigma) = 1 - \delta.$$

Furthermore, it is reasonable to assume that $\partial l/\partial \pi \leqslant 0$, implying

$$L_2 + L_3 \geqslant 0.$$

A. *Stability*

The stability of the third order system (12.26), and (12.27) can, in principle, be determined using the Routh–Hurwitz conditions; see Samuelson (1947). Unfortunately, given the complexity of the model, these turn out to be extremely complicated and consequently not very enlightening. We therefore find it more satisfactory to proceed by considering the two limiting cases of fixed expectations ($\rho \to 0$), and perfect foresight ($\rho \to \infty$). Both of these cases reduce the dynamics to second-order systems, which although not simple, are at least manageable.

The necessary and sufficient conditions for the local stability of the system for these two cases are given in the Appendix. In neither case are there any obviously simple or intuitively appealing conditions that will guarantee stability. Therefore, rather than try and extract some complicated, but not very intuitive sufficiency conditions, we find it more useful to confine our comments to identifying some of the stabilizing and destabilizing elements in the model.

Various approaches have been adopted to analyse the balance of payments and these focus on different elements in their analyses of stability. As the present model is in some sense a synthesis of these approaches, its stability properties tend to reflect the different factors considered by previous writers. The early discussions of stability emphasized the elasticities of demand, identifying the Marshall–Lerner condition as being the crucial stability condition; see for instance Stern (1973). In our expanded model this is obviously no longer critical, although it nevertheless still plays a role; see Section 2 of the Appendix. Indeed, polar cases can be obtained in which the Marshall–Lerner condition is actually necessary and sufficient for stability, yielding results quite similar to the early findings of Laursen and Metzler (1950).

Keynesian analyses generally identify leakages from the 'circular flow of income' via savings, imports, and taxes as being stabilizing; see Alexander (1952) and also Stern (1973). Noting that a low value of H_1 means a high value of M_1 and/or S_1, this result tends to hold in our model as well. The more recent monetary approaches often focus on the role of inflationary expectations and the parameters of the money demand function. For example, Shinkai (1973) finds that destabilizing factors include rapidly adjusting expectations, expectations-sensitive demand for money, and the interaction of the weight of domestic goods in the domestic cost-of-living index with expectational parameters. The same applies in our model, with the qualification that in a few instances, two parameters interact so as to constitute a stabilizing influence, even though each is destabilizing elsewhere.

Real interest rate effects on spending and savings have ambiguous consequences for stability, as do wealth effects on domestic expenditure on domestic goods. However, wealth effects on savings, and the inflation tax on wealth are both stabilizing. Indeed if one takes the limiting case $S_3 = p = 0$ we see that the system will be *unstable* even if expectations remain fixed.

Since, as we discuss below, $p = q$ in the steady state and is therefore exogenously given, we deduce that a *necessary* condition for stability in a non-inflationary world is that $S_3 < 0$. The essential destabilizing element which needs to be offset is the interest payment on government debt. This result is in general agreement with the corresponding proposition obtained for fixed prices; see Chapter 11.

B.   *General observations on the short run*
         (12.26a)–(12.26d) determine an instantaneous equilibrium of the system in the variables Z, Y^D, p, and n, for *given* values of V, σ, and π. It is apparent that this subsystem is quite similar to many of the models presented in the course of the extensive discussion of the 'assignment problem'. This literature is short run and the essential features of it are summarized in Chapters 9, 10. Below we analyse (12.26a)–(12.26d) more closely in order to bring out the corresponding aspects of the present model. We also examine the short-run effects of an external inflationary shock, comparing it to the analysis of Chapter 10.

On the details of relationships between the various approaches to the assignment problem and the instantaneous equilibrium of our model, the following points should be noted.

(i) The appropriate explanation of the capital and interest accounts of the balance of payments soon emerged as a central issue of the assignment-problem debate. There was increasing theoretical and empirical support for the proposition that capital movements are a once-for-all, stock-adjustment process rather than a permanent flow phenomenon, at least in a non-growing world; see Kouri and Porter (1974). Furthermore, the level of output was allowed to play a proximate role in the explanation of capital flows, and this role was increasingly associated with the transactions demand for money. Finally, some of the later papers explicitly included the flow of interest payments associated with internal indebteness; see Levin (1972). It is evident that the present model incorporates these developments.

(ii) Some of the later treatments (see e.g. Helliwell (1969)) included an equation which was tantamount to a short-run Phillips curve. However, aggregate price movements were allowed to interact with the rest of the system in a limited way, and the results of the earlier fixed-price analyses were not qualitatively revised as a consequence of this extension. (12.26a)–(12.26d) turns out to have the same property.

(iii) Simple Keynesian models in general, and the assignment-problem models in particular, tend to require output and disposable income always to move together. Our model allows for divergent movements although this turns out to be unimportant as far as the relationship between the assignment-problem discussion and our short-run model is concerned.

(iv) In the light of these points we should expect to obtain the standard results associated with the perfect capital mobility assumption: expansionary fiscal policy improves the balance of payments (or the level of reserves; comparative-static analysis cannot clearly distinguish between a change in the level of a variable and a change in its rate of change), and monetary policy has no effect on output.

As noted above as well as in previous chapters, the questions of external balance and the effects of domestic monetary policy have been major issues of the discussion. It will be observed from (12.26) that the system as currently specified does not explicitly include variables which pertain to these issues. Hence in order to deal with them we require some reformulation of the model. This turns out to be quite minor and can be achieved quite simply by noting that the real money supply, expressed in terms of cost of living units, consists of a domestic component (d), and the level of foreign reserves (f), so that

$$V = d + f + n. \tag{12.9'}$$

Thus we can treat d as the instrument of domestic monetary policy and let f measure the external balance objective. These variables can be incorporated into the instantaneous equilibrium (12.26) by eliminating n from the above expression for real wealth.

The monetary instrument d has thus been expressed in real terms. From a long-run point of view, this is the only feasible specification of monetary policy for a stable, small country operating under a fixed exchange rate in a stationary world. As we have argued in Chapter 8, if portfolio balance is to be maintained in long-run equilbrium, l must converge to some constant level. From the identity $l = d + f$ it follows that d must similarly be constant in the long-run equilibrium, for otherwise foreign reserves would either be accumulated, or decumulated without limit.

C.   *Fiscal policy, monetary policy and imported inflation in the short run*
     We now discuss the comparative statics of the instantaneous system, recalling that feedbacks from savings, changing terms of trade, and changing inflationary expectations are disregarded, as has been the usual practice in the discussion of the assignment problem. Monetary policy is characterized by an open market operation (specified by a change in d). Initially we assume that any government deficit created by a change in government expenditure is bond-financed, so that the effects of a change in G_d are those associated with a pure fiscal policy. Concerning the treatment of external inflationary shocks, an increase in the foreign inflation rate will presumably be eventually accompanied by an increase in the exogenously given foreign interest rate r^*. For simplicity we abstract from this in our analysis of the instantaneous equilibrium. In contrast, this effect is fully accounted for in our steady-state analysis.

Differentiating the set of equilibrium relationships (12.26), together with the definitional equation (12.9'), and applying the normalization $\sigma = \phi(\sigma) = 1$, the effects of fiscal policy, monetary policy and foreign inflation are summarized in the matrix equation

$$
\begin{pmatrix}
1 & -H_1 & 0 & 0 \\
-(1-u) & 1 & 0 & (1-u)r^* \\
L_1 & 0 & 0 & -1 \\
\gamma_1 & 0 & 1 & 0
\end{pmatrix}
\begin{pmatrix}
dZ \\
dY^D \\
dp \\
df
\end{pmatrix}
=
\begin{pmatrix}
dG_d \\
-(1-u)r^*d\bar{d} \\
d\bar{d} \\
\gamma_3 dq
\end{pmatrix}
$$

$$(12.28)$$

where $\bar{d}$ denotes the fact that d is assumed to be chosen exogenously. The Jacobian of this system is positive; this may be deduced directly from our prior restriction on parameter values. Alternatively it can be deduced from our first condition for local stability of the fixed-rate system in the limiting case of fixed expectations (see conditions in Appendix below).

The effects of fiscal and monetary policy (as defined above) on the level of domestic output are

$$
\frac{\partial Z}{\partial G_d} > 0, \quad \frac{\partial Z}{\partial \bar{d}} = 0.
$$

These results are quite consistent with those obtained in Chapters 9 and 10 for the more conventional short-run model. Output is increased by expansionary fiscal policy; the relevant multiplier is more complicated than usual, owing to interest income and inflation-tax leakages. Monetary policy has no effect because in a world of perfect capital mobility, open market operations cannot influence how the private sector chooses to allocate its wealth between money and bonds.

With regard to the external objective, we obtain

$$
\frac{\partial f}{\partial G_d} = L_1 \frac{\partial Z}{\partial G_d} > 0, \quad \frac{\partial f}{\partial \bar{d}} = -1.
$$

Expansionary fiscal policy improves the balance of payments as domestic residents sell bonds in order to augment transactions balances. An open market purchase of bonds by the authorities is completely offset by a matching private sector purchase of bonds from abroad; the level of reserves therefore declines. Again these results are consistent with those obtained previously.

The impact multipliers for the effects of fiscal and monetary policy on the other two endogenous variables, disposable income and the rate of inflation are also readily calculated. They are given by

$$
\frac{\partial Y^D}{\partial G_d} \gtrless 0, \quad \frac{\partial Y^D}{\partial \bar{d}} = 0
$$

$$
\frac{\partial p}{\partial G_d} = \gamma_1 \frac{\partial Z}{\partial G_d} > 0, \quad \frac{\partial p}{\partial \bar{d}} = 0.
$$

Interpretation of these results is straightforward and we do not dwell on them.

One point which should be emphasized however, is that the effect of an increase in government expenditure on the internal economy (Z, p, Y^D) is in fact *independent* of the mode of deficit financing chosen by the government. This follows directly from the facts, established above, that in a world of perfect capital mobility $\partial Z/\partial \bar{d} = \partial p/\partial \bar{d} = \partial Y^D/\partial \bar{d} = 0$. As a consequence any monetary expansion associated with financing the government deficit does not give rise to any induced monetary effects on the economy.

The effects of an external inflationary shock are summarized by

$$\frac{\partial Y^D}{\partial q} = \frac{\partial Z}{\partial q} = \frac{\partial f}{\partial q} = 0, \quad \frac{\partial p}{\partial q} = \gamma_3 < 1.$$

Instantaneously, the only impact of an increase in the foreign rate of inflation is to raise the domestic rate of inflation. It has no other effects on any of the other endogenous variables. These responses are much simpler than the corresponding results discussed in connection with our short-run inflationary model developed in Chapter 10. The reason is that the instantaneous equilibrium treats the terms of trade and money supply as given, thereby abstracting from two of the crucial channels through which inflation was shown to be imported; see Chapter 10. In other words, the 'instantaneous' equilibrium is simply too short to provide an accurate indication of short-run impacts. They need to be integrated over a finite time horizon and for this purpose it is more convenient to consider the first period effects of a discrete-time analysis; see also the comments in Chapter 7.

Note, however, that as in Chapter 10, the concept of imported inflation discussed here is that of an inflationary 'shock' which at least instantaneously is not accompanied by a higher nominal foreign interest rate. The results become indeterminate if such adjustment is permitted.

D. General observations on the steady state

On the assumption that the system is stable, we now examine some of its steady-state properties. From the stationarity conditions to the dynamic equations (12.27), together with (12.18c), we deduce that in equilibrium

$$S(Y^D, r^* - \pi, V) = 0 \tag{12.29}$$

$$p = \pi = p_1 = q. \tag{12.30}$$

That is, steady-state savings are zero; all disposable income is spent either on domestic goods or imports. Furthermore, the rate of inflation of domestically produced goods must converge to the exogenously given world rate of inflation. This in turn means that both the domestic cost of living, and domestic residents' expectations of it, must also grow at the same rate. In summary, all rates of inflation are tied to the world rate.

It follows further from (12.15) that in the steady state

$$\frac{b_c + g_c}{W} = \frac{\dot{L} + \dot{N}}{L + N} = q \qquad (12.31)$$

where

$$b_c = \frac{X(\sigma) - \sigma(M + G_m)}{\phi(\sigma)} + (r^* + e)(n - a) \qquad (12.32a)$$

$$g_c = \frac{G_d + \sigma G_m - uZ}{\phi(\sigma)} + (r^* + e)(a - un). \qquad (12.32b)$$

That is, b_c is the real balance of payments on current account; analogously g_c is defined as the real domestic government deficit on current account (both deflated by P). Of course, in the present context $e \equiv 0$, but as the quantities b_c, g_c occur in the flexible case below, we prefer to define them generally. This result can be compared with the corresponding condition under fixed prices. In that case it was shown that perfect capital mobility yields the equilibrium condition $b_c + g_c = 0$; see Chapter 11. The accumulation of assets *in real terms* must cease; their nominal quantity, however, will grow at the world rate of inflation.

Substituting (12.29) into (12.18b), it is an immediate consequence that

$$(1 - \alpha_2 - \alpha_3)q = \alpha_0 + \alpha_1(Z - \bar{Z}). \qquad (12.33)$$

It therefore follows that the steady-state level of domestic output, and hence employment, is determined solely by the world rate of inflation, together with the parameters characterizing the domestic wage—price sector. Differentiating (12.33) with respect to q, we obtain

$$\text{sgn} \frac{\partial Z}{\partial q} = \text{sgn}(1 - \alpha_2 - \alpha_3).$$

If $1 - \alpha_2 - \alpha_3 > 0$, then an increase in foreign inflation will raise domestic output; in the limiting case $1 = \alpha_2 + \alpha_3$, there is no effect.[8]

The striking conclusion to emerge from these results is that under fixed exchange rates the domestic government has no control over the steady-state output and rate of inflation. Neither increases in government expenditure, nor any monetary policy, are able to influence the level of domestic output.[9] Furthermore, any once-and-for-all devaluation of the currency will be ineffective. All it will do is increase the price of domestic output by the same proportion, leaving σ, and everything else, unchanged. The only way the domestic government can affect the steady-state output is by changing the parameters of the wage—price sector. If this is impossible, then the small economy must simply adapt to the given world rate of inflation. All of these results are in marked contrast to the conventional conclusions derived from short-run Keynesian type models discussed in Chapters 9, 10. The conclusions of these short-run models, like those of the instantaneous equilibrium of the present model, do not carry over to the steady state.

The finding that the steady-state rate of domestic inflation and level of output is independent of domestic monetary and fiscal policy is a direct consequence of the specification we have chosen for the domestic Phillips curve. If this were to be modified, then these conclusions need not hold. For example, one might quite plausibly specify that in the long run $\bar{Z}$ is responsive to σ. In this case, while the equilibrium value for $(Z - \bar{Z})$ would still be determined solely by q, Z itself could now respond to other factors, and in particular monetary and fiscal policies.

E.   *Fiscal policy, monetary policy and imported inflation in the steady state*

Equations (12.29), (12.30) and (12.33), together with (12.26a)– (12.26c) determine the steady state of the system in Z, Y^D, p, p_1, n, V, σ, and π. Here we analyse this equilibrium more closely in order to obtain further properties of the steady state and to compare them with our findings for the case of given values of V, σ, and π.

In view of the fact we regard the comparative statics of external balance as of more interest than the stock of bonds held by domestic residents, we use (12.9') to replace n by f in the equilibrium equations. The reason for working in terms of n rather than f in the stability analysis is simply that when specified in this way, the dynamics of the system and hence its equilibrium is completely determined without specifying any government policy for financing its deficits or monetary policy. That is not so as far as the level of foreign reserves is concerned. While the equilibrium values of V, n and hence $d + f$ are independent of government policy, it can be readily seen from (12.9') that this is obviously not true of the separate components d, f. In particular, to determine f, we must explain the behaviour of the domestic component of the monetary base d. As in our short-run discussion, this is done by simply postulating that the real domestic monetary base is pegged by the authorities; that is to say $d = \bar{d}$. In this sense, government expenditure is said to be bond financed, although as we shall demonstrate for the same reasons as in the short run, the effects of changes in government expenditure on internal economic variables, are independent of the method of deficit financing. In connection with our flexible exchange rate section below, we argue that our definition is reasonable; here we merely note that it is the counterpart of the conventional, fixed-price approach. A final point before we turn to the comparative statics: for simplicity we eliminate p, p_1, and π directly, using (12.30).

The effects of fiscal policy, monetary policy, and imported inflation are summarized in the matrix equation[10]

$$
\begin{pmatrix}
S_3 & 0 & 0 & S_1 & 0 \\
0 & 0 & -\alpha_1 & 0 & 0 \\
-H_4 & -(H_3 + X') & 1 & -H_1 & 0 \\
q-(1-u)r^* & (1-u)(1-\delta)Z & -(1-u) & 1 & r^*(1-u) \\
L_4 & 0 & L_1 & 0 & -1
\end{pmatrix}
\begin{pmatrix}
dV \\
d\sigma \\
dZ \\
dY^D \\
df
\end{pmatrix}
$$

$$
=
\begin{pmatrix}
-S_2(\partial r^*/\partial q - 1)dq \\
(\alpha_2 + \alpha_3 - 1)dq \\
dG_d + H_2(\partial r^*/\partial q - 1)dq \\
-(1-u)r^* d\bar{d} + [(1-u)n\partial r^*/\partial q - V]dq \\
d\bar{d} - [L_2 . \partial r^*/\partial q - (L_2 + L_3)]dq
\end{pmatrix}
\qquad (12.34)
$$

Note that in considering dq, we have taken account of the fact that an increase in the foreign inflation rate will presumably affect the exogenously given foreign nominal interest rate r^* as well.[11]

We have already seen that $\partial Z/\partial G_d = \partial Z/\partial \bar{d} = 0$. Considering some of the other multipliers, we can show that provided the system is stable.

$$
\frac{\partial \sigma}{\partial G_d} < 0, \quad \frac{\partial \sigma}{\partial \bar{d}} = 0.
$$

With domestic output given, an increase in government expenditure on domestic goods forces up the price of domestic goods relative to the price of imports (terms of trade). An open market purchase of bonds, as in the short run, affects neither the magnitude nor the composition of domestic portfolios. Thus, neither the terms of trade, nor, as is shown below, disposable income and wealth are affected by this policy:

$$
\frac{\partial Y^D}{\partial G_d} > 0, \quad \frac{\partial Y^D}{\partial \bar{d}} = 0, \quad \frac{\partial V}{\partial G_d} = -\frac{S_1}{S_3} \cdot \frac{\partial Y^D}{\partial G_d} > 0, \quad \frac{\partial V}{\partial \bar{d}} = 0.
$$

Expansionary fiscal policy increases disposable income and wealth, essentially because of the improvement in the terms of trade resulting from this policy. More precisely, an increase in government expenditure on domestic output will tend to force up the price of domestic goods relative to imports. This lowers σ and raises the relative price P_1/P. For fixed Z this increases real disposable income (measured in terms of the overall cost of living P). A further effect of this is to increase savings and hence equilibrium real wealth.

The fact that $\bar{d}$ has no effect on any of the internal variables (Z, p, σ, V, Y^D) is an immediate consequence of the fact that the stability of the system and its equilibrium when specified in terms of n (rather than d and f) is independent of any domestic monetary policy. Thus, as in the short run, the induced monetary effects from any money-financed government deficit are zero. From this we conclude that the effects of an increase in government expenditure are independent of the financial mix chosen by the government and always have the signs indicated above.

When varying terms of trade are taken into consideration, external balance has at least *two* dimensions; the level of reserves as measured in domestic and in foreign cost of living units. Insofar as the authorities seek 'adequate backing' for the domestic money supply, the former is relevant; insofar as purchasing power over imports is the criterion of reserve adequacy, the latter is important. The effects of fiscal and monetary policy on the former measure are indicated by

$$\frac{\partial f}{\partial G_d} = L_4 \frac{\partial V}{\partial G_d} > 0, \quad \frac{\partial f}{\partial \bar{d}} = -1.$$

These results are related to those established for the short run. Fiscal expansion improves the level of reserves since domestic residents sell bonds abroad because of increased 'wealth' demand for real balances. The effect of monetary expansion is exactly the same as in the short run.

Let f^* denote the level of reserves as measured in foreign cost of living units. Then the bridge relationship connecting f and f^* is

$$f^* \equiv \phi(\sigma)\sigma^{-1}f,$$

whence

$$\frac{\partial f^*}{\partial G_d} = \frac{\partial f}{\partial G_d} - \delta f \frac{\partial \sigma}{\partial G_d} > 0, \quad \frac{\partial f^*}{\partial \bar{d}} = -1.$$

Evidently, therefore, it is unnecessary to distinguish between the different measures of the 'real' level of reserves when one is considering the qualitative effects of fiscal and monetary expansion.

Taking stock of the overall effects of fiscal expansion, it might seem that the policy is more advantageous than one would intuitively expect, even allowing for the assumption of perfect capital mobility. Perhaps it is as well to point out here that the scope for this policy is limited by our stability conditions. *Ceteris paribus,* the system is unstable unless the direct substitution effect on output of a terms-of-trade change outweighs the indirect income effect of such a change, via disposable income. If a large proportion of output is purchased by the government, then the former effect is reduced, while a low income-tax rate increases the latter effect (see (iii) on p. 300.).

We now consider the effects of an increase in the foreign inflation rate. It turns out that incomplete adjustment of the foreign nominal interest rate, i.e., $\partial r^*/\partial q < 1$, is associated with comparative-static results which are indeterminate and difficult to interpret. (Thus we have a parallel to the short-run situation, where it was found that more than zero adjustment has the same consequence.) For this reason, and also because the hypothesis that complete adjustment eventually occurs is of intrinsic interest (that is, the rest of the world is 'Fisherian'; see Chaper 7), we confine attention to this case. Also, the results are sharpened by confining attention to the case of a natural rate of unemployment, $1 = \alpha_2 + \alpha_3$. Then it is a trivial consequence of the latter restriction that $\partial Z/\partial q = 0$, and we can also establish

$$- \text{sgn} \, \frac{\partial \sigma}{\partial q} = \text{sgn} \, \frac{\partial Y^D}{\partial q} = \text{sgn} \, \frac{\partial V}{\partial q} = \text{sgn} \left(\epsilon_\pi - \frac{(l + un)q}{r^*(1 - u)l} \right) \quad (12.35)$$

where

$$\epsilon_\pi \equiv \pi L_3 / l > 0.$$

Given full interest-rate adjustment and a natural rate of unemployment, a sufficient condition for an increase in foreign inflation to worsen the terms of trade and lower disposable income and wealth is that the elasticity of demand for real balances with respect to expected inflation be less than the ratio of the exogenous world rate of inflation to the nominal world rate of interest. This condition is almost certainly likely to be satisfied, at least during moderate inflation, and also on the basis of the available empirical evidence on ϵ_π; see Chapter 6. The explanation of this result is that an increased rate of inflation tax lowers disposable income. But increased (expected) inflation also induces a switch from non-interest-earning money to interest-earning bonds, offsetting the direct loss of disposable income to some extent. Suppose, for example, that all wealth were held in real balances, a frequent simplification in the literature. Then an increase in foreign inflation would unambiguously worsen the terms of trade − cf. (Shinkai (1973)).

The presumption that the elasticity of demand with respect to expected inflation is less than the ratio of the inflation rate to the interest rate is sufficient, but not necessary, for determining the sign of the change in real reserves with respect to a change in foreign inflation − regardless of which of the two suggested measures of 'real reserves' is used. This is because increased expected inflation has a direct negative effect on the demand for real balances, and hence reserves, which reinforces the indirect negative effect via wealth and the terms of trade.

4.   Flexible exchange rate

The flexible exchange rate regime turns out to be considerably more complicated to analyse than the fixed rate case we have just been considering. The principal complication arises from the fact that this system is not fully specified until one postulates some sort of policy describing how the government finances its deficit and this imposes a further dynamic relationship on the system.

Just as in Section 3, we reduce the set of equations further, this time to

$$Z - H(Y^D, r^* + e - \pi, \sigma, V) - X(\sigma) - G_d = 0 \quad (12.36a)$$

$$Y^D - (1 - u) \left(\frac{Z}{\phi(\sigma)} + (r^* + e) \right) (V - l) + \pi V = 0 \quad (12.36b)$$

$$l - L(Z, r^* + e - \pi, -\pi, V) = 0 \qquad (12.36c)$$

$$p - \gamma_0 - \gamma_1(Z - \bar{Z}) - \gamma_2\pi - \gamma_3(q + e) = 0. \qquad (12.36d)$$

While we have eliminated n, we now have an extra endogenous variable, e, the rate of depreciation of the domestic currency. These four equations can be viewed as determining Z, Y^D, p, e, for given values of V, σ, π, l.

The dynamic equations for V, σ, π, remain as before, modified only by the inclusion of e

$$\dot{V} = S(Y^D, r^* + e - \pi, V) + (\pi - p)V \qquad (12.37a)$$

$$\dot{\sigma} = [q + e - \alpha_0 - \alpha_1(Z - \bar{Z}) - \alpha_2\pi - \alpha_3(q + e)]\sigma \qquad (12.37b)$$

$$\dot{\pi} = \rho(p - \pi). \qquad (12.37c)$$

To close the system it becomes necessary to specify some policy for the stock of real money l. With a flexible exchange rate there is no accumulation of foreign reserves; $\dot{F} \equiv 0$, implying $\dot{D} \equiv \dot{L}$ (see 12.14)). It is also clear that any government policy describing the evolution of $\dot{l}$ must satisfy the government budget constraint (12.11). Transforming this to real terms, it becomes

$$\dot{l} + \dot{a} = g_D \qquad (12.38)$$

where
$$g_D = g_T + (r^* + e)(a - un) - p(a + l) = g_c - p(a + l).$$

Thus, g_D differs from g_T (see (12.19b)) and also $(g_c$ (see (12.32b)) in that it accounts for both interest payments and capital gains. We shall describe it as the *real* deficit.

Given that asset demands have been described in real terms it is convenient to specify government financial policy in real terms as well. The comments we made in this regard in Chapters 7 and 8, therefore apply here as well. As in previous chapters we shall define the government deficit to be *purely bond financed* if $\dot{l} = 0$, so that

$$\dot{a} = g_D. \qquad (12.39)$$

At the other extreme, we shall define the deficit to be *purely money financed* if $\dot{a} = 0$, and

$$\dot{l} = g_D. \qquad (12.40)$$

These two extreme cases turn out to have rather different implications for the dynamics of the model. Consider first the pure bond finance case. Real domestic money supply l is held constant at $\bar{l}$ say, while the real stock of bonds issued by the domestic government is specified by (12.34). Since a does not appear either in the instantaneous equations (12.36), or in the other dynamic equations (12.37), the dynamics of a can simply be ignored. Being a small country, and with capital being perfectly mobile, the domestic government can continue to issue bonds indefinitely. These will be absorbed by the rest of the world, with no feedback on the domestic economy. The upshot is that for this extreme case, the system is fully described by equations (12.36) and (12.37), with $l = \bar{l}$. But it is important to stress the two assumptions we are making which permit this simplification. These are (i) the small country assumption, (ii) perfect capital mobility. This case is discussed in detail in Subsections 4.A–4.E below.

With pure money financing, things are more complicated. Since l appears in the rest of the system, its dynamics must be taken into account. The reason for this is that since only domestic residents hold domestic money, any increases in its real quantity must be absorbed in their portfolios and will clearly affect their decisions, and feedback on the rest of the domestic system. Consequently, in this case the dynamics become a fourth order system, consisting of equations (12.37), together with (12.40). Moreover, this continues to be the case in the intermediate case where the government finances its deficit partially by bonds and partially by money. As long as *some* fraction – no matter how small – of the government deficit is money financed, the real domestic money supply will be changing, so that its dynamics will need to be taken into account. This second extreme is therefore much more characteristic of the general case which is discussed briefly towards the end of Subsection F below.

A.   Stability

In our discussion of local stability under fixed rates, for tractability we resorted to two limiting cases of the formation of inflationary expectations. Tractability is a more severe problem in the flexible-rate version of the model. In the case of pure bond financing, the system can be reduced to a second-order one also; but the domestic interest rate remains endogenous, which complicates the analysis substantially. In the case of pure or partial money financing, the system is third order, even when the limiting cases just mentioned are introduced. It is virtually an impossible task to analyse systematically the stability of this case. In summary, it turns out that it is not particularly enlightening to attempt a systematic treatment of the flexible-rate case along the lines of the previous section. We do refer to stability considerations in this section, however, when the need arises to sign Jacobians.

B.   General observations on the short run

Equations (12.36a)–(12.36d) determine an instantaneous equilibrium of the system in the variables Z, Y^D, p, and e, for *given* values of V, σ, π, and l. As we shall discuss below, in many respects this system resembles the standard short-run model of a *closed* economy (such as that discussed in Chapter 6) more than it does in the typical static model dealing with the assignment problem of an economy under a flexible exchange rate. Below we analyse the effects of fiscal and monetary policy on internal and external balance and compare our results both with those typical of the assignment-problem literature (see e.g. Chapters 9, 10) and also the typical short-run closed economy model (such as those presented in Chapters 2 and 6). We also examine the effects of an external inflationary shock.

On the details of the relationship between the various approaches to the assignment problem, simple *IS–LM* models, and the instantaneous equilibrium of our model, we note:

(i) By contrast to the fixed rate case, there is an important difference between our view of the relationship between the domestic and foreign interest rate and that taken by the assignment-problem literature. There it is assumed that investors ignore actual and prospective exchange rate movements in their choices between securities denominated in different currencies. That is to say, investors are assumed to ignore capital gains and losses due to exchange rate changes, at least in the short run.[12] The perfect capital mobility assumption then yields $r = r^*$. This contrasts with our present approach where, on the assumption that exchange rate changes are perfectly anticipated, we have shown that the perfect capital mobility assumption yields $r = r^* + e$.

(ii) Our specification of perfect capital mobility with $r = r^* + e$ illustrates a kind of symmetry between the roles of nominal interest rates and exchange depreciation rates in liquidity preference and disposable income. Thus, if one's 'short-run' is long enough for interest rates to have an effect, then the same should be true of exchange depreciation rates. This leads us to the observation that the interest rate in simple closed-economy models plays the same role as the exchange depreciation rate in (12.36a)–(12.36d), except of course in the Phillips curve.

(iii) Simple Keynesian models of closed and open economies sometimes include an equation tantamount to a Phillips curve. As in these models, and also our short-run model of the fixed-rate case, it turns out that the qualitative results of earlier, fixed-price analyses are not upset here as a consequence of feedbacks from that relation. By contrast to these cases, however, the split between output and disposable income in our model does make a difference to the comparative statics. This is because the exchange depreciation rate – which equals, up to a parametric constant, the domestic interest rate – is free to vary. But this leads to indeterminacies rather than sign reversals.

(iv) As we have shown, the assignment-problem literature generally leads to the conclusion that with perfect capital mobility, fiscal policy has no effect on the output of a small country under a flexible rate. This result stems directly from the fact, noted in (i), that this literature describes the assumption of perfect capital mobility by setting $r = r^*$. By contrast, our specification of perfect capital mobility, which allows the domestic interest rate to deviate from the fixed world rate by the endogenously determined rate of exchange depreciation, enables the economy to once again be responsive to domestic fiscal policy. In this respect a flexible exchange rate restores some of the characteristics of the closed economic model.

C.   *Fiscal policy, monetary policy and imported inflation in the short run*

We now discuss the comparative statics of (12.36a)–(12.36d), recalling that our short run is specified by the absence of feedbacks from $\dot{V}$, $\dot{\sigma}$, and $\dot{\pi}$. Our specifications of short-run fiscal policy, monetary policy, and an external inflationary shock have been set forth in the fixed-rate counterpart of this section. Differentiating the set of equilibrium relationships (12.36a)–(12.36d), and applying the normalization $\sigma = \phi(\sigma) = 1$, the effects of these shift parameters are summarized in the matrix equation

$$
\begin{pmatrix}
1 & -H_1 & 0 & -H_2 \\
-(1-u) & 1 & 0 & -n(1-u) \\
L_1 & 0 & 0 & L_2 \\
-\gamma_1 & 0 & 1 & -\gamma_3
\end{pmatrix}
\begin{pmatrix}
dZ \\
dY^D \\
dp \\
de
\end{pmatrix}
=
\begin{pmatrix}
dG_d \\
-(r^* + e)(1-u)d\bar{l} \\
d\bar{l} \\
\gamma_3 dq
\end{pmatrix}.
$$

$$(12.41)$$

Prior restrictions on parameter values imply that a sufficient condition for the Jacobian of (12.41) to be positive is

(IS): $\Omega \equiv H_1 n(1-u) + H_2 < 0$.

This also turns out to be the necessary and sufficient condition for the *IS* curve to have a negative slope.[13] Accordingly we have denoted this condition by (IS). Stability is more likely if (IS) holds. More generally, we can show that the Jacobian of (12.41) is simply the flexible-rate counterpart of the first condition for local stability of the fixed exchange rate system in the case $\rho = 0$ (see above). A necessary condition for stability is that this be positive, which we henceforth assume.

The usual calculations yield

$$
\frac{\partial Z}{\partial G_d} > 0, \quad \text{sgn} \left(\frac{\partial Z}{\partial \bar{l}} \right) = -\text{sgn} \left[\Omega - L_2 H_1 (r^* + e)(1-u) \right] \gtreqless 0
$$

Output is increased by expansionary fiscal policy. The relevant multiplier is similar to that obtained in the fixed exchange rate case and simple Keynesian models generally. One difference in comparison with the fixed rate case, however, is that the domestic interest rate is free to move upwards in response to expansionary fiscal policy, thus augmenting disposable income. This particular effect has, of course, been recognized in the recent development of fiscal policy in closed economic models; see Chapters 4, 7, 8. It is also responsible for our ambiguous result for the effect of monetary policy on output. In *IS–LM* terms, it is possible here (unless (IS) holds) that the *IS* curve is upward-sloping, or that monetary expansion shifts the *IS* curve to the left more than it shifts the LM curve to the right. In either event, monetary expansion could lower output. However, such outcomes tend to be associated with instability.

With regard to the impact on the rate of exchange depreciation (the external objective), we obtain

$$\frac{\partial e}{\partial G_d} > 0, \quad \frac{\partial e}{\partial \bar{l}} < 0.$$

Expansionary fiscal policy increases the rate of exchange depreciation whereas expansionary monetary policy lowers it. Given the symmetry between the rate of exchange depreciation and the nominal interest rate observed above, these results can be interpreted in terms of the *IS–LM* model of a closed economy, as simply being a restatement of the usual propositions concerning the effects of fiscal and monetary policy on the domestic interest rate; see (4.6).

On the other hand these two sets of results appear to be somewhat inconsistent with the analogous results obtained for the conventional short-run model of the economy under flexible exchange rates and summarized in Chapter 9. There it was shown that with the perfect capital mobility, an increase in G_d will have no effect on domestic output and will lower the exchange rate. Under the same limiting assumption, an increase in the money supply will raise both domestic output and the exchange rate. The apparent discrepancy between these propositions can be readily reconciled. The difference in the effect on output is simply due to the fact that the conventional approach (i) abstracts from the rate of exchange depreciation in its definition of the rate of return on bond holdings, (ii) excludes interest income in its definition of disposable income. Once these two elements are incorporated into the conventional model (or omitted from the present), the results become consistent.

The external effects are also in fact really not contradictory. The traditional static model deals with the effects on the *level* of the exchange rate; the present analysis is in terms of the *rate* of exchange *depreciation*. As noted above, this is dimensionally much more closely related to the nominal interest rate, and once this is recognized, the two sets of results can again be reconciled. While the domestic interest rate was shown to be independent of monetary and fiscal policy in the conventional model (see (9.31)), this was again a consequence of omitting factors (i) and (ii) mentioned above. Once these are taken into account consistency is again obtained.

By way of completeness, we present the impact multipliers for the effects of fiscal and monetary policy on disposable income and the rate of inflation

$$\frac{\partial Y^D}{\partial G_d} > 0, \quad \frac{\partial Y^D}{\partial \bar{l}} \gtreqless 0$$

$$\frac{\partial p}{\partial G_d} > 0, \quad \frac{\partial p}{\partial \bar{l}} \gtreqless 0.$$

Interpretation of these results is straightforward and we do not dwell on them.

Finally, we consider the effects of an external inflationary shock, on the assumption that the foreign interest rate does not respond. The relevant instantaneous effects are summarized by

$$\frac{\partial Z}{\partial q} = \frac{\partial Y^D}{\partial q} = \frac{\partial e}{\partial q} = 0, \quad 0 < \frac{\partial p}{\partial p} < 1$$

which are identical to those obtained in the fixed-rate case. Note, that unlike our model of Chapter 10, perfect insulation from foreign inflationary pressures is not achieved in the present model as it was there. The reason for the difference is once again due to the two factors mentioned above.

D.   *General observations on the steady state*
       From the stationary solutions to the pair of dynamic equations (12.37b), (12.37c), and the cost of living equation (12.18c), it follows that in the steady state

$$p = \pi = p_1 = q + e. \tag{12.42}$$

All prices in terms of domestic currency, as well as domestic inflationary expectations, must grow at the same rate. But this rate may deviate from the exogenously given world inflation rate, by the rate of exchange depreciation. Since e is endogenous to the model, it follows that the steady-state rate of domestic inflation is also endogenously determined. Under a flexible-rate system, a small country is *not* tied to the world rate of inflation. Finally, we note that the relationship $p = q + e$ may be regarded as simply a statement of the 'relative' version of the purchasing power parity theory.

An alternative expression for the steady-state rate of inflation is obtained from the condition $\dot{V} = 0$. Using this relationship we have

$$\frac{\dot{L} + \dot{N}}{L + N} = \frac{\dot{L}}{L} = \frac{b_c + g_c}{V} = p = q + e. \tag{12.43}$$

This equation is analogous to (12.31) for the fixed-rate case. The domestic rate of inflation equals the rate of accumulation of domestic assets, in nominal terms. This, of course, does not mean that domestic nominal asset accumulation *causes* domestic inflation, rather, it is more accurate to view it as jointly determined with the domestic inflation rate.

E.   *Fiscal policy, monetary policy, and imported inflation in the steady state*
       Substituting conditions (12.42) into (12.36) and (12.37), the steady state of the system is described by

$$S(Y^D, r^* - q, V) \qquad\qquad\qquad = 0 \quad (12.44a)$$

$$(1 - \alpha_2 - \alpha_3)(q + e) - \alpha_0 - \alpha_1(Z - \bar{Z}) = 0 \quad (12.44b)$$

$$Z - H(Y^D, r^* - q, \sigma, V) - X(\sigma) - G_d = 0 \quad (12.44c)$$

$$Y^D - (1 - u)\left(\frac{Z}{\phi(\sigma)} + (r^* + e)(V - \bar{I})\right) - (q + e)V = 0 \quad (12.44d)$$

$$\bar{I} - L[Z, r^* - q, -(q + e), V] \qquad\qquad = 0 \quad (12.44e)$$

(12.44a) and (12.44b) are just the stationary solutions to (12.37a) and (12.37b) respectively, while (12.44c)–(12.44e) are just the steady-state versions of (12.36a)–(12.36c). These equations yield the steady-state solutions for V, σ, Z, Y^D, e; the steady-state rate of domestic inflation can then be immediately obtained from (12.42). The fact that the real money stock is held constant throughout, is denoted by the bar.

Taking total differentials of (12.44) as $G_d, \bar{I}, q$ vary, the resulting changes in the endogenous variables are summarized by

$$
\begin{pmatrix}
S_3 & 0 & 0 & S_1 & 0 \\
0 & 0 & -\alpha_1 & 0 & 1-\alpha_2-\alpha_3 \\
-H_4 & -(H_3 + X') & 1 & -H_1 & 0 \\
(q + e)-(1-u)(r^*+e) & (1-u)Z(1-\delta) & -(1-u) & 1 & \bar{I} + un \\
-L_4 & 0 & -L_1 & 0 & L_3
\end{pmatrix}
\begin{pmatrix}
dV \\
d\sigma \\
dZ \\
dY^D \\
de
\end{pmatrix}
$$

$$
=
\begin{pmatrix}
-S_2(\partial r^*/\partial q - 1)dq \\
-(1 - \alpha_2 - \alpha_3)dq \\
dG_d + H_2(\partial r^*/\partial q - 1)dq \\
[n\partial r^*/\partial q - V]dq - (1 - u)rd\bar{I} \\
-[-L_2\partial r^*/\partial q + L_2 + L_3]dq - d\bar{I}
\end{pmatrix}
\cdot \quad (12.45)
$$

Denote the Jacobian of (12.45) by Δ. Then stability of the system, when dynamized only by non-zero savings, requires $\Delta > 0$, given conventional assumptions about the effects of relative price changes.[14]

The partial derivatives contained in (12.45) yield several interesting conclusions. First, it is readily shown that

$$\frac{\partial p}{\partial G_d} = \frac{\partial e}{\partial G_d} = \frac{\alpha_1 L_4 S_1(1 - u)Z(1 - \delta)}{\Delta} > 0. \quad (12.46)$$

That is, any increase in government expenditure on domestic output will raise the rate of depreciation (or lower the rate of appreciation) of the domestic currency, leading to a higher rate of domestic inflation. This is the same as the short-run result. However, the mechanism is somewhat different. It is clear from (12.46) that feedbacks from savings and changing terms of trade, ruled out in our short run, are necessary for the multiplier to be non-zero.

The effect of the increased government activity on output is given by

$$\frac{\partial Z}{\partial G_d} = \left(\frac{1 - \alpha_2 - \alpha_3}{\alpha_1}\right) \frac{\partial p}{\partial G_d} \geq 0. \tag{12.47}$$

provided $1 - \alpha_2 - \alpha_3 > 0$, implying a steady-state trade-off between domestic inflation and domestic excess demand, the government is able to increase output through increases in G_d. If $1 = \alpha_2 + \alpha_3$, however, the steady-state level of output is determined by the 'natural rate' $\bar{Z}$ and is therefore independent of any increases in government expenditure. As noted in our short-run discussion, the result typically obtained in the assignment problem literature is $\partial Z/\partial G_d = 0$. Our steady state may also yield this result. Again, however, the mechanism is rather different, for the elements in the usual short-run analyses which yield it are fixed exchange-depreciation expectations and the absence of 'wealth' effects in the demand for money.

The effect of an increase in G_d on the relative price σ differs from that of the fixed exchange rate case in an interesting way. There are now two offsetting effects. If $1 = \alpha_2 + \alpha_3$, output is fixed at $\bar{Z}$, implying that any increase in G_d must be matched by a reduction in H or X. This reduction in private demand is achieved by a rise in the price of domestic goods relative to imports, that is by a fall in σ. However, if $1 - \alpha_2 - \alpha_3 > 0$, then the increase in G_d will also increase Z; see (12.47). The extent to which this occurs will tend to reduce the relative price of domestic goods, i.e., to raise σ. The overall effect turns out to be ambiguous, depending upon how close the economy is to having a natural rate (i.e. the magnitude of $1 - \alpha_2 - \alpha_3$). This same indeterminacy appears in the expressions for $\partial Y^D/\partial G_d$, $\partial V/\partial G_d$.

Now consider the effects of an increase in $\bar{l}$, that is to say, a real open market operation. In order to obtain clear-cut results we confine attention to the case $\alpha_2 + \alpha_3 = 1$. An immediate consequence of this restriction is $\partial Z/\partial \bar{l} = 0$. We can also establish, provided that the parameters of the system are such that it is stable under fixed and flexible rates,

$$\frac{\partial e}{\partial \bar{l}} = \frac{\partial r}{\partial \bar{l}} = \frac{\partial p}{\partial \bar{l}} = \frac{\Gamma}{\Delta} < 0$$

$$- \text{sgn} \frac{\partial \sigma}{\partial \bar{l}} = \text{sgn} \frac{\partial Y^D}{\partial \bar{l}} = \text{sgn} \frac{\partial V}{\partial \bar{l}} = \text{sgn} \left(\frac{(\bar{l} + un)p}{r(1 - u)\bar{l}} - \epsilon_\pi\right)$$

where Γ denotes the third condition for stability of the fixed-rate system (see p. 300.).

Our short-run findings for the qualitative effects of monetary expansion on the exchange depreciation and interest rates carry over to the steady state. The mechanism is more complicated and it would be tedious to expound it at length. However, we note that the propensity to save out of disposable income and the negative association between the nominal interest rate and the demand for money are still involved, as in the simplest of *IS–LM* models.

One important difference is that here the inflation, exchange depreciation and interest rates differ only by parametric constants. Thus, while the short-run effect of monetary expansion on inflation is unclear, in the steady state that policy is unambiguously deflationary.

At first sight, this proposition might seem to conflict with familiar monetarist notions that increases in the money supply result in higher rates of inflation. But it should be realized that increasing the real money stock is *not* the same as increasing the rate of nominal monetary expansion. On the contrary, in our steady state there is an inverse association between these variables. The rationale for the result can be seen most simply from the money market equilibrium conditions (12.44e). Differentiating it with respect to $\bar{l}$, and recalling that under the constraint $\alpha_2 + \alpha_3 = 1$, $\partial Z/\partial \bar{l} = 0$, we have

$$L_3 \frac{\partial e}{\partial \bar{l}} = -\left(1 - L_4 \frac{\partial V}{\partial \bar{l}}\right).$$

The stability conditions ensure that the induced wealth effect resulting from the increase in the real quantity of money generates insufficient demand for real money balances to match the increased real supply. The only way equilibrium in the money market can be restored is if demand is stimulated, and with the real rate of return on holding bonds fixed exogenously at $r^* - q$ the only way this can occur is if the real rate of return on holding money is to increase. That is the rate of exchange depreciation must fall, resulting in a corresponding reduction in the rate of domestic inflation.

We have seen that with flexible rates the domestic government is able to regain control over crucial domestic variables such as output and domestic inflation. This, of course, does not mean that flexible exchange rates completely insulate the domestic economy from inflationary pressures abroad. On the contrary, all the endogenous domestic variables will, in general, still be affected by q. The important point is that, by contrast to the fixed exchange rate regime, the domestic government is able to offset foreign inflationary effects, by appropriate policy measures.

The fact that the domestic economy is not, in general, fully insulated from the rest of the world can be readily seen from (12.45). Suppose that the foreign nominal interest rate does *not* fully reflect the foreign rate of inflation, so that

$$\frac{\partial r^*}{\partial q} < 1.$$

In this case, an increase in the foreign rate of inflation will reduce the real rate of interest, thereby reducing savings. The only way that savings can be restored to its equilibrium level of zero is if disposable income increases, and/or domestic wealth decreases. An increase in disposable income will increase domestic demand, increasing the domestic rate of inflation. All of these effects will impinge on the financial sector, which in turn will feed back onto the rest of the economy. The ultimate impacts turn out to be rather complex and we do not report them in detail.[15]

But this raises the following interesting question: when, if ever, will a flexible exchange rate yield perfect insulation for the domestic economy from foreign inflation? The answer is simple. *For arbitrarily specified parameters, a flexible exchange rate system will insulate the domestic economy perfectly from foreign inflation if and only if the foreign nominal interest rate fully reflects the foreign rate in inflation;* i.e., if and only if

$$\frac{\partial r^*}{\partial q} = 1. \tag{12.48}$$

This is immediately apparent from (12.45). Inserting (12.48) into the right hand side of (12.45) we find

$$\frac{\partial V}{\partial q} = \frac{\partial Z}{\partial q} = \frac{\partial \sigma}{\partial q} = \frac{\partial Y^D}{\partial q} = \frac{\partial p}{\partial q} = 0 \tag{12.49a}$$

$$\frac{\partial e}{\partial q} = 1. \tag{12.49b}$$

Under these conditions, any increase in foreign inflation will be exactly offset by an equal appreciation of the domestic exchange rate, leaving the rest of the system unaffected.[16]

It thus becomes clear that under a flexible exchange rate system the crucial mechanism whereby inflation may be imported from abroad is through the real rates of return on assets. If, as in a Fisherian world, these are independent of the rate of inflation, perfect insulation is possible. But if the world is non-Fisherian, then any increase in foreign inflation will have an impact domestically, as people seek to adjust their portfolios and expenditures in response to the changes in the real rates of return as these occur.

F.   *Steady-state properties: money financing*
        Our treatment of this case shall be brief. The steady-state rate of inflation still satisfied equation (12.42) and substituting this into (12.36) and (12.37) again yields the five steady-state equations (12.44). The only difference is that with money financing, l is now endogenous, leaving us with six variables V, σ, Z, Y^D, e and also l. In the polar case of pure money financing (i.e., $\dot{a} = 0$), the steady-state equation is the stationary solution to equation (12.40), namely

$$g_c = (\bar{a} + l)p \tag{12.50}$$

where $\bar{a}$ denotes the fact that the real stock of government bond debt remains constant. Rewriting (12.50) in the form

$$p = \frac{g_c}{l + \bar{a}} = \frac{\dot{L} + \dot{A}}{L + A} \tag{12.51}$$

we see that the steady-state rate of inflation equals the rate of growth of *nominal* government debt. Domestic inflation can be explained by a kind of generalized quantity theory. This equation is the analogue to (7.32e′) and (8.48g′) obtained for the closed economy.

The steady-state properties of the model can be derived by differentiating (12.44) and (12.50) with respect to the various exogenous factors. We do not discuss specific results, except to note that an increase in G_d does not have an unambiguously inflationary effect. This arises from the fact that one partial effect of an increase in G_d is to raise σ. To the extent that this may occur, the real value of the current government deficit and therefore, the rate of domestic inflation, will tend to be reduced. However, we hasten to add that this is only one partial effect and is presumably dominated by the usual expansionary and inflationary effects of increased government expenditure.

Another matter to which attention should be drawn is the fact that our conclusions regarding perfect insulation of the domestic economy under flexible exchange rates continue to hold. Invoking the Fisherian condition $\partial r^*/\partial q = 1$, it can be readily verified that once again the set of equations (12.49) is obtained.

We conclude by showing how the equilibrium we have just been discussing generalizes to the intermediate case of partial bond and partial money deficit financing. This case is described by

$$\dot{l} = \theta g_D \qquad 0 < \theta < 1 \qquad (12.52a)$$

$$\dot{a} = (1-\theta)g_D. \qquad (12.52b)$$

Integrating these two equations yields

$$(1-\theta)(l-l_0) = \theta(a-a_0) \qquad (12.53)$$

where a_0, l_0 denote the initial values of a, l. The dynamics of government debt accumulation can therefore be summarized by (12.52a) and (12.53).[17] The steady state of the system in this case thus consists of equations (12.44) (with l unconstrained), the stationary solution to (12.52a), and equation (12.53). These seven equations will determine the equilibrium values of V, σ, Z, Y^D, p, l, a. In particular, the steady-state rate of inflation is given by

$$p = \frac{g_c}{l+a}. \qquad (12.51')$$

This is virtually the same as (12.52); the only difference is that a is no longer fixed, but is determined by (12.53).

The nature of the steady state for the intermediate case $0 < \theta < 1$ is basically the same as for the polar case $\theta = 1$. In particular, our conclusions regarding the perfect insulation of flexible exchange rates continue to apply.

5. Concluding observations

Despite the length of this chapter, the main conclusions can be fairly readily summarized.

We systematically examined the stability of the fixed exchange rate system, posulating constant world inflation and interest rates, and constant domestic government-spending and income-tax rates. The possibility of instability of the domestic economy in this setting certainly cannot be dismissed. Most of the stabilizing and destabilizing factors can be reconciled with those identified in earlier analyses. Thus, the Marshall—Lerner condition, Keynesian leakages, the adjustment speed of inflationary expectations, the elasticity of demand for real balances with respect to inflationary expectations, and interest payments on government debt, all play their accustomed roles. One surprising implication of the necessary conditions, however, is that if the nominal rate of interest is positive and wealth has no effect on domestic savings, then the system is stable only in an inflationary world. *Ceteris paribus,* the world inflation rate is an automatic stabilizer.

We specified a short run of the fixed-rate system by disregarding feedbacks from savings, changing terms of trade, and changing inflationary expectations. In this instantaneous equilibrium, monetary and fiscal policies have effects on internal and external objectives which are familiar from the discussion of the assignment problem for the case of perfect capital mobility. Expansionary monetary policy has no effect on the internal economy; in particular it leaves the level of domestic output unaffected. As a consequence the effects of an increase in government expenditure on the internal economy are all independent of the method of debt financing employed by the government; in particular it has an expansionary effect on domestic output. The level of reserves is increased by fiscal expansion and lowered by monetary expansion. An external inflationary shock, specified as an increase in the foreign inflation rate with no change in the foreign interest rate, spurs domestic inflation. Disposable income, output and reserves are unaffected by this disturbance, at least instantaneously.

Provided the system is stable, savings, changing terms of trade and changing inflation expectations drive the system towards a steady state. In that state, the rates of inflation of domestically produced goods and the domestic cost of living, together with the expected rate of inflation, must all converge to the exogenously given world rate. The level of output is then determined by that rate, and/or by the parameters describing the domestic wage—price sector. The domestic government has no control over the steady-state rate of inflation and the only way it can affect output is by altering the parameters of the wage—price sector, if that is possible. Nominal wealth is accumulated at the world inflation rate. A devaluation merely increases the price of domestic output by the same proportion, leaving the terms of trade, and everything else, unchanged.

Thus, fiscal and monetary policies have no effect on steady-state output.

The short-run results no longer apply. However, the qualitative short-run results for the effects of fiscal and monetary policy on reserves do carry over, regardless of whether reserves are measured in terms of either domestic or foreign purchasing power. With regard to the effects of foreign inflation, it turns out that it is necessary to resort to more specialized cases in order to obtain clear-cut results. Thus, provided that the foreign interest rate fully adjusts to changes in the foreign inflation rate, the domestic economy has a natural rate of unemployment, and presuming that the elasticity of demand for real balances with respect to expected inflation is less than the ratio of the inflation rate to the nominal interest rate, an increase in foreign inflation worsens the terms of trade and lowers disposable income, wealth and reserves.

We turn now to the main conclusions for the case of flexible exchange rates. We found that stability is too complex to be analysed in a systematic yet illuminating way. In the short run, fiscal and monetary policies have qualitative effects on internal and external objectives which in many respects resemble the implications of simple Keynesian models of a closed economy. Thus, fiscal expansion stimulates output; monetary expansion also stimulates output, provided that interest-income effects are sufficiently weak. Fiscal expansion increases the domestic interest rate — and the exchange depreciation rate, for the two are equal up to a parametric constant; monetary expansion lowers those rates. On the other hand, these results appear to be somewhat at variance with the analogous results obtained for the conventional short-run flexible exchange rate models. These apparent inconsistencies are readily reconciled; they arise solely due to differences in specification. An external inflationary shock has the same qualitative effects as in the fixed-rate case.

By contrast to the fixed-rate case, the steady state depends crucially upon how the government finances its real deficit. If it is purely bond financed, the domestic inflation rate must equal the rate of accumulation of nominal domestic wealth, just as in the fixed-rate case. Fiscal expansion raises the domestic interest rate, the rate of exchange depreciation, and the rate of domestic inflation. It also increases the level of domestic output, unless the economy has its steady-state output determined by the 'natural rate' $\bar{Z}$. With regard to the effects of monetary policy, it turns out that it is useful to resort to the specialized case considered formerly for the situation of an increase in foreign inflation under fixed rates. In that case, the qualitative effects on monetary contraction are the same as the qualitative effects of an increase in foreign inflation under fixed rates. Monetary expansion (an increase in the steady-state stock of real balances, not to be confused with an increase in the rate of nominal monetary expansion) has the same qualitative effect on interest and exchange depreciation rates as in the short run. The domestic inflation rate is lowered by this policy.

If the deficit under flexible rates is financed at least partially by printing money, the steady state is quite different. For then there is a direct link between the current deficit, expressed as a fraction of outstanding government debt, and the inflation rate. The inflation rate must equal the rate of growth of nominal debt. The only way the domestic government can reduce the steady-state rate of domestic inflation is by reducing the rate of growth of its nominal debt. And that is possible if and only if the government current deficit, expressed as a fraction of outstanding government debt, is reduced. Furthermore, under either mode of financing, while the government can, in general, regain control of domestic inflation and output under flexible rates, this does not mean that the domestic economy will be fully insulated from foreign inflation. In general it is not. In both the short run and the steady state, perfect insulation occurs if and only if the foreign nominal interest rate is fully adjusted for the foreign rate of inflation. If this is so any random change in the foreign inflation rate will be exactly offset by the exchange depreciation rate, leaving the internal economy undisturbed.

We conclude this discussion by briefly relating these findings to the monetary approach. Some authors have suggested that the essential difference between monetarism and Keynesianism is that of the time horizon. In particular it has been suggested that the steady state of a properly specified Keynesian model should resemble the equilibrium of a monetary model.[18] In several respects our results support this view. In particular they support the proposition that in a stable fixed exchange rate world, national inflation rates tend to converge; there is a 'natural distribution of specie', where 'specie' consists of real outside financial wealth. Devaluation is neutral. In a stable floating exchange rate world the movement of the exchange rate conforms to the purchasing power parity theory and, with at least some money financing, the home steady-state rate of inflation is governed by a kind of generalized quantity theory. Under either kind of exchange regime, inflation can be represented as a taxation mechanism and revenues generated within a given country accrue to both home and foreign governments. These are all characteristically monetarist propositions. However, there are some differences. Under both fixed and flexible rates, the possibility of involuntary, nonfrictional unemployment − central to Keynesian theory − is retained. In addition, under flexible rates there is a steady-state, as well as a short-run tradeoff between inflation and unemployment, unless the economy has a natural rate of unemployment. If this is so, steady-state output is fixed, again in keeping with monetary notions.

Appendix
1.   *Savings and the Marshall−Lerner condition*

In this appendix we wish to derive the relationship between the Marshall−Lerner condition and the restrictions implied by the domestic disposable income constraint. Equation (12.21) can be written in the form

$$Y^D = \frac{H(Y^D, r^* - \pi, \sigma, W) + \sigma I(Y^D, r^* - \pi, \sigma, W)}{\phi(\sigma)}$$

$$+ S(Y^D, r^* - \pi, W). \qquad (12.A.1)$$

Differentiating both sides with respect to σ, and invoking the normalization $\sigma = \phi(\sigma) = 1$, it can be seen that our assumption $\partial S / \partial \sigma = 0$ implies

$$(\delta - 1)H + H_3 + \delta I + I_3 = 0. \qquad (12.A.2)$$

The M−L condition is

$$\frac{\partial}{\partial \sigma}(X - \sigma I) > 0$$

where initially $X = \sigma I (= I)$. Applying our normalization, this yields

$$X' - I - I_3 > 0. \qquad (12.A.3)$$

(12.A.2) can be written as

$$[(H_3 + X') - (1 - \delta)(H + X)] + (X - X' + I_3) = 0 \qquad (12.A.4)$$

from which we deduce that the M−L condition holds if and only if

$$(H_3 + X') > (1 - \delta)(H + X). \qquad (12.A.5)$$

Converted to elasticity form, we can assert

$$\partial S / \partial \sigma = 0 \Leftrightarrow (\eta_1 + \eta_2 \geqslant 1 \Leftrightarrow \eta_3 \geqslant 1 - \delta) \qquad (12.A.6)$$

where

η_1 = price elasticity of demand for the domestic good by the rest of the world,

η_2 = price elasticity of demand for the foreign good by the domestic private sector,

η_3 = price elasticity of demand for the domestic good by the rest of the world and the domestic private sector combined,

$1 - \delta$ = price elasticity of disposable income, or an index of the 'terms-of-trade effect on real income', or the weight of the foreign good in the domestic cost-of-living index;

Thus, M−L holds if and only if the price elasticity of demand for the domestic good, η_3, exceeds the 'terms-of-trade effect' $1 - \delta$, provided savings are independent of relative prices. In order to see the role of M−L in our stability discussion it is necessary merely to note that $H_3 + X' \equiv (H + X)\eta_3$. Finally, lest there is confusion, we point out that the above price elasticities of demand are compensated rather than uncompensated expressions. Furthermore, they are 'cost-of-living' compensated, rather than the Slutsky-compensated expressions frequently employed in the literature on the pure theory of international trade. In the special case of Cobb−Douglas functions at home and abroad (see Section 2A), the elasticities are Hicks-compensated.

2. *Conditions for local stability of fixed exchange rate systems*

Sufficient conditions for the local stability of the fixed exchange rate for the two polar cases of fixed expectations and perfect foresight are as follows.

(a) *Fixed expectations* ($\rho = 0$)

(i) $1 - H_1(1 - u) + H_1 r^*(1 - u)L_1 + \gamma_1 VH_1 > 0$

(ii) $\alpha_1 [(H_3 + X' - H_1(1 - u)Z(1 - \delta)] + \gamma_1 V [(S_1 H_4 - S_3 H_1)$
$+ H_4 + r(1 - u)(1 - L_4)H_1 - H_1 p] - S_3 [1 - H_1(1 - u)$
$+ H_1 r^*(1 - u)L_1] + S_1 [-(1 - u)(1 - L_1 r^*)H_4 + p$
$- r^*(1 - u)(1 - L_4)] > 0.$

(iii) $Z(1 - u)(1 - \delta)(S_1 H_4 - S_3 H_1)\alpha_1$
$+ (H_3 + X')\{S_3 - S_1 [p - r^*(1 - u)(1 - L_4)]\}\alpha_1 < 0.$

(b) *Perfect foresight* ($\rho = \infty$)

(i) $(1 - \gamma_2)[1 - H_1(1 - u) + L_1 r^*(1 - u)H_1]$
$- \gamma_1 [H_1 r^*(1 - u)(L_2 + L_3) - (H_2 + H_1 V)] > 0$

(ii) $\alpha_1 [(H_3 + X') - H_1(1 - u)Z(1 - \delta)]$
$+ \gamma_1 \langle S_3 [H_1 r^*(1 - u)(L_2 + L_3) - (H_2 + H_1 V)]$
$- S_2 \{H_4 + [H_1(1 - L_4)r^*(1 - u) - p]\} - S_1 \{H_4 r^*(1 - u)(L_2 + L_3)$
$- H_4 V + H_2 [r^*(1 - u)(1 - L_4) - p]\}\rangle$
$+ (1 - \gamma_2)\{-S_3 [1 - H_1(1 - u) + H_1 r^*(1 - u)L_1]$
$+ S_1 [-(1 - L_1 r^*)(1 - u)H_4 + p - r^*(1 - u)(1 - L_4)]\}\} > 0$

(iii) $Z(1 - u)(1 - \delta)(S_1 H_4 - S_3 H_1)\alpha_1$
$+ (H_3 + X')\{S_3 - S_1 [p - r^*(1 - u)(1 - L_4)]\}\alpha_1 < 0.$

The set of necessary conditions for local stability is given by the corresponding weak inequalities.

PART III. STABILIZATION POLICIES

13

AN INTRODUCTION TO STABILIZATION THEORY AND POLICY

1.   Introduction

With a few exceptions (most notably Chapter 7, Section 7; Chapter 9, Sections 7, 8; Chapter 11, Section 5), the first two parts of this book have treated the government policy variables as being exogenously determined, or restricted their endogenous adjustment to that necessary to satisfy certain financing constraints. In particular, apart from the exceptions noted above, we have treated government expenditure as exogenously given and analysed its effects over various time horizons under alternative assumptions regarding the financing of the government deficit. Depending upon what form of financing is being assumed, the money supply or stock of government bonds were then allowed to vary endogenously in accordance with the requirements of the government budget constraint.

As we first commented in Chapter 7, the government is unlikely to hold its policy variables, such as government expenditure, fixed over long periods. On the contrary, it is likely to adjust these variables in response to changing economic conditions, in order to stabilize the economy. If unemployment gets too high, it is likely to increase government expenditure or the rate of growth of the money supply; if the rate of inflation gets too high it will tend to revert to contractionary policies. The point is that the government is likely to use its policy instruments for active stabilization purposes and not react merely passively as we have so far been assuming.

The theory of economic stabilization is a broad one and we can deal only with certain central issues in this volume. For more detailed discussion of the subject the reader is referred to some of the recent specialized texts in this area.[1]

The theory of stabilization is discussed in several different senses in the literature. At the simplest level there is a theory dealing with the stabilization of static, non-stochastic, systems. In this instance the problem is a relatively straightforward one; if one were unkind, one might even say that it is trivial. Secondly, there is a body of theory dealing with the stabilization of static stochastic systems. Stabilization in this context refers to minimizing the random fluctuations of the system in some specified sense. Thirdly, the stabilization problem is sometimes discussed in terms of controlling dynamic, non-stochastic, systems. Here the concern may be with the fluctuations in the time path of the variable of concern, which unlike those of the second case are non-random and entirely predictable. Fourthly, one can combine cases two and three and analyse the stabilization problem of a dynamic system which is also subject to stochastic disturbances.

Throughout the next two chapters we shall consider these questions progressively. The present chapter is devoted to reviewing some of the more basic issues, while Chapter 14 discusses the more general problems associated with the optimal stabilization of dynamic and stochastic systems.

2.   Static Tinbergen theory of stabilization

The theory of economic policy originated with Tinbergen's important book, *On the Theory of Economic Policy,* first published in 1952. In it he proved the now classic proposition stating that under certainty, and provided certain conditions to be discussed below are met, the policy maker need use only as many policy variables as he has target variables in order to achieve any desired values for these target variables.

To see this, consider the following linear system

$$y = Ax \tag{13.1}$$

where

$y = n \times 1$ vector of target variables,
$x = m \times 1$ vector of policy instruments, under the direct control of the policy maker,
$A = n \times m$ vector of constant coefficients.

Equation (13.1) thus describes a static linear system relating the target variables, which are the ultimate concern of the policy maker, to the policy instruments, which are under his direct control. Suppose also that the policy maker has chosen a vector $y = y^*$ of desired (target) values for y. The question first raised by Tinbergen, concerning the number of instruments, necessary to achieve $y = y^*$, can be answered from this equation, using some elementary properties of linear algebra. First, if the number of targets exceed the number of instruments (i.e., $n > m$), it is in general impossible to achieve the desired target vector y^* with the available instruments. Secondly if $n = m$, the target objective in general can be achieved by means of a unique choice of instruments. In this case A is a square matrix, and provided that it is non-singular, we can solve (13.1) for

$$x^* = A^{-1}y^*, \tag{13.2}$$

the unique values x^* of the policy variables. Thirdly, if $m > n$, the target objective can be attained by use of less than the available number of instruments. The policy maker can achieve y^* by the appropriate choice of n instruments, setting the remaining $m - n = 0$. To see this suppose that the matrix A is partitioned so that

$$y = (A_1 \quad A_2) \begin{pmatrix} x_1 \\ x_2 \end{pmatrix}$$

$$= A_1 x_1 + A_2 x_2 \qquad\qquad (13.3)$$

where

x_1 denotes the first n instruments,

x_2 denotes the remaining $(m - n)$ instruments,

A_1 is accordingly an $n \times n$ matrix,

A_2 is an $n \times (n - m)$ matrix.

Without any essential loss of generality we can suppose A is non-singular, in which case, $y = y^*$ can be achieved by setting

$$x_1^* = A_1^{-1} y^*$$

$$x_2^* = 0. \qquad\qquad (13.4)$$

For example, if we have one target and two instuments, related by

$$y = a_1 x_1 + a_2 x_2$$

where y, x_1, x_2 are now scalar quantities, any combination of the two instruments lying on the line

$$a_1 x_1 + a_2 x_2 = y^*$$

will achieve the objective. In particular, the use of one policy variable will suffice.

Any static system for which there exist sufficient policy instruments so as to achieve any desired values for the target variables y is said to be *statically controllable*. The above conditions which ensure this property can be summarized more formally by the following *static controllability* condition:

The static system $y = Ax$ is statically controllable if and only if $r(A) = n$, (where r denotes the rank of the matrix).

The analogous concept applicable to dynamic systems, namely that of *dynamic controllability*, also exists and will be introduced in Chapter 14.

Apart from dealing with a linear, static system, the Tinbergen proposition implicitly makes two other assumptions. The first is the absence of any costs associated with adjusting the policy instruments. Intuitively it seems plausible that if the adjustment of instruments is associated with increasing costs then no matter how many instruments there are in excess of the number of targets it will always pay the policy maker to use as many instruments as are available, thereby spreading the costs among them. This proposition is in fact correct and is taken up in Section 4.

Secondly, the Tinbergen proposition assumes a world of perfect certainty. As first shown by Brainard (1967), the proposition ceases to apply once multiplicative stochastic disturbances are introduced. We now turn to a discussion of the Brainard model.

3. Stabilization in the presence of stochastic disturbances

A. One instrument – one target case

Brainard's analysis begins with the one target – one instrument problem. The target y and instrument x are related by the stochastic linear relation

$$y = ax + u \tag{13.5}$$

where y, x are now scalar quantities and a, u are random variables with[2]

$$E(u) = \bar{u}, \quad E(a) = \bar{a},$$

$$Var(u) = \sigma_u^2, \quad var(a) = \sigma_a^2,$$

Thus according to (13.5), the relationship between target and instrument contains both an additive random disturbance (one that is independent of the level of the policy variable) and a multiplicative one (one which is proportional to the level at which the instrument is operated). Viewing (13.5) as a reduced form equation between say, the money supply (x) and the level of income (y), the multiplicative disturbance arises through random disturbances in the coefficients of the system. Consequently, the marginal impact of the policy variable becomes stochastic. As we shall see it is this multiplicative disturbance which is the critical one in causing the modification to the Tinbergen results.

The policy maker is assumed to have chosen some target vector y^*. Given this chosen value, the stabilization problem as formulated by Brainard is to choose x so as to keep y as close to y^* on average as possible. This can be formalized by postulating say a quadratic cost function associated with having y away from y^*.

Formally then the problem is to choose x to

$$\text{Min } E(u) \equiv E[(y - y^*)^2]$$

$$\text{subject to } y = ax + u. \tag{13.6}$$

Substituting (13.5) into (13.6), yields

$$E[(ax + u - y^*)^2] \tag{13.7}$$

and taking expected values we obtain

$$E[U] = \sigma_a^2 x^2 + \sigma_u^2 + 2\rho\sigma_a\sigma_u x + (\bar{a}x + \bar{u} - y^*)^2 \tag{13.8}$$

where ρ denotes the correlation coefficient between a and u.

Minimizing (13.8) with respect to x, yields

$$x_u = \frac{\bar{a}(y^* - \bar{u}) - \rho\sigma_a\sigma_u}{\bar{a}^2 + \sigma_a^2} \tag{13.9}$$

which expresses the optimal policy for x under uncertainty, denoted by x_u, in terms of the target y^* and the parameters characterizing the probability distributions of u, a. Note that if we have a world of certainty, $\sigma_a = \sigma_u = 0$, in which case

$$x_c = \frac{(y^* - \bar{u})}{\bar{a}} \tag{13.9'}$$

which is clearly the required adjustment according to the Tinbergen proposition.[3]

Thus in general we see that the policy adjustment under uncertainty, x_u, in general differs from what it would be under certainty, x_c. This, however, depends crucially on $\sigma_a \neq 0$. If the only random disturbance is the additive term u, then $x_u = x_c$; that is, the policy under uncertainty is identical to that under certainty. This invariance of the policy to additive disturbances is a well established result, dating back to Theil (1958). It is often referred to as a 'certainty equivalence' result; see Chapter 14.

The interesting differences between x_u and x_c therefore arise through the presence of multiplicative disturbances. To discuss these further, let us assume for the moment that $\sigma_u = 0$. In this case

$$x_u = \frac{\bar{a}(y^* - \bar{u})}{\bar{a}^2 + \sigma_a^2} = \frac{\bar{a}^2}{\bar{a}^2 + \sigma_a^2} x_c \tag{13.10}$$

so that $|x_u| < |x_c|$, implying a more conservative response on the part of the policy maker. This makes quite sound intuitive sense. If $\sigma_a^2 > 0$, the policy maker is uncertain as to the marginal increment of his instrument. He will therefore adjust it more cautiously than if he were certain of its effects. Moreover, the more uncertain he is, (the larger σ_a^2), the smaller relatively will be the adjustment.

Inserting the optimal policy (13.10) into (13.5) (with $u = \bar{u}$ since $\sigma_u^2 = 0$) we find the corresponding value of the target to be

$$y = \frac{a\bar{a}(y^* - \bar{u})}{\bar{a}^2 + \sigma_a^2} + \bar{u}$$

from which we deduce

$$E(y) - y^* = \frac{\sigma_a^2(\bar{u} - y^*)}{\bar{a}^2 + \sigma_a^2}. \tag{13.11}$$

Without any loss of generality we can assume $y^* > \bar{u}$ in which case, as long as $\sigma_a^2 \neq 0$, the target variable will on average *undershoot* its desired value. On the other hand, if $\sigma_a^2 = 0$, while $\sigma_u^2 \neq 0$, it can be shown by an analogous argument that $E(y) = y^*$, so that y will fluctuate randomly about its target value.

These results remain intact even in the presence of additive disturbances, provided that they are uncorrelated with a. A non-zero correlation, however, complicates the results. The relationship between x_u and x_c is now given by

$$x_u = \frac{\bar{a}^2}{\bar{a}^2 + \sigma_a^2} x_c - \frac{\rho \sigma_a \sigma_u}{\bar{a}^2 + \sigma_a^2} . \tag{13.10'}$$

If $\rho > 0$, the adjustment in x_u is reduced.

It is now even possible for the direction of further adjustment to be reversed from what it would be under certainty. By contrast, if the additive and multiplicative disturbances are negatively correlated, the adjustment of x_u is increased, even to the extent that the target variable may *overshoot* its goal (on average).

B.   *Two instruments – one target case*

Let us now consider the situation where the policy maker has two instruments available to meet his objective. This can be described by

$$y = a_1 x_1 + a_2 x_2 + u \tag{13.12}$$

where

$$E(a_i) = \bar{a}_i, \quad i = 1, 2, \quad E(u) = \bar{u}$$

$$\text{Var}(a_i) = \sigma_i^2, \quad i = 1, 2, \quad \text{Var}(u) = \sigma_u^2,$$

and now for simplicity we assume a zero correlation between the multiplicative and additive disturbances. However, we shall allow a_1 and a_2 to be correlated, denoting their correlation coefficiency by γ.

Assuming that the objective is, as before, to minimize (13.6), subject now to (13.12), the formal problem is the choice of x_1, x_2 to minimize

$$\sigma_1^2 x_1^2 + \sigma_2^2 x_2^2 + \sigma_u^2 + 2\sigma_1 \sigma_2 \gamma x_1 x_2$$
$$+ (\bar{a}_1 x_1 + \bar{a}_2 x_2 + \bar{u} - y^*)^2 . \tag{13.13}$$

Performing the optimization yields the solutions

$$\sigma_1^2 x_1 + \sigma_1 \sigma_2 \gamma x_2 + \bar{a}_1 (\bar{a}_1 x_1 + \bar{a}_2 x_2 + \bar{u} - y^*) = 0$$
$$\sigma_1 \sigma_2 \gamma x_1 + \sigma_2^2 x_2 + \bar{a}_2 (\bar{a}_1 x_1 + \bar{a}_2 x_2 + \bar{u} - y^*) = 0. \tag{13.14}$$

Note that if $\sigma_1^2 = \sigma_2^2 = 0$ – that is the marginal impacts of the policy instruments are known with certainty – both equations (13.14) reduce to the *same* equation

$$\bar{a}_1 x_1 + \bar{a}_2 x_2 + \bar{u} - y^* = 0.$$

This is precisely the same as the Tinbergen policy-adjustment rule obtained under certainty, in which case either x_1 or x_2 may be chosen arbitrarily. This of course is as it should be.

For $\sigma_1^2 \neq 0$, $\sigma_2^2 \neq 0$, so that both instruments are operated with uncertainty, equation (13.14) will in general yield *unique* values for x_1, x_2, implying that it will be optimal to use *both* instruments simultaneously. The solution to (13.14) will be unique provided

$$\begin{vmatrix} \sigma_1^2 + \bar{a}_1^2 & \sigma_1\sigma_2\gamma + \bar{a}_1\bar{a}_2 \\ \sigma_1\sigma_2\gamma + \bar{a}_1\bar{a}_2 & \sigma_2^2 + \bar{a}_2^2 \end{vmatrix} \neq 0.$$

It can be shown that this will certainly be met provided $-1 \leqslant \gamma < 1$, so that the two instruments are not perfectly positively correlated. Even if $\gamma = 1$, it will still be met unless

$$\frac{\sigma_1}{\bar{a}_1} = \frac{\sigma_2}{\bar{a}_2}$$

in which case the two disturbances have identical coefficients of variation.

The relative intensity of the two instruments can be easily obtained from (13.14) as

$$\frac{x_1}{x_2} = \frac{\sigma_2(\bar{a}_1\sigma_2 - \sigma_1\gamma\bar{a}_2)}{\sigma_1(\bar{a}_2\sigma_1 - \sigma_2\gamma\bar{a}_1)}. \tag{13.15}$$

In particular, if $\gamma = 0$, we see that

$$\frac{x_1}{x_2} = \frac{\bar{a}_1}{\bar{a}_2}\frac{\sigma_2^2}{\sigma_1^2}. \tag{13.15'}$$

The relative intensity of the two instruments will vary inversely with their respective variances — again a perfectly plausible result.

While we have focused on ony two instruments, it is clear that the above analysis generalizes to any number of instruments and targets. The general conclusion to emerge from the model is the conclusion that, with the effects of policies subject to multiplicative stochastic disturbances, the policy maker should use all available instruments at his disposal, rather than just one. The reason is that by diversifying in this way, the associated risks can be reduced.

4. Costs of instrument adjustment

Thus far we have assumed that all policy instruments can be adjusted as much as desired at zero costs. This may, or may not, be the case. Some policy instruments, such as the money supply, may be relatively costless to adjust. Others, such as the tax rate, and the level of government expenditure are not so freely adaptable. Typically they can be adjusted only within small ranges at any instant of time, and then only after appropriate legislation has been passed. These restraints on the rate at which the instrument can be changed are what are often broadly referred to as 'adjustment costs'. For simplicity we shall assume that they are a quadratic function of the *rate of change* of the instrument. While we do not pretend that the quadratic cost of adjustment is necessarily realistic, it does yield the essential feature of increasing marginal costs of adjustment. Most people would agree that small tax changes, say, involve less costs, administrative and otherwise, than large reforms. This aspect of costs is captured by the quadratic function.

A. *One instrument – one target case*

The problem of policy adjustment we shall consider is specified by the following optimization problem

$$\text{Min } W = \int_0^\infty [m(y - y^*)^2 + n\dot{x}^2] e^{-rt} dt \qquad \begin{aligned} m &> 0 \\ n &> 0 \end{aligned} \qquad (13.16a)$$

subject to

$$y = ax \qquad (13.16b)$$

where x denotes the time derivative of x. This is the familiar one instrument – one target problem, in which y and x are related by the non-stochastic relationship (13.16b), and as before y^* is the desired target for y. The quantities $m > 0$, $n > 0$ indicate the relative costs associated with having the target variable away from its goal on the one hand, and changing the instrument on the other. Note that presence of adjustment costs – i.e. costs associated with *changing* the instrument – introduce an essential dynamic element into the problem, even though the basic relationship (13.16b) is static. Hence it becomes crucial to weigh up these costs over time, with the discount rate r reflecting the social rate of discount.

Substituting (13.16b) into (13.16a), the problem can be reformulated as choosing x to minimize

$$W = \int_0^\infty [m(ax - y^*)^2 + n\dot{x}^2] e^{-rt} dt. \qquad (13.17)$$

This is a very simple problem in the calculus of variations, the solution methods for which are well known; see e.g., Bryson and Ho (1969). Denoting the integrand by H

$$H(x, \dot{x}) \equiv [m(ax - y^*)^2 + n\dot{x}^2] e^{-rt}$$

the optimal level of x at each point of time t is determined by solving the Euler equation[4]

$$\frac{\partial H}{\partial x} = \frac{d}{dt} \left(\frac{\partial H}{\partial \dot{x}} \right).$$

Performing this calculation we find that x must satisfy the second order differential equation

$$n\ddot{x} - nr\dot{x} - ma(ax - y^*) = 0. \qquad (13.18)$$

The optimal stationary value for x, which we shall denote by x^*, is obtained when $\ddot{x} = \dot{x} = 0$, and is therefore given by

$$ax^* - y^* = 0. \qquad (13.19)$$

This of course is precisely the Tinbergen solution. It is an immediate implication of (13.18) that unless $n = 0$ (i.e. no adjustment costs), x will not in general be at its stationary value. In other words there will be a dynamic adjustment path for x. To obtain this involves solving equation (13.18). Applying the standard methods of solution (see e.g. Kaplan (1958)), yields

$$x - x^* = A_1 e^{\lambda_1 t} + A_2 e^{\lambda_2 t} \tag{13.20}$$

where λ_1, λ_2 are the two roots of the quadratic equation

$$n\lambda^2 - nr\lambda - ma = 0 \tag{13.21}$$

and A_1, A_2 are arbitrary constants. One can immediately infer from (13.21) that the two roots λ_1, λ_2 are of opposite sign. Suppose $\lambda_1 < 0, \lambda_2 > 0$. In order to ensure that the adjustment path for x converges to the optimal stationary value $x = x^*$, the constant A_2 must be set equal to zero. (This is a consequence of the so-called transversality conditions, see e.g. Athans and Falb (1966)).

The optimal adjustment rule thus becomes

$$x - x^* = A_1 e^{\lambda_1 t} \tag{13.20'}$$

where

$$\lambda_1 = \frac{nr - (n^2 r^2 + 4nma)^{1/2}}{2n} < 0. \tag{13.21'}$$

Differentiating (13.20'), the adjustment rule can be written in the equivalent form

$$\dot{x} = \lambda_1(x - x^*). \qquad \lambda_1 < 0 \tag{13.22}$$

Hence along the optimal path, the policy instrument is continually adjusted so as to close some proportion of the gap between its present value and its optimal stationary value. The speed with which this adjustment occurs is given by λ_1 defined in (13.21').

From (13.21') one can readily ascertain how λ_1 responds to the parameters m, n, r, say. These are given by

$$\frac{\partial \lambda_1}{\partial m} < 0 \tag{13.23a}$$

$$\frac{\partial \lambda_1}{\partial n} > 0 \tag{13.23b}$$

$$\frac{\partial \lambda_1}{\partial r} > 0. \tag{13.23c}$$

Realizing that $\lambda_1 < 0$, these results are all as one would expect. An increase in the costs of having the target variable away from its desired value will lead to more rapid policy adjustment. On the other hand an increase in adjustment costs will slow down the adjustment. Taking limiting values one can show that as $n \to 0$, one gets instantaneous adjustment, while as $n \to \infty$, $\lambda_1 \to 0$, and adjustment tends to cease. Finally, an increase in the social rate of discount tends to slow down the rate of adjustment. The less future deviations from the optimum matter, the slower will the adjustment proceed – again a perfectly plausible result.

B.   *Two instruments – one target case*

Let us now turn to the one target – two instrument case. To keep the analysis as simple as possible, we shall assume a zero discount rate so that $r = 0$. The problem now is

$$\text{Min } W = \int_0^\infty [m(y - y^*)^2 + n_1 \dot{x}_1^2 + n_2 \dot{x}_2^2] dt \qquad (13.24a)$$

subject to

$$y = a_1 x_1 + a_2 x_2 \qquad (13.24b)$$

where n_1, n_2 are now the adjustment costs associated with the two instruments x_1, x_2 respectively. Substituting for y into (13.24a) yields

$$W = \int_0^\infty [m(a_1 x_1 + a_2 x_2 - y^*)^2 + n_1 \dot{x}_1^2 + n_2 \dot{x}_2^2] dt$$

as the criterion to be minimized with respect to x_1, x_2. Again denoting the integrand by H, it is seen that H depends upon $x_1, \dot{x}_1, x_2, \dot{x}_2$. The optimality conditions are given by the direct generalization of the previous Euler condition, namely

$$\frac{\partial H}{\partial x_1} = \frac{d}{dt} \left(\frac{\partial H}{\partial \dot{x}_1} \right)$$

$$\frac{\partial H}{\partial x_2} = \frac{d}{dt} \left(\frac{\partial H}{\partial \dot{x}_2} \right).$$

Carrying out these calculations, yields the optimality conditions

$$n_1 \ddot{x}_1 - ma_1(a_1 x_1 + a_2 x_2 - y^*) = 0 \qquad (13.25a)$$

$$n_2 \ddot{x}_2 - ma_2(a_1 x_1 + a_2 x_2 - y^*) = 0. \qquad (13.25b)$$

The stationary values for x_1, x_2, denoted by x_1^*, x_2^* are obtained by setting $\ddot{x}_i = \dot{x}_i = 0, i = 1, 2$. In this case (13.25a) and (11.25b) define the same relationship

$$a_1 x_1^* + a_2 x_2^* = y^* \qquad (13.26)$$

between the optimal stationary values of the two instruments. This result seems to imply that there is an infinity of pairs of optimal stationary values lying on a straight line, but as we now show, the optimal stationary pair is uniquely determined by the initial condition.

To see this we must solve equations (13.25). Using the fact that the instruments are required to converge to finite optimal stationary values, the solution must take the form[5]

$$x_1(t) - x_1^* = A_1 e^{\lambda_1 t} \tag{13.27a}$$

$$x_2(t) - x_2^* = A_1 \frac{a_2 n_1}{a_1 n_2} e^{\lambda_1 t} \tag{13.27b}$$

$$\lambda_1 = -\left[m(a_2^2 n_1 + a_1^2 n_2)/n_1 n_2 \right]^{1/2} \tag{13.27c}$$

$$x_2^* = (y^* - a_1 x_1^*)/a_2. \tag{13.27d}$$

Equation (13.27d) is just a restatement of (13.26). Substituting the expression for x_2^* into (13.27b) and letting $t = 0$ we can use (13.27a) and (13.27b) to determine x_1^* and A_1. Thus in order to assure that the optimal path for each instrument passes through its initial value we must set x_1^* and therefore x_2^* appropriately.

The adjustment equations themselves can be written in an infinite number of ways, once x_1^* and x_2^* are determined. They are

$$\dot{x}_1 = B_{11}(x_1 - x_1^*) + B_{12}(x_2 - x_2^*) \tag{13.28a}$$

$$\dot{x}_2 = B_{21}(x_1 - x_1^*) + B_{22}(x_2 - x_2^*) \tag{13.28b}$$

where

$$B_{11} = \lambda_1 - B_{12} \frac{a_2 n_1}{a_1 n_2},$$

$$B_{21} = \frac{a_2 n_1}{a_1 n_2} (\lambda_1 - B_{22}).$$

We are free to choose arbitrarily one of the B_{ij} in each of the equations (13.28a) and (13.28b).

Thus in contrast to the case of zero adjustment costs under certainty, both instruments must be adjusted during the transition to equilibrium. Since adjustment costs vary with the square of the change in each of the instruments, it is better to adjust many instruments rather than one more intensively at each instant of time. Thus in the presence of adjustment costs the policy maker is better off when many instruments are available, even under certainty.

It is possible to extend the above discussion to the situation of risk. This has in fact been done by Henderson and Turnovsky (1972). Briefly, they show how the optimal stationary solution is essentially the same as Brainard's static optimum discussed in Section 3. They also consider the properties of the dynamic adjustment path to the long-run optimum and determine how it varies with the degree of uncertainty. This problem is extended further by Ali and Greenbaum (1976) to allow for the impacts of fixed costs on the choice of instrument.

5. **Review of basic multiplier–accelerator models**

So far, the analysis has assumed the relationships between the target and instrument variables to be static. In contrast, early work by Phillips (1954, 1957) focused on the problems of stabilization policy as arising from the existence of lags in the economic system. His work is rightly often regarded as marking the beginnings of dynamic stabilization theory.

The Phillips analysis was based on the dynamic multiplier–accelerator model, which had been developed before him by Samuelson (1939), Hicks (1950) and summarized most conveniently by Allen (1956). There are numerous versions of this model and we shall consider the simplest formulation used by Phillips. He worked with continuous-time dynamic systems, but essentially the same conclusions can be reached using discrete time.

The aggregate demand of the economy at time t, $Z(t)$ is defined by

$$Z(t) = C(t) + I(t) + G(t) \tag{13.29}$$

where as usual

    $C(t)$ denotes consumption,
    $I(t)$ denotes investment,
    $G(t)$ denotes government expenditure.

The model can be dynamized in various ways. One method used by Phillips is to introduce a product market disequilibrium relationship. This is described by

$$\dot{Y}(t) = \alpha[Z(t) - Y(t)] \qquad \alpha > 0 \tag{13.30}$$

where $Y(t)$ denotes aggregate supply at time t. This equation asserts that if demand exceeds supply, producers increase supply at a rate proportional to the rate of excess demand. If $Z(t) < Y(t)$, the adjustment is reversed. Integrating (13.30) we can write

$$Y(t) = \alpha \int_{-\infty}^{t} e^{-\alpha(t-s)} Z(s)ds \tag{13.30'}$$

from which we see that supply is an exponentially declining weighted average of past demands.

In order to complete the model, some behavioural hypotheses must be introduced for consumption and investment. The simplest of these is to specify

$$C(t) = cY(t) \qquad 0 < c < 1 \tag{13.31}$$

and I constant. In this case if G is constant as well, substituting (13.29), (13.31) into (13.30) yields the first order linear differential equation determining output

$$\dot{Y} = \alpha[(c-1)Y + I + G]. \tag{13.32}$$

This model is of course the familiar dynamic multiplier model. Note that in this case the only dynamic element is the product market equilibrium adjustment mechanism (13.30); if this were lacking the model would reduce to the simplest static multiplier model; see Chapter 2.

Phillips' essential contribution was to endogenize G in various ways to be discussed in Section 6 below. Much of his work was developed, and can be discussed, in terms of this simple model. However, most of the literature, as well as much of Phillips own contributions, did endogenize investment by means of the accelerator theory, which can be shown to generate a much richer array of patterns of behaviour for Y than is yielded by (13.32).

For example, consider the flexible accelerator model described by

$$K^*(t) = vY(t) \tag{13.33a}$$

$$\dot{K}(t) = \delta[K^*(t) - K(t)]. \tag{13.33b}$$

Equation (13.33a) defines the desired capital stock to be proportional to income, while (13.33b) defines the lagged adjustment of capital stock to its desired level. Noting the fact that I, K are related by

$$I = \dot{K}$$

one can eliminate I from (13.32) and obtain the following differential equation for Y

$$\ddot{Y} - [\alpha(c-1) + \alpha\delta v - \delta]\dot{Y} - \delta\alpha(c-1)Y = \alpha\delta G + \alpha\dot{G}. \tag{13.34}$$

This is capable of generating cyclical behaviour, which may be either stable or unstable. If $\delta \to \infty$, so that the accelerator operates instantaneously this system simplifies to

$$(1 - \alpha v)\dot{Y} - \alpha(c-1)Y = \alpha G.$$

These two equations represent typical formulations of the dynamic multiplier–accelerator model. In either case, it is clear that due to the accelerator component, a dynamic system is obtained even if $\alpha \to \infty$ so that continuous product market equilibrium prevails.

Much of the work analysing multiplier–accelerator models is formulated in discrete time. The essential dynamic elements here arise through lags in the underlying behavioural relationships. For example, the Hicks–Samuelson approach is based on

$$C_t = cY_{t-1} \tag{13.35a}$$

$$I_t = v(Y_{t-1} - Y_{t-2}) \tag{13.35b}$$

according to which consumption depends upon last period's income, while investment adjusts fully to lagged changes in income. Assuming product market equilibrium to hold in each period

$$Y_t = C_t + I_t + G_t$$

gives rise to the second order difference equation for output,

$$Y_t = (c + v)Y_{t-1} - vY_{t-2} + G_t. \tag{13.36}$$

This equation provided the basis for Hicks' important work on the trade cycle many years ago.

The approach prior to the work of Phillips was to study the dynamic properties of equations such as (13.32), (13.34) or (13.36) on the assumption that government expenditure is held constant. This is a simple exercise for these low order systems, but soon can become tedious when the order of the system is increased through the introduction of additional lags. The main purpose to which equations such as (13.36) were put was to the analysis of business cycles. But unfortunately, although this class of models is capable of generating cyclical behaviour for Y_t, it proved unsatisfactory as an explanation of them. Apart from the obvious over-simplification due to the abstraction of financial sectors and the other elements discussed in Parts I and II, these models suffer from the problem that they can generate only *linear* cyclical behaviour. That is, the cycles they yield must ultimately either die out, or explode. They *cannot* regenerate themselves. To achieve this some kind of non-linearity is required. Hicks accomplished this by introducing a floor and a ceiling to the capacity of the economy. Other authors such as Goodwin (1951) and Kalecki (1935) achieved the necessary non-linearity in other ways.

For our purpose, we do not propose to discuss these issues in any further detail. An excellent survey is contained in Allen (1956), to which the interested reader should refer.

6. **The Phillips stabilization policies**

As indicated above, Phillips' stabilization analysis can be discussed most conveniently with reference to equation (13.32). However, before discussing the policies he introduced, we should briefly consider the properties of this equation. With I, G given, it is a linear first order differential equation in Y. Provided $0 < c < 1$, it is clearly stable and income Y will converge to the stationary equilibrium level $\bar{Y}$

$$\bar{Y} = \frac{1 + G}{1 - c}. \tag{13.32'}$$

This will be recognized as being the equilibrium level of income for the simplest static linear macroeconomic model. Indeed it is precisely the solution to (2.7) in the simplest model of Chapter 2 for the case where the consumption function is linear.

Within this simple framework, Phillips' important contribution was to treat government expenditure G as a policy variable, which was continually adjusted in order to meet certain specified objectives. In his analysis, he emphasized the lags associated with adjusting the policy instrument. These might be called the *policy lags* and reflect lags in implementing decisions. They are quite distinct from lags such as those embodied in the produce market disequilibrium relationship, or in the accelerator (13.33). These latter lags are inherent in the system and can appropriately be described as *system lags*. These two kinds of lags are also frequently referred to as *inside lags* and *outside lags* respectively.

Phillips assumed that the actual policy implemented adjusts with an exponential lag to past policy decisions. Thus, if $G^d(t)$ is the desired value of the policy variable chosen at time t (the policy decision), the actual adjustment of $G(t)$ is described by

$$\dot{G}(t) = \beta[G^d(t) - G(t)] \qquad \beta > 0. \tag{13.37}$$

The desired value of the policy variable $G^d(t)$ is related according to certain rules to the ultimate target objective, in this case national income. Phillips postulated three such policy adjustment rules: namely the proportional, integral, and derivative policies. We shall now discuss these in turn.

A. *Proportional policy*

This was specified by Phillips to be

$$G^d = -\gamma(Y - Y^*) \qquad \gamma > 0 \tag{13.38}$$

where Y^* is the target level of output. If $Y > Y^*$, then $G^d < 0$; if $Y > Y^*$, $G^d < 0$. That is, the desired level of government expenditure is proportional, but opposite, to the deviation between current and the desired level of income. If for simplicity, one assumes an infinitely fast adjustment of G to G^d (i.e. the absence of policy lags), $\beta \to \infty$ so that

$$G(t) = G^d(t).$$

The dynamics of income, when the policy (13.38) is introduced, and no policy lags exist, is given by

$$\dot{Y} = \alpha[(c-1)Y + I - \gamma(Y - Y^*)] \tag{13.39}$$

which is again a first order linear differential equation. This is stable if and only if

$$(1-c) + \gamma > 0 \tag{13.40}$$

which is certainly met if the marginal propensity to consume is less than one. But now it is seen that the economy may still be stabilized even if $c > 1$. In other words provided $\gamma > 0$, the policy provides a generally stabilizing effect.[6]

The equilibrium level of income $\bar{Y}$ is obtained by setting $\dot{Y} = 0$ in (13.39) and is given by

$$\bar{Y} = \frac{I + \gamma Y^*}{1 - c + \gamma} \neq Y^*. \tag{13.41}$$

That is, in general the desired level of income will ultimately *not* be attained. This was taken by Phillips to be an undesirable feature of the proportional policy, but in fact it may also be viewed as reflecting an inadequate specification of the rule as given by (13.38). This formulation ignores the fact that given the behaviour of the private sector, as reflected by C, I, the government must choose an appropriate level of expenditure, G^* if it wishes to attain Y^* in the steady state equilibrium. This appropriate level is determined by the stationary solution

$$Y^* = cY^* + I + G^* \tag{13.42}$$

By choosing G^*, in accordance with (13.42), the government can be assured that any chosen level of Y^* can in fact be sustained indefinitely.

Once this fact is recognized, it becomes much more natural to modify (13.38) (with $G^d \equiv G$) to

$$G - G^* = -\gamma(Y - Y^*) \qquad \gamma > 0 \tag{13.38'}$$

In this case we find that current government expenditure is adjusted above its steady state level when income is below its target, and is adjusted below otherwise. Inserting (13.38') into (13.32) and noting (13.42), we now obtain

$$\dot{Y} = \alpha(c - 1 - \gamma)(Y - Y^*) \tag{13.39'}$$

The stability for this equation is again determined by (13.40), but now, provided this condition is met, income will in fact converge to its long run optimum value Y^*.

Let us now introduce the existence of policy lags into the adjustment. Following Phillips, and assuming these are of the form (13.37), the system is now modified to

$$Z = cY + I + G$$
$$\dot{Y} = \alpha(Z - Y)$$
$$G^d - G^* = -\gamma(Y - Y^*)$$
$$Y^* = cY^* + I + G^*$$
$$\dot{G} = \beta[G^d - G]$$

where we have chosen to specify the proportional adjustment rule by (13.38') rather than by the original expression. By substitution, this system can be written as a pair of differential equations in Y, G, namely

$$\begin{pmatrix} \dot{Y} \\ \dot{G} \end{pmatrix} = \begin{pmatrix} \alpha(c-1) & \alpha \\ -\beta\gamma & -\beta \end{pmatrix} \begin{pmatrix} Y - Y^* \\ G - G^* \end{pmatrix} \tag{13.43}$$

which will be stable if and only if[7]

$$\alpha(c - 1) - \beta < 0$$

$$\alpha\beta[\gamma + 1 - c] > 0.$$

For $\alpha > 0, \beta > 0, 0 < c < 1, \gamma > 0$, these two conditions will be met, ensuring that the policy will be stable and will converge to the desired optimum pair (Y^*, G^*). However, whereas in the absence of policy lags (i.e., $\beta \to \infty$) the convergence would be monotonic, now the possibility of cyclical adjustment arises. This will occur if

$$[\alpha(c - 1) + \beta]^2 - 4\alpha\beta\gamma < 0.$$

The fact that lags may induce cycles is hardly surprising. With the implementation of chosen policies taking time to be put into effect, by the time $G^d(t)$ may be yielding its actual impact, economic conditions which led to that decision may have changed. The policy $G(t)$ actually implemented may in fact now be inappropriate and may cause the economy to overadjust.

B.   Integral policy

As an alternative policy, Phillips introduced the possibility that G^d is determined by the integral (sum) of past deviations in income from its target, rather than only the current deviation. This can be formulated by

$$G^d(t) = -\gamma \int_{-\infty}^{t} [Y(s) - Y^*] ds. \qquad \gamma > 0 \qquad (13.44)$$

Abstracting from lags in government policy, this becomes

$$G(t) = -\gamma \int_{-\infty}^{t} [Y(s) - Y^*] ds$$

and differentiating with respect to t, can be written as

$$\dot{G}(t) = -\gamma[Y(t) - Y^*]. \qquad (13.45)$$

This form of the integral policy will be recognized as being identical to the kind of policy adjustment rule specified by Mundell and others and discussed in connection with the assignment problem; see Chapters 9, 11.

Coupling (13.45) with (13.32), yields the dynamic system

$$\dot{Y} = -\alpha[(1 - c)Y - I - G]$$

$$\dot{G} = -\gamma(Y - Y^*).$$

Equilibrium is attained when $\dot{G} = \dot{Y} = 0$, so that

$$Y = Y^* \qquad (13.46a)$$

$$G = (1 - c)Y^* - I. \qquad (13.46b)$$

Note that the adjustment rule (13.45) forces Y to Y^* in equilibrium. The product market equilibrium condition (13.46b) then defines the appropriate equilibrium level of government expenditure. In this respect, this hypothesis resembles our modified proportional policy, specified by (13.38'). There is a difference, however, in that (13.32) and (13.45) define a second order system, even when there are no lags in implementing the policy. Writing the system as

$$\begin{pmatrix} \dot{Y} \\ \dot{G} \end{pmatrix} = \begin{pmatrix} -\alpha(1-c) & \alpha \\ -\gamma & 0 \end{pmatrix} \begin{pmatrix} Y-Y^* \\ G-G^* \end{pmatrix} \tag{13.47}$$

we see that the stability conditions

$$\alpha(1-c) > 0$$

$$\alpha\gamma > 0$$

will be met, so that the equilibrium level of Y^*, G^* will be attained. Cyclical adjustment however, is a possibility and will occur if

$$\alpha^2(1-c)^2 - 4\alpha\gamma < 0.$$

While the adjustment is monotonic if γ is small, a large adjustment can induce cycles into the economy. The reason is quite apparent and is similar to that given for the proportional policy where there were lags in the implementation of the government decision. The current policy is based on past as well as recent discrepancies between Y and Y^*. These may have now been corrected but nevertheless the policy is still reacting to them.

As a further step one can introduce lags into the implementation of this policy. As one might expect the result is a third-order differential equation. Cyclical behaviour now becomes more likely and indeed the possibility of instability is now introduced.

C.   *Derivative policy*
The third policy introduced by Phillips is of the form

$$G^d = -\gamma\dot{Y} \qquad \gamma > 0. \tag{13.48}$$

That is government expenditure is dependent upon the rate of change of income. It will be recognized as an offsetting accelerator. Assuming $G^d \equiv G$ and substituting into (13.32), yields the dynamic equation

$$\dot{Y} = \frac{-\alpha[1-c)Y - I]}{1+\alpha\gamma}. \tag{13.49}$$

It can be seen from this equation that this policy has a stabilizing effect, but it will not succeed in driving income to its desired level Y^*.

Phillips considered combining these three policies by postulating e.g.

$$G^d = -\gamma_1(Y-Y^*) - \gamma_2 \int_{-\infty}^{t} [Y(s) - Y^*]ds - \gamma_3\dot{Y}$$

One can show that the various desirable features of the individual policies are preserved. For example, the presence of the integral component ensures that (with proportional policy as specified) income converges to Y^*. On the other hand the possibility of cyclical adjustment associated with this policy is likely to be reduced with the simultaneous use of proportional adjustment. Finally, we should also comment that Phillips introduced these policies into more complex models which include an accelerator determined investment function. For further discussion of this see Phillips (1954), Allen (1956).

These three policy adjustment rules introduced by Phillips are postulated on the grounds of their plausibility. They are not in general optimal, although they sometimes do appear as components of an optimal policy; see Chapter 14. In any event, they have provided an extremely important basis for subsequent developments in stabilization theory. We have already drawn attention to the application of the integral adjustment rule in the 'assignment problem' literature. Furthermore, while the Phillips model has been presented in the context of a model in which the stabilization instrument is a ficsal instrument, government expenditure, the general approach has also been applied to problems of monetary stabilization policy; see, e.g., Sargent (1971a), Lovell and Prescott (1968). Furthermore, recent simulation studies of various monetary policies base their analysis on the class of proportional and derivative policies; see Cooper and Fischer (1974).

7.   Introduction to stabilization of dynamic stochastic systems

Some years ago, Baumol (1961) considered the stability properties of the discrete-time multiplier–accelerator model, in which the time path of income is described by an equation of the form

$$Y_t + aY_{t-1} + bY_{t-2} = G_t \qquad (13.50)$$

where a, b are constants, and government expenditure, G_t, is generated by the class of stabilization rules of the form

$$G_t = g_1 Y_{t-1} + g_2 Y_{t-2} + B_t \qquad (13.51)$$

with g_1, g_2 constant. Rewriting the policy (13.51) as

$$G_t = (g_1 - g_2)(Y_{t-1} - \bar{Y}_t) - g_2(Y_{t-1} - Y_{t-2}) \qquad (13.52)$$

It can be seen to be a mixture of a proportional and a derivative policy, so that in many respects Baumol's work can be viewed as a discrete-time analogue of the Phillips' analysis.

Inserting (13.51) into (13.50) and assuming for simplicity that $B_t = \bar{B}$ is constant over time, the time path of income can be written as

$$Y_t + (a - g_1)Y_{t-1} + (b - g_2)Y_{t-2} = \bar{B} \qquad (13.53)$$

As in Section 5, the time path of Y_t depends upon the policy parameters

g_1, g_2. The complete solution for (13.53) is given by

$$Y_t = \frac{\bar{B}}{1-(a-g_1)-(b-g_2)} + A_1\lambda_1^t + A_2\lambda_2^t, \qquad t = 1, 2, \ldots$$

(13.54)

where λ_1, λ_2 are the roots to the characteristic equation

$$\lambda^2 + (a-g_1)\lambda + (b-g_2) = 0 \tag{13.55}$$

and A_1, A_2 are arbitrary constants determined by initial conditions. If the characteristic roots of (13.55) are complex (13.54) may be written in trigonometric form.

The necessary and sufficient conditions for the roots λ_1, λ_2 to be within the unit circle (i.e. $|\lambda_i| < 1$) and hence for the solution (13.54) to be stable, are given by[8]

$$1 + a + b - g_1 - g_2 > 0$$

$$1 - a + b + g_1 - g_2 > 0 \tag{13.56}$$

$$1 - b + g_2 \qquad\quad > 0.$$

If these conditions are met, Y_t will ultimately converge to

$$\bar{Y} = \frac{\bar{B}}{1-(a-g_1)-(b-g_2)}.$$

From a consideration of (13.53), Baumol concluded that 'policies — automatic or not — which appear to be properly designed may very well turn out to aggravate fluctuations'. In other words, the injudicious choice of the policy parameters g_1, g_2 may induce fluctuations, and even instability, into the time path of Y_t. It is clear from (13.54) that the appropriate signs of g_1, g_2 are insufficient to ensure stability. Attention must also be given to their magnitudes. For example interpreting the g_2 coefficient in (13.52) as describing a derivative policy so that $g_2 > 0$ it is clear from (13.54) that g_2 cannot be too large; too much derivative control can induce instability.

Some years later, Howrey (1967) extended the Baumol analysis to include stochastic disturbances in the underlying dynamic equation (13.50). He considered the system

$$Y_t + aY_{t-1} + bY_{t-2} = G_t + u_t \tag{13.57}$$

where u_t is a random disturbance, which was assumed to have the following properties

$$E(u_t) = 0$$

$$\mathrm{Var}(u_t) = \sigma^2$$

$$E(u_t, u_t') = 0 \qquad t \neq t';$$

that is it has mean zero, constant variance and is independently distributed through time. He also introduced a stochastic disturbance into the government stabilization policy equation (13.51), but this is not essential.

Combining (13.57) with (13.51) (with $B_t = \bar{B}$) yields

$$Y_t + (a - g_1)Y_{t-1} + (b - g_2)Y_{t-2} = \bar{B} + u_t \qquad (13.58)$$

which is now a *stochastic* difference equation. The complete solution for Y_t is given by

$$Y_t = \frac{\bar{B}}{1 - (a - g_1) - (b - g_2)} + A_1\lambda_1^t + A_2\lambda_2^t + \sum_{j=0}^{t-1} \alpha_j u_{t-j} \qquad t = 1, 2, \ldots$$

$$(13.59)$$

where λ_1, λ_2 are the roots to the characteristic equation (13.55), A_1, A_2 are arbitrary constants, and

$$\alpha_j = \frac{\lambda_1^{j+1} - \lambda_2^{j+1}}{\lambda_1 - \lambda_2}.$$

The important point to observe is that, as well as including the components of the deterministic solution (13.54), the stochastic solution also includes a random component. Provided the stability conditions (13.56) are met, the transient component $A_1\lambda_1^t + A_2\lambda_2^t$ will tend to zero so that ultimately

$$Y_t = \frac{\bar{B}}{1 - (a - g_1) - (b - g_2)} + \sum_{j=0}^{\infty} \alpha_j u_{t-j} \qquad (13.60)$$

That is, asymptotically the system will *fluctuate* about the stationary equilibrium $\bar{B}/[1 - (a - g_1) - (b - g_2)]$ rather than converge to it, as before.

From equation (13.58) it can be shown that the asymptotic variance of Y_t about $\bar{Y}$, is given by

$$\sigma_y^2 = \frac{\sigma_u^2[1 + b + g_2]}{[1 - (b + g_2)]\{[1 + (b + g_2)]^2 - (a + g_1)^2\}} \qquad (13.61)$$

This quantity measures the degree of long-run variability in Y_t. Note that this quantity will be finite if and only if the stability conditions (13.56) are met.

The main point of Howrey's contribution is the observation that since the stochastic response is an integral part of the solution, it is inappropriate to evaluate alternative stabilization policies in a stochastic system on the basis of their effect on the transient response alone. Indeed he shows how in certain instances such a procedure may be quite misleading. For example, he shows how attempts to make the system more stable in the sense of reducing the time for the transient response to dampen out, may actually *increase* the asymptotic variance σ_y^2.

One final observation concerns the asymptotic variance σ_y^2. It is given above for arbitrary g_1, g_2. In much of our discussion of Chapter 14 we shall be concerned with policies which minimize the asymptotic variance. In the present context this involves choosing g_1, g_2 so as to minimize (13.61). Performing this calculation it is seen that the optimal policy in this sense is to set

$$g_1^* = -a$$

$$g_2^* = -b$$

that is

$$G_t = -aY_{t-1} - bY_{t-2} \tag{13.62}$$

in which case the solution is

$$Y_t = \bar{Y} + u_t \tag{13.63}$$

and

$$\sigma_y^2 = \sigma_u^2.$$

The optimal policy thus requires the government policy to be chosen to completely offset the autoregressive structure of the system. In this case income will fluctuate about $\bar{Y}$ with a variance σ_u^2, which is the irreducible minimum that can be achieved. It is impossible to reduce the variability of Y_t below that of u_t (unless there are other offsetting random disturbances). This is sometimes referred to as being a case where 'perfect stabilization' is possible; see Fischer and Cooper (1973).

However, it should be clearly understood that it is only under very special assumptions that perfect stabilization is achievable. First, by minimizing σ_y^2, we are implicitly attaching zero costs to adjusting the policy instrument. Secondly, the introduction of stochastic components into the coefficients a, b also makes perfect stabilization in the above sense, impossible to achieve. These issues will be taken up in our discussion of optimal stochastic stabilization to which we now turn.

14

OPTIMAL STABILIZATION THEORY

We have so far dealt mainly with some of the more traditional issues in stabilization theory. Much of our discussion, particularly with regard to dynamic models, has focused on what one might call *descriptive* stabilization policy. That is, it has considered the properties of various specified plausible, but generally non-optimal, policies. The task of the present chapter is to survey some of the recent developments in the *optimal* stabilization of both deterministic and stochastic dynamic linear systems and to illustrate briefly these methods by means of a simple example. In expositing these theories we shall restrict ourselves to discrete-time systems. Not only are these less difficult analytically, but they are also typically more convenient for analysing short-run stabilization problems. Nevertheless, it should be realized that an analogous set of results exist which are applicable to systems specified using continuous time.

1. Theil static optimal stabilization policy

The first systematic treatment of optimal stabilization policies can probably be attributed to Theil (1958, 1964).[1] While much of this approach has now been superseded by modern control theory methods it is nevertheless very important and serves as a convenient starting point.

Beginning with the static control problem, Theil assumes the policy maker to be endowed with a quadratic utility function

$$U(x, y) = a'x + b'y + \tfrac{1}{2}(x'Ax + y'By + x'Cy + y'C'x) \qquad (14.1)$$

where

x is a vector of m policy instruments,

y is a vector of n target variables,

a, b, A, B, C are vectors and matrices of appropriate order with fixed elements; A and B are also assumed to be symmetric matrices; primes denote the vector transpose.

The vectors x, y are connected by the linear constraint

$$y = Rx + s \qquad (14.2)$$

where R, s, are a matrix and vector of appropriate order. Equation (14.2) is the analogue to (13.1), although in discussing the Tinbergen theory we did not bother to include any additive component s.

Assuming perfect certainty, the stabilization problem as formulated by Theil is to maximize $U(x, y)$ subject to (14.2). This can be expressed in the Lagrangean form as the minimization of

$$U(x, y) - \lambda'(y - Rx - s) = a'x + b'y + \tfrac{1}{2}(x'Ax + y'By + x'Cy + y'Cx)$$
$$- \lambda'(y - Rx - s) \tag{14.3}$$

where λ is a column of n Lagrangean multipliers. Differentiating (14.3) with respect to x, y, λ, the first order conditions for the optimum can be written as

$$\begin{pmatrix} A & C & R' \\ C' & B & -I \\ R & -I & 0 \end{pmatrix} \begin{pmatrix} x \\ y \\ \lambda \end{pmatrix} = \begin{pmatrix} -a \\ -b \\ -s \end{pmatrix}. \tag{14.4}$$

These $m + 2n$ equations in the $m + 2n$ variables x, y, λ can be solved, provided the matrix on the left hand side is non-singular. Moreover, in order to ensure that (14.4) yields a maximum (and not a minimum) it is required that appropriate second order conditions be met. As Theil shows, it is sufficient that the principal minors of order $n + 1, \ldots, n + m$ of the matrix of second partial derivatives of the preference function $U(x, y)$, bordered with the corresponding n rows and columns of the multiplicative coefficients $[R \quad -I]$ of the constraints, have alternating signs, the first being $(-1)^{n+1}$. In this case the matrix in (14.4) is also non-singular and the solution for (x, y, λ) can be obtained.

Theil extends this basic framework in two directions. First, he shows that if the additive term s in the constraints (14.2) is stochastic, but everything else is known with certainty, the optimal policy can be obtained by simply replacing the random variable s by its expected value. In essence one solves the *deterministic* optimization problem (14.3) by treating $E(s)$ as if it occurred with certainty. This is the principle of certainty equivalence mentioned in Chaper 13. It applies only to the additive term s and does not apply if say R was stochastic. This is not too surprising in view of our results obtained in Chapter 13, Section 3, which in many ways can be viewed as a scalar version of the Theil system.

The second extension by Theil is to a multiperiod time horizon. The most significant result here is what he calls the 'first period certainty equivalence' result. That is, he shows that under appropriate assumptions, the first period decision to a multiperiod stabilization problem can be obtained by replacing the additive disturbances in the constraints by their expected values and optimizing the multiperiod objective function with respect to the decision variables for all periods and then solving for the first period subvector. The decisions for subsequent periods will later be modified as more information becomes available. Since subsequent developments in linear control theory provide more powerful techniques for solving these multiperiod stabilization problems, we prefer not to pursue this approach any further; for further elaboration see Theil (1964; Chapter 4), as well as Theil (1957), Simon (1956).

2.   **Formulation of dynamic stabilization theory: the deterministic case**
        Consider the following first order dynamic system

where
$$Y_t = AY_{t-1} + BX_t \tag{14.5}$$

$Y_t = n \times 1$ vector of target (state) variables,

$X_t = m \times 1$ vector of policy instruments (control variables),

A is an $n \times n$ matrix, B is an $n \times m$ matrix, both having constant elements.

Equation (14.5) is a dynamic generalization of (13.1) in that the target variables depend not only on the current policy variables, but also on their own values in the previous period. As in Chapter 13, we shall assume that the policy maker has in mind some equilibrium desired levels of the target variables Y^*, together with a set of long-run desired values of the policy instruments X^* which he wishes to attain. These two sets of long-run objectives chosen by the policy maker are assumed to be consistent with the system. Consequently they are required to satisfy equation (14.5) so that

$$Y^* = AY^* + BX^*. \tag{14.6}$$

Note that if $m = n$ and the matrix B is non-singular, then for given target objectives Y^*, (14.6) defines a unique long-run policy X^*. Otherwise, this equation provides a set of conditions which the desired values of the target and instruments, however chosen, must satisfy in order to be consistent with long-run equilibrium. We have taken X^*, Y^* to be constant. It is possible to extend the theory to allow for time-dependent values of X^*, Y^*.

As in Chapter 13, we assume that the objective of the policy maker is to control the economy so as to keep the target variables as close to equilibrium as possible over some finite planning horizon T say. We shall assume that the costs of being away from equilibrium can be adequately measured by the quadratic cost function

$$C = \sum_{t=1}^{T} (Y_t - Y^*)'M(Y_t - Y^*).$$

The cost matrix M is taken to be positive semi-definite, meaning that the policy maker attributed non-negative costs to having each of the target variables away from their respective equilibrium. This means that some of the target variables may have zero costs attached to them. If the policy maker attributes independent positive costs to each of the target variables, then strict positive definiteness of M is required.[2]

In addition there may be control costs associated with having the instruments away from their respective long-run equilibrium values. In many cases, such as those associated with government expenditure, the nature of these costs is clear enough. But in other cases, the rationale for including control costs is less clear. For example, there are no obvious direct costs associated with having the money supply away from its long-run equilibrium. What effects are incurred are more likely to be felt via the impacts on the other target variables. Taking instrument costs into account, total costs become

$$\sum_{t=1}^{T} (Y_t - Y^*)'M(Y_t - Y^*) + \sum_{t=1}^{T} (X_t - X^*)'N(X_t - X^*) \qquad (14.7)$$

where N is the costs associated with the instrument variables. We shall assume that N is positive semi-definite, allowing for the possibility that some policy variables are costless.

By adopting a quadratic cost function, we are following the conventional practice of modern stabilization theory. Its main advantage in the present context is that, given the linearity of the basic dynamic relationships (14.5), it leads to linear optimal decision rules. However, as we mentioned in Chaper 13, the quadratic loss function may not be appropriate in all respects and should be treated only as an approximation. One of its major drawbacks is the cost symmetry it implies between positive and negative deviations of equal amounts. For example, if the target rate of unemployment is 4% say, it implies that the loss of having unemployment at 3% equals that incurred when unemployment is at 5%. For obvious reasons, this may be an inaccurate reflection of the social costs incurred in these two cases. Some attempts have been made to introduce asymmetric loss functions; in particular see Friedman (1972, 1975a).

We should also clarify a notational point at this stage. For convenience, and where there is no risk of confusion, we shall denote a positive semi-definite matrix X say by the weak inequality $X \geqslant 0$. If X is strictly positive definite we write $X > 0$. These inequalities do *not* mean that X has all non-negative or strictly positive elements.

The dynamic optimal stabilization problem we shall consider is to choose X_t at each time t to minimize (14.7) subject to (14.5). Subtracting (14.6) from (14.5) and defining the *deviation* variables

$$y_t = Y_t - Y^*$$
$$x_t = X_t - X^*$$

the optimal stabilization problem can be expressed more conveniently as being to minimize

$$\sum_{t=1}^{T} (y_t'My_t + x_t'Nx_t) \qquad M \geqslant 0, \quad N \geqslant 0 \qquad (14.8)$$

subject to

$$y_t = Ay_{t-1} + Bx_t. \tag{14.9}$$

Despite the fact that the dynamics has been written as a first order system (i.e. y_t depends only on y_{t-1} and not on more distant lags), the formulation is in fact quite general. Any higher order system can be written as an augmented first order system. For example, the dynamic system

$$y_t = A_1 y_{t-1} + A_2 y_{t-2} + B_0 x_t + B_1 x_{t-1}$$

can be written as

$$z_t \equiv \begin{pmatrix} y_t \\ y_{t-1} \\ x_t \end{pmatrix} = \begin{pmatrix} A_1 & A_2 & B_1 \\ I & 0 & 0 \\ 0 & 0 & 0 \end{pmatrix} \begin{pmatrix} y_{t-1} \\ y_{t-2} \\ x_{t-1} \end{pmatrix} + \begin{pmatrix} B_0 \\ 0 \\ I \end{pmatrix} v_t \tag{14.10}$$

which with appropriate redefinition is of the form (14.9). The cost functions can be adjusted similarly; see Turnovsky (1974a).

Returning to the stabilization problem postulated in (14.8) and (14.9), before any stabilization is possible we require that the system (14.9) be *dynamically controllable* over some time period $(0, T)$. By this it is meant that it is possible to find a sequence of values of the policy (control) variables such that it is possible to move the target (state) variables y_t from any initial state y_0, to any arbitrary state y_T in T time periods.

A necessary and sufficient condition for this to be so is given by the following *dynamic controllability* condition:

The system $y_t = Ay_{t-1} + Bx_t$ is dynamically controllable over the period $T \geqslant n$ if and only if $r[B, AB, \ldots, A^{n-1}B] = n$.[3]

While this condition yields a necessary and sufficient condition for controllability over a time horizon at least as long as n periods, it may also be possible to attain the chosen state y_T in less than n periods.

Proof: Suppose y_0 is given, then y_T is obtained recursively from (14.9) and is given by

$$y_T = Bx_T + ABx_{T-1} + \ldots + A^{T-1}Bx_1 + A^T y_0$$

which we can rewrite as

$$y_T = [B, AB, \ldots, A^{T-1}B] \begin{pmatrix} x_T \\ x_{T-1} \\ \cdot \\ \cdot \\ \cdot \\ x_1 \end{pmatrix} + A^T y_0 \tag{14.11}$$

The system is dynamically controllable over the period $(0, T)$ if and only if it is possible to find a sequence of instruments $x_1, \ldots, x_T$, so that given y_0, any y_T can be achieved at time T. Essentially this involves being able to solve (14.11) for the vector $(x_T, \ldots, x_1)'$. This will also be so, if and only if

$$r[B, AB, \ldots, A^{T-1}B] = n.$$

But by the Cayley–Hamilton theorem on matrices (see, e.g., Bellman (1960)) any square matrix of order n must satisfy its characteristic equation and must therefore satisfy an nth order polynomial

$$A^n + c_1 A^{n-1} + c_2 A^{n-2} + \ldots + c_1 A + c_0 = 0$$

where c_i are constants. This implies that the columns of $A^T B$ for $T \geqslant n$ are linearly dependent in the previous columns. Hence $r[B, AB, \ldots, A^{T-1}B] = r[B, AB, \ldots, A^{n-1}B] = n$, establishing the result.

The dynamic controllability condition is the dynamic extension of the Tinbergen proposition relating the number of instruments to the number of targets. Note that if one is prepared to allow the transition from one state to another to take place over a number of periods, this can be achieved by *fewer* instruments than there are targets. For example, the system

$$\begin{pmatrix} y_{1t} \\ y_{2t} \end{pmatrix} = \begin{pmatrix} a_{11} & a_{12} \\ a_{21} & 0 \end{pmatrix} \begin{pmatrix} y_{1,t-1} \\ y_{2,t-1} \end{pmatrix} + \begin{pmatrix} 1 \\ 0 \end{pmatrix} x_t$$

is dynamically controllable, even though there is only one instrument for two targets, so that it is not statically controllable. The topic of dynamic controllability is a highly complex one and a more detailed treatment of it is beyond our scope. For further discussion, the interested reader is referred to Athans and Falb (1966), Preston (1974), Preston and Sieper (1976).

3. **Optimal stabilization policy: deterministic systems**

The formal stabilization problem we wish to consider is to minimize

$$\sum_{t=1}^{T} (y_t' M y_t + x_t' N x_t) \tag{14.8}$$

subject to

$$y_t = A y_{t-1} + B x_t. \tag{14.9}$$

This is a standard problem in control theory and is well documented in the relevant literature. For our purposes it suffices merely to quote the solution; the proofs are involved and are available in books such as Astrom (1970), Kushner (1971).

Under the assumptions stated in Section 2, the solution to the stabilization problem specified by (14.8) and (14.9) is given by

$$x_t = R_t y_{t-1} \tag{14.12a}$$

where

$$R_t = -[N + B'S_tB]^{-1}[B'S_tA] \tag{14.12b}$$

and S_t is generated by the equation

$$S_{t-1} = M + R'_tNR_t + (A + BR_t)'S_t(A + BR_t) \tag{14.12c}$$

with the boundary condition

$$S_T = M. \tag{14.12d}$$

There are several comments we wish to make about this solution.[4] First, the set of equations (14.12) yields what is known as a *linear feedback control law*, whereby the policy maker may compute the optimal policy x_t given the immediate past state of the system. It may be viewed as a generalized form of the Phillips proportional adjustment policy, although the generalized constant of proportionality is a function of time.

It should be emphasized that the optimal stabilization policy is proportional to the state, *however* that state is defined. Thus if (14.9) is in fact an augmented first order system, obtained from some other higher order system, then these higher order lags would appear in (14.12a). For example, the optimal feedback solution for (14.10) would be of the form

$$v_t = R_t z_{t-1}$$

or

$$x_t = R_{1t}y_{t-1} + R_{2t}y_{t-2} + R_{3t}x_{t-1}$$

so that the more distant lags would also appear in the solution.

To take another example, we can infer that the simple scalar proportional policy proposed by Phillips will be optimal provided (14.9) is a first order scalar system. Moreover if (14.9) is of the form

$$y_t = a_1y_{t-1} + a_2y_{t-1} + bx_t$$

where y_t, x_t are scalars, the optimal policy will be of the form

$$x_t = r_1y_{t-1} + r_2y_{t-2}$$
$$= (r_1 + r_2)y_{t-1} - r_2(y_{t-1} - y_{t-2})$$

which is the sum of a proportional plus derivative policy. Thus, these policies can emerge as optimal, for very special cases.

Secondly, provided the matrix $[N + B'S_tB]$ is non-singular the solution (14.12b) will not only exist, but also from the recursive formula (14.12c) it will be unique. As long as N is strictly positive definite (i.e. $N > 0$) this will certainly be the case, irrespective of the number of target variables and instruments. However, under our weaker assumption of $N \geqslant 0$, it is possible for the inverse not to exist. To take an extreme example, suppose there are no control costs (i.e. $N = 0$). Then from the definitions of B, S_t a necessary condition for the existence of the inverse $(B'S_tB)^{-1}$ is that $n \geqslant m$, that is the number of instruments cannot exceed the number of targets. But this condition is weakened if, as is typically the case, (14.9) is obtained from some higher order system; see Turnovsky (1974a).

However, even if $(N + B'S_tB)$ is singular, an optimal solution to the control problem can still exist although it will no longer be unique. To obtain the solution, the matrix $[N + BS_tB]^{-1}$ is simply replaced by its generalized inverse; see Preston (1976). For our purposes we can take the existence of the inverse for granted.

One special case worthy of mention occurs if control is costless ($N = 0$); the number of instruments equals the number of targets, and B is non-singular. With these assumptions, the solution (14.12b) simplifies to

$$R_t = -B^{-1}A \tag{14.13}$$

and substituting (14.13) into the dynamic equation (14.9), this implies

$$y_t = 0. \tag{14.14}$$

Thus the optimal policy calls for the destruction of the autoregressive structure, causing the target variables to be maintained at their desired equilibrium values. This property can also be shown to generalize to dynamic systems involving higher order lags; see Turnovsky (1976b).

The system of equations (14.12) yields a recursive procedure for determining the optimal policy. Beginning with $S_T = M$, (14.12b) implies a value for R_T and feeding this into (14.12c) we obtain

$$S_{T-1} = M + R'_T NR_T + (A + BR_T)'S_T(A + BR_T).$$

Substituting for S_{T-1} into (14.12b) yields R_{T-1} and hence u_{T-1}. Inserting R_{T-1}, S_{T-1} into (14.12c) we can determine S_{T-2} etc. and thus working successively backwards we can generate all the S_ts, R_ts and hence the feedback control laws. Note that the control laws are linear and that they depend upon the stochastic components of the coefficients. Unfortunately the computation suffers from one difficulty in that the control law of immediate interest, namely that for the first period, requires solutions for S_1 and R_1. These are extremely tedious to calculate, being obtained at the Tth stage of this recursion procedure, so that a numerical solution is inevitable, even for simple scalar systems.[5]

Note further that the solutions for S_t are all positive semi-definite being strictly so if $M > 0$. This can be immediately established by induction. Since $M \geqslant 0, N \geqslant 0$, it follows that $S_t \geqslant 0$ implies $S_{t-1} \geqslant 0$. Since $S_T = M \geqslant 0$, it thus follows $S_t \geqslant 0$ for all t.

The positive definiteness of S_t plays a crucial role in establishing the stability properties of the optimal policies. It can be shown that provided $S_t > 0$, for all t, the optimally controlled system y_t given by (14.12) will be stable so that the deviation y_t will converge to zero. Hence x_t, being given by (14.12a) must also converge to zero. But the assumptions we have made on the cost matrices, $M \geqslant 0, N \geqslant 0$, are *not* sufficient to ensure $S_t > 0$; they imply only $S_t \geqslant 0$. Hence the possibility of part of the system being unstable cannot be dismissed, without strengthening these cost conditions; see Turnovsky (1974a).

One case which has attracted some attention is that of 'instrument instability'; see Holbrook (1972). This term described the possibility which may arise when the optimal stabilization of the target variable requires a continual increase in the magnitude of the adjustment of the policy variables so as to offset the effects of past policies. In other words, the adjustment path of the control variables u_t is unstable. This may occur if $N = 0$, although as long as $N > 0$, it can be ruled out. Moreover, when the coefficients are stochastic, the possibility of instrument instability becomes quite remote, even if $N = 0$. The reason for this is that the existence of stochastic elements exerts an inhibiting influence on the adjustment of policy instruments, making it optimal to adjust them more cautiously. Thus the adjustment path of u_t is dampened down, making it stable; for further discussion see Turnovsky (1974a).

Suppose now that the planning horizon $T \to \infty$. Then provided that the matrix equation (14.12c) converges, (14.12) implies the following constant limiting control law for the infinite horizon case,

where
$$x_t = R y_{t-1} \tag{14.15a}$$
$$R = -[N + B'SB]^{-1}[B'SA] \tag{14.15b}$$

and S is the unique positive semi-definite solution to the equation

$$S = M + R'NR + (A + BR)'S(A + BR). \tag{14.15c}$$

Note that as before the optimal stabilization policy is a linear feedback control law. The only difference is that now the matrix determining the intensity of control, R, is constant over time. Moreover, S is no longer obtained recursively but is calculated by solving a set of quadratic equations. Finally, we see that if (14.15c) possesses a solution $S \geqslant 0$ and if $M > 0$, then in fact we must have $S > 0$; that is S must be *strictly* positive definite.

4. Optimal stabilization policies: stochastic systems

We now extend the previous discussion to the case where the dynamic system is subject to stochastic disturbances. Parallel to our treatment of the static Brainard system we shall introduce both multiplicative disturbances (i.e. random coefficients) and additive disturbances, although initially we shall assume that these two sets of random variables are uncorrelated with one another. While in some cases this assumption can be justified, in others it cannot, especially when we interpret the variables of the system as being in deviation form. Suppose, as we have done above, one begins with an underlying set of equations specified in the form of *levels*, and in the course of deriving the solution is required to transform the system to *deviations*. If the multiplicative and additive disturbances are uncorrelated with one another in the original levels equation, they will *necessarily* be correlated in the transformed deviations equation. The consequences of this correlation and the modifications it introduces to the stabilization policies are taken up in Section 4B below.

Before proceeding with the formal solution it may be useful to give a brief guide to the literature in this area. It would be fair to say that most of the formulation and development of the underlying theory has been undertaken by engineers and control theorists, with the contributions by economists being more on the applied aspects. Comprehensive surveys of the theoretical contributions are contained in Astrom (1970), Athans (1972), Kushner (1971). These authors deal with the case where the coefficients are deterministic, so that the only disturbances are additive. For analysis of the stochastic coefficient case, using continuous time, in which all probability distributions are known, see Wonham (1963, 1967, 1968, 1969). Some discussion of the discrete-time stochastic coefficient case is given by Caines and Mayne (1970, 1971). The introduction of learning processses with respect to the probability distributions is a much more difficult problem and thus far no analytical solutions for the optimal policies have been obtained.

While, as we have said, most of the contributions by economists in this area have been rather applied, they have, nevertheless provided some theoretical contributions as well. Early work by economists in the area of stochastic control theory includes the seminal papers by Simon (1956) and Theil (1957). For more recent contributions by economists on the more theoretical aspects of the subject see for example, Chow (1970, 1972, 1973a, 1973b), Pagan (1975), Prescott (1971, 1972), Turnovsky (1974a, 1976b). See also some of the papers in the National Bureau of Economic Research conferences on Stochastic Control Theory, published in the October 1972, January 1974, Spring 1975 and Spring 1976, issues of the *Annals of Economic and Social Measurement*. Brief reference to some of the areas of economic application is given in Section 7.

The statement of the results we shall give is taken from Turnovsky (1976b). This is in turn a modification of the Wonham results to a discrete-time system, although the results are generalized to allow for correlation among the various classes of random disturbances. We shall restrict our discussion to the infinite horizon case, in which the policy maker's objective is to choose his policy instruments so as to minimize an asymptotic cost function. This problem is less general than the finite horizon case, but for a variety of reasons it is important and merits the attention we are giving it.

First, this criterion is not new to economics. It has been used quite extensively by a number of authors using both control theory and less sophisticated techniques.[6] Indeed we have already encountered it in our introduction to dynamic stochastic stabilization policy in Chapter 13, Section 7. Secondly, as shown below it leads to precisely the same control laws as those obtained in the limit of the finite time horizon problem as the time horizon tends to infinity. Consequently, it can be viewed as an approximation to the case of a long finite planning horizon, so that it is much less restrictive than may at first appear.

Thirdly — and this is the most important point — the asymptotic case with stochastic coefficients gives rise to problems pertaining to the existence of feasible feedback control policies, issues which do not arise with a finite time horizon. More specifically, it can be shown that the asymptotic control problem with stochastic coefficients may not possess a feasible solution if the random disturbances of the coefficients are too severe (in a sense to be defined more precisely below); see Turnovsky (1976b). This fact is of some economic significance. For example, it implies that any attempts at optimal control may be useless if there is too much parameter uncertainty.

A.   *Uncorrelated multiplicative and additive disturbances*
        The stochastic control problem we shall consider is to minimize the asymptotic expected value

$$E(y_t'My_t + x_t'Nx_t) \tag{14.16}$$

subject to

$$y_t = (A + V_t)y_{t-1} + (B + W_t)x_t + u_t \tag{14.17}$$

where
   A, B are constant matrices describing the deterministic components of the coefficients describing the system,
   $V_t = (v_{ijt})$, $W_t = (w_{ijt})$ are matrices denoting the random components of the coefficients.

This is a straightforward stochastic generalization of our previous model specified by (14.8) and (14.9). But before we can solve the system, it is necessary to specify the stochastic assumptions being made, more fully. For the present we assume:
   (i) The elements of the random matrices V_t, W_t, and the random vector u_t, are independently distributed through time with zero means and finite second moments, assumed to be constant through time.
   (ii) The probability distributions governing these random variables are assumed to be given at the beginning of the planning horizon and to remain unchanged throughout.
   (iii) The elements of V_t are correlated.
   (iv) The elements of W_t are correlated.
   (v) The elements of V_t are correlated with those of W_t.
   (vi) Both V_t and W_t are uncorrelated with u_t.
As indicated above in Section 4B, assumption (vi) is dropped. The analysis can also be extended to allow for the possibility of the additive disturbances being autocorrelated; see Pagan (1975), Turnovsky (1976b).

The derivation of the optimal policies for this stochastic case is a rather arduous task and only the outline of the solution is given.

As originally shown by Wonham, one important difference between the deterministic stabilization problem and the stochastic stabilization problem is that in the latter case there may in fact be no optimal policy. To ensure that such a policy does exist, two restrictions are required. The first is, that the pair of matrices (A, B) appearing in the dynamic system (14.17) be what is known as *stabilizable*. By this it is meant that there exists a matrix K, such that the matrix $(A + BK)$ is stable; that is, all its eigenvalues lie within the unit circle. This amounts to assuming that one can find a feedback control law

$$x_t = Ky_{t-1} \tag{14.18}$$

so that when this is applied, the resulting dynamic system

$$y_t = (A + BK)y_{t-1} \tag{14.19}$$

will be stable. This is a mild restriction and can reasonably be assumed to hold. Indeed, unless it is satisfied, one cannot find any stable control policy, in which case the problem of finding an optimal feedback law makes very little sense.

The second restriction is more stringent. This is known as the *stochastic stabilizability* condition. It is required in order to ensure that the equation (14.21c) below, in which we solve for the positive semi-definite matrix S, does indeed possess a solution for $S \geq 0$. As originally shown by Wonham (1967, 1969), the stochastic system (14.17) is *stochastically stabilizable* if the matrix pair (A, B) is stabilizable and

$$\inf_{R} \| \sum_{n=0}^{\infty} [(A + BR)']^n E\{(V + WR)'(V + WR)\} [A + BR]^n \| < 1 \tag{14.20}$$

where $\| \quad \|$ is the Euclidean operator norm, and inf denotes infimum.[7] Basically, this condition asserts that a feasible stochastic stabilization policy exists, provided the disturbances in the parameters are not too great. It imposes restrictions upon the intensity of parameter uncertainty. The condition is independent of any additive noise and will certainly be satisfied under deterministic conditions.

Thus provided the dynamic system (14.17) satisfies the stochastic stabilizability condition (14.20), and that the stochastic assumptions (i)–(vi) stated above are met, the solution to the asymptotic stabilization problem, specified by (14.16) and (14.17) exists, and is of the form

$$x_t = Ry_{t-1} \tag{14.21a}$$

where

$$R = -[N + B'SB + E(W'SW)]^{-1} [B'SA + E(WSV)] \tag{14.21b}$$

and S is a positive semi-definite solution to the equation

$$S = M + R'NR + (A + BR)'S(A + BR) + E[(V + WR)'S(V + WR)].$$

(14.21c)

For notational simplicity we have deleted the time subscript from the random variables. If further, M is strictly positive definite, then S is strictly positive definite, implying uniqueness of the optimal stabilization policy. We should make it clear however, that the additional restriction stated to ensure $S > 0$ and uniqueness is only sufficient, and certainly not necessary. It is possible, and indeed quite likely that $S > 0$ and unique even if we impose only our weaker assumptions that $M \geqslant 0, N \geqslant 0$.

The analogy between (14.21) and the deterministic analogue (14.15) is immediate. The one difference is that, as one would expect, the optimal stabilization policy under stochastic conditions depends upon the variances of the stochastic disturbances in the parameters (but not on the additive disturbances) and that if these are zero, the two solutions coincide. The fact that the solution is independent of the additive disturbances is consistent with the results of Chapter 13, and is also a restatement of the Theil 'certainty equivalence' result referred to in Section 1 above.

But there is one further important difference between deterministic and stochastic systems and that pertains to the nature of the stability of the system. With stochastic elements present the deterministic notion of stability is inapplicable and must be modified. In fact various concepts of *stochastic* stability, having varying degrees of stringency, have been defined and the positive definiteness of the matrix S can be shown to play an analogous role to that played in the deterministic case. Specifically, provided $S > 0$, the optimally controlled system will be stable in the presence of additive disturbances, in the sense that the asymptotic expected value (14.16) will be finite. If the only disturbances are multiplicative, the system will satisfy the stronger conditions of being asymptotically stable with probability one (w.p.1).[8]

B.   *Correlated multiplicative and additive stochastic disturbances*
        It will be recalled that we have interpreted the variables y_t, x_t to be *deviations* about some desired (constant) target values. The dynamics of the system have thus been specified in deviation form, with the coefficients of these deviations being stochastic and uncorrelated with the additive disturbances.

While we are perfectly at liberty to begin directly with a specification as (14.17) in deviation form, in most economic applications it is more natural to postulate an underlying relationship in *levels* and to transform the system to deviations in the process of deriving the solution. In this case, if the multiplicative and additive disturbances are uncorrelated in the original levels equation, they are necessarily correlated in the derived deviations equation;

the transformation to deviations induces a correlation between them. This can be seen as follows.

Let

$$Y_t = (A + V_t)Y_{t-1} + (B + W_t)X_t + u_t \qquad (14.22)$$

be a first order system, where Y_t, X_t denote *levels* of the state of control variables respectively, and V_t, W_t, u_t are stochastic disturbances. These are assumed to satisfy the conditions (i)–(vi) above; in particular both V_t and W_t are uncorrelated with u_t. The equilibrium values of Y, X, which we denote by Y^*, X^* respectively satisfy the stationary equation

$$Y^* = AY^* + BX^*. \qquad (14.23)$$

Subtracting (14.23) from (14.22) and letting $y_t = Y_t - Y^*, x_t = X_t - X^*$ (as we have been doing), we obtain the following equation in deviation form

$$y_t = (A + V_t)y_{t-1} + (B + W_t)x_t + u_t + V_t Y^* + W_t X^*. \qquad (14.24)$$

The crucial point to observe is that the additive disturbance in (14.24) becomes a composite one, containing as components $V_t Y^*, W_t X^*$, and given our assumptions this will necessarily be correlated with the stochastic components of the coefficients.

By a similar argument, our specification (14.17), which starts out with the deviation equation in which multiplicative and additive disturbances are uncorrelated, has implications for the underlying levels equation. Thus adding equations (14.17) and (14.23) together, yields;

$$Y_t = (A + V_t)Y_{t-1} + (B + W_t)X_t + u_t - V_t Y^* - W_t X^* \qquad (14.25)$$

implying a levels equation with a composite error term which is correlated with the multiplicative disturbances. Thus the stochastic specification we have adopted in earlier sections is perfectly valid, provided one is willing to accept a levels equation having the properties of (14.25).

It becomes clear from this discussion that it is important to extend the theory to allow for correlation between additive and multiplicative disturbances. Rather than restrict ourselves to the very specific correlation implied by (14.24), we shall give a general treatment. Thus the formal problem is to minimize (14.16) subject to (14.17), the only difference being that now u_t may be correlated with both V_t and W_t. Assuming that the conditions which ensured the solution (14.21) are satisfied, with the exception that now u_t is correlated with both V_t and W_t, the solution to the stabilization problem specified by (14.16) and (14.17) exists, and is of the form

$$x_t = Ry_{t-1} + p \qquad (14.26a)$$

where

$$R = -[N + B'SB + E(W'SW)]^{-1}[B'SA + E(W'SV)] \qquad (14.26b)$$

$$p = -[N + B'SB + E(W'SW)]^{-1}[B'k + E(W'Su)] \qquad (14.26c)$$

and S is a positive semi-definite solution to

$$S = M + R'NR + (A + BR)'S(A + BR)$$
$$+ E[(V + WR)'S(V + WR)] \qquad (14.26d)$$

and k is the solution to

$$k = (A + BR)'k + E[(V + WR)'Su]. \qquad (14.26e)$$

By strengthening the condition on M to $M > 0$ the strict positive definiteness of S and the uniqueness of the optimal control policy can be established.

The optimal policy is seen to consist of a feedback component R, together with a fixed component p. It is interesting to observe that the expression for the former is *identical* to that given in (14.21), so that the endogenous part of the policy adjustment is independent of any correlation between the additive and multiplicative disturbances. On the other hand, the fixed component p depends crucially upon these correlations; if they are zero this term vanishes leaving us with the feedback component alone.

One further interesting aspect of the control law is the fact that even if in period $(t - 1)$ the system is at its desired target, so that $y_{t-1} = 0$, nevertheless due to the correlation between the additive and multiplicative disturbances, it will be optimal to adjust x_t. In other words, because of these correlations the system will be regulated to a stationary level which *differs from* the desired targets. Whether it undershoots or overshoots depends upon the sign of these correlations and an example of the former is given in Section 7. As we discussed in Chapter 13, this proposition was first demonstrated by Brainard (1967) for a purely static scalar system so that the present result can be viewed as a dynamic analogue of his analysis.

5.   A scalar example

It is clear that it is virtually impossible to investigate analytically the properties of the optimal policy for the matrix systems considered in Sections 3 and 4. Therefore, in order to obtain a more precise idea of the properties of the optimal policies, and in particular of the issues raised by the introduction of stochastic disturbances into the coefficients, we shall simplify to the case of a scalar system.

Consider the problem

$$\min E(my_t^2 + nx_t^2) \quad \text{where} \quad m > 0, \quad n \geqslant 0 \qquad (14.27)$$

subject to

$$y_t = (a + v_t)y_{t-1} + (b + w_t)x_t + u_t. \qquad (14.28)$$

All quantities appearing in (14.27) and (14.28) are now scalars.[9] Equation (14.28) describes a stochastic control system where the policy instrument operates with a Koyck lag. The coefficients a, b are deterministic, describing the mean of the lag coefficient and the expected short-run impact of x_t on y_t respectively. An increase in $|a|$ increases the expected lag, while the expected short run impact varies directly with $|b|$. The stochastic components v_t, w_t are independently distributed through time, having zero means, variances σ_v^2, σ_w^2, and correlation coefficient ρ. Hence σ_v^2, σ_w^2 may be used to parameterize the variability in the length of lag and in the short-run effect of control respectively. Finally, the additive disturbance u_t is also independently distributed through time, with mean zero, variance σ_u^2, and is uncorrelated with v_t or w_t. Thus for simplicity we are focusing on the scalar analogue to the system treated in Section 4A.

Applying the optimal control law (14.21) yields the policy[10]

$$x_t = r y_{t-1} \tag{14.29a}$$

where

$$r = \frac{-(ab + \sigma_v \sigma_w \rho)s}{n + (b^2 + \sigma_w^2)s} \tag{14.29b}$$

and with $m > 0$, s is the unique positive solution to the quadratic equation

$$s = m + (a^2 + \sigma_v^2)s - \frac{(ab + \sigma_v \sigma_w \rho)^2 s^2}{n + (b^2 + \sigma_w^2)s} \tag{14.29c}$$

This last equation can be expressed more conveniently in the form

$$[(1 - a^2 - \sigma_v^2)(b^2 + \sigma_w^2) + (ab + \sigma_v \sigma_w \rho)^2] s^2$$
$$+ [n(1 - a^2 - \sigma_v^2) - m(b^2 + \sigma_w^2)] s - mn = 0 \tag{14.29c'}$$

Before analysing the optimal policy itself, we shall deal with the existence issue, discussed at length in Section 4. From our previous discussion it is clear that this turns upon the equation (14.29c') in fact possessing a positive solution for s. First, observe that the stabilizability requirement is satisfied essentially trivially. For any a, b, such that $b \neq 0$, one can always find a value of k such that $-1 < a + bk < 1$, thereby satisfying the requirement. Secondly note that if $\sigma_v = \sigma_w = 0$, so that the parameters are non-stochastic, equation (14.29c') simplifies to

$$b^2 s^2 + [n(1 - a^2) - mb^2] s - mn = 0. \tag{14.30}$$

It can be readily verified that this equation *always* possesses a unique solution $s > 0$.

A necessary and sufficient condition for (14.29c') to have a unique positive solution is that the coefficient of s^2 in (14.29c') be positive, that is

$$\theta \equiv (1 - a^2 - \sigma_v^2)(b^2 + \sigma_w^2) + (ab + \sigma_v \sigma_w \rho)^2 > 0 \tag{14.31}$$

This inequality traces out a relationship describing the tolerable amounts of variability in the two parameters, given the parameters of the system, and need not be satisfied for all values of these parameters. Taking the special case $\rho = 0$, (14.30) can be written in the form

$$\sigma_v^2 < 1 - a^2 + \frac{a^2 b^2}{b^2 + \sigma_w^2} \tag{14.32}$$

indicating how in that case, the amount of admissible variability in v_t varies inversely with the amount of variability in w_t. Note, however, that if the two coefficients are allowed to be correlated, then it is possible for an increase in the uncertainty in w_t to actually allow an increase in the admissible variability in v_t.

One simple sufficient condition that ensures inequality (14.31) will be met is

$$1 - a^2 - \sigma_v^2 > 0. \tag{14.33}$$

This condition can be shown to be a sufficient condition for the uncontrolled linear system

$$y_t = (a + v_t)y_{t-1} + u_t$$

to have a finite variance. It is not the scalar analogue of the stochastic stabilizability condition given in (14.20), which as shown in footnote 11 is a good deal more complicated.[11]

As mentioned in Section 4, one of the important policy implications of the existence criterion is the restriction it may impose on the range of policy instruments available to the policy maker. Different degrees of uncertainty associated with different instruments may mean that he is able to use some instruments but not others. This point can be illustrated with the following example.[12]

Consider the two control systems,

$$y_t = (a + v_t)y_{t-1} + (b + w_t)r_t + u_t \tag{14.34a}$$

$$y_t = (a + v_t)y_{t-1} + g_t + u_t. \tag{14.34b}$$

These may be viewed as two pure multiplier models, where consumption depends stochastically upon lagged income. In (14.34a), the government controls income y_t, by choosing the interest rate r_t, thereby influencing investment and activity. The stochastic coefficient $(b + w_t)$ indicates the responsiveness of investment to changes in the interest rate. Equation (14.34) assumes zero or constant investment and instead supposes that the government controls the economy by varying government expenditure g_t.

The conditions for the existence of control in the two cases are respectively

$$\sigma_v^2 < 1 + \frac{\sigma_v^2 \sigma_w^2 \rho^2 + 2ab\sigma_v\sigma_w\rho - a^2\sigma_w^2}{b^2 + \sigma_w^2} \tag{14.35a}$$

$$\sigma_v^2 < 1. \tag{14.35b}$$

If $\rho = 0$, (14.35a) implies a more stringent constraint on σ_v^2, than does (14.35b) with the implication that for σ_v^2 in the range

$$1 - \frac{a^2 \sigma_w^2}{b^2 + \sigma_w^2} < \sigma_v^2 < 1$$

an optimal government expenditure policy will exist, even though no feasible interest rate control policy is available.

This example has another interesting implication. It may seem reasonable that if the direct effects of one policy instrument are subject to variability while the direct effects of an alternative instrument are known with certainty, then in order to compensate for this difference in uncertainty the use of the former policy instrument will tolerate less variability in the lagged effects than will the latter. This is certainly the case when $\rho = 0$, but in general it need not be true. As can be seen from (14.35a), if $ab\rho > 0$, it is possible for the r_t policy to allow *more* variability in v_t than does the g_t policy, despite the fact that the immediate impact of r_t on y_t is uncertain. This conclusion is perhaps rather surprising and illustrates the importance of allowing for correlation in assessing control policies.

With $s > 0$, it is seen from (14.29b) that the sign of the feedback control law varies inversely with that of $(ab + \sigma_v \sigma_w \rho)$. It is clear that if $\sigma_v \sigma_w \rho$ is sufficiently large in magnitude then parameter uncertainty may cause a reversal in sign of the control. Moreover, a passive policy – that is, one in which nothing is done – is optimal if and only if

$$\rho = \frac{-ab}{\sigma_v \sigma_w}$$

We now turn to the question of how welfare (as measured by the asymptotic cost function (14.27) is affected by the introduction of parameter uncertainty. In the scalar case, the expression for the welfare costs incurred when the optimal policy is applied, reduces to $s\sigma_u^2$. Hence given σ_u^2, the problem reduces to determining the effects of σ_v, σ_w on s.

The main result of interest is th.. increase in parameter uncertainty may actually increase welfare (or reduce losses). This can be most simply demonstrated for the special case of zero control costs. Setting $n = 0$, the asymptotic costs, corresponding to the optimal policy, C_0 say, can be shown to be (see Turnovsky (1976c))

$$C_0 = s\sigma_u^2 = \frac{m(b^2 + \sigma_w^2)\sigma_u^2}{(1 - a^2 - \sigma_v^2)(b^2 + \sigma_w^2) + (ab + \sigma_v \sigma_w \rho)^2} \quad (14.36)$$

Furthermore, we shall assume $1 - a^2 - \sigma_v^2 > 0$, ensuring the existence of a solution. Differentiating (14.36) with respect to σ_v, σ_w yields

$$\frac{\partial C_0}{\partial \sigma_v} = \sigma_u^2 \frac{\partial s}{\partial \sigma_v} = \frac{-2(b^2 + \sigma_w^2)}{\theta^2}[(ab + \sigma_v \sigma_w \rho)\sigma_w \rho - \sigma_v(b^2 + \sigma_w^2)]m\sigma_u^2$$

$$(14.37a)$$

$$\frac{\partial C_0}{\partial \sigma_w} = \sigma_u^2 \frac{\partial s}{\partial \sigma_w} = \frac{2(ab + \sigma_v \sigma_w \rho)(\sigma_w a - b\sigma_v \rho)m\sigma_u^2}{\theta^2} \qquad (14.37b)$$

where θ is defined in (14.31). Both of these expressions can be negative for values of $\rho \neq 0$, implying the rather paradoxical result that an increase in parameter variability may actually reduce expected costs, provided the two stochastic parameters are appropriately correlated. This result cannot be obtained if only one parameter is uncertain or if the two parameters are independently distributed in which case increasing parameter variability will always add to welfare costs.[13] Furthermore, while it is tedious to show, this pattern of results continues to hold when positive control costs are introduced.

Related to this issue, it is also of interest to calculate the gains to be obtained from applying optimal control over simply applying a passive policy and to see how these gains are affected by the lag structure and its uncertainty. Assuming a passive policy,

$$y_t = (a + v_t)y_{t-1} + u_t$$

the asymptotic costs of which are

$$C_p = \frac{m\sigma_u^2}{1 - a^2 - \sigma_v^2} \geqslant s\sigma_u^2. \qquad (14.38)$$

Hence the gains from applying optimal stochastic control are given by

$$G = C_p - C_0 = \frac{s^2(ab + \sigma_v \sigma_w \rho)^2 \sigma_u^2}{[n + (b^2 + \sigma_w^2)s](1 - a^2 - \sigma_v^2)} \qquad (14.39)$$

which are always positive except in the one case when the passive policy is in fact optimal. In considering how these gains are affected by the means and variances of the coefficients, we shall, for simplicity, restrict ourselves to uncorrelated stochastic parameters. Thus assuming $\rho = 0$, we find unambiguously that

$$\frac{\partial G}{\partial a} > 0 \qquad (14.40a)$$

$$\frac{\partial G}{\partial \sigma_v^2} > 0. \qquad (14.40b)$$

That is, an increase in the expected length or variability of the system lag increases the potential gains from applying optimal stochastic control. On the one hand an increase in a or σ_v^2 increases the costs of the optimally controlled system. At the same time, it is clear from (14.38) that an increase in a or σ_v^2 increases the costs of the uncontrolled system as well, and at an apparently even faster rate. Note, however, that,

$$\lim_{n \to \infty} \frac{\partial G}{\partial \sigma_v^2} = 0 = \lim_{n \to \infty} \frac{\partial G}{\partial a}$$

so that as the control costs become infinitely large, the marginal gains from control tend to zero.

Similarly it can be shown that

$$\frac{\partial G}{\partial \sigma_w^2} = - \sigma_u^2 \frac{\partial s}{\partial \sigma_w^2} < 0. \tag{14.41}$$

That is, an increase in the uncertainty of the direct effects of control will lead to a reduction in the gains from control – a perfectly reasonable result. On the other hand the sign of $\partial G / \partial b$ is ambiguous and will depend among other things upon the magnitude of ρ. If control costs are zero, an increase in the expected impact effect of policy increases the gains from control, which is once again a plausible result.

Turning to an analysis of the effects of these parameter changes on the control law itself, it is again necessary, because of the complexity of the expressions, to treat the case where v_t and w_t are uncorrelated. Setting $\rho = 0$, the intensity of the feedback law in that case is given by the expression

$$r = - \frac{abs}{n + (b^2 + \sigma_w^2)s}. \tag{14.42}$$

Differentiating (14.42) with respect to a and σ_v^2, we obtain

$$\frac{\partial r}{\partial a} = - \frac{bs}{n + (b^2 + \sigma_w^2)s} - \frac{abn}{[n + (b^2 + \sigma_w^2)s]^2} \frac{\partial s}{\partial a} \tag{14.43a}$$

$$\frac{\partial r}{\partial \sigma_v^2} = - \frac{abn}{[n + (b^2 + \sigma_w^2)s]^2} \frac{\partial s}{\partial \sigma_v^2}. \tag{14.43b}$$

Using the fact that when $\rho = 0$, $\partial s / \partial a > 0$, $\partial s / \partial \sigma_v^2 > 0$, and assuming without any essential loss of generality that $a > 0$, $b > 0$, we immediately deduce

$$\frac{\partial r}{\partial a} < 0 \tag{14.44a}$$

$$\frac{\partial r}{\partial \sigma_v^2} < 0. \tag{14.44b}$$

Hence since under these same assumptions $r < 0$, we conclude that the intensity of control, as measured by $|r|$ will increase with both the expected system lag and its variability.[14]

Uncertainty in the impact of control is slightly more complicated. Differentiating (14.42) with respect to σ_w^2 yields

$$\frac{\partial r}{\partial \sigma_w^2} = \frac{-ab}{[n + (b^2 + \sigma_w^2)s]^2} \left(n \frac{\partial s}{\partial \sigma_w^2} - s^2 \right). \tag{14.45}$$

By differentiating (14.29c') with respect to σ_w^2, the term in brackets can be shown to be negative, implying

$$\operatorname{sgn} \frac{\partial r}{\partial \sigma_w^2} = \operatorname{sgn} ab = -\operatorname{sgn} r. \qquad (14.46)$$

Thus an increase in the variability of the impact of the control variable will induce the policy maker to decrease the intensity of his control. However, the effect of an increase in b or r is ambiguous. This can be seen most clearly by setting $n = 0$, in which case the control law simplifies to

$$r = -\frac{ab}{b^2 + \sigma_w^2} \qquad (14.42')$$

with

$$\frac{\partial r}{\partial b} = -\frac{a}{(b^2 + \sigma_w^2)^2} \, [\sigma_w^2 - b^2]. \qquad (14.47)$$

Thus whether an increase in the expected impact effect increases or decreases the intensity of control, depends upon whether the coefficient of variation of $(b + w_t)$, σ_w/b, exceeds, or is less than, unity.

It needs to be stressed that the above results depend crucially upon the assumption of zero correlation between the stochastic coefficients. The effects of parameter uncertainty on the control law can be quite different when the correlation is taken into account. To see this consider the case when $n = 0$. The feedback law now simplifies to

$$r = -\left(\frac{ab + \sigma_v \sigma_w \rho}{b^2 + \sigma_w^2} \right) \qquad (14.42'')$$

from which we immediately obtain

$$\frac{\partial r}{\partial \sigma_v} = \frac{-\rho \sigma_w}{b^2 + \sigma_w^2} \qquad (14.48a)$$

$$\frac{\partial r}{\partial \sigma_w} = \frac{-(2\sigma_w r + \sigma_v \rho)}{b^2 + \sigma_w^2} \qquad (14.48b)$$

indicating the crucial role the sign of the correlation coefficient can play in determining how the policy maker should respond to increasing parameter variability.

To summarize this scalar example, we see that it provides considerable insight into the general characteristics of the class of stochastic control problems being considered in this chapter. First, it clearly illustrates the nature of the existence problem and allows us to consider quite explicitly the kinds of constraints it imposes on the degree of admissible variability in the stochastic coefficients. Secondly it shows how different policy instruments may tolerate different amounts of variability in the underlying parameters, so that in fact only some subset of the available instruments may be actually feasible. In this connection it is possible for a policy instrument, the direct effects of which are stochastic, to tolerate more uncertainty in the length of its lags than some other instrument, the direct impact of which is known with perfect certainty. This will occur if the two stochastic parameters v_t, w_t are appropriately correlated (depending upon the sign of a, b).

This example also illustrates some of the interesting implications of parameter uncertainty for the optimal control policies and associated welfare losses. An increase in the uncertainty in either parameter may actually reduce losses, provided the two parameters are appropriately correlated. If they are uncorrelated, additional parameter uncertainty will always imply additional welfare losses. With one exception, the gains from applying the optimal stochastic control policy over using a simple passive policy are shown to be strictly positive. The exception arises in the one instance in which the two policies coincide. Moreover, these gains increase with both the length and variability in the lag, provided that this is uncorrelated with the impact effect. Likewise, the gains decrease with increased uncertainty in the direct impact of the instrument, provided again that v and w are uncorrelated. By contrast an increase in the expected impact effect has an ambiguous effect on the gains. Furthermore, maintaining the assumption that v and w are uncorrelated, the intensity of the optimal feedback control policy (the stabilization policy) is shown to increase with both the expected lag and its variability; an increase in the variability of the direct impact will tend to have the opposite effect, while that of an increase in the expected impact effect is indeterminate. However, if the two stochastic parameters are correlated, all effects became indeterminate and depend (among other things) upon the sign of this correlation coefficient.

6.   Rules versus discretionary stabilization policies

One issue which has been the subject of some debate during recent years concerns the relative merits of discretionary stabilization policies as compared to fixed policy rules. This discussion was begun by Milton Friedman (1961) who advanced the proposition that due to the length and variability of lags in the effects of monetary policy, the monetary authorities should abandon discretionary monetary management and instead should allow the money supply to grow at a fixed rate. This proposition, being somewhat controversial, has stimulated extensive research on various aspects of monetary control. In the first place, a good deal of effort has been devoted to analysing the empirical evidence available on the lag structure of monetary policy; see e.g. Tanner (1969), Hamburger (1971). Secondly, some of the theoretical effects of monetary policy on the stability of income have been investigated by means of small *IS–LM* type macroeconomic models; see Tucker (1966), Howrey (1969), Moore (1972). Thirdly, recent work has applied linear control theory to consider the effects of various specified (but not necessarily optimal) stabilization policies on the stability of the system as measured by the variance of income; see Cooper and Fischer (1972a, 1973).

The kind of stochastic stabilization framework developed in the foregoing sections provides a useful framework for a theoretical analysis of this question. The present section is therefore devoted to a brief discusssion of it, for the one instrument / one target (scalar) case considered in Section 5.

We have seen from (14.29b) that with one exception a passive policy is never optimal; that is a judiciously chosen discretionary control will always be superior. However, this can hardly be taken as a refutation of the Friedman view. To determine and implement the optimal policy involves substantial amounts of information; in particular it assumes that the policy makers must possess complete and perfect information on all underlying probability distributions. In practice, of course, they are unlikely to have such knowledge and are therefore unlikely to apply the true optimal policy. It is this lack of information upon which the Friedman view is based. Hence, in order to address ourselves to this question it is appropriate to examine the scope for discretionary, but non-optimal policy adjustment. This can be done by considering the extent to which an arbitrary policy will be preferable to a passive policy and seeing how this is affected by the length and variability of the lags in the system.

Consider now an arbitrary discretionary policy which we write in the alternative forms

$$x_t = \mu y_{t-1} = \lambda r y_{t-1}. \tag{14.49}$$

The coefficient μ measures the absolute intensity of the arbitrary discretionary policy, while λ measures its intensity relative to the optimal policy r. Substituting the arbitrary policy (14.49) into the system equation (14.28) and calculating the asymptotic variance (14.27), the cost associated with the non-optimal feedback policy (14.53) is

$$C_n = \frac{(m + nr^2\lambda^2)\sigma_u^2}{1 - (a + b\lambda r)^2 - (\sigma_v^2 + \lambda^2 r^2 \sigma_w^2 + 2\lambda r \sigma_v \sigma_w \rho)} \tag{14.50}$$

where r is given by (14.29). Thus the issue involves determining the range of λ (or equivalently μ) over which the inequality

$$\frac{(m + nr^2\lambda^2)\sigma_u^2}{1 - (a + b\lambda r)^2 - (\sigma_v^2 + \lambda^2 r^2 \sigma_w^2 + 2\lambda r \sigma_v \sigma_w \rho)} - \frac{m\sigma_u^2}{1 - a^2 - \sigma_v^2} < 0 \tag{14.51}$$

holds. Simplifying (14.51) we can show that this inequality holds as long as

$$0 < \lambda < \lambda^* \tag{14.52}$$

where

$$\lambda^* = \frac{2m[n + (b^2 + \sigma_w^2)s]}{n(1 - a^2 - \sigma_v^2) + ms(b^2 + \sigma_w^2)} \tag{14.53}$$

Taking the case of zero control costs, $\lambda^* = 2$, so that (14.52) becomes

$$0 < \lambda < 2. \tag{14.52'}$$

Thus an arbitrary feedback policy will be preferable to no policy, provided the intensity of the policy lies within 100 per cent on either side of the optimal policy. This would indicate a significant range over which discretionary control is to be preferred. Moreover, when $n > 0$, the relative scope for discretionary policy increases further. From (14.38), we have $m > (1 - a^2 - \sigma_v^2)s$, so that substituting into (14.53) yields

$$\lambda^* > 2.$$

The absolute intensity over which discretionary control is preferable can be obtained by substituting μ for λr directly in (14.51). Restricting ourselves to negative feedback control policies, we obtain an analogous range

$$0 > \mu > \mu^* \tag{14.54}$$

where

$$\mu^* = \frac{-2m(ab + \sigma_v \sigma_w \rho)}{n(1 - a^2 - \sigma_v^2) + m(b^2 + \sigma_w^2)}. \tag{14.55}$$

The magnitude $|\mu^*|$ gives the maximum intensity of a discretionary feedback control law which will be preferable to a passive policy.

To consider how the scope for discretionary control responds to various parameters, we take the special case $\rho = 0$. In this case we have

$$\frac{\partial \mu^*}{\partial n} > 0 \tag{14.56a}$$

$$\frac{\partial \mu^*}{\partial m} < 0 \tag{14.56b}$$

$$\frac{\partial \mu^*}{\partial \sigma_v^2} < 0 \tag{14.56c}$$

$$\frac{\partial \mu^*}{\partial \sigma_w^2} > 0 \tag{14.56d}$$

$$\frac{\partial \mu^*}{\partial a} < 0 \tag{14.56e}$$

$$\frac{\partial \mu^*}{\partial b} \gtrless 0. \tag{14.56f}$$

The first five results are as one would expect. The absolute scope for discretionary control varies inversely with control costs and positively with the target variable costs; its scope varies positively with the length of the system lag and its uncertainty; it varies inversely with the uncertainty in the impact effect. The effect of an increase in the mean impact effect on the scope for discretionary control is, however, ambiguous, even in the simplest cases. For example, if there are no control costs

$$\text{sgn}\, \frac{\partial \mu^*}{\partial b} = \text{sgn}\, (b^2 - \sigma_w^2)$$

so that the effects depend purely upon the coefficient of variation of $b + w_t$. If the coefficient of variation exceeds unity (i.e., $\sigma_w/b > 1$), the scope for discretionary control is increased with an increase in the expected impact effect.

Again it should be realized that these results are obtained for $\rho = 0$. Correlation between a_t, b_t may lead to a reversal of these results, but these calculations are left as exercises.

As a final comment, it will be recalled from our discussion of the Phillips stabilization model in Chapter 13, that in general we can identify *two* types of lags. These are, first, the lags inherent in the system – the *system* lag. Secondly, there may be lags in the adjustment in the policy variable itself – what can be referred to as the *policy* lag. It should be apparent that in this chapter, and in particular in the present discussion, we have focused only on lags of the former type. That is, any policy becomes fully operational within the period it is chosen. On the other hand, the Friedman proposition is presumably concerned with the latter class of lags as well. This problem can be analysed using the analysis of the present chapter, and in fact we have done so in detail elsewhere; see Turnovsky (1976c). There it is shown that if the only lags are those due to the adjustment of the policy instrument, and if the additive disturbances are independently distributed over time (as we have assumed here), the passive policy becomes optimal. That is, an arbitrary policy adjustment of the form (14.49) is always dominated by a purely passive policy. This result is quite intuitive. In a situation in which there are (a) no system lags; (b) no autocorrelation in the additive disturbances, the sytem will, if left to its own devices, ultimately fluctuate about its desired equilibrium with the minimum attainable variance σ_u^2. It is clear that if the only uncertainties are those inherent in the policies themselves, there is no point in introducing them, as all they can do is add to this uncertainty. The scope for discretionary stabilization is re-established, however, once either assumption (a) or (b) is relaxed.

7. An application to the stabilization of a multiplier–accelerator model

The problem of macroeconomic stabilization policy has provided a natural area for the application of the techniques we have been discussing. In the first place, building on the Phillips (1954, 1957) contributions, several authors, e.g. Holt (1962), Sengupta (1970), Turnovsky (1973), have applied linear control theory to very simple (continuous-time) multiplier–accelerator type models. A second related body of literature has tended to focus on monetary stabilization policy and on such things as the choice of monetary instrument (e.g. see Sargent (1971a), Moore (1972), Turnovsky (1975a, 1977b)), although in many ways these can be regarded as simple extension of the basic multiplier–accelerator models. Analytical solutions have been obtained for only the crudest aggregate models and recently attention has been devoted to deriving numerical solutions to larger systems; see Pindyck (1973), Cooper and Fischer (1972b, 1974).

In this section we shall apply some of the results obtained in preceding sections to the stabilization of a simple multiplier–accelerator model. The model is a stochastic version of that specified in (13.36).

The basic model we shall consider is

$$C_t = c_0 + (c + v_{1t})Y_{t-1} + u_{1t} \qquad 0 < c < 1 \tag{14.57a}$$

$$I_t = h_0 + (h + v_{2t})(Y_{t-1} - Y_{t-2}) + u_{2t} \qquad h > 0 \tag{14.57b}$$

$$Y_t = C_t + I_t + G_t \tag{14.57c}$$

where

C_t = real consumption

I_t = real investment

Y_t = real income

G_t = real government expenditure

$v_{it}, i = 1, 2$ are stochastic disturbances in parameters, assumed to have zero means, finite variances σ_c^2, σ_h^2, respectively, and to be independently distributed through time.

$u_{it}, i = 1, 2$ are additive stochastic disturbances assumed to have zero means, finite variances σ_1^2, σ_2^2 respectively, and to be independently distributed through time.

Equation (14.51a) specifies a consumption function having a one period lag. The investment function, described in (14.51b), is a simple accelerator, which also operates with a single period lag. Both the marginal propensity to consume, and the magnitude of the acceleration coefficient are subject to stochastic disturbances.

Substituting (14.51a) and (14.51b) into the product market equilibrium condition (14.57c) we obtain the following equation generating the dynamics of income

$$Y_t = (c_0 + h_0) + (c + v_{1t})Y_{t-1} + (h + v_{2t})(Y_{t-1} - Y_{t-2})$$

$$+ G_t + u_t. \tag{14.58}$$

From the above assumptions, the additive disturbance $u_t = u_{1t} + u_{2t}$, has mean zero and finite variance denoted by σ_u^2. For simplicity we assume that v_{1t}, v_{2t}, u_t, are all uncorrelated with one another.

The policy maker is assumed to have chosen a target level of income Y, which is viewed as desirable. The control problem we shall consider is to choose G_t so as to minimise the asymptotic variance of income about the target level,

$$E(Y_t - \bar{Y})^2$$

subject to the dynamics specified by (14.58). Note that for simplicity, we are excluding any costs being associated with the control variable G_t.

In order to derive the optimal policy, it is convenient to transform the system to deviation form. Corresponding to the target level of income $\bar{Y}$, (14.58) implies an equilibrium level of government expenditure $\bar{G}$, defined by

$$\bar{Y} = (c_0 + h_0) + c\bar{Y} + \bar{G} \qquad (14.59)$$

$\bar{G}$ defines the level of government expenditure need to achieve $\bar{Y}$ on average. Subtracting (14.59) from (14.58), we obtain the system in deviation form

$$y_t = (c + v_{1t})y_{t-1} + (h + v_{2t})(y_{t-1} - y_{t-2}) + g_t + u_t + v_{1t}\bar{Y} \qquad (14.60)$$

where
$$y_t = Y_t - \bar{Y},$$
$$g_t = G_t - \bar{G}.$$

Transforming to a first order system, the formal optimization problem can be stated as being to choose g_t so as to minimize

$$E(y_t^2) \qquad (14.61)$$

subject to

$$\begin{pmatrix} y_t \\ z_t \end{pmatrix} = \begin{pmatrix} c + h + v_{1t} + v_{2t} & -(h + v_{1t}) \\ 1 & 0 \end{pmatrix} \begin{pmatrix} y_{t-1} \\ z_{t-1} \end{pmatrix}$$
$$+ \begin{pmatrix} 1 \\ 0 \end{pmatrix} g_t + \begin{pmatrix} u_t + v_1 \bar{Y} \\ 0 \end{pmatrix}. \qquad (14.62)$$

In terms of the notation introduced in Section 4, we let

$$A = \begin{pmatrix} c + h & -h \\ 1 & 0 \end{pmatrix}, \quad v_t = \begin{pmatrix} v_{1t} + v_{2t} & -v_{2t} \\ 0 & 0 \end{pmatrix}$$

$$B = \begin{pmatrix} 1 \\ 0 \end{pmatrix} \quad W_t = \begin{pmatrix} 0 \\ 0 \end{pmatrix}, \quad M = \begin{pmatrix} 1 & 0 \\ 0 & 0 \end{pmatrix} \quad N = 0 \qquad (14.63)$$

$$\mathsf{IS} = \begin{pmatrix} S_{11} & S_{12} \\ S_{12} & S_{22} \end{pmatrix} \quad u_t^* = \begin{pmatrix} u_t + v_1 \bar{Y} \\ 0 \end{pmatrix}.$$

Two things should be noted. First, because of $v_{1t}\bar{Y}$, the composite disturbance u_t^* is correlated with v_t. Secondly, again because of term $v_{1t}\bar{Y}$, the additive disturbance vector, is not quite of the form expressed in (14.17) although this turns out not to affect the application of the theorem.

Applying (14.26), the optimal government expenditure policy is a linear feedback law of the form

$$g_t = r_1 y_{t-1} + r_2 z_{t-1} + p \qquad (14.64)$$

where evaluating (14.26b), (14.26c), we have

$$r_1 = -(c + h) - S_{12}/S_{11} \tag{14.65a}$$

$$r_2 = h \tag{14.65b}$$

$$r = -k_1/S_{11} \tag{14.65c}$$

and from (14.26e)

$$k_1 = \frac{S_{11} \bar{Y} \sigma_c^2}{1 + S_{12}/S_{11}} \tag{14.65d}$$

The matrix $S = (S_{ij})$, a positive semi-definite solution to (14.26d), turns out to be unique and to be given by

$$\begin{pmatrix} \dfrac{1}{(1 - \sigma_h^2)^2 - \sigma_c^2} & \dfrac{-\sigma_h^2}{(1 - \sigma_h^2)^2 - \sigma_c^2} \\ \dfrac{-\sigma_h^2}{(1 - \sigma_h^2)^2 - \sigma_c^2} & \dfrac{\sigma_h^2}{(1 - \sigma_h^2)^2 - \sigma_c^2} \end{pmatrix} \tag{14.66}$$

Details of these calculations are straightforward but tedious, and are omitted.

There are two points regarding S worth noting. First, the requirement that $S \geqslant 0$, and therefore that an optimal linear policy exist, imposes the inequality constraints

$$(1 - \sigma_h^2)^2 - \sigma_c^2 > 0 \tag{14.67a}$$

$$1 \geqslant \sigma_h^2 \geqslant 0. \tag{14.67b}$$

Secondly, it is clear that provided $1 > \sigma_h^2 > 0$, S will be in fact strictly positive definite, even though the cost matrices satisfy the much weaker conditions $M \geqslant 0, N = 0$.

The two pairs of inequalities (14.67a), (14.67b) imposes restrictions on the amount of uncertainty in the stochastic parameters c, h, which the system will tolerate and still yield an optimal policy. They indicate a trade-off between the noise intensities (as measured by variances) in the two coefficients. As $\sigma_h^2 \to 1$, (14.67a) implies that $\sigma_c^2 \to 0$, in order for there to be an optimal policy; likewise if $\sigma_h^2 \to 0$, the constraint on σ_c^2 is correspondingly weakened.

The optimal policy itself is obtained by substituting appropriate elements of S given in (14.66) into (14.65). Observing that $z_{t-1} = y_{t-2}$, this yields the policy

$$g_t = [\sigma_h^2 - (c + h)] y_{t-1} - h y_{t-2} - \frac{\bar{Y} \sigma_c^2}{1 - \sigma_h^2} \tag{14.68}$$

or in the terms of original levels variables

$$G_t - \bar{G} = -(c - \sigma_h^2)(Y_{t-1} - \bar{Y}) - h(Y_{t-1} - Y_{t-2}) - \frac{\bar{Y} \sigma_c^2}{1 - \sigma_h^2}. \tag{14.69}$$

There are several aspects of this equation worthy of comment. Written in this way, we see that the policy consists of two components. The first, includes the first two terms on the right hand side of (14.69) and shows how government expenditure is adjusted to past levels of income. The first of these terms describes a proportional policy, which provided $c - \sigma_h^2 > 0$, will be negative or counter-cyclical. While the fact that $0 < c < 1$, and the restrictions on σ_h^2 given in (14.67) suggest that this inequality will in all probability be met, nevertheless we cannot rule out the possibility of pro-cyclical government expenditure if the acceleration coefficient has a sufficiently large variance. The second term describes a negative derivative control policy, in which government expenditure is required to exactly offset the deterministic part of investment generated by the accelerator. Secondly, there is the constant component, $- \bar{Y}\sigma_c^2/(1 - \sigma_h^2)$, due to the correlation between the composite additive disturbance and v_{1t}. This term is always negative.

Substituting (14.68) into (14.60), we see that the asymptotic value towards which $E(Y_t)$ tends is given by

$$E(Y_t) = \bar{Y} - \frac{\bar{Y}\sigma_c^2}{(1 - \sigma_h^2)^2} < \bar{Y}.$$

That is, the effect of the correlation between the two sets of disturbances is to cause output to be directed to a value below its long-run target. The amount by which it undershoots the desired objectives varies directly with the amount of uncertainty in both the marginal propensity to consume and the acceleration coefficient.

The linear control laws of this example turn out to be exceedingly simple. Note that the feedback component is independent of σ_c^2, which affects only the constant, although this does play a role in determining the existence of a feasible policy; that is in determining the conditions under which S will be positive semi-definite. Part of the reason for the extreme simplicity of the control law stems from the fact that control costs have been excluded ($N = 0$) and also from the fact that the impact effect of the control G_t on the state Y_t is not subject to any random fluctuations. Modifying either of these assumptions complicates enormously the computation of the optimal policy — even in a simple model such as this.

8.   Conclusion

The example we have just been discussing has been considered purely for illustrative purposes — in order to provide some feel for the kinds of issues raised in the optimal stabilization of stochastic systems. Any model which is meant to provide serious policy guidance will require the introduction of additional sectors and control variables, and in general would need to incorporate some of the issues we have been stressing in earlier chapters. Such models are obviously much more difficult to solve. First they are typically inherently nonlinear, but even after linearization they can be solved only by using numerical methods. Some work on obtaining numerical solutions for optimal stabilization policies in reasonably large deterministic systems has been done by Pindyck (1973), Norman (1971) and others, and further work in this area is proceeding. Attempts to extend this to stochastic systems are only just beginning. Most of the existing work on the stabilization of larger scale stochastic systems involves simulating the effects of alternative specified policies, frequently some combination of 'proportional' and 'derivative' adjustment rules, see e.g. Cooper and Fischer (1972c). But these policies will in general not be optimal. The next step is to obtain numerical solutions for the kinds of optimal stochastic control laws we have been considering in this chapter. In any event, the general area of optimal stabilization policy is an extremely active one currently,[15] and we look forward to continuing progress in its application over the coming years.

NOTES

Notes to chapter 2

1 There are many good text books available dealing with the conventional static macroeconomic model. See e.g., Branson (1972), Crouch (1972).
2 See Branson and Klevorick (1969).
3 Throughout this book, where no ambiguity can arise, we shall adopt the convention of letting primes denote total derivatives and denoting partial derivatives by appropriate subscripts. Time derivatives will be denoted by dots above the variable concerned. Thus we shall let

$$f'(x) \equiv \frac{df}{dx}; \quad f_i(x_1, \ldots, x_n) \equiv \frac{\partial f}{\partial x_i} \qquad i = 1, \ldots, n,$$

$$f_{ij}(x_1, \ldots, x_n) \equiv \frac{\partial^2 f}{\partial x_i \partial x_j} \text{ etc.}, \quad \dot{x} \equiv \frac{dx}{dt}$$

The application of a bar to a letter is used to denote either a stationary equilibrium value to a dynamic system, or the fact that the variable to which it is applied is fixed exogenously. The intended meaning should be quite clear from the particular context.

4 The fact that nominal taxes are typically levied on nominal income, implies that real taxes cannot be written as a function of real income alone unless the tax structure is proportional or the rates are changed in response to price changes (i.e. indexed). Since tax indexation is a relatively new phenomenon which at the present time is not widely implemented, we shall assume that the rates remain fixed and focus on the former case. In this case letting Z denote nominal income, and P be the aggregate price level, we have

$$Z = PY.$$

Assuming nominal taxes, T_n, are levied according to the relationship

$$T_n = T(Z) = T(PY),$$

real taxes are of the form $T(PY)/P$. These will be a function of Y alone; if, and only if,

$$\frac{d}{dP} \left(\frac{T(PY)}{P} \right) = 0$$

i.e. if, and only if,

$$Z\frac{dT}{dZ} = T(Z).$$

Integrating this equation with respect to Z, we have

$$T_n = kZ = kPY$$

which establishes the assertion. In particular, if taxes are progressive, then $T(PY)/P$ can certainly not be written in terms of Y alone. This forms difficulties in our discussion of inflation in later chapters.

5 See in particular, the seminal works of Duesenberry (1948), Friedman (1957), Ando and Modigliani (1963). The formulation (2.10) is closest to the Ando–Modigliani version of the consumption function, although the three approaches have many common elements. Typical consumption functions exclude the interest rate, mainly on the grounds of statistical insignificance. Some recent work by Weber (1970) suggests however, that this may have been due to misspecifying the way the interest rate enters the consumption function. Most early analyses included it linearly, finding it to be insignificant. Weber, on the other hand introduces it non-linearly, consistent with the underlying theory and obtains quite significant results.

6 See Branson (1972, Chapter 11).

7 See Jorgenson (1963, 1965). The investment function (2.12) is also consistent with that recently developed by Foley and Sidrauski (1971).

8 This was first recognized by Baumol (1952).

9 See Tobin (1969) who derives a demand for money function of the form (2.15). This also leads into the literature dealing with portfolio behaviour under risk and uncertainty. According to this, asset demand functions such as (2.15) should be derived from some form of expected utility maximization. However, this has yet to be adequately incorporated into macroeconomic theory.

10 Specifically, the utility function has the property

$$U_1 > 0, \quad U_2 > 0$$

$$U_{11} < 0, \quad U_{22} < 0, \quad U_{11}U_{22} - U_{12}^2 > 0.$$

Notes to chapter 3

1 For a very good and more complete discussion of the balance sheets of the various sectors within the economy and a derivation of their respective net wealth, see Crouch (1972).

2 See, for example, Barro (1974) for a recent discussion of this issue and further references to the literature.

3 For simplicity we assume that all profits earned by firms are distributed to the households who own them. Hence we are ruling out the possibility that firms finance their investments through retained earnings. This assumption is made purely for convenience and does not involve any essential loss of generality.

4 This may be contrasted with what is sometimes called 'beginning-of-period equilibrium'. According to this notion, households adjust their demands to achieve equilibrium at the beginning of the period, given the existing stocks of assets. For a detailed discussion of these concepts and the difference between them, see Foley (1975), Turnovsky and Burmeister (1977).

5 For example, one frequently sees consumption functions of the form

$$C = C(Y, V) \qquad 0 < C_1 < 1, \quad C_2 > 0$$

where both C and V refer to the same instant t. In making the above comment, we are interpreting C as describing *plans*. This would seem to be the appropriate interpretation, in view of the fact that such models typically also include $Y = C + I + G$ as an equilibrium relationship. If one interprets C as being *actual* behaviour, then (3.27) below suggests that the partial derivative C_2 should be *negative*. The reason is that an increase in wealth is the *result* of more saving and less consumption.

    One case where the inclusion of wealth contemporaneously can be justified is if one views C as being obtained by aggregating over individuals with varying planning horizons, some of which are less than one unit in length.

6 For further discussion of these points see Branson (1972).

7 As mentioned in Chapter 2, some macro models consider the four markets – output, labour, money, and bonds – and use Walras' law to eliminate bonds. We could add in the labour market, but this is not necessary for the points we wish to make. For a statement of Walras' law which also includes the labour market, see Hansen (1970).

8 For further discussion of this point see May (1970), Foley (1975).

9 The development of Sections 7–12 is based extensively on Turnovsky (1977a). The material is somewhat more difficult and can be omitted on a first reading. The results from these sections are not used until Chapter 8.

10 In general, in defining flows we shall adopt the notational convention

$$x(t + h, t) = \int_t^{t+h} x(\tau, t)\, d\tau$$

and we shall define $x(t, t) \equiv x(t)$. An exception is planned investment $I(t + h, t)$ which is defined in (3.30) below.

11 For further discussion of the weak consistency axiom, see Burmeister and Turnovsky (1976); Turnovsky and Burmeister (1977). They also define a *strong* consistency axiom, which is equivalent to the notion of perfect myopic foresight. See also Chapter 8.

12 For simplicity we assume that households and firms hold identical expectations.

13 Since we are only concerned with letting $h \to 0$ through positive values, we are, strictly speaking, dealing only with right-hand derivatives.

14 In a recent paper, Meyer (1975) identifies what he calls three conservation principles for each sector in a stock–flow model. These include (i) the budget constraint, (ii) the balance sheet constraint, (iii) the financing constraint. There is clearly only one such constraint (the budget constraint (3.14) in discrete time. As we have seen this gives rise to two constraints, namely the balance sheet constraint (3.38) and the financing constraint (3.39) when one transforms to continuous time.

15 Institutionally this could be carried out by offering a 'rights' issue to existing shareholders. That is, giving the firm's shareholders the priviledge of purchasing the new issues of common stock at a fixed subscription price; see Levy and Sarnat (1972, pp. 39–43).

16 The alternative assumption that all new shares are issued at par, in which case $E \equiv K$, so that $p_e^* = p_k^* = q^*$ say, implies the firms' budget constraint

$$K^d(t + h, t) - K(t) = I(t + h, t).$$

This yields an aggregate constraint identical to (3.35) provided the household sector's budget constraint is written as

$$M(t) + B(t) + q(t)K(t) + [q^*(t + h,t) - q(t)] K(t)$$

$$+ [q^*(t + h, t) - 1] I(t + h, t) + r(t)B(t)h + Y(t + h, t)$$

$$= M^d(t + h, t) + B^d(t + h, t) + q^*(t + h, t)K^d(t + h, t)$$

$$+ C(t + h, t) + U(t + h, t)$$

and includes the capital gains resulting from the revaluation of the new investment.

17 Recalling (3.40b), y^D is defined by

$$y^D = y + p^*_{e,1} E + rB - u.$$

It therefore follows that $s_B \neq s_E \neq s_M$ and strictly speaking one should consider separate derivatives for the different components of V. This point is ignored in (3.68), although the different expressions can be easily calculated.

18 Meyer (1975) argues that even in discrete time the adding up conditions (3.65) hold. Presumably he must be considering an infinitesimally short planning horizon.

19 See also Levhari and Patinkin (1968). The definition (3.69) will be consistent with $s(t) = \dot{V}(t)$ if transfer payments equal to $\dot{M}/P$ are continually paid by the government to the private sector; (3.70) will satisfy the condition if zero transfer payments are made.

Notes to chapter 4

1 For examples of macroeconomic models focusing on the dynamics resulting from the government budget constraint see Ritter (1955–56), Ott and Ott (1965), Christ (1967, 1968, 1969), Steindl (1971), Silber (1970), Blinder and Solow (1973). The present analysis is in some respects a discrete time version of the Blinder–Solow analysis and draws heavily on Turnovsky (1975b).

2 To avoid confusion time intervals must be defined carefully. All transactions are assumed to take place at the discrete points of time $t = 0, 1, 2$ etc. The time subscript on stocks therefore refers to quantity at time t. For flows, the time subscript t refers to period t, that is the unit time interval $(t - 1, t)$.

3 M in our analysis therefore refers to 'high powered money'.

4 Throughout our analysis we assume tax rates to remain fixed. Once we allow tax rates to vary we open up a much wider range of policies. Many of these have been considered at length by Christ (1967, 1969).

5 A sufficient condition for the multiplier in (4.14) to exceed that in (4.6a) is that $(1 - c)(1 - u) - i > 0$ and $\theta \neq 0$.

   The former condition, which occurs at various stages in our analysis, is mildly stronger than (4.4).

6 One further point worth noting is that if we assume variable interest rate bonds, the value of which is B, the appropriate wealth variable is $(M_{t-1} + B_{t-1})$.

7 It is clear that with this more general formulation, the restriction (4.4) now becomes $1 - c_1(1 - u) - i > 0$.

8 The system is considered to be in equilibrium when Y, r are constant. With wealth effects and interest payments present, this can easily be shown to require $\Delta M_t = \Delta B_t = 0$. When wealth effects are absent from both the output and money markets and interest payments are ignored (the case considered in Section 3) we need only have $\Delta M_t = 0$. B_t need not be constant, as any

changes in B_t are fully absorbed by the demand for bonds without affecting the rest of the system.

9

$$\Delta M_1 + \frac{\Delta B_1}{r_2} = \Delta M_1 + \frac{\Delta B_1}{r_1(1 + \Delta r_2/r_1)} \doteq \Delta M_1 + \frac{\Delta B_1}{r_1} \quad \text{to the first order}$$

Hence, taking limits

$$\frac{\partial M_1}{\partial B_1} + \frac{1}{r_2} \doteq \frac{\partial M_1}{\partial B_1} + \frac{1}{r_1} > 0.$$

10 That is, $K = G + (1 - u)B$.
11 Indeed even if (4.33) is not met, the system may still be stable. In this case however, the possibility of instability cannot be ruled out.
12 $\Delta'x$ refers to changes in equilibrium levels; it must not be confused with $\Delta x_t = x_t - x_{t-1}$.
13 See Christ (1969, p. 698).
14 This may seem unusual, but it is a consequence of condition (4.37) which introduces a singularity into the dynamic system. That is, M_t, B_t are not allowed to adjust independently, but are constrained to the line defined by (4.37).
15 The comments made in note 11 apply here as well.
16 This can be most easily seen for a continuous-time system although the analogous argument applied in the discrete-time case. The continuous-time analogue of (4.37) is

$$\frac{dB}{r} = \left(\frac{(1-\theta)}{\theta}\right)dM.$$

Denote the initial equilibrium by 0 and the new equilibrium by 1. Then,

$$\int_0^1 \frac{dB}{r} = \left(\frac{(1-\theta)}{\theta}\right) \quad \int_0^1 dM = \left(\frac{(1-\theta)}{\theta}\right)\Delta'M.$$

Integrating, the left hand side by parts yields

$$\int_0^1 \frac{dB}{r} = \left(\frac{B}{r}\right)\Big|_0^1 + \int_0^1 \frac{B}{r^2}\,dr$$

$$\doteq \frac{\Delta'B}{r} - \frac{B\Delta'r}{r^2} + \int_0^1 \frac{B}{r^2}\,dr.$$

But to the first order, the second and third terms are equal yielding

$$\frac{\Delta'B}{r} = \left(\frac{(1-\theta)}{\theta}\right)\Delta'M.$$

Notes to chapter 5

1 For a survey of this early literature see Bronfenbrenner and Holzman (1963).
2 For a summary of many of these studies see Bodkin, Bond, Reuber and Robinson (1966).
3 For a detailed study using vacancy data see Dow and Dicks-Mireaux (1958).

4 Several essays dealing with various aspects of these issues are contained in
   Phelps (1970).
5 An early attempt to deal with the problem by means of the notions of 'key
   groups' and 'wage rounds' was undertaken by Eckstein and Wilson (1962).
   More recently Hamermesh (1970) and Sparks and Wilton (1971) have
   attempted to take into account the institutional realities of bargaining by
   analysing samples of contracts directly.
6 Another early integrated theory of the wage–price sector is developed by
   Pitchford (1957, 1963).
7 These data have now been used to test various macroeconomic propositions
   involving expectations. For a brief description of them see Turnovsky (1970).
8 Recently, Sargent (1973b) has tested the natural rate hypothesis within a
   complete macroeconomic model, but his results are inconclusive. For a test of
   the hypothesis under the assumption of 'rational expectations' see Lucas
   (1972).

Notes to chapter 6

1 This chapter draws heavily on, and is an extension of, Turnovsky (1974b).
2 See, for example, Gibson (1970), Pyle (1972), Sargent (1969), Yohe and
   Karnosky (1969).
3 The role of inflationary expectations has also been given somewhat less
   treatment in other areas of macroeconomics. For example, it has been introduced into investment functions by Jorgenson and Siebert (1968) and Ando,
   Modigliani, Rasche and Turnovsky (1974). The importance of price expectations on the demand for money has been investigated by Smith and Winder
   (1971) using Canadian data. Overall, the empirical results obtained in these
   two areas are somewhat mixed in quality. This, no doubt, reflects at least in
   part the difficulty of obtaining adequate proxies for price expectations, but it
   may also be due to the relative stability of prices over most of the relevant
   time horizons.
4 Some years ago Mundell (1963) analysed the Fisherian proposition within a
   kind of modified *IS–LM* framework. Recently, Sargent (1972) has reconsidered the proposition using a linearized, dynamic model and in some respects
   the present model is a short-run version of his. However, as seen below, there
   are many differences in that we focus on a much wider range of issues, and
   allow price expectations to enter the system through a variety of channels.
5 Strictly speaking this statement may apply to the short run only. In the longer
   run tax rates are likely to be adjusted in the light of actual inflation.
6 As noted in footnote 14 below, most of the interesting results continue to
   hold if we generalize the consumption and investment functions to
   $C(Y - T, r - \pi), I(Y, r - \pi)$.
7 See, for example, Jorgenson (1963), Ando, Modigliani, Rasche and Turnovsky
   (1974).
8 See Friedman (1956).
9 Since we are concerned with a single time period, we drop the time subscript
   where possible.
10 More precisely, $k = -1/\bar{N}F'(\bar{N})$.
11 A sufficient condition for (6.15) to be strictly positive is that $M - \theta P(G - T)$
   > 0. From (6.14d) this condition can be written as $M_{-1} + m > 0$ a condition
   which will surely be met under any reasonable conditions.
12 A typical estimate of the short run elasticity of the demand for money is
   about -0.03, while $0 \leqslant b \leqslant 1$. There is much less evidence on e_π, and we take

the Smith–Winder estimate of -0.01. Assuming $r = 0.04$, $\pi = 0.02$, (the average for the sample periods of most of the existing studies and therefore of the data upon which these estimates are based), we obtain $e_r/r = -0.75$, $e_\pi/\pi = -0.50$. If further we assume $G \geqslant T$, we deduce that $\Omega < 0$ for *all* feasible values of b. Note that our assumptions do not eliminate the possibility of $\partial r/\partial \pi < 0$, although for any reasonable set of parameter values this is *most* unlikely to occur.

However, these estimates were obtained over periods of relative price stability, when r and π were low relative to their recent values and b also tended to be low. Recent empirical evidence would suggest that values of b close to unity occur in periods of high inflation. For example, taking $r = 0.08$, $\pi = 0.08$ as more representative of recent experience, and doubling e_π to say -0.02, we find that Ω could quite plausibly become positive as b approaches 1.

13 Other factors, particularly those included in the Jacobian J, will influence the magnitude of the responses in (6.16). Thus for example, like Sargent (1969) whose analysis always implies $\partial r/\partial \pi < 1$ in the short run, we find that the adequacy of the approximation $\partial r/\partial \pi = 1$ improves with the speed of adjustment of commodity prices and the interest elasticity of investment demand with respect to the real rate of interest. In our model the accuracy of the approximation will vary inversely with the interest elasticity of the demand for money only if the inflationary expectations elasticity of the demand for money is sufficiently small.

Mundell's model also implies $\partial r/\partial \pi < 1$, due to the fact that inflation reduces real money balances resulting in a decline in wealth which stimulates an increase in saving.

14 These results hold if $C = C(Y, r - \pi)$, $I = I(Y, r - \pi)$. The only difference is that I' in (6.16a), (6.16c) is replaced by $(C_2 + I_2)$ and $(1 - C')$ becomes $(1 - C_1 - I_1)$.

15 See for example, Yohe and Karnosky (1969) and Gibson (1970). By contrast Pyle (1972) uses semi-annual data and obtains expectations coefficients quite close to unity. This suggests that an alternative reason for the low estimates obtained in the previous studies may be a statistical one, due to severe observational errors being introduced into the proxy expectational variable. This may arise from the fact that this variable is typically calculated by taking changes of quarterly or monthly data, in which rounding errors become relatively much more important.

16 Another argument providing a possible explanation of these low estimates is developed by Sargent (1971b). The usual procedure in estimating expectations effects is to construct (often only implicitly) proxy expectations variables by taking weighted sums of past actual inflation, with weights summing to unity. The coefficient of this constructed variable, is then interpreted as an expecations coefficient. As Sargent points out, it is not necessarily rational to assume that these weights add to unity and indeed under certain conditions it is most reasonable to assume that they add to less than unity. In this case the expectations coefficient estimated on the basis that these weights add to unity will be an underestimate of the true effect.

17 For further conjectures attempting to explain these differences see Taylor, Turnovsky and Wilson (1973, Chapter 9).

18 To see this one must compare the Jacobian J with what it would be in the absence of the price adjustment relationship.

19 Note that this analysis abstracts from the fact that in the longer run tax rates tend to get adjusted in the light of inflation.

20 It should be noted that the linear tax function has the undesirable property of implying negative tax receipts for very low levels of income. However, it should be realized that it is intended to apply only as an approximation for a restricted range of X, over which $T_n > 0$. The main advantage in using this formulation is its convenience in parameterizing base and marginal tax rates.

   Note also that one could write (6.23) in the equivalent form $T_n = t(X - X_b)$ where X_b is the base taxable income. However, written in this way the effects of a change in the marginal tax rate becomes much more complicated to determine due to the fact that it enters multiplicatively with both X and X_b.

21 Note that we are assuming workers to have zero 'tax illusion'. As an alternative hypothesis, one might posulate that they seek only partial compensation of their money wages for taxes, attempting to maintain $(WQ - uT)/P^*$, $0 \leqslant u \leqslant 1$, are constant. This case can be analysed in a similar manner to that considered here and yields essentially similar results.

22 The tax rate will of course exert an indirect effect on p, through its impact on excess demand $(Y - \bar{Y})$.

23 For further discussion of this effect see Hansen (1971).

24 From (6.29e) $M - \theta GP + \theta t_1 X = M_{-1} + m - \theta t_0 > 0$.

25 If the tax structure is proportional or regressive then $t_0 \geqslant 0$ and an increase in the supply of money is unambiguously inflationary.

26 Some of the earlier discussions took place in the December 1969 and June 1971 issues of the *American Economic Review*. In particular, see the papers by Eisner (1969) and Hansen (1971).

27 For an analysis of the inflationary effects of taxes in the context of the bargaining model outlined in Chaper 3 Section 7 see Pitchford and Turnovsky (1976). There it is shown how in the context of that model, the income claims effect will not be purely transitory as it is in the present analysis.

Notes to chapter 7

1 This chapter is adapted from Pyle and Turnovsky (1976).

2 An equilibrium in which K is growing is precisely analogous to the notion of a 'quasi-equilibrium' as it has been termed by Hansen (1970) — a steady state in which prices are growing at a constant rate.

3 See, e.g., Bhatia (1972) and McElroy and Poindexter (1975). The estimate we have cited refers to consumption out of *accrued* capital gains, since these are the relevant component of disposable income.

4 As first shown by Modigliani and Miller, under appropriate assumptions the firm's average cost of capital is invariant with respect to its capital structure.

5 Equation (7.19c) is obtained by dividing (7.16) by K and noting that $\dot{m} = \dot{M}/K - m(p + \dot{k})$ and $\dot{b} = \dot{B}/K - b(p + \dot{k})$.

6 Other specifications of government expenditure policy are possible. For example, Tobin and Buiter (1976) take the expenditure policy variable to include interest payments on government debt. Alternatively one could treat the deficit to be the policy variable and to allow expenditure to adjust endogenously.

7 This portfolio balance condition follows from our assumption that asset demand functions are homogeneous of degree one in wealth. Optimum portfolio rules in which asset demand is proportional to wealth are obtained when individuals are presumed to maximize expected utility with utility functions which display constant proportional risk aversion. See, e.g., Hakansson (1970) and Merton (1971).

8 For the evaluation of the various partial derivatives, it is useful to note that

$$L_Y + J_Y = -N_Y = (1 - n_s)R'/r_e > 0$$

$$L_r + J_r = -N_r = -n_3 + n_s \, b/r^2 > 0$$

$$L_{r_e} + J_{r_e} = -N_{r_e} = -n_2 - (1 - n_s)\frac{R}{r_e^2} > 0$$

$$L_\pi + J_\pi = -N_\pi = -n_3 - n_4 > 0.$$

9 The restrictions imposed on the various derivatives in Section 3 are specified for the unscaled functions. It is clear that identical properties apply to the normalized functions.

10 While the strict inequalities in (7.24) are also necessary for the stability of the associated linearized system to (7.23), they are not necessary for the *local* stability of (7.23); the corresponding *weak* inequalities are the appropriate necessary conditions. This point is discussed further in Chapter 9, note 8.

11 See e.g., Burmeister and Dobell (1970).

12 In this connection it is felt that Blinder and Solow may be excessively confident in concluding $\partial y/\partial b > 0$. They deduce this by claiming that $\partial y/\partial b$ is analogous to an ordinary multiplier for transfer payments, which the US empirical evidence suggests is between 1 and 2. But this analogy is not entirely correct. It is certainly true that one effect of an increase in b is to increase disposable income and in this respect it is similar to an increase in transfer payments. But the increase in b has wealth effects, not shared by transfer payments, and these are what create the indeterminacy.

For $\partial y/\partial m \geqslant \partial y/\partial b > 0$, we also require that the quantity $(1 - u - p - i)$ is non-negative which is surely the case for the US.

13 In particular (7.39') and (7.43) give answers to the Blinder–Solow question 'Does fiscal policy matter?' in the context of our model. The analysis of (7.43) suggests that there are plausible circumstances in which bond-financed fiscal policy matters more than money-financed fiscal policy.

14 It is, of course, entirely possible that the government chooses inflation and output objectives which do *not* lie in the long-run Phillips curve. In this case it will need to introduce an additional policy directed at *shifting* the Phillips curve so as to render its targets feasible.

Notes to chapter 8

1 See e.g. the reference to the Livingston survey data, given in Chaper 5. If weak consistency did not hold, the appropriate definition of $\pi/t, t - h)$ would be

$$\frac{[P^*(t, t - h) - P^*(t - h, t - h)]}{hP^*(t - h, t - h)} .$$

2 The rate of taxation is assumed to be fixed throughout.

3 See Chapter 2, Section 11.

4 For a statement of the Routh–Hurwitz conditions see Samuelson (1947).

5 For a proof of this proposition see e.g. Henderson and Quandt (1971).

6 Tax receipts are $T = uY$. Since in the steady state $\dfrac{\partial Y}{\partial u} = 0$, it follows that an

incremental effect of an increase in u is to raise steady state tax receipts by an amount Y.

Notes to chapter 9

1 Major contributions in this area are contained in Mundell (1968).
2 See e.g. Takayama (1972), Stern (1973), Mundell (1968), Caves and Jones (1973).
3 See Krueger (1965), Helliwell (1969), Takayama (1969) for examples of the basic model we are considering. A recent taxonomic discussion within this static framework is conducted by Shinkai (1975).
4 For a discussion of the elasticity approach to the analysis of devaluation see e.g. Stern (1973, Chapter 7).
5 See e.g. Kindleberger (1963, pp. 656–8).
6 See e.g. Johnson (1966), Krueger (1965), Takayama (1969).
7 The model of Sections 5 and 6 are essentially minor variants of the Mundell (1962, 1964) – Fleming (1962) models.
8 The strict inequalities in (9.35) which are necessary and sufficient for the linearized system (9.34) to be stable are also sufficient for the associated non-linear system to be locally stable. Necessary conditions for local stability require the absence of instability of the associated linearized system (9.34) and this will be met provided the weak inequalities

$$\alpha_{11} F_1 + \alpha_{12} G_1 + \alpha_{21} F_2 + \alpha_{22} G_2 \leqslant 0$$

$$(\alpha_{11}\alpha_{22} - \alpha_{12}\alpha_{21})(F_1 G_2 - F_2 G_1) \geqslant 0$$

hold. The weaker inequalities are due to the fact that because of higher order terms, a non-linear system can be locally stable even when its first order approximation is in a state of neutral stability; see Samuelson (1947, p. 301).
9 For further comments along these lines see Tsiang (1975).

Notes to chapter 10

1 This chapter is a somewhat revised version of the paper by Turnovsky and Kaspura (1974). We have taken this opportunity to correct a number of minor errors contained in that paper.
2 An early analysis of imported inflation is contained in Pitchford (1963). For a survey of the more recent literature, including a discussion of the so-called 'Scandinavian' model see Caves (1973).
3 This assumption is also made by Shinkai (1973). Empirical evidence supporting it is discussed by Michaely (1972). It seems the most natural open-economy extension of the traditional Keynesian model, which usually assumes only a single commodity is produced. As another extreme possibility, one could consider a 'pure small country' case where export prices as well as import prices are determined abroad. This case can be readily analysed along the lines of this chapter. On the other hand, the case where export prices are determined partly domestically and partly abroad is extremely difficult. Now export prices will not be the same as the prices of domestically produced non-traded goods and to analyse how these two prices are determined involves constructing a complete general equilibrium model. With prices in our model being determined by a disequilibrium adjustment process, this is clearly rather complicated to do and is not attempted here.
4 It is straightforward to relax these assumptions. But this obscures the workings of the model, without changing the basic results.
5 The overall rate of domestic inflation is defined by p in equation (10.4') below.

6 Since we are concerned with a single time period, we drop the time subscript where possible.

7 See, for example, Bodkin, Bond, Reuber and Robinson (1966), Pitchford (1968), Lipsey and Parkin (1970), Taylor, Turnovsky and Wilson (1973).

8 For further elaboration of this point see Taylor, Turnovsky and Wilson (1973,, Chapter 2). It must be noted that we are interpreting these international competitive influences rather broadly, since domestic producers do not produce the imported good, and therefore do not compete directly with foreign producers in its production. Nevertheless, the basic idea would seem to apply in the present context. As the price of foreign goods rise, domestic producers can raise the price of domestic goods without finding that they suffer a loss in demand. Where imported inputs are allowed, the variable $\Delta(QE)/(QE)_{-1}$ will reflect cost effects, as well as the international competitive influences.

9 More generally, but still without going to a complete stock model, the capital inflow term is frequently postulated as $K(Y, \bar{Y}, r - \bar{r})$ where $\bar{Y}, \bar{r}$ denote the foreign level of income and rate of interest respectively making capital flows responsive to the interest differential. A small country can take these foreign factors as given enabling us to write $K(Y, r)$. Despite the fact that we are dealing with an inflationary situation it is the nominal interest rate which is relevant, as the inflationary component cancels. The inflow of domestically owned capital will depend upon $(r - \pi) - (\bar{r} - \pi) = r - \bar{r}$, likewise the inflow of foreign owned capital will depend upon $(r - \bar{\pi}) - (\bar{r} - \bar{\pi})$, where $\bar{\pi}$ denotes inflationary expectations abroad, and which again reduces to $(r - \bar{r})$.

10 Thus we could analyse the short-run effect of an increase in inflationary expectations on the system. This could be done using the identical procedure to that adopted in Chaper 6 for the closed economy and is left as an exercise.

11 See Chapter 9. As discussed there, the Marshall—Lerner condition has been developed for models which abstract from capital movements. We are therefor interpreting them as applying to the balance of trade component of the balance of payments.

12 More explicitly, the feedbacks originating with say the demand effects are obtained by calculating the impacts of an incremental shift in the demand function. This is done by replacing the right hand side vector of (10.18) by $(1, 0, 0, 0, 0)'$ and solving the system of equations for the vector $(\partial Y/\partial H^*,$ $\partial r/\partial H^*, \partial B/\partial H^*, \partial p_1/\partial H^*, \partial p/\partial H^*)'$ (where the prime denotes vector transpose). The other feedbacks are obtained similarly, with the unit term appearing in the position corresponding to the effect being considered.

13 For example Taylor, Turnovsky and Wilson (1973) obtain a short run estimate of a_2 for Canada of about 0.4. Pitchford's (1968) estimates for Australia are slightly lower (somewhat less than 0.3).

14 The impact of foreign inflation on the terms of trade is obtained by calculating the derivative

$$\frac{\partial}{\partial q} \left(\frac{(1 + p_1)}{E(1 + q)} \right).$$

15 See Chapter 13. The Tinbergen proposition regarding the numbers of targets and instruments holds only under very special assumptions. It ceases to apply as soon as one introduces risk; see Brainard (1967). However, even in a deterministic context it will not be true if there are costs of adjustment associated with the different instruments; see Henderson and Turnovsky (1972).

In either case, it will pay policy makers to use all available instruments. These issues are discussed further in Part III.

16 One could take the domestic inflation target to be p_1 rather than p. This yields virtually identical results to those we obtain. If the policy makers wish to control p_1 and p, then of course a fourth instrument will be required. One might also wish to express the balance of payments target in real rather than nominal terms.

17 See Dunn (1970).

18 For example, if the exchange rate enters currently in all equations except the pricing equation, where it enters with a distributed lag, one can readily show that in general the derivatives reported in (10.27a). will not be zero.

Notes to chapter 11

1 This chapter is a revised version of Turnovsky (1976a).

2 See Chapter 9 for a summary of much of this literature.

3 Throughout this analysis we abstract from growth in the capital stock and technological change.

4 As in previous chapters we abstract from a fractional reserve banking system so that L refers to the monetary base or the volume of 'high powered money'.

5 This assumption is stronger than necessary. The reason for making it relates to having private bonds in the domestic economy. If such bonds exist, and domestic bonds are imperfect substitutes for foreign bonds, the foreign holding of domestic private bonds needs to be netted out in the definition of domestic private wealth. This causes unnecessary complications in the analysis. Alternatively, we can permit domestic private bonds if we add the assumption that none of them are held by foreigners. In any event, there are no restrictions on the nature of the foreign bonds.

6 This specification of the demand functions for bonds is similar to that adopted by Kouri and Porter (1974) in their study of international capital flows and portfolio equilibrium. It should be noted that V^* contains A^F/r. By treating V^* as exogenous, we are assuming either that this constitutes a negligible fraction of foreign wealth, or that any changes in A^F/r are offset by changes in the other components of foreign wealth.

7 Symmetry may suggest postulating $L^d = L(Y, r, V, r^*)$; with r^* determined abroad; this immediately reduces to (11.2).

8 It is clear that this equation imposes the following constraints on the derivatives of the asset demand functions; see Chapter 3.

$$L_i + J_i^D + N_i = 0 \qquad i = 1, 2,$$

$$L_3 + J_3^D + N_3 = 1.$$

9 We are assuming that interest income earned abroad is taxed solely by the domestic government. In practice a portion of this may be taxed by the foreign government, with the domestic government granting a credit for the amount of tax paid abroad.

10 In two papers, Oates (1966) and McKinnon (1969) consider the limiting case of zero capital mobility, when B is simply the balance of trade T, and treat $g + T = 0$, as the equilibrium condition. But it is clear that their argument regarding equilibrium does not depend upon that polar assumption. In another paper, McKinnon and Oates (1966) assume perfect capital mobility and again postulate $g + T = 0$ as the equilibrium condition. As we show below, it is only in very special circumstances that the equilibrium conditions in the two cases

will be the same. Even then they differ somewhat from (11.13). The relevant equilibrium condition is actually $g + b = 0$, where b equals the balance of payments on current account (balance of trade plus interest payments on outstanding debt). However, as these authors ignore interest payments in their analysis, the condition $g + b = 0$ is essentially equivalent to the McKinnon–Oates equilibrium.

11   The equilibrium is not identical to (11.13) however; see note 10 above.

12   For discussion of this point see Chapter 9 note 8.

13   For a discussion of this borderline case see for example, Kaplan (1958, p. 422).

14   This requirement follows immediately from the fact that the condition for a linear system $Ax = b$ to have a consistent solution for x is that $r(A) = r(A, b)$ where r denotes rank.

15   The estimates of H_1, H_3 are based on the following considerations. Typical estimates of the total marginal propensity to consume (including imports) are about 0.9, while Ando and Modigliani (1963) estimated the wealth effect in consumption to be about 0.06. The breakdown we have chosen between domestic goods and imports, while arbitrary, does not seem unreasonable.

16   In this case $g_1 + b_1 = [T_1(1 - u) - u] \dfrac{\partial Y}{\partial L} < 0.$

17   This can be seen from the constraints given in note 8.

18   It is of interest to compare the stability result of this section with that obtained by Aghevli and Borts (1973). Their analysis is based on perfect capital mobility and abstracts from wealth effects. Furthermore they assume complete debt financing of the government budget deficit ($\theta = 0$) and throughout most of their paper have no sterilization policy ($s = 1$). With these assumptions they establish that the adjustment in the total balance of payments (B) is stable, tending towards an equilibrium value $B = 0$. The stability analysis of this section is totally consistent with, and indeed generalizes, the Aghevli–Borts results. First, setting $\theta = 0$ in (11.23"), our equilibrium also implies $B = 0$ for complete debt financing, although as we have pointed out above, this conclusion does not extend to the case $\theta \neq 0$. Secondly, that they obtain stability in the absence of wealth effects, while we do not, is due to the fact that they also abstract from interest payments, which as we have shown are the essential destabilizing element in the adjustment process.

19   An equilibrium in which both $\dot{A}$ and $\dot{L}$ equal zero requires $b = g = 0$.

20   This formulation can be easily modified to follow the conventional approach of treating B rather than F as the external policy objective.

21   Stability conditions can be obtained from the Routh–Hurwitz conditions. For a general statement which can be applied to the 4 × 4 case see for example, Samuelson (1947, p. 434).

Notes to chapter 12

1   This chapter is adapted with substantial revision and modification from Kingston and Turnovsky (1976).

2   This is the assumption also made in Chapter 10, where it is discussed in more detail. McKinnon (1963) is responsible for popularizing an alternative assumption which allows the simplicity of the traditional two-good model to be retained. He suggests classifying domestic output into traded and non-traded goods with the price of the former being determined abroad, and the price of the latter determined endogenously. This case can be readily analysed along the lines of this chapter.

The analysis becomes almost identical if one assumes further (i) no domestic consumption of the exportable; (ii) the foreign currency prices of tradeables move in proportion; (iii) the price of a 'representative basket' of domestic output is the same as the domestic cost of living. In this formulation domestic output of the traded good is supply rather than demand determined, and the key relative price is the cost of living (cost of production) at home relative to that abroad, rather than the terms of trade.

3 In comparing two price situations, the true cost-of-living index is 'the ratio of the cost of the cheapest bundle of goods at the price of the second situation which will yield satisfaction equivalent to that of the initial situation to the cost of the initial bundle and the initial prices'. (Samuelson (1947)). The proposition asserted above is well known and has been proved most recently by Samuelson and Swamy (1974).

4 These assumptions could easily be relaxed by postulating adaptive schemes similar to the equation describing inflationary expectations introduced below.

5 If one adopts the net-of-tax specification, the following points need to be noted. Provided the domestic government taxes capital gains on foreign exchange rate changes at the same rate as interest income, then with perfect capital mobility we again obtain the interest parity condition (12.7). However, if the government taxes interest income and exchange-rate capital gains at different rates then parity cannot hold in general. In that event home and foreign government securities cannot be perfect substitutes; that is to say, an investor distinguishes between domestic and foreign bonds for reasons other than net rates of return in the investor's home currency. To see this, suppose that capital gains are not taxed and that $u \neq u^*$, where u and u^* are the domestic and foreign rates of taxation respectively. Then the interest rate parity theory implies that home investors engage in arbitrage resulting in $r(1-u) = r^*(1-u) + e$, and foreign investors do the same, resulting in $r^*(1-u^*) = r(1-u^*) - e$. This implies $r = r^*$ and $e = 0$; these conditions, implausible in a flexible-rate world, are the only ones under which both home and foreign investors can achieve perfect arbitrage.

6 As in previous chapters we abstract from a fractional reserve banking system so that L refers to the 'monetary base', with D and F being its domestic and foreign components respectively.

7 The case of constant, exogenous growth of capacity output can be readily incorporated if one assumes further (i) capacity output in the home country and the rest of the world grows at the same rate; (ii) demand functions are homogeneous of degree one in real quantities; (iii) $(Z - \bar{Z})/\bar{Z}$ replaces $(Z - \bar{Z})$ in (12.5); (iv) $K/\bar{Z}$ is constant. For related approaches see, e.g., Mundell (1971), Johnson (1973).

8 Most empirical evidence would seem to suggest $1 > \alpha_2 + \alpha_3$.

9 This fairly obvious implication of the open economy Phillips curve has been recognized by previous authors. It is the central conclusion of Waterman (1966) and is also noted in Fleming (1971). However, these authors paid little attention to stability.

10 There is also the question of uniqueness of equilibrium. Unfortunately this is extremely difficult to determine in general and we do not attempt to pursue it further here. A sufficient condition for uniqueness is that the matrix on the left hand side of (12.34) be a P-matrix; see Chapter 2.

11 Our export function should, strictly speaking, be extended so as to include an argument for the real interest rate whenever we allow the foreign real interest rate to vary. For simplicity, this is omitted; none of our steady-state conclusions are affected by this.

12 See e.g., Mundell (1964), Helliwell (1969). There have been exceptions. Argy and Porter (1972) contains a systematic analysis of the consequences of non-fixed exchange-rate expectations, and gives references to the relevant literature.

13 This can be seen by substituting for Y^D into (12.36a) and calculating $\partial r / \partial Z$ for given V, σ, π.

14 Specifically, let us impose the purchasing power parity and perfect myopic foresight conditions summarized in (12.42). Furthermore, presume that *either* the direct substitution effect on output of a relative price change outweighs the indirect, income ('terms-of-trade') effect via the effect of a relative price change on disposable income; *or* that the Marshall–Lerner condition holds, together with the condition that government purchases of the domestic good are less than or equal to income-tax revenues. Then the first-order differential equation described by $\dot{V} = S(Y^D, r^* - q, V)$, together with (12.44b)–(12.44c), is stable.

15 Boyer (1975) considers the question of relative insulation under fixed and flexible exchange rates in a static monetary model. His main conclusion is that flexible rates provide better, but not perfect, insulation.

16 These propositions regarding perfect insulation carry over to the case where investors are concerned with the after-tax rate of return $(r^* + e)(1 - u) - (q + e)$, discussed in note 5.

17 Thus (12.53) embodies the assumption that g_D is continuous with respect to time over the interval (t_0, t).

18 This point would seem to be implicit in some comments made by Ando (1974).

Notes to chapter 13

1 In particular see Fox, Sengupta, and Thorbecke (1973), Culbertson (1968).

2 E( ) denotes the expectation operator, while Var( ) denotes variance.

3 From Section 2, under certainty the model is

$$y = \bar{a}x + \bar{u}$$

and y^* is attained by setting $x = (y^* - \bar{u})/\bar{a}$.

4 These conditions are analogous to the usual first order conditions obtained from the calculus. There are also second order conditions to be met, which ensure that the optimum is a minimum. These can be rather complex, but are assured providing $H(x, \dot{x})$ is convex in x, $\dot{x}$ as is the case here.

5 For methods of solving sets of simultaneous linear differential equations see Kaplan (1958). The characteristic equation for the pair of differential equations (13.25) is

$$n_1 n_2 \lambda^4 + m(a_1^2 n_2 + a_2^2 n_1)\lambda^2 = 0$$

the only negative root of which is λ_1 given in (13.27).

6 By the same token if $0 < c < 1$, it is possible for the government to *destabilize* the system if it chooses $\gamma < 0$ and adjusts its expenditure the wrong way.

7 The stability conditions for the second order system (13.43) require (i) tr $\Delta < 0$, (ii) det $\Delta > 0$ where Δ denotes the matrix in (13.43), tr denotes the trace, and det denotes the determinant.

8 See Samuelson (1947, Appendix).

Notes to chapter 14

1 See also Theil (1957), Simon (1956).

2 For example if

$$M = \begin{pmatrix} 1 & -1 \\ -1 & 1 \end{pmatrix}$$

then

$$C = \sum_{t=1}^{T} [(Y_{1t} - Y_1^*) - (Y_{2t} - Y_2^*)]^2$$

where Y_{1t}, Y_{2t} are the components of Y_t. M is thus only positive semi-definite and the costs are defined in terms of the differences between these two components and not in terms of each independently.

3 $r(A)$ denotes the rank of the matrix A.

4 With the finite horizon case, the assumptions that the matrices A, B, M, N are constant over time are not necessary. Identical optimal policies are obtained if these matrices over time are dependent, the only difference being that they will have a time subscript attached to them. On the other hand, for the asymptotic case we shall consider below, the assumption that these matrices be time-invariant *is* necessary.

5 In the scalar case, the recursive solution for s_t can be obtained in the form

$$s_{t-1} = m + a^2 s_t - \frac{a^2 b^2 s_t^2}{n + b^2 s_t}, \quad s_T = 0,$$

where all quantities denoted by lower case letters are the scalar analogues of the matrices defined in the text. At this point it suffices to observe that as long as $n > 0$, to solve for s_1 is an extremely arduous task. If $n = 0$, however, this equation simplifies to

$$s_{t-1} = m \qquad \text{for all } t.$$

6 See for example, Chow (1970), Cooper and Fischer (1972a, 1973), Sargent (1971), Turnovsky (1975a).

7 The quantity $\|x\|$ where x is a vector, is defined by

$$\Sigma x_i^2 = 1.$$

For a matrix A, $\|A\|$ is taken to be the Euclidean operator norm and is defined as

$$\|A\| = \max [\|Ax\| : \|x\| = 1]$$

The infimum of a set is defined to be the least upper bound.

8 For a detailed discussion of stochastic stability see Kushner (1967). Asymptotic stability w.p.1 is extremely strong, being a direct extension of the deterministic definition. It requires the random function to ultimately converge to the non-stochastic equilibrium and cannot be satisfied in the presence of an additive disturbance with constant variance.

9 Note that with a single state variable it would make no sense to permit $m = 0$: hence the restriction in (14.27).

10 The work in this section is somewhat similar to the interesting papers by Cooper and Fischer, (1972a, 1973) who analyse in great detail the relationship between the lag structure and the effectiveness of certain specified policy rules. The rules they consider are simple proportional and derivative policies,

rather than fully optimal feedback policies and their objective function is to minimize the asymptotic variance of y_t rather than a more general quadratic cost function. Moreover, they consider only one stochastic coefficient and therefore they are unable to consider the effects of correlated disturbances in the parameters. In these respects their approach is less general than that given here. On the other hand, the dynamic equation they specify is more general than (14.28), allowing for more flexible lags than the simple first order system we consider.

11 The scalar analogue to the stochastic stabilizability condition (14.20) is

$$\inf_{n=0}^{\infty} \sum (a + br)^{2n}(\sigma_v^2 + 2\sigma_v\sigma_w\rho r + \sigma_w^2 r^2), \quad \text{such that} \quad |a + br| < 1.$$

That is, there exists an r such that

$$\frac{\sigma_v^2 + 2\sigma_v\sigma_w\rho r + \sigma_w^2 r^2}{1 - (a + br)^2} < 1 \quad \text{and} \quad |a + br| < 1.$$

Suppose $|a + br| < 1$ and set $\theta = (a + br)$. The above inequality can be written

$$(b^2 + \sigma_w^2)\theta^2 + 2(a\sigma_w^2 - \sigma_v\sigma_w\rho b)\theta + b^2(\sigma_v^2 - 1) + a^2\sigma_w^2 - 2\sigma_v\sigma_w\rho ab < 0$$

and $|\theta| < 1.$

In general, the quadratic $x^2 - 2\theta x + \alpha < 0$ for some x, $|x| < 1$ if and only if $|\beta| - \sqrt{(\beta^2 \alpha)} < 1$. Applying this condition yields the following sufficient condition for (14.24) to have an optimal policy.

$$(b^2 + \sigma_w^2) - |a\sigma_w^2 - \sigma_v\sigma_w\rho b| > -\{(a\sigma_w^2 - \sigma_v\sigma_w\rho b)^2$$

$$- (b^2 + \sigma_w^2)[b^2(\sigma_v^2 - 1) + a^2\sigma_w^2 - 2\sigma_v\sigma_w\rho ab]\}^{1/2}.$$

12 One example of this kind of problem which has recently been receiving the attention of monetary economists is the so-called 'instrument problem' which consider whether the monetary authorities should attempt to use the interest rate or money supply as their control variable; see Poole (1970), Sargent (1971), Turnovsky (1975).

13 This last statement is essentially analagous to the Cooper–Fischer (1972a) finding that increased variability in the system lags will always increase the minimum attainable variance. However, our results suggest that their conclusion is extremely sensitive to their assumption of including only one stochastic parameter (the system lag).

14 This result for $\partial r/\partial \sigma_v^2$ may appear to contradict a result obtained in the Cooper–Fischer paper. Their general conclusion is that an increase in the variability of the system lag will tend to imply less vigorous control. However, not surprisingly, the difference is due to differences in model specification. The way they formulate their lags, an increase in the variability of lags will increase both σ_v^2, σ_w^2 (in our notation). Since we find increases in these two parameters to have opposite effects, the apparent inconsistency is resolved.

15 For a comprehensive survey of recent applications of control theory to macroeconomics see Kendrick (1976).

REFERENCES

Aghelvi, B.B., and G.H. Borts, 'The Stability and Equilibrium of the Balance of Payments Under a Fixed Exchange Rate', *Journal of International Economics,* 3 (1973), 1–20.

Alexander, S.S., 'Effects of a Devaluation on a Trade Balance', *IMF Staff Papers,* 2 (1952), 263–78.

Ali, M.M. and S.J. Greenbaum, 'Stabilization Policy, Uncertainty and Instrument Proliferation', *Economic Inquiry,* 14 (1976), 105–15.

Allen, P.R., 'A Portfolio Approach to International Capital Flows', *Journal of International Economics,* 3 (1973), 135–60.

Allen, R.G.D., *Mathematical Economics,* Macmillan, London (1956).

Allen, R.G.D., *Macro-Economic Theory,* Macmillan, London (1967).

Almon, S., 'The Distributed Lag Between Capital Appropriations and Expenditures', *Econometrica,* 33 (1965), 178–96.

Ando, A.K., 'Some Aspects of Stabilization Policies, the Monetarist Controversy, and the MPS Model', *International Economic Review,* 15 (1974), 541–71.

Ando, A.K. and F. Modigliani, 'The "Life-Cycle" Hypothesis of Saving: Aggregate Implications and Tests', *American Economic Review,* 53 (1963), 55–84.

Ando, A., F. Modigliani, R. Rasche and S.J. Turnovsky, 'On the Role of Expectations of Price and Technological Change in an Investment Function', *International Economic Review,* 15 (1974), 384–414.

Argy, V. and M.G. Porter, 'The Forward Exchange Market and the Effects of Domestic and External Disturbances Under Alternative Exchange Rate Systems', *IMF Staff Papers* (1972), 503–32.

Astrom, K.J., *Introduction to Stochastic Control Theory,* Academic Press, New York (1970).

Athans, M., 'The Discrete Time Linear–Quadratic–Gaussian Stochastic Control Problem', *Annals of Economic and Social Measurement,* 1 (1972), 449–92.

Athans, M. and P. Falb, *Optimal Control,* McGraw-Hill, New York (1966).

Barro, R.J., 'Are Government Bonds Net Wealth?', *Journal of Political Economy,* 82 (1974), 1095–1118.

Baumol, W.J., 'Pitfalls in Contracyclical Policies: Some Tools and Results', *Review of Quarterly Journal of Economics,* 66 (1952), 545–56.

Baumol, W.J., 'Pitfalls in Contrayclinical Policies: Some Tools and Results', *Review of Economics and Statistics,* 43 (1961), 21–6.

Bellman, R., *Stability Theory of Differential Equations,* McGraw-Hill, New York (1960).

Bhatia, K.B., 'Capital Gains and the Aggregate Consumption Function, *American Economic Review,* 62, (1972), 866–79.

Bischoff, C.W. 'The Effects of Alternative Lag Distributions', in G. Fromm (ed.), *Tax*

Incentives and Capital Spending, Brookings Institution Washington, DC (1971).

Black, S.W. and H.H. Kelejian, 'The Formulation of the Dependent Variable in the Wage Equation', *Review of Economic Studies,* 39 (1972), 55–60.

Blinder, A.S. and R.M. Solow, 'Does Fiscal Policy Matter?', *Journal of Public Economics,* 2 (1973), 319–38.

Bodkin, R.G., E.P. Bond, G.L. Reuber and T.R. Robinson, *Price Stability and High Employment: The Options of Canadian Economic Policy; an Econometric Study,* Queens Printer, Ottawa (1966).

Boyer, R.S., 'Fixed Rates, Flexible Rates and the International Transmission of Inflation, International Monetary Research Programme, London School of Economics (April 1975).

Brainard, W., 'Uncertainty and the Effectiveness of Policy', *American Economic Review, Proceedings,* 57 (1967), 411–25.

Brainard, W. and J. Tobin, 'Pitfalls in Financial Model Building', *American Economic Review, Proceedings,* 58 (1968), 99–122.

Branson, W.H., *Macroeconomic Theory and Policy,* Harper and Row, New York (1972).

Branson, W.H., 'Monetarist and Keynesian Models of the Transmission of Inflation', *American Economic Review, Papers and Proceedings,* 65 (1975), 115–19.

Branson, W.H. and A.K. Klevorick, 'Money Illusion and the Aggregate Consumption Function', *American Economic Review,* 59 (1969), 832–49.

Bridge, J.L., *Applied Econometrics,* North-Holland, Amsterdam (1971).

Bronfenbrenner, M. and F.D. Holzman, 'Survey of Inflation Theory', *American Economic Review,* 53 (1963), 593–661.

Bryson, A.E. and Y.C. Ho, *Applied Optimal Control,* Blaisdell, Waltham, Mass. (1969).

Burmeister E. and A.R. Dobell, *Mathematical Theories of Economic Growth,* Macmillan, New York (1970).

Burmeister, E. and S.J. Turnovsky, 'The Specification of Adaptive Expectations in Continuous Time Dynamic Economic Models', *Econometrica,* 44 (1976), 879–905.

Cagan, P., 'The Monetary Dynamics of Hyperinflation', in M. Friedman (ed.), *Studies in the Quantity Theory of Money,* University of Chicago Press, Chicago (1956).

Caines, P.E. and D.Q. Mayne, 'On the Discrete Time Matrix Riccati Equation of Optimal Control', *International Journal of Control,* 12 (1970), 785–94.

Caines, P.E. and D.Q. Mayne, 'On the Discrete Time Matrix Riccati Equation of Optimal Control – a Correction', *International Journal of Control,* 14 (1971), 205–7.

Caves, R.E., 'Looking at Inflation in the Open Economy., Discussion Paper No. 286, Harvard Institute of Economic Research (March 1973).

Caves, R.E. and R.W. Jones, *World Trade and Payments,* Little, Brown and Company, Boston (1973).

Chow, G.C., 'Optimal Stochastic Control of Linear Economic Systems', *Journal of Money, Credit and Banking,* 2 (1970), 291–302.

Chow, G.C., 'Optimal Control of Linear Econometric Systems with Finite Time Horizon', *International Economic Review,* 13 (1972), 16–25.

Chow, G.C. 'Effect of Uncertainty on Optimal Control Policies', *International Economic Review,* 14 (1973a), 632–45.

Chow, G.C., 'Problems of Economic Policy from the Viewpoint of Optimal Control', *American Economic Review,* 63 (1973b), 825–37.

Christ, C.F., 'A Short-Run Aggregate-Demand Model of the Interdependence and Effects of Monetary and Fiscal Policies with Keynesian and Classical Interest Elasticities', *American Economic Review, Proceedings,* 57 (1967), 434–43.

Christ, C.F., 'A Simple Macroeconomic Model with a Government Budget Restraint', *Journal of Political Economy,* 76 (1968), 53–67.

Christ, C.F., 'A Model of Monetary and Fiscal Policy Effects on the Money Stock, Price Level, and Real Output', *Journal of Money, Credit and Banking,* 1 (1969) 683–705.

Coen, R.M., 'The Effect of Cash Flow on the Speed of Adjustment', in G. Fromm (ed.), *Tax Incentives and Capital Spending*, Brookings Institution, Washington, DC (1971).

Cooper, J.P. and S. Fischer, 'Stabilization Policy and Lags: Summary and Extension', *Annals of Economic and Social Measurement*, 1 (1972a), 407–18.

Cooper, J.P. and S. Fischer, 'Simulation of Money Rules in the FRB–MIT–Penn Model', *Journal of Money, Credit and Banking*, 4 (1972b), 384–96.

Cooper, J.P. and S. Fischer, 'Stochastic Simulation of Monetary Rules in Two Macroeconomic Models', *Journal of the American Statistical Association*, 67 (1972c), 750–60.

Cooper, J.P. and S. Fischer, 'Monetary and Fiscal Policy in the Fully Stochastic St Louis Econometric Model', *Journal of Money, Credit and Banking*, 6 (1974), 1–22.

Cooper, R.N., 'Macroeconomic Policy Adjustment in Interdependent Economies', *Quarterly Journal of Economics*, 83 (1969), 1–24.

Cramer, J.S., *Empirical Econometrics*, North-Holland, Amsterdam (1971).

Crouch, R.L., *Macroeconomics*, Harcourt, Brace, Jovanovich, New York (1972).

Culbertson, J.M., *Macroeconomic Theory and Stabilization Policy*, McGraw-Hill, New York (1968).

Debreu, G., 'Excess Demand Functions', *Journal of Mathematical Economics*, 1 (1974), 15–21.

Desai, M., 'Growth Cycles and Inflation in a Model of the Class Struggle', *Journal of Economic Theory*, 6 (1973), 527–45.

Desai, M., 'The Phillips Curve: A Revisionist Interpretation', *Economica*, 42 (1975), 1–19.

Dornbusch, R., 'Devaluation, Money and Nontraded Goods', *American Economic Review*, 63 (1973), 871–80.

Dow, J.C.R. and L.A. Dicks-Mireaux, 'Excess Demand for Labour', *Oxford Economic Papers*, 10 (1958), 1–33.

Duesenberry, J.S., *Income, Saving, and the Theory of Consumer Behavior*, Harvard University Press, Cambridge, Mass. (1948).

Dunn, R.M., 'Flexible Exchange Rates and Oligopoly Pricing: A Study of Canadian Markets', *Journal of Political Economy*, 78 (1970), 140–51.

Eckstein, O., 'A Theory of the Wage–Price Process in Modern Industry', *Review of Economic Studies*, 31 (1964), 267–86.

Eckstein, O., and R. Brinner, 'The Inflation Process in the United States', Joint Economic Committee, US Government Printing Office, Washington, DC (1972).

Eckstein, O. and G. Fromm, 'The Price Equation', *American Economic Review*, 58 (1968), 1159–83.

Eckstein, O. and T.A. Wilson, 'The Determination of Money Wages in American Industry', *Quarterly Journal of Economics*, 76 (1962), 379–414.

Eisner, R., 'Fiscal and Monetary Policy Reconsidered', *American Economic Review*, 59 (1969), 897–905.

Evans, M.K., *Macroeconomic Activity*, Harper and Row, New York (1969).

Fischer, S. and J.P. Cooper, 'Stabilization Policy and Lags', *Journal of Political Economy*, 81 (1973), 847–77.

Fisher, I., *The Theory of Interest*, Macmillan, New York (1930).

Fleming, J.M. 'Domestic Financial Policies under Fixed and Floating Exchange Rates', *IMF Staff Papers*, 9 (1962), 369–379.

Fleming, J.M., 'On Exchange Rate Unification', *Economic Journal*, 81 (1971), 467–88.

Floyd, J., 'Monetary and Fiscal Policy in a World of Capital Mobility', *Review of Economic Studies*, 36 (1969) 503–18.

Foley, D.K., 'On Two Specifications of Asset Equilibrium in Macroeconomic Models', *Journal of Political Economy*, 93 (1972), 305–24.

Foley, D.K. and M. Sidrauski, 'Portfolio Choice, Investment, and Growth', *American*

Economic Review, 60 (1970), 44–63.

Foley, D.K. and M. Sidrauski, *Monetary and Fiscal Policy in a Growing Economy,* Macmillan, New York (1971).

Fox, K.A., J.K. Sengupta and E. Thorbecke, *The Theory of Quantitative Economic Policy,* North-Holland, Amsterdam (2nd ed.) (1973).

Friedman, B., 'Optimal Economic Stabilization Policy, An Extended Framework', *Journal of Political Economy,* 80 (1972), 1002–22.

Friedman, B., *Economic Stabilization Policy,* North-Holland, Amsterdam (1975a).

Friedman, B., 'Rational Expectations are Really Adaptive After All', Harvard University Discussion Paper No. 430 (1975b).

Friedman, M., 'The Quantity Theory of Money: A Restatement', in M. Friedman ed., *Studies in the Quantity Theory of Money,* University of Chicago Press, Chicago (1956).

Friedman, M., *A Theory of the Consumption Function,* Princeton University Press, Princeton, New Jersey (1957).

Friedman, M., 'The Lag in Effect of Monetary Policy', *Journal of Political Economy,* 69 (1961), 447–66.

Friedman, M., 'The Role of Monetary Policy', *American Economic Review,* 58 (1968), 1–17.

Friedman, M., 'A Theoretical Framework for Monetary Analysis', *Journal of Political Economy,* 78 (1970), 193–238.

Gale, D. and H. Nikaido, 'The Jacobian Matrix and Global Univalence of Mappings', *Mathematische Annalen,* 129 (1965), 81–93.

Gibson, W., 'Price Expectations Effects on Interest Rates', *Journal of Finance,* 25 (1970).

Goldfeld, S.M., 'The Demand for Money Revisited', *Brookings Papers on Economic Activity,* 3 (1973), 577–646.

Goodwin, R.M., 'The Non-linear Accelerator and the Persistence of Business Cycles', *Econometrica,* 19 (1951), 225–39.

Gordon, R.J., 'Inflation in Recession and Recovery', *Brookings Papers on Economic Activity,* 1 (1970), 8–47.

Gould, J.P., 'Adjustment Costs in the Theory of Investment of the Firm', *Review of Economic Studies,* 35 (1968), 447–66.

Gould, J.P., 'The Use of Endogenous Variables in Dynamic Models of Investment', *Quarterly Journal of Economics,* 83 (1969), 580–99.

Hakansson, N.H., 'Optimal Investment and Consumption Strategies for a Class of Utility Functions, *Econometrica,* 38 (1970), 587–607.

Hamburger, M., 'The Lag in the Effect of Monetary Policy – a Survey of Recent Literature', *Federal Reserve Bank of New York* (1971).

Hamermesh, D.S., 'Wage Bargains, Threshold Effects and the Phillips Curve', *Quarterly Journal of Economics,* 84 (1970), 501–17.

Hansen, B., *A Survey of General Equilibrium Systems,* McGraw-Hill, New York (1970).

Hansen, B., 'Fiscal and Monetary Policy Reconsidered: Comment', *American Economic Review,* 61 (1971) 444–7.

Helliwell, J.F., 'Monetary and Fiscal Policies for an Open Economy', *Oxford Economic Papers,* 21 (1969), 35–55.

Henderson, D.W. and S.J. Turnovsky, 'Optimal Macroeconomic Policy Adjustment Under Conditions of Risk', *Journal of Economic Theory,* 4 (1972), 58–71.

Henderson, J.M. and R.E. Quandt, *Microeconomic Theory,* McGraw-Hill, New York (2nd ed.) (1971).

Hicks, J.R., *A Contribution to the Theory of the Trade Cycle,* Oxford University Press, Oxford (1950).

Holbrook, R.S. 'Optimal Economic Policy and the Problem of Instrument Instability', *American Economic Review,* 62 (1972), 57–65.

Holt, C.C., 'Linear Decision Rules for Economic Stabilization and Growth', *Quarterly Journal of Economics*, 76 (1962), 20–45.

Howrey, E.P., 'Stabilization Policy in Linear Stochastic Models', *Review of Economics and Statistics*, 49 (1967), 404–11.

Howrey, E.P., 'Distributed Lags and the Effectiveness of Monetary Policy: Note', *American Economic Review*, 59 (1969), 997–1001.

Johnson, H.G., 'Some Aspects of the Theory of Economic Policy in a World of Capital Mobility', in Antonio Milani Gabiotti, ed., *Essays in Honour of Marco Fanno*, Padova (1966).

Johnson, H.G. 'The Monetary Approach to Balance of Payments Theory', in Conolly, M.B. and A.K. Swoboda, *International Trade and Money*, George Allen and Unwin, London (1973), 206–24.

Johnston, J., 'A Model of Wage Determination Under Bilateral Monopoly', *Economic Journal*, 82 (1972), 837–52.

Jones, R.W., 'Monetary and Fiscal Policy for an Economy with Fixed Exchange Rates', *Journal of Political Economy*, 76 (1968), 921–43.

Jorgenson, D.W., 'Capital Theory and Investment Behavior', *American Economic Review, Proceedings*, 53 (1963), 247–59.

Jorgenson, D.W., 'Anticipations and Investment Behavior', in J.S. Duesenberry, G. Fromm, L.R. Klein, and E. Kuh (eds.), *The Brookings Quarterly Econometric Model of the United States*, Rand McNally, Chicago (1965).

Jorgenson, D.W. and C.D. Siebert, 'Optimal Capital Accumulation and Corporate Investment Behavior', *Journal of Political Economy*, 76 (1968), 1123–51.

Kalecki, M., 'A Macrodynamic Theory of Business Cycles', *Econometrica*, 3 (1935), 327–44.

Kaplan, W., *Ordinary Differential Equations*, Addison-Wesley, Reading, Mass. (1958).

Kendrick, D.A., 'Applications of Control Theory to Macroeconomics', *Annals of Economic and Social Measurement*, 5 (1976), 171–90.

Kindleberger, C., *International Economics*, Irwin, Homewood, Illinois, 3rd edition (1963).

Kingston, G.H. and S.J. Turnovsky, 'Imported Inflation and Government Policies in a Dynamic Macroeconomic Model Under Alternative Exchange Rate Policies', unpublished manuscript, ANU (1976).

Kouri, P. and M.G. Porter, 'International Capital Flows and Portfolio Equilibrium', *Journal of Political Economy*, 82 (1974), 443–68.

Krueger, A.O., 'The Impact of Alternative Government Policies Under Varying Exchange Systems', *Quarterly Journal of Economics*, 79 (1965), 195–208.

Kuh, E. and R.L. Schmalensee, *An Introduction to Applied Macroeconomics*, North-Holland, Amsterdam (1973).

Kushner, H.J., *Stochastic Stability and Control*, Academic Press, New York (1967).

Kushner, H.J., *Introduction to Stochastic Control*, Holt, Rinehart and Winston, New York (1971).

Laidler, D.E.W. and J.M. Parkin, 'Inflation – A Survey', *Economic Journal*, 85 (1975), 741–809.

Laursen, S. and L.A. Metzler, 'Flexible Exchange Rates and the Theory of Employment', *Review of Economics and Statistics*, 32 (1950), 281–99.

Levhari, D. and D. Patinkin, 'The Role of Money in a Simple Growth Model', *American Economic Review*, 58 (1968), 713–53.

Levin, J.H., 'International Capital Mobility and the Assignment Problem', *Oxford Economic Papers*, 24 (1972), 54–67.

Levy, H. and M. Sarnat, *Investment and Portfolio Analysis*, Wiley, New York (1972).

Lipsey, R.G., 'The Relation between Unemployment and the Rate of Change of Money Wage Rates in the United Kingdom 1862–1957: A Further Analysis', *Economica*,

27 (1960), 1–31.

Lipsey, R.G. and J.M. Parkin, 'Incomes Policy' – A Re-appraisal', *Economica,* 37 (1970), 115–38.

Lovell, M.C., *Macroeconomics: Measurement, Theory and Policy,* Wiley, New York (1975).

Lovell, M.C. and E. Prescott, 'Money Multiplier Accelerator Interaction', *Southern Economic Journal,* 35 (1968), 60–72.

Lucas, R.E., 'Optimal Investment Policy and the Flexible Accelerator', *International Economic Review,* Vol. 8 (1967), 78–85.

Lucas, R.E., 'Econometric Testing of the Natural Rate Hypothesis', in *The Econometrics of Price Determination,* Federal Reserve Board (1972).

McElroy, M.B. and J.C. Poindexter, 'Capital Gains and the Aggregate Consumption Function: A Comment', *American Economic Review,* 65 (1975), 700–3.

McKinnon, R.I., 'Optimum Currency Areas', *American Economic Review,* 53 (1963), 717–24.

McKinnon, R.I., 'Portfolio Balance and International Payments Adjustment' in R.A. Mundell and A.K. Swoboda (eds.) *Monetary Problems of the International Economy,* University of Chicago Press, Chicago (1969).

McKinnon, R.I. and W.E. Oates, 'The Implications of International Economic Integration for Monetary, Fiscal and Exchange-Rate Policy', *Princeton Studies in International Finance,* No. 16 (1966).

Machlup, F., 'The Terms of Trade Effects of Devaluation upon Real Income and the Balance of Trade', *Kyklos,* 9 (1956), 417–52.

May, J., 'Period Analysis and Continuous Analysis in Patinkin's Macroeconomic Model', *Journal of Economic Theory,* 2 (1970), 1–9.

Merton, R.C., 'Optimum Consumption and Portfolio Rules in a Continuous-Time Model', *Journal of Economic Theory,* 3 (1971), 373–413.

Meyer, L.H., 'The Balance Sheet Identity, the Government Financing Constraint and the Crowding-Out Effect', *Journal of Monetary Economics,* 1 (1975), 65–78.

Michaely, M., *Concentration in International Trade,* North-Holland, Amsterdam (1962).

Modigliani, F. and R. Brumberg, 'Utility Analysis and the Consumption Function: An Interpretation of Cross-Section Data', in K.K. Kurihara, ed., *Post Keynesian Economics,* Rutgers University Press, New Brunswick, New Jersey (1954).

Modigliani, F. and M.H. Miller, 'The Cost of Capital, Corporation Finance, and the Theory of Investment', *American Economic Review,* 48 (1958) 261–97.

Moore, B.J., 'Optimal Monetary Policy', *Economic Journal,* 82 (1972), 116–29.

Mundell, R.A., 'Inflation and Real Interest', *Journal of Political Economy,* 71 (1963), 280–3.

Mundell, R.A., 'The Appropriate Use of Monetary and Fiscal Policy for Internal and External Stability', *IMF Staff Papers,* 9 (1962), 70–9.

Mundell, R.A., 'A Reply: Capital Mobility and Size', *Canadian Journal of Economics and Political Science,* 30 (1964), 421–31.

Mundell, R.A., *International Economics,* Macmillan, New York (1968).

Mundell, R.A. *Monetary Theory: Inflation, Interest and Growth in the World Economy,* Goodyear Publishing Co., California (1971).

Mundell, R.A., 'The Optimum Balance of Payments Deficit', in E. Claassen and P. Stalin (eds.), *Stabilization Policies in Interdependent Economies,* North-Holland, Amsterdam–London, (1972), 69–87.

Muth, J.F., 'Rational Expectations and the Theory of Price Movements', *Econometrica,* 129 (1961), 315–35.

Nerlove, M., 'Adaptive Expectations and Cobweb Phenomena', *Quarterly Journal of Economics,* 73 (1958), 227–40.

Nordhaus, W.D., 'Recent Developments in Price Dynamics', in *The Econometrics of*

Price Determination, Federal Reserve Board (1972).

Norman, A.L., 'Control Theory and Econometric Models', *IEEE Conference on Decision and Control* (1971), 85–95.

Oates, W.E., 'Budget Balance and Equilibrium Income: A Comment on the Efficiency of Fiscal and Monetary Policy in an Open Economy', *Journal of Finance,* 21 (1966), 489–98.

Okun, A., *The Political Economy of Prosperity,* Norton, New York (1970).

Ott, D.J. and A. Ott, 'Budget Balance and Equilibrium Income', *Journal of Finance,* 20 (1965), 71–7.

Pagan, A.R., 'Optimal Control of Econometric Models with Autocorrelated Disturbance Terms', *International Economic Review,* 16 (1975), 258–63.

Patinkin, D., *Money, Interest and Prices, 2nd edition,* Harper and Row, New York (1965).

Patrick, J.D., 'Establishing Convergent Decentralized Policy Assignment', *Journal of International Economics,* 3 (1973), 37–52.

Perry, G.L., 'The Determinants of Wage Rate Changes and the Inflation–Unemployment Trade-Off for the United States', *Review of Economic Studies,* 31 (1964), 287–303.

Pesek, B.P. and T.R. Saving, *Money, Wealth, and Economic Theory,* Macmillan, New York (1967).

Phelps, E.S., 'Money-Wage Dynamics and Labor-Market Equilibrium', *Journal of Political Economy,* 76 (1968), 678–711.

Phelps, E.S. (ed.), *Microeconomic Foundations of Employment and Inflation Theory,* Norton, New York (1970).

Phillips, A.W., 'Stabilisation Policy in a Closed Economy', *Economic Journal,* 64 (1954), 290–323.

Phillips, A.W., 'Stabilisation Policy and the Time Form of Lagged Responses', *Economic Journal,* 67 (1957), 265–77.

Phillips, A.W., 'The Relation between Unemployment and the Rate of Change of Money Wage Rates in the United Kingdom, 1861–1957', *Economica,* 25 (1958), 283–99.

Pindyck, R.S., *Optimal Planning for Economic Stabilization,* North-Holland, Amsterdam (1973).

Pitchford, J.D., *A Study of Cost and Demand Inflation,* North-Holland, Amsterdam (1963).

Pitchford, J.D., 'Cost and Demand Elements in the Inflationary Process', *Review of Economic Studies,* 24 (1957), 139–48.

Pitchford, J.D. 'An Analysis of Price Movements in Australia 1947–68', *Australian Economic Papers,* 7 (1968), 111–35.

Pitchford, J.D., 'The Phillips Curve and the Minimum Rate of Inflation' in *Essays in Honour of A.W. Phillips,* Wiley, London (forthcoming) (1977).

Pitchford, J.D. and S.J. Turnovsky, 'Some Effects of Taxes on Inflation', *Quarterly Journal of Economics,* 90 (1976), 523–37.

Poole, W., 'Optimal Choice of Monetary Policy Instruments in a Simple Stochastic Macro Model', *Quarterly Journal of Economics,* 84 (1970), 197–216.

Prescott, E.C., 'Adaptive Decision Rules for Macroeconomic Planning', *Western Economic Journal,* 9 (1971), 369–78.

Prescott, E.C., 'The Multi-period Control Problem Under Uncertainty', *Econometrica,* 40 (1972), 1043–58.

Preston, A., 'A Dynamic Generalization of Tinbergen's Theory of Policy', *Review of Economic Studies,* 41 (1974), 65–74.

Preston, A., 'Existence, Uniqueness and Stability of Linear Optimal Stabilization Policies', in J.D. Pitchford and S.J. Turnovsky, (eds.) *Applications of Control Theory to Economic Analysis,* North-Holland, Amsterdam (1976), 255–92.

Preston, A., and E. Sieper, 'Policy Objectives and Instrument Requirements for a Dynamic Theory of Policy', in J.D. Pitchford and S.J. Turnovsky (eds.) *Applications of Control Theory to Economic Analysis*, North-Holland, Amsterdam (1976), 215–53.

Pyle, D.H., 'Observed Price Expectations and Interest Rates., *Review of Economics and Statistics*, 54 (1972), 275–80.

Pyle, D.H. and S.J. Turnovsky, 'The Dynamics of Government Policy in an Inflationary Economy: An "Intermediate-Run" Analysis', *Journal of Money, Credit and Banking*, 8 (1976).

Ritter, L.S., 'Some Monetary Aspects of Multiplier Theory and Fiscal Policy', *Review of Economic Studies*, 23 (1955–56), 126–31.

Robichek, A.A. and S.C. Myers, *Optimal Financing Decisions*, Prentice-Hall, Englewood Cliffs, New Jersey (1965).

Sakakibara, E., 'A Dynamic Approach to Balance of Payment Theory', *Journal of International Economics*, 5 (1975), 31–54.

Samuelson, P.A., 'Interaction between the Multiplier Analysis and the Principle of Acceleration', *Review of Economic Statistics*, 21 (1939), 75–8.

Samuelson, P.A., *The Foundations of Economic Analysis*, Harvard University Press, Cambridge, Mass. (1947).

Samuelson, P.A. and S. Swamy, 'Invariant Economic Index Numbers and Canonical Duality: Survey and Synthesis', *American Economic Review*, 64 (1974), 566–93.

Sargent, T.J., 'Commodity Price Expectations and the Interest Rate', *Quarterly Journal of Economics*, 83 (1969), 127–40.

Sargent, T.J., 'The Optimum Monetary Instrument Variable in a Linear Economic Model', *Canadian Journal of Economics*, 4 (1971a), 50–60.

Sargent, T.J., 'A Note on the "Accelerationist" Controversy', *Journal of Money, Credit and Banking*, 3 (1971b), 721–5.

Sargent, T.J., 'Anticipated Inflation and the Nominal Rate of Interest', *Quarterly Journal of Economics*, 86 (1972), 212–25.

Sargent, T.J., 'Interest Rates and Prices in the Long Run', *Journal of Money, Credit and Banking*, 5 (1973a), 385–449.

Sargent, T.J., 'Rational Expectations, the Real Rate of Interest, and the Natural Rate of Unemployment', *Brookings Papers on Economic Activity*, 2 (1973b), 429–72.

Sengupta, J.K., 'Optimal Stabilization Policy with a Quadratic Criterion Function', *Review of Economic Studies*, 37 (1970), 127–46.

Shell, K., M. Sidrauski, and J.E. Stiglitz, 'Capital Gains, Income and Saving', *Review of Economic Studies*, 36 (1969), 15–26.

Shinkai, Y., 'A Model of Imported Inflation', *Journal of Political Economy*, 81 (1973), 962–71.

Shinkai, Y., 'Stabilization Policies for an Open Economy', *International Economic Review*, 16 (1975) 662–81.

Silber, W.L., 'Fiscal Policy in IS–LM Analysis – A Correction', *Journal of Money, Credit and Banking*, 2 (1970), 461–72.

Simon, H.A., 'Dynamic Programming Under Uncertainty with a Quadratic Criterion Function', *Econometrica*, 24 (1956), 74–81.

Smith, L.B. and J.W.L. Winder, 'Price and Interest Expectations and the Demand for Money in Canada', *Journal of Finance*, 26 (1971), 671–82.

Sohmen, E., 'Fiscal and Monetary Policies under Alternative Exchange Rate Systems', *Quarterly Journal of Economics*, 81 (1967), 515–23.

Solow, R.M., 'A Contribution to the Theory of Economic Growth', *Quarterly Journal of Economics*, 70 (1956), 65–94.

Solow, R.M., 'Recent Controversy on the Theory of Inflation: An Eclectic View', in S.W. Rousseas (ed.), *Inflation: Its Causes, Consequences and Control*, Kazanjian Economic Foundation, Wilton, Conn. (1968).

Sonnenschein, H., 'Market Excess Demand Functions', *Econometrica,* 40 (1972), 549–63.

Sparks, G.R. and D.A. Wilton, 'Determinants of Negotiated Wage Increases: An Empirical Analysis', *Econometrica,* 39 (1971), 739–50.

Stein, J.L., 'Neoclassical and "Keynes–Wicksell" Monetary Growth Models', *Journal of Money, Credit, and Banking,* 1 (1969), 153–71.

Steindl, F.G., 'A Simple Macroeconomic Model with a Government Budget Restraint: A Comment', *Journal of Political Economy,* 79 (1971), 675–9.

Stern, R.M., *The Balance of Payments: Theory and Economic Policy,* Aldine, Chicago (1973).

Takayama, A., 'The Effects of Fiscal and Monetary Policies Under Flexible and Fixed Exchange Rates', *Canadian Journal of Economics,* 2 (1969), 190–209.

Takayama, A., *International Trade,* New York (1972).

Tanner, J.E., 'Lags in the Effects of Monetary Policy: A Statistical Investigation', *American Economic Review,* 59 (1969), 794–805.

Taylor, L.D., S.J. Turnovsky and T.A. Wilson, *The Inflationary Process in North American Manufacturing,* Information Canada, Ottawa (1973).

Teigen, R.L., 'Demand and Supply Functions for Money in the United States: Some Structure Estimates', *Econometrica,* 32 (1964), 476–509.

Theil, H., *Linear Aggregation and Economic Relations,* North-Holland, Amsterdam (1954).

Theil, H., 'A Note on Certainty Equivalence in Dynamic Planning', *Econometrica,* 25 (1957), 346–9.

Theil, H., *Economic Forecasts and Policy,* North-Holland, Amsterdam (1958).

Theil, H., *Optimal Decision Rules for Government and Industry,* North-Holland, Amsterdam (1964).

Tinbergen, J., *On the Theory of Economic Policy,* North-Holland, Amsterdam (1952).

Tobin, J., 'The Neutrality of Money in Growth Models: A Comment', *Economica,* 34 (1967), 69–72.

Tobin, J., 'A General Equilibrium Approach to Monetary Theory', *Journal of Money, Credit and Banking,* 1 (1969), 15–29.

Tobin, J., 'Inflation and Unemployment', *American Economic Review,* 62 (1972), 1–18.

Tobin, J. and W. Buiter, 'Long-Run Effects of Fiscal and Monetary Policy on Aggregate Demand', in J.L. Stein (ed.), *Monetarism,* North-Holland, Amsterdam, (1976), 273–309.

Tower, E., 'The Short-Run Effects of Monetary and Fiscal Policy Under Fixed and Flexible Exchange Rates', *Economic Record,* 48 (1972), 411–23.

Treadway, A.B., 'On Rational Entrepreneurial Behaviour and the Demand for Investment', *Review of Economic Studies,* 36 (1969), 227–39.

Trevithick, J.A. and C. Mulvey, *The Economics of Inflation,* Robertson, London (1975).

Tsiang, S.C., 'Capital Flows, Internal and External Balance', *Quarterly Journal of Economics,* 89 (1975), 195–214.

Tucker, D.P., 'Dynamic Income Adjustment to Money Supply Changes', *American Economic Review,* 56 (1966), 433–49.

Turnovsky, S.J., 'Some Empirical Evidence on the Formation of Price Expectations', *Journal of the American Statistical Association,* 65 (1970), 1441–54.

Turnovsky, S.J., 'The Expectations Hypothesis and the Aggregate Wage Equation: Some Empirical Evidence for Canada', *Economica,* 39 (1972), 1–17.

Turnovsky, S.J., 'Optimal Stabilization Policies for Deterministic and Stochastic Linear Economic Systems', *Review of Economic Studies,* 40 (1973), 79–96.

Turnovsky, S.J., 'The Stability Properties of Optimal Economic Policies', *American Economic Review,* 64 (1974a), 136–48.

Turnovsky, S.J. 'On the Role of Inflationary Expectations in a Short-Run

Macroeconomic Model', *Economic Journal*, 84 (1974b), 317–37.

Turnovsky, S.J., 'Optimal Choice of Monetary Instrument in a Linear Economic Model with Stochastic Coefficients', *Journal of Money, Credit and Banking*, 7 (1975a), 51–80.

Turnovsky, S.J., 'Monetary Policy, Fiscal Policy and the Government Budget Constaint', *Australian Economic Papers*, 14 (1975b), 197-215.

Turnovsky, S.J., 'The Dynamics of Fiscal Policy in an Open Economy', *Journal of International Economics*, 6 (1976a), 115–42.

Turnovsky, S.J., 'Optimal Control of Linear Systems with Stochastic Coefficients and Additive Disturbances', in J.D. Pitchford and S.J. Turnovsky eds., *Applications of Control Theory to Economic Analysis*, North-Holland, Amsterdam (1976b), 293–335.

Turnovsky, S.J., 'On the Scope of Optimal and Discretionary Policies in the Stabilisation of Stochastic Linear Systems', in J.D. Pitchford and S.J. Turnovsky, eds., *Applications of Control Theory to Economic Analysis*, North-Holland, Amsterdam (1976c), 337–63.

Turnovsky, S.J., 'On the Formulation of Continuous Time Macroeconomic Models with Asset Accumulation', *International Economic Review*, 18 (1977a), 1–28.

Turnovsky, S.J., 'Stabilization Policies and the Choice of Monetary Instrument in a Small Open Economy', in *Essays in Honour of A.W. Phillips*, Wiley and Sons, New York (1977b).

Turnovsky, S.J. and E. Burmeister, 'Perfect Foresight, Expectational Consistency and Macroeconomic Equilibrium', *Journal of Political Economy*, 85 (1977).

Turnovsky, S.J. and A. Kaspura, 'An Analysis of Imported Inflation in a Short-Run Macro-economic Model', *Canadian Journal of Economics*, 7 (1974), 355–80.

Turnovsky, S.J. and J.D. Pitchford, 'Expectations and Income Claims in Wage–Price Determination: An Aspect of the Inflationary Process', in *Essays in Honour of A.W. Phillips*, Wiley, London, (1977).

Turnovsky, S.J. and M.L. Wachter, 'A Test of the "Expectations Hypothesis" Using Directly Observed Wage and Price Expectations', *Review of Economics and Statistics*, 54 (1972), 47–54.

Vanderkamp, J., 'Wage Adjustment, Productivity and Price Change Expectations', *Review of Economic Studies*, 39 (1972), 61–72.

Waterman, A.M.C., 'Some Footnotes to the "Swan Diagram" – or How Dependent is a Dependent Economy', *Economic Record*, 42 (1966), 447–64.

Weber, W.E., 'The Effect of Interest Rates on Aggregate Consumption', *American Economic Review*, 60 (1970), 491–600.

Wonham, W.M., *Stochastic Problems in Optimal Control*, RIAS Technical Report 63–14 (May 1963).

Wonham, W.M. 'Optimal Stationary Control of a Linear System with State-Dependent Noise, *SIAM Journal of Control*, 5 (1967), 486–500.

Wonham, W.M., 'On a Matrix Riccati Equation of Stochastic Control', *SIAM Journal of Control*, 6 (1968), 681–97.

Wonham, W.M., 'Random Differential Equations in Control Theory', in A.T. Barucha-Reid, (ed.), *Probabilistic Methods in Applied Mathematics*, II, Academic Press, New York (1969).

Wonnacott, P., *Macroeconomics*, Irwin, Homewood, Illinois (1974).

Yaari, M.E., 'On the Consumer's Lifetime Allocation Process', *International Economic Review*, 5 (1964), 304–17.

Yohe, W.P. and D.S. Karnosky, 'Interest Rates and Price Level Changes, 1952–69', *Review of the Federal Reserve Bank of St Louis*, 51 (1969), 18–38.

INDEX

adding up constraints, 62–4, 136, 271–2, 367, 370
Aghevli, B.B., 216, 230, 242, 262
Alexander, S.S., 278
Ali, M.M., 317
Allen, P.R., 242
Allen, R.G.D., 3, 318, 320, 325
Almon, S., 99
Ando, A., 1, 360, 364, 371, 373
Argy, V., 373
assignment problem, 208–16, 232–4, 262–4
Astrom, K.J., 334, 338
asymptotic variance, 327, 339
Athans, M., 315, 334, 338

balance
    external 208, 213, 214, 230, 262–4
    internal, 208, 212, 214, 230, 262–4
balanced budget, 71, 80, 180
balanced budget multiplier, 26, 180
balance of payments
    defined, 201–3, 222, 247, 273
    current account, 250, 283
    monetary approach, 217, 301–2
balance of trade, 249, 274
Barro, R.J., 360
basic macro model, 11–35, 69–71
    fiscal policy in, 21–6, 72–3
    monetary policy in, 21–6, 71
Baumol, W.J., 325, 360
Bellman, R., 334
Bhatia, K.B., 366
bilateral bargaining elements in wage–price determination, 102–3
Bischoff, C.W., 1
Black, S.W., 91
Blinder, A.S., 5, 23, 41, 82, 85, 129, 131, 132, 133, 150, 177, 241, 255, 367
Blinder–Solow model, 130–2
Bodkin, R.G., 100, 363, 369
Bond, E.P., 100, 363, 369

bonds
    government 36–8, 48
    private, 36–8
    perpetuities, 37
    variable interest rate, 36
Borts, G.H., 216, 230, 242, 262, 371
Boyer, R.S., 373
Brainard, W., 63, 309, 369
Branson, W.H., 2, 3, 217, 359, 360, 361
Bridge, J.L., 3
Brinner, R., 101
Bronfenbrenner, M., 363
Brumberg, R., 1
Bryson, A.E., 314
Buiter, W., 41, 132, 165, 366
Burmeister, E., 3, 52, 138, 360, 361, 367

Cagan, P., 99
Caines, P.E., 338
capital accumulation, 131–2, 139–40, 172
capital flows, 202, 222, 249, 273, 369
capital gains, 46, 34, 65, 135, 167, 272
capital mobility
    perfect, 202, 205, 207, 232, 233, 256–62, 270–1
    zero, 251–6
Caves, R.E., 5, 368
Chow, G.C., 338, 374
Christ, C.F., 4, 41, 68, 69, 72, 80, 83, 84, 85, 255, 362
classical model, 26–9
Coen, R.M., 170
comparative statics, 7, 32–4
consistent macro model, 36–67, 275–6
consumption
    actual, 48–9, 54, 361
    plans, 14–15, 46, 196–7, 218, 243, 268
continuous-time analysis, 43–4, 52–66, 159–64
control costs, 332

controllability
  dynamic, 333
  static, 309
Cooper, J.P., 325, 328, 350, 353, 358, 374, 375
Cooper, R.N., 215
correspondence Principle, 34
cost of adjustment, 313–17
Cramer, J.S., 3
Crouch, R.L., 359, 360
crowding out, 84–5, 130–1
Culbertson, J.M., 373

Debreu, G., 2
devaluation, 201, 204–5, 231–4, 283
Desai, M., 90, 102
Dicks-Mireaux, L.A., 363
discrete-time analysis, 4, 43–51
disposable income, 15, 42, 48–9, 54, 66, 167, 246, 272
Dobell, A.R., 3, 367
domestic cost of living: related to price of domestically produced goods, 220, 269
Dornbusch, R., 217, 269
Dow, J.C.R., 363
Duesenberry, J.S., 1, 360
Dunn, R.M., 370
dynamics of macro system, 3–7, 68–85, 131, 137–40, 170–2, 174–5, 208–16, 250–1, 255–6, 262–4, 272–5, 277, 313–28, 353–7

Eckstein, O., 90, 92, 93, 101, 364
Eisner, R., 366
elasticity of substitution, 182–4
endogenous government policy, 155–6, 208–16, 307–58
equities
  held in portfolios, 36–40, 50, 55–6, 58–60
  rate of return on, 137, 168
  relationship to physical capital, 47, 58–60, 169
  value, 58, 168, 171
Euler conditions, 316, 373
Evans, M.K., 2, 3
exchange rate
  as policy instrument, 231–5
  expectations, 271
  fixed, 203–6, 217–34, 241–66, 277–87
  flexible, 203, 206–7, 235–7, 287–98
expectations
  adaptive, 99, 137–8, 159–64, 275
  as exogenous parameter, 104–28, 141–3, 217–40, 277–82, 287–93
  equilibrium relationship, 151–2, 176, 282, 293
  extrapolative, 99

rational, 123–4
  specification, 45
'Expectations hypothesis', 94–101, 109–113
  empirical testing, 98–101
export demand, 198, 219

Falb, P., 315, 334
feedback control law
  defined, 242
  existence of, 339, 340
financial sector, 136, 165, 242–4, 270–2
firms' budget constraint, 39–40, 50, 55–6, 138, 171
first order system:
  as reduction of higher order system, 333
fiscal policy
  long-run effects of, 81–4, 151–4, 179–84, 186–9, 255, 262, 284–6, 293–8
  short-run effects of, 21–6, 72–3, 76–7, 78–9, 113–14, 118–20, 144, 204–5, 207, 231–2, 280–2, 291–3
Fischer, S., 325, 328, 350, 353, 358, 374, 375
Fisher, I., 104, 154
Fisherian proposition, 111, 141–3, 154–5, 183–4, 296–7
Fleming, J.M., 368, 372
flow constraint, 53–8, 66, 166, 276
flow variables:
  specification, 46
Floyd, J., 241
Foley, D.K., 47, 56, 64, 67, 360, 361
foreign reserves, 199–200, 221–2, 243, 262–4, 273
foresight
  imperfect, 44–51
  perfect, 47
  perfect myopic foresight, 52
Fox, K.A., 373
Friedman, B., 160, 329
Friedman, M., 1, 94, 96, 106, 107, 133, 350, 360, 364
Fromm, G., 93

Gale, D., 33
Gibson, W., 364, 365
Goldfeld, S.M., 183
Goodwin, R.M., 320
Gould, J.P., 1, 170
Gordon, R.J., 100
government bonds
  as wealth, 38
government budget constraint, 40–2, 50–1, 57, 66, 68–85, 108, 130–2, 138, 171, 222, 247, 272, 288
government debt, 41, 146, 149

government deficit
  bond-financed, 131, 140, 148–50, 152–4, 186–9, 288
  comparison of bond and money financing, 153–4, 189–91
  mixed financing, 71–85, 219, 245, 286, 295; 222, 248, 289, 298
  money-financed, 131, 141, 146–8, 150–4, 177–86, 288, 297–8
Greenbaum, S.J., 317

Hakansson, N.H., 366
Hamburger, M., 350
Hamermesh, D.S., 364
Hansen, B., 361, 366
Helliwell, 214, 216, 217, 279, 368, 373
Henderson, D.W., 317, 369
Henderson, J.M., 367
Hicks, J.R., 318
Ho, Y.C., 314
Holbrook, R.S., 337
Holt, C.C., 353
Holzman, F.D., 363
household sector budget constraint, 38–40, 45–50, 53–5, 65
Howrey, E.P., 326, 327, 350
Hume, D., 217

imports, 196–9, 219, 249, 273
imputed market price of capital, 47, 59, 171
income distribution
  impact of government expenditure on, 183
income tax
  effects of changes in, 120–2, 186, 189
  interaction with inflationary expectations, 114–8
inflation
  as tax, 179, 181, 188, 272
  general, 86–90, 129–56, 159–91
  international transmission of, 217–40, 267–303
  related to rate of growth of financial assets, 151, 177, 283, 293, 297–8
inflationary accounting, 64–6
inflationary expectations, 99, 105–28, 141–3, 170, 219–23, 268–75
instantaneous equilibrium, 139, 141–6, 174, 249, 251–2, 256–7, 277, 280–2, 287–8, 291–3
instrument instability, 337
insulation from foreign inflation under flexible exchange rates, 235–6, 296–8
interest payments
  as component of capital flows, 246, 270
  on government debt, 40, 50, 73–5, 138, 171, 247, 272

interest rate parity, 271, 290
intermediate-run equilibrium, 150–5
intermediate-run model, 129–58
investment
  actual, 50, 167
  plans, 14–15, 50, 55, 131, 137, 172, 196–7
IS curve, 16

Jacobian, 32
Jacobian matrix, 33
Johnson, H.G., 215, 217, 368, 372
Johnston, J., 102
Jones, R.W., 5, 215, 368
Jorgenson, D.W., 1, 16, 170, 360, 364

Kalecki, M., 320
Kaplan, W., 315, 371, 373
Karnosky, D.S., 364, 365
Kaspura, A., 217, 368
Kelejian, H.H., 91
Kendrick, D.A., 375
Keynes, J.M., 17
Keynesian rigidities, 30–2
Kindleberger, C., 368
Kingston, G.H., 270, 371
Klevorick, A.K., 359
Kouri, R., 279, 370
Krueger, A.O., 216, 368
Kuh, E., 3
Kushner, H.J., 328, 332, 334, 338, 374

Labour market, 26–32, 169–70, 220–1
Laidler, D.E.W., 87
Laursen, S., 278
Levhari, D., 362
Levin, J.H., 214, 215, 279
Levy, H., 361
linear systems
  deterministic, 308–9, 313–17, 329–31, 331–7
  dynamic, 318–24, 325–8, 331–58
  static, 308–13, 329–31
  stochastic, 310–13, 325–8, 337–58
Lipsey, R.G., 89, 90, 369
Livingston, J.A., 100
LM curve, 19
Lovell, M.C., 2, 325
long-run model, 159–91
Lucas, R.E., 1

McElroy, M.B., 366
McKinnon, R.I., 241, 247, 370, 371
Machlup, F., 269
marginal physical product of capital
  defined, 169
  relationship to real rate of return on equity, 58–60, 168–9, 246
mark-up pricing, 88, 92

Marshall–Lerner condition, 201–2,
    204–5, 207, 225, 277, 301–2
May, J., 43, 44, 54, 361
Mayne, D.Q., 338
Merton, R.C., 366
methodology, 6–7
Metzler, L.A., 278
Meyer, L.H., 361, 362
Michaely, M., 368
Miller, M.H., 135, 366
Modigliani, F., 1, 135, 360, 364, 366, 371
Modigliani and Miller theorem 135
monetarist debate, 84–5
monetary base, 18
monetary instrument problem, 375
monetary policy
    long-run effects of, 79–81, 151–4,
        186, 284–7
    short-run effects of, 21–6, 71, 75–6,
        77, 113–14, 118–20, 205–6, 207,
        231–2, 280–2, 291–3
money illusion, 14, 29–30, 94
money market
    specification, 17–20, 135–6,
        199–201, 221, 243
money supply
    relationship to base money, 18–19
Moore, B.J., 350, 353
multiplier–accelerator models, 318–20,
    353–7
Mulvey, C., 87, 94
Mundell, R.A., 5, 208, 210, 215, 217, 230,
    234, 262, 364, 368, 372, 373
Muth, J.F., 124
Myers, S.C., 37

national income identity, 12
natural rate of unemployment, 96, 97,
    151, 177, 178, 283, 287
neoclassical growth models
    stability of, 179
Nerlove, M., 99
Nikaido, H., 33
Nordhaus, W.D., 93
Norman, A.L., 358

Oates, W.E., 241, 247, 370
Okun's law, 94
open market operation, 18, 70, 76, 78, 80,
    144–5, 184–6, 230
optimal stabilization policies, 331–50
Ott, A., 4, 41, 68, 69, 72, 84, 85, 362
Ott, D.J., 4, 41, 68, 69, 72, 84, 85, 362
output market, 13–17, 60–2, 105–6,
    135, 167, 196–9, 219, 243, 268

P-matrix, 33
Pagan, A.R., 338, 339
Parkin, J.M., 87, 369

Patinkin, D., 2, 39, 43, 362
Patrick, J.D., 211, 230
Perry, G.L., 90
Pesek, B.P., 38
Phelps, E.S., 2, 94, 98, 133, 364
Phelps hypothesis, 98
Phillips, A.W., 61, 87, 88, 89, 318, 322,
    323, 325, 335, 353
Phillips curve, 87–102, 106–8, 135, 151,
    170, 177, 221, 270
Pindyck, R.S., 353, 358
Pitchford, J.D., 102, 364, 366, 368, 369
Poindexter, J.C., 366
policy adjustment rules
    derivative, 324, 335, 358
    integral, 323–4
    proportional, 321–3, 335, 349–50,
        352, 358
policy instruments, 208–211, 264,
    308–17, 329
Poole, W., 375
Porter, M.G., 279, 370, 373
portfolio balance, 135, 140, 164–5,
    172–3, 244, 280
Prescott, E.C., 325, 338
Preston, A., 334, 336
principle of effective market classification,
    210, 212, 214, 262
production function, 93, 107, 169–70
product market disequilibrium, 60-2,
    166–7, 172
profits
    role in wage determination, 90, 92
purchasing power parity, 282, 293
Pyle, D.H., 364, 365, 366

quadratic cost function, 310, 314, 316,
    329, 331–2
Quandt, R.E., 367

Rasche, R., 364
rate of change: relationship between
    anticipated and actual, 52
rate of interest
    nominal, 15–18, 106, 110, 135
    real, 106, 110, 135, 166
restrictions imposed by budget
    constraints, 62–4
Reuber, G.L., 100, 363, 369
Ritter, L.S., 362
Robichek, A.A., 37
Robinson, T.R., 100, 363, 369
Routh–Hurwitz conditions, 175, 278
rules versus discretionary control, 350–3

Sakakibara, E., 242
Samuelson, P.A., 34, 89, 318, 367, 368,
    371, 372, 373
Sargent, T.J., 133, 154, 155, 353, 364,
    365, 374, 375

Sarnat, M., 371
Saving, T.R., 38
savings
    actual, 48, 54, 276, 282
    planned, 48, 53, 276, 282
    relationship to wealth accumulation,
        42–4, 48, 54
Schmalensee, R.L., 3
Sengupta, J.K., 353, 373
Shell, K., 64
Shinkai, Y., 278, 287, 368
short-run equilibrium, 20–32, 32–4,
        75–9, 104–28, 141–6, 174, 203–7,
        218–33, 249, 256, 277, 279–80,
        287–8, 289–90
short-run model, 195–216, 217–40,
        241–66
Sidrauski, M., 64, 67, 360
Siebert, C.D., 364
Sieper, E., 331
Silber, W.L., 362
Simon, H.A., 331, 338, 373
Smith, L.B., 364, 365
Sohmen, E., 215
Solow, R.M., 5, 23, 41, 82, 85, 100, 129,
        131, 132, 133, 150, 177, 241, 255,
        362, 367
Sonnenschein, H., 2
Sparks, G.R., 364
stability, 32–4, 79, 82, 83, 146–50, 175,
        179, 187, 208–16, 251–5,
        258–61, 262–3, 278–9, 289, 303,
        368, 373
stabilizability, 340
stabilization policies, 208–16, 261–3,
        307–58
steady state 79–83, 150–5, 175–7, 247,
        254–5, 259, 282–4, 293
Stein, J.L., 64
Steindl, F.G., 362
sterilization of changes in foreign reserve,
        200, 222, 248
Stern, R.M., 5, 278, 368
Stiglitz, J.E., 64
stochastic control, 325–8, 337–51
stochastic stability, 341, 364
stochastic stabilizability, 340, 375
stock adjustment, 62, 172
stock constraint, 53, 65, 136, 164–5, 245,
        271

strong consistency axiom, 163
Swamy, S., 372

Takayama, A., 5, 205, 215, 216, 217, 368
Tanner, J.E., 350
target variables, 208–11, 264, 308–17,
        329
Taylor, L.D., 91, 94, 365, 369
Teigen, R.L., 18, 19
terms of trade: defined, 196
Theil, H., 2, 311, 329, 330, 331, 338, 373
Thorbecke, E., 373
Tobin, J., 2, 37, 41, 47, 60, 63, 64, 90,
        106, 132, 133, 135, 136, 142, 165,
        176, 360, 366
Tower, E., 238, 241
Treadway, A.B., 1
Trevithick, J.A., 87, 94
Tsiang, S.C., 368
Tucker, D.P., 350
Turnovsky, S.J., 37, 41, 52, 91, 94, 100,
        101, 102, 112, 138, 160, 217, 270,
        317, 333, 336, 337, 338, 339, 346,
        353, 360, 361, 362, 364, 365, 366,
        368, 369, 370, 371, 374, 375

unanticipated policy changes, 123–6
unemployment rate: defined, 89
unit labour costs, 88

vacancies, 89
Vanderkamp, J., 100

Wachter, M.L., 100, 101, 112
wage-price sector, 86–103, 107–8, 169,
        269–70
Walras' law, 11, 42, 51
Waterman, A.M.C., 372
weak consistency axiom, 48, 160
wealth, 36–8, 40–2, 53, 73–5, 135–7,
        166, 245–6, 271
Weber, W.E., 182, 360
Winder, J.W.L., 364, 365
Wilson, T.A., 90, 91, 94, 364, 365, 369
Wilton, D.A., 364
Wonham, W.J., 338, 340
Wonnacott, P., 2

Yaari, M.E., 1
Yohe, W.P., 364, 365